PATTERNS
IN
WRITING **THIRD EDITION**

HOLT

RINEHART

AND

WINSTON

New York

HOLT,

RINEHART

AND

WINSTON

New York · Chicago · San Francisco

PATTERNS IN WRITING

THIRD EDITION

ROBERT B. DOREMUS

EDGAR W. LACY

GEORGE BUSH RODMAN

UNIVERSITY OF WISCONSIN

Preface

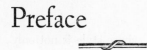

WE BELIEVE that a college course in composition should have three primary aims:

1. to give the student instruction and practice in the art and craft of writing;
2. to provide him opportunity and guidance for intelligent and accurate reading;
3. to enlarge his understanding and improve his power of thought.

No one of these three can be slighted. But paradoxically the first is the most easily overlooked.

We do not believe that technique and technique alone is important. We do not believe that one can study style and ignore content. We know that students must learn both to read well and to write well, and that they are more apt to do both if their minds are stimulated by what they read and by what they write about. The mere setting before a student, however, of material for reading and of subject matter for thinking does not automatically lead him to see that whatever he is reading and thinking about is also a case history in the problem of writing. Hence in compiling this book of readings and in constructing the critical apparatus which follows each selection, we have firmly observed the principle that above all we ought to provide examples of effective writing, and that our primary purpose should be to point out to the student how other authors have solved—or sometimes failed to solve—their particular problems in communication.

Since writing is done at a great many different levels and for a great many different ends, our selections cover a wide range of subject, tone, and degree of stylistic sophistication. The book is divided into seven parts, and within each part except the sixth the selections are arranged in a roughly progressive order according to their complexity in style, structure, and thought. All of them, however, illustrate a useful or effective type of writing at some level. They range in style from the seeming casualness of Clarence Day or Mark Twain to the conscious rhetoric of Winston Churchill; in purpose, from an explanation of the weather to a defense of reading poetry; in tone, from the sober argument of Walter Lippmann to the tongue-in-cheek needling of Morris Bishop and David L. Cohn. We have tried to keep a judicious balance throughout, but if we must confess any bias, it is in favor of authors who have not only intelligence but wit, whose style is not only clear but sparkling.

The selections have been grouped primarily on the basis of their purpose. Since an author may have several purposes in mind, it is not possible to establish categories that are mutually exclusive and admit of no overlap; but we have placed selections according to what seems to be their dominant aim and attitude. Thus the passages in Part I, EXPERIENCE AND OBSERVATION, are those which attempt to convey to the reader what the author has seen and done, either in his own person or vicariously by observing others. Although this is by no means the simplest kind of writing, it is a good one for students to begin with in their own compositions, since the material is readily at hand within their own experience. Part II, EXPLANATION, contains examples of a number of different kinds of simple exposition. Here the author's intent is to furnish information or instruction, to tell what, how, or why. The third part, EVALUATION, introduces writing which not only expounds but appraises, not only presents information but weighs and judges it and sometimes draws conclusions from it. In the following group, PERSUASION, are those selections wherein the author not only has evaluated his material but is engaged in a more or less determined attempt to persuade others to his way of thinking about it. Part V, RESEARCH, presents an example of that kind of writing so frequently encountered by the college student because it is so widely used in making available the advances of knowledge in the sciences, the social studies, and the humanities. Here the author has been examining his subject, carefully collecting or discovering facts about it, and drawing inductive conclusions for whose underlying evidence he furnishes accurate documentation.

Parts VI and VII, THE CRAFT OF WRITING and NARRATION, have a different though none the less important relationship to the student's own composition. The first of these contains a number of discussions—in varying moods—of how words and sentences should and should not be used. In the second are nine short stories. Though only a few students may want to try writing stories themselves, nearly all will profit by seeing how the writer of fiction uses the tools of his craft for a particular effect.

When we suggest that the readings in this book have been chosen primarily for their value as models and examples of writing, we do not mean that the average college writer will be able to produce something exactly like them. We do mean that by looking carefully at these selections, the student can discover what it is that makes writing "good"— that is, efficient in fulfilling its purpose of communicating with the reader and having the desired effect upon him—and can apply these techniques in his own writing according to his own needs and purposes.

To write effectively, to read understandingly, to think fruitfully —these are the skills which the student ought to learn from his college course in composition. And the first, though it cannot really flourish without the other two, is still the most important to remember, because it is the most easily slighted and because as a technical craft it is the hardest to learn. That is why we have so constantly emphasized it. When it is not so emphasized, it tends to slip out of sight and the balance is spoiled. To develop in the college writer all three of these skills together is the task and responsibility of the composition instructor. To provide a set of readings which will make easier the fulfillment of that task and that responsibility has been our aim in this book.

R.B.D.
E.W.L.
G.B.R.

Madison, Wisconsin

Contents

PART FOUR
Persuasion   369

PART FIVE
Research   497

PATTERNS
IN
WRITING THIRD EDITION

PART ONE

Experience
and Observation

WE LIVE IN A WORLD OF IDEAS ONLY PART OF THE TIME. DURING most of our waking hours we are constantly aware of the world of things and people: the world we can see and hear, touch and be a living part of. That is the world we enjoy and worry about the most, the world of— where to eat dinner? which movie to see? how to earn a living? That is the world we chatter about between classes and write about in our letters to friends. From that very real world comes the stuff that makes each of us just a little different from all other individuals in our way of talking and of living in the breakfast-to-breakfast cycle.

Strangely we sometimes close our eyes to that world when we scratch a pen on the paper of a formal assignment. But we write best and most easily when we make use of what we know best and are most spontaneous about. True, little of our writing for academic ends can be composed entirely of our observations and experiences, but what we have seen and lived through can give the color of individuality to any type of writing. Hence it is well to analyze and be able to present observations and experiences for themselves alone. Only in that way can we as writers learn that we have a wealth of detail always available to us.

All but one of the following ten selections are biographical or autobiographical in whole or in part. Each author presents what he himself or some other person has seen and lived through. To do this, he has had to learn—as you must learn—to write only about something observed accurately or remembered intimately. Although the observations are concrete and the experiences have the effect of immediacy, they are placed in a framework which makes them meaningful to the reader. A

1

perennial subject of satire is the man who cannot stick to the point when telling a story. To stick to his point, each one of these authors has had to decide what items to include and what to omit, where to begin and where to end. By getting his purpose clearly in mind, he has found a definite principle of organization. Otherwise his observations and experiences would have been so many bright stones scattered on an endless beach. A writer must know where he is going and why.

The Feel

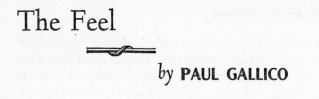

by PAUL GALLICO

A CHILD WANDERING through a department store with its mother, is admonished over and over again not to touch things. Mother is convinced that the child only does it to annoy or because it is a child, and usually hasn't the vaguest inkling of the fact that Junior is "touching" because he is a little blotter soaking up information and knowledge, and "feel" is an important adjunct to seeing. Adults are exactly the same, in a measure, as you may ascertain when some new gadget or article is produced for inspection. The average person says: "Here, let me see that," and holds out his hand. He doesn't mean "see," because he is already seeing it. What he means is that he wants to get it into his hands and feel it so as to become better acquainted.

2. As suggested in the foregoing chapter, I do not insist that a curiosity and capacity for feeling sports is necessary to be a successful writer, but it is fairly obvious that a man who has been tapped on the chin with five fingers wrapped up in a leather boxing glove and propelled by the arm of an expert knows more about that particular sensation than one who has not, always provided he has the gift of expressing himself. I once inquired of a heavyweight prizefighter by the name of King Levinsky, in a radio interview, what it felt like to be hit on the chin by Joe Louis, the King having just acquired that experience with rather disastrous results. Levinsky considered the matter for a moment and then reported: "It don't feel like nuttin'," but added that for a long while afterwards he felt as though he were "in a transom."

3. I was always a child who touched things and I have always had a tremendous curiosity with regard to sensation. If I knew what playing a game felt like, particularly against or in the company of experts, I was better equipped to write about the playing of it and the problems of the men and women who took part in it. And so, at one time or another, I have tried them all, football, baseball, boxing, riding, shooting, swimming, squash, handball, fencing, driving, flying, both land and sea planes, rowing, canoeing, skiing, riding a bicycle, ice-skating, roller-skating, tennis, golf, archery, basketball, running, both the hundred-yard dash and the mile, the high jump and shot put, badminton, angling, deep-sea, stream-, and surf-casting, billiards and bowling, motorboating

3

and wrestling, besides riding as a passenger with the fastest men on land and water and in the air, to see what it felt like. Most of them I dabbled in as a youngster going through school and college, and others, like piloting a plane, squash, fencing, and skiing, I took up after I was old enough to know better, purely to get the feeling of what they were like.

4. None of these things can I do well, but I never cared about becoming an expert, and besides, there wasn't time. But there is only one way to find out accurately human sensations in a ship two or three thousand feet up when the motor quits, and that is actually to experience that gone feeling at the pit of the stomach and the sharp tingling of the skin from head to foot, followed by a sudden amazing sharpness of vision, clear-sightedness, and coolness that you never knew you possessed as you find the question of life or death completely in your own hands. It is not the "you" that you know, but somebody else, a stranger, who noses the ship down, circles, fastens upon the one best spot to sit down, pushes or pulls buttons to try to get her started again, and finally drops her in, safe and sound. And it is only by such experience that you learn likewise of the sudden weakness that hits you right at the back of the knees after you have climbed out and started to walk around her and that comes close to knocking you flat as for the first time since the engine quit its soothing drone you think of destruction and sudden death.

5. Often my courage has failed me and I have funked completely, such as the time I went up to the top of the thirty-foot Olympic diving-tower at Jones Beach, Long Island, during the competitions, to see what it was like to dive from that height, and wound up crawling away from the edge on hands and knees, dizzy, scared, and a little sick, but with a wholesome respect for the boys and girls who hurled themselves through the air and down through the tough skin of the water from that awful height. At other times sheer ignorance of what I was getting into has led me into tight spots such as the time I came down the Olympic ski run from the top of the Kreuzeck, six thousand feet above Garmisch-Partenkirchen, after having been on skis but once before in snow and for the rest had no more than a dozen lessons on an indoor artificial slide in a New York department store. At one point my legs, untrained, got so tired that I couldn't stem (brake) any more, and I lost control and went full tilt and all out, down a three-foot twisting path cut out of the side of the mountain, with a two-thousand-foot abyss on the left and the mountain itself on the right. That was probably the most scared I have ever been, and I scare fast and often. I remember giving myself up for lost and wondering how long it would take them to retrieve my body and whether I should be still alive. In the meantime the speed of the descent was increasing. Somehow I was keeping my feet and negotiating

turns, how I will never know, until suddenly the narrow patch opened out into a wide, steep stretch of slope with a rise at the other end, and *that* part of the journey was over.

6. By some miracle I got to the bottom of the run uninjured, having made most of the trip down the icy, perpendicular slopes on the flat of my back. It was the thrill and scare of a lifetime, and to date no one has been able to persuade me to try a jump. I know when to stop. After all, I am entitled to rely upon my imagination for something. But when it was all over and I found myself still whole, it was also distinctly worth while to have learned what is required of a ski runner in the breakneck *Abfahrt* or downhill race, or the difficult *slalom*. Five days later, when I climbed laboriously (still on skis) halfway up that Alp and watched the Olympic downhill racers hurtling down the perilous, ice-covered, and nearly perpendicular *Steilhang*, I knew that I was looking at a great group of athletes who, for one thing, did not know the meaning of the word "fear." The slope was studded with small pine trees and rocks, but half of the field gained precious seconds by hitting that slope all out, with complete contempt for disaster rushing up at them at a speed often better than sixty miles an hour. And when an unfortunate Czech skidded off the course at the bottom of the slope and into a pile of rope and got himself snarled up as helpless as a fly in a spider's web, it was a story that I could write from the heart. I had spent ten minutes getting myself untangled after a fall, *without* any rope to add to the difficulties. It seems that I couldn't find where my left leg ended and one more ski than I had originally donned seemed to be involved somehow. Only a person who has been on those fiendish runners knows the sensation.

7. It all began back in 1922 when I was a cub sports-writer and consumed with more curiosity than was good for my health. I had seen my first professional prizefights and wondered at the curious behavior of men under the stress of blows, the sudden checking and the beginning of a little fall forward after a hard punch, the glazing of the eyes and the loss of locomotor control, the strange actions of men on the canvas after a knockdown as they struggled to regain their senses and arise on legs that seemed to have turned into rubber. I had never been in any bad fist fights as a youngster, though I had taken a little physical punishment in football, but it was not enough to complete the picture. Could one think under those conditions?

8. I had been assigned to my first training-camp coverage, Dempsey's at Saratoga Springs, where he was preparing for his famous fight with Luis Firpo. For days I watched him sag a spar boy with what seemed to be no more than a light cuff on the neck, or pat his face with what looked like no more than a caressing stroke of his arm, and the fellow would

come all apart at the seams and collapse in a useless heap, grinning vacuously or twitching strangely. My burning curiosity got the better of prudence and a certain reluctance to expose myself to physical pain. I asked Dempsey to permit me to box a round with him. I had never boxed before, but I was in good physical shape, having just completed a four-year stretch as a galley slave in the Columbia eight-oared shell.

9. When it was over and I escaped through the ropes, shaking, bleeding a little from the mouth, with rosin dust on my pants and a vicious throbbing in my head, I knew all that there was to know about being hit in the prize-ring. It seems that I had gone to an expert for tuition. I knew the sensation of being stalked and pursued by a relentless, truculent professional destroyer whose trade and business it was to injure men. I saw the quick flash of the brown forearm that precedes the stunning shock as a bony, leather-bound fist lands on cheek or mouth. I learned more (partly from photographs of the lesson, viewed afterwards, one of which shows me ducked under a vicious left hook, an act of which I never had the slightest recollection) about instinctive ducking and blocking than I could have in ten years of looking at prizefights, and I learned, too, that as the soldier never hears the bullet that kills him, so does the fighter rarely, if ever, see the punch that tumbles blackness over him like a mantle, with a tearing rip as though the roof of his skull were exploding, and robs him of his senses.

10. There was just that—a ripping in my head and then sudden blackness, and the next thing I knew, I was sitting on the canvas covering of the ring floor with my legs collapsed under me, grinning idiotically. How often since have I seen that same silly, goofy look on the faces of dropped fighters—and understood it. I held onto the floor with both hands, because the ring and the audience outside were making a complete clockwise revolution, came to a stop, and then went back again counter-clockwise. When I struggled to my feet, Jack Kearns, Dempsey's manager, was counting over me, but I neither saw nor heard him and was only conscious that I was in a ridiculous position and that the thing to do was to get up and try to fight back. The floor swayed and rocked beneath me like a fishing dory in an off-shore swell, and it was a welcome respite when Dempsey rushed into a clinch, held me up, and whispered into my ear: "Wrestle around a bit, son, until your head clears." And then it was that I learned what those little love-taps to the back of the neck and the short digs to the ribs can mean to the groggy pugilist more than half knocked out. It is a murderous game, and the fighter who can escape after having been felled by a lethal blow has my admiration. And there, too, I learned that there can be no sweeter sound than the bell that calls a halt to hostilities.

11. From that afternoon on, also, dated my antipathy for the spectator at prizefights who yells: "Come on, you bum, get up and fight! Oh, you big quitter! Yah yellow, yah yellow!" Yellow, eh? It is all a man can do to get up after being stunned by a blow, much less fight back. But they do it. And how a man is able to muster any further interest in a combat after being floored with a blow to the pit of the stomach will always remain to me a miracle of what the human animal is capable of under stress.

12. Further experiments were less painful, but equally illuminating. A couple of sets of tennis with Vinnie Richards taught me more about what is required of a top-flight tournament tennis-player than I could have got out of a dozen books or years of reporting tennis matches. It is one thing to sit in a press box and write caustically that Brown played uninspired tennis, or Black's court covering was faulty and that his frequent errors cost him the set. It is quite another to stand across the net at the back of a service court and try to get your racket on a service that is so fast that the ear can hardly detect the interval between the sound of the server's bat hitting the ball and the ball striking the court. Tournament tennis is a different game from week-end tennis. For one thing, in average tennis, after the first hard service has gone into the net or out, you breathe a sigh of relief, move up closer and wait for the cripple to come floating over. In big-time tennis second service is practically as hard as the first, with an additional twist on the ball.

13. It is impossible to judge or know anything about the speed of a forehand drive hit by a champion until you have had one fired at you, or, rather, away from you, and you have made an attempt to return it. It is then that you first realize that tennis is played more with the head than with the arms and the legs. The fastest player in the world cannot get to a drive to return it if he hasn't thought correctly, guessed its direction, and anticipated it by a fraction of a second.

14. There was golf with Bob Jones and Gene Sarazen and Tommy Armour, little Cruickshank and Johnny Farrell, and Diegel and other professionals; and experiments at trying to keep up in the water with Johnny Weissmuller, Helene Madison, and Eleanor Holm, attempts to catch football passes thrown by Benny Friedman. Nobody actually plays golf until he has acquired the technical perfection to be able to hit the ball accurately, high, low, hooked or faded and placed. And nobody knows what real golf is like until he has played around with a professional and seen him play, not the ball, but the course, the roll of the land, the hazards, the wind, and the texture of the greens and the fairways. It looks like showmanship when a top-flight golfer plucks a handful of grass and lets it flutter in the air, or abandons his drive to march two hundred yards down to the green and look over the situation. It isn't.

It's golf. The average player never knows or cares whether he is putting with or across the grain of a green. The professional *always* knows. The same average player standing on the tee is concentrated on getting the ball somewhere on the fairway, two hundred yards out. The professional when preparing to drive is actually to all intents and purposes playing his *second* shot. He means to place his drive so as to open up the green for his approach. But you don't find that out until you have played around with them when they are relaxed and not competing, and listen to them talk and plan attacks on holes.

15. Major-league baseball is one of the most difficult and precise of all games, but you would never know it unless you went down on the field and got close to it and tried it yourself. For instance, the distance between pitcher and catcher is a matter of twenty paces, but it doesn't seem like enough when you don a catcher's mitt and try to hold a pitcher with the speed of Dizzy Dean or Dazzy Vance. Not even the sponge that catchers wear in the palm of the hand when working with fast-ball pitchers, and the bulky mitt are sufficient to rob the ball of shock and sting that lames your hand unless you know how to ride with the throw and kill some of its speed. The pitcher, standing on his little elevated mound, looms up enormously over you at that short distance, and when he ties himself into a coiled spring preparatory to letting fly, it requires all your self-control not to break and run for safety. And as for the things they can do with a baseball, those major-league pitchers . . . ! One way of finding out is to wander down on the field an hour or so before game-time when there is no pressure on them, pull on the catcher's glove, and try to hold them.

16. I still remember my complete surprise the first time I tried catching for a real curve-ball pitcher. He was a slim, spidery left-hander of the New York Yankees, many years ago, by the name of Herb Pennock. He called that he was going to throw a fast breaking curve and warned me to expect the ball at least two feet outside the plate. Then he wound up and let it go, and that ball came whistling right down the groove for the center of the plate. A novice, I chose to believe what I saw and not what I heard, and prepared to catch it where it was headed for, a spot which of course it never reached, because just in front of the rubber, it swerved sharply to the right and passed nearly a yard from my glove. I never had a chance to catch it. That way, you learn about the mysterious drop, the ball that sails down the alley chest high but which you must be prepared to catch around your ankles because of the sudden dip it takes at the end of its passage as though someone were pulling it down with a string. Also you find out about the queer fade-away, the slow curve, the fast in- and out-shoots that seem to be timed almost as delicately as

shrapnel, to burst, or rather break, just when they will do the most harm
—namely, at the moment when the batter is swinging.

17. Facing a big-league pitcher with a bat on your shoulder and trying to hit his delivery is another vital experience in gaining an understanding of the game about which you are trying to write vividly. It is
one thing to sit in the stands and scream at a batsman: "Oh, you bum!"
for striking out in a pinch, and another to stand twenty yards from that
big pitcher and try to make up your mind in a hundredth of a second
whether to hit at the offering or not, where to swing and when, not to
mention worrying about protecting yourself from the consequences of
being struck by the ball that seems to be heading straight for your skull
at an appalling rate of speed. Because, if you are a big-league player,
you cannot very well afford to be gun-shy and duck away in panic from
a ball that swerves in the last moment and breaks perfectly over the
plate, while the umpire calls: "Strike!" and the fans jeer. Nor can you
afford to take a crack on the temple from the ball. Men have died from
that. It calls for undreamed-of niceties of nerve and judgment, but you
don't find that out until you have stepped to the plate cold a few times
during batting practice or in training quarters, with nothing at stake
but the acquisition of experience, and see what a fine case of the jumping jitters you get. Later on, when you are writing your story, your imagination, backed by the experience, will be able to supply a picture of
what the batter is going through as he stands at the plate in the closing
innings of an important game, with two or three men on base, two out,
and his team behind in the scoring, and fifty thousand people screaming
at him.

18. The catching and holding of a forward pass for a winning touchdown on a cold, wet day always make a good yarn, but you might get an
even better one out of it if you happen to know from experience about
the elusive qualities of a hard, soggy, mud-slimed football rifled through
the air, as well as something about the exquisite timing, speed, and courage it takes to catch it on a dead run, with two or three 190-pound men
reaching for it at the same time or waiting to crash you as soon as your
fingers touch it.

19. Any football coach during a light practice will let you go down
the field and try to catch punts, the long, fifty-yard spirals and the tricky,
tumbling end-over-enders. Unless you have had some previous experience, you won't hang on to one out of ten, besides knocking your fingers
out of joint. But if you have any imagination, thereafter you will know
that it calls for more than negligible nerve to judge and hold that ball
and even plan to run with it, when there are two husky ends bearing
down at full speed, preparing for a head-on tackle.

20. In 1932 I covered my first set of National Air Races, in Cleveland, and immediately decided that I had to learn how to fly to find out what that felt like. Riding as a passenger isn't flying. Being up there all alone at the controls of a ship is. And at the same time began a series of investigations into the "feel" of the mechanized sports to see what they were all about and the qualities of mentality, nerve, and physique they called for from their participants. These included a ride with Gar Wood in his latest and fastest speedboat, *Miss America X*, in which for the first time he pulled the throttle wide open on the Detroit River straightaway; a trip with the Indianapolis Speedway driver Cliff Bergere, around the famous brick raceway; and a flip with Lieutenant Al Williams, one time U. S. Schneider Cup race pilot.

21. I was scared with Wood, who drove me at 127 miles an hour, jounced, shaken, vibrated, choked with fumes from the exhausts, behind which I sat hanging on desperately to the throttle bar, which after a while got too hot to hold. I was on a plank between Wood and his mechanic, Johnson, and thought that my last moment had come. I was still more scared when Cliff Bergere hit 126 on the Indianapolis straightaways in the tiny racing car in which I was hopelessly wedged, and after the first couple of rounds quite resigned to die and convinced that I should. But I think the most scared I have ever been while moving fast was during a ride I took in the cab of a locomotive on the straight, level stretch between Fort Wayne, Indiana, and Chicago, where for a time we hit 90 miles per hour, which of course is no speed at all. But nobody who rides in the comfortable Pullman coaches has any idea of the didoes cut up by a locomotive in a hurry, or the thrill of pelting through a small town, all out and wide open, including the crossing of some thirty or forty frogs and switches, all of which must be set right. But that wasn't sport. That was just plain excitement.

22. I have never regretted these researches. Now that they are over, there isn't enough money to make me do them again. But they paid me dividends, I figured. During the great Thompson Speed Trophy race for land planes at Cleveland in 1935, Captain Roscoe Turner was some eight or nine miles in the lead in his big golden, low-wing, speed monoplane. Suddenly, coming into the straightaway in front of the grandstands, buzzing along at 280 miles an hour like an angry hornet, a streamer of thick, black smoke burst from the engine cowling and trailed back behind the ship. Turner pulled up immediately, using his forward speed to gain all the altitude possible, turned and got back to the edge of the field, still pouring out that evil black smoke. Then he cut his switch, dipped her nose down, landed with a bounce and a bump, and rolled up to the line in a perfect stop. The crowd gave him a great cheer as he

climbed out of the oil-spattered machine, but it was a cheer of sympathy because he had lost the race after having been so far in the lead that had he continued he could not possibly have been overtaken.

²³· There was that story, but there was a better one too. Only the pilots on the field, all of them white around the lips and wiping from their faces a sweat not due to the oppressive summer heat, knew that they were looking at a man who from that time on, to use their own expression, was living on borrowed time. It isn't often when a Thompson Trophy racer with a landing speed of around eighty to ninety miles an hour goes haywire in the air, that the pilot is able to climb out of the cockpit and walk away from his machine. From the time of that first burst of smoke until the wheels touched the ground and stayed there, he was a hundred-to-one shot to live. To the initiated, those dreadful moments were laden with suspense and horror. Inside that contraption was a human being who any moment might be burned to a horrible, twisted cinder, or smashed into the ground beyond all recognition, a human being who was cool, gallant, and fighting desperately. Every man and woman on the field who had ever been in trouble in the air was living those awful seconds with him in terror and suspense. I, too, was able to experience it. That is what makes getting the "feel" of things distinctly worth while.

COMMENTARY AND QUESTIONS

This selection is a chapter from *Farewell to Sport*. As Paul Gallico tells you here, in 1922 he was a cub sports-writer. From then until 1938, when he published *Farewell to Sport*, he spent most of his time observing and writing about sports events.

1. Does the fact that Gallico alludes to events of the 1920's and 1930's make it difficult for you to understand his central point?
2. What is his central point?
3. Beginning with par. 7 Gallico discusses a series of sports. What are the sports? What relation does this discussion have to the central point?
4. Are the first six paragraphs essential to the writer's purpose? Does the first paragraph have anything to do with sports?
5. In the last two paragraphs Gallico contrasts two reactions to an event. Is this the same contrast that he has made in pars. 11 and 17 between the spectator and the player?
6. Is the style of this selection different, or should it be different, from that found on the average sports page? Consider, for example, this sentence in par. 8: "I watched him sag a spar boy with what seemed to be no more than a light cuff on the neck, or pat his face with what

looked like no more than a caressing stroke of his arm, and the fellow would come all apart at the seams and collapse in a useless heap, grinning vacuously or twitching strangely."

SUGGESTIONS FOR WRITING

1. Select a particular sport which you know well and make it the basis for a discussion of the difference between the player's and the spectator's point of view.
2. Draw on your experiences or observations outside the realm of sports for material to use in demonstrating the importance of "the feel." For example, you might like to contrast what you had thought about the life of a farmer with what you learned by working on a farm for a summer.
3. Have you ever been in danger because you were doing something for which you lacked training and experience? Write about your sensations during this incident, making sure that your account has a "point" to give it a principle of organization.

The Turtle

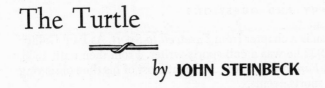

by JOHN STEINBECK

THE CONCRETE HIGHWAY was edged with a mat of tangled, broken, dry grass, and the grass heads were heavy with oat beards to catch on a dog's coat, and fox-tails to tangle in a horse's fetlocks, and clover burrs to fasten in sheep's wool; sleeping life waiting to be spread and dispersed, every seed armed with an appliance of dispersal, twisting darts and parachutes for the wind, little spears and balls of tiny thorns, and all waiting for animals and for the wind, for a man's trouser cuff or the hem of a woman's skirt, all passive but armed with appliances of activity, still, but each possessed of the anlage of movement.

2. The sun lay on the grass and warmed it, and in the shade under the grass the insects moved, ants and ant lions to set traps for them,

grasshoppers to jump into the air and flick their yellow wings for a second, sow bugs like little armadillos, plodding restlessly on many tender feet. And over the grass at the roadside a land turtle crawled, turning aside for nothing, dragging his high-domed shell over the grass. His hard legs and yellow-nailed feet threshed slowly through the grass, not really walking, but boosting and dragging his shell along. The barley beards slid off his shell, and the clover burrs fell on him and rolled to the ground. His horny beak was partly open, and his fierce, humorous eyes, under brows like fingernails, stared straight ahead. He came over the grass leaving a beaten trail behind him, and the hill, which was the highway embankment, reared up ahead of him. For a moment he stopped, his head held high. He blinked and looked up and down. At last he started to climb the embankment. Front clawed feet reached forward but did not touch. The hind feet kicked his shell along, and it scraped on the grass, and on the gravel. As the embankment grew steeper and steeper, the more frantic were the efforts of the land turtle. Pushing hind legs strained and slipped, boosting the shell along, and the horny head protruded as far as the neck could stretch. Little by little the shell slid up the embankment until at last a parapet cut straight across its line of march, the shoulder of the road, a concrete wall four inches high. As though they worked independently the hind legs pushed the shell against the wall. The head upraised and peered over the wall to the broad smooth plain of cement. Now the hands, braced on top of the wall, strained and lifted, and the shell came slowly up and rested its front end on the wall. For a moment the turtle rested. A red ant ran into the shell, into the soft skin inside the shell, and suddenly head and legs snapped in, and the armored tail clamped in sideways. The red ant was crushed between body and legs. And one head of wild oats was clamped into the shell by a front leg. For a long moment the turtle lay still, and then the neck crept out and the old humorous frowning eyes looked about and the legs and tail came out. The back legs went to work, straining like elephant legs, and the shell tipped to an angle so that the front legs could not reach the level cement plain. But higher and higher the hind legs boosted it, until at last the center of balance was reached, the front tipped down, the front legs scratched at the pavement, and it was up. But the head of wild oats was held by its stem around the front legs.

³· Now the going was easy, and all the legs worked, and the shell boosted along, waggling from side to side. A sedan driven by a forty-year old woman approached. She saw the turtle and swung to the right, off the highway, the wheels screamed and a cloud of dust boiled up. Two wheels lifted for a moment and then settled. The car skidded back onto the road, and went on, but more slowly. The turtle had jerked into its shell, but now it hurried on, for the highway was burning hot.

4. And now a light truck approached, and as it came near, the driver saw the turtle and swerved to hit it. His front wheel struck the edge of the shell, flipped the turtle like a tiddly-wink, spun it like a coin, and rolled it off the highway. The truck went back to its course along the right side. Lying on its back, the turtle was tight in its shell for a long time. But at last its legs waved in the air, reaching for something to pull it over. Its front foot caught a piece of quartz and little by little the shell pulled over and flopped upright. The wild oat head fell out and three of the spearhead seeds stuck in the ground. And as the turtle crawled on down the embankment, its shell dragged dirt over the seeds. The turtle entered a dust road and jerked itself along, drawing a wavy shallow trench in the dust with its shell. The old humorous eyes looked ahead, and the horny beak opened a little. His yellow toe nails slipped a fraction in the dust.

COMMENTARY AND QUESTIONS

This selection is the third chapter of *The Grapes of Wrath*. The chapters of this novel fall into two types: those containing the story proper, and those containing observations and commentaries about experiences and events relevant, directly or obliquely, to the story proper and its theme. This chapter may be interpreted to have a symbolic significance for the novel as a whole, but it also has a unity of its own.

1. In par. 2 Steinbeck presents a great many details about the turtle and its activities. By what simple method does he tie these details together? In this paragraph what obstacles or dangers does the turtle overcome?

2. What connection does par. 1 have with pars. 2 and 4? Could par. 3 be combined with one of the other paragraphs or be omitted entirely?

3. Does Steinbeck indicate what attitude he wants you to take toward the turtle? What, for example, would be the effect if this statement, in the next-to-last sentence of par. 4, were changed from "The old humorous eyes looked ahead" to "The tired old eyes drooped"?

4. Do you think Steinbeck based this selection on his observation of a particular turtle at a particular time?

SUGGESTION FOR WRITING

Here is a topic you might develop in a way similar to that used by Steinbeck in par. 3: a woman, packages in arms, getting on a bus. Whatever method you use for organizing details, remember that you can write accurately only about what you have observed carefully. If you haven't developed an eye for details, go out and look before you begin to write.

Cub-Pilot

by MARK TWAIN

I The Boys' Ambition

WHEN I WAS A BOY, there was but one permanent ambition among my comrades in our village[1] on the west bank of the Mississippi River. That was, to be a steamboatman. We had transient ambitions of other sorts, but they were only transient. When a circus came and went, it left us all burning to become clowns; the first negro minstrel show that ever came to our section left us all suffering to try that kind of life; now and then we had a hope that, if we lived and were good, God would permit us to be pirates. These ambitions faded out, each in its turn; but the ambition to be a steamboatman always remained.

2. Once a day a cheap, gaudy packet arrived upward from St. Louis, and another downward from Keokuk. Before these events, the day was glorious with expectancy; after them, the day was a dead and empty thing. Not only the boys, but the whole village, felt this. After all these years I can picture that old time to myself now, just as it was then: the white town drowsing in the sunshine of a summer's morning; the streets empty, or pretty nearly so; one or two clerks sitting in front of the Water Street stores, with their splint-bottomed chairs tilted back against the walls, chins on breasts, hats slouched over their faces, asleep—with shingle-shavings enough around to show what broke them down; a sow and a litter of pigs loafing along the sidewalk, doing a good business in watermelon rinds and seeds; two or three lonely little freight piles scattered about the "levee"; a pile of "skids" on the slope of the stone-paved wharf, and the fragrant town drunkard asleep in the shadow of them; two or three wood flats at the head of the wharf, but nobody to listen to the peaceful lapping of the wavelets against them; the great Mississippi, the majestic, the magnificent Mississippi, rolling its mile-wide tide along, shining in the sun; the dense forest away on the other side; the "point" above the town, and the "point" below, bounding the river-glimpse and turning it into a sort of sea, and withal a very still and brilliant and lonely one. Presently a film of dark smoke appears above one of those remote "points"; instantly a negro drayman, famous for his quick eye and pro-

From *Life on the Mississippi* by Mark Twain. Reprinted by permission of Harper & Row, Publishers, New York.

---

[1] Hannibal, Missouri.

digious voice, lifts up the cry, "S-t-e-a-m-boat a-comin'!" and the scene changes! The town drunkard stirs, the clerks wake up, a furious clatter of drays follows, every house and store pours out a human contribution, and all in a twinkling the dead town is alive and moving. Drays, carts, men, boys, all go hurrying from many quarters to a common center, the wharf. Assembled there, the people fasten their eyes upon the coming boat as upon a wonder they are seeing for the first time. And the boat *is* rather a handsome sight, too. She is long and sharp and trim and pretty; she has two tall, fancy-topped chimneys, with a gilded device of some kind swung between them; a fanciful pilot-house, all glass and "ginger-bread," perched on top of the "texas" deck behind them; the paddle-boxes are gorgeous with a picture or with gilded rays above the boat's name; the boiler-deck, the hurricane-deck, and the texas deck are fenced and ornamented with clean white railings; there is a flag gallantly flying from the jack-staff; the furnace doors are open and the fires glaring bravely; the upper decks are black with passengers; the captain stands by the big bell, calm, imposing, the envy of all; great volumes of the blackest smoke are rolling and tumbling out of the chimneys—a hus-banded grandeur created with a bit of pitch-pine just before arriving at a town; the crew are grouped on the forecastle; the broad stage is run far out over the port bow, and an envied deck-hand stands picturesquely on the end of it with a coil of rope in his hand; the pent steam is scream-ing through the gauge-cocks; the captain lifts his hand, a bell rings, the wheels stop; then they turn back, churning the water to foam, and the steamer is at rest. Then such a scramble as there is to get aboard, and to get ashore, and to take in freight and to discharge freight, all at one and the same time; and such a yelling and cursing as the mates facilitate it all with! Ten minutes later the steamer is under way again, with no flag on the jack-staff and no black smoke issuing from the chimneys. After ten more minutes the town is dead again, and the town drunkard asleep by the skids once more.

3. My father was a justice of the peace, and I supposed he possessed the power of life and death over all men, and could hang anybody that offended him. This was distinction enough for me as a general thing; but the desire to be a steamboatman kept intruding, nevertheless. I first wanted to be a cabin-boy, so that I could come out with a white apron on and shake a table-cloth over the side, where all my old com-rades could see me; later I thought I would rather be the deck-hand who stood on the end of the stage-plank with the coil of rope in his hand, because he was particularly conspicuous. But these were only day-dreams—they were too heavenly to be contemplated as real pos-sibilities. By and by one of our boys went away. He was not heard of

for a long time. At last he turned up as apprentice engineer or "striker" on a steamboat. This thing shook the bottom out of all my Sunday-school teachings. That boy had been notoriously worldly, and I just the reverse; yet he was exalted to this eminence, and I left in obscurity and misery. There was nothing generous about this fellow in his greatness. He would always manage to have a rusty bolt to scrub while his boat tarried at our town, and he would sit on the inside guard and scrub it, where we all could see him and envy him and loathe him. And whenever his boat was laid up he would come home and swell around the town in his blackest and greasiest clothes, so that nobody could help remembering that he was a steamboatman; and he used all sorts of steamboat technicalities in his talk, as if he were so used to them that he forgot common people could not understand them. He would speak of the "labboard" side of a horse in an easy, natural way that would make one wish he was dead. And he was always talking about "St. Looy" like an old citizen; he would refer casually to occasions when he was "coming down Fourth Street," or when he was "passing by the Planter's House," or when there was a fire and he took a turn on the brakes of "the old Big Missouri"; and then he would go on and lie about how many towns the size of ours were burned down there that day. Two or three of the boys had long been persons of consideration among us because they had been to St. Louis once and had a vague general knowledge of its wonders, but the day of their glory was over now. They lapsed into a humble silence, and learned to disappear when the ruthless "cub"-engineer approached. This fellow had money, too, and hair-oil. Also an ignorant silver watch and a showy brass watch-chain. He wore a leather belt and used no suspenders. If ever a youth was cordially admired and hated by his comrades, this one was. No girl could withstand his charms. He "cut out" every boy in the village. When his boat blew up at last, it diffused a tranquil contentment among us such as we had not known for months. But when he came home the next week, alive, renowned, and appeared in church all battered up and bandaged, a shining hero, stared at and wondered over by everybody, it seemed to us that the partiality of Providence for an undeserving reptile had reached a point where it was open to criticism.

4. This creature's career could produce but one result, and it speedily followed. Boy after boy managed to get on the river. The minister's son became an engineer. The doctor's and the postmaster's sons became "mud clerks"; the wholesale liquor dealer's son became a barkeeper on a boat; four sons of the chief merchant, and two sons of the county judge, became pilots. Pilot was the grandest position of all. The pilot, even in those days of trivial wages, had a princely salary—from a hun-

dred and fifty to two hundred and fifty dollars a month, and no board to pay. Two months of his wages would pay a preacher's salary for a year. Now some of us were left disconsolate. We could not get on the river— at least our parents would not let us.

5. So, by and by, I ran away. I said I would never come home again till I was a pilot and could come in glory. But somehow I could not manage it. I went meekly aboard a few of the boats that lay packed together like sardines at the long St. Louis wharf, and humbly inquired for the pilots, but got only a cold shoulder and short words from mates and clerks. I had to make the best of this sort of treatment for the time being, but I had comforting day-dreams of a future when I should be a great and honored pilot, with plenty of money, and could kill some of these mates and clerks and pay for them.

II *I Want to Be a Cub-Pilot*

6. Months afterward the hope within me struggled to a reluctant death, and I found myself without an ambition. But I was ashamed to go home. I was in Cincinnati, and I set to work to map out a new career. I had been reading about the recent exploration of the river Amazon by an expedition sent out by our government. It was said that the expedition, owing to difficulties, had not thoroughly explored a part of the country lying about the headwaters, some four thousand miles from the mouth of the river. It was only about fifteen hundred miles from Cincinnati to New Orleans, where I could doubtless get a ship. I had thirty dollars left; I would go and complete the exploration of the Amazon. This was all the thought I gave to the subject. I never was great in matters of detail. I packed my valise, and took passage on an ancient tub called the *Paul Jones,* for New Orleans. For the sum of sixteen dollars I had the scarred and tarnished splendors of "her" main saloon principally to myself, for she was not a creature to attract the eye of wiser travelers.

7. When we presently got under way and went poking down the broad Ohio, I became a new being, and the subject of my own admiration. I was a traveler! A word never had tasted so good in my mouth before. I had an exultant sense of being bound for mysterious lands and distant climes which I never have felt in so uplifting a degree since. I was in such a glorified condition that all ignoble feelings departed out of me, and I was able to look down and pity the untraveled with a compassion that had hardly a trace of contempt in it. Still, when we stopped at villages and wood-yards, I could not help lolling carelessly upon the railings of the boiler-deck to enjoy the envy of the country boys on the bank. If they did not seem to discover me, I presently sneezed to attract

their attention, or moved to a position where they could not help seeing me. And as soon as I knew they saw me I gaped and stretched, and gave other signs of being mightily bored with traveling.

8. I kept my hat off all the time, and stayed where the wind and the sun could strike me, because I wanted to get the bronzed and weather-beaten look of an old traveler. Before the second day was half gone I experienced a joy which filled me with the purest gratitude; for I saw that the skin had begun to blister and peel off my face and neck. I wished that the boys and girls at home could see me now.

9. We reached Louisville in time—at least the neighborhood of it. We stuck hard and fast on the rocks in the middle of the river, and lay there four days. I was now beginning to feel a strong sense of being a part of the boat's family, a sort of infant son to the captain and younger brother to the officers. There is no estimating the pride I took in this grandeur, or the affection that began to swell and grow in me for those people. I could not know how the lordly steamboatman scorns that sort of presumption in a mere landsman. I particularly longed to acquire the least trifle of notice from the big stormy mate, and I was on the alert for an opportunity to do him a service to that end. It came at last. The riotous pow-wow of setting a spar was going on down on the forecastle, and I went down there and stood around in the way—or mostly skipping out of it—till the mate suddenly roared a general order for somebody to bring him a capstan bar. I sprang to his side and said: "Tell me where it is—I'll fetch it!"

10. If a rag-picker had offered to do a diplomatic service for the Emperor of Russia, the monarch could not have been more astounded than the mate was. He even stopped swearing. He stood and stared down at me. It took him ten seconds to scrape his disjointed remains together again. Then he said impressively: "Well, if this don't beat h——l!" and turned to his work with the air of a man who had been confronted with a problem too abstruse for solution.

11. I crept away, and courted solitude for the rest of the day. I did not go to dinner; I stayed away from supper until everybody else had finished. I did not feel so much like a member of the boat's family now as before. However, my spirits returned, in instalments, as we pursued our way down the river. I was sorry I hated the mate so, because it was no[t] in (young) human nature not to admire him. He was huge and muscular, his face was bearded and whiskered all over; he had a red woma[n] and a blue woman tattooed on his right arm—one on each side of a bl[ue] anchor with a red rope to it; and in the matter of profanity he was s[ub]lime. When he was getting out cargo at a landing, I was always whe[re I] could see and hear. He felt all the majesty of his great position, and m[ade]

the world feel it, too. When he gave even the simplest order, he discharged it like a blast of lightning, and sent a long, reverberating peal of profanity thundering after it. I could not help contrasting the way in which the average landsman would give an order with the mate's way of doing it. If the landsman should wish the gang-plank moved a foot farther forward, he would probably say: "James, or William, one of you push that plank forward, please"; but put the mate in his place, and he would roar out: "Here, now, start that gang-plank for'ard! Lively, now! *What* 're you about! *snatch* it! *snatch* it! There! there! Aft again! aft again! Don't you hear me? Dash it to dash! are you going to *sleep* over it! 'Vast heaving. 'Vast heaving, I tell you! Going to heave it clear astern? WHERE 're you going with that barrel! *for'ard* with it 'fore I make you swallow it, you dash-dash-dash-*dashed* split between a tired mud-turtle and a crippled hearse-horse!"

12. I wished I could talk like that.

13. When the soreness of my adventure with the mate had somewhat worn off, I began timidly to make up to the humblest official connected with the boat—the night watchman. He snubbed my advances at first, but I presently ventured to offer him a new chalk pipe, and that softened him. So he allowed me to sit with him by the big bell on the hurricane-deck, and in time he melted into conversation. He could not well have helped it, I hung with such homage on his words and so plainly showed that I felt honored by his notice. He told me the names of dim capes and shadowy islands as we glided by them in the solemnity of the night, under the winking stars, and by and by got to talking about himself. He seemed over-sentimental for a man whose salary was six dollars a week —or rather he might have seemed so to an older person than I. But I drank in his words hungrily, and with a faith that might have moved mountains if it had been applied judiciously. What was it to me that he was soiled and seedy and fragrant with gin? What was it to me that his grammar was bad, his construction worse, and his profanity so void of art that it was an element of weakness rather than strength in his conversation? He was a wronged man, a man who had seen trouble, and that was enough for me. As he mellowed into his plaintive history his tears dripped upon the lantern in his lap, and I cried, too, from sympathy. He said he was the son of an English nobleman—either an earl or an alderman, he could not remember which, but believed was both; his father, the nobleman, loved him, but his mother hated him from the cradle; and so while he was still a little boy he was sent to "one of them old, ancient colleges"—he couldn't remember which; and by and by his father died and his mother seized the property and "shook" him, as he phrased it. After his mother shook him, members of the nobility with whom he was

acquainted used their influence to get him the position of "loblolly-boy in a ship"; and from that point my watchman threw off all trammels of date and locality and branched out into a narrative that bristled all along with incredible adventures; a narrative that was so reeking with bloodshed, and so crammed with hair-breadth escapes and the most engaging and unconscious personal villainies, that I sat speechless, enjoying, shuddering, wondering, worshiping.

14. It was a sore blight to find out afterward that he was a low, vulgar, ignorant, sentimental, half-witted humbug, an untraveled native of the wilds of Illinois, who had absorbed wildcat literature and appropriated its marvels, until in time he had woven odds and ends of the mess into this yarn, and then gone on telling it to fledglings like me, until he had come to believe it himself.

III   A Cub-Pilot's Experience

15. What with lying on the rocks four days at Louisville, and some other delays, the poor old *Paul Jones* fooled away about two weeks in making the voyage from Cincinnati to New Orleans. This gave me a chance to get acquainted with one of the pilots, and he taught me how to steer the boat, and thus made the fascination of river life more potent than ever for me.

16. It also gave me a chance to get acquainted with a youth who had taken deck passage—more's the pity; for he easily borrowed six dollars of me on a promise to return to the boat and pay it back to me the day after we should arrive. But he probably died or forgot, for he never came. It was doubtless the former, since he had said his parents were wealthy, and he only traveled deck passage because it was cooler.[2]

17. I soon discovered two things. One was that a vessel would not be likely to sail for the mouth of the Amazon under ten or twelve years; and the other was that the nine or ten dollars still left in my pocket would not suffice for so impossible an exploration as I had planned, even if I could afford to wait for a ship. Therefore it followed that I must contrive a new career. The *Paul Jones* was now bound for St. Louis. I planned a siege against my pilot, and at the end of three hard days he surrendered. He agreed to teach me the Mississippi River from New Orleans to St. Louis for five hundred dollars, payable out of the first wages I should receive after graduating. I entered upon the small enterprise of "learning" twelve or thirteen hundred miles of the great Mississippi River with the easy confidence of my time of life. If I had really

---

[2] "Deck" passage—*i. e.,* steerage passage.

known what I was about to require of my faculties, I should not have
had the courage to begin. I supposed that all a pilot had to do was to
keep his boat in the river, and I did not consider that that could be much
of a trick, since it was so wide.

18. That boat backed out from New Orleans at four in the afternoon,
and it was "our watch" until eight. Mr. Bixby, my chief, "straightened
her up," plowed her along past the sterns of the other boats that lay at
the Levee, and then said, "Here, take her; shave those steamships as
close as you'd peel an apple." I took the wheel, and my heartbeat fluttered up into the hundreds; for it seemed to me that we were about to
scrape the side off every ship in the line, we were so close. I held my
breath and began to claw the boat away from the danger; and I had my
own opinion of the pilot who had known no better than to get us into
such peril, but I was too wise to express it. In half a minute I had a wide
margin of safety intervening between the *Paul Jones* and the ships; and
within ten seconds more I was set aside in disgrace, and Mr. Bixby was
going into danger again and flaying me alive with abuse of my cowardice. I was stung, but I was obliged to admire the easy confidence with
which my chief loafed from side to side of his wheel, and trimmed the
ships so closely that disaster seemed ceaselessly imminent. When he
had cooled a little he told me that the easy water was close ashore and
the current outside, and therefore we must hug the bank, up-stream, to
get the benefit of the former, and stay well out, down-stream, to take
advantage of the latter. In my own mind I resolved to be a down-stream
pilot and leave the up-streaming to people dead to prudence.

19. Now and then Mr. Bixby called my attention to certain things.
Said he, "This is Six-Mile Point." I assented. It was pleasant enough information, but I could not see the bearing of it. I was not conscious that
it was a matter of any interest to me. Another time he said, "This is Nine-
Mile Point." Later he said, "This is Twelve-Mile Point." They were all
about level with the water's edge; they all looked about alike to me; they
were monotonously unpicturesque. I hoped Mr. Bixby would change the
subject. But no; he would crowd up around a point, hugging the shore
with affection, and then say: "The slack water ends here, abreast this
bunch of China trees; now we cross over." So he crossed over. He gave
me the wheel once or twice, but I had no luck. I either came near chipping off the edge of a sugar-plantation, or I yawed too far from shore,
and so dropped back into disgrace again and got abused.

20. The watch was ended at last, and we took supper and went to bed.
At midnight the glare of a lantern shone in my eyes, and the night
watchman said:

21. "Come, turn out!"

²². And then he left. I could not understand this extraordinary procedure; so I presently gave up trying to, and dozed off to sleep. Pretty soon the watchman was back again, and this time he was gruff. I was annoyed. I said:

²³. "What do you want to come bothering around here in the middle of the night for? Now, as like as not, I'll not get to sleep again to-night."

²⁴. The watchman said:

²⁵. "Well, if this ain't good, I'm blessed."

²⁶. The "off-watch" was just turning in, and I heard some brutal laughter from them, and such remarks as "Hello, watchman! ain't the new cub turned out yet? He's delicate, likely. Give him some sugar in a rag, and send for the chambermaid to sing 'Rock-a-by Baby,' to him."

²⁷. About this time Mr. Bixby appeared on the scene. Something like a minute later I was climbing the pilot-house steps with some of my clothes on and the rest in my arms. Mr. Bixby was close behind, commenting. Here was something fresh—this thing of getting up in the middle of the night to go to work. It was a detail in piloting that had never occurred to me at all. I knew that boats ran all night, but somehow I had never happened to reflect that somebody had to get up out of a warm bed to run them. I began to fear that piloting was not quite so romantic as I had imagined it was; there was something very real and worklike about this new phase of it.

²⁸. It was a rather dingy night, although a fair number of stars were out. The big mate was at the wheel, and he had the old tub pointed at a star and was holding her straight up the middle of the river. The shores on either hand were not much more than half a mile apart, but they seemed wonderfully far away and ever so vague and indistinct. The mate said:

²⁹. "We've got to land at Jones's plantation, sir."

³⁰. The vengeful spirit in me exulted. I said to myself, "I wish you joy of your job, Mr. Bixby; you'll have a good time finding Mr. Jones's plantation such a night as this; and I hope you never *will* find it as long as you live."

³¹. Mr. Bixby said to the mate:

³². "Upper end of the plantation, or the lower?"

³³. "Upper."

³⁴. "I can't do it. The stumps there are out of water at this stage. It's no great distance to the lower, and you'll have to get along with that."

³⁵. "All right, sir. If Jones don't like it, he'll have to lump it, I reckon."

³⁶. And then the mate left. My exultation began to cool and my wonder to come up. Here was a man who not only proposed to find this plantation on such a night, but to find either end of it you preferred. I

dreadfully wanted to ask a question, but I was carrying about as many short answers as my cargo-room would admit of, so I held my peace. All I desired to ask Mr. Bixby was the simple question whether he was ass enough to really imagine he was going to find that plantation on a night when all plantations were exactly alike and all of the same color. But I held in. I used to have fine inspirations of prudence in those days.

³⁷· Mr. Bixby made for the shore and soon was scraping it, just the same as if it had been daylight. And not only that, but singing:

"Father in heaven, the day is declining," etc.

It seemed to me that I had put my life in the keeping of a peculiarly reckless outcast. Presently he turned on me and said:

³⁸· "What's the name of the first point above New Orleans?"

³⁹· I was gratified to be able to answer promptly, and I did. I said I didn't know.

⁴⁰· "Don't *know?*"

⁴¹· This manner jolted me. I was down at the foot again, in a moment. But I had to say just what I had said before.

⁴²· "Well, you're a smart one!" said Mr. Bixby. "What's the name of the *next* point?"

⁴³· Once more I didn't know.

⁴⁴· "Well, this beats anything. Tell me the name of *any* point or place I told you."

⁴⁵· I studied awhile and decided that I couldn't.

⁴⁶· "Look here! What do you start out from, above Twelve-Mile Point, to cross over?"

⁴⁷· "I—I—don't know."

⁴⁸· "You—you—don't know?" mimicking my drawling manner of speech. "What *do* you know?"

⁴⁹· "I—I—nothing, for certain."

⁵⁰· "By the great Caesar's ghost, I believe you! You're the stupidest dunderhead I ever saw or ever heard of, so help me Moses! The idea of *you* being a pilot—*you!* Why, you don't know enough to pilot a cow down a lane."

⁵¹· Oh, but his wrath was up! He was a nervous man, and he shuffled from one side of his wheel to the other as if the floor was hot. He would boil awhile to himself, and then overflow and scald me again.

⁵²· "Look here! What do you suppose I told you the names of those points for?"

⁵³· I tremblingly considered a moment, and then the devil of temptation provoked me to say:

⁵⁴· "Well to—to—be entertaining, I thought."

⁵⁵· This was a red rag to the bull. He raged and stormed so (he was

crossing the river at the time) that I judged it made him blind, because
he ran over the steering-oar of a trading-scow. Of course the traders
sent up a volley of red-hot profanity. Never was a man so grateful as
Mr. Bixby was; because he was brimful, and here were subjects who
could *talk back*. He threw open a window, thrust his head out, and such
an irruption followed as I never had heard before. The fainter and farther away the scowmen's curses drifted, the higher Mr. Bixby lifted his
voice and the weightier his adjectives grew. When he closed the window
he was empty. You could have drawn a seine through his system and not
caught curses enough to disturb your mother with. Presently he said to
me in the gentlest way:

56. "My boy, you must get a little memorandum-book; and every time
I tell you a thing, put it down right away. There's only one way to be
a pilot, and that is to get this entire river by heart. You have to know
it just like A B C."

57. That was a dismal revelation to me; for my memory was never
loaded with anything but blank cartridges. However, I did not feel discouraged long. I judged that it was best to make some allowances, for
doubtless Mr. Bixby was "stretching." Presently he pulled a rope and
struck a few strokes on the big bell. The stars were all gone now, and
the night was as black as ink. I could hear the wheels churn along the
bank, but I was not entirely certain that I could see the shore. The voice
of the invisible watchman called up from the hurricane-deck:

58. "What's this, sir?"

59. "Jones's plantation."

60. I said to myself, "I wish I might venture to offer a small bet that
it isn't." But I did not chirp. I only waited to see. Mr. Bixby handled the
engine-bells, and in due time the boat's nose came to the land, a torch
glowed from the forecastle, a man skipped ashore, a darky's voice on the
bank said: "Gimme de k'yarpet-bag, Mass' Jones," and the next moment
we were standing up the river again, all serene. I reflected deeply
awhile, and then said—but not aloud—"Well, the finding of that plantation was the luckiest accident that ever happened; but it couldn't happen again in a hundred years." And I fully believed it *was* an accident,
too.

61. By the time we had gone seven or eight hundred miles up the
river, I had learned to be a tolerably plucky up-stream steersman, in daylight; and before we reached St. Louis I had made a trifle of progress in
night work, but only a trifle. I had a note-book that fairly bristled with
the names of towns, "points," bars, islands, bends, reaches, etc.; but the
information was to be found only in the note-book—none of it was in my
head. It made my heart ache to think I had only got half of the river set
down; for as our watch was four hours off and four hours on, day and

night, there was a long four-hour gap in my book for every time I had
slept since the voyage began.

62. My chief was presently hired to go on a big New Orleans boat,
and I packed my satchel and went with him. She was a grand affair.
When I stood in her pilot-house I was so far above the water that I
seemed perched on a mountain; and her decks stretched so far away,
fore and aft, below me, that I wondered how I could ever have considered the little *Paul Jones* a large craft. There were other differences, too.
The *Paul Jones's* pilot-house was a cheap, dingy, battered rattle-trap,
cramped for room; but here was a sumptuous glass temple; room enough
to have a dance in; showy red and gold window-curtains; an imposing
sofa; leather cushions and a back to the high bench where visiting pilots
sit, to spin yarns and "look at the river"; bright, fanciful "cuspidores,"
instead of a broad wooden box filled with sawdust; nice new oilcloth on
the floor; a hospitable big stove for winter; a wheel as high as my head,
costly with inlaid work; a wire tiller-rope; bright brass knobs for the
bells; and a tidy, white-aproned, black "texas-tender," to bring up tarts
and ices and coffee during mid-watch, day and night. Now this was
"something like"; and so I began to take heart once more to believe that
piloting was a romantic sort of occupation after all. The moment we
were under way I began to prowl about the great steamer and fill myself
with joy. She was as clean and as dainty as a drawing-room; when I
looked down her long, gilded saloon, it was like gazing through a splendid tunnel; she had an oil-picture, by some gifted sign-painter, on every
stateroom door; she glittered with no end of prism-fringed chandeliers;
the clerk's office was elegant, the bar was marvelous, and the barkeeper
had been barbered and upholstered at incredible cost. The boiler-deck
(*i. e.*, the second story of the boat, so to speak) was as spacious as a
church, it seemed to me; so with the forecastle; and there was no pitiful
handful of deck-hands, firemen, and roustabouts down there, but a whole
battalion of men. The fires were fiercely glaring from a long row of furnaces, and over them were eight huge boilers! This was unutterable
pomp. The mighty engines—but enough of this. I had never felt so fine
before. And when I found that the regiment of natty servants respectfully "sir'd" me, my satisfaction was complete.

IV *Perplexing Lessons*

63. At the end of what seemed a tedious while, I had managed to
pack my head full of islands, towns, bars, "points," and bends; and a
curiously inanimate mass of lumber it was, too. However, inasmuch as I
could shut my eyes and reel off a good long string of these names with-

out leaving out more than ten miles of river in every fifty, I began to
feel that I could take a boat down to New Orleans if I could make her
skip those little gaps. But of course my complacency could hardly get
start enough to lift my nose a trifle into the air, before Mr. Bixby would
think of something to fetch it down again. One day he turned on me
suddenly with this settler:

⁶⁴· "What is the shape of Walnut Bend?"

⁶⁵· He might as well have asked me my grandmother's opinion of
protoplasm. I reflected respectfully, and then said I didn't know it had
any particular shape. My gun-powdery chief went off with a bang, of
course, and then went on loading and firing until he was out of adjectives.

⁶⁶· I had learned long ago that he only carried just so many rounds of
ammunition, and was sure to subside into a very placable and even re-
morseful old smoothbore as soon as they were all gone. That word "old"
is merely affectionate; he was not more than thirty-four. I waited. By and
by he said:

⁶⁷· "My boy, you've got to know the *shape* of the river perfectly. It is
all there is left to steer by on a very dark night. Everything else is
blotted out and gone. But mind you, it hasn't the same shape in the night
that it has in the daytime."

⁶⁸· "How on earth am I ever going to learn it, then?"

⁶⁹· "How do you follow a hall at home in the dark? Because you know
the shape of it. You can't see it."

⁷⁰· "Do you mean to say that I've got to know all the million trifling
variations of shape in the banks of this interminable river as well as I
know the shape of the front hall at home?"

⁷¹· "On my honor, you've got to know them *better* than any man ever
did know the shapes of the halls in his own house."

⁷²· "I wish I was dead!"

⁷³· "Now I don't want to discourage you, but—"

⁷⁴· "Well, pile it on me; I might as well have it now as another time."

⁷⁵· "You see, this has got to be learned; there isn't any getting around
it. A clear starlight night throws such heavy shadows that, if you didn't
know the shape of a shore perfectly, you would claw away from every
bunch of timber, because you would take the black shadow of it for a
solid cape; and you see you would be getting scared to death every fifteen minutes by the watch. You would be fifty yards from shore all the
time when you ought to be within fifty feet of it. You can't see a snag in
one of those shadows, but you know exactly where it is, and the shape of
the river tells you when you are coming to it. Then there's your pitch-
dark night; the river is a very different shape on a pitch-dark night from
what it is on a star-light night. All shores seem to be straight lines, then,

and mighty dim ones, too; and you'd *run* them for straight lines, only you know better. You boldly drive your boat right into what seems to be a solid, straight wall (you knowing very well that in reality there is a curve there), and that wall falls back and makes way for you. Then there's your gray mist. You take a night when there's one of these grisly, drizzly, gray mists, and then there isn't *any* particular shape to a shore. A gray mist would tangle the head of the oldest man that ever lived. Well, then, different kinds of *moonlight* change the shape of the river in different ways. You see—"

76. "Oh, don't say any more, please! Have I got to learn the shape of the river according to all these five hundred thousand different ways? If I tried to carry all that cargo in my head it would make me stoop-shouldered."

77. "*No!* you only learn *the* shape of the river; and you learn it with such absolute certainty that you can always steer by the shape that's *in your head,* and never mind the one that's before your eyes."

78. "Very well, I'll try it; but, after I have learned it, can I depend on it? Will it keep the same form and not go fooling around?"

79. Before Mr. Bixby could answer, Mr. W. came in to take the watch, and he said:

80. "Bixby, you'll have to look out for President's Island, and all that country clear away up above the Old Hen and Chickens. The banks are caving and the shape of the shores changing like everything. Why, you wouldn't know the point above 40. You can go up inside the old syca-more snag, now."[3]

81. So that question was answered. Here were leagues of shore chang-ing shape. My spirits were down in the mud again. Two things seemed pretty apparent to me. One was, that in order to be a pilot a man had got to learn more than any one man ought to be allowed to know; and the other was, that he must learn it all over again in a different way every twenty-four hours.

82. That night we had the watch until twelve. Now it was an ancient river custom for the two pilots to chat a bit when the watch changed. While the relieving pilot put on his gloves and lit his cigar, his partner, the retiring pilot, would say something like this:

83. "I judge the upper bar is making down a little at Hale's Point; had quarter twain with the lower lead and mark twain[4] with the other."

84. "Yes, I thought it was making down a little, last trip. Meet any boats?"

---

[3] It may not be necessary, but still it can do no harm to explain that "inside" means between the snag and the shore.

[4] Two fathoms. Quarter twain is 2¼ fathoms, 13½ feet. Mark three is three fathoms.

^{85.} "Met one abreast the head of 21, but she was away over hugging the bar, and I couldn't make her out entirely. I took her for the *Sunny South*—hadn't any skylights forward of the chimneys."

^{86.} And so on. And as the relieving pilot took the wheel his partner[5] would mention that we were in such-and-such a bend, and say we were abreast of such-and-such a man's woodyard or plantation. This was courtesy; I supposed it was *necessity*. But Mr. W. came on watch full twelve minutes late on this particular night—a tremendous breach of etiquette; in fact, it is the unpardonable sin among pilots. So Mr. Bixby gave him no greeting whatever, but simply surrendered the wheel and marched out of the pilot-house without a word. I was appalled; it was a villainous night for blackness, we were in a particularly wide and blind part of the river, where there was no shape or substance to anything, and it seemed incredible that Mr. Bixby should have left that poor fellow to kill the boat, trying to find out where he was. But I resolved that I would stand by him anyway. He should find that he was not wholly friendless. So I stood around, and waited to be asked where we were. But Mr. W. plunged on serenely through the solid firmament of black cats that stood for an atmosphere, and never opened his mouth. "Here is a proud devil!" thought I; "here is a limb of Satan that would rather send us all to destruction than put himself under obligations to me, because I am not yet one of the salt of the earth and privileged to snub captains and lord it over everything dead and alive in a steamboat." I presently climbed up on the bench; I did not think it was safe to go to sleep while this lunatic was on watch.

^{87.} However, I must have gone to sleep in the course of time, because the next thing I was aware of was the fact that day was breaking, Mr. W. gone, and Mr. Bixby at the wheel again. So it was four o'clock and all well—but me; I felt like a skinful of dry bones, and all of them trying to ache at once.

^{88.} Mr. Bixby asked me what I had stayed up there for. I confessed that it was to do Mr. W. a benevolence—tell him where he was. It took five minutes for the entire preposterousness of the thing to filter into Mr. Bixby's system, and then I judge it filled him nearly up to the chin; because he paid me a compliment—and not much of a one either. He said:

^{89.} "Well, taking you by and large, you do seem to be more different kinds of an ass than any creature I ever saw before. What did you suppose he wanted to know for?"

^{90.} I said I thought it might be a convenience to him.

^{91.} "Convenience! D——nation! Didn't I tell you that a man's got to know the river in the night the same as he'd know his own front hall?"

---

[5] "Partner" is technical for "the other pilot."

⁹². "Well, I can follow the front hall in the dark if I know it *is* the front hall; but suppose you set me down in the middle of it in the dark and not tell me which hall it is; how am *I* to know?"

⁹³. "Well, you've *got* to, on the river!"

⁹⁴. "All right. Then I'm glad I never said anything to Mr. W."

⁹⁵. "I should say so! Why, he'd have slammed you through the window and utterly ruined a hundred dollars' worth of window-sash and stuff."

⁹⁶. I was glad this damage had been saved, for it would have made me unpopular with the owners. They always hated anybody who had the name of being careless and injuring things.

⁹⁷. I went to work now to learn the shape of the river; and of all the eluding and ungraspable objects that ever I tried to get mind or hands on, that was the chief. I would fasten my eyes upon a sharp, wooded point that projected far into the river some miles ahead of me, and go to laboriously photographing its shape upon my brain; and just as I was beginning to succeed to my satisfaction, we would draw up toward it and the exasperating thing would begin to melt away and fold back into the bank! If there had been a conspicuous dead tree standing upon the very point of the cape, I would find that tree inconspicuously merged into the general forest, and occupying the middle of a straight shore, when I got abreast of it! No prominent hill would stick to its shape long enough for me to make up my mind what its form really was, but it was as dissolving and changeful as if it had been a mountain of butter in the hottest corner of the tropics. Nothing ever had the same shape when I was coming down-stream that it had borne when I went up. I mentioned these little difficulties to Mr. Bixby. He said:

⁹⁸. "That's the very main virtue of the thing. If the shapes didn't change every three seconds they wouldn't be of any use. Take this place where we are now, for instance. As long as that hill over yonder is only one hill, I can boom right along the way I'm going; but the moment it splits at the top and forms a V, I know I've got to scratch to starboard in a hurry, or I'll bang this boat's brains out against a rock; and then the moment one of the prongs of the V swings behind the other, I've got to waltz to larboard again, or I'll have a misunderstanding with a snag that would snatch the keelson out of this steamboat as neatly as if it were a sliver in your hand. If that hill didn't change its shape on bad nights there would be an awful steamboat graveyard around here inside of a year."

⁹⁹. It was plain that I had got to learn the shape of the river in all the different ways that could be thought of—upside down, wrong end first, inside out, fore-and-aft, and "thort-ships"—and then know what to do on

gray nights when it hadn't any shape at all. So I set about it. In the course
of time I began to get the best of this knotty lesson, and my self-compla-
cency moved to the front once more. Mr. Bixby was all fixed, and ready
to start it to the rear again. He opened on me after this fashion:

100. "How much water did we have in the middle crossing at Hole-in-
the-Wall, trip before last?"

101. I considered this an outrage. I said:

102. "Every trip, down and up, the leadsmen are singing through that
tangled place for three-quarters of an hour on a stretch. How do you
reckon I can remember such a mess as that?"

103. "My boy, you've got to remember it. You've got to remember the
exact spot and the exact marks the boat lay in when we had the shoalest
water, in every one of the five hundred shoal places between St. Louis
and New Orleans; and you mustn't get the shoal soundings and marks of
one trip mixed up with the shoal soundings and marks of another, either,
for they're not often twice alike. You must keep them separate."

104. When I came to myself again, I said:

105. "When I get so that I can do that, I'll be able to raise the dead,
and then I won't have to pilot a steamboat to make a living. I want to
retire from this business. I want a slush-bucket and a brush; I'm only fit
for a roustabout. I haven't got brains enough to be a pilot; and if I had I
wouldn't have strength enough to carry them around, unless I went on
crutches."

106. "Now drop that! When I say I'll learn[6] a man the river, I mean it.
And you can depend on it, I'll learn him or kill him."

V   *Continued Perplexities*

107. There was no use in arguing with a person like this. I promptly
put such a strain on my memory that by and by even the shoal water and
the countless crossing-marks began to stay with me. But the result was
just the same. I never could more than get one knotty thing learned before another presented itself. Now I had often seen pilots gazing at the
water and pretending to read it as if it were a book; but it was a book
that told me nothing. A time came at last, however, when Mr. Bixby
seemed to think me far enough advanced to bear a lesson on water-
reading. So he began:

108. "Do you see that long, slanting line on the face of the water? Now,
that's a reef. Moreover, it's a bluff reef. There is a solid sand-bar under it
that is nearly as straight up and down as the side of a house. There is

---

[6] "Teach" is not in the river vocabulary.

plenty of water close up to it, but mighty little on top of it. If you were to hit it you would knock the boat's brains out. Do you see where the line fringes out at the upper end and begins to fade away?"

109. "Yes, sir."

110. "Well, that is a low place; that is the head of the reef. You can climb over there, and not hurt anything. Cross over, now, and follow along close under the reef—easy water there—not much current."

111. I followed the reef along till I approached the fringed end. Then Mr. Bixby said:

112. "Now get ready. Wait till I give the word. She won't want to mount the reef; a boat hates shoal water. Stand by—wait—*wait*—keep her well in hand. *Now* cramp her down! Snatch her! snatch her!"

113. He seized the other side of the wheel and helped to spin it around until it was hard down, and then we held it so. The boat resisted, and refused to answer for a while, and next she came surging to starboard, mounted the reef, and sent a long, angry ridge of water foaming away from her bows.

114. "Now watch her; watch her like a cat, or she'll get away from you. When she fights strong and the tiller slips a little, in a jerky, greasy sort of way, let up on her a trifle; it is the way she tells you at night that the water is too shoal; but keep edging her up, little by little, toward the point. You are well up on the bar now; there is a bar under every point, because the water that comes down around it forms an eddy and allows the sediment to sink. Do you see those fine lines on the face of the water that branch out like the ribs of a fan? Well, those are little reefs; you want to just miss the ends of them, but run them pretty close. Now look out—look out! Don't you crowd that slick, greasy-looking place; there ain't nine feet there; she won't stand it. She begins to smell it; look sharp, I tell you! Oh, blazes, there you go! Stop the starboard wheel! Quick! Ship up to back! Set her back!"

115. The engine bells jingled and the engines answered promptly, shooting white columns of steam far aloft out of the 'scape-pipes, but it was too late. The boat had "smelt" the bar in good earnest; the foamy ridges that radiated from her bows suddenly disappeared, a great dead swell came rolling forward, and swept ahead of her, she careened far over to larboard, and went tearing away toward the shore as if she were about scared to death. We were a good mile from where we ought to have been when we finally got the upper hand of her again.

116. During the afternoon watch the next day, Mr. Bixby asked me if I knew how to run the next few miles. I said:

117. "Go inside the first snag above the point, outside the next one, start out from the lower end of Higgins's woodyard, make a square crossing, and—"

[118.] "That's all right. I'll be back before you close up on the next point."

[119.] But he wasn't. He was still below when I rounded it and entered upon a piece of the river which I had some misgivings about. I did not know that he was hiding behind a chimney to see how I would perform. I went gaily along, getting prouder and prouder, for he had never left the boat in my sole charge such a length of time before. I even got to "setting" her and letting the wheel go entirely, while I vaingloriously turned my back and inspected the stern marks and hummed a tune, a sort of easy indifference which I had prodigiously admired in Bixby and other great pilots. Once I inspected rather long, and when I faced to the front again my heart flew into my mouth so suddenly that if I hadn't clapped my teeth together I should have lost it. One of those frightful bluff reefs was stretching its deadly length right across our bows! My head was gone in a moment; I did not know which end I stood on; I gasped and could not get my breath; I spun the wheel down with such rapidity that it wove itself together like a spider's web; the boat answered and turned square away from the reef, but the reef followed her! I fled, but still it followed, still it kept—right across my bows! I never looked to see where I was going, I only fled. The awful crash was imminent. Why didn't that villain come? If I committed the crime of ringing a bell I might get thrown overboard. But better that than kill the boat. So in blind desperation, I started such a rattling "shivaree" down below as never had astounded an engineer in this world before, I fancy. Amidst the frenzy of the bells the engines began to back and fill in a curious way, and my reason forsook its throne—we were about to crash into the woods on the other side of the river. Just then Mr. Bixby stepped calmly into view on the hurricane-deck. My soul went out to him in gratitude. My distress vanished; I would have felt safe on the brink of Niagara with Mr. Bixby on the hurricane-deck. He blandly and sweetly took his toothpick out of his mouth between his fingers, as if it were a cigar— we were just in the act of climbing an overhanging big tree, and the passengers were scudding astern like rats—and lifted up these commands to me ever so gently:

[120.] "Stop the starboard! Stop the larboard! Set her back on both!"

[121.] The boat hesitated, halted, pressed her nose among the boughs a critical instant, then reluctantly began to back away.

[122.] "Stop the larboard! Come ahead on it! Stop the starboard! Come ahead on it! Point her for the bar!"

[123.] I sailed away as serenely as a summer's morning. Mr. Bixby came in and said, with mock simplicity:

[124.] "When you have a hail, my boy, you ought to tap the big bell three times before you land, so that the engineers can get ready."

125. I blushed under the sarcasm, and said I hadn't had any hail.

126. "Ah! Then it was for wood, I suppose. The officer of the watch will tell you when he wants to wood up."

127. I went on consuming, and said I wasn't after wood.

128. "Indeed? Why, what could you want over here in the bend, then? Did you ever know of a boat following a bend up-stream at this stage of the river?"

129. "No, sir—and *I* wasn't trying to follow it. I was getting away from a bluff reef."

130. "No, it wasn't a bluff reef; there isn't one within three miles of where you were."

131. "But I saw it. It was as bluff as that one yonder."

132. "Just about. Run over it!"

133. "Do you give it as an order?"

134. "Yes. Run over it!"

135. "If I don't, I wish I may die."

136. "All right; I am taking the responsibility."

137. I was just as anxious to kill the boat, now, as I had been to save it before. I impressed my orders upon my memory, to be used at the inquest, and made a straight break for the reef. As it disappeared under our bows I held my breath; but we slid over it like oil.

138. "Now, don't you see the difference? It wasn't anything but a *wind* reef. The wind does that."

139. "So I see. But it is exactly like a bluff reef. How am I ever going to tell them apart?"

140. "I can't tell you. It is an instinct. By and by you will just naturally *know* one from the other, but you never will be able to explain why or how you know them apart."

141. It turned out to be true. The face of the water, in time, became a wonderful book—a book that was a dead language to the uneducated passenger, but which told its mind to me without reserve, delivering its most cherished secrets as clearly as if it uttered them with a voice. And it was not a book to be read once and thrown aside, for it had a new story to tell every day. Throughout the long twelve hundred miles there was never a page that was void of interest, never one that you could leave unread without loss, never one that you would want to skip, thinking you could find higher enjoyment in some other thing. There never was so wonderful a book written by man; never one whose interest was so absorbing, so unflagging, so sparklingly renewed with every reperusal. The passenger who could not read it was charmed with a peculiar sort of faint dimple on its surface (on the rare occasions when he did not overlook it altogether); but to the pilot that was an *italicized* pas-

sage; indeed, it was more than that, it was a legend of the largest capitals, with a string of shouting exclamation-points at the end of it, for it
meant that a wreck or a rock was buried there that could tear the life
out of the strongest vessel that ever floated. It is the faintest and simplest
expression the water ever makes, and the most hideous to a pilot's eye.
In truth, the passenger who could not read this book saw nothing but all
manner of pretty pictures in it, painted by the sun and shaded by the
clouds, whereas to the trained eye these were not pictures at all, but
the grimmest and most dead-earnest of reading-matter.

142. Now when I had mastered the language of this water, and had
come to know every trifling feature that bordered the great river as
familiarly as I knew the letters of the alphabet, I had made a valuable
acquisition. But I had lost something, too. I had lost something which
could never be restored to me while I lived. All the grace, the beauty,
the poetry, had gone out of the majestic river! I still kept in mind a certain wonderful sunset which I witnessed when steamboating was new
to me. A broad expanse of the river was turned to blood; in the middle
distance the red hue brightened into gold, through which a solitary log
came floating, black and conspicuous; in one place a long, slanting mark
lay sparkling upon the water; in another the surface was broken by boiling, tumbling rings, that were as many-tinted as an opal; where the
ruddy flush was faintest, was a smooth spot that was covered with graceful circles and radiating lines, ever so delicately traced; the shore on our
left was densely wooded, and the somber shadow that fell from this
forest was broken in one place by a long, ruffled trail that shone like
silver; and high above the forest wall a clean-stemmed dead tree waved
a single leafy bough that glowed like a flame in the unobstructed splendor that was flowing from the sun. There were graceful curves, reflected
images, woody heights, soft distances; and over the whole scene, far and
near, the dissolving lights drifted steadily, enriching it every passing
moment with new marvels of coloring.

143. I stood like one bewitched. I drank it in, in a speechless rapture.
The world was new to me, and I had never seen anything like this at
home. But as I have said, a day came when I began to cease from noting
the glories and the charms which the moon and the sun and the twilight
wrought upon the river's face; another day came when I ceased altogether to note them. Then, if that sunset scene had been repeated, I
should have looked upon it without rapture, and should have commented upon it, inwardly, after this fashion: "This sun means that we
are going to have wind to-morrow; that floating log means that the river
is rising, small thanks to it; that slanting mark on the water refers to a
bluff reef which is going to kill somebody's steamboat one of these

nights, if it keeps on stretching out like that; those tumbling 'boils' show a dissolving bar and a changing channel there; the lines and circles in the slick water over yonder are a warning that that troublesome place is shoaling up dangerously; that silver streak in the shadow of the forest is the 'break' from a new snag, and he has located himself in the very best place he could have found to fish for steamboats; that tall dead tree, with a single living branch, is not going to last long, and then how is a body ever going to get through this blind place at night without the friendly old landmark?"

144. No, the romance and beauty were all gone from the river. All the value any feature of it had for me now was the amount of usefulness it could furnish toward compassing the safe piloting of a steamboat. Since those days, I have pitied doctors from my heart. What does the lovely flush in a beauty's cheek mean to a doctor but a "break" that ripples above some deadly disease? Are not all her visible charms sown thick with what are to him the signs and symbols of hidden decay? Does he ever see her beauty at all, or doesn't he simply view her professionally, and comment upon her unwholesome condition all to himself? And doesn't he sometimes wonder whether he has gained most or lost most by learning his trade?

COMMENTARY AND QUESTIONS

These autobiographical experiences first appeared in *The Atlantic Monthly* in 1875. Later they were incorporated by the author in a book, *Life on the Mississippi*. The five sections here reprinted are chapters 4-6 and 8-9 of that book.

1. Show how in each one of the five sections there is an increase or a decrease (or both) in the fascination of river life. How would you distinguish the attitude of the boy at the beginning of section I from that of the cub-pilot at the end of section V? The title of the selection is not the author's. Suggest a title to replace "Cub-Pilot."
2. Does the author in this selection take the same attitude toward actual experience as Paul Gallico does in "The Feel" (pp. 3-12)?
3. In pars. 19 and 37-57 one topic is considered; in pars. 28-36 and 57-60, another topic. Do you think the author should have completed his treatment of one before going on to the other?
4. Par. 107 serves as an introduction to section V and as a transition from the preceding section. If you were dividing the rest of section V into sub-sections, what paragraphs would you group together? What titles or headings would you give each of the sub-sections? How is par. 107 related to your final sub-section?
5. What technique has been used to achieve a humorous effect in these

four passages: "He would boil awhile to himself, and then overflow and scald me again" (par. 51); "You could have drawn a seine through his system and not caught curses enough to disturb your mother with" (par. 55); ". . . my memory was never loaded with anything but blank cartridges" (par. 57); ". . . the barkeeper had been barbered and upholstered at incredible cost" (par. 62)? Can you find other examples in this selection?

SUGGESTIONS FOR WRITING

1. In par. 2 the author presents two contrasting pictures of Hannibal, Missouri. Use the same technique in writing about a particular place, for example, a football stadium.
2. In par. 144 the question is asked whether a doctor "has gained most or lost most by learning his trade." Do you think a yes-or-no answer is possible? Draw examples from your own experiences in developing your discussion. One of these topics may prove helpful:
   (a) Those whom the gods love die young.
   (b) Where would we be without doctors?
   (c) Keeping a sense of wonder without remaining naïve.

Pilot's Progress

by JAMES MORRIS

ALMOST ANYWHERE on its lower reaches the Mississippi is lined with a narrow wilderness. There are thick trees, with their roots in the water, and tall grasses, jumping insects, the cries of improbable birds, an occasional deer, mosquitoes, brambles, and sometimes a turtle sunning itself on the mud. It is a lonely little jungle, but if you manage to push your way through it, and emerge on the bank of the river itself, you are unlikely to preserve your solitude for long; before an hour is past you will almost certainly hear the distant pounding of engines, and see the long

Reprinted from *As I Saw the U.S.A.* (English title: *Coast to Coast*) by James Morris, by permission of Pantheon Books and Faber and Faber Ltd. (London). Copyright © 1956 by Pantheon Books Inc.

line of a Mississippi tow creeping downstream. The river has become a tremendous industrial artery, and there is a ceaseless flow of traffic on it, winter and summer. Few Americans know how important the Mississippi is to them, for they have been brought up to believe that river traffic was killed by roads and railways, and they think of the Mississippi instinctively in nostalgic terms of stern-wheelers, gamblers, ornate steamboat captains, Huckleberry Finns and log rafts. It is true that passenger traffic is all but dead (despite many brave attempts to revive it) and there are probably fewer craft on the river than there were in the brassy days— in 1849 there were more than 1,000 packet boats on the Mississippi; but the tonnage carried is immeasurably greater than ever before. There are a few stern-wheelers on the river still, things of dignity, with black funnels belching smoke, and white upperworks, and great paddles churning up the muddy water; but most Mississippi boats are now steam or diesel screw-driven craft, very trim and sturdy, and they push (not pull) enormous loads of modern barges anywhere from Pittsburgh to Texas. These are the boats you will see go by from your vantage point among the brambles. They are powerful and well-tended, generally spruce, with company crests emblazoned proudly on their funnels, and radar screens and wireless masts on their superstructures. Sometimes they push a miscellaneous collection of barges, lashed together shapelessly, piled high with coal or yellow sulphur; sometimes a line of "integrated" barges, made to fit each other, and generally containing oil. Occasionally you may see a triple-decker barge, looking rather like a waffle, carrying cars downstream from Detroit.

2. Sometimes the towboats move mammoth loads, in weight as in length. It is common for a string of barges to be as long as the *Queen Elizabeth*, and such a tow often carries 6,500,000 gallons of oil. The heaviest tow recorded was pushed by a mighty stern-wheeler, the steamboat *Sprague*, which now lies in honored retirement at Vicksburg, a beloved and familiar personality. On her big day she moved sixty barges, with a deck area of six-and-a-half acres; in them there were 67,307 tons of coal.

3. All this traffic moves in an unceasing stream from the industrial regions southwards, and from the southern oilfields up to the Middle West. Pittsburgh, on the upper Ohio, is an important river port, and so is St. Paul, more than 2,000 miles from the Gulf of Mexico. There is river traffic on the Missouri, the Tennessee, the Allegheny, the Cumberland, and many other famous tributary rivers, and some barges go by canal eastward into Florida, or westward into Texas. A towboat can be 1,000 miles from its home port, and as isolated as any Atlantic liner; for the boats sail inexorably, day and night, never putting in at the river

towns they pass, nor picking up passengers at stages, nor stopping for wood as the old packets used to, nor delivering the mail to riverside plantations. From the banks of the Mississippi they seem totally cut off from life along its shores, as if they were part of the river, and cognizant of all its moods and manners.

4. Because I wanted to learn more about these boats, pounding by so head-in-air, I stood alone one hot summer southern evening at a landing stage on the banks of the Mississippi. I had arranged a passage on the towboat *White Gold,* and the landing stage had been arranged as a rendezvous, where a motorboat from the tow would pick me up. The stage was on a subsidiary channel of the Mississippi, and in the distance I could see the occasional light of a craft on the river proper. Behind me, on a bluff, the town of Vicksburg was all asleep, and usually there were only the noises of shunting trains and mosquitoes. Once a tug came close past me on the channel, its engines thudding; there were a few dim lights on its bridge, and a couple of shadowy figures, and I could hear muffled and desultory voices. Presently, away over the bluffs, I saw the repeated flash of a searchlight, and heard the distant beat of diesels; and soon my motorboat arrived out of the darkness, with a cloud of spray. Two jolly deckhands heaved my luggage aboard, there was a roar of motors, and we were away, scudding down to the river, with the man at the wheel shouting at me: "Cap'n says sorry we're late, we got held up at Natchez, he reckons we'll make it up between here and Greenville."

5. The Mississippi at night is the very quintessence of blackness. The tangled jungle banks are all black, and so is the water, and only occasionally could we see looming past the motorboat a floating trunk or a mass of jumbled branches. We kept our eyes on the flashing searchlight, though, and soon made out the long dark line of the barges. The *White Gold* was bound for Chicago from Louisiana, with a cargo of oil, and she had an integrated tow of five barges. As she approached, we swung around in a great arc to run alongside her. The motorboat's engines were cut off, a hoist lifted us out of the water, and a moment later we stood on one of the barges, still sweeping through the water, with the sound of slapping waves, and the lights of the towboat's pilothouse far astern. Such clandestine embarkations are often arranged, for crewmen who have to go ashore for emergencies, and join the tow again later on its voyage; or for the rare stranger who manages, despite the death of the passenger packets, to contrive a Mississippi passage.

6. There is (as I had suspected) a quality of supreme remoteness about the life aboard a Mississippi towboat. Hour after hour, day after day the silent banks slip by, with scarcely a sign of life on them; and you feel entirely separate from affairs behind the levees. Gradually the

river encloses you, and when you pass a river town you examine it as you might a picture show, or a toy town, or something in a museum. There is something hypnotic about such an experience. From the glass windows of the pilothouse the yellow oozy water seems to stretch away endlessly. The sun is scorching and the sky cloudless, so that the decks of the barges shimmer, and the bare backs of the deckhands shine. Only rarely do you glimpse an old merchant town through a gap in the levee; a long hot main street, a few Negroes lounging on the pavement, a mule and buggy kicking up the dust. Sometimes, down by the water there is a crooked shanty boat, swarming with children, with a sun-tanned old philosopher idling his days away on its balcony. More often there is nothing at all but the merciless sun, the river, and the dark and desolate wooded banks.

7. In the pilothouse, though, there is always an underlying sense of tension, for navigating a Mississippi boat is still one of the most exacting tasks in the world. The master and pilot of the *White Gold* was Captain Robert Shelton. He was 27, and characteristic of the modern breed of Mississippi pilots. The modern towboat does not have a wheel, but instead a light touch on a polished metal bar steers the tow; and there Shelton would sit, one hand on his lever, his feet on a ledge in front of him, talking easily of anything from Tennessee Williams to French politics, sipping coffee brought at very frequent intervals by a willing deckhand, but always with a keen eye on the river and its banks. The Mississippi pilot still has to know more than any man has the right to know (as Mark Twain put it). Every foot of river and bank must be familiar to him, and he must recognize it in an instant. It is constantly altering, never looking the same twice, and he must notice any change instinctively and summon at once the necessary reflexes. He must know the name of every light on the river bank, anywhere from New Orleans to Pittsburgh. He must know where to find slack water in the treacherous currents, where to sail in midstream and where to hug the banks (festooned with wild tree trunks). He must foresee a thousand and one perilous tricks of the river. He is utterly responsible for the towboat and its valuable cargo, night and day, often half a continent and several weeks from home. The good pilot is handsomely paid, and he is never unemployed; if he leaves one company, within a day or two there will be others bidding for his services. The days of the old gaudy steamboat pilots are over, and Shelton (whose grandfather was one of them) sometimes regrets those times of silk hats, diamond pins, embroidered waistcoats, and kid gloves; but the Mississippi pilot is a man of stature still.

8. It is queer to spend a morning in a towboat's pilothouse, for though you feel very much alone with the waters, to the pilot every moment brings some familiar landmark into view. Here we come up to

Opossum Chute, where Joe Daniels ran his tow on a sand bar. There's the light on Sarah Island, above Poverty Point. See that channel there? That's Bunch's Cutoff, where the river used to run up to Pilcher's Point Landing. There's the 575-mile mark. Over that bluff's where a town called Napoleon used to be, a big town in Mark Twain's time, 30,000 people or more, but it died when the river changed and made this cutoff. (*More coffee, Joe!*) Sometimes a tow will pass in the opposite direction, and the pilot is almost sure to know it. There will be an exchange of blasts on the sirens, and a deckhand will wave lethargically. Sometimes there will be a call on the radio, from head office in New Orleans, perhaps, like a voice from another world: "Bob? Bob, you'd oblige me by calling on Ted Harris, when you get to Chicago, and tell him we fixed what he wanted, like he asked. OK? How's everything?" Or a friendly engineer's boat may call up with some advice (you can probably see its upperworks over the levee at the next bend, and the voice on the radio comes very loud and clear): "Keep way inshore past Salem Bar, cap'n. We've been moving the buoys there. Real hot, ain't it?"

9. Sometimes the towboat captain gives a hand to a friend in trouble. Very early one morning, as we moved upstream, we overtook a big steamboat struggling with a heavy load. It was a difficult bend in the river, where the current ran especially strongly, and the towboat was making slow progress. Shelton recognized it at once, and knew its pilot, and very gingerly we approached to help. The *White Gold*'s barges were 800 feet long, the other towboat's more than 1,000; and these two huge strings of barges, each as long as an Atlantic liner, had to be joined in midstream, without pausing, in a place wrecked by eddies and cross-currents, so that the towboats could combine their energies. When I climbed up to the pilothouse (bleary-eyed and unshaven, for it was only just dawn) I found it charged with a routine excitement. The steersman, a sort of apprentice pilot, stood tensely in a corner. Shelton was cool and poised at his twin tillers. Far down on the barges two deckhands waited with hawsers. From the portholes of the other boat a few sleepy heads emerged, one of them in curlers (for many Mississippi boats carry women cooks, laundresses and stewardesses). Slowly, slowly, the tows approached each other, and the two pilots exchanged glances through their windows, and the porthole heads craned a little farther, and the deckhands gathered their ropes for the throw; until with a scarcely perceptible bump the barges touched, the hawsers were cast, and the two tows became one. Shelton handed the tillers to his steersman, and the rest of us sauntered across to the other tow for a gossip and a taste of someone else's coffee.

10. Sometimes during our voyage Shelton passed the tillers to me. It is a disconcerting experience to handle a Mississippi tow for the first

time. The atmosphere of the pilothouse is at once placid and nerve-racking, for it has the silence of an operating theater, only broken by the quiet click-click of the tillers, and a few murmured remarks from any off-duty deckhand who has chosen to come and sit on the high leather bench at the back. You are instructed to keep the head of the tow on such-and-such a sandbank, or such-and-such a tree; but soon, in the hot haze of the river, one bank merges with another, and the shape of the tree changes, and the horizon becomes blurred and featureless. When you touch your tillers gently, you find that the whole immense tow swings suddenly and alarmingly, so that for a moment you are afraid the barges will be swept broadside on to the current, and carried away helplessly in the opposite direction. "Keep her well inshore," says the pilot indulgently, and if you are timid about it he will tell you again, and again, and again, until the barges are barely escaping the roots of trees, and the gloomy overhanging foliage is brushing the upperworks of the towboat. The Mississippi pilot pursues his profession with great dash and *élan*. The emergencies are generally slow—a gradual swinging with the current, so that the leading barge hits the pillar of a bridge, or an inch-by-inch movement toward collision; but the dangers are very real. (Sometimes, indeed, the perils are less leisurely; in flood time a tow may have to be maneuvered downstream, through all the intricate, shifting, treacherous difficulties of the river, at fifteen or twenty miles an hour.)

11. For the deckhands, life on a towboat seems invitingly tranquil. During the long days on the river there is really very little to do, and they spend much of their time keeping the boat spick and span, painting its upperworks and polishing its brass. Often and again they saunter back to the galley for a cup of the coffee that is constantly on the boil. Or, leaning against the sternrail in the sunshine, they watch the frothy churning of the screw (they call it the "wheel," so strong is the Mississippi tradition) and swap mildly vulgar anecdotes. They need have no worry about currents and shore lights. Some of them have no idea where they are, measuring their progress only in terms of days out of port. There are unpredictable handicaps, of course—not long ago sixteen men were drowned when a towboat hit an Ohio bridge, and one of the *White Gold's* barges has a buckled front because of an oil explosion; but in general the deckhand lives an easy life, enjoyably.

12. His quarters, if the towboat is modern, are excellent, with comfortable bunks and showerbaths, and his food is comparable with that in one of the less penurious London clubs. On the *White Gold*, master, mate, chief engineer and all sat together at a high counter and were served by a Filipino cook with a dry sense of humor; and the choice of the dishes was enviable. Mississippi River food has always been good.

Here is the dinner menu on board the steam packet *Monarch*, sailing between Cincinnati and New Orleans, on 31 March 1861:

BILL OF FARE

Steamer Monarch, Cincinnati, Memphis and New Orleans
Union Line Passenger Packet

J. A. Williamson, Master   A. D. Armstrong, Clerk

Soup

Green Turtle   Oyster a la Plessey

Fish

Barbecued Red a la Maitre Decate
Trout a la Vortpre

Roast

| Beef | Pork | Pig | Mutton |
| Turkey | Chuck Veal | | Chicken |

Hot Entrees

Scallop of Chicken with Mushrooms and Green Corn
Vol au Vent of Oysters a la Buchmer
Tendons of Veal a la Dumpling and Green Peas
Fillets of Fowl with Truffle Supreme Sauce
Curbancedes of Mutton Garnished with New Potatoes
Vegetables of the Season

Cold Dishes

Potted Fowl and Tongue Ornamented With Jelly
Boned Turkey, Champagne Jelly
Cream with Apple Jelly

Boiled

| Mutton | Country Ham | Corned Beef |
| Turkey | Tongue | Chicken |

Condiments

Radishes	Oyster Catsup	Green Onions
Spanish Olives	Worcestershire Sauce	John Bull Sauce
Lettuce	Chow Chow	French Mustard
Raw Tomatoes	Chives Horseradish	Cucumbers
Shrimp Paste	Cold Slaw	Celery
Pickles	Pickled Onions	

Game

Pate Chaud of Pigeon a la Chausseur
Teal Duck Braised a la Madeira

Pastry and Desserts
(Pies)

| Apple | Whortleberry | Peach | Cherry |

Gooseberry and Mince
(Tarts)
Apple and Gooseberry
(Puffs)
Chocolate
(Miscellaneous)

Cabinet Pudding, Custard Sauce   Lemon Ice Cream
Russian Cream   Apple Tarts with Quince Macaroons
Jelly Pie Ornaments   Boiled Custard   Apple Meringue
Naples Biscuit   Boston Cream Cake   Orange Jelly
Almonds   Cheese   Cake   Cocoanut Cream

Cakes
Pound   Fruit   Jelly   Sponge   Plum   Cloud

Confectionery
Candy Kisses   Golden Molasses   Cocoanut Drops
Cream Figs   French Kisses   Lemon Drops   Gum Drops

Nuts and Fruits
Raisins   Almonds   Prunes   Brazil Nuts   Pecans
Peanuts   Filberts   English Walnuts   Pineapple
Oranges   Bananas   Figs   Apples   Dates
Coffee

D. H. Kendalle, Steward

("Cold Slaw," among the condiments, is the most interesting entry here. It is a salad of grated cabbage, and it was introduced to America by the Dutch of New Amsterdam. They called it *koolsla—kool*, cabbage, *sla*, salad—which became in English "cole-slaw"; but simple Americans, to this day, insist on further Anglicizing it as Mr. Kendalle did on board the *Monarch*.)

13. Such memories of the grand old days of the river color the thoughts of the modern Mississippi boatman. He lives in a silent, self-sufficient, introspective world, and as the months and years go by, and the tangled banks float past, so slowly he merges his identity with the Mississippi's water. He becomes, indeed, like the boats and barges, a part of the river. Having seen a little of this process for myself, I left my towboat one evening at dusk, and the motorboat dropped me at a disused landing stage in Arkansas, near a bridge and a lonely highway. I said good-by to my friends, shouldered my baggage, and set off up a dusty track over the levee; and at the top of the embankment I looked

back. There was the tow still streaming by, her engines beating, her searchlight flickering and flashing and feeling the banks, like a restless finger; as if she could no more stop, or pause in her progress, than the river currents themselves, swirling under the piers of the bridge.

COMMENTARY AND QUESTIONS

This selection is an excerpt from a book, *As I Saw the U. S. A.*, by an Englishman who has had many assignments as a special correspondent for *The Times* of London. While holding a Commonwealth Fund Fellowship during 1953-54, James Morris traveled throughout different sections of the United States gathering material. In his book, as part of his discussion of the South, he stresses the continuing importance of the Mississippi River, and describes the struggle of engineers to prevent flood damage and to improve navigation on the river. In our excerpt we have omitted the opening sentence of the first paragraph, a transitional sentence referring to the earlier discussion of the work done by engineers.

1. What factual material is presented in pars. 1-3 to substantiate the statement that the "river has become a tremendous industrial artery"?

2. In pars. 4-5 Morris describes the process of being picked up by a motorboat and of being taken aboard the towboat *White Gold*. In pars. 7-10 he gives details about life in the pilothouse. How does par. 6 serve as a transition between pars. 4-5 and 7-10?

3. Some of the details used by Morris in par. 6 are similar to those used by Mark Twain in par. 2 (pp. 15-16) of "Cub-Pilot." In these two paragraphs do the two authors use the details to substantiate the same or a different generalization about river life? In Morris's paragraph the river and shore are seen from the boat. Is this true in Mark Twain's paragraph? In each paragraph is there any connection between the place from which details are viewed and the kind of generalization made?

4. Morris states that a pilot on the Mississippi still faces many of the problems described almost a century earlier by Mark Twain. How does Morris's method of presenting material differ from Mark Twain's? Compare, for example, par. 10 of "Pilot's Progress" with pars. 18-19 (p. 22) or with pars. 107-140 (pp. 31-34) of "Cub-Pilot."

5. In pars. 11-12 Morris comments on the life of the deckhand as less strenuous than that of the pilot. In par. 12 how does Morris use material from an earlier period of time to substantiate obliquely his picture of the life of the deckhand given in par. 11 and at the beginning of par. 12?

6. In par. 13 the reader is given information about Morris's leaving the towboat. In this paragraph and in earlier paragraphs (for example, in pars. 3, 4, and 10) has it been the author's purpose to present himself

in a way to arouse a strong reaction from the reader—a strong reaction like that desired by Mark Twain for the presentation of himself in "Cub-Pilot"?

7. In the opening sentence of par. 6 Morris speaks of the "quality of supreme remoteness about the life aboard a Mississippi towboat." What details are used in the selection to emphasize this quality of remoteness? Consider, for example, the description of the shore in par. 1; the reference to an Atlantic liner in par. 3; the description of embarkation in par. 5; the calls on the radio in par. 8; the final view of the *White Gold* in par. 13.

8. The next-to-last sentence of par. 3 ends with a series of participial phrases: "never putting in at the river towns they pass, nor picking up passengers at stages, nor stopping for wood as the old packets used to, nor delivering the mail to riverside plantations." Point out examples of parallelism in par. 6.

SUGGESTION FOR WRITING

Compare and contrast "Pilot's Progress" with "Cub-Pilot" (pp. 15-36), making clear how each author's purpose is reflected in content and technique.

Father Teaches Me

to Be Prompt

by CLARENCE DAY

FATHER MADE A GREAT POINT of our getting down to breakfast on time. I meant to be prompt, but it never occurred to me that I had better try to be early. My idea was to slide into the room at the last moment. Consequently, I often was late.

2. My brothers were often late, too, with the exception of George. He

was the only thoroughly reliable son Father had. George got down so early, Father pointed out to me, that he even had time to practice a few minutes on the piano.

3. The reason George was so prompt was that he was in a hurry to see the sporting page before Father got hold of the newspaper, and the reason he then played the piano was to signal to the rest of us, as we dressed, which team had won yesterday's ball game. He had made up a code for this purpose, and we leaned over the banisters, pulling on our stockings and shoes, to hear him announce the results. I don't remember now what the titles were of the airs he selected, but the general idea was that if he played a gay, lively air it meant that the Giants had won, and when the strains of a dirge or lament floated up to us, it meant that Pop Anson had beaten them.

4. As Father didn't approve of professional baseball, we said nothing to him about this arrangement. He led his life and we led ours, under his nose. He took the newspaper away from George the moment he entered the room, and George said good morning to him and stepped innocently into the parlor. Then, while Father watched him through the broad doorway and looked over the political headlines, George banged out the baseball news for us on the piano. Father used to admonish him with a chuckle not to thump it so hard, but George felt that he had to. We were at the top of the house, and he wanted to be sure that we'd hear him even if we were brushing our teeth. George always was thorough about things. He not only thumped the piano as hard as he could but he hammered out the tune over and over besides, while Father impatiently muttered to himself, *"Trop de zèle."*

5. Upstairs, there was usually some discussion as to what kind of news George was sending. He had not been allowed to learn popular tunes, which it would have been easy for us to recognize, and the few classic selections which were available in his little music book sounded pretty much alike at a distance. George rendered these with plenty of good will and muscle but not a great deal of sympathy. He regarded some of the rules of piano-playing as needlessly complicated.

6. The fact remained that he was the one boy who was always on time, and Father was so pleased by this that he bought a watch for him with "George Parmly Day, Always on Time" engraved on the back. He told me that as I was the eldest he had meant to give me a watch first, and he showed me the one he had bought for me. It was just like George's except that nothing had been engraved on it yet. Father explained that to his regret he would have to put it away for a while, until I had earned it by getting down early to breakfast.

7. Time went on, without much improvement on my part. Dawdling

had got to be a habit with me. Sometimes my lateness was serious. One morning, when breakfast was half over and I had nothing on but a pair of long woolen drawers, Father called up from the front hall, napkin in hand, that he wouldn't stand it and that I was to come down that instant. When I shouted indignantly that I wasn't dressed yet, he said he didn't care. "Come down just as you are, confound it!" he roared. I was tempted to take him at his word, but thought there might be some catch in it and wouldn't, though I hurried, of course, all I could. Father ate his usual hearty breakfast in a stormy mood, and I ate my usual hearty breakfast in a guilty and nervous one. Come what might, we always ate heartily. I sometimes wished afterward that I hadn't, but it never seemed to hurt Father.

8. Mother told Father that if he would give me the watch, she was sure I'd do better. He said that he didn't believe it, and that that was a poor way to bring a boy up. To prove to him that he was wrong, Mother at last unlocked her jewel box and gave me a watch which had belonged to one of her elderly cousins. It was really too valuable a watch for a boy to wear, she said, and I must be very careful of it. I promised I would.

9. This watch, however, turned out to be painfully delicate. It was old, I was young. We were not exactly made for each other. It had a back and front of thin gold, and as Mother had had the former owner's monogram shaved off the front cover, that cover used to sink in the middle when pressed. Also, the lid fitted so closely that there was barely room for the glass crystal over the face. Such a very thin crystal had to be used that any pressure on the lid broke it.

10. I didn't press on the lid, naturally, after the first time this happened. I was careful, and everything would have gone well enough if other boys had been careful, too. It was not practicable, however, for me to make them be careful enough. When I had a fight, friendly or otherwise, I used to ask my opponent if he would be so kind as not to punch me on the left side of my stomach. He might or might not listen. If he and I were too excited and kept on long enough, the watch crystal broke anyway. There was never time to take off my watch first, and anyhow there was no place to put it. A watch that goes around the streets in a boy's pocket has to take life as it comes. This watch had never been designed for any such fate.

11. The first two crystals I broke Mother paid for, as Father disapproved of the whole business and would have nothing to do with it. Mother was always short of small change, however, and I hated to trouble her—and she hated to be troubled, too. "Oh, Clarence, dear! You haven't broken your watch again?" she cried when I opened the cover the second time, to show her the shattered fragments. She was so upset

that I felt too guilty to tell her the next time it happened, and from then on I was reduced to the necessity of paying for the damage myself.

¹²· My pocket money never exceeded a dollar a month. Every new crystal cost twenty-five cents. It was a serious drain.

¹³· Wrestling and rolling around on the floor with Sam Willets, my watch quite forgotten, I would suddenly hear a faint tinkle and know that I was once more insolvent. I would pick out the broken glass and leave the watch with no crystal till I had twenty-five cents on hand, but these delays made me nervous. I knew that Mother wanted to feel sure I was taking good care of the watch, and that she might look at it any evening. As soon as I had the money, I hurried over to Sixth Avenue, where two old Germans kept a tiny watch shop, and left it there to be fixed. One of my most dismal memories is of that stuffy little shop's smell of sauerkraut, and how tall the glass counter then seemed, and the slowness of those two old Germans. When I got there late and they made me leave the watch overnight, I didn't have one easy moment until I got it back the next day. Again and again I argued with them that twenty-five cents was too much, especially for a regular customer, but they said it didn't pay them to do the work even for that, because those thin old-fashioned crystals were hard to get.

¹⁴· I gave up at last. I told Mother I didn't want to wear the watch any more.

¹⁵· Then I found, to my amazement, that this way out of my troubles was barred. The watch was an heirloom. And an heirloom was a thing that its recipient must value and cherish. No good Chinese, I read later on in life, fails to honor his ancestors; and no good boy, I was told in my youth, fails to appreciate heirlooms.

¹⁶· I left Mother's room in low spirits. That night, as I wound up my watch with its slender key, I envied George. Father had selected the right kind for George; he knew what a boy needed. It had a thick nickel case, it had an almost unbreakable crystal, and it endured daily life imperturbably, even when dropped in the bathtub.

¹⁷· It seemed to me that I was facing a pretty dark future. The curse of great possessions became a living thought to me, instead of a mere phrase. The demands that such possessions made on their owners for upkeep were merciless. For months I had had no money for marbles. I couldn't even afford a new top. In some way that I didn't fully understand I was yoked to a watch I now hated—a delicate thing that would always make trouble unless I learned to live gingerly.

¹⁸· Then I saw a way out. All this time I had kept on being late for breakfast at least once a week, out of habit, but it now occurred to me that if I could reform, perhaps Father might relent and give me that

reliable nickel watch he had bought. I reformed. I occasionally weakened in my new resolution at first, but every time that crystal got broken I was spurred on to fresh efforts. When I had at length established a record for promptness that satisfied Father, he had my name engraved on the watch he had bought, and presented it to me. He was a little surprised at the intense pleasure I showed on this occasion, and as he watched me hopping around the room in delight he said "There, there" several times. "Don't be so excited, confound it," he added. "You'll knock over that vase."

19. Mother said she couldn't see why Father should give me a nickel watch when I had a gold one already, but he laughed and told her that "that old thing" was no kind of a watch for a boy. She reluctantly laid it away again to rest in her jewel box.

20. Her parting shot at Father was that anyhow she had been right; she had said all along that a watch was what I needed to teach me how to be prompt.

COMMENTARY AND QUESTIONS

A good many people can look back on a childhood spent in a lively family. Somewhat fewer can write about the members of such a family so effectively as to make them as interesting to outsiders as they were to each other. Among those who have done so is the author of this selection. The passage here reprinted is a complete chapter from *Life with Father*, in which (as in its companion volume, *Life with Mother*) Clarence Day recreated for his readers a boyhood in the New York of the 1880's.

1. Reminiscences, oral or written, are apt to become chaotic and therefore boring unless they are arranged in some kind of satisfying pattern. Clarence Day has woven all the details of this chapter into what is essentially one unified incident or anecdote. Why did he introduce the word *prompt* into par. 1, par. 20, and the title?

2. Pars. 2-6 develop a contrast between Clarence and his brother George. The contrast is amusing in itself, but is this Day's chief reason for introducing it? Why is there no mention of watches until par. 6?

3. Another contrast developed in the telling of the incident is that between two kinds of watch: the nickel watch selected by Father for George, and the gold watch given by Mother to Clarence. By what means does Day convey this contrast to the reader? What reason might he have had for arranging the details so that the emphasis is first on the nickel watch, then on the gold, and finally on the nickel again?

4. The more successful writers of childhood reminiscences have been able to convey to their readers simultaneously the vividness of a child's

experience and an adult's understanding of its significance. Among the added dimensions which maturity finds in experience is a recognition of the ironic contrasts between things as they seem and things as they are. Much of the force of Clarence Day's way of writing about his family comes from a good-natured but constantly alert recognition of these ironies. How, for example, does he make the reader smilingly recognize the following contrasts:

a. between Father's interpretation of George's promptness and George's real motives?
b. between Father's interpretation of George's thoroughness and zeal in piano-playing and its real motives?
c. between Mother's criteria of value in watches and Clarence's?
d. between Father's reasons for giving the nickel watch and Clarence's for getting it?
e. between Mother's interpretation of the incident and Father's?
f. between either of their interpretations and the reader's?

5. What other examples of ironic wording can you find in this selection? Would you say that for his irony to be successful an author necessarily has to "raise his voice" very much?

6. The bare outline of this anecdote could be told very briefly. But it is the skillful use of appropriate and imaginative detail that makes it come alive. For example, despite the brevity of the chapter, both Father and Mother emerge with very distinct personalities, not at all alike. Point out concrete details used by the author to convey these personalities. How does Day substantiate his statement about Father: "He led his life and we led ours, under his nose"?

7. Which versions of the following sentences are superior?
a. "He regarded some of the rules of piano-playing as needlessly complicated" or "He played the piano rather carelessly"?
b. "A watch that goes around the streets in a boy's pocket has to take life as it comes" or "A boy's watch must stand a great deal of abuse"?

SUGGESTIONS FOR WRITING

1. Parents need glasses.
2. Doing the right thing for the wrong reason.
3. The curse of great possessions.
4. My musical career.

Surveyor
in the Woods

by KENNETH ANDLER

I

I WANT TO TELL YOU about a woodsman, what he was like, what his work was, and what it meant. His name was Alfred D. Teare and he came originally from Nova Scotia, but all the time I knew him his home was in Berlin, New Hampshire. Probably the best surveyor of old lines in New England, he was—in his way—a genius.

2. I saw him for the first time when I was a boy of twelve; he was visiting my stepfather, a lawyer, who was then engaged in litigation involving boundary lines. Mr. Teare, a wonderful story-teller, held our family entranced with his tales of the woods. He conjured up a marvelous land of mountains, rivers, and lakes, peopled it with lumberjacks, rivermen, timber cruisers, Maine guides, and plenty of bears and moose for good measure. Just the expression "the Maine woods," as he used it, tingled along my spine. He visited our house several times after that and always brought my stepfather a bundle of pipe-lighters, little sticks about a foot long, taken from the roots of an old-growth pine windfall, for use with an open fire. They smelled good; they had the woods in them as a sea shell has the roar of the sea.

3. The summer I was fourteen, in 1918, I had a chance to work as a chainer for Mr. Teare, who then was running lines near Reading and Plymouth, Vermont; and I spent several seasons with him thereafter.

4. At that time he was nearing sixty years of age. Over average height in spite of a pronounced stoop to his shoulders and quite heavily set, he appeared to be coming at you aggressively with his head lowered like a buffalo. Although his back was quite bent he had powerful arms and shoulders, and somehow he seemed stronger that way than if he had been erect, particularly when he carried an enormous pack by means of a tumpline.

5. He had a forceful, weatherbeaten, almost leathery face; a dewlap like a bulldog's; a bald pate bounded by a horseshoe of black hair turning gray; blue eyes, and short, strong, even teeth with spaces between them. One of the curious little tricks he delighted in, when occasion re-

quired, was biting a fish line in two with hardly more than one snap. His hands, remarkably square with large blunt fingers, were tough and work-hardened with skin like brown leather. A mosquito never could drill through this hide of his, and often, when one tried, Mr. Teare would watch it with a tolerant amusement until it staggered off bewildered.

6. He took a peculiar pride in his eyesight; but he must have been farsighted like many outdoor men, for he had a sturdy pair of glasses which hung from a fish line about his neck and nestled snugly under his shirt in the abundant hair on his chest. To use them, he always hauled them up through his open shirt, and taking them by one end with his blunt fingers, perched them on his nose. He had the characteristic habit of always sitting on his left foot, his left leg bent under him, his right leg out straight. He was nimble enough to do this as long as he lived and it provided him a cushion of sorts on ground no matter how cold or wet. When he made his survey notes he would seat himself thus, affix his glasses with a kind of clumsy ease and write laboriously in a red-covered notebook with a hard smudgeless drawing pencil which seemed lost in his great, rough paw.

7. Summer or winter he always wore heavy woolen socks, and in summer, ankle-height moccasins, half-soled and hobnailed (really the best footgear imaginable), trousers of heavy khaki, a faded blue denim work shirt, and a slouch hat. He never would wear corduroy as he said corduroy gets wet two weeks before a rain.

8. Of Scottish descent and old-fashioned in manner, he used rare and almost obsolete expressions seldom if ever heard nowadays. He used "gran'sir" for "grandfather," spoke of building up a good fire "against the night," and was the only person I ever heard use the archaic "an" for "if." One favorite expression he coined himself, I believe: of an honest man he would say, "He's as square as ninety degrees."

9. Of course, he reeked with ordinary woods lore. He pointed out to me what a widow-maker was: the dead top of a tree which would come crashing down when an axeman started to cut at the base. A fool-killer, equally dangerous, was a live tree bent over by a fallen one so that when an unwary chopper drove an axe into it the tremendous tension, suddenly released, sent the tree splitting and charging up to catch him under the chin. A smudge of brakes warded off mosquitoes, of course, but it was news to me that only a bright fire would stop midges or "no-see-ums," for they'd fly right into it. Nothing in the world could stop an onslaught of black flies while we were at work on the line, although the best protection was a smudge pot and smearing our faces and hands with tobacco juice. Mr. Teare advised these things for our sakes; insects didn't irritate him. When we got soaked from a sudden shower, as we often did, and came tramping back to camp through water-laden brush, Mr. Teare said

we wouldn't catch cold if we let our clothes dry on us. We always took his advice and slogged around camp like saturated dishrags while we built up a fire, but we never did catch cold from our wettings.

10. He was ingenious to a degree and a wizard with an axe. When a tree became lodged, he employed what he called a "Samson Pole" to make it fall in a different direction. This was a strong pole which he held upright, in a notch of which another strong pole fitted, running as a cross bar to a notch in the recalcitrant tree, and with this device he could exert a tremendous leverage. If an axe handle got cracked he fixed it by binding a fish line tightly about it in a manner few could duplicate. He always had in camp an awl with waxed ends with which he could sew up his moccasins, and if he was far enough back in the woods and the need arose, he would tap them, sometimes using bark for leather.

11. He was full of lore and ideas of his own concerning the curative properties of herbs. For bronchial trouble he advised the sticky gum which exudes from cherry trees. Balsam blisters were also good. If he had a bad enough cough he mixed up a mysterious concoction which someone called "spruce gum and blue vitriol," and he downed it with a bearlike roar of distaste. When I cut my fingers deeply near the knuckles with an axe he rushed to my side where I was leaning against a tree, faint from loss of blood in July heat, and mopping up the gash with a handkerchief, he told me to wiggle my fingers. They wiggled; he could see the cords move, and he acted relieved. Then he took his plug of tobacco, chewed up a piece to a soft cud and placed it in the gash. He bound up my fingers with a splint and a handkerchief to keep in the tobacco. No infection set in, thanks to the nicotine, and although some stitches would have been a good idea, none were taken. The cut healed perfectly, though I shall always bear the scar.

12. His medicinal theories carried more weight with me when I learned that, many years before, when a doctor had given him six months to live because of his weakened, and I gathered, consumptive condition, he had struck out for the woods where he slept on the ground and gulped a prodigious number of raw eggs every day. He came out of it all right and throughout the rest of his years was as rugged as an old gnarled oak.

II

13. He was not by any means simply a backwoodsman. He had traveled extensively throughout the United States; his work brought him into contact with the executives of large companies; but most of his life

he spent in the woods. They were really home to him although he had a conventional home, a remarkable wife, and five grownup children.

14. While I worked with him we usually camped out in a lean-to tent, open on one side, and before this side we built with huge flat rocks a fireplace in which on chilly nights we kept a fire of four-foot wood. Sometimes we threw into the fire great pieces of punk, a fungus black on the outside, reddish within, which grows in nubs on old birch trees, and then we'd have coals for the morning. We made our bed on the ground from the tips of fir branches, set upright very close together and then pushed backward at an angle.

15. At the opening of the tent we had a bench made from saplings, or from a board if we had one, which Mr. Teare called the "deacon seat." Sometimes where a tent would be a nuisance and we weren't going to stay long we built a bark lean-to, and often we reveled luxuriously in deserted and almost ruined farmhouses.

16. Although the company furnished us a cook one summer in Vermont when we had two timber cruisers with us, almost all the time I was with him, Mr. Teare did the cooking. He was very good at it, too. When we got in from work he would don a white apron (at least it had been white originally), mix up a batch of biscuits on a table of saplings covered with birch bark, put them in his little tin baker which faced the open fire, fry some meat, turn out a rice pudding to which we helpers contributed raspberries or blueberries in season, brew tea, and in no time produce an excellent meal. He delighted in baking beans in the ground, fried excellent doughnuts and a somewhat similar product which he called "doughgods."

17. We always carried our lunch for the noon meal together with a nest of metal cups and a tin tea pail. Invariably we would stop by a spring or brook and build a fire. Mr. Teare would sit on his left foot, hunched forward and intent, holding the pail over the fire on a long pole, and he never paid the slightest attention if the smoke engulfed him. When the water boiled, he would swing the pail out for one of us to toss in a handful of good black tea, and then he'd swing it back over the fire for a momentary re-boiling in the interest of strength and power. Our pail had seen so much service that merely boiling water in it produced stronger tea than most people would care to drink.

18. After lunch Mr. Teare would get out his long-bladed jackknife, pare off some shavings from his strong plug tobacco, and with the knife still held, blade upright, between thumb and forefinger of his right hand (lest more paring be necessary) he'd work the tobacco with a semicircular motion, between the palms of his hands—grist between millstones —then fill and light his pipe. He never, never used a match for this pur-

pose if a fire were going, principally, I think, because he regarded matches in the woods as precious. He always took a brand from the fire, blew on it prodigiously to bring it to a bright coal, and lighted up with that. Often he would have only embers to choose from and these too he used, holding one somehow in his tough paw. He would press the ignited tobacco down with an impervious thumb and then, when the smoke rolled out, he would settle back to spellbind us with some yarn. The whole business of the noon meal was a never-varied rite.

19. He worked summer and winter on every passably workable day. In the winter, if camping out, he used a square tent with a stove in it. He wore ordinary snowshoes for fairly level country but bearpaws for rough and hilly terrain. As our lunch always froze we toasted our sandwiches over the fire. When Mr. Teare knocked the icy clods from his snowshoes, stood them up in the snow, and hunched over to start a fire with birch bark and dry sticks, he seemed as integral a part of winter in the woods as the snow upon the ground.

20. Sometimes he would stay at farmhouses instead of camping out. During the last forty years of his life, he worked mostly for such large corporations as the International Paper Company, the Mt. Tom Sulphite & Pulp Company, the Draper Corporation, the Brown Company and others. He traveled extensively through the back country of northern New England and stayed at literally hundreds of isolated farmhouses, using them either to work from directly or as bases from which he could pack his "wangan" into the woods for a camp. Lonely farm families whose homes he had previously visited looked forward eagerly to his coming, for he brought to their routine existence an inexhaustible store of adventure tales and to their drab lives a fresh and lively color.

III

21. The problem of surveying in the timberland of northern New England is one of the most difficult and fascinating things in the world. It's difficult because it consists largely of re-locating the old lines of original lots and ranges run by pioneers with crude compasses as much as one hundred and seventy-five years ago. The early surveyors blazed or spotted the trees along these lines, and for corners set posts, marked trees, or piled up stones. They also blazed trees about the corners for "witnesses." Succeeding surveyors have respotted the lines infrequently, perhaps not oftener than once in twenty years, and in many instances the original lines have not been renewed at all.

22. When a tree is spotted with an axe the wood grows over the blaze

in a few years and leaves nothing on the bark but a scar which only an experienced woodsman can recognize. A novice either notices no spot at all or thinks that every scar he sees is a spot whether it's a hedgehog mark, a wind-gall, or just a natural blemish.

23. The original lots, laid out by the proprietors of each township, classified by number in ranges and divisions, usually contained about one hundred acres each and were described quite accurately and specifically by the early surveyors, who gave points of compass and definite distances in the title deeds; but as these lots were either split up or amalgamated with other lots, people grew very careless when conveying real estate, and fell into the habit of bounding land by the names of the adjoining owners, as in the classic example Mr. Teare used to quote from a Vermont deed: "Bounded on the North by Brother Jim, on the West by Brother Bill, on the South by Sister Sal, and on the East by Mother."

24. With the migration of farmers to the West, or to the cities, immense areas of rural farm land reverted to the wilderness. Even many New Englanders do not realize how far this went and how extensively the forests have crept in over once-tilled fields. We have seen sites of villages silent in the woods, crumbling cellar holes through which great trees are growing, once proud highways which are now only dim trails, and even a graveyard in Vermont from which three crops of pulp wood have been cut. Gone are the people who owned these farms, their most lasting works faded like old ink, their names nothing but an echo in the land records.

25. Consequently, in these abandoned districts, now merely a wilderness, a reference in an old deed such as "bounded on the North by land of Abijah Davis," which may have been perfectly plain to the contracting parties in 1860, means very little now. A surveyor must trace the title deeds in the registry, draw tentative diagrams and fit them together like a jigsaw puzzle, and somehow or other get the chain of title back to the older deeds where references to compass courses and distances provide something definite to work on. By this research one may discover that Abijah Davis owned Lot Number 2 in the 3d Range and 1st Division and that the line in question was originally "North 85° East 88 Rods and 17 Links."

26. To his task Mr. Teare brought very peculiar educational equipment. He never went beyond the seventh grade in school as he had to leave and go to work, but in his early years he had followed the sea and had become skipper of a three-masted schooner, and thus he had learned navigation.

27. As a surveyor he brought this navigation inland. It was really dead reckoning on land. A college-trained engineer would have thought

his methods rule of thumb, but where such an engineer would have seen only woods, Mr. Teare could read them like an open book. For instance, he would go up to some old spruce on which, once he'd pointed it out, you could see a small scar, then taking an axe he'd swing with great true blows; and as large flying chips began to litter the ground he would lay open the white flesh of the tree in a larger and larger gash. After a while he would begin to strike more slowly and carefully, now and then peering into the opening, until finally he had disclosed an old blaze, black and flat with the original axemarks in it.

28. Then he would fish up his glasses from his shirt and holding them to his eyes would count the annual rings of growth. More than once I have seen him cut out spots made more than a hundred years before, and he once found spots on the old Masonian curved line, run in 1751 by Joseph Blanchard—the first line surveyed in New Hampshire. Mr. Teare had a spiritual affinity with the pioneer surveyors. He saw at a glance what they'd done, what they meant by their marks. He would sometimes look at a spot which definitely had been made with an axe, glance around and growl: "Not a line, just a trapper's trail."

29. He could follow not only the original spotted lines but the "lines of occupancy" as well, such as the trail of an old brush fence, all obvious remnants of which had disappeared at least twenty-five years before. This he would do by noting the crooked growth of trees here and there along its course, or a stretch of hazel bushes (which are likely to grow up along the remains of a brush fence), or piles of moss-covered stones in which fence posts had once been set. Whenever Mr. Teare, scattering the leaf mould near one of these stone heaps, uncovered a split ash rail, he would pick it up and fondle it lovingly. "They never rot," he would say with a solid approval of the wood itself and of the pioneer farmer who had taken pains to use it.

30. For equipment he used an open-sight compass with about a five-inch needle. There was no telescope on it but sight vanes instead with slits in them, and this compass rested not on a tripod, which would be too awkward in the woods, but rather on a single staff called a "Jacob staff." That was the kind of compass George Washington and Abraham Lincoln used when they were land surveyors, but Mr. Teare's was considerably more accurate. He referred affectionately to his compass as "Mary Jane" and almost always called it an "instrument" instead of a "compass."

31. When I first went with him he used a Gunter's chain, two rods in length, but in later years a steel tape of the same length. The Gunter's chain is an actual chain with real links and it can be folded up instead of rolled. It is very durable; it can be used to help a man go down over

steep ledges, and will perform a hundred and one odd jobs that it would be sacrilege to force on a tape, which couldn't do them anyhow. He never wanted a chain or tape longer than two rods because the ground he had to work on was so hilly and rough. Somehow or other the Gunter's chain seemed to fit him better than a tape.

32. This type of surveying, difficult and requiring an analytical mind as well as woodcraft, is a fascinating pursuit—a sort of treasure hunt for old lines and corners. The problem was posed more than a century ago by men who marked those lines and corners in the wilderness and left cryptic directions on how to find them. In deserted areas it is a search through a forest-buried civilization as dead as the bottom layer of an Egyptian city. The fascination of it for Mr. Teare never left him.

33. I can see him now hunched over his compass while the needle settles on the proper course, then standing behind it and shouting directions to his axemen, while the two chainers bring up the rear. He is full of anticipation at what he may find at a given distance where he thinks a corner ought to be. He assiduously examines the trees alongside the line to see if he is following the old spotting, and now and then breaks into some rollicking song. His joy in living radiates around him.

34. Mr. Teare's genius, true to the proverb, consisted largely in his capacity for taking infinite pains. He would always make sure of a starting point that could not be questioned. Once he ran twenty-four miles of trail line to locate one corner. Furthermore, he would never let an obstacle or a series of them block him. If a swamp were deep and cold he crossed it nevertheless, if towering cliffs barred his way he scaled them, if blown down trees strewed his path he slashed his way through, if a swollen river cut across a line he felled a tree for a bridge and kept on going. He was absolutely indomitable and he followed an old line as a hound follows a fox.

35. He hated to see the woods cut by the companies for which he was working, even though he well knew that timber like other crops must be harvested. Often people asked him what he considered the most beautiful thing he had seen and he always gave them the same reply—sunset over the Adirondacks and Lake Champlain, from Mt. Mansfield. He worked most of a lifetime in the woods of northern New England and in spite of hardships and privation he never lost his love for these wild and wooded hills, for the silence of the deep forest in winter, the splendor of the mountains in the winey tang of autumn days.

36. The infinite variety of his daily scenes of activity pleased him. One day he might stand among tall spruces high up on some mountain, sighting, far below, an isolated farmhouse on which he could take a "triangulation shot"; another day he might be following a hardwood

ridge of beech and maple, or working in the bear-wallow sort of land that often lies atop a mountain, or following the stone walls of abandoned fields. Often he made a traverse survey of the great roaring brooks which come tumbling out of mountain ponds and cut their resounding way down deep ravines; he loved to drive a canoe across a lake or down a river through white water.

37. Often he would pause at the summit of some hill. Then with his Jacob staff, he would point out to us the mountains and hills as they rolled away into blue distance, calling them by name and referring to certain jobs he had done on each. He knew them all as a father knows his children.

IV

38. The thing that staggers me when I get to thinking about Mr. Teare is the stupendous amount of work he accomplished in his long career. He surveyed thousands upon thousands of acres in Maine, New Hampshire, and Vermont. And he did not work merely for a monthly pay check; a craftsman, he labored so that his work would endure.

39. Many if not most surveyors in timberlands leave few marks or monuments. Some of them figure that they'll soon be hired to resurvey the land if the lines become easily lost. Most make a half-hearted attempt to mark their lines and corners, but their work is like snow upon the desert, for the resurgent life in New England woods is almost tropical, as anyone knows who has tried to keep brush out of a field.

40. Mr. Teare, on the other hand, when he was sure a line was finally right—and if he was sure it was right, it *was*—would have the axemen blaze almost every tree along the whole line. One that stood exactly on line he'd spot on both sides, while a tree that stood off a little way to one side or the other he'd blaze with "quarter spots," that is, blazes which were quartered on the bole, not centered, and these faced toward the line.

41. He made his blazes deep enough to take out a shaving of the wood, and they were large man-size spots, not boy's work. Some foresters and engineers complained that every tree would die but Mr. Teare knew better and he was right. He knew one great primary truth: you can't mark a line in New England's fast-growing woods a bit too plain.

42. Iron rods are impractical to carry in the woods and also a menace to the compass, so for a corner he set a large wooden post, fashioned from a suitable tree nearby, hewn flat on three sides or four as circumstances demanded, sharpened at the bottom and topped at an angle for

a "roof." He never pounded it into the ground as that would soften the top and let the rain in, but instead forced it in with its own weight. Around it he piled rocks. He stripped the bark off so it would last longer and with a timber scribe—a fascinating little instrument with which he could carve letters almost as fast as one can print on paper—he marked the names of the adjoining owners, the date, and his mark which was two parallel lines with a circle between them. He always said with a twinkle in his eye when he finished a corner and straightened up from piling stones, "There, that'll stand till Gabriel calls all good surveyors home."

43. About the corner he blazed witness trees in a circle facing the post and inscribed on them the date and his mark. These words, figures, and symbols, being only in the bark, never grow over. One could stand at a corner and, looking back into the woods, see the line stretching straight and true and well brushed out, its blazes shining new and startlingly clear. Few things give one quite the sense of accomplishment that this does—to go forth to a tract of land as nebulous in location as the scene of a fantasy, to find the old lines and corners, and to leave them well marked and definite.

44. These lines of Mr. Teare's, reaching for hundreds of miles in the aggregate through the deep woods of northern New England, live on today as I can testify, for while working as a land surveyor myself and later while abstracting titles, I have followed many of them. One of the companies had Mr. Teare respot its lines at seven-year intervals and, of course, these are exceptionally plain. But I have followed easily, and without a compass, lines which he had established thirty-five years before and which had never been touched since. The wooden corner posts needed renewing, yes, but that was easily accomplished. One can follow his lines even through the areas devastated by the hurricane of September, 1938, where the blazed trees, no longer upright, lie in a tangled snarl upon the ground.

45. In scores, even hundreds of towns in northern New England, his lines form a reliable basic network from which almost any survey of land in their general neighborhood would be started today. The local people, farmers, timber operators, and investors would no more think of questioning his lines than they would the law of gravitation. More than once when I have told some timber buyer that several lines of a proposed tract had been run by Mr. Teare I have seen his face light up—he knew that *those* boundaries would be distinct, at any rate. Quite often I have heard one of Mr. Teare's old friends use the expression, "Why, it's as plain as one of Teare's lines."

46. Whenever I happen to come upon one of his corners now that he

is gone and, in the solemn hush of the forest, see the post in its cairn standing there, the trees about it alive with dates of those years when we worked together, and with his mark and perhaps the initials of the old crew members, I feel an ineffable sadness not only because he is gone but because everything in those woods seems to inquire for him—and he would be enjoying himself so much if he were there.

47. But he did his work well and it survives him. No more can a mortal really ask. His lines are impressed into the living forest, his corners stand in wooded solitudes silently eloquent of his skill, and his witness trees bear witness not only to them but to him. Wherever he worked he brought order out of confusion and established a lasting thing.

COMMENTARY AND QUESTIONS

1. The author of this selection, an attorney by profession, grew up in New England. What autobiographical details appear here?
2. Is the first sentence an adequate statement of what the writer intends to do? Is it an effective opening sentence?
3. If the first three paragraphs of section I are considered introductory, on what basis could the other paragraphs in the section be divided into two groups?
4. What heading or title do you think might be given to pars. 14-18?
5. If pars. 21-31 were divided into three groups (21-25, 26-29, 30-31), what heading would you give each group? How are the three groups related?
6. What purpose do the last two sentences in par. 27 serve? Can you find other examples in this selection?
7. Why do you think Andler waits until section IV to give a detailed account of Mr. Teare's lines, with their blazes and corners?
8. Why does Andler explain some of the following words or phrases but not others: *tumpline* (par. 4); *dewlap* (par. 5); *widow-maker* (par. 9); *fool-killer* (par. 9); *Samson Pole* (par. 10); *punk* (par. 14); *deacon seat* (par. 15); *doughgods* (par. 16); *quarter spots* (par. 40); *bole* (par. 40)?

SUGGESTIONS FOR WRITING

1. A woodsman I have known.
2. A man who respects his work.
3. In par. 26 Andler explains that Mr. Teare had "peculiar educational equipment." Write about somebody you have known well who also has peculiar educational equipment for his job.

It's a Democracy, Isn't It?

by ALISTAIR COOKE

I WAS STANDING on the corner of Lexington Avenue on a Sunday in May waiting for a bus. It was a gorgeous day, hot and golden, and there were not many people around. Sunday is more than a bearable day in New York because for one thing there are about a million less cars than usual. No trucks. Suburbanites in for the day pointing up and down and walking with their feet out. A couple of cabs parked outside a lunch-room, the drivers gone in for a beer. A family or two hand in hand, taking the children off to the park. A well-dressed upper-crust couple coming across from Park Avenue also hand in hand—a very common sight in New York, for Americans are not much concerned in such matters with what looks proper or what the neighbors will think. A good day—the sort of day when, for all the panicky newspaper headlines, your faith in people, and their needs and inclinations, is restored.

2. Suddenly, I heard a ghost. It was a familiar ghost, an invisible man somewhere in mid-air saying in a brisk monotone—"Strike. The count is two and two. Runners on first and third." This lingo, or the language of which this is a snatch, is something you would hear in a hundred places—homes, cafés, saloons, cars—from then till the end of the first week in October. It is a radio sports announcer covering a ball game—a ball game being, as you probably know, a baseball game.

3. The voice was coming from nowhere. A young Negro couple, arm in arm, was ambling towards me. But the man's free arm carried a little box. Of course, it was a portable radio. They went down the subway steps, and as they pattered down into the darkness the voice went on floating up, more excited now: "A base hit to left field. Fuselli's in, Rodgers coming into third." Nobody else on the street seemed to notice or to care. But if you had cared, and wanted for one day to get away from radio, I don't know where you could have gone. Out at Coney Island, thousands of bodies would be lying in close proximity not only to thousands of other bodies but to hundreds of other little boxes, tuned high. And the air would be so full of "He's out" and "The bases are loaded"

Reprinted from One Man's America by Alistair Cooke, by permission of Alfred A. Knopf, Inc. Copyright 1952 by Alistair Cooke.

and "Full count," that you'd have had quite a time knowing what the wild waves were saying.

⁴· This little picture is meant to produce a shudder in you. If it doesn't, then Britons are not what they used to be, and their passion for privacy, and what's more for respecting the next man's privacy, is dead and gone. Don't misunderstand me. I approve myself very strongly of this feeling. I share it. But it makes me all the less of an American. Only a week ago, I heard a plonking sound, allied to music, quite faint, coming up through the living-room floor. It was a neighbor in our apartment house who is either six years of age and a promising pianist or forty years of age and a dope . . . because she—why do I say "she," I wonder —has been stuck on that same piece for a month or two now. I grumbled about the sameness of her repertory, and my twelve-year-old daughter, idling over a book, said, "Relax, Pop, you don't have to hear it if you don't want to."

⁵· By this simple remark my daughter didn't mean that I could get up and go downstairs and start a riot, or that I could call the police or take out an injunction. She simply meant I should shut my mind to the sound. I made sure this is what she meant, because when I played aloud with the idea of strangling our tinkling neighbor, she said, "I don't think that's very nice. She paid *her* rent too, you know."

⁶· Now, I should like to say that I am proud of my daughter and usually turn to her for a response that is commonsensical and unshocked (by, so far as I can make out, anything in life). But I wasn't aware she had acquired so young a fundamental mood or attitude of what Americans call democracy. In Britain, one of the minor duties of good citizenship is not to disturb the private life of other citizens. In this country, it's the other way around—not to disturb other citizens who are enjoying their private life in public. That, as you see, is a heavily loaded interpretation of an attitude that is universal among Americans. And there are limits. Just the same, the decision of a Washington court of appeal not to let advertisers broadcast in public buses only shows how far you can go in America without being stopped.

⁷· Americans regard most of us born in Britain as dull, decent, amiable people but given to being rather testy about our rights. So "Relax, Pop," says my daughter and goes back to reading her book with one third of her mind, listening to the pianist downstairs with another lobe, and at the same time dreaming on all cylinders about some absent male of the species. Quite aside from the principle involved, this attitude entails a considerable physical feat. It is the ability not to hear what you don't want to hear, what the most famous radio critic in America calls "selective deafness." He says it is a faculty essential to an enjoyment of

American radio, and it is a faculty that most visiting Britons would rather not develop. Because they soon learn, as Mr. Crosby—John, not Bing—remarks, that the advertising people are aware of this conditioned reflex and so from year to year, like drug addicts, they increase the dose of the sales talk they cut into the programs. Still, nobody hearing his favorite comedian or forum discussion or symphony concert bothers to turn off the "plug." He lets it chatter on about some soap that "atomizes dirt" or a toothpaste that is "kind to gums but murder on film." And then the ecstatic announcer stops, and so back to Bob Hope or "Whither Europe?" or the Second Symphony of Beethoven.

8. To watch an American on a beach, or crowding into a subway, or buying a theater ticket, or sitting at home with his radio on, tells you something about one aspect of the American character: the capacity to withstand a great deal of outside interference, so to speak: a willing acceptance of frenzy which, though it's never self-conscious, amounts to a willingness to let other people have and assert their own lively, and even offensive, character. They are a tough race in this. You are expected —far beyond what other peoples would say were the restraints of manners—to assume that one man's opinion is as good as another's. The expert is an American idol, but only in certain understood fields. He is safe from contradiction if his expertness is in a science—in medicine, technology, industrial research, or in making something with his hands (better, if he uses somebody else's hands, because that shows he has mastered a process which can be left to drones): such things as an automobile, a waterproof watch, or a non-riding girdle. But when it comes to ideas about life and love and religion and education and architecture and painting and music, indeed all forms of pleasure, there is a national conviction that an expert is a phony, or "wants to be different," and that what matters is you should know what you like and—this is a democracy, isn't it?—speak up and say your piece. It may well be born from generations of living close to many races and many prejudices and temperaments and having to strike a livable compromise that may not be as smooth as some other societies; but at least it is a society, a going concern, which had to be built not out of a theory but out of the urgent practical need to get along at all.

9. At any rate, if you want to live here in any spiritual comfort you have to allow for a wide variety of temperament in your friends and neighbors and approve a sharp clash of tastes. An insistence on privacy in such a society looks, as it would not look in Britain, like a form of conceit or neurosis, a refusal to admit the status quo by which you all live. So if the issue ever came up in argument, I think most Americans would say that it is merely elementary good manners and good citizenship to

look on yourself as only one member of the community, whether that community is a town, a party, or a family.

10. It may be what makes Americans so easy-going about their children. I don't know if anyone has ever taken a statistical count, and there may be just as many nagging parents here as anywhere else, but my impression is that if you are what they used to call a severe disciplinarian with children, you get known to the neighbors as a crank. There is a sort of cheerful, unstated assumption that children will grow up and be polite soon enough and that there's no sense for the first fifteen years or so in pretending they are anything but inhabitants of the jungle. (There is a certain family pride in seeing your child become king or queen of the jungle.) The children themselves are of course not aware of being particularly bad or violent or ill-mannered. They have no other system to compare themselves with, and like all children don't even know that any other system exists. Remembering this, you can appreciate that if a six- or a ten- or a fifteen-year-old passes you on the street, looks up and says, "Hi!" he is paying you far more the respect of genuine liking than if he said, "Good morning, sir"—which would be a very alien, not to say sarcastic, sound in these parts.

11. The same sort of tolerance explains too, I think, such a seemingly irrelevant thing as the variety of men's clothes in a big city. There is not among Americans anything remotely resembling the uniform of the English city businessman. They dress for themselves, with their own tastes in ties, shirts, shoes; and this gives to an American street a color, often a garishness, and it makes it pretty impossible for a foreigner to guess at the occupation of the other men around. With women, it is even more difficult. A flock of girls comes into a restaurant and you can't tell the débutante from the shop girl. I remember a Swedish girl on a skiing party watching the swirl of people in the snow and saying, "Which are the nice people? Who are my kind? Give me a sign." There are signs. But they are small and subtle and would take her years to learn. And if she stayed here long, she would insensibly shed the signs she sought.

12. I was taking an Englishman the other night up to my apartment, and as we approached the entrance of the apartment house, I saw a man who lives in the building polishing the radiator of his car. I hissed to call my friend's attention to him as we came close. "Tell me quick," I said, "what sort of an American is this—I mean is he a banker, a real-estate agent, a baseball player or what?—look him over." My friend leered politely at him sideways. He was a middle-aged dark man, with a black mustache and big eyes. He was hatless. He had on a blue sports coat, slacks of a different color, a button-down collar, and a bright tie. He was polishing away and coughing smoke all over the radiator. Then

he bent down to start on the wheels. Standing genially over him was the janitor, saying the utterly meaningless sentence, as we came on it: "No, sir, not for my money . . . but some guys are that crazy, I reckon." When we got inside I looked at my friend.

13. "Oh, I don't know," he said, "I should say an advertising man or perhaps the owner of a chain of drugstores."

14. "That," I said, as we went into the elevator, "is a dethroned Archduke."

15. He was dethroned by the bullet that shot his great-uncle and started the First World War.

COMMENTARY AND QUESTIONS

Alistair Cooke is an Englishman who has spent many years in the United States making reports to his countrymen on the American scene. (Many of these reports have appeared in the *Manchester Guardian.*) This essay was originally a radio talk, one of a series prepared for the British Broadcasting Corporation. The author selected some of the talks for publication in a book, titled in England *Letters from America* and here *One Man's America.* Except for some changes in vocabulary and sentence construction and, as Cooke says, "a little trimming and polishing," the talks were published as delivered.

1. In pars. 2 and 3 the author refers to people listening to a baseball game, but he does not mention baseball again in the essay. In what way is listening to a baseball game related to the central point of the essay?

2. In pars. 12-15 the author presents the incident of the visiting Englishman and his guess about the man polishing the radiator of his car. Does the incident strike you initially as a kind of digression? How closely is it related to the central point of the essay?

3. Cooke begins his essay with the incident of the baseball game and ends it with the incident of the visiting Englishman and his guess about the dethroned Archduke. All of Cooke's generalizations about Americans' feelings with regard to privacy come in the middle section of the essay. What advantage does Cooke gain by this structural arrangement?

4. In par. 6 the author states that one of the duties of good citizenship in the United States is "not to disturb other citizens who are enjoying their private life in public." In the last sentence of par. 9 occurs a positive counterpart of this negative statement. Should pars. 6 and 9 be combined and pars. 7 and 8 be omitted?

5. In his preface for the American reader, the author identifies his type of writing as the radio essay, a form especially appealing to British listeners if it is well done. He compares the composing of such an

essay to writing for blind men: "Thoughtfulness must be entertaining. Any meandering must be artful. Casualness must be calculated; if it is the real thing, it is dreadful." On what basis do you think Cooke would defend the inclusion of each of these items: the description of a May Sunday in New York City (par. 1); the discussion of a neighbor's piano-playing (par. 4); the explanation of the way in which American children are brought up (par. 10); the analysis of the clothes Americans wear (par. 11)?

6. In what way does the construction of certain sentences in par. 1 suggest that this selection was originally a talk?

7. Do you think Cooke is being careless or inconsistent in allowing his choice of words to range from *upper-crust* and *phony* to *neurosis* and *insensibly?* Why is *dreaming on all cylinders* (par. 7) appropriate in its context?

8. In par. 6 Cooke recognizes that his daughter has acquired "a fundamental mood or attitude of what Americans call democracy." Has she also acquired the idiomatic phrasing that an American child would use when she says, "Relax, Pop, you don't have to hear it if you don't want to" (par. 4)?

SUGGESTIONS FOR WRITING

1. Alistair Cooke attempts to interpret an American attitude for his own countrymen. Interpret the attitude or manners of a group (for example, your own family or a social organization of which you are a member) to someone outside the group.

2. Privacy *vs.* membership in a group.

3. Conditions in a dormitory that make for tolerance.

4. In par. 8 Cooke makes the statement that the expert is an American idol; then he limits this generalization with another statement. "But when it comes to ideas about life and love and religion and education and architecture and painting and music, indeed all forms of pleasure, there is a national conviction that an expert is a phony, or 'wants to be different,' and that what matters is you should know what you like and—this is a democracy, isn't it?—speak up and say your piece." Do you think these generalizations about American life are accurate? Offer examples from your own observations which seem to prove or disprove the statements; or, if you think the statements accurate, point out possible dangers for American life which might result.

The Pleasures
and Uses of Bankruptcy

by JOHN KENNETH GALBRAITH

SINCE THE END of World War II, we have been coming for the summer
to an old farm in southeastern Vermont. Once here, the days lengthen
perceptibly. There is magic in the late evening mist on our meadows and
the way the early morning sun comes through the maples. Life acquires
a new tranquillity. So, we think, do the children. The pay, entertainment
allowances and other perquisites of a professor compare badly with those
of industry, law and harness racing. But it is hard to regret an occupation which enables one to spend three or four months of each year on
the edge of paradise. Many others yearn for such privileged surroundings
and therein lies the story.

2. As a teacher of economics, I am visited each summer by a certain
number of my professional friends and colleagues. Without exception,
they inquire about the economic underpinning of this part of Vermont.
Some are being polite; some may even wish to know. I have found the
line of thought which these questions set in motion to be troublesome.
The hills and narrow valleys north of the Massachusetts line and between
the Green Mountains and the Connecticut look reasonably prosperous
but they are without visible means of support. There are no important
industries—fortunately. The valleys have a few dairy farms, but it is
northern Vermont which fattens on the revenues and suffers the vicissi-
tudes of the Boston milkshed. Some people work in the forests which
have largely retrieved the stony and never very fertile cropland. But this
is too rigorous an occupation for many of my neighbors. French Cana-
dians are considered better suited to such toil. For a year or two, as this
is written, a considerable number have been employed in building two
large federal flood-control dams in the neighborhood, but people were
fairly prosperous before the Army Engineers made things better. Many
local residents have always worked on the roads—scraping them and re-
pairing winter damage in the summer and plowing the snow in the winter. But my best-informed neighbor says that all of the money so earned

goes back in taxes for keeping up the roads. I haven't checked his calculations, but he is a reliable man.

3. Then there are the part-time residents—on the whole, we would rather be called "part-time residents" than "summer people" because, as compared with Maine or Martha's Vineyard, we arrive earlier in the summer and stay much later in the autumn, so we are really part of the community. But this is not a fashionable area, and the migratory population consists either of professors or businessmen who share the interests of their academic friends, including an interest in not wasting money. We contribute something to the economic life, but we are no gold mine.

II

4. But gradually I have become aware of another source of revenue which is important. And those who supply it add greatly to the comfort, convenience and pleasure of country life and may even make it tolerable. These are the people who systematically disburse their savings, money they have inherited or whatever they can borrow, on enterprises conducted for the public good. They grow things, make useful articles or (most important of all) render valuable services which one could never obtain on a purely commercial basis. Their prices are not always low, but since they are always selling below cost, no one can complain. The community benefits not only from the goods and services they supply but also from the rent or interest they pay, the purchases they make, and the payrolls they meet. To be sure, the day comes when the rent, interest, bills and payroll become troublesome or can no longer be met. But, invariably others come along. The competition to serve the public at a loss is rather keen. In a town not far from here is an inn which has failed decisively in the financial sense not once but twice in the past five years. It is now up for sale at the highest price yet. The chances of getting the asking price or something close are excellent. On the basis of this and other cases, it is my belief that service generally improves with each bankruptcy.

5. Inns provide the best example of capital consumption, to give this admirable phenomenon its technical name. In the course of an autumn holiday, to offer what economists call a synthetic model of reality, a man and his wife from New Canaan take a leisurely motor trip to Montreal. They are fond of the country, which is why they live in Fairfield County and why they choose this particular trip. Somewhere between Brattleboro and Montpelier they spend a night at a village inn on a secondary road—not a motel, but the real thing with elms and maples all but hiding

the small Shell station across the way. What peace! What a contrast between the life of the innkeepers and their own! Independence and serenity as against the daily penance on the New Haven, the obscene struggle on the subway and the crushing pressures of organization.

6. The travelers have talked of getting off the rat-race. Could it really happen? It won't happen to many people, but it could happen to them. This husband has about fifteen years before actuarial decrepitude, the sense to know it, and a keen desire to enjoy the years that remain. His wife is younger and a good companion. They have some money. They have something even more precious, which is imagination and courage and a knowledge of how to cook.

7. Vaguely, perhaps more than vaguely, they know that the trend is away from the great corporations. The small entrepreneur has always been morally superior—a true child of freedom. Liberal Democrats support him to the hilt. He is not the sort of man Ike had to the White House in the heyday of modern Republicanism. But he is esteemed by *Fortune* which regularly publishes vignettes of small business ingenuity, enterprise and success. Quite a number of these tell of men who found fulfillment and success by starting on their own very late in life. None tells of failure. Those of us who profit from the savings of people who are going broke are profoundly indebted to these and similar success stories and the overtones of community stature, moral fiber, social responsibility and easy money which they contain. The couple returns to the village and searches out the real estate man. He is not hard to find.

8. "Yes, there is a good small inn for sale." It turns out to be the one at which they stopped. This is no coincidence; nearly all small country inns are for sale. Being from New York and therefore experienced in the tools of modern management, the husband has a good hard look at the books. He finds that it has been losing money. Perceptively and quite correctly, he attributes the losses to bad management. What he does not know is that such enterprises never make enough money to give the impression even of indifferent management.

9. So the previous owners go back to New Jersey. For four years, they have furnished jobs and modest wages to the community. They have bought meat and frozen vegetables from the local grocer and quite a bit of liquor from the state store. There were moments when it seemed possible that the liquor might put them in the black and other less commercial interludes when it eased toil and softened anxiety. The part-time residents have had a place with atmosphere and home cooking at which to dine and, on occasion, to deposit a redundant guest. During the two-week deer season and the week before Labor Day, business was always amazing—several times what could be accommodated. The total cost of

so benefiting the community was $13,600. It would have been more but, because of the competition to serve, they are selling out at a considerable capital gain. They have also provided us with considerable unpaid labor, although it is the capital that really counts.

10. The future is also bright. The local carpenter and his two men can look forward to the busiest autumn since the other couple from New Jersey converted their barn into a full-time furniture factory. For the new owners of the inn have unhesitantly identified better management with modernizing the kitchen, refurnishing the bedrooms, adding two baths, and making the former woodshed into a cozy new bar. These improvements will make the inn a better place to leave or take guests and more of an all-round community asset.

III

11. Lest anyone think this story contrived, let me return to strict matters of experience. For years, we have been eating meals at a succession of inns that were being endowed by their owners. The owners were from the city. All were able to bring a modest amount of capital to our service. We always guessed that they were spending money on us and this could have meant—there are some subtle differences here between average and marginal costs—that each visit absorbed some of their capital. Nonetheless, we always felt that our patronage was a real favor and so did they. We were always sorry to see them go, as eventually they did, but we were comforted by the knowledge that others would take their place, and others always have.

12. Until last year, our plumbing was done by a man from Long Island, who left suddenly for (I believe) Montana. We have some excellent and very inexpensive furniture from a former furniture factory. I owe a dollar and fifty cents for some white gladioli to a man who also disappeared and before I could pay him. A nice neighbor left his job in New York to drill artesian wells. We would have patronized him, but unhappily he went out of business just before we ran out of water. Some time ago, I negotiated for a piece of property with a former Army colonel who had left his job on Wall Street to enter the local real estate business. When I suggested that the price was too high, he said I had mortally insulted his professional honor as a West Pointer, and the deal fell through. He is now back in a bond house. We used to sell our hay to a horse farm which provided an excellent market while it lasted. We get firewood from people—they change frequently—who believe that their forest is a real resource. A neighbor from New York is supplying us with

potatoes. He is an encouraging departure, for he is not using savings or an inheritance but has one foot in an advertising agency. The list of such benefactors could be extended almost indefinitely.

IV

13. The notion of an economic system in which everyone works hard, saves his money, and then disperses it by running useful enterprises for the common good is very attractive. However, the local Vermonters do not participate to any extent. They have a strong preference for profitable activity. This means they are rarely to be found running country inns, making furniture, growing African violets (an especially imaginative current venture) or raising horses or potatoes. U.S. Route 5 makes its way along the eastern border of the state through a hideous neon-lighted tunnel walled by motels, antique shops, roadside furniture shops featuring not Vermont but North Carolina craftsmanship and, of course, service stations and restaurants. Quite a few local people are to be found here for they have discovered that the Humbert Humberts patronize this garish bazaar in preference to the lovely local villages, as does almost everyone else. There are no New Yorkers on Route 5. One can hardly trade the rat race for a multiple-lane highway.

14. As a nation, we owe much to subsidies. They built the railroads, and also the airlines. Advocates of protection have never wavered in their belief that it was tariff subsidies—as distinct from, say, free competition —which made our country industrially great. Our merchant marine is kept afloat by a subsidy, and so, we may recall, was Richard Nixon in his salad days. Evidently, therefore, we need feel no shame that our pleasant countryside is subsidized by aspiring small enterprisers. And as subsidies go, this is an excellent one. Unlike farm support prices, it requires no federal appropriations and brings no charges that we are living too well at the taxpayers' expense. Unlike the depletion allowances enjoyed by the oilmen, it brings no complaints, quite justified, of fantastic favoritism. Our subsidy is perfectly reliable, for as I have noted, when one entrepreneur has exhausted his capital and credit, another is always ready and eager to take his place. The very best journals proclaim the virtue of such sacrifice on our behalf. It is a demonstration of worth, an affirmation of faith in the system. A recession or depression would, one imagines, increase the number of people seeking the serenity of the country and the security of their own business. The outlays must have a certain cogency to the individuals involved, but this has nothing to do with the great impersonal sweep of economic forces.

COMMENTARY AND QUESTIONS

In this selection Galbraith is slyly making fun of an attitude of mind (the inconsistency of those who righteously accept the benefits of subsidies for themselves while condemning the theory of subsidies for others) and is suggesting with ironic innocence an unorthodox theory of economy (that money and energy spent on unprofitable enterprises are subsidies for the common good). He develops his point by devoting the major part of his essay to a carefully circumstantial portrayal of the actions of people whom he observed as a Harvard professor summering in Vermont.

1. In pars. 1-3 Galbraith, among other things, states his profession, reveals what attracts him and his family to Vermont for vacations, and identifies the type of people who visit them in Vermont. What use is made of the fact that these visitors are "professional friends and colleagues"?

2. In pars. 4-10 Galbraith presents as a cause for praise and approval something normally regarded as a cause for pity or castigation: people escaping from the city and going bankrupt trying to run unprofitable enterprises. Who is it that benefits from these enterprises?

3. Pars. 5-8 form a unit. How is this unit related to par. 4 and to pars. 9 and 10?

4. In par. 9 Galbraith restates some of the points given in par. 4. Why does the restatement not seem like mere repetition?

5. In light of what Galbraith does in pars. 5-8, explain the phrase "a synthetic model of reality" (which appears in the second sentence of par. 5). Is Galbraith's statement at the beginning of par. 11 ("let me return to strict matters of experience") intended to suggest that the description in pars. 5-8 is not based on the author's observations?

6. How is par. 12 related to par. 11?

7. Why, in par. 13, does Galbraith introduce "the local Vermonters"?

8. Should the defense of subsidies in par. 14 have been made at the beginning of the essay?

9. In par. 7 reference is made to articles in *Fortune* (Galbraith himself was once on the board of editors of that magazine) which praise the small business man: stressing his opportunity for success, not failure. Does the statement in par. 14 about "the very best journals" contradict or reinforce the point made in par. 7?

10. The tone of the essay is exemplified in this sentence from par. 4: "The competition to serve the public at a loss is rather keen." Point out other sentences or phrases which echo this tone.

11. In the context of the essay explain the meaning and evaluate the stylistic use of these expressions: "the obscene struggle on the sub-

way" (par. 5); "actuarial decrepitude" (par. 6); "trade the rat race for a multiple-lane highway" (par. 13).

SUGGESTIONS FOR WRITING

1. The pleasures and uses of failure (to make the team; to be valedictorian; to be pledged to a fraternity).
2. Another example of self-delusion (paralleling the city man who tries to earn a living in the country).

The Bird
and the Machine
by LOREN EISELEY

I SUPPOSE their little bones have years ago been lost among the stones and winds of those high glacial pastures. I suppose their feathers blew eventually into the piles of tumbleweed beneath the straggling cattle fences and rotted there in the mountain snows, along with dead steers and all the other things that drift to an end in the corners of the wire. I do not quite know why I should be thinking of birds over the *New York Times* at breakfast, particularly the birds of my youth half a continent away. It is a funny thing what the brain will do with memories and how it will treasure them and finally bring them into odd juxtapositions with other things, as though it wanted to make a design, or get some meaning out of them, whether you want it or not, or even see it.

2. It used to seem marvelous to me, but I read now that there are machines that can do these things in a small way, machines that can crawl about like animals, and that it may not be long now until they do more things—maybe even make themselves—I saw that piece in the

Times just now. And then they will, maybe—well, who knows—but you read about it more and more with no one making any protest, and already they can add better than we and reach up and hear things through the dark and finger the guns over the night sky.

3. This is the new world that I read about at breakfast. This is the world that confronts me in my biological books and journals, until there are times when I sit quietly in my chair and try to hear the little purr of the cogs in my head and the tubes flaring and dying as the messages go through them and the circuits snap shut or open. This is the great age, make no mistake about it; the robot has been born somewhat appropriately along with the atom bomb, and the brain they say now is just another type of more complicated feedback system. The engineers have its basic principles worked out; it's mechanical, you know; nothing to get superstitious about; and man can always improve on nature once he gets the idea. Well, he's got it all right and that's why, I guess, that I sit here in my chair, with the article crunched in my hand, remembering those two birds and that blue mountain sunlight. There is another magazine article on my desk that reads "Machines Are Getting Smarter Every Day." I don't deny it, but I'll still stick with the birds. It's life I believe in, not machines.

4. Maybe you don't believe there is any difference. A skeleton is all joints and pulleys, I'll admit. And when man was in his simpler stages of machine building in the eighteenth century, he quickly saw the resemblances. "What," wrote Hobbes, "is the heart but a spring, and the nerves but so many strings, and the joints but so many wheels, giving motion to the whole body?" Tinkering about in their shops it was inevitable in the end that men would see the world as a huge machine "subdivided into an infinite number of lesser machines."

5. The idea took on with a vengeance. Little automatons toured the country—dolls controlled by clockwork. Clocks described as little worlds were taken on tours by their designers. They were made up of moving figures, shifting scenes and other remarkable devices. The life of the cell was unknown. Man, whether he was conceived as possessing a soul or not, moved and jerked about like these tiny puppets. A human being thought of himself in terms of his own tools and implements. He had been fashioned like the puppets he produced and was only a more clever model made by a greater designer.

6. Then in the nineteenth century, the cell was discovered, and the single machine in its turn was found to be the product of millions of infinitesimal machines—the cells. Now, finally, the cell itself dissolves away into an abstract chemical machine—and that into some intangible, inexpressible flow of energy. The secret seems to lurk all about, the

wheels get smaller and smaller, and they turn more rapidly, but when you try to seize it the life is gone—and so, by popular definition, some would say that life was never there in the first place. The wheels and the cogs are the secret and we can make them better in time—machines that will run faster and more accurately than real mice to real cheese.

7. I have no doubt it can be done, though a mouse harvesting seeds on an autumn thistle is to me a fine sight and more complicated, I think, in his multiform activity, than a machine "mouse" running a maze. Also, I like to think of the possible shape of the future brooding in mice, just as it brooded once in a rather ordinary mousy insectivore who became a man. It leaves a nice fine indeterminate sense of wonder that even an electronic brain hasn't got, because you know perfectly well that if the electronic brain changes, it will be because of something man has done to it. But what man will do to himself he doesn't really know. A certain scale of time and a ghostly intangible thing called change are ticking in him. Powers and potentialities like the oak in the seed, or a red and awful ruin. Either way, it's impressive; and the mouse has it, too. Or those birds, I'll never forget those birds—yet before I measured their significance, I learned the lesson of time first of all. I was young then and left alone in a great desert—part of an expedition that had scattered its men over several hundred miles in order to carry on research more effectively. I learned there that time is a series of planes existing superficially in the same universe. The tempo is a human illusion, a subjective clock ticking in our own kind of protoplasm.

8. As the long months passed, I began to live on the slower planes and to observe more readily what passed for life there. I sauntered, I passed more and more slowly up and down the canyons in the dry baking heat of midsummer. I slumbered for long hours in the shade of huge brown boulders that had gathered in tilted companies out on the flats. I had forgotten the world of men and the world had forgotten me. Now and then I found a skull in the canyons, and these justified my remaining there. I took a serene cold interest in these discoveries. I had come, like many a naturalist before me, to view life with a wary and subdued attention. I had grown to take pleasure in the divested bone.

9. I sat once on a high ridge that fell away before me into a waste of sand dunes. I sat through hours of a long afternoon. Finally, as I glanced beside my boot an indistinct configuration caught my eye. It was a coiled rattlesnake, a big one. How long he had sat with me I do not know. I had not frightened him. We were both locked in the sleep-walking tempo of the earlier world, baking in the same high air and sunshine. Perhaps

he had been there when I came. He slept on as I left, his coils, so ill discerned by me, dissolving once more among the stones and gravel from which I had barely made him out.

10. Another time I got on a higher ridge, among some tough little wind-warped pines half covered over with sand in a basin-like depression that caught everything carried by the air up to those heights. There were a few thin bones of birds, some cracked shells of indeterminable age, and the knotty fingers of pine roots bulged out of shape from their long and agonizing grasp upon the crevices of the rock. I lay under the pines in the sparse shade and went to sleep once more.

11. It grew cold finally, for autumn was in the air by then, and the few things that lived thereabouts were sinking down into an even chillier scale of time. In the moments between sleeping and waking I saw the roots about me and slowly, slowly, a foot in what seemed many centuries, I moved my sleep-stiffened hands over the scaling bark and lifted my numbed face after the vanishing sun. I was a great awkward thing of knots and aching limbs, trapped up there in some long, patient endurance that involved the necessity of putting living fingers into rock and by slow, aching expansion bursting those rocks asunder. I suppose, so thin and slow was the time of my pulse by then, that I might have stayed on to drift still deeper into the lower cadences of the frost, or the crystalline life that glistens pebbles, or shines in a snowflake, or dreams in the meteoric iron between the worlds.

12. It was a dim descent, but time was present in it. Somewhere far down in that scale the notion struck me that one might come the other way. Not many months thereafter I joined some colleagues heading higher into a remote windy tableland where huge bones were reputed to protrude like boulders from the turf. I had drowsed with reptiles and moved with the century-long pulse of trees; now, lethargically, I was climbing back up some invisible ladder of quickening hours. There had been talk of birds in connection with my duties. Birds are intense, fast-living creatures—reptiles, I suppose one might say, that have escaped out of the heavy sleep of time, transformed fairy creatures dancing over sunlit meadows. It is a youthful fancy, no doubt, but because of something that happened up there among the escarpments of that range, it remains with me a lifelong impression. I can never bear to see a bird imprisoned.

13. We came into that valley through the trailing mists of a spring night. It was a place that looked as though it might never have known the foot of man, but our scouts had been ahead of us and we knew all about the abandoned cabin of stone that lay far up on one hillside. It had been built in the land rush of the last century and then lost to the cattlemen again as the marginal soils failed to take to the plow.

14. There were spots like this all over that country. Lost graves marked by unlettered stones and old corroding rim-fire cartridge cases lying where somebody had made a stand among the boulders that rimmed the valley. They are all that remain of the range wars; the men are under the stones now. I could see our cavalcade winding in and out through the mist below us: torches, the reflection of the truck lights on our collecting tins, and the far-off bumping of a loose dinosaur thigh bone in the bottom of a trailer. I stood on a rock a moment looking down and thinking what it cost in money and equipment to capture the past.

15. We had, in addition, instructions to lay hands on the present. The word had come through to get them alive—birds, reptiles, anything. A zoo somewhere abroad needed restocking. It was one of those reciprocal matters in which science involves itself. Maybe our museum needed a stray ostrich egg and this was the payoff. Anyhow, my job was to help capture some birds and that was why I was there before the trucks.

16. The cabin had not been occupied for years. We intended to clean it out and live in it, but there were holes in the roof and the birds had come in and were roosting in the rafters. You could depend on it in a place like this where everything blew away, and even a bird needed some place out of the weather and away from coyotes. A cabin going back to nature in a wild place draws them till they come in, listening at the eaves, I imagine, pecking softly among the shingles till they find a hole and then suddenly the place is theirs and man is forgotten.

17. Sometimes of late years I find myself thinking the most beautiful sight in the world might be the birds taking over New York after the last man has run away to the hills. I will never live to see it, of course, but I know just how it will sound because I've lived up high and I know the sort of watch birds keep on us. I've listened to sparrows tapping tentatively on the outside of air conditioners when they thought no one was listening, and I know how other birds test the vibrations that come up to them through the television aerials.

18. "Is he gone?" they ask, and the vibrations come up from below, "Not yet, not yet."

19. Well, to come back, I got the door open softly and I had the spotlight all ready to turn on and blind whatever birds there were so they couldn't see to get out through the roof. I had a short piece of ladder to put against the far wall where there was a shelf on which I expected to make the biggest haul. I had all the information I needed just like any skilled assassin. I pushed the door open, the hinges squeaking only a little. A bird or two stirred—I could hear them—but nothing flew and there was a faint starlight through the holes in the roof.

20. I padded across the floor, got the ladder up and the light ready, and slithered up the ladder till my head and arms were over the shelf.

Everything was dark as pitch except for the starlight at the little place back of the shelf near the eaves. With the light to blind them, they'd never make it. I had them. I reached my arm carefully over in order to be ready to seize whatever was there and I put the flash on the edge of the shelf where it would stand by itself when I turned it on. That way I'd be able to use both hands.

21. Everything worked perfectly except for one detail—I didn't know what kind of birds were there. I never thought about it at all, and it wouldn't have mattered if I had. My orders were to get something interesting. I snapped on the flash and sure enough there was a great beating and feathers flying, but instead of my having them, they, or rather he, had me. He had my hand, that is, and for a small hawk not much bigger than my fist he was doing all right. I heard him give one short metallic cry when the light went on and my hand descended on the bird beside him; after that he was busy with his claws and his beak was sunk in my thumb. In the struggle I knocked the lamp over on the shelf, and his mate got her sight back and whisked neatly through the hole in the roof and off among the stars outside. It all happened in fifteen seconds and you might think I would have fallen down the ladder, but no, I had a professional assassin's reputation to keep up, and the bird, of course, made the mistake of thinking the hand was the enemy and not the eyes behind it. He chewed my thumb up pretty effectively and lacerated my hand with his claws, but in the end I got him, having two hands to work with.

22. He was a sparrow hawk and a fine young male in the prime of life. I was sorry not to catch the pair of them, but as I dripped blood and folded his wings carefully, holding him by the back so that he couldn't strike again, I had to admit the two of them might have been more than I could have handled under the circumstances. The little fellow had saved his mate by diverting me, and that was that. He was born to it, and made no outcry now, resting in my hand hopelessly, but peering toward me in the shadows behind the lamp with a fierce, almost indifferent glance. He neither gave nor expected mercy and something out of the high air passed from him to me, stirring a faint embarrassment.

23. I quit looking into that eye and managed to get my huge carcass with its fist full of prey back down the ladder. I put the bird in a box too small to allow him to injure himself by struggle and walked out to welcome the arriving trucks. It had been a long day, and camp still to make in the darkness. In the morning that bird would be just another episode. He would go back with the bones in the truck to a small cage in a city where he would spend the rest of his life. And a good thing,

too. I sucked my aching thumb and spat out some blood. An assassin has to get used to these things. I had a professional reputation to keep up.

^{24.} In the morning, with the change that comes on suddenly in that high country, the mist that had hovered below us in the valley was gone. The sky was a deep blue, and one could see for miles over the high out-croppings of stone. I was up early and brought the box in which the little hawk was imprisoned out onto the grass where I was building a cage. A wind as cool as a mountain spring ran over the grass and stirred my hair. It was a fine day to be alive. I looked up and all around and at the hole in the cabin roof out of which the other little hawk had fled. There was no sign of her anywhere that I could see.

^{25.} "Probably in the next county by now," I thought cynically, but before beginning work I decided I'd have a look at my last night's capture.

^{26.} Secretively, I looked again all around the camp and up and down and opened the box. I got him right out in my hand with his wings folded properly and I was careful not to startle him. He lay limp in my grasp and I could feel his heart pound under the feathers but he only looked beyond me and up.

^{27.} I saw him look that last look away beyond me into a sky so full of light that I could not follow his gaze. The little breeze flowed over me again, and nearby a mountain aspen shook all its tiny leaves. I suppose I must have had an idea then of what I was going to do, but I never let it come up into consciousness. I just reached over and laid the hawk on the grass.

^{28.} He lay there a long minute without hope, unmoving, his eyes still fixed on that blue vault above him. It must have been that he was already so far away in heart that he never felt the release from my hand. He never even stood. He just lay with his breast against the grass.

^{29.} In the next second after that long minute he was gone. Like a flicker of light, he had vanished with my eyes full on him, but without actually seeing even a premonitory wing beat. He was gone straight into that towering emptiness of light and crystal that my eyes could scarcely bear to penetrate. For another long moment there was silence. I could not see him. The light was too intense. Then from far up some-where a cry came ringing down.

^{30.} I was young then and had seen little of the world, but when I heard that cry my heart turned over. It was not the cry of the hawk I had captured; for, by shifting my position against the sun, I was now seeing further up. Straight out of the sun's eye, where she must have been

soaring restlessly above us for untold hours, hurtled his mate. And from far up, ringing from peak to peak of the summits over us, came a cry of such unutterable and ecstatic joy that it sounds down across the years and tingles among the cups on my quiet breakfast table.

[31.] I saw them both now. He was rising fast to meet her. They met in a great soaring gyre that turned to a whirling circle and a dance of wings. Once more, just once, their two voices, joined in a harsh wild medley of question and response, struck and echoed against the pinnacles of the valley. Then they were gone forever somewhere into those upper regions beyond the eyes of men.

[32.] I am older now, and sleep less, and have seen most of what there is to see and am not very much impressed any more, I suppose, by anything. "What Next in the Attributes of Machines?" my morning headline runs. "It Might Be the Power to Reproduce Themselves."

[33.] I lay the paper down and across my mind a phrase floats insinuatingly: "It does not seem that there is anything in the construction, constituents, or behavior of the human being which it is essentially impossible for science to duplicate and synthesize. On the other hand . . ."

[34.] All over the city the cogs in the hard, bright mechanisms have begun to turn. Figures move through computers, names are spelled out, a thoughtful machine selects the fingerprints of a wanted criminal from an array of thousands. In the laboratory an electronic mouse runs swiftly through a maze toward the cheese it can neither taste nor enjoy. On the second run it does better than a living mouse.

[35.] "On the other hand . . ." Ah, my mind takes up, on the other hand the machine does not bleed, ache, hang for hours in the empty sky in a torment of hope to learn the fate of another machine, nor does it cry out with joy nor dance in the air with the fierce passion of a bird. Far off, over a distance greater than space, that remote cry from the heart of heaven makes a faint buzzing among my breakfast dishes and passes on and away.

COMMENTARY AND QUESTIONS

In this essay an anthropologist presents a group of personal experiences, drawn largely from the time when he was a young scientist, to explain his dismay at the reverence shown machines and their capabilities, and to suggest something else. "It's life," says Eiseley, "I believe in, not machines."

1. In pars. 1-3 Eiseley refers to articles in various types of publications which report the current accomplishments of machines and hint at

an even more important future. How does the attitude expressed toward this information help to explain why Eiseley includes a historical survey in pars. 4-6?

2. In par. 7 Eiseley refers to the time when he was a young man, part of a large scientific expedition in a remote and lonely region, and introduces the two sets of remembered experiences that comprise the bulk of the essay: the second set (pars. 13-31) centers on the pair of hawks; from the first set (pars. 8-12) he says he learned the lesson of time. Does the nature of the observation made about time determine why more than one form of life is discussed in pars. 8-12?

3. The word *bird* appears in the title of the essay. But not until par. 13 does Eiseley begin his presentation of the incidents involving the hawks. How has he maintained suspense? (Comment on the references to birds in pars. 1, 3, 7, 10, and 12.)

4. In pars. 13-23 Eiseley, among other things, explains the reason for trying to catch the birds, details his own preparations, and describes the struggle with and ultimate capture of the male hawk. Three times (in pars. 19, 21, and 23) he labels himself as playing the role of assassin: why this emphasis?

5. In pars. 24-31 he reveals what he did with the hawk on the morning following the capture. What is the significance of the observation (in par. 24) that it "was a fine day to be alive"?

6. In pars. 32-35 Eiseley returns to the present time and to the articles on machines mentioned in the opening paragraphs of the essay. The initial sentence of par. 32 serves as a transitional sentence, but it also echoes the initial sentence of par. 30. Is the attitude toward life reflected in the two sentences similar or altogether different?

7. Eiseley begins par. 35 with the same quoted phrase ("On the other hand . . .") that ends par. 33. Does he, by the use of the phrase in par. 35, imply something different from the implication of the same phrase in par. 33? How do the comments in par. 35 pick up the discussion of the machine mouse in par. 7 and the reference to machines in par. 2?

8. At the end of par. 7 Eiseley identifies the lesson of time he learned on the expedition: "I learned there that time is a series of planes existing superficially in the same universe. The tempo is a human illusion . . ." (In the paragraphs immediately following he speaks of the "century-long pulses of trees" and "the sleep-walking tempo of the earlier world"—represented by the rattlesnake—and says that birds might be described as reptiles "that have escaped out of the heavy sleep of time.") Earlier in par. 7 Eiseley comments on man: "A certain scale of time and a ghostly intangible thing called change are ticking in him." With the aim of explaining why Eiseley includes in the same essay the two sets of remembered experiences—one having to do with the lesson of time, the other with the hawks—evaluate the following sentence as a statement of Eiseley's central idea:

"Because living matter in any form—but represented at any given moment by forms living at different levels—is capable of change whereas machines cannot change except as man determines a change, life—represented in its essence by the cry of joy of the reunited hawks and by the watcher's awareness and memory of that joy— transcends any machine."

9. In par. 7 Eiseley suggests a positive and a negative direction of change possible in man's future: "Powers and potentialities like the oak in the seed, or a red and awful ruin." Do you think the digression on the future in pars. 17-18 picks up the positive or the negative direction? Do you think the reader, after finishing the essay, is intended to be left with a positive or a negative impression?

10. One way Eiseley achieves unity of effect is by weaving patterns with details. How is the *blue mountain sunlight* (in par. 3) picked up in pars. 24, 27, 28, 29, and 30? How are the *cogs* (in par. 3) and *wheels* (in par. 4) picked up in par. 6 and par. 34? How is *a wind* (in par. 24) picked up in par. 27? How is *breakfast* (in par. 1) picked up in pars. 3, 30, and 35? Find other examples of such patterns.

SUGGESTION FOR WRITING

Select some event from your own experience that has a significant bearing on your way of thinking. Develop the presentation of the event in such a way that the reader gets the full flavor of the actual experience and the wider meaning or significance that it has for you now.

A Matter of Proportion

by R. B. ROBERTSON

IN DESCRIBING WHALES, and especially that greatest of them all—*Sibbaldus musculus*, the blue whale, or sulphur-bottom—one quickly runs out of adjectives, or, rather, never finds a single adequate one. Huge, immense, enormous, titanic, mighty, vast, stupendous, monstrous, gigantic, elephantine, colossal, Cyclopean, Gargantuan—these are about the only adjectives that Roget can find to help, and not only are they all incapable of conveying an idea of the bulk of the blue whale to a person who has never seen one but some are downright misleading. "Elephantine," for instance, is a pygmy adjective, giving an utterly false impression of this greatest of all monsters of all time, for the blue whale has the bulk and weight of fifty elephants. Like most people, I imagine, I had always mentally accepted the fact that a whale is big, but I had never realized how its bigness transcended adjectives until I saw one close at hand three years ago, when I spent eight months serving as senior medical officer on a British whaling factory ship in the antarctic. A whaling factory ship is a hulking brute of a vessel, four hundred or more feet long, with a gaping tunnel, or skidway, leading from open water at the stern to a spacious deck area amidships, and when I saw my first blue whale— nearly a quarter as long as the ship itself—being dragged up that skidway in order to be stripped, or flensed, of its blubber on the open deck, it became clear that no word in Roget's section on bigness would ever mean the same to me again.

2. I have before me some statistics concerning a fairly large (hundred-and-twenty-ton) but far from record-breaking blue whale that was measured and then weighed, piece by piece, at the Stromness whaling station, on South Georgia Island, in the antarctic, on November 8, 1926, the day after it was killed. In presenting these figures, I shall try to correlate them with commonplace objects that may help make them more intelligible. The length of this whale, then, was eighty-nine feet, or a bit more than that of a Pullman car; its height was nine feet and its girth forty-six feet—dimensions that also correspond fairly closely with those

of a Pullman car. An elephant could have walked through the arch of its upended jawbone without touching it at any point, for it was twenty-three feet long and proportionately wide. Each fin—nine and a half feet long and weighing a ton—was the size and weight of a substantial marble banquet table, and its eighteen-foot flukes would have made a pair of wings for a fighter plane. Its twenty-six tons of blubber would have kept all the votive candles in St. Peter's, in Rome, burning for a century or more, and its fifty-six tons of meat would have provided a hamburger (and a good one, too) for every person in Boston, Massachusetts. Its tongue alone weighed three tons, and six very strong men would have been needed to lift its half-ton heart. Its skull was the size and weight of an automobile (and the brain it contained was not much bigger than the automobile's carburetor). Its blood would have filled seven thousand quart milk bottles. Its liver and lungs weighed a ton apiece, and its kidneys and stomach half a ton. All in all, a monster. Its value today would be about five thousand dollars. Not long ago, in reading a book about a voyage of the famous Charles W. Morgan, the last of the New Bedford whaleships, I came across this statement: "We continued our cruise for some six weeks longer and took whales enough to make us about two hundred and fifty barrels [of oil]." The single whale anatomized on South Georgia Island gave up a total of a hundred and sixty-two barrels of oil, from its blubber, meat, and bones. But its carcass had been stripped and dissected and boiled down by techniques and machines the old whalemen never dreamed of, and, furthermore, it was a blue whale—the mightiest whale of all, and a species that, because of its speed, was practically invulnerable in the days of sails and oars and hand harpoons.

3. On one perfectly ordinary day at the peak of the season in the whaling grounds, near the antarctic pack ice, we had twelve such whales in tow behind our factory ship and two more alongside. I saw them that evening, when I took a recess from my duties in the sick bay and went above to see how the whaling business was progressing. They had been killed by one or another of our whale catchers, the small, speedy harpoon vessels that ranged the ocean and did our hunting, and they had been towed back to the factory by our two corvettes, similar little ships that provided a fast shuttle service between the widespread catchers and us. The two whales alongside the factory served as fenders, because in the tossing, heaving antarctic seas no small ship, unless held off by a cushion, could have made fast to our big ship without being smashed to bits, and no fender ever devised by man provides half so good a cushion as the rubbery, springy, mountainous bulk of a whale. As I made my way to my favorite point of observation, on the after winch deck, overlooking the vast working area on the main deck, the bosun of the factory

ship, a huge and grandfatherly Shetland Islander named Adamson, passed me on his way to check up on his winchmen. "We'll easily stow this lot before morning," he said. I stayed up all night to watch them do it.

4. By international law, every whale that is not being used for a fender must be on the deck of the factory ship within thirty-three hours after it is killed. Anyone who has smelled a whale that has been dead longer than that and who realizes that whales are killed for food, among other things, can understand the wisdom of this law, but carrying it out on a bucking and rolling factory ship in the short, freezing antarctic night is another matter. The twelve free whales, moored by their tails with wire rope, floated in the sea astern of us, looking uncomfortably pathetic and ridiculous as they tossed about in the glare of the ship's floodlights. A few hours before, they had been the masters of the ocean, the mightiest animals that ever knew life on this planet, and now they were just so many tons of dead organic matter, waiting their turn to be converted into margarine and poultry feed.

5. Adamson began the business of getting the whales aboard, and I settled down to watch a show of seamanship that even the oldest hands on a factory ship never tire of seeing. The whales are dragged, tail first, up the skidway from the waterline at the stern by a great steel "grab," a clawlike instrument that weighs ten tons and is cunningly shaped to fit over and grasp the whale's tail, and getting it into position to do its work is no job for a tyro. Under Adamson's direction, it was raised from the deck and, by skillful teamwork between five powerful stern and center-deck winches, was carried, suspended in the air, down the skidway. Arriving in position over the tail of the first whale, which was lashing about in the seas that broke into the lower end of the skidway, the grab hovered there for a moment or two, following, as if it had eyes, the wild movements of the tail. It crept closer, its jaws wide open. Suddenly, at an instant when it was directly over the tail, it seemed to pounce, and, with a crash of iron that could be heard throughout the ship, the jaws slammed together. A hundred tons of whale were now secure, and ready to be pulled on board. The first time I saw the grab in action, it had seemed to me to have a brain and consciousness of its own, enabling it to pursue the wildly heaving tail and leap on it at precisely the moment when the motions of the sea and the ship were favorably synchronized. But as I sat there that night, I knew that the brain and consciousness were those of Adamson, far below me in the floodlights. He was quietly leaning over a rail halfway down the skidway, in the only place where he could be seen by all five winch operators at once, and with barely perceptible movements of his hands and head he was starting, stopping, slacking, and otherwise controlling the slightest move-

ments of the guy ropes attached to the grab. He directed his winchmen, dispersed hundreds of feet away from him, like a suave and undemonstrative orchestra conductor, and, indeed, the rhythmic advance of the grab and the grand climax when it secured the whale seemed to demand a musical accompaniment. Once the grab was firmly in position, I saw Adamson jerk his right thumb sharply upward once. Then he walked away, and as another and even more powerful set of winches amidships went into action, the great whale began to move up the skidway toward the deck of the factory. I felt like applauding, and it seemed as if Adamson ought to come back and take at least one bow, but he was already down among a snapping tangle of wire ropes at the stern, coaxing the next ninety-foot monster to the lower end of the skidway.

6. The first whale glided smoothly and steadily upward. Its arrival at the top of the skidway was the signal for the appearance of the chief flenser, a sombre and aloof Norwegian. (Most of the whaling specialists on our expedition, including the gunners and flensers, were Norwegians; most of the men who were concerned with the navigation, maintenance, and machinery of the ship and the catchers were British.) This man, as far as I know, never once spoke to a soul aboard during the entire eight months of the expedition. In fact, in all those eight months I never saw him without his flensing knife—a wicked-looking article shaped like a hockey stick —in his hand, attending to his specialty. I never found out his name, or what he did in his spare time, or where he disappeared to when he was not at work. As a flenser, he was just about peerless; the other officers of the expedition, some of whom had sailed with him many times before, regarded him as the most talented practitioner in the antarctic. But they knew no more about him than I did. They called him the Gaunt Stranger. Now, weighing and balancing his curved knife in its four-foot shaft, he looked much like a surgeon about to commence a major operation. He did not wait for his hundred-ton patient to be placed on the operating table before starting his first incision; as the whale emerged from the skidway, he stuck his knife into it and made a long, precise cut through the six-inch thickness of the blubber as the whale was drawn past him by the winches. Then, the whale having come to rest, he neatly carved out steps in its carcass, as a mountaineer does on a perpendicular ice slope, and, with their help, climbed atop it. Once there, though the ship was pitching heavily, he balanced in his spiked boots and made some more long, sure slices in the blubber, sometimes cutting out a chunk and kicking it off onto the deck, sometimes drawing twisting and turning slashes here and there. Then, like race horses let out of the gate, the other flensers leaped at the whale. They sliced and hacked with what seemed to be random fury, but actually every cut was deliberate, and was the

same sort of cut that the same man had been making on the same type of whale during all the years of his experience.

7. Now wire ropes began descending from derricks overhead. A flenser was waiting for each rope as it swung down, and upon catching it he fixed it to a toggle he had inserted in a hole cut in the blubber. Then more winches steamed up, and great slabs of blubber, which would have taken hours to remove by the old methods, were stripped from the whale as easily as peeling an orange—or so it seemed. There could, however, be no margin of error among the flensers; one false cut or one loose shackle and there would have been blood other than whale blood sluicing over the pitching, slippery deck. A flenser who did not fully appreciate the dangers of his job could not survive for a month in the midst of that maelstrom of whirring machinery, straining ropes, and razor-sharp knives. While at first glance there appeared to be a state of complete confusion among the flensers as they dashed about slashing at the blubber, I had watched them before and I could see that every man among them was being both extremely methodical and extremely careful. Even at the height of the melee, not one of the knife blades was ever turned in the direction of a fellow-flenser; every wire rope lying on the deck was walked around as warily as one would walk around a rattlesnake; and each flenser before signalling to his winch operator to haul away took a sharp look about him to make sure that his mates were standing clear.

8. There are two particularly dangerous steps in the blubber-stripping process. The first is the ceremony of the turning of the whale. After the blubber has been stripped from one side of the animal, the carcass must be turned over to allow the flensers to attack the other side. This is done by running a wire rope through a pulley fixed to one edge of the deck by a shackle, passing it over the top of the whale, and securing it to the base of the farther fin. Then a donkey engine musters all its power, and the wire rope and shackle begin to take up the strain. At this point, every flenser leaves the deck to stand in the mouth of one of the alleyways leading off it. The first time I saw the operation, I leaned far out over the rail of the winch deck for a better view, and Adamson, seeing me, shouted, "Get back, for Christ sake! You bloody fool!" I did indeed get back, and quickly, because I knew there must be good reason for such a blast of strong language from the most quiet-spoken and courteous man on the ship. As soon as the whale had been turned on that occasion, Adamson heaved himself up the ladder to the winch deck to apologize. "That's the most dangerous time of the flensing process, Doctor," he said. "The whole weight of the whale is taken by that one shackle on the deck, and there never was a shackle made yet that won't give way sooner or later. When it does give way—and I've seen it happen several

times—it acts like a slingshot. The shackle is the shot, and the wire rope is the sling, and anyone who happens to be standing or leaning inside the arc made by the rope will have to be scraped off the deck with a shovel. Sorry if I was rude, but you were right in line with the shackle, and there wasn't time to do anything but bawl you out." I thanked the old man for his warning, and now, later in the season, I needed no bosun's shout to make me seek shelter as the whale was turned over. Standing several cautious paces back, I watched the rope tightening until it and the shackle began to make that groaning, protesting noise that sailors respect, for it means that the rope is what they call "bar tight" and that both rope and shackle have nearly reached the limit of their endurance. But the whale gave first, and, with a slithering smack that shook the whole ship, crashed over. The flensers immediately darted out from their places of shelter and attacked it again. The first of the two most dangerous moments was past.

⁹· The second comes when the tons of baleen—the bony plates that fill the top of the blue whale's mouth cavity and strain its diet of small crustaceans out of the water—are removed and dumped overside. A century ago, in the days of corsets and kepis, baleen, or whalebone, was the most valuable part of the whale, but in this age of steel and plastics it is not worth its passage home, and is therefore jettisoned as so much junk. To remove it, a wire rope from a derrick overhead is fixed securely to the mass with tongs. A winchman takes a heavy strain on this rope, pulling the whalebone upward and outward. As he does so, the chief flenser slices down the length of the whale's upper jaw, toward the juncture of the jawbones. The winchman increases the strain as the chief flenser cuts more and more baleen loose. Just before making his last cut, to sever the appalling cartilaginous mass from the whale, the chief flenser cries "*Barde!*"—Norwegian for "Baleen!" The men around him take up the cry, and everybody except the chief flenser dives for cover. Then the last cut is started. The winch, keeping pace with the flenser's knife, accelerates, and the *barde,* with a wrenching tear, parts from the whale, swings wildly up, and is deftly turned outboard by the winchman, just grazing the bulwarks. For half a second, it is suspended there; then the winchman releases the tongs, and the tons of baleen, which would smash to pulp anyone beneath them, plunge down toward the sea. That, at any rate, is the theory. But occasionally the ship will roll at just the wrong moment, and the great, jagged lump of bony matter will come crashing inboard again. "I've seen maybe five or six men killed by the *barde,*" Adamson told me. "I'd advise you, Doctor, if you're anywhere in the vicinity and you hear the cry of '*Barde!*,' don't stop to look around and see where it is, but get under some kind of cover, or fall down flat on

your face." Later in the voyage, when a man was brought to me in the sick bay who looked as though he hadn't a whole bone left in his body and who was barely able to mutter, "I no hear them shout 'Bardel,'" I realized the wisdom of the old bosun's advice.

10. Fortunately, no such accident occurred this time. After the baleen was safely overboard and the whale was flensed completely, the blubber was cut into slivers eighteen inches wide and ten feet long. These strips were seized upon by the "blubber boys," a motley collection of ragamuffins ranging in age from eighteen to eighty, who fixed their whale hooks in them and hauled them to round, iron-rimmed holes in the deck that belched forth steam and fritters of boiling fat. These holes, the size of manholes, led down to a battery of modern pressure cookers on the factory deck below. I watched the blubber boys awhile as they stuffed ton after ton of oily fat into the maws of the cookers, and admired the dexterity with which each of them wielded his whale hook—a simple tool consisting of a piece of iron about two feet long with a sharp hook at one end and a wooden handgrasp at the other. The whale hook has been an essential whaling implement ever since the first whaleman tried to handle a slippery piece of blubber. A blubber boy without a hook in his hand is a sorry and useless lump of sailordom, but with it he is a prestidigitator of the first order. He is seen at his best in his battles with the flensers. Flensers as a class for some reason hate blubber boys. I have often seen a flenser cut out a five-pound chunk of blubber in order to insert a toggle, and then catch up the slimy mass on the end of his knife and hurl it venomously at the nearest blubber boy. Sometimes he scores a hit, but equally often the blubber boy, without even seeming to look up, retaliates by diverting the course of the projectile with his whale hook and sending it along to smack in the face of the nearest flenser beyond, who may be as much as twenty yards away. There is a legend that blubber boys eat with their whale hooks and darn their socks with them. That is not strictly true, but it is true that they put the hooks to a variety of uses for which they were never designed. Let a blubber boy reach for a rope, and he will reach with his hook. Let him open a door, lift a lid, or steady himself as the ship rolls, and he will always use his dexterous third arm in preference to the two God gave him. Hopping around the deck in a ring on the outskirts of the flensing team, the blubber boys are like nothing so much as a horde of Captain Hooks playing outfield in some odd nautical game.

11. When the blubber was all flensed, cut up, and stowed, the Gaunt Stranger stood back, still solemn, still silent, and surveyed his work. He looked now not so much like a surgeon as like a priest standing in silent prayer over the remains of a sacrifice. Then he nodded curtly and walked

off the scene. His nod was seen by two winchmen fully two hundred feet forward on the ship. Wire ropes tightened, all hands stood clear and formed little groups by the bulwarks, lighting their pipes or sharpening their knives, and the skinned whale, now a pink-and-white mountain of flesh and blood and bone, began to slide slowly through an archway amidships. This archway, known inevitably as Hell's Gates because of the steam and blood and noise that filled it, led to the lemming deck forward, where the lemmers, the expert anatomists of the ship, awaited it.

12. These lemmers—nobody knows the origin of their title—use the same type of knife as the flensers, but they also have heavy, steam-driven bone saws to assist them. Thus armed, they dismember the carcass and sort out its huge and ghastly sections into various categories. From my position on the after winch deck, I could see little of this dissection, so, curiosity overcoming my terror of the contorting and straining wire ropes and the mysterious objects swinging in the air overhead, I ventured forward to the archway, as I had not summoned up the courage to do until that night. The steam and noise on the lemming deck were ten times as great as they had been on the flensing deck, and the diabolic tempo at which the lemmers worked made the flensers seem slow and awkward. For a while, I stood in dazed uncertainty at Hell's Gates, not sure whether to retreat or to plunge forward into the steam and blood and noise and take my chances among the demons who were rushing about there with flashing, blood-stained knives. Then in the midst of the grotesque charade I suddenly saw a cheerful, familiar face and a beckoning arm. It was a bone-saw man named Hamish, whom I had talked with on many off-duty occasions. He had a magnificent bristling black beard and the confident bearing of a man who is on a job that he understands as well as anyone else on earth. I dived through the steam toward him and found a place of comparative safety behind his saw. "You've never been forrard here to see us working yet, have you, Doc?" he shouted in my ear. "Well, wait ere I fix this bluidy backbone, and then I'll tell you what's going on."

13. "Fixing the bluidy backbone" looked dead easy as Hamish did it, but I could see that it was in fact a miracle of coöperation between many brains and much machinery. By this time, the lemmers had sliced the tons of flesh from the back of the whale as neatly as a butcher cuts a rump steak, and this vast quantity of meat had gone down into a special hole in the deck. The rib casing—every rib bigger than a man—had been cut away and hauled up overhead, and now swung suspended from the derricks like a giant's feast of pork chops. In a moment, it, too, would be carved up and stowed in the cookers. The innards of the whale had been heaved out, and lay, each anatomical pile in its proper place on the deck, awaiting consignment to the factory deck below or rejection into the sea. Only the massive backbone remained, and it was Hamish's turn.

14. First, a chain was passed under the great ligaments, as thick and tough as a warship's anchor cables, that ran along the millstone-size vertebrae. With a horrid rending noise, similar to that made by a dog crunching a bone but amplified a thousand times, the ligaments were ripped free from the spine. Then a wire rope from a winch beside Hamish's bone saw was passed around a bollard and attached by a heavy iron double hook to the tail of the vertebral column. Hamish gave a toss of his head as the signal to heave away, and the winchman brought the great mass of bone and tendon whizzing across the deck to a point right under the saw. Hamish dropped the heavy, steam-driven fifteen-foot blade in exactly the right place to cut off a chunk just big enough to go down a four-foot hole to the cookers. Then he lifted the blade and wagged his beard, and at this sign eight men who had been scattered about nearby knew precisely what to do. Four darted in with whale hooks, seized the severed piece, and hauled it off to the cooker hole; the fifth thrust the double hook from the winch deep into the next vertebra; the sixth, the winchman, opened his throttle and pulled the backbone another couple of feet along the deck; and the seventh and eighth, two little gnomelike lemmers, scurried out of the steam and made some intricate cuts in the backbone with their knives, so that it would sit properly under the saw. The ninth man present, Hamish himself, brought his immense saw blade slamming down for the next cut, and the tenth man, the doctor, cowered a bit closer against the bulwarks behind the saw.

15. It took about three minutes to reduce the backbone to lumps of a size that could be pushed down into the cookers. Then Hamish had a few moments in which to light his pipe and disparage the dangers of his job to me. "It's the same as Andy MacTavish, our village butcher in Peterhead, killin' and sawin' up a cattle beast," he said. "There's nae mair to whalin' than there is tae Andy's job, except the beasts are bigger an' the slaughterhouse is in a kinda inconvenient place down here in the ice. It's all a matter of proportion. Andy's just as likely tae have an accident wi' his bone saw as I am wi' mine, but when he does, he'll lose a finger or two, whilst if I make a mistake, as like as not I'll nick the head off that little lemmer there."

16. Hamish turned to tinker with his saw blade, and I ventured forth to observe some of the other operations that were going on in the gigantic butchery. I found that the liver of the whale, weighing nearly a ton, had been hauled to a corner of the deck, where a man was engaged in chopping it into chunks and popping them into a hole that led to the "liver plant" below. The stomach and intestines had also been hauled aside—not to a hole in the deck but to a break in the bulwarks, through which they were to be cast into the sea. (They are the only parts of the whale other than the flukes and the baleen to be thrown away.) Before

they were heaved overboard, however, Adamson arrived on the scene, armed with a flensing knife. He split the stomach open and spilled its contents, a hundred-weight or so of little red shrimps, out onto the deck, and then drew a notebook from his trousers pocket and wrote something down with a stub of pencil. I asked him what on earth he was doing, taking notes in such a setting. "The law insists that we do this," he said. "I'm writing down the contents of the stomach, which we've got to do for every whale we take. The biologist boys reckon they can work out something about the migrations of whales from what we find they've been eating. Any old whalemen will tell them they're wrong, of course."

17. "Are ye finished with these guts yet, Bosun?" an irritated voice broke in from the surrounding steam as I was asking Adamson more questions; it was clear from the tone that I was guilty of the major crime aboard a whaleship—holding up production.

18 "Aye!" replied Adamson, and with that a winch clanked in the distance, a rope tightened close at hand, and a mountain of whale innards slid toward the ship's side and dropped into the sea far below.

19. I leaned over the rail to see the fate of these parts of the whale for which man has no use. It was not long in coming. Hundreds of black-and-white Cape pigeons gathered around the filthy mess, and in a few moments each one had ripped off a small piece and was swimming about in the ocean, tearing at his dinner. An occasional albatross glided down on his ten-foot wings, chased off some of the shrilly complaining pigeons, and made a silent and dignified meal before starting a long run on the water to rise and glide off. And all the while a cloud of Wilson's petrels fluttered above the mess; every few minutes one of them would dart down to take a tiny beakful of the rich fodder, and then rise into the air again to digest it.

20. But the birds did not get the entire feast, by any means. Five killer whales, the most voracious animals in the Southern Ocean, showed up for their share, and a large share it was. They were from twenty to thirty feet long, and their huge black dorsal fins rose rhythmically from the water as they advanced upon their meal. From time to time, they revealed their evil black-and-white snouts and their malignant, fang-filled jaws; only hyenas on land and vultures in the air can convey the same sense of remorseless ill will against all creation. These killer whales were about five hundred yards out when I first saw them rise to blow, scarcely rippling the water as they did so. Each of them puffed once, then slid below the surface again, its horrible sickle-shaped fin riding it like a hunchback's hump. About ten seconds later, the performance was repeated a hundred yards closer in. Then the last appearance, fifty yards off, and this time I could see their cold, black little eyes. Again they slid

below, and now suddenly all the birds that had gathered around the offal rose squawking into the air. There was a great swirling of water, and chunks of the stuff began to disappear beneath the water, half a ton or so at a time. One of the killers, evidently made overconfident by the lavishness of the feast, pushed his snout above the water to grab a hundred-pound tidbit floating high on the sea. He never drew his meal below the surface. From the wing of the bridge overhead, where Mark, the ship's chief officer, was on duty, came the sharp crack of a rifle. The killer, drilled neatly behind the eyes by a heavy bullet, leaped half out of the water in his death spasm and then sank in a whirl of spray and blood. "There's Mark at his favorite sport again!" someone remarked at my shoulder. "He hates killer whales with a loathing quite out of proportion to the damage they do to him and his bonus, though it's true they tear out the tongues and the best part of the oil from half the whales we catch. He'll be happy all night now he's killed that one."

21. By morning, as Adamson had promised, all fourteen whales had been disposed of. Just as the early antarctic dawn was breaking, iron covers were hauled over the cooker holes and clamped down, and the steam straightway vanished. The winchmen heaved in their loose ropes and shut off their winches. A gang of men appeared and hosed down the decks. A young cadet officer went up to a platform on the starboard side and checked over the stores, spare harpoons, and ropes laid out for the next catcher that might need them. Hamish was greasing his saw and tuning it up for the next lot of whales. And the hundred-odd men who had been slaving all night on the deck were slipping off to their cabins or messrooms. In something less than an hour after the last whale had been hauled up the skidway, not a vestige of the fourteen remained abovedecks, except their blood, which lay about in slippery clots.

22. Just before I left the deck of the now apparently lifeless ship, I heard another burst of rifle fire from the bridge overhead, and I knew that one other person was still wide awake. Mark, whiling the time away as he conned our huge ship through the freezing dawn, was indulging his hatred of the killer whales.

COMMENTARY AND QUESTIONS

Few people have had much contact with whales. Robertson has. His first-hand knowledge gives him an advantage in securing the interest and attention of his readers. But this advantage is not in itself enough to maintain that interest and attention. As a writer, Robertson has had to select from the mass of information he has gained through long observation just those significant details which he can present in an attractive and comprehensible pattern.

1. In par. 1 Robertson states that for eight months he served "as senior medical officer on a British whaling factory ship in the antarctic." This statement identifies the writer as one who has first-hand information. How does the material in the rest of this paragraph and in par. 2 indicate Robertson's awareness of the unusual nature of his subject?

2. Beginning with par. 5, Robertson describes what takes place on a whaling factory ship. By what method does he organize this material? What groupings of paragraphs can you make within pars. 5-20?

3. If a writer follows any method of organization mechanically, he may lose his reader's interest. How does information introduced in pars. 8, 9, 10, for example, offer a variation in Robertson's pattern?

4. How is par. 21 related to par. 3?

5. The full report of Robertson's voyage appeared as a book (*Of Whales and Men*) soon after portions of the report had been published in a different form in *The New Yorker*. In the book version this selection is called "Brobdingnagian Butcher's Shop." What particular incident might suggest this title? Do you think that it is more or less effective than the title "A Matter of Proportion"?

6. A process can be described without introducing any information about the observer or the workers involved in the process. What is gained by introducing such information here? What details are given to make Adamson, the Gaunt Stranger, Hamish, and Mark each a distinct person?

7. Remembering the peculiar writing problem faced by Robertson, tell what principle underlies the following comparisons:
   a. ". . . his flensing knife—a wicked-looking article shaped like a hockey stick" (par. 6).
   b. "These holes, the size of manholes, led down to a battery of modern pressure cookers on the factory deck below" (par. 10).
   c. "With a horrid rending noise, similar to that made by a dog crunching a bone but amplified a thousand times, the ligaments were ripped from the spine" (par. 14).

8. In *Moby Dick* (published in 1851) Herman Melville describes how the blubber was stripped from a whale a century ago. The dead whale was not hauled aboard, and after the blubber had been stripped by means of ropes and tackles attached to the mast of the ship, the carcass of the whale was allowed to float free. Compare the following description by Melville (from Chapter LXIX of *Moby Dick*) with pars. 19-20 of "A Matter of Proportion." Aside from factual differences, would it be possible to substitute the passage by Melville for the one by Robertson?

> The vast tackles have now done their duty. The peeled white body of the beheaded whale flashed like a marble sepulchre; though changed in hue, it has not perceptibly lost anything in bulk. It is still colossal.

Slowly it floats more and more away, the water round it torn and splashed by the insatiate sharks, and the air above vexed with rapacious flights of screaming fowls, whose beaks are like so many insulting poniards in the whale. The vast white headless phantom floats further and further from the ship, and every rod that it so floats, what seem square roods of sharks and cubic roods of fowls, augment the murderous din. For hours and hours from the almost stationary ship that hideous sight is seen. Beneath the unclouded and mild azure sky, upon the fair face of the pleasant sea, wafted by the joyous breezes, that great mass of death floats on and on, till lost in infinite perspectives.

There's a most doleful and most mocking funeral! The sea-vultures all in pious mourning, the air-sharks all punctiliously in black or speckled. In life but few of them would have helped the whale, I ween, if peradventure he had needed it; but upon the banquet of his funeral they most piously do pounce. Oh, horrible vulturism of earth! from which not the mightiest whale is free.

SUGGESTION FOR WRITING

Describe the functioning of a group of workers as they go about their business (for example, firemen at a burning building, a rescue team at an overturned boat, a crew unloading a circus train).

PART TWO

Explanation

TO PROVIDE SOMEONE ELSE WITH INFORMATION IS ONE OF THE commonest reasons for writing. The kinds of information and the reasons for providing it may of course be infinite in variety. The man who writes down the facts of history in a textbook is doing this kind of writing; so is the author of a magazine article telling his readers what new advance has been made in science, or why the corn crop is so large or so small this year, or how to build a boat. The function, then, of this sort of writing—to which in this book we have given the name *explanation*—is to explain, to instruct, to inform; and its emphasis is not on personal experience, as in the selections of Part I, nor on personal opinion and appraisal, as in those of Part III, nor on converting others to a point of view, as in those of Part IV, but on setting forth facts and ideas objectively and without bias. The qualities of an author's mind and heart always affect what he writes, but for many purposes it is more important that he provide information than that he parade his opinions or persuade others to adopt them.

To do this job properly, explanatory writing must have clarity, completeness, and accuracy. Accuracy means precision of statement as well as of fact. Completeness means giving all the pertinent facts or concepts that are necessary for the intended reader's understanding of the subject. Clarity in itself implies precision and thoroughness of statement and thought. But clarity also demands that material be presented in a logical and comprehensible order, and that it have readability. For writing cannot really be called clear, even though it may be accurate and thorough, if the reader finds it unnecessarily difficult—difficult, that is,

99

not through any inherent complexity in the facts and ideas but because of the author's lack of skill in presenting them. A style that is lively and forceful—provided that the liveliness and force are not gained at the expense of accuracy and completeness—is essentially clearer than one that is turgid and dull. For the aim of explanatory writing is to convey facts and ideas from the mind of the author to the mind of the reader, and whatever facilitates that process without annoying the reader is an aid to clarity.

A few sentences back we mentioned the "intended reader." This phrase is important. Not all authors write for the same set of readers, and not all readers are alike. A style that is clear and simple to one reader may be a bore to another, while what is lively and stimulating to some may be over the heads of the rest. A wise author is therefore very careful to consider what class of readers he is aiming at, and what his purpose is in writing for them. The selections which follow show a considerable variety of intended audience and purpose, and consequently a considerable range of style and method. All, however, are intent on solving the same problem: to convey information from writer to reader. Each one is a profitable case-study in how well, and by what means, the writer solved his particular form of the problem.

The Kick
of an Electric Eel

by CHRISTOPHER W. COATES

I

THERE ARE SO-CALLED lower creatures on earth today which can accomplish electrical feats beyond those of our most advanced laboratories. These living dynamos are all fishes and they hail from Africa, South America, and the temperate and tropical seas. How long they have been electrocuting their enemies and prey is unknown, but fossil fishes from deposits laid down over a hundred million years ago have organs so similar to the electric ones of living forms that there is no doubt they, too, possessed electric powers.

2. Of all the electric fishes, the best known, both by scientists and by laymen, is the electric eel, and as self-appointed press agent to that fish I have extolled and demonstrated its powers to so many people that I have come to look upon it with paternalistic affection. Our first meeting was not auspicious, however, for in 1929, when I saw my first electric eel sluggishly swimming about at the old New York Aquarium and read on the label that such a four-foot animal could "knock down a horse," I was more than a little dubious. How could *one* animal produce a current? Where did the current go in the water and why didn't it electrocute the fish itself?

3. The scientific literature on the subject did not dispel my doubts either. Although such illustrious scientists as Galen, Lord Cavendish, Sir Humphry Davy, and Michael Faraday had all worked on electric fishes, none of them offered a satisfactory explanation of the fishes' powers or even a measurement of their potency. Faraday did determine that externally the current from an electric eel flows from head to tail, but that was about all. I hoped I could do better.

4. My chance came a few years later when, as a member of the Aquarium staff and armed with assorted wires and lamps, I set out to trap the eel's current. I learned the hard way, first by being literally knocked off my feet when I attempted to pick up the fish in a net. Maybe

it could down a horse! I gingerly noosed a bit of wire around the front part of the fish's elongate body, carefully holding on to the insulated portion, and did likewise with its tail. Now a lamp joining these two wires should light most brightly. But when I introduced the lamp into the circuit nothing at all happened, not even the slightest glow. With my first two fingers I touched the ends of the wires, but did not feel anything until I gently prodded the eel with a dry wooden handle of a net. The tingle in my hand proved that the fish was giving off electricity, but there was still not a sign of response from the lamp. What kind of electricity was this?

5. From here on my investigations took a most discouraging turn. I was convinced that until I could measure the eel's electricity, or at least prove that it *was* electricity, I was in no position to approach some hard-working physicist or biochemist and request that he devote some of his time to my pet interest. Nothing worked. Voltmeters, ammeters, and galvanometers either burned out or failed to register any "juice" at all, while electric lights both in water and out reacted not one bit. It seemed as if the only way to gauge this strange power was to feel it—a nerve-racking process. To the detriment of my pocketbook and the chagrin of my friends (who had lent me some of the instruments) I continued this unsuccessful experimenting intermittently for over a year.

6. Everyone who came into contact with the eel swore that it was electric—in fact many simply swore. One time I was trying to unload a whole hogshead of eels stored 'tween decks of a steamer. I had on a pair of heavy rubber gloves and we tried to move the hogshead towards the hatchway but made no progress at all, because the container was much too heavy for me to handle alone, and when the longshoremen tried to help, their bare hands were continually subject to shock. One of them, a giant of a man, said he would fix it and, hooking in his dog hook, gave a mighty heave. Over went the hogshead, out came the water and the eels in a slithery, slimy cascade, and up and down went all the people in a mad dance to get their feet off the steel deck. Imagine fourteen writhing giant eels—some of them nine feet long—all giving off several hundred volts of electricity at the same time. I am still not sure how we managed to get them back into the hogshead and finally into the Aquarium.

7. The turning point in my investigations came one Saturday afternoon. I was trying out a new kind of lamp, a neon one—not the kind employed for advertising, but a small bulb or pip such as is used for a night light. The laboratory floor was liberally splashed with water and was covered by a maze of wires. Things were both literally and figuratively at loose ends, for the electric eel that was the subject of the experi-

ments had been behaving badly. At times like these I try to remember the "Harvard law of animal behavior"[1] and laugh the trouble off, but this afternoon I was tired and discouraged and careless. Suddenly, I received the full shock of the eel, was thrown several feet into the air, and at the same time saw the neon pip burst into a dull orange glow. So intense was the jolt that I suspected the glow to be an illusion caused by the shock.

[8.] None too hopefully I traced out the circuit. Apparently, the pip was in simple direct circuit with the fish. I disturbed the eel with a rubber-gloved hand and again the light flickered on and off. All at once it dawned on me why I had been unable to register the current before. Ordinary electrical apparatus has an appreciable warm-up time, or lag, as it is called, before it begins to operate; commercial incandescent lamps have a lag of about one fiftieth of a second, for example. The electric eel's discharge was powerful enough, but of such short duration that it failed to excite the usual instruments and lights. I now also knew that the potential was at least eighty volts, because that was the minimum necessary to light such a neon pip.

II

[9.] *Electrophorus electricus,* as ichthyologists call it, looks like a caricature of an eel, being eel-shaped but completely lacking the sinuous grace and streamlined contours of the common fish-market variety. It is a much stouter creature, a specimen forty-eight inches long having a girth of over a foot. From its bluntly rounded head to the tip of its clumsy tail it is a more or less uniform dull gray in color, with the exception of an expanse of salmon red on its throat and chin. This area is yellowish green in eels from Venezuela. The Amazonian variety, which I am here describing, belongs to the same species. Its skin is naked and wrinkled, with small flattened papillae irregularly distributed over it. Two absurd little round fins stick out on either side of its head like the ears on a cartoon character. No fins at all are to be found on its back, but one long continuous fin stretches along the posterior four fifths of its underside. By undulating this the eel moves about, seemingly as easily backwards as forwards.

[10.] Practically nothing is known about the life history of the electric eel. For example, we are not absolutely positive whether the fish lays eggs or gives birth to live young, although our anatomical investigations

---

[1] That animals under the most exactly controlled experimental conditions do exactly as they please.

strongly point to the former method of reproduction. No one has yet seen an electric eel's egg with the embryo eel developing in it.

11. Very small eels have never been brought to this country, but collectors in South America have reported finding specimens an inch or so long at the ebb of flood waters towards the end of the rainy season. They are reported as accompanying an adult fish, sex unknown, swimming in a more or less compact group of from fifty to five hundred about the head of the presumed parent. At this size they can produce a discernible amount of electricity, although no more than enough to tingle the cupped hands in which they are held. The collectors are quite certain that the adults swim over the inundated lowlands during the wet season to spawn, not returning to the streams and rivers until the receding floods force them back. Fish six or eight inches long apparently have left the parental brood and seem to be on their own. At this stage of development the amount of electricity per unit length of eel is higher than at any other, for while the average voltage per centimeter of a large eel may be eight or ten, that of a small one is nearer thirty for each centimeter of electric tissue. Since any voltage smaller than this would be inadequate to discourage enemies or to immobilize food, it seems reasonable to assume that the young eels remain under the care of their parent until they are large enough to protect themselves with their own discharges.

12. My first device for actually measuring the electricity of the eel was a simple series of neon pips connected with different resistances. With these I was able to make good estimates of the fish's voltage and found that it ranged to over three hundred and that Faraday had correctly determined the direction of the flow of current—from head to tail outside the body of the fish. Now I felt I had sufficient tangible evidence to approach some specialist for aid in further investigations. But biophysicists or physicists interested in animate things are few and far between, and I "peddled" my eel at a number of different institutions before I discovered one sufficiently interested in "eel-electricity" to work with me on it. Dr. Richard T. Cox, at that time Professor of Physics at New York University, was already up to his ears in nuclear physics, but he agreed to come down to the old Aquarium and try out on the eel the new portable model Cathode Ray Oscillograph he had recently received.

13. Like a neon light, the oscillograph has no appreciable lag, and this made it suitable for picking up the eel's discharges; best of all, it gave a graphic picture of them, providing the means whereby the electricity drew a picture of itself on a fluorescent screen. We came up with some amazing results. We recorded voltages up to 550 and found that the average discharge in water amounted to about forty watts—more

than enough to stun a man or a horse. Each discharge lasted only two one-thousandths of a second, but the eel could send out four hundred or more per second!

III

14. That a creature of flesh and blood could energize so much seemed fantastic. However, we soon learned that the eel was largely composed of a very special kind of flesh: electric tissue. All its vital organs—stomach, intestine, liver, and so forth—are confined to the front fifth of its body, and even its vent is located under the chin; the remainder of its elongate body is principally occupied by three pairs of electric organs. Measured by volume, nearly half of the fish is electric tissue. These organs are, in turn, made up of smaller units, which are separated by thin walls of electrically resistant tissue and act very similarly to cells in a storage battery. They are the producers of the electricity, each one creating about one tenth of a volt. It is by hooking these tiny batteries together in series, so to speak, that the eel builds up its powerful discharge. Just how it does this, throwing thousands of "switches" on and off hundreds of times a second, we do not know. That is another of the mysteries of the electric eel.

15. The electric organs of the eel are in three pairs: the Large Organs, the Bundles of Sachs, and the Organs of Hunter. The Large Organs are apparently so called for want of a better name; the Bundles of Sachs were named for Dr. Carl Sachs, the naturalist and Amazon explorer, who devoted much time to the study of the eel in the 1870's; the Organs of Hunter were first described by Dr. John Hunter, the eighteenth-century anatomist. The first of these is functionally the most important, and begins at about one fifth of the length of the fish behind the snout, continuing unchanged to a point about two-thirds the length of the fish behind the snout. From this place on, it tapers off and the resulting space is taken up by the Bundles of Sachs, which grow in size as the Large Organs diminish. The Bundles are responsible for the small discharges apparently used for locating food. The third pair of organs, those of Hunter, start at the same level as do the Large Organs and run to the end of the tail. In cross-section these are very small and their discharge is irregular and appears to be a function of that of the Large Organs. In relation to the area of the whole cross-section of the fish at a point midway from head to tail the electric organs occupy about 55 per cent. The appearance of electric tissue is different from any other. It is a flaccid whitish jelly and, by analysis, is composed of 92 per cent water.

16. Another mystery of the electric eel is its sensitivity to electric

currents. When I finally got the fourteen eels—the ones that had been spilled out of their hogshead on the steamer deck—into a tank at the Aquarium, I noticed that the fish were aware of each other's discharges. (This was apparently the first time anyone had made any observations on more than one eel at a time—at least anyone who cared to talk about it.) The natural food of electric eels consists of fishes and other small aquatic animals which they stun before swallowing whole. Although they can be taught in captivity to eat cut-up raw fish and strips of beef, when first caught they will eat only live fish. While feeding these fourteen eels I discovered that when one fish discharged, stunning its prey, all the others in the tank came over, apparently to see what was going on, and they always went to the spot where the feeding eel had discharged, even if it had subsequently moved away. Apparently, eels were not only aware of one another's discharges but could nicely judge whence the current came.

17. Later on, Professor Cox and I "electrolyzed" a tankful of eels by dropping an electrode at each end of their tank and passing a strong current through the water. All the eels then gathered at the anode or positive pole. This was reasonable, because the head of a discharging eel is always positive in respect to the body behind it, and the head would be exactly where a hungry eel would want to go, when he sensed his brother eel shocking some prey.

18. We now wanted to find out whether captive electric eels behaved like wild ones, since our researches were more or less based on the proposition that what the fish did in the Aquarium's tanks and laboratory was "normal." For this purpose Professor Cox established headquarters at the Goeldi Museum in Para at the mouth of the Amazon.[2] What he found confirmed our supposition: eels in Brazil behaved no differently from those in New York. However, he also discovered some electrical activity we hadn't noticed before. When lying quietly on the bottom, only moving occasionally to come to the surface for a gulp of air—the fish is an air-breather and drowns if kept under water—electric eels give off no electricity at all, but while "cruising about" they emit a series of weak discharges having a voltage of the order of fifty and at a rate of about fifty per second.

19. We first believed that these were warning discharges by which the eel kept potential enemies at a distance, and we were supported in this view by some observations on the eel's closest relatives. These are fishes of the family of gymnotid eels of which the electric eel is a member

---

[2] A popular account of this expedition is to be found in Shelby Shackleford's *Electric Eel Calling* (Scribner's, New York, 1941).

—elongate fishes, not at all related to the true, edible eel, but rather to the infamous piranhas of South American rivers and the radiant neon tetras of tropical-fish fame. Their popular name is knife fish, and a triangular carving knife, minus its handle, gives a good approximation of their body shape. None of these "cousins" to the electric eel has any electric powers, and all of them are more or less likely to have their long tails nipped off in the course of growing up. In fact, in some species it is almost impossible to find an intact specimen. Electric eels, on the other hand, almost never show such mutilations.

20. Undoubtedly the electric eel's discharges protect it, but the steady repetitions of minor discharges which it emits while swimming serve another purpose, quite as utilitarian. We discovered this use by carefully observing the behavior of a lone eel. Adult electric eels are virtually blind, since they develop cataracts when quite young, undoubtedly as a consequence of either their own electric shocks or those of their fellows. Nevertheless, when a food fish was put into its tank, the lone eel unerringly made for it. That the eel could see through the clouded lenses of its eyes seemed unbelievable; yet to be positive that sight was not being utilized, we repeated the test in nearly total darkness. Not only did the eel easily find the food fish in the dark, but it could even distinguish between a dead floating food fish and a piece of floating wood of approximately the same size.

21. Was the eel using its weak discharges to locate the fish? We couldn't stop the eel from broadcasting its current, so perhaps we could stop it from receiving that current back, and this we did. Arranged in definite patterns on both sides and the top of an electric eel's head are series of prominent pits. No such development is found in other gymnotids; therefore we thought these might in some way be associated with electric powers. We painted the head of our eel with an insulating lacquer, thus sealing off the pits from any possible electric impulses. Sure enough, that fish now failed to find any prey, living or dead, dropped into its tank, and simply swam aimlessly around. If the food fish was placed on its lips, however, it would gulp the meal down; and when the lacquer was removed, the eel once again easily located its food.

22. The details of this wonderfully acute eel "radar" have yet to be worked out; we believe it operates something like this. The minor discharges of the eel radiate out in all directions from the rear portion of its tail, the area in which they are produced. Whenever they come into contact with some solid object in the water, they are reflected back towards the sensory pits on the eel's head. By turning its head and discharging again, the eel can so orient itself that both left and right sides receive the reflected pulses simultaneously. Then it is pointed towards

the reflecting object. When we realize that this locating of an object is done through a complex "background" of reflected impulses (from the walls of the tank, for example); that although the impulses travel at the speed of light, the eel can differentiate between differences of a few inches; and that the eel can make allowance for its own movement as well as that of living prey, the truly amazing character of this behavior is apparent. Nothing I have ever learned about this incredible creature has astounded me more.

IV

23 Electric fishes in general have played a long role in medical history, if not always an honorable one. No one knows how long the Indians of Surinam have employed the discharge of the electric eel in the treatment of disease. Even today in Brazil its flesh is considered by some to be a cure for rheumatism. One learned rheumatic doctor, however, told Professor Cox that he had eaten eel meat and, of the two, he considered rheumatism the more bearable. Dr. Peter Kellaway of McGill University has made a thorough study of the use of electric fishes in medicine, and the first record he found of the therapeutic use of these creatures' electric powers was in A.D. 46 when one Scribonius Largus, a Roman physician, claimed the shock of the torpedo to be a cure for headache and gout.

> For any type of gout, a live black torpedo should, when the pain begins, be placed under the feet. The patient must stand on a moist shore washed by the sea and he should stay like this until his whole foot and leg up to the knee is numb. This takes away present pain and prevents pain from coming on if it has not already arisen.

24. The discharge of electric catfishes, too, has been utilized since ancient times by African tribes as a cure for various ailments, and one Moslem physician of the eleventh century thought that to place a live electric catfish on the brow of a person suffering an epileptic fit was beneficial. Electrotherapy was all the rage in Europe during the eighteenth century, and electric fishes vied successfully with Leyden jars and other shocking machines. When many electric eels were imported for this purpose, people flocked to them for relief from gout, rheumatism, and other ills. One London advertisement of 1777 gives a price of two shillings and sixpence per treatment of "natural" electricity from a "torporific eel."

25. The importance of the electric eel in present-day medical science rests not with its use as a shocking machine, but with its physiology. The

physico-chemical reactions that take place in a nerve whenever an impulse passes over it are of prime importance to physiologists, and books have been written on this subject alone. A nerve is so small, however, that to determine quantitatively just what chemical reactions are taking place inside it is next to impossible. But the discharge of an electric eel is identical in nature with the passage of an impulse over a nerve, and since thousands of times more tissue is involved, the chemical changes can be much more easily measured.

26. Briefly, this is how such an investigation is made. A tiny piece of electric tissue is removed from a resting eel; then the fish is made to discharge and the amount of electricity produced is carefully recorded. Another small piece of electric tissue is now taken out. By chemically analyzing these two pieces, the changes which took place in the electric organ during the electric discharges are determined. This amount of change is then correlated with the amount of electricity produced. Studies like this have enabled Dr. David Nachmansohn of the College of Physicians and Surgeons to confirm certain basic theories on the nature of nervous activity—a matter of fundamental importance to biologists, physicians, neurologists, and psychologists. And lest it be thought that such treatment of an eel injures it, let me point out that not only is the fish apparently unaware of the operation, since it does not discharge during the process, but so great are its regenerative capabilities that in less than a month not even a scar remains where the pieces of tissue were removed.

27. One of the key substances in the production of electric energy in electric fishes, and in the production of a nervous impulse too, is cholinesterase. During the war, it became necessary to obtain large amounts of this rare chemical, which cannot yet be synthetically produced but must be extracted from living tissue. Ounce for ounce, the electric organs of the eel are far richer in cholinesterase than any other known tissue; so when the Chemical Warfare Service called for large amounts of it in order to study the effects of a new, deadly nerve gas they were investigating, scores of eels were sacrificed to provide them with the precious substance.

28. Not only is the electric eel well known to scientists these days; it is familiar to laymen as well. Thousands of people witnessed a demonstration of its powers in the New York Zoological Society's building at the World's Fair, and even more now come to the Lion House in the Zoological Park in the Bronx to see it. But tall tales die hard: the one Humboldt told about the electric eel still circulates around, even in some high-class encyclopedias and natural history books. Humboldt reported that South American Indians capture the eels by driving horses into water contain-

ing the fish. When the eels have exhausted themselves shocking the horses, the Indians harpoon them and remove them from the water with impunity. Our investigations have proved that this notion is tommyrot, because an electric eel can't be exhausted so easily. If kept moist, so that it can breathe properly, it will discharge intermittently all day long without showing appreciable fatigue.

²⁹· Even after giving off electric shocks at its greatest rate, for twenty minutes, a five-minute rest is all that is needed to bring its activity back to normal. In fact, one of our leading battery manufacturers has been studying the eel, trying to pick up some pointers on current-production. One of the company's experts wistfully remarked to me the other day: "If we only could make batteries that would operate as efficiently as that eel!"

COMMENTARY AND QUESTIONS

The satisfaction of reader curiosity is the legitimate purpose of a good deal of explanatory writing. Most people have heard of electric eels without knowing very much about them. In this essay Christopher W. Coates, drawing on his experiences as curator and aquarist of the New York Aquarium, satisfies a certain amount of public curiosity in a lively example of informal exposition.

1. What is the significance of the questions Coates asked himself on first seeing an electric eel (par. 2)? Were his reactions the ones to be expected of other people? Why does he mention the failure of earlier scientists (par. 3)? Why does he emphasize the contrast, or seeming paradox, in pars. 5 and 6? Why is there so much narrative in pars. 2-8? Is the author's primary purpose to tell a story or to transmit information by telling how he himself discovered the information?

2. Why is par. 8 logically the end paragraph in the first section? What new kind of information is introduced in section II? Why does the author put this in section II instead of beginning with it in section I? Why are the exact measurements of eel voltage and current reported in the closing paragraphs of section II instead of immediately following par. 8? How is par. 12 connected with par. 11? Section III with section II? How is par. 16 linked to earlier paragraphs?

3. What is the dominant subject of section III? What method does the author use in pars. 16-21 to convey his information to the reader and make it seem lively? What is the dominant subject of section IV of the essay? Why is this information presented here instead of, say, in section II? Is there anything in par. 29 that echoes something in par. 1? Was this echo accidental?

4. What kind of reader is the author writing for? How much technical knowledge does he assume in the reader? Although the same person

might well enjoy both essays, do you think that Coates and Robertson (pp. 85-95) were aiming at precisely the same level of interest? Defend your answer. Compare the styles of the two essays. In what ways do the vocabulary, tone, sentence structure, and attitude of each author differentiate the two selections?

SUGGESTIONS FOR WRITING

1. If at some time you have been sufficiently interested in an unusual plant or animal to make an investigation of your own, explain for the benefit of those lacking your knowledge what makes the plant or animal unusual.
2. Seeing an electric eel in an aquarium led Coates to make his investigation. Describe an event which resulted, perhaps unexpectedly, in your becoming interested in something new to you: it may have been an enforced visit to a museum or merely reading a suggested book.

The Art
of the Hoax

by GILBERT HIGHET

BLUE, GOLD, white, gold, and blue. Blue skies, golden sun, white foam flying; white uniforms, gold epaulets, and the solid, confident blue of the Royal Navy. Above, bright strings of signal flags snapping in the breeze: the pennant of an admiral and the white ensign of the Royal Navy. Below, the British Channel Fleet in review order showing its full strength in the year 1910. It lay at anchor at Weymouth, a disciplined mass of huge gray ships, their paint spotless, their decks blinding, their brasswork dazzling: little dispatch boats weaving a net of white curving wakes across the blue among them. On the Admiral's quarter-deck, one discordant note to spoil the splendid harmony: a small group of foreign-

From *Horizon*, January, 1961. By permission of the publishers. Copyright © 1960 by American Horizon, Inc.

ers, with black faces and cocoa beards and huge rolling yellow eyes, speaking an ugly and incomprehensible language, and sloppily dressed in robes and turbans which might be intended to be formal but which looked like old curtains and carpets and rugs and towels. The men and their gabble and their robes were a stain on the trim *Dreadnought*. The stain was, no doubt, inevitable, but it was temporary. It would remove itself in a few hours. Meanwhile it had to be endured. It was an emperor, with his suite. The emperor was the guest of the Foreign Office; his realm, Abyssinia, was a strategically interesting and potentially rich area in northeastern Africa, and so a visit to the Channel Fleet had been specially arranged for the Emperor of Abyssinia and his suite.

2. The battleship was dressed. The crew was mustered. The guard of honor—Royal Marines in red and blue parade uniforms—presented arms and was inspected by His Majesty. The band struck up a ceremonial march. The great guns were raised and lowered and turned, as though the *Dreadnought* were a powerful half-tamed animal showing its teeth and claws, ready for a fight to the death. The Emperor watched and remained impassive. His courtiers and attendants rolled their liquid amber eyes and wagged their beards in astonishment. "Entaqui, mahai, kustufani!" they said to one another; and every moment they looked more frightened, more and more deeply impressed.

3. Nothing ruffles the courtesy of the Royal Navy. Although neither he nor any of his staff could speak Amharic, the Admiral still contrived to converse cordially and diplomatically with the Emperor. Through an interpreter whom His Majesty had brought with him—an immensely tall and gawky German who appeared to be about to despair of his all but impossible task—the Admiral explained that the Marines who wore red were gunners and the Marines who wore blue were foot soldiers. The interpreter assimilated this information. He thought for a while, moving his lips, and then he explained. "Tahli bussor ahbat tahl aesque miss," he said, and the emperor nodded gravely. "Erraema, fleet use, fert queré fert, queso ror!" Enlightenment dawned in the hooded eyes of the monarch. He gazed at the Marine guard. It was clear that the distinctive hues of their uniforms had already caught his eye; and now he realized that it was not merely a whim or a phenomenon of Western barbarism. It had a meaning. He nodded and slowly, meditatively belched. It was a sign of profound satisfaction.

4. At length, after several hours of slow progress through the inwards of H.M.S. *Dreadnought*, the imperial visit drew to a close. Would His Majesty care to take lunch with the Admiral and his senior officers? Alas, no. It was quite impossible. His Majesty's religious beliefs prevented him from touching any food whatever which had not been pre-

pared in the strictest accordance with ancestral ritual. With expressions of gratitude for the Admiral's courtesy, the monarch and his suite took their leave. Boatswains' pipes split the air. The Marine guard presented arms. The ship's band, having been unable to find the national anthem of Abyssinia, broke into the national anthem of Zanzibar. The Admiral's launch accepted its august crew and sped towards shore. Only one contretemps marred the final minutes of the imperial visit. As the launch approached Weymouth dock, a picket boat crossed its bow. It is of course the grossest discourtesy to cross the bow of a vessel carrying royalty, and the young officer in command ought to have known that, for he had some connections with royalty, being called Battenberg (later Mountbatten); but he was summoned by his captain and severely reprimanded. Otherwise, the visit was successfully concluded. The Emperor's attendants tipped the launch's crew magnificently and offered a gorgeous decoration to its young commander, which he dutifully declined as against naval etiquette; and then the entire party disappeared into the imperial compartment on the London train, smiling ivory smiles and saying to one another, "Heia age! rumpe moras!"

5. The Admiral and his staff sat down to dinner in the wardroom, congratulating themselves on having got through a rather sticky afternoon without too much bobbery. Speeding back to London, the Emperor and his aides were also felicitating one another. They had found the visit a complete success. At times they had almost despaired of carrying it through, but now that it was over they could scarcely believe that they had managed it all with such superb aplomb, such resolute refusal to falter before the power and prestige of the Navy, and such amazing fluency in the Ethiopian language. For the Admiral and his officers it had been a diplomatic ordeal. For the Emperor and his suite it had been a magnificent hoax. They were not Ethiopians. They were not even foreigners. They were all English. The Emperor of Abyssinia was a handsome young man called Anthony Buxton. His escort, putatively from the Foreign Office, was the greatest of modern English jokers, Horace de Vere Cole, wearing a superbly diplomatic morning coat and top hat. His interpreter, Kauffmann, was a Bloomsbury intellectual who had been a little embarrassed on the quarter-deck when he thought that his six-foot-five-inch stature and unmistakable features would surely be recognized by various friends and relatives among the *Dreadnought's* crew. Cole's suite were all young men with good family connections and a strong sense of humor—except one, who was a girl. They knew her as the interpreter's sister, Virginia Stephen; the world knew her later as Virginia Woolf.

6. It had been easy, unexpectedly easy, for Cole and his friends to

be received by the Admiral. They had simply sent him a telegram warning him that the Emperor was arriving, and appended to it the name of
the head of the Foreign Office. Their costumes had been rented from the
best London theatrical costumer, Clarksons; and Clarkson himself had
secured their beards and stained their faces. The language had been a
serious problem. The ever inventive Cole had tried to teach "Kauffmann"
some words of Swahili, in the hope that they could be extrapolated; but
poor Kauffmann, when he had to explain why some Marines wore red
and others blue, was forced to fall back on the only foreign language he
knew really well. At school he had learned many hundreds of lines of
Homer and Vergil by heart, and at the crisis of the Marines' uniforms,
he began, slightly distorting and misplacing the syllables and accents,
the pathetic description of Dido's desperate pleas to the lover who is
deserting her:

> *Talibus orabat talesque*
> *miserrima feetus fertque*
> *refertque soror. . . .*

7. Surely that was the perfect hoax, unique and incomparable?
Probably; yet consider. In the years before 1914, if there was one single
military force which was prouder than the British Royal Navy, it was
undoubtedly the German army. Its devotion to duty was ascetic. Its
officers were aristocrats by birth, by selection, by training, and even by
appearance. Its ambitions embraced and dominated the entire world. No
one could despise it, and woe to that man who dared to ridicule it. And
yet not only the German army but the German Reich and the hard,
exact, cold bureaucracy which supported it were shown to be obtuse,
mechanical, and absurd. They were converted briefly into the laughing-
stock of Europe, not by a humiliating defeat, nor by a painful scandal
like the Dreyfus case, nor even by a joke like the *Dreadnought* hoax, but
by an act of desperation committed by a petty crook who for one day
became a genius.

8. In the autumn of 1906 the township of Köpenick, an ancient and
peaceful foundation which had become a suburb of Berlin, was digesting
its lunch and looking forward to its dinner. Two squads of German soldiers, marching smartly through its streets, did not disturb it. On the
contrary, they reassured it, as a visible symbol of German might and
German discipline. The Captain marching at their head, with his spiked
helmet, his long field-gray overcoat, his heavy saber, and his air of high
resolve, recalled the military efficiency of General von Moltke and the
personal majesty of the Kaiser Wilhelm II. Even when the soldiers, with

fixed bayonets, took up their positions in front of the Town Hall, even when the Captain posted a local policeman at its door and strode inside, the citizens of Köpenick were not alarmed: they were only curious and perhaps a little anxious in case, among the innumerable regulations and ordinances of the new Germany, they had transgressed (through oversight, not through failure of will power, still less through contumacy) one of them. Slowly, buttoning their waistcoats and brushing their mustaches, they began to gather before the Town Hall, gazing with respect and admiration at the impassive faces and heavy uniforms and glistening bayonets of the guard.

9. Meanwhile the Captain, followed by six grenadiers and a fusilier, mounted the staircase. He went first to the office of the Secretary.

10. "You are the Secretary of the Town Council?"

11. "Yes, Captain."

12. "Prepare yourself. You are being sent to Berlin."

13. "Very good, Captain."

Next, he went to the office of His Honor, the Mayor.

14. "You are the Mayor of Köpenick?"

15. "Yes, Captain."

16. "Prepare yourself. You are being sent to Berlin."

17. "Captain, may one enquire why?"

18. "I do not know. It is not part of my mission."

19. "Very good, Captain."

Next, he went to the office of the Chief of Police. The Chief of Police was snoozing deliciously in his chair, enjoying the peristaltic motion of his prandial pork and potatoes. Here the Captain really made his authority felt. Hastily buttoning his uniform, the Chief of Police was harshly reprimanded for dereliction of duty and sent home to take a bath which would clear his fat, dirty, sleepy, louse-ridden head.

Finally, he went to the office of the Town Treasurer.

20. "Clear your accounts and close your books. You are being sent to Berlin."

21. "Very good, Captain. I have here the sum of four thousand marks which has been paid in today, and which I have not yet entered. Will the Captain take charge of them, and give me a receipt?"

22. "Certainly."

23. "Here in the safe there are an additional two million marks. Will the Captain assume the responsibility for these also?"

24. For a moment the Captain seemed to interrogate himself. Then, with military promptness and the assurance which comes of long training, he decided.

25. "Not necessary. Close the safe. Take the key."

26. Signing the receipt, the Captain thrust the four thousand marks

into his overcoat pocket and left the Treasurer to make his preparations. Outside, a crowd of officials had gathered. All wanted answers to their questions, decisions on outstanding problems, clear, firm, authoritative guidance. In a few sentences the Captain resolved all their anxieties and gave them a final encouragement.

27. "The administration of this town is now in my hands. For everything that happens, I am responsible."

28. With relief and with admiration, they bowed and parted as the Captain moved to the door of the Town Hall. He returned the salutes of the policeman and the rigid military guard standing outside and strode away. Ten minutes later he was on the suburban train for Berlin. An hour later he was sitting in a café, wearing ordinary civilian clothes, drinking a glass of blond beer, and waiting for the papers to come out with the news from Köpenick.

29. He was not a Captain. He had never been in the army. He was an ex-convict named Wilhelm Voigt, who was approaching sixty years of age and had spent about half his life in prison. When Voigt worked, he was a shoe machinist; but because of his prison record, which had begun in his poverty-stricken youth, he could never find or keep settled employment. The efficient and ruthless German police were constantly making inquiries about him, checking his papers, and asking him to move on, from one city to another, from one state to another, until at last he determined to leave Germany altogether and settle in Austria or some other more peaceful, less interfering country. But to leave Germany, he needed a passport. An ex-convict would never be given a passport. How could Voigt ever obtain one? Never by entreaty, only by authority. What authority did all Germans recognize? That of the army, the uniform, the spiked helmet, the air of command, and the squad of armed automata. Therefore Voigt procured a uniform and took command of the first squad of soldiers he met in the street; and the rest followed with elegant, drill-like precision. He made only one mistake: he went to Köpenick because he thought it was an efficient little town which would have every kind of blank document in its Town Hall—so that he need only get rid of the top officials on some pretext and then make out his own passport. It was inside the Town Hall that he realized his blunder. He had not underestimated the obedience and naïveté of German officials, but he had forgotten their passion for complexity and departmentalization. Passports were not issued by the police offices of towns and cities but by the police offices of administrative districts, and Köpenick was not the capital of an administrative district. Poor Voigt pocketed his four thousand marks (at least they would be eating-money), ignored the two million marks (which would have sent him to jail for the rest of his life), and vanished.

30. (By the way, do you notice anything familiar in the story? The poverty-stricken youth, with the long years in prison, the loneliness? The bold assumption of power without training? The rapid and summary abrogation of all civil authority? The hypnotic domination of long-experienced and legally appointed officials? The superb arrogance of the ultimate declaration: "For everything that happens, I am responsible?" Yes, the Captain of Köpenick was the immediate predecessor of Adolf Hitler.)

31. Wilhelm Voigt was soon arrested. Another ex-convict remembered hearing him say, in prison, "You can always get what you want in Germany by picking up a few soldiers in the street and requisitioning it." He was tried, and found guilty of fraud, impersonation, larceny, etc., and sentenced to four years in prison; but he was set free on the personal orders of His Imperial Majesty Kaiser Wilhelm II. We can scarcely imagine that His Majesty wished to confer an imperial favor on the man who had successfully mimicked one of his own officers and bamboozled several hundreds of his own subjects. Either he felt that Voigt, after nearly thirty years in jail, was not quite sane; or else he heard the waves of laughter which were wafted into Germany on every breeze, realized that the Captain of Köpenick had made the German army and German officialdom ridiculous, and determined, instead of being vindictive, to be magnanimous. Within Germany, Voigt's act was a complex of crimes. Outside Germany, it appeared to be a hoax. Which was it?

32. In 1944 an elderly British lieutenant called Clifton James, who had been a rather unsuccessful actor before the war, was picked out of a routine job in the desk-bound Army Pay Corps and given a special mission. He was to impersonate Field Marshal Viscount Montgomery. Physically, he looked very like his model: spare frame, keen birdlike face, brisk nervous manner. Spiritually, he was almost the exact reverse of that mystical martinet. But he was shown many motion pictures of Montgomery; he was seconded to Montgomery's personal staff in order to register the timbres of Montgomery's voice and observe his mannerisms; he was trained to fly without being airsick; he was fitted with a replica of Montgomery's highly individual uniform—beret, medal-ribbons, gold chain across the chest, and all—and finally he talked for some time with Montgomery himself, face to face. After this training, he was briefed, and he became Montgomery. First, he was flown out to Gibraltar, where he was received by the Governor with a guard of honor and closely observed by a number of German agents using Spanish cover. He then proceeded to Allied headquarters in North Africa, where he was seen in public for an entire week. Then he returned to

Britain in utter secrecy and vanished. This impersonation was so successful that it deceived Admiral Canaris and his German intelligence staff. It was one element in the enormous and multiplex deception worked out by Allied intelligence officers in order to conceal from the Germans the time and place of the main D-day landings and, in particular, to make them believe that a massive blow, under Montgomery's command, would soon be delivered across the Mediterranean at southern France. This, like the rest of the magnificent D-day deception, was brilliantly successful. Was it a hoax?

33. Now, it is here that most books on famous hoaxes and famous hoaxers fail. A hoax is not an exaggeration or a lie told and acted for profit. A hoax is an exaggeration or a lie told and acted for amusement, for the sake of sheer mischief, for the sake of art. There is a fine anthology of swindles collected by Professor Curtis MacDougall, recently published in a second edition (*Hoaxes*, Dover Publications, 1958); but although it is rich in material, it spoils the appreciation of a delicate art by confusing elegant hoaxes with vulgar frauds and grimly serious deceptions. What connection is there between a vicious propaganda fabrication such as the *Protocols of the Elders of Zion*, a greedy series of forgeries like those seen in the career of Ivar Kreuger, and a neat, farcical, and virtually harmless mystification, as when Hugh Troy and a few friends dug up Fifth Avenue at Fifty-fourth Street and left the hole surrounded by signs saying MEN AT WORK.

34. It is the purpose and the effect that distinguish a hoax from other forms of deception. The swindler wants to get something. The hoaxer wants to create a work of art. The swindler wants either money, or power, or prestige, or revenge. The hoaxer wants to comment, to criticize, or to re-interpret. The swindler is a thief. The hoaxer is a satirist.

35. Now, look at the three impersonations again. When Lieutenant James pretended to be Field Marshal Montgomery, he was in deadly earnest. If he succeeded, his deception would help to save the lives of thousands of Allied soldiers; and we now know that all phases of the grand deception succeeded. When Hannibal drove a huge cattle herd along an Italian mountainside, with burning torches tied to their horns, to convince the Romans that his entire army was on the move, he was not hoaxing them; nor were the Japanese hoaxing when in the midst of diplomatic discussions and without a declaration of war, they attacked the United States fleet in Pearl Harbor.

36. The case of the Captain of Köpenick is more complex. The German army, administration, and police took his deception very seriously. But for the rest of the world, to whom it displayed in full bloom certain German characteristics which members of other nations find both absurd and repellent, it was a hoax. In effect it was the equivalent of a

satire on German authoritarianism, German militarism, German accuracy, and the awful quality which the Germans believe to be unflinching loyalty but others call porcine obtuseness.

37. And what of the Emperor of Abyssinia and his visit to the British Channel Fleet? We might put it down simply as a prank, like putting a cow in the college chapel or giving a man the number of the zoo and telling him to call Mr. Wolf. But in fact it went deeper. The Admiral and his officers were derided for being taken in. When they went ashore, small boys followed them, shouting Abyssinian words such as "Bunga, bunga!" Questions were asked in Parliament. The entire thing had started as an attempt by one young British officer to pull the leg of another (the chief of the Admiral's staff); but it developed into a first-class satire. It exposed the uncritical readiness of the British government and of the Royal Navy to entertain any odd-looking foreigner without inquiring closely into his character and background and to do him the honors so thoroughly that he went away awed and happy and pro-British. That kind of diplomatic courtesy helped to build up an enormous empire and to keep many spheres of influence in orbit. The *Dreadnought* hoax was a mocking exposure of its shallowness and insincerity. Thus, the silly little blackface impersonation by half a dozen unemployed youngsters proved to be a satire on the entire British imperial system.

38. In drawing and painting, a hoax corresponds to caricature; in music, literature, and drama, to parody. What the "Emperor of Abyssinia" and his suite did to the Royal Navy with their official visit, Gilbert and Sullivan had done some years earlier with *H.M.S. Pinafore*. (It looks and sounds innocuous enough nowadays, dear old *Pinafore*; but when it was produced, its satire was felt to be so acid that Disraeli himself said it "made him quite sick" with mortification.)

39. Artists are not concerned with gaining power or making money. They are trying to interpret the world. Some see it and show it as tragic, some as comic, some as romantic or fantastic. But some see it as pretentious, ridiculous, occasionally repulsive: these are the satirists. With all the pomp and circumstance of an epic poet, Juvenal describes the cruel and foolish Emperor Domitian convoking an emergency meeting of his cabinet to determine how to cook a vast circular turbot, too big for any of the imperial pots. In a single black-and-white drawing, the British cartoonist David Low shows a little man with a ridiculous mustache and a railway official's uniform defying the Creator of the universe and threatening to destroy mankind. Using all the resources of a full orchestra, Ernst von Dohnanyi builds up an atmosphere full of hideous menace: vast blocks of sound move through the air as though some unchallengeable portent were being brought to birth, cellos groan and trombones roar like beasts of the primeval slime, the music swells to a

fearful climax and falls silent. Then, with one finger, the pianist plays "Baa, baa, black sheep, have you any wool?"

40. It is in this realm of art, the only realm which combines the sublime and the ridiculous, that the hoax belongs. When Horace de Vere Cole strewed horse droppings (procured with considerable difficulty and expense from mainland Italy) about the center of that horseless city, Venice, and then watched the Venetians gazing with a wild surmise first at the pavement of the Piazza di San Marco and then at the sky above, where nothing has yet been seen to fly but pigeons and airplanes, he was enjoying the purest pleasure of art—which combines criticism, creation, and appreciation.

COMMENTARY AND QUESTIONS

To explain the nature of an object, an act, or an idea is to define it. Definition may be accomplished in many ways; one of the commonest and most effective is to present illustrative examples. By well chosen examples a writer can show vividly both what a thing is, and what it is not. In this essay Gilbert Highet uses such a method to define the nature and justification of the hoax.

1. The greater part of Highet's essay consists of three incidents, all (and especially the first two) presented in considerable detail. The word *hoax* does not appear (except in the title of the essay) until par. 5; no immediate answer is given to the question which ends par. 31; and no formal definition of a hoax is presented until par. 33. What advantages does Highet gain by such an arrangement?

2. Why do you think Highet arranged the three major incidents presented in pars. 1-32 in this particular order? Why does he reverse the order when he discusses them in pars. 35-37? What advantage does Highet gain by passing from narration of the specific incidents of pars. 1-32 to the generalized discussion of pars. 33-34 and then back to an analysis of the specific incidents again in pars. 35-37? What word, occurring in pars. 33, 34, and 40, and implied by pars. 38 and 39, connects all these paragraphs and is essential to Highet's concept of the hoax?

3. Discuss the appropriateness of the short additional examples of hoaxes and non-hoaxes appearing in pars. 33-40, and their arrangement and placement: for example, the probable principle governing the choice of those in par. 35, and the possible advantages of the particular order used for those in par. 33 and those in par. 39. What statements in pars. 33, 34, and 39 make the absurdity of the hoax described in par. 40 so peculiarly appropriate? Would you have ended the essay with a different example?

4. Highet's style is full of skillful rhetorical devices. For example, there is conscious parallelism of construction in the opening description of par. 1 and in the careful distinctions of par. 34. Find other examples. When it is judiciously used, alliteration can be an effective stylistic device, as in the phrase *mystical martinet* occurring in par. 32. Find an elaborate alliterative expression in par. 19. Is alliteration the only virtue of these particular two phrases?

5. What irony underlies the following:
   a. "one discordant note to spoil the splendid harmony" (par. 1).
   b. "his all but impossible task" (par. 3).
   c. "with military promptness and the assurance which comes of long training" (par. 24).
   d. "The ship's band, having been unable to find the national anthem of Abyssinia, broke into the national anthem of Zanzibar" (par. 4).
   e. "they were . . . perhaps a little anxious in case, among the innumerable regulations and ordinances of the new Germany, they had transgressed (through oversight, not through failure of will power, still less through contumacy) one of them" (par. 8).

   The first three of these quotations exploit an irony of situation, a comic contrast of appearance with reality. Show how the last two involve a different sort of irony, not merely intensifying the comic situation but also suggesting the satiric judgments on human folly made by these two hoaxes: consider, for example, these two quotations in connection with pars. 36 and 37. Find other examples of irony in the essay. Why is there no irony in par. 32?

6. This essay appeared originally in the pages of an expensive periodical designed for sophisticated (but not solemn) readers. Such an audience might be expected to appreciate, without need of elaborate explanation, the allusions to history and literature which appear in Highet's text. Can you explain the allusions to *Mountbatten* (par. 4), *Bloomsbury* (par. 5), *Dreyfus case* (par. 7), *Ivar Kreuger* (par. 33), *gazing with a wild surmise* (par. 40), and *Piazza di San Marco* (par. 40)? What would Highet have gained or lost by omitting these references or explaining them? *Heia age! rumpe moras!* (par. 4) is a quotation from a section of the *Aeneid* just a little beyond the lines explained at the end of par. 6. The god Mercury, having just warned Aeneas in a dream that if he delays leaving Carthage the angry Dido will use her fleet to attack and burn his ships, adds this urgent command, which may be translated "Come away! Cease delay!" Is there a double meaning in *ivory smiles?*

7. In par. 5 Highet mentions Virginia Woolf; when you read "Mr. Bennett and Mrs. Brown" (pp. 479-494) see whether you detect there any of the same sense of humor which led the youthful Virginia Stephen to take part in the *Dreadnought* hoax.

1. To hoax or not to hoax.
2. Practical jokes vs. hoaxes.
3. In defense of the absurd.

Winds That Blow Straight Up

by WOLFGANG LANGEWIESCHE

I

A PUFF OF WIND comes down the street. An old newspaper stirs in the gutter, jumps up on the sidewalk, spirals up to second-story height and flaps about there for a moment; then, with a new burst of energy, it sweeps upward again, and when you last see it, it is soaring high above the roof tops, turning over and over, blinking in the sunlight.

2. The wind has picked up a piece of paper and blown it away. What of it? A generation ago, in philosophical discourse, one might have chosen this as an example of an event completely void of significance, completely chance. But not in the air age. The tiny occurrence demonstrates an important fact concerning the air ocean—one that is only now becoming the practical knowledge of practical airfaring men: there are winds which blow neither east nor west, neither north nor south, but in the third dimension: straight up.

3. These upward currents run in all sizes and strengths. Sometimes they are barely able to lift pieces of paper and bits of dust, and not very high at that. Sometimes they do not blow at all. Sometimes they are upward hurricanes which blow clear up to the stratosphere and would be strong enough to lift a man. There is a story going around the airports now that a man was caught in such an updraft, after bailing out of a

disabled airplane; and that the updraft carried him up and killed him by cold and lack of oxygen before he came down far from the scene of the wreck. The story is probably apocryphal; it is told sometimes of Europe, sometimes of the South Pacific, and can't be pinned down. But it is not impossible; the laws of chance say that it will happen someday.

4. These upward winds answer an amazing variety of questions— some of them vague questions perhaps, but some of them very old.

5. The soaring of birds, for example—how does an eagle, a buzzard, a hawk manage to fly on out-stretched wings, without flapping, apparently without effort? Now in retrospect one wonders that this puzzle did not drive men crazy. Yet the answer is simple. The bird seeks out one of these upward winds and lets himself be blown upward, precisely as that piece of paper was blown upward.

6. Had Leonardo da Vinci seen the plain evidence of these upward winds—the flying leaves, the soaring birds—the air age might have begun in his time, and the airplane developed along with the sailing vessel. For these upward winds also explain the soaring of gliders. And a glider is nothing but a wood-and-fabric replica of a hawk; there is nothing in it that Leonardo could not have designed, built, and flown. It used to be that motorless airplanes could fly only over carefully selected sites, where a steep hillside faced a strong wind and deflected it upward. But today, with no new equipment but a clear mental image of these upward winds, men can fly without motors for hundreds of miles across country, even across flat plains, without machine power of any kind, riding on these updrafts.

7. The updrafts also are an important ingredient of all weather. In fact, it is but a small exaggeration to say that they *are* the weather. They explain why some days are clear, others smoky, still others showery. They account for cloud shapes; one kind of cloud particularly—the white puffy kind you find on a summer afternoon—is nothing but an updraft become visible. And the updrafts explain thunderstorms: by modern understanding, a thunderstorm is nothing but an updraft of terrific strength; the rain and the hail, the thunder and the lightning are merely by-products of this upward rush of air. Thus the puff of wind which lifts a piece of paper is nothing but a thunderstorm in embryo.

II

8. What makes the air rise in these updrafts is heat. The air is not being blown from below, nor being sucked from above; it rises because it is warmer than the surrounding air and hence less dense and hence buoyant—it *bubbles* up. You have seen those shimmering, trembling

"heat waves" over a sun-heated pavement: those waves are really blobs of air that have been heated by contact with the warm ground, have thus become light and are ballooning away; and this sort of air is the stuff which feeds those upward winds.

9. These winds themselves—if we could see them, perhaps on a summer afternoon when they are most nicely developed—would appear as giant columns, mile-high, standing all over the countryside at intervals of miles; chimney-like shapes within which warm air is flowing upward. One such chimney might stand over a little town, draining the warm-air bubbles off its pavements and roofs. Another might stand over a sunny hillside; still another above some dark, plowed field; any particularly hot spot of ground is likely to cause an updraft. One chimney might stop spouting for a while and fade out. Another might form nearby and start blowing. But always these winds would be, not a general widespread upward drift of all the air, but narrow, fast-blowing jets.

10. That's why pilots did not become clearly conscious of these updrafts until the middle '30's, although anyone who rides in an airplane will feel these updrafts often. On a day when the updrafts blow, an airplane is bound simply by chance to run into one every minute or so. It then gets an upward shove, felt by the occupants as a bump. But because the updraft is so narrow, the airplane flies out of it, usually a couple of seconds later. The sudden fading of lift then makes the occupants feel as if they were dropping. People used to call that an "air pocket," and used to imagine that they had fallen into a hole in the air. Thus, through three decades of flying there had been plenty of experience with updrafts. Any old-timers remembered some quite powerful, big updrafts: "There I was, with my throttle clear back and my nose down, and still going up a thousand feet per minute!" And they knew also that certain types of clouds tended to suck you in as you passed underneath. But pilots, proud of their motors, did not see any use in such commotions, nor any pattern; they were merely annoyed by them and called them "rough air."

11. As for the glider enthusiasts, they were indeed always looking for updrafts that would hold them up. But they looked for them over sites where an ordinary wind—a level-blowing wind—was caught in a trick configuration of terrain and forced to flow up a steep hillside. Such "slope soaring" had first been proved possible by Orville Wright, in a little-known exploit in 1911, 12 years before the famous German gliding meets on the Rhone, when he soared a glider for 13 minutes over the dunes of Kitty Hawk. In the '20's it was proved again and again, and pilots stayed up in such slope winds literally for days. It finally ceased to make much sense, even as a sport, for it was easy as shooting fish,

and you could fly, by this technique, only back and forth, back and forth over some carefully selected hill.

12. But all the time the hawks and buzzards knew better. The trick by which the soaring bird plays the updrafts is amazingly simple: when he enters an updraft, he has sense enough not to fly out on the other side. Instead, he banks around and circles—thus staying within the updraft. This technique is particularly obvious in the case of the turkey buzzards of the South because they do their hunting at low altitude, and at low altitude the updrafts are narrowest so that the bird can sometimes stay within them only by flying quite steeply banked, in tight and accurate circles. Higher up, where hawks and eagles fly, the updrafts are wider, so that those birds' circling is less steeply-banked and less regular.

13. Not until the early '30's did glider pilots begin to see the light: that a glider, too, flown by a hawk's technique, can fly on these heat-updrafts, and that it therefore can fly anywhere, even over plains, on any day when the updrafts are blowing. Today, a sailplane is launched from any ordinary airport. An automobile pulls it into the air with a long rope, much as a boy launches a kite by running with it against the wind. At 800 feet or so, the pilot pulls a lever which releases the tow rope. He then glides along, steadily losing altitude of course, just as an airplane glides with the engine throttled; and he hopes to hit a bump. If he fails to hit one, he keeps on coming down for a forced landing; and then is towed up for another try. If he does hit one—it may be so gentle that it can't be felt but only shown by a sensitive instrument—he lays the sail-

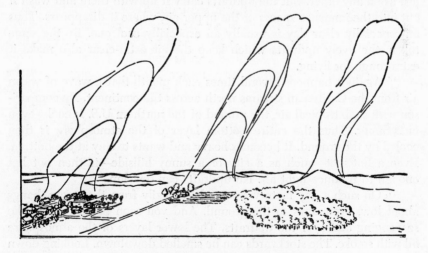

*Warm air bubbles up from heated areas to
make giant invisible columns a mile high.*

plane over into a steeply-banked turn and then jockeys so as to stay within the updraft. Thus, circling like a hawk, he is slowly, steadily carried upward. And so new is the idea of these currents, even today, that his delight is flavored with a strong admixture of unbelief.

III

14. The updrafts don't blow every day all day. They depend on the weather, just as they are in turn the weather's most important mechanism.

15. For example, it happens several times each month (in the course of world-wide, almost rhythmical commotions of the air ocean) that a flood of cold air from the polar regions sweeps southward across the northern United States, when the pavements, the fields, and the woods are still warm from a previous warm spell. Then the whole country acts as one giant hot-spot; the ground everywhere warms the air which comes in contact with it. The entire bottom layer of the atmosphere becomes light and buoyant, and updrafts bubble up everywhere, practically at random. On such a day you can see factory smoke being caught in the updrafts. Instead of flowing away in a smooth trail, it breaks up into individual puffs which bubble upward as they drift away with the wind. That's how those extra-clear days come about: the smoke from forest fires, factories, railroad yards, and kitchens pours forth on such a day just as on any other. But the updrafts carry it up with them and wash it out into the immense spaces of the upper air, where it disappears. Thus an especially clear day is usually an especially cool one. By the same token, the lively updrafts which keep the air extra-clear also make it extra-rough for flying.

16. Again it happens several times each month that a wave of warm air from the Caribbean streams north across the continent. By comparison with such tropical air, the ground of the northern U.S. is cool—even in summer. Thus the entire bottom layer of the atmosphere is then cooled by the ground. It becomes heavy and wants to stay at the bottom. Even a hot-spot—such as a city or a sunny hillside—is then not hot enough to produce light air. No updrafts can develop.

17. On such a day factory smoke drifts lazily from the stacks, hangs about low, even sinks to the ground. And you soon begin to miss the scavenging action of the updrafts. The lower layers of the atmosphere fill with smoke. The stockyards can be smelled downtown. Looking down a city street you can see the bottom-heaviness of the air—motor fumes and dust are thick at street level, making a bluish-gray, ill-smelling haze, while even at 10th-story height the air is clearer.

¹⁸· Three days of such up-and-down calm in the atmosphere, and you can't quite tell whether the day really means to be "good" or "bad." Straight up, the sky may be blue, but toward the horizon it is gray or yellow. A solid week of up-and-down calm—a rare occurrence—and the air becomes so smoke-laden that your eyes smart. The sun seems yellow. Most flying stops. The "smog" of St. Louis comes about largely that way, and so does the traditional London fog.

¹⁹· In the South, such days are less likely to develop—at least in summer. The ground is warmer, and updrafts do develop, even in this tropical air, during the hot hours of the day. They clear the air of smoke and water vapor, keep the sky blue, and toward afternoon make big, puffy clouds, showers, and thunderstorms. That's why the Southern summer, even though hotter, is actually so much more pleasant than the steamy season of New York, Pittsburgh, or St. Louis.

²⁰· Another typical sort of day is caused by an "inversion": the ground is warm enough and the air is cool enough to *start* updrafts. But a few thousand feet aloft there lies some warmer air; and such a warm layer forms an invisible lid which stops the updrafts short.

²¹· You have seen an updraft run against such a lid and die. The peculiarly-shaped smoke cloud of Mt. Vesuvius—so often photographed and painted—is caused by just that condition. This smoke is, of course, nothing but a very hot updraft rising from an unusual sort of hot-spot. On most days it rises practically straight up in the narrow, chimney-like shape typical of updrafts to a height of a few thousand feet above the mountain's top. At that height it stops rising abruptly and spreads out level across the Bay of Naples. The explanation is simple: on most days the lower air layers in that region consist of cool, Mediterranean Sea air; compared to such cool air the smoke is warm, has good buoyancy, and rises briskly. The higher air layers consist of warm African desert air; compared to such warm air the smoke is cool, has no buoyancy, and cannot rise.

²²· This condition is called an inversion because normally, and on the average, the higher up you go the colder the air. That's why mountain resorts are cool, and why aviators wear fur clothing. A layer of relatively warm air aloft is thus a reversal, locally at that altitude, of this general arrangement.

²³· Such inversions are almost always present at some altitude. If you watch for them, you will often see ordinary U. S. working smoke assume the Mt. Vesuvius pattern. Sometimes the inversion is very low. During a summer night, for example, the ground cools off and in turn cools the lowest layer of air. At daybreak, then, the smoke from the kitchen fire may rise only 20 feet above the roof of a farm, and there hit that invisible lid and spread. This "morning inversion" has recently

caused some concern at Wichita, Kansas. Normally Wichita burns natural gas which is smokeless. But in the new housing, hastily built for B-29 workers, coal ranges had to be installed because of wartime shortages. First thing you knew, the smoke from innumerable breakfast fires, spreading out underneath the morning inversion, formed a low blanket across the airport. The airliners had to pass up their stops, and the B-29's had to postpone their morning's test flying.

24. These morning inversions are tenuous things, broken up by the wind and the sun before most people are up and around. More persistent inversions often lie a mile or so up in the air, for days at a time. Such an inversion is characteristic, for example, of the tropical, moist air masses which spread from the Caribbean Sea across the U. S.—in summer our typical summer air. It is what makes the usual summer days of the Atlantic seaboard—those hot, muggy days which are almost gray in the morning, turn blue and a little clearer in the early afternoon, and gray and smoky again at night. It is that mile-high inversion holding down the industrial smoke, the dust, and the moisture. Only during the early afternoon is the ground heated enough so that it starts updrafts hot enough to pierce that inversion and thin out the pollution a little. And the whole stagnant condition won't break until an entirely new air mass, cooler and without a strong inversion, sweeps the old one away.

25. From the ground, you feel that high-up, oppressive blanket more than you see it. But from the air a strong inversion sometimes makes a dramatic sight. It looks like a lake. A flat, sharp, grayish surface spreads in all directions all the way out to the horizon, completely, mathematically level. This is the top surface of the murk. Sometimes this haze level is so clearly defined that you can let your plane wheels trail in the smoke, as you might let your hand into the water from a rowboat, while the rest of your airplane is in the clear air. Looking down through the smoke, you see the ground dimly, as you might see the bottom of a lake. Above you, the air is clear and the sky dark blue, almost black; just because all the smoke, dust, and vapor is being held down, the upper air is almost completely clean.

IV

26. Even on a day with no such lid aloft, the updrafts still don't keep going up and up, mile after mile. Every updraft has a built-in brake which tends to bring it to a stop.

27. As soon as each warm air bubble starts away from the ground, it begins to cool. What cools it is not, as one might think, its contact with

the cooler air aloft. Warm air and cool air never mix well, and never heat or cool each other appreciably. That's why there is such a thing as a cool draft in a heated room: some cool air current stubbornly refuses to mix with the rest of the air, or to be warmed by its warmth. In the same way, the updraft-air stubbornly remains a separate entity. What cools it is a process akin to mechanical refrigeration. Each updraft bubble, as it balloons upward, runs into lower and lower atmospheric pressures. Hence it expands, and this expansion cools it. This is another general fact about air—it always heats up when you compress it, and cools when you let it expand. You know this if you have ever felt a tire pump get hot, or if you have ever released pressure from a tire and felt the icy coldness of the escaping air.

28. The soaring pilot experiences both—the expansion and the cooling. The expansion, by making the updrafts bigger in diameter, makes them easier to find, easier to stay in than they are near the ground. Once a soaring pilot has climbed a few thousand feet, he can easily hop from updraft to updraft, and thus fly across country. As for the cooling, it soon makes him shiver, and it also makes him wonder. Though the currents he is riding are technically warm air chimneys, they can feel mighty cool.

29. This sounds like a paradox, but it isn't. The same climb which expands the updraft air and cools it also takes it up into the colder air layers aloft. Compared to this colder air, even the cooled-off updraft is then still warm and still has lift. Near the ground, it was hot air rising through warm air. Higher up, it is cool air rising through cold air. Still higher up, it may be cold air rising through ice-cold air. But eventually, the expansion cooling wins out. Eventually the rising air finds itself cooled to the same temperature as the air which then surrounds it. It loses its lift and comes to a stop—usually about a mile or so above the ground. The brake has worked.

30. And a good thing, too. If all the updrafts always kept going up and up, mile after mile, the atmosphere would be a witches' cauldron of perpetual thunderstorms and the earth would be uninhabitable.

31. But sometimes the brake is taken off. And then—look out.

V

32. It begins mildly enough with a little cloud. The updraft consists of moist air, and somewhere on its way up, expansion makes it so cool that it can no longer hold all the water vapor which it held easily when it was warm, near the ground. The water condenses out in the form of tiny droplets, so small that they don't fall, but float like dust. These

droplets, dancing on the updraft and glistening white in the sun—that's a cloud.

33. Thus on a bright, blue summer morning about 10 o'clock, puffs of white cloud often appear quite suddenly all over the sky, all at the same altitude. Those are the updrafts reaching, after a morning's climb, the altitude where they start clouding; and from then on, until late afternoon, they keep growing bigger and higher.

34. Each of these clouds, then, is the top-most visible spearhead of an updraft. At the seashore or on the Great Lakes on a typical summer day banks of white, towering clouds build up everywhere inland; but over the water the sky is blue all day. That's because the land is hot and sends up updrafts, but the water is cool and does not.

35. Right here, another of those old, vague puzzles explains itself— the long ocean voyages of some Pacific islanders. How do they manage to find a tiny island, across hundreds of miles of ocean, without sextants, chronometers, or star tables? Here is the answer: The ocean is cool and sends up no updrafts. In it the island, sun-heated, forms a hot-spot. Moist ocean air which flows across it heats up, becomes light, bubbles up and turns into cloud. Thus a bank of cumulus clouds floats high above the island throughout the day, while the surrounding sky is clear. A low, palm-studded island is visible to a man in a boat for perhaps 8 miles; but the cloud acts as a beacon, and marks the location of the island for perhaps 80 miles around!

36. Now, as a cloud, the updraft is still an updraft. True, it is now cool, foggy air; but the clear air which surrounds it up there is downright cold. Compared to this cold air, the cloud is warm. It is buoyant. It still wants to go up.

37. On some days the clouds can't make it. On some days the clouds run out of moisture and die. On some days they run into a strong inversion and flatten out. On some days they form so close to one another that they make a solid deck which then keeps the sun from the ground. A pilot knows as many varieties of cumulus as a botanist knows of orchids. There is *cumulus humilis, c. castellatus, c. mammatus, fracto-cumulus, strato-cumulus, cirro-cumulus, cumulo-nimbus* and so forth. But one thing all these clouds have in common: They *want* to go up. For this account, we pick a day with warm, moist air and no very strong inversion.

38. On such a day, the clouds keep growing upward until by midafternoon they are towering mountains. Looking up straight from the ground you may not appreciate just how high they are, because in that perspective you see only the base. But they show up clearly out toward the horizon, where you see them in side view. The typical cumulus cloud

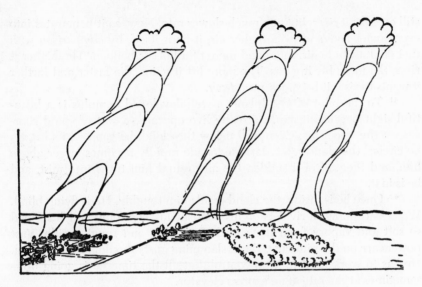

*Puffs of white cloud appear all at the same level,
on the invisible columns of rising wind.*

has a mathematically flat base—and the bases of all the clouds in the sky are at exactly the same height. That is the level at which the updraft-air turns foggy. Above that level, each cumulus cloud looks remarkably like the billows of smoke rising from a bonfire. And that's not chance. What the two air shapes have in common is that hot, live air is pushing its way up through cold, inert air.

39. For something paradoxical happens to the updraft once it has turned into cloud: it develops heat within itself. It is as if a fire had been lit within the cloud, *driving* it upward. This invisible fire is really sun-heat—but old, preserved sun-heat. Weeks ago the sun shone on some tropical sea or on some hot, moist field, and evaporated bits of water into the air. In this hidden form, then, as water vapor, sun-heat is contained in the air, although you can't feel it as warmth. The air is then caught in an updraft, and expansion-cooled by its rise. The vapor is turned back into water and in the process the sun-heat is freed again and now, as actual feelable warmth, goes back into the air. It isn't enough to make the air actually warmer; but it is enough to keep it from getting as cold as its expansion-cooling would otherwise make it.

40. And that means the brake is now off! Up to the clouding stage the updraft was continually being braked to a stop by its own internal expansion-cooling. Now that the cloud-making has begun, the uncorking of this preserved sun-heat counteracts the expansion-cooling. The cloud

still cools as it rises, but at a much slower rate. Now, as it penetrates into even cooler layers of even higher air, it finds itself, by *comparison* with that cold altitude air, more and more of a hot air balloon. The higher it rises, the more lift it gains. The more lift it gains, the faster and farther it wants to rise: it becomes a runaway.

41. To the pilot of a sailplane, a well-developed cumulus is a beautiful sight because it marks a really live updraft—a sort of spiral staircase to the upper air. Even well below the cloud, he can feel its lift. As he circles, the cloud's flat, dark underside rapidly becomes larger above him, and then all of a sudden the air around him turns into mist, and he is in it.

42. Once he is inside, the cloud mauls him roughly. He is flying blind. Water is running in rivulets on his windshield. The thing which seemed so soft and vapory from the outside is vicious and rough inside. Vast powers are on the rampage. Hard, slamming gusts shoulder him upward. He has to work hard to keep control, but all the time he is going up—sometimes at the rate of an express elevator.

43. If a cumulus cloud grows high enough, it produces a shower. "Yes, sure," you might think, "with all that vapor turning back to water, it's bound eventually to drop out." But it isn't so simple—nothing about the weather is simple. The water droplets which make up the cloud are much too small for rain. It takes ten thousand of them to make one raindrop. And for fundamental reasons of physics, having to do with vapor pressure, surface tension, etc., the droplets of a cloud do not run together voluntarily or even by chance. They stay apart. Considering their minute size, they are almost as far apart as the moon from the earth.

44. Yet the cloud does eventually drop out a lot of rain, and drops it with a bang, suddenly. Here is how. As the up-flowing air reaches higher and higher, clouding as it goes, it finally becomes so cold that it no longer makes cloud droplets. Instead, ice crystals materialize directly out of the air. In summertime the updraft has to go at least three miles up before it will be so cold. It is then *still* a hot-air current—for the clear air around it up there is way below freezing.

45. And the ice crystals do it. As the cloud's turbulence mixes crystals and droplets together, the water droplets which could not coalesce with one another can adhere to the much colder ice. Each ice crystal becomes the nucleus of a raindrop; and heavy with the water adhering to it, it drops.

46. That's why a shower comes so suddenly: just as there was one certain moment when the updraft first turned into cloud, so there is one certain moment when it reaches the crystal-making level. And at that moment, the rain breaks loose.

VI

47. The final, most spectacular stage of an updraft is the thunderstorm.

48. Seen from the ground as it goes over you, a thunderstorm is merely a confused sequence of events—low, dark clouds, puffs of wind, rain and hail, thunder and lightning. But sometimes you can see one on the horizon, in side view. Or you may see one from the air—clear of the low cloud-scud which usually hides the storm-cloud itself from the ground observer. Then you see that a thunderstorm is really one monstrous thing—a thing which has its own characteristic shape—just as a breaking wave, a tornado, a flame each has a shape of its own. It is a cumulus cloud of gigantic proportions and ferocious energy.

49. What drives this giant cloud upward is the same invisible fire which drives an ordinary cumulus cloud; the hidden heat, contained in water vapor, suddenly turned back into actual heat.

50. What makes it so ferocious is a particular set of conditions. The most important of these is that the air be warm and muggy. If it were warm and *dry*, it would not contain enough of that hidden heat-energy, because it would not contain enough water vapor. If it were moist, but *cool*, it would not actually contain much water. That's why thunderstorms occur almost always in warm, muggy air.

51. Thus in a thunderstorm this heat comes flowing in such vast waves and so suddenly that the driving fire resembles more nearly an explosion. A motion picture of a thundercloud's growth, reeled off in fast motion, actually looks remarkably like a slow-motion picture of an explosion!

52. Essentially then, what happens in a thunderstorm is the story you already know. The characteristic difference lies in the incredible violence of the updraft. The usual shower mechanism triggers off a violent rain, but the updraft catches many of the raindrops and won't let them fall. That is, the drop keeps falling and falling through the air; but the air itself rushes upward about as fast as the drop can fall.

53. But a raindrop, falling through air, is not a stable thing. When it first starts falling, it takes on a nice streamlined shape—the "tear drop" shape which much resembles an airplane's fuselage. Thus it slips easily through the air and picks up speed. But at the higher speed, the air then presses it out of shape. It flattens out, becomes short and squat. For that shape it is then falling too fast: it splatters itself into bits.

54. This tearing of rain from rain has an effect which is electrically analogous to pulling a sweater off yourself, or a cellophane wrapper off

a cigarette package: as you tear apart what had been together, the small, split-off fragments of each raindrop come away charged with "negative" electricity; the main part of each drop itself keeps the "positive" charge. The small fragments, being lighter, are blown back up into the cloud. The main parts of the drops, being heavier, soar around in the lower part of the cloud and eventually fall to the ground. Thus high tension is built up between the upper and lower parts of the cloud, and between the cloud and the ground. Lightning then jumps across as a gigantic spark.

55. Often the updraft inside a thunderstorm is so strong that the raindrops are blown clear up into the icy top of the cloud—perhaps 4 miles above the ground. Up in that sub-zero region, the drop freezes into a chunk of solid ice—a hailstone. The stone finally is kicked out of the lively part of the updraft and starts falling. But further down in the cloud, in the rainy part, it is often caught again in a renewed upward gust and soars upward again. Meteorologists have dissected freshly-fallen hailstones and found that they consist of many layers, onion-like. This suggests that a hailstone must have taken many trips up into the ice zone to freeze, down into the water zone of the cloud to pick up more water, and up again to freeze the water on as another coat. That's how the big ones are made that kill sheep and wreck car roofs. Wind tunnel tests show that to make an object of such weight and size soar upward takes a wind of 200 mph—straight up!

56. That's the dynamite packed in the puff of wind which picks up a piece of paper.

COMMENTARY AND QUESTIONS

To explain complex scientific or technical facts and processes in terms that the untrained layman can understand is not easy. It requires that the explainer understand not only the technicalities of the subject but also the techniques of making himself clear. Wolfgang Langewiesche has written a number of articles on aviation and weather which demonstrate that he has this firm grip on both facts and prose.

In writing about the winds that blow straight up, Langewiesche has one marked disadvantage and one marked advantage. The disadvantage is that the physical processes of the weather are distinctly complicated, demanding for full scientific explanation a knowledge of hydrostatics, thermodynamics, and higher mathematics; so that to make them understandable to the general public requires an immense and judicious simplification. The advantage is that everyone has actually observed the weather at close range; it is an everyday phenomenon. Notice what skillful use the author of this essay makes of the reader's own observation and experience to illuminate and make simple the essentially complicated processes he is explaining.

1. What is the purpose of section I? Is the introduction to the subject made by general statement or by concrete example? How does the author suggest the amount of power latent in winds that blow straight up? At what points in this opening section does the author appeal to the reader's direct experience of the effects of these upward winds?

2. What is the relation of par. 4 to pars. 5, 6, and 7? Of pars. 4 and 5 to section II? Of par. 7 to sections III, IV, V, and VI? In section II the author first explains the cause of updrafts. Why is the explanation here instead of in section I? In what section does the author continue his explanation by showing what makes updrafts keep going or slow down? Why is this continuation put where it is instead of earlier or later? Give two good reasons for putting the section on thunderstorms last: one connected with the logical order of explanation and one with the need for climax. Can you find similar reasons for the order of topics within section VI?

3. What connects the last paragraph of section I with the first, and the last paragraph of the essay with both? What is the effect of these connections? Why does the word *updrafts* appear in either the first or second sentence of every section from II through VI? Why doesn't it occur in the first paragraph? Would this article have been more likely to attract readers if it had been called "Updrafts"?

4. The author of this essay makes very good use of metaphors and similes —comparison, implied or expressed, between what he is explaining and something vivid in the reader's experience. For example, heated air is said to *bubble* up and to go *ballooning* away (par. 8); the updrafts are called *columns, chimneys,* and *fast-blowing jets* (par. 9). Find a few other such comparisons and consider their effectiveness in making the author's explanations clear and vivid.

5. Is the author of this article trying to write a textbook chapter in meteorology? What is he trying to do? How successful is he? Defend your answer.

SUGGESTIONS FOR WRITING

1. What happens when a lake freezes.
2. The effects of a severe storm in my home town.
3. How an automobile engine works.
4. How a plant grows.

The Old Gentleman

by GILBERT HIGHET

THE OLD GENTLEMAN was riding round his land. He had retired several years ago, after a busy career; but farming was what he liked, and he knew that the best way to keep farms prosperous was to supervise them in person. So, although he was approaching 70, he rode round his property for four or five hours, several days each week. It was not easy for him, but it was not difficult either. He never thought whether a thing was easy or difficult. If it ought to be done, it would be done. Besides, he had always been strong. Although his hair was white and his eyes were dimming, he stood a good six feet and weighed 210 pounds. He rose at four every morning. It was December now, Christmas was approaching, snow was in the air, frost and snow on the ground. This month he had been away from home on a toilsome but necessary trip; and in the hard weather he had been able to ride over his farms very seldom. Still, he liked to see them whenever he could. The land was quiet; yet a deal of work remained to be done.

2. There was much on the old gentleman's mind. His son had come home from college in some kind of disturbance and uneasiness, unwilling to go back again. Perhaps he should be sent elsewhere—to Harvard, or William and Mary? Perhaps he should have a private tutor? . . . Meanwhile, in order to teach him habits of quiet and undistracted industry, 'I can [the old gentleman wrote to a friend], and I believe I do, keep him in his room a certain portion of the twenty-four hours.' But even so, nothing would substitute for the boy's own will power, which was apparently defective. The grandchildren, too, were sometimes sick, because they were spoiled. Not by their grandmother, but by their mother. The old gentleman's wife never spoiled anyone: indeed, she wrote to Fanny to warn her, saying emphatically, 'I am sure there is nothing so pernisious as over charging the stomack of a child.'

3. He also thought hard and long about the state of the nation. Although he had retired from politics, he was often consulted, and he kept closely in touch. One advantage of retirement was that it gave him time to think over general principles. Never an optimist, he could usually see important dangers some time before they appeared to others. This December, as he rode over the stiff clods under the pale sky, he was think-

From *People, Places, and Books* (New York: Oxford University Press, Inc., 1953). By permission of the publishers. Copyright 1952 by Gilbert Highet.

ing over two constant threats to his country. One was the danger of disputes between the separate States and the central government. (Congress had just passed a law designed to combat sedition, and two of the States had immediately denounced it as unconstitutional. This could lead only to disaster.) The other problem was that respectable men were not entering public life. They seemed to prefer to pursue riches, to seek their private happiness, as though such a thing were possible if the nation itself declined. The old gentleman decided to write to Mr. Henry, whom he considered a sound man, and urge him to re-enter politics: he would surely be elected if he would consent to stand; and then, with his experience, he could do much to bridge the gap between the federal government and the States.

4. The old gentleman stopped his horse. With that large, cool, comprehensive gaze which every visitor always remembered, he looked round the land. It was doing better. Five years ago his farms had been almost ruined by neglect and greed. During his long absence the foremen had cropped them too hard and omitted to cultivate and fertilize, looking for quick and easy profits. Still, even before retiring, he had set about restoring the ground to health and vigor: first, by feeding the soil as much as possible, all year round; second, by 'a judicious succession of crops'; and third, most important of all, by careful regularity and constant application. As he put it in a letter, 'To establish good rules, and a regular system, is the life and the soul of every kind of business.' Now the land was improving every year. It was always a mistake to expect rapid returns. To build up a nation and to make a farm out of the wilderness, both needed long, steady, thoughtful, determined application; both were the work of the will.

5. Long ago, when he was only a boy, he had copied out a set of rules to help in forming his manners and his character—in the same careful way as he would lay out a new estate or survey a recently purchased tract of land. The last of the rules he still remembered. *Keep alive in your breast that little spark of celestial fire called Conscience.* Some of the philosophers said that the spark from heaven was reason, the power of the intellect, which we share with God. The old gentleman did not quarrel with them, but he did not believe them. He knew that the divine fire in the spirit was the sense of duty, the lawfulness which orders the whole universe, the power of which a young poet then alive was soon to write

> Thou dost preserve the stars from wrong;
> And the most ancient heavens, through Thee,
> are fresh and strong.

6. His mind turned back over his long and busy life. He never dreamed or brooded, but he liked to note things down, to plan them and record them. Now, on this cold December day, he could recall nearly every Christmas he had ever spent: sixty at least. Some were peaceful, some were passed in deadly danger, many in war, some in strange lonely places, some in great assemblies, some in happiness and some in anguish of soul, none in despair.

7. One of the worst was Christmas Day of twenty-one years before. That was early in the war, a bad time. It snowed four inches on Christmas. His men were out in the open, with no proper quarters. Although he started them on building shelters, an aggressive move by the enemy made them stand to arms and interrupt all other work for nearly a week. And they had no decent uniforms, no warm coats, no strong shoes, no regular supplies, two days without meat, three days without bread, almost a quarter of his entire force unfit for duty. He was receiving no supplies from the government, and he was actually meeting opposition from the locals. They had sent up a protest against keeping the troops in service during the winter. Apparently they thought you could raise an army whenever you needed one—not understanding that this little force was the only permanent barrier between them and foreign domination. He had replied with crushing energy to that protest. In a letter to the President of Congress, he wrote:

> I can assure those gentlemen that it is a much easier and less distressing thing to draw remonstrances in a comfortable room by a good fire side than to occupy a cold, bleak hill, and sleep under frost and snow without clothes or blankets. However, although they seem to have little feeling for the naked and distressed soldiers, I feel superabundantly for them, and from my soul I pity those miseries which it is neither in my power to relieve or prevent.

He ended with his well-known, strongly and gracefully written signature, *G. WASHINGTON.*

8. The year before that, 1776, things had been nearly as bad—the same difficulty about uniforms and supplies. Late in December he wrote earnestly from his camp, 'For godsake hurry with the clothing as nothing will contribute more to facilitate the recruiting service than warm & comfortable clothing to those who engage . . . The Commissary informs me that he cannot prevail on the millers to grind; & that the troops in consequence are like to suffer for want of flour . . . This must be reme-

died by fair or other means.' However, his chief concern then was not supplies, nor discipline, nor defense, but attack. On Christmas Day, long before dawn, he was crossing the Delaware River at McKonkey's Ferry, with a striking force of over two thousand men. He spent Christmas morning marching to Trenton. Next day he attacked Colonel Rahl and his Hessians. Half of them were sleeping off their Christmas liquor, and nearly all were paralyzed with drowsiness and astonishment. Hungry and hopeful, the Americans burst in on them like wolves among fat cattle. The surprise was complete. The victory, prepared on Christmas Day, was the first real success of the war.

9. Two winters later at Christmas time, Washington was in Philadelphia to discuss the plans for next year's campaign with a Congressional committee. People were very civil; they called him the Cincinnatus of America; and some of them made an effort to take the war seriously. But many did not. He would rather have been in winter quarters with his men. A few days before Christmas 1778 he wrote to Mr. Harrison that, as far as he could see, most people were sunk in 'idleness, dissipation, and extravagance . . . Speculation, peculation, and an insatiable thirst for riches seem to have got the better of every other consideration and almost of every order of men.'

10. Year after year he was in winter quarters at Christmas time, usually in a simple farmhouse, 'neither vast nor commodious,' in command of a starving and bankrupt army. In 1781, after Yorktown, things were a trifle better, and he had dinner with his wife and family at Mr. Morris's in Philadelphia amid general rejoicing. But the following Christmas was the blackest ever. He had thought of asking for leave, to look after his 'long neglected private concerns'; but the army was very close to mutiny, which would have meant the final loss of the war and the probable collapse of the entire nation. It was not only the enlisted men now, it was the officers: they were preparing to make a formal protest to Congress with a list of their grievances; and only the personal influence of Washington himself, only his earnest pleading and his absolute honesty and selflessness, kept the little force in being through that winter.

11. Yet by Christmas the next year, in 1783, it was all over. Washington said farewell to his officers, and then, on December 23rd, he resigned his commission. His formal utterance still stands, grave as a monument:

> Happy in the confirmation of our Independence and Sovereignty, and pleased with the opportunity afforded the United States of becoming a respectable nation, I resign, with satisfaction, the appointment I accepted with diffidence: a diffidence in my abilities to accomplish so arduous a task, which, however, was superceded by a confidence in the rectitude of our cause, the support of the supreme power of the Union, and the patronage of Heaven.

So he said. And the President of Congress replied, in terms which, although still balanced and baroque, are more emotional and almost tender:

> We join you in commending the interests of our dearest country to the Almighty God, beseeching him to dispose the hearts and minds of its citizens, to improve the opportunity afforded them of becoming a happy and respectable nation. And for you, we address to him our earnest prayers, that a life so beloved may be fostered with all his care; that your days may be happy as they have been illustrious; and that he will finally give you that reward which this world cannot give.

Next day Washington left for Mt. Vernon, and spent Christmas 1783 at home in peace.

^{12.} Some years passed. December was always busy. Washington was on horseback nearly every day, riding round his place, directing the operations which kept the land alive and fed all those who lived on it, ditching, threshing, hog-killing, repairing walls, lifting potatoes, husking corn. And it was a poor December when he did not have at least half a dozen days' hunting, though in that thickly wooded country he often lost his fox and sometimes hounds too. For Christmas after Christmas in the 'eighties, his diary shows him living the life of a peaceful squire, and on the day itself usually entertaining friends and relatives. On Christmas Eve 1788, Mr. Madison stayed with him, and was sent on to Colchester next day in Washington's carriage.

^{13.} Again a change. Christmas 1789 saw him as the first President of the United States, living in New York, the capital of the Union, and receiving formal calls from diplomats and statesmen. In the forenoon he attended St. Paul's Chapel; in the afternoon Mrs. Washington received visitors, 'not numerous, but respectable'; and next day Washington rode out to take his exercise. (He and Theodore Roosevelt were probably the finest horsemen of all our Presidents; those who knew him best liked to think of him on horseback, the most graceful rider in the country.) But for years thereafter his exercise was cut short and his days were swallowed up in the constant crowding of business. He rarely saw his land and seldom visited his home. His Christmases were formal and public; brilliant, but not warm; not holidays.

^{14.} But now, after his final retirement, he had time to look back on earlier Christmases. Some of them were very strange. Christmas of 1751

he had spent at sea. His elder brother Lawrence, frail and overworked, sailed to Barbados for a winter cruise, and George accompanied him. On November 3rd, they landed at Bridgetown, and were invited to dine next day with Major Clarke, O.C. British forces. Washington observed gravely to his diary: 'We went,—myself with some reluctance, as the smallpox was in his family.' Less than two weeks later Washington was down with smallpox, which kept him in bed for nearly a month; but he recovered with very few marks. By December 25th he and his brother were sailing back, past the Leeward Islands. As he liked to do all through his life, he noted the weather ('fine, clear and pleasant with moderate sea') and the situation ('latitude 18°30''); and, with a youthful exuberance which he soon lost, he adds: 'We dined on a fat Irish goose, Beef, &ca &ca, and drank a health to our absent friends.'

15. Five years later, he was a colonel engaged in one of the wars that helped to make this continent Anglo-Saxon instead of Latin: the war to keep the French, pressing downward along the Ohio from Canada and upward along the Mississippi from New Orleans, from encircling the British colonies in an enclave along the coast and cutting them off forever from the wealth of the plains, the rivers, and the distant, fabulous Pacific. Those two Christmases Washington could recall as a time of profound depression, filled with the things he hated most: anarchic competition and anarchic indiscipline. He commanded a Virginia regiment; and Captain Dagworthy of the Maryland troops at Fort Cumberland would not supply him. He despised drunkenness and slack soldiering; and he would not tolerate the attempts by the liquor trade to batten on his troops and run local elections by handing out free liquor. His enemies beat him temporarily, not by bending his will, but by wrecking his health. Christmas 1757 saw him on leave after a physical collapse which looked very like an attack of consumption, involving hemorrhage, fever, and a certain hollowness of the chest which never quite left him. He bore up as well as he could under the barrage of slander which his enemies poured in upon him, including the foulest of all, that he was accepting graft; but he had been ill for months when he finally broke down. (Years later, when he was appointed Commander-in-Chief, he was offered a regular salary, but refused to accept it. Instead, he asked Congress to pay his expenses; he kept the accounts scrupulously; and he presented them without extras at the end of the war. Slanders are always raised about great men; but this one slander was never leveled at Washington again.)

16. He looked back beyond that to one of the hardest Christmases in his memory. That was the Christmas of 1753, when he was only 21. Governor Dinwiddie had determined to stop the encirclement of Virginia.

The French were building forts on the Ohio, and arresting traders from the British colonies who penetrated that territory. Soon there would be nothing westward except a ring of hostile Indians supported by arrogant French officers. Isolated by land, the colonies could later have been cut off by sea, too, and the seed would have withered almost before it struck firm root.

[17.] The governor commissioned young Major Washington to make his way to the French fort, to deliver a letter from him to the French commandant, and to bring back both a reply and an estimate of the situation. He did; but he was very nearly killed. Not by the French. Or not directly. They merely told him that they were absolutely determined to take possession of the Ohio territory, and returned a diplomatic but unsatisfactory reply to the governor's letter. Still, Major Washington had at least the substance of a good intelligence report, for he had inspected the fort and his men had observed how many canoes the French were building. He had only to return. The French, however, endeavored to persuade him to go up and interview the governor of French Canada; and, that failing, set about bribing the Indians in his party with liquor and guns either to leave him altogether or to delay until the worst of the winter, when travel would be impossible for months. But Washington had a good guide; he was friendly with the Indian chief; and he had a tireless will. He set off on the return journey about the third week in December, when snow was already falling heavily mixed with rain. Six days were spent on a river full of ice. The canoes began to give out. The horses foundered. The rest of the party went more and more slowly. Major Washington 'put himself in Indian walking dress' and pushed on, on foot. On Christmas Day he was making his way toward the Great Beaver Creek. Next day he left the entire party to follow with horses, money, and baggage, and set out alone with the guide, Christopher Gist.

[18.] Next day a lone Indian who pretended to know the territory, but who was evidently a French agent, spent some hours leading the two men off their route, and finally shot at the young officer from close range. Gist would have killed him; but Washington would not allow it: they kept him for several hours, and then let him go. Then they pressed on eastward. They had to cross the swollen, ice-jammed Allegheny River. They built a raft; but they could force it only halfway through the roaring current and the hammering ice-blocks. That night they spent freezing on an island in midstream. In the morning, they struggled across on the ice, and pressed on again. In his journal the guide recorded that the major was 'much fatigued.' But still he kept going: eighteen miles a day with a gun and a full pack, over rough territory, threatened by hostile

Indians, in mid-December, with snow and rain falling from the sky and lying thick on the ground.

[19.] Now, over a period of forty-five years, he looked back on that Christmas. It had been, he remembered, 'as fatiguing a journey as it is possible to conceive'—and still a necessary one. It was the first of his many services to his country, to keep it from being surrounded and strangled from without or poisoned from within. And he reflected that it is not necessary to try to be brave, or clever, or generous, or beloved, or even happy. It is necessary simply to do one's duty. All else flows from that. Without that, all else is useless.

[20.] Darkness closed in early in these winter days. It was getting toward Christmas of the year 1798. General Charles Pinckney and his lady were expected for Christmas dinner. The old gentleman finished looking over the land, and turned homeward. He paid no heed to the cold.

BIBLIOGRAPHY

R. G. Adams (ed.), *Journal of Major George Washington* (Scholars' Facsimiles, New York, 1940).

C. H. Ambler, *George Washington and the West* (Chapel Hill, 1936).

W. S. Baker, *Itinerary of General Washington* (Lippincott, 1892).

W. S. Baker, *Washington after the Revolution* (Lippincott, 1898).

G. W. P. Custis, *Recollections and Private Memoirs of Washington* (ed. B. J. Lossing, Derby & Jackson, New York, 1860).

J. C. Fitzpatrick (ed.), *Diaries of George Washington, 1748-1799* (Houghton Mifflin, 1925).

J. C. Fitzpatrick (ed.), *Writings of George Washington* (U.S. Government Printing Office, 1931-44).

D. S. Freeman, *George Washington* (Scribner, 1948—).

P. L. Haworth, *George Washington, Country Gentleman* (Bobbs Merrill, 1925).

D. M. Larrabee (ed.), *Journal of George Washington* (Allegheny College, 1924).

T. Lear, *Letters and Recollections of George Washington* (Doubleday, Page, 1906).

J. M. Toner (ed.), *Daily Journal of Major George Washington* (Munsell, Albany, 1892).

COMMENTARY AND QUESTIONS

Biography is an attempt to explain to the reader exactly what sort of man or woman the subject of the biography is or was: how he looked.

what he did, and which traits of character and personality distinguished him from others and made him worth remembering. Like all explanation, successful biographical writing requires a judicious selection and ordering of facts.

1. In this biographical essay, Gilbert Highet is not writing a complete life of Washington but singling out certain highlights of his character and career and presenting them in a carefully planned arrangement. By means of what unusual technical device is he able to select representative actions or situations from a long span of Washington's lifetime and yet give them all a formal connection with one another?

2. Each of the first five paragraphs presents details which emphasize Washington's sense of duty and strength of will. Point out these details. The quotation in par. 5 is from Wordsworth's "Ode to Duty." What is the function of par. 6? What reasons might Highet have had for not revealing the name of his subject until the end of par. 7?

3. Pars. 7-11 form a natural unit. What is the basis for this unity? Why does this group begin with a paragraph on Valley Forge rather than observing strict chronology? In what way is this group related to the facts about Washington presented in pars. 1-5? In what way are pars. 12 and 13, taken together, related to both groups?

4. The order of pars. 14-18 is not chronological. What is the basis of arrangement? What reasons might Highet have had for placing this group of paragraphs here rather than before par. 7?

5. The first and last paragraphs of the essay present Washington riding over his lands at Mount Vernon. Both paragraphs mention the cold. Is this merely a touch of climatic verisimilitude?

6. In par. 2 Highet introduces the first of a number of quotations from Washington's letters and diaries. How does he make them seem a natural part of his text, and what does he gain by using them?

7. Nowhere in this essay does Highet make a formal summary of Washington's distinguishing traits. How, then, is the reader able to gain so clear an idea of his character?

SUGGESTION FOR WRITING

Write a biographical essay, either about a historical figure you know from books, or about someone you know personally. Decide before you write what principles you are going to use as your basis for selecting details and how you are going to organize these details into a satisfying essay.

Crash!

by FREDERICK LEWIS ALLEN

I

EARLY IN SEPTEMBER the stock market broke. It quickly recovered, however; indeed, on September 19th the averages as compiled by the *New York Times* reached an even higher level than that of September 3rd. Once more it slipped, farther and faster, until by October 4th the prices of a good many stocks had coasted to what seemed first-class bargain levels. Steel, for example, after having touched 261¾ a few weeks earlier, had dropped as low as 204; American Can, at the closing on October 4th, was nearly twenty points below its high for the year; General Electric was over fifty points below its high; Radio had gone down from 114¾ to 82½.

2. A bad break, to be sure, but there had been other bad breaks, and the speculators who escaped unscathed proceeded to take advantage of the lesson they had learned in June and December of 1928 and March and May of 1929: when there was a break it was a good time to buy. In the face of all this tremendous liquidation, brokers' loans as compiled by the Federal Reserve Bank of New York mounted to a new high record on October 2nd, reaching $6,804,000,000—a sure sign that margin buyers were not deserting the market but coming into it in numbers at least undiminished. (Part of the increase in the loan figure was probably due to the piling up of unsold securities in dealers' hands, as the spawning of investment trusts and the issue of new common stock by every manner of business concern continued unabated.) History, it seemed, was about to repeat itself, and those who picked up Anaconda at 109¾ or American Telephone at 281 would count themselves wise investors. And sure enough, prices once more began to climb. They had already turned upward before that Sunday in early October when Ramsay MacDonald sat on a log with Herbert Hoover at the Rapidan camp and talked over the prospects for naval limitation and peace.

3. Something was wrong, however. The decline began once more. The wiseacres of Wall Street, looking about for causes, fixed upon the collapse of the Hatry financial group in England (which had led to much forced selling among foreign investors and speculators), and upon the bold refusal of the Massachusetts Department of Public Utilities to allow

the Edison Company of Boston to split up its stock. They pointed, too, to the fact that the steel industry was undoubtedly slipping, and to the accumulation of "undigested" securities. But there was little real alarm until the week of October 21st. The consensus of opinion, in the meantime, was merely that the equinoctial storm of September had not quite blown over. The market was readjusting itself into a "more secure technical position."

II

⁴· In view of what was about to happen, it is enlightening to recall how things looked at this juncture to the financial prophets, those gentlemen whose wizardly reputations were based upon their supposed ability to examine a set of graphs brought to them by a statistician and discover, from the relation of curve to curve and index to index, whether things were going to get better or worse. Their opinions differed, of course; there never has been a moment when the best financial opinion was unanimous. In examining these opinions, and the outgivings of eminent bankers, it must furthermore be acknowledged that a bullish statement cannot always be taken at its face value: few men like to assume the responsibility of spreading alarm by making dire predictions, nor is a banker with unsold securities on his hands likely to say anything which will make it more difficult to dispose of them, unquiet as his private mind may be. Finally, one must admit that prophecy is at best the most hazardous of occupations. Nevertheless, the general state of financial opinion in October, 1929, makes an instructive contrast with that in February and March, 1928, when, as we have seen, the skies had not appeared any too bright.

⁵· Some forecasters, to be sure, were so unconventional as to counsel caution. Roger W. Babson, an investment adviser who had not always been highly regarded in the inner circles of Wall Street, especially since he had for a long time been warning his clients of future trouble, predicted early in September a decline of sixty or eighty points in the averages. On October 7th the Standard Trade and Securities Service of the Standard Statistics Company advised its clients to pursue an "ultra-conservative policy," and ventured this prediction: "We remain of the opinion that, over the next few months, the trend of common-stock prices will be toward lower levels." Poor's *Weekly Business and Investment Letter* spoke its mind on the "great common-stock delusion" and predicted "further liquidation in stocks." Among the big bankers, Paul M. Warburg had shown months before this that he was alive to the dangers of the

situation. These commentators—along with others such as the editor of the *Commercial and Financial Chronicle* and the financial editor of the *New York Times*—would appear to deserve the 1929 gold medals for foresight.

6. But if ever such medals were actually awarded, a goodly number of leather ones would have to be distributed at the same time. Not necessarily to the Harvard Economic Society, although on October 19th, after having explained that business was "facing another period of readjustment," it predicted that "if recession should threaten serious consequences for business (as is not indicated at present) there is little doubt that the Reserve System would take steps to ease the money market and so check the movement." The Harvard soothsayers proved themselves quite fallible: as late as October 26th, after the first wide-open crack in the stock market, they delivered the cheerful judgment that "despite its severity, we believe that the slump in stock prices will prove an intermediate movement and not the precursor of a business depression such as would entail prolonged further liquidation." This judgment turned out, of course, to be ludicrously wrong; but on the other hand the Harvard Economic Society was far from being really bullish. Nor would Colonel Leonard P. Ayres of the Cleveland Trust Company get one of the leather medals. He almost qualified when, on October 15th, he delivered himself of the judgment that "there does not seem to be as yet much real evidence that the decline in stock prices is likely to forecast a serious recession in general business. Despite the slowing down in iron and steel production, in automobile output, and in building, the conditions which result in serious business depressions are not present." But the skies, as Colonel Ayres saw them, were at least partly cloudy. "It seems probable," he said, "that stocks have been passing not so much from the strong to the weak as from the smart to the dumb."

7. Professor Irving Fisher, however, was more optimistic. In the newspapers of October 17th he was reported as telling the Purchasing Agents Association that stock prices had reached "what looks like a permanently high plateau." He expected to see the stock market, within a few months, "a good deal higher than it is today." On the very eve of the panic of October 24th he was further quoted as expecting a recovery in prices. Only two days before the panic, the *Boston News Bureau* quoted R. W. McNeel, director of McNeel's Financial Service, as suspecting "that some pretty intelligent people are now buying stocks." "Unless we are to have a panic—which no one seriously believes—stocks have hit bottom," said Mr. McNeel. And as for Charles E. Mitchell, chairman of the great National City Bank of New York, he continuously and enthusiastically radiated sunshine. Early in October Mr. Mitchell was positive that,

despite the stock-market break, "The industrial situation of the United States is absolutely sound and our credit situation is in no way critical. . . . The interest given by the public to brokers' loans is always exaggerated," he added. "Altogether too much attention is paid to it." A few days later Mr. Mitchell spoke again: "Although in some cases speculation has gone too far in the United States, the markets generally are now in a healthy condition. The last six weeks have done an immense amount of good by shaking down prices. . . . The market values have a sound basis in the general prosperity of our country." Finally, on October 22nd, two days before the panic, he arrived in the United States from a short trip to Europe with these reassuring words: "I know of nothing fundamentally wrong with the stock market or with the underlying business and credit structure. . . . The public is suffering from 'brokers' loanitis.'"

8. Nor was Mr. Mitchell by any means alone in his opinions. To tell the truth, the chief difference between him and the rest of the financial community was that he made more noise. One of the most distinguished bankers in the United States, in closing a deal in the early autumn of 1929, said privately that he saw not a cloud in the sky. Habitual bulls like Arthur Cutten were, of course, insisting that they were "still bullish." And the general run of traders presumably endorsed the view attributed to "one large house" in mid-October in the *Boston News Bureau's* "Broad Street Gossip," that "the recent break makes a firm foundation for a big bull market in the last quarter of the year." There is no doubt that a great many speculators who had looked upon the midsummer prices as too high were now deciding that deflation had been effected and were buying again. Presumably most financial opinion agreed also with the further statement which appeared in the "Broad Street Gossip" column on October 16th, that "business is now too big and diversified, and the country too rich, to be influenced by stock-market fluctuations"; and with the editorial opinion of the *News Bureau*, on October 19th, that "whatever recessions (in business) are noted, are those of the runner catching his breath. . . . The general condition is satisfactory and fundamentally sound."

9. The disaster which was impending was destined to be as bewildering and frightening to the rich and the powerful and the customarily sagacious as to the foolish and unwary holder of fifty shares of margin stock.

III

10. The expected recovery in the stock market did not come. It seemed to be beginning on Tuesday, October 22nd, but the gains made during the day were largely lost during the last hour. And on Wednes-

day, the 23rd, there was a perfect Niagara of liquidation. The volume of trading was over six million shares, the tape was 104 minutes late when the three-o'clock gong ended trading for the day, and the *New York Times* averages for fifty leading railroad and industrial stocks lost 18.24 points—a loss which made the most abrupt declines in previous breaks look small. Everybody realized that an unprecedented number of margin calls must be on their way to insecurely margined traders, and that the situation at last was getting serious. But perhaps the turn would come tomorrow. Already the break had carried prices down a good deal farther than the previous breaks of the past two years. Surely it could not go on much longer.

11. The next day was Thursday, October 24th.

12. On that momentous day stocks opened moderately steady in price, but in enormous volume. Kennecott appeared on the tape in a block of 20,000 shares, General Motors in another of the same amount. Almost at once the ticker tape began to lag behind the trading on the floor. The pressure of selling orders was disconcertingly heavy. Prices were going down. . . . Presently they were going down with some rapidity. . . . Before the first hour of trading was over, it was already apparent that they were going down with an altogether unprecedented and amazing violence. In brokers' offices all over the country, tape-watchers looked at one another in astonishment and perplexity. Where on earth was this torrent of selling orders coming from?

13. The exact answer to this question will probably never be known. But it seems probable that the principal cause of the break in prices during that first hour on October 24th was not fear. Nor was it short selling. It was forced selling. It was the dumping on the market of hundreds of thousands of shares of stock held in the name of miserable traders whose margins were exhausted or about to be exhausted. The gigantic edifice of prices was honeycombed with speculative credit and was now breaking under its own weight.

14. Fear, however, did not long delay its coming. As the price structure crumbled there was a sudden stampede to get out from under. By eleven o'clock traders on the floor of the Stock Exchange were in a wild scramble to "sell at the market." Long before the lagging ticker could tell what was happening, word had gone out by telephone and telegraph that the bottom was dropping out of things, and the selling orders redoubled in volume. The leading stocks were going down two, three, and even five points between sales. Down, down, down. . . . Where were the bargain-hunters who were supposed to come to the rescue at times like this? Where were the investment trusts, which were expected to provide a cushion for the market by making new purchases at low prices? Where were the big operators who had declared that they were still bullish?

Where were the powerful bankers who were supposed to be able at any moment to support prices? There seemed to be no support whatever. Down, down, down. The roar of voices which rose from the floor of the Exchange had become a roar of panic.

15. United States Steel had opened at 205½. It crashed through 200 and presently was at 193½. General Electric, which only a few weeks before had been selling above 400, had opened this morning at 315—now it had slid to 283. Things were even worse with Radio: opening at 68¾, it had gone dismally down through the sixties and the fifties and forties to the abysmal price of 44½. And as for Montgomery Ward, vehicle of the hopes of thousands who saw the chain store as the harbinger of the new economic era, it had dropped headlong from 83 to 50. In the space of two short hours, dozens of stocks lost ground which it had required many months of the bull market to gain.

16. Even this sudden decline in values might not have been utterly terrifying if people could have known precisely what was happening at any moment. It is the unknown which causes real panic.

17. Suppose a man walked into a broker's branch office between twelve and one o'clock on October 24th to see how things were faring. First he glanced at the big board, covering one wall of the room, on which the day's prices for the leading stocks were supposed to be recorded. The LOW and LAST figures written there took his breath away, but soon he was aware that they were unreliable: even with the wildest scrambling, the boys who slapped into place the cards which recorded the last prices shown on the ticker could not keep up with the changes: they were too numerous and abrupt. He turned to the shining screen across which ran an uninterrupted procession of figures from the ticker. Ordinarily the practiced tape-watcher could tell from a moment's glance at the screen how things were faring, even though the Exchange now omitted all but the final digit of each quotation. A glance at the board, if not his own memory, supplied the missing digits. But today, when he saw a run of symbols and figures like

R   WX
6.5½.5.4.   9.8⅞¾½¼.8.7½.7.

he could not be sure whether the price of "6" shown for Radio meant 66 or 56 or 46; whether Westinghouse was sliding from 189 to 187 or from 179 to 177. And presently he heard that the ticker was an hour and a half late; at one o'clock it was recording the prices of half-past eleven! All this that he saw was ancient history. What was happening on the floor now?

18. At ten-minute intervals the bond ticker over in the corner would

hammer off a list of selected prices direct from the floor, and a broker's clerk would grab the uncoiling sheet of paper and shear it off with a pair of scissors and read the figures aloud in a mumbling expressionless monotone to the white-faced men who occupied every seat on the floor and stood packed at the rear of the room. The prices which he read out were *ten or a dozen or more points below those recorded on the ticker*. What about the stocks not included in that select list? There was no way of finding out. The telephone lines were clogged as inquiries and orders from all over the country converged upon the Stock Exchange. Once in a while a voice would come barking out of the broker's rear office where a frantic clerk was struggling for a telephone connection: "Steel at ninety-six!" Small comfort, however, to know what Steel was doing; the men outside were desperately involved in many another stock than Steel; they were almost completely in the dark, and their imaginations had free play. If they put in an order to buy or to sell, it was impossible to find out what became of it. The Exchange's whole system for the recording of current prices and for communicating orders was hopelessly unable to cope with the emergency, and the sequel was an epidemic of fright.

[19.] In that broker's office, as in hundreds of other offices from one end of the land to the other, one saw men looking defeat in the face. One of them was slowly walking up and down, mechanically tearing a piece of paper into tiny and still tinier fragments. Another was grinning shamefacedly, as a small boy giggles at a funeral. Another was abjectly beseeching a clerk for the latest news of American & Foreign Power. And still another was sitting motionless, as if stunned, his eyes fixed blindly upon the moving figures on the screen, those innocent-looking figures that meant the smash-up of the hopes of years. . . .

GL.   AWW.   JMP.
  8.7.5.2.1.90.89.7.6.   3.2½.2.   6.5.3.2½.

[20.] A few minutes after noon, some of the more alert members of a crowd which had collected on the street outside the Stock Exchange, expecting they knew not what, recognized Charles E. Mitchell, erstwhile defender of the bull market, slipping quietly into the offices of J. P. Morgan & Company on the opposite corner. It was scarcely more than nine years since the House of Morgan had been pitted with the shrapnel-fire of the Wall Street explosion; now its occupants faced a different sort of calamity equally near at hand. Mr. Mitchell was followed shortly by Albert H. Wiggin, head of the Chase National Bank; William Potter, head of the Guaranty Trust Company; and Seward Prosser, head of the Bankers Trust Company. They had come to confer with Thomas W. Lamont of the Morgan firm. In the space of a few minutes these five men, with George F. Baker, Jr., of the First National Bank, agreed in behalf of their respective institutions to put up forty millions apiece to shore up the stock market. The object of the two-hundred-and-forty-million-dollar pool thus formed, as explained subsequently by Mr. Lamont, was not to hold prices at any given level, but simply to make such purchases as were necessary to keep trading on an orderly basis. Their first action, they decided, would be to try to steady the prices of the leading securities which served as bell wethers for the list as a whole. It was a dangerous plan, for with hysteria spreading there was no telling what sort of *débâcle* might be impending. But this was no time for any action but the boldest.

21. The bankers separated. Mr. Lamont faced a gathering of reporters in the Morgan offices. His face was grave, but his words were soothing. His first sentence alone was one of the most remarkable understatements of all time. "There has been a little distress selling on the Stock Exchange," said he, "and we have held a meeting of the heads of several financial institutions to discuss the situation. We have found that there are no houses in difficulty and reports from brokers indicate that margins are being maintained satisfactorily." He went on to explain that what had happened was due to a "technical condition of the market" rather than to any fundamental cause.

22. As the news that the bankers were meeting circulated on the floor of the Exchange, prices began to steady. Soon a brisk rally set in. Steel jumped back to the level at which it had opened that morning. But the bankers had more to offer the dying bull market than a Morgan partner's best bedside manner.

23. At about half-past one o'clock Richard Whitney, vice-president of the Exchange, who usually acted as floor broker for the Morgan interests, went into the "Steel crowd" and put in a bid of 205—the price of the last previous sale—for 10,000 shares of Steel. He bought only 200 shares and left the remainder of the order with the specialist. Mr. Whitney then went to various other points on the floor, and offered the price of the last previous sale for 10,000 shares of each of fifteen or twenty other stocks, reporting what was sold to him at that price and leaving the remainder of the order with the specialist. In short, within the space of a few minutes Mr. Whitney offered to purchase something in the neighborhood of twenty or thirty million dollars' worth of stock. Purchases of this magnitude are not undertaken by Tom, Dick, and Harry; it was clear that Mr. Whitney represented the bankers' pool.

24. The desperate remedy worked. The semblance of confidence returned. Prices held steady for a while; and though many of them slid off

once more in the final hour, the net results for the day might well have been worse. Steel actually closed two points higher than on Wednesday, and the net losses of most of the other leading securities amounted to less than ten points apiece for the whole day's trading.

25. All the same, it had been a frightful day. At seven o'clock that night the tickers in a thousand brokers' offices were still chattering; not till after 7:08 did they finally record the last sale made on the floor at three o'clock. The volume of trading had set a new record—12,894,650 shares. ("The time may come when we shall see a five-million-share day," the wise men of the Street had been saying twenty months before!) Incredible rumors had spread wildly during the early afternoon—that eleven speculators had committed suicide, that the Buffalo and Chicago exchanges had been closed, that troops were guarding the New York Stock Exchange against an angry mob. The country had known the bitter taste of panic. And although the bankers' pool had prevented for the moment an utter collapse, there was no gainsaying the fact that the economic structure had cracked wide open.

IV

26. Things looked somewhat better on Friday and Saturday. Trading was still on an enormous scale, but prices for the most part held. At the very moment when the bankers' pool was cautiously disposing of as much as possible of the stock which it had accumulated on Thursday and was thus preparing for future emergencies, traders who had sold out higher up were coming back into the market again with new purchases, in the hope that the bottom had been reached. (Hadn't they often been told that "the time to buy is when things look blackest"?) The newspapers carried a very pretty series of reassuring statements from the occupants of the seats of the mighty; Herbert Hoover himself, in a White House statement, pointed out that "the fundamental business of the country, that is, production and distribution of commodities, is on a sound and prosperous basis." But toward the close of Saturday's session prices began to slip again. And on Monday the rout was under way once more.

27. The losses registered on Monday were terrific—17½ points for Steel, 47½ for General Electric, 36 for Allied Chemical, 34½ for Westinghouse, and so on down a long and dismal list. All Saturday afternoon and Saturday night and Sunday the brokers had been struggling to post their records and go over their customers' accounts and send out calls for further margin, and another avalanche of forced selling resulted. The prices at which Mr. Whitney's purchases had steadied the leading stocks

on Thursday were so readily broken through that it was immediately clear that the bankers' pool had made a strategic retreat. As a matter of fact, the brokers who represented the pool were having their hands full plugging up the "air-holes" in the list—in other words, buying stocks which were offered for sale without any bids at all in sight. Nothing more than this could have been accomplished, even if it could have been wisely attempted. Even six great banks could hardly stem the flow of liquidation from the entire United States. They could only guide it a little, check it momentarily here and there.

28. Once more the ticker dropped ridiculously far behind, the lights in the brokers' offices and the banks burned till dawn, and the telegraph companies distributed thousands of margin calls and requests for more collateral to back up loans at the banks. Bankers, brokers, clerks, messengers were almost at the end of their strength; for days and nights they had been driving themselves to keep pace with the most terrific volume of business that had ever descended upon them. It did not seem as if they could stand it much longer. But the worst was still ahead. It came the next day, Tuesday, October 29th.

29. The big gong had hardly sounded in the great hall of the Exchange at ten o'clock Tuesday morning before the storm broke in full force. Huge blocks of stock were thrown upon the market for what they would bring. Five thousand shares, ten thousand shares appeared at a time on the laboring ticker at fearful recessions in price. Not only were innumerable small traders being sold out, but big ones, too, protagonists of the new economic era who a few weeks before had counted themselves millionaires. Again and again the specialist in a stock would find himself surrounded by brokers fighting to sell—and nobody at all even thinking of buying. To give one single example: during the bull market the common stock of the White Sewing Machine Company had gone as high as 48; on Monday, October 28th, it had closed at 11⅛. On that black Tuesday, somebody—a clever messenger boy for the Exchange, it was rumored—had the bright idea of putting in an order to buy at 1—and in the temporarily complete absence of other bids he actually got his stock for a dollar a share! The scene on the floor was chaotic. Despite the jamming of the communication system, orders to buy and sell— mostly to sell—came in faster than human beings could possibly handle them; it was on that day that an exhausted broker, at the close of the session, found a large waste-basket which he had stuffed with orders to be executed and had carefully set aside for safe-keeping—and then had completely forgotten. Within half an hour of the opening the volume of trading had passed three million shares, by twelve o'clock it had passed eight million, by half-past one it had passed twelve million, and when

the closing gong brought the day's madness to an end the gigantic record of 16,410,030 shares had been set. Toward the close there was a rally, but by that time the average prices of fifty leading stocks, as compiled by the *New York Times*, had fallen nearly forty points. Meanwhile there was a near-panic in other markets—the foreign stock exchanges, the lesser American exchanges, the grain market.

³⁰· So complete was the demoralization of the stock market and so exhausted were the brokers and their staffs and the Stock Exchange employees, that at noon that day, when the panic was at its worst, the Governing Committee met quietly to decide whether or not to close the Exchange. To quote from an address made some months later by Richard Whitney: "In order not to give occasion for alarming rumors, this meeting was not held in the Governing Committee Room, but in the office of the president of the Stock Clearing Corporation directly beneath the Stock Exchange floor. . . . The forty governors came to the meeting in groups of two and three as unobtrusively as possible. The office they met in was never designed for large meetings of this sort, with the result that most of the governors were compelled to stand, or to sit on tables. As the meeting progressed, panic was raging overhead on the floor. . . . The feeling of those present was revealed by their habit of continually lighting cigarettes, taking a puff or two, putting them out and lighting new ones—a practice which soon made the narrow room blue with smoke. . . ." Two of the Morgan partners were invited to the meeting and, attempting to slip into the building unnoticed so as not to start a new flock of rumors, were refused admittance by one of the guards and had to remain outside until rescued by a member of the Governing Committee. After some deliberation, the governors finally decided not to close the Exchange.

³¹· It was a critical day for the banks, that Tuesday the 29th. Many of the corporations which had so cheerfully loaned money to brokers through the banks in order to obtain interest at 8 or 9 per cent were now clamoring to have these loans called—and the banks were faced with a choice between taking over the loans themselves and running the risk of precipitating further ruin. It was no laughing matter to assume the responsibility of millions of dollars' worth of loans secured by collateral which by the end of the day might prove to have dropped to a fraction of its former value. That the call money rate never rose above 6 per cent that day, that a money panic was not added to the stock panic, and that several Wall Street institutions did not go down into immediate bankruptcy, was due largely to the nerve shown by a few bankers in stepping into the breach. The story is told of one banker who went grimly on authorizing the taking over of loan after loan until one of his subordinate

officers came in with a white face and told him that the bank was insolvent. "I dare say," said the banker, and went ahead unmoved. He knew that if he did not, more than one concern would face insolvency.

32. The next day—Wednesday, October 30th—the outlook suddenly and providentially brightened. The directors of the Steel Corporation had declared an extra dividend; the directors of the American Can Company had not only declared an extra dividend, but had raised the regular dividend. There was another flood of reassuring statements—though by this time a cheerful statement from a financier fell upon somewhat skeptical ears. Julius Klein, Mr. Hoover's Assistant Secretary of Commerce, composed a rhapsody on continued prosperity. John J. Raskob declared that stocks were at bargain prices and that he and his friends were buying. John D. Rockefeller poured Standard Oil upon the waters: "Believing that fundamental conditions of the country are sound and that there is nothing in the business situation to warrant the destruction of values that has taken place on the exchanges during the past week, my son and I have for some days been purchasing sound common stocks." Better still, prices rose—steadily and buoyantly. Now at last the time had come when the strain on the Exchange could be relieved without causing undue alarm. At 1:40 o'clock Vice-President Whitney announced from the rostrum that the Exchange would not open until noon the following day and would remain closed all day Friday and Saturday—and to his immense relief the announcement was greeted, not with renewed panic, but with a cheer.

33. Throughout Thursday's short session the recovery continued. Prices gyrated wildly—for who could arrive at a reasonable idea of what a given stock was worth, now that all settled standards of value had been upset?—but the worst of the storm seemed to have blown over. The financial community breathed more easily; now they could have a chance to set their houses in order.

34. It was true that the worst of the panic was past. But not the worst prices. There was too much forced liquidation still to come as brokers' accounts were gradually straightened out, as banks called for more collateral, and terror was renewed. The next week, in a series of short sessions, the tide of prices receded once more—until at last on November 13th the bottom prices for the year 1929 were reached. Beside the figures hung up in the sunny days of September they made a tragic showing. [See table.]

35. The *New York Times* averages for fifty leading stocks had been almost cut in half, falling from a high of 311.90 in September to a low of 164.43 on November 13th; and the *Times* averages for twenty-five leading industrials had fared still worse, diving from 469.49 to 220.95.

	High Price Sept. 3, 1929	Low Price Nov. 13, 1929
American Can	181⅞	86
American Telephone & Telegraph	304	197¼
Anaconda Copper	131½	70
General Electric	396¼	168⅛
General Motors	72¾	36
Montgomery Ward	137⅞	49¼
New York Central	256⅜	160
Radio	101	28
Union Carbide & Carbon	137⅞	59
United States Steel	261¾	150
Westinghouse E. & M.	289⅞	102⅝
Woolworth	100⅜	52¼
Electric Bond & Share	186¾	50¼

36. The Big Bull Market was dead. Billions of dollars' worth of profits —and paper profits—had disappeared. The grocer, the window-cleaner, and the seamstress had lost their capital. In every town there were families which had suddenly dropped from showy affluence into debt. Investors who had dreamed of retiring to live on their fortunes now found themselves back once more at the very beginning of the long road to riches. Day by day the newspapers printed the grim reports of suicides.

37. Coolidge-Hoover Prosperity was not yet dead, but it was dying. Under the impact of the shock of panic, a multitude of ills which hitherto had passed unnoticed or had been offset by stock-market optimism began to beset the body economic, as poisons seep through the human system when a vital organ has ceased to function normally. Although the liquidation of nearly three billion dollars of brokers' loans contracted credit, and the Reserve Banks lowered the rediscount rate, and the way in which the larger banks and corporations of the country had survived the emergency without a single failure of large proportions offered real encouragement, nevertheless the poisons were there: overproduction of capital; overambitious expansion of business concerns; overproduction of commodities under the stimulus of installment buying and buying with stock-market profits; the maintenance of an artificial price level for many commodities; the depressed condition of European trade. No matter how many soothsayers of high finance proclaimed that all was well, no matter how earnestly the President set to work to repair the damage with soft words and White House conferences, a major depression was inevitably under way.

38. Nor was that all. Prosperity is more than an economic condition; it is a state of mind. The Big Bull Market had been more than the climax of a business cycle; it had been the climax of a cycle in American mass

thinking and mass emotion. There was hardly a man or woman in the country whose attitude toward life had not been affected by it in some degree and was not now affected by the sudden and brutal shattering of hope. With the Big Bull Market gone and prosperity going, Americans were soon to find themselves living in an altered world which called for new adjustments, new ideas, new habits of thought, and a new order of values. The psychological climate was changing; the ever-shifting currents of American life were turning into new channels.

   [39.] The Post-war Decade had come to its close. An era had ended.

COMMENTARY AND QUESTIONS

"Crash!" is the next to last chapter in Frederick Lewis Allen's lively and informative book about that extraordinary American decade of the 1920's, which began with the "return to normalcy" after the First World War and ended with the country falling downhill fast into the bog of the Great Depression. In this chapter Allen does two things. He first of all explains how the Big Bull Market came to an end—how its disastrous toboggan-slide began, what kept it going, and how far it went. But he is also explaining the effect of this slide on the sliders—the citizens of the country—and making clear why he says at the end of this chapter that "an era had ended."

1. The basic structure of this chapter is obviously chronological. It is not, however, merely a simple sequence of facts, for at several points the author interrupts the chronological flow with passages of necessary explanation. Tell why the following such passages are placed where they are and explain what each one accomplishes: pars. 4-9, 13, 17-19, 36-39. What is the effect of the short sentence that begins the chapter? Notice that although a good many of the paragraphs are moderately long (but not at all ponderous), the author once in a while uses a very short one—perhaps only a single sentence. What is accomplished by the extreme brevity of the following paragraphs: pars. 9, 11, 16, 39?

2. Since nearly every reader of this chapter knows that there was a stock market crash in 1929, followed by a depression, the author cannot depend for interest and suspense on the simple desire to "know how the story comes out." He does, however, play skillfully on the reader's desire to know just how complete and spectacular the collapse was. What details does the author choose to point up the unbelievable and nightmarish quality of the autumn of 1929? How does he keep hinting that worse is yet to come? Note how the author heightens the effect by a liberal use of irony—that is, a contrast between the surface meaning of a set of words and their real meaning, or between what is said and what the reader knows is really true: for example, the last sentence of par. 8. Find other places in which irony is made to rein-

force the reader's sense that the men of 1929 could not believe what was happening because they had so thoroughly and fatuously deluded themselves.

3. The style of this selection is marked by a number of lively expressions and plays on words: for example, the last sentence of par. 22 and the remark in par. 32 about John D. Rockefeller's pouring "Standard Oil upon the waters." Find other such expressions. There are also in this selection a number of rather well worn phrases, such as "nor was Mr. Mitchell by any means alone in his opinions" (par. 8), "the gigantic edifice of prices was honeycombed with speculative credit" (par. 13). Can you find other examples? Compare Allen's choice of words with that of Dixon Wecter when you read the next selection.

SUGGESTIONS FOR WRITING

1. How to get poor quick.
2. Explain the effect some outside event or series of events had on your immediate circle of friends or on your family.
3. Allen makes ironic use of the self-deluding statements of certain leaders at the time of the crash. Contrast an actual event within your range of experience—for example, the unexpected outcome of an election with the mistaken prophecies that preceded it.

From Riches

to Rags

by DIXON WECTER

IN MID-OCTOBER, 1929, the average middle-class American saw ahead of him an illimitable vista of prosperity. A newly inaugurated president, Herbert Hoover, had announced soberly in the previous year that the conquest of poverty was no longer a mirage: "We have not yet reached the goal, but given a chance to go forward with the policies of the last

Reprinted with permission of the publisher from *The Age of the Great Depression 1929-1941* by Dixon Wecter. Copyright 1948 by the Macmillan Company.

eight years, and we shall soon with the help of God be within sight of the day when poverty will be banished from the nation."[1] This was the economic promise interwoven with what a popular historian soon would call the American Dream. More complacently, Irving Fisher and other economists in the confidence of Wall Street assured the citizen that he was dwelling upon "a permanently high plateau" of prosperity.

2. This upland of plenty—more tangible than the Beulahland dear to the old Protestant hymnal—appeared to be the final triumph of a great industrial development dating from the Civil War. The aftermath of America's latest war had seen the arrival in strength of mass production, to compound the wonders of the new technology. Even now, in this third week of October, 1929, with the president and other notables in attendance, Henry Ford was sponsoring the "Golden Jubilee of Light," honoring Edison and the fiftieth birthday of the incandescent lamp. Motor cars, bathtubs, electric refrigerators, radios, were the touchstones of progress. Keeping up with the Joneses, under the spur of fashion and advertisement, demanded nothing less than the latest model. Pressures of salesmanship urged even the duplication of luxuries—two cars in every garage—in a consumer's market already displaying symptoms of surfeit, not because all Americans were gorged with worldly goods, but because buying power was unevenly distributed.

3. The nation's policies and institutions were closely enmeshed with the prosperous middle class. "The suburban community is the dominant American group," one observer wrote in the summer of 1929. The increasing stress upon the solidarity and good fellowship of certain organizations —fraternal orders, business men's luncheon clubs, Legion conventions— and the moral meddlesomeness of others like the Anti-Saloon League bred a regimentation which he feared as foreshadowing "the group from which the Fascisti of the future will be drawn, if there are Fascisti." That Babbitt might ever doff his natty silk shirt for one of brown or black was problematical; but the cult of conformity, in so far as it boosted material success, was in the saddle. Cotton Mather, Ben Franklin, Peter Parley and Horace Greeley would have understood the spirit of the times, even though old maxims of drudgery and penny pinching seemed to have been by-passed for quicker ways to wealth.

4. *Time*, liveliest weekly of the decade, in January, 1929, hailed Walter P. Chrysler as "Man of the Year," because during the past twelvemonth he had introduced the public to Plymouth and DeSoto cars,

---

[1] Speech accepting the nomination of the Republican party, *N. Y. Times,* Aug. 12, 1928. With omission of "yet" and "soon" and "with the policies of the last eight years," Hoover stoutly repeated these words in the depths of the Depression, in his Madison Square Garden speech of October 31, 1932. Herbert Hoover, *State Papers* (W. S. Myers, ed., N. Y., 1934), II, 426-427.

bought out Dodge Brothers for one hundred and sixty million dollars and begun to build "the world's tallest skyscraper, a 68-story colossus."[2] Now, on the cover of *Time* for October 14, 1929, appeared the face of William Wrigley, jr., to be followed in successive weeks by Harry F. Guggenheim, Ivar Kreuger, Samuel Insull and Thomas W. Lamont—heroes all. The last issue before the Wall Street crash carried a triple-page announcement of the new magazine *Fortune*, at the "unique price of $10 a year," which proclaimed the "generally accepted commonplace that America's great achievement has been Business." Other large advertisements featured Babson's *Reports* ("Your Dollars—Are They Continuously and Efficiently at Work?"), the Hamilton watch ("Can you tell a successful man by the time he carries?"), Robert I. Warshow's new book *The Story of Wall Street* ("These giants march through its pages . . . like the adventurers of the middle ages . . . Daniel Drew, Jim Fisk, Jay Gould, Vanderbilt, Hill, Harriman . . . and the many others whose exploits have astounded the nation"), and the investment services of a firm to collapse in 1932 leaving millions in defaulted bonds, S. W. Straus & Co. ("He invests his modest earnings in good sound securities"). They represented the stimuli which beat incessantly upon the mind of the average magazine reader.

5. Masses of Americans who bought their first bonds in the liberty loans of 1918 had lately turned to more speculative issues. Advertisements flaunting high prices instead of bargains—from $45,000 apartments on Park Avenue and bathrooms equipped with "Crane Louis XVI Trianon Fittings Gold-Plated," down to $2.50 lipsticks and razor blades at three for fifty cents—set the sumptuary scale for a generation of easy money. To keep abreast of the traffic in this climb to the highlands of permanent prosperity, the stock market was the obvious vehicle. In 1920 there had been 29,609 stockbrokers in the United States; within ten years they had jumped to 70,950. It was commonly observed that a great many citizens no longer read the front page of their newspaper, but turned hurriedly to the financial columns. Tabloid papers and tip sheets offered investment advice to amateurs. Over the radio flowed the voice of the "Old Counselor," steady as a deacon, intoning the wisdom of Samuel Insull's own brokers.[3]

---

[2] As announced in January, 1930, "Man of the Year" was Owen D. Young, author of the Young Plan for the payment of German reparations and also endowed with the glamour of great wealth; but *Time's* choice for the following year, by significant contrast, was Mahatma Gandhi.

[3] The identity of this famous character was a minor mystery. While the head of Halsey, Stuart & Co., his sponsors, told a Senate committee that the "Old Counselor" was a University of Chicago professor paid $50 a week to read their script, the president of NBC, M. H. Aylesworth, testified that he was an actor. Ruth Brindze, *Not to Be Broadcast* (N. Y., 1937), 40-41.

6. Popular interest was growing about the mystery of business cycles. Whether they were ruled by overproduction or underproduction, banking operations, innovations in method, hysterias of hope or panic, or perhaps sun spots, was not clear. Guessing was garbed in the robes of prophecy. Wishfulness took priority over planning. Optimists believed that the old laws of economics had been arrested; others conceded that rainy days might come, but after every storm the skies must clear—if everybody, as the season's most popular song exhorted, would keep his sunny side up. Above all, recession was the abnormal thing. Prosperity needed no explanation. Nor was it the monopoly of so-called leisured classes, or the Republican party, despite their effort to claim all the credit.

> If a man saves $15 a week, and invests in good common stocks, and allows the dividends and rights to accumulate, at the end of twenty years he will have at least $80,000 and an income from investments of around $400 a month. He will be rich. And because income can do that, I am firm in my belief that anyone not only can be rich, but ought to be rich.

So declared John J. Raskob, chairman of the Democratic national committee, in the summer of 1929. Employees were encouraged to invest in the stocks and bonds of their employers—a system regarded somewhat vaguely as the American equivalent of profit sharing, or perhaps social security.

7. Much of this buying of stocks was on margin, which meant that investors, including the small fry with little cash but big hopes, put up about a fourth of the price. The broker advanced the rest by borrowing from banks. This precarious credit structure of brokers' loans had trembled in February, 1929, when the Federal Reserve Board ordered member banks not to lend money for such speculative purposes. But private bankers, led by Charles E. Mitchell, had promptly unlocked their millions for speculation and given a further fillip to the great bull market and the age of confidence upon which it was built. This caused another spasm of activity, unwarranted by any such tangibles as consumer demand, gains in productive efficiency or real earning of the stocks in question. While the rich were growing richer, several million citizens with small incomes were raiding their savings, reducing their immediate purchasing power and mortgaging their future in order to speculate. Ninety per cent of these market transactions in the twenties, it has been estimated, were gambling ventures rather than permanent investments.

8. Almost imperceptibly a shift had occurred in economic control, from the industrial capitalism of an earlier day to finance capitalism.

Exploitation of investors and frequent duplicity in bookkeeping were among the less lovely traits of the new order. The holding company— an avatar which sprang from the slain dragon of the "trusts" late in the previous century—now flourished mightily. It permitted control by a small group of stockholders over a widely scattered empire of interlocking or even loosely related interests, like Samuel Insull's three-billion-dollar domain in utilities. The power exercised by the holding company, particularly in the utility field, was often so disproportionate to its size that Franklin D. Roosevelt as president well described it as "a ninety-six-inch dog being wagged by a four-inch tail."

9. These concerns were sometimes pyramided one upon another, towers of Babel reaching to the skies and equally tremulous at the base. Not infrequently they were used to mask the true state of corporate finances from the eyes of regulatory authorities or the public. A New York state bank called Bank of United States, in January, 1930—almost a year before its spectacular failure brought down the roof upon nearly half a million depositors—concealed its growing weakness by creating a dummy company, the Bolivar Development Corporation, capitalized at one hundred dollars, to buy and sell the stock of still another dummy conjured by the Bank into making the motions of prosperity. Deceived by this solemn farce, the outsider was slow to suspect that many a façade of granite and marble had become a hollow shell of indebtedness and precarious bookkeeping.

10. Another development in the pathology of Wall Street was the mushrooming in the latter twenties of so-called investment trusts, whose function was to invest moneys loaned to them and to distribute the net return to their stockholders or beneficiaries. Some were "rigid," *i.e.* confined to a restricted list of securities, but many were "flexible," which meant that the selection of securities for investment was left wide open. In practice they were little better than gambling establishments in which the innocent patron intrusted his stakes not even to a fellow player picked at random but to the croupier—whose main interest, of course, was to represent "the house." Four and a half million Americans, it was reported, handed over part or all their savings to investment trusts, eventually losing about a third of their capital, or a total of three billion dollars.

11. The overexpansion of credit was a prime cause of the disasters that followed 1929. The First World War began a process which reckless financing continued to accelerate. In the background loomed the huge structure of long-term debt in the United States—a public debt, federal, state and municipal, of thirty-three billion dollars, and corporate and individual debts of one hundred billion—which demanded expanding

markets and world prosperity for successful carrying. A relatively small reduction in buying power, or backsliding of prices, could send tremors along the whole length of this mountain chain. The grand operations of credit, a new force of such power that one economist likened it to the prime movers of physics, were still imperfectly understood and recklessly abused. The average American in 1929 had little notion of credit on the imperial scale, such as the growth of international financing dependent upon a constant transfusion of credit from have to have-not nations, nor even the magnitude of eight billion dollars' credit in the form of brokers' loans which Wall Street recorded at its all-time crest of September 3, 1929.

12. The common man knew more about overexpansion of credit in such homely shapes as installment buying. Intensive campaigns to break down "sales resistance"—often insufficient purchasing power among small citizens—led to new extensions of the time-payment plan for cars, clothes, electric washers, refrigerators, furniture, jewelry. In effect it was a loan from producer to consumer, because the latter lacked cash, and the former, with his urgent need for sales, preferred this method to that of increasing mass purchasing power by cutting prices and boosting wages. By 1929 felicity on the installment plan had lured its tens of millions. In the harsh light of the Great Depression, such aspects of the system as inflated prices and exorbitant carrying charges, along with misrepresentation of the product, would become all too plain. Certain state laws, like those of New York and Kentucky, held a still more pernicious trap, sprung during the early thirties, by which a debtor's entire wages could be attached until the account was cleared.

13. Meanwhile important business enterprises were being concentrated in fewer hands. The forging of chain stores all over the nation was no less significant than recent big mergers in the automotive industry. Centralized industry made every metropolis the center of a regional web, and each of these networks fitted into a national pattern for making, selling and distributing commodities. The economy of a continent had never been so highly integrated, nor its equilibrium so sensitive. The frontier, the farm, the village and Middletown had at last been engulfed by the rise of the city. As never before, urban industrialism called the tune. In 1870 wage and salary workers had made up about half the working population; now they composed four fifths. An interdependence unknown to old-fashioned America had become the basic economic fact. The fabric of industrial and corporate life, joined to the structure imposed by labor unions and labor legislation, had imperceptibly altered the flexibility of *laissez faire* into something more rigid, less accommodating.

14. These sweeping changes had hardly entered the consciousness of the average citizen. In his own mind he was never more loyal than in 1929 to the doctrine of individualism and unhampered private enterprise. Clashes between theory and practice, like the potential friction of capital and labor, remained almost inaudible so long as the nation's economic mechanism ran with the oil of prosperity.

15. Not, indeed, that the prosperity of the twenties was consistently sound. To the later view it resembled a hectic flush rather than the bloom of health. Agriculture still groaned from its dropsical overexpansion in 1917-1918. Along with bituminous coal mining and textiles, it belonged to a clinical ward known as the "sick industries." Great was the industrial turnover; a sense of insecurity about jobs had been rising for several years. Even in 1926 the unemployed were estimated at 1,500,000; by 1929 their number had swelled to upwards of 1,800,000.[4] Unperceived by the optimists, joblessness and poverty had come to be chronic social problems in the United States—neither a passing crisis nor one readily met by efforts of private charity. The ratio of private to public funds for such purposes was diminishing, as public relief expenditures gradually mounted. Sixteen major cities which in 1911 had spent $1,500,000 on public charity were by 1928 spending $20,000,000 annually.

16. Flaws in banking practice might also have been suspected. During the six years prior to the October crash of 1929 bank failures occurred at an average rate of nearly two a day, but since the delinquents were minor institutions, chiefly in small towns, scant publicity resulted. Nor was the output of goods commensurate with the capacity to produce. At least twenty per cent of the country's resources were not being utilized, to the loss of about fifteen billion dollars in national income, or one fourth of the goods and services it was actually producing.

17. Yet beyond question the major shortcomings of the American economy lay not with production but consumption. Already in the early autumn of 1929 financial pages gloomed over "heaviness" in automobiles and radios, slackening of the building trades, disappointment along the new frontiers of aviation. Much of America's productive effort and income had lately gone into luxuries and durable goods, whose purchase could be postponed without affecting daily needs. At the first storm warnings these goods would pile up in warehouses, causing wheels to stop turning and huge areas of joblessness to appear. This was one reason

---

4 R. R. Nathan, *Estimates of Unemployment in the United States, 1929-1935* (Geneva, 1936), gives the higher computation of 2,860,000 by March, 1929—a figure accepted by Harry L. Hopkins, *Spending to Save* (N. Y., 1936), 13. Generally speaking, liberals tended to estimate unemployment in the twenties and early thirties at higher figures than did the Hoover administration and the majority of conservatives.

why the Depression following 1929 was unparalleled for severity and duration.

[18.] Even in 1929 the purchasing power of the American people looked ill-balanced, an anomaly soon to be pointed up by quotation of Carlyle's phrase, "poverty in the midst of plenty." Between 1923 and 1928, while the index of speculative gains rose from 100 to 410, the index of wages advanced from 100 to a mere 112. Naturally enough, too little income went for consumer goods in proportion to the torrents that flowed into investment channels and the call-money market, into the making of new capital equipment for future production and into the savings of the well-to-do. Never before had so large a share of the national income been saved and invested as in this decade, nor had current production ever outstripped current consumption so spectacularly. The National Survey of Potential Product Capacity later described the period from 1923 to 1929 as an "orgy of saving" among the rich.

[19.] Two thirds of the country's savings were made by families with incomes over $10,000 a year. Those with less than $1500, comprising forty per cent of the population, actually paid out more than they earned. Six million families, one fifth of the nation, fell below even $1000. Making provision for a rainy day seemed less than feasible when one was already drowning. Up to the income bracket of $5000, American families had to spend a disproportionate amount merely to get sufficient food; hence among those nine out of ten families "not in a position to enjoy a liberal diet," substantial savings could hardly be expected.[5] In presenting the extremes of the economic spectrum a study by the Brookings Institution observed that the twenty-four thousand families which received over $100,000 apiece in 1929 enjoyed a total income three times as great as that of the six million poorest families. In other words, the average income among the top group was six hundred and thirty times that in the bottom one.

[20.] Orthodox economists argued that savings led to more capital equipment and superior efficiency and, in turn, to lower production costs, lower prices and greater purchasing power for the masses. It was plain by 1929, however, that this chain of causation had developed weak links. Mass buying power was unable to absorb the nation's output, not alone because wages had advanced comparatively little but because retail prices took virtually no cut between 1922 and 1929. Savings

---

[5] Maurice Leven and others, *America's Capacity to Consume* (Wash., 1934), 93, 123. At 1929 prices an adequate diet for the average family was estimated to cost $800; $2000 was reckoned the minimum for basic necessities of living. A summary of statistics on this subject for 1929 and later will be found in S. C. Menefee, "Standard of Living," *Survey*, LXXIII (1937), 281-282.

achieved by improved technologies were not being handed on to the consumer in the form of lower prices. They were diverted into dividends, reserves, bigger salaries and bonuses. Various shapes of monopoly, like trusts in disguise, mergers, combinations in mining and manufacturing, helped keep prices up, even while new machinery, better production methods and services of "efficiency experts" increased the over-all output of American labor by more than a third in the decade after the First World War. In some trades, like automobiles, productive efficiency was reported to have tripled.

21. But from this plenitude the average consumer gathered only the crumbs, and even the producer reaped merely a shortsighted advantage. To reckon profit not for a day or season, but upon a broad and long-term base of buying power, might have proved wiser. Posterity would probably agree with the retrospective view of Hoover who, after praise for the technologists, remarked:

> When we fully understand the economic history of the 'twenties, we shall find that the débâcle which terminated another apparently highly prosperous period was largely contributed by a failure of industry to pass its improvement (through labor-saving devices) on to the consumer.

22. Some others were less inclined to praise the engineers than to damn them. Their ingenuity, it was charged, had supplanted men with machines. The effect of invention in upsetting group equilibrium was, of course, no novelty. In the past, management had sometimes shown reluctance to scrap old equipment for new; more often, labor feared the "immigration of iron men." Naturally at the first threat of spreading unemployment the machine was indicted, for this generation was less apt than its forefathers to accept all calamities as mysterious visitations of Providence. Soon, in the wake of apprehensions that technology had done its job too well, came a flock of ideas about social engineering. Could not the same magic which had rid the factory of waste and inefficiency do the same for society? This hope—newer to American life than the invincible faith in applied science—led from Hoover the "Great Engineer" to Technocracy, the National Recovery Administration, the Tennessee Valley Authority, the National Resources Committee and other concepts of a managed economy. Few could have foreseen in 1929 all the paths of this projection. Nevertheless in that year the fundamental balances of a vast industrial civilization were slipping: the precarious relations between wages and prices, production and consumption, machines and man power.

23. Upon this world of uneasy prosperity the first blow fell in late October. Like the sound of gunshot which starts an Alpine avalanche,

a minor panic on the New York Stock Exchange began on the twenty-third among stocks that speculators had pushed to fantastic heights. The next day, "Black Thursday," saw hysteria rampant. Brokers wept and tore off their collars trying to keep abreast selling orders; sightseers jammed the Wall Street district, ogled the arrival of great bankers in their limousines before the House of Morgan, and under the rumor of mass suicide gathered to watch an ordinary workman on a scaffolding in morbid expectation of his plunge.

24. At first it appeared that the magicians of finance had arrested disaster, but just as the public cheered them and breathed more easily, another sickening lurch sent the market to new depths, spreading conviction that these wizards had merely propped the falling timbers long enough to get out from under. October 29 set a lurid record for sales, a total of 16,410,000 shares. At the month's close fifteen billion dollars in market value had been wiped out, and before the end of the year losses reached an estimated forty billion.

25. After the first shock official optimism took over. A generation taught to be "a bull on the United States" was conditioned to respond. Upon feeling the initial jolt, many seemed as incredulous about the real gravity of the situation as the passengers of a luxury liner ripped below decks by an iceberg: the boat listed only a trifle at first while the band played on. Manhattan's dapper mayor, "Jimmy" Walker, asked the movies to show nothing but cheerful pictures. The patient was recommended to try the hair of the dog that bit him: *True Story Magazine* ran big advertisements in the newspapers urging wage-earners to buy more luxury items on credit. "Wall Street may sell stocks, but Main Street is buying goods," came a cheery assurance from the *Saturday Evening Post*. A Manhattan jeweler in early November put on display a "$750,000 pearl necklace," while the Shuberts revealed plans for a $15,000,000 theater-hotel on Broadway. "Forward America, Nothing Can Stop U. S.," shouted the nation's billboards. And over the radio Julius Klein, assistant secretary of commerce, announced that only four per cent of the people had been adversely affected. A tuneful hit called "Happy Days Are Here Again" was copyrighted on November 7 for one of the new talking pictures appropriately named "Chasing Rainbows"; three years later it would become the campaign song of the New Deal. And early in 1930, with skies growing blacker, makers of a cheap radio brought out a "prosperity model."

26. The solvent of American humor began early to attack the crisis. Grim jokes arose about the complimentary revolver given with every share of Goldman Sachs, or the room clerk's query of every registrant, "For sleeping or jumping?" A little later, when mass unemployment began to steal the headlines from Wall Street, bravado succeeded flip-

pancy. Billboards began to ask, "Wasn't the Depression Terrible?" The departing owner of a ruined shop scrawled upon the door "Opened by mistake" if he were a humorist, or "Busted and disgusted" if possessed by the blues. Trained in the cult of the stiff upper lip, of singing in the rain, Americans hated to admit that things were not as they had always been. The International Association of Lions Clubs observed the week of October 19, 1930, as Business Confidence Week. Prosperity was just around the corner; perhaps the corner was one already turned.

27· For a while the momentum of the great bull market carried certain enterprises. The year 1931, for example, saw the opening of the world's finest luxury hotel, the new Waldorf-Astoria in Manhattan, and completion of the tallest of all skyscrapers, the Empire State Building of one hundred and two stories topped by a "mooring mast" for airships —but functionally as useless as the metallic needle surmounting its nearest rival, the new Chrysler Building. Many floors in each of these grandiose business palaces remained spectrally vacant in the times ahead. The same year saw publication of architects' plans for New York's most impressive cluster of buildings, Rockefeller Center, which the next two years consummated. Housing broadcasting studios, ornate movie and music halls, foreign-trade syndicates and other business enterprises upon a scale never before attempted, this group culminated in the austere gray seventy-story shaft of the R. C. A. building.

28· Some critics of architecture prophesied that these would be the last dinosaurs of America's metropolitan era, convinced that such vainglory had overreached itself, promoting little save congested traffic, overcrowding and colossal debts. Like many other vanities of the century, perhaps the skyscraper too was bankrupt. At any rate, the nation's outlay for new construction fell sixty per cent between 1931 and 1932 as the momentum of prosperity ground to a dead stop. By 1933 architects were doing less than a seventh of the business they had enjoyed in 1928.

29· Gala openings and soothing statements no longer fitted the temper of the times; the smile of official optimism slowly froze into something that resembled a *risus sardonicus*. In 1931 Edward Angly garnered the more fulsome assurances of Wall Street and Washington into a little book with the derisive title *Oh Yeah!* Early in the following year appeared a new magazine called *Ballyhoo*, its first issue packaged in cellophane as a touch of commercial parody. Within six months it rocketed to a two-million circulation largely by debunking the specious salesmanship of the twenties.[6]

---

[6] Its creator was a disillusioned Manhattan editor and artist, Norman Anthony, but the name which *Ballyhoo* made famous was that of a fictional high-powered advertising man, one Elmer Zilch. In a chapter called "Jackpot!" Anthony gave the history of this magazine in *How to Grow Old Disgracefully* (N. Y., 1946).

[30.] The public, seeking a scapegoat for its bitterness, found one with the help of a shrewd publicist hired by the Democratic party, Charles Michelson. Old newspapers were called "Hoover blankets," jack rabbits "Hoover hogs" and the shanties of starvation rising on outskirts of cities "Hoovervilles." A large share of popular odium also fell upon the shoulders of rich and weary Andrew Mellon, lately toasted by business as the "greatest secretary of the treasury since Alexander Hamilton." In February, 1932, Mellon was glad enough to relinquish his portfolio and be kicked upstairs as ambassador to Britain.

[31.] As President Coolidge had said in the palmy days, the business of America has indeed been business. But now the luxuries and amusements, the bustling sense of power which cloaked life's essential materialism for the prosperous urban or suburban citizen, were suddenly stripped away. This greatest of economic reverses gave millions of citizens the jolt of taking a downward step in the dark when expecting an upward one. A nation used to regarding prosperity as a habit found itself startled, then incredulous, more than a little helpless and finally resentful. It made the situation no easier that the adversary was invisible, and unlike a domestic or foreign foe, invulnerable to ridicule, ballots or bullets.

[32.] But the reality of this enemy admitted no doubt. His unseen stature could be measured by the two yardsticks of income and employment. The loss of earnings, chiefly paper profits, had first taken the spotlight. A few moths had singed their wings; so what? But as early as the spring of 1930, when the Federal Council of Churches set aside April 27 as "Unemployment Sunday," the crisis had assumed breadth as well as depth. Soon, lowered income and unemployment were seen in constant interaction, forcing the national economy into a descending spiral. White-collar workers began to take salary cuts, laborers to find discharge slips in pay envelopes. The city felt the shock first. Initial symptoms were not ostentatious: postponement in buying that new car, or breaking ground for a new home; surrender of small apartments by young couples moving in with parents; a drop in pleasure travel and theater attendance; more business for the cleaner, invisible mender, shoe-repair man, less for tailor and haberdasher.

[33.] A few grimmer signs appeared early, upon a small scale. In late February, 1930, Seattle, Los Angeles and Chicago witnessed minor demonstrations of the unemployed, in which Communists usually had a hand. In the same month bread lines in the Bowery were drawing two thousand daily. In March Milwaukee opened a municipal soup kitchen. The summer of 1930, as happened seasonally through the Depression, brought a measure of relief. Food was fresher, more plentiful and cheaper; clothing, fuel and shelter offered problems less acute. But the descent of winter in 1930-1931 inaugurated harder times, with New York City appropriating a million dollars for direct relief and Lloyd's of London announcing that for the first time on record they were selling riot and civil-commotion insurance in quantity to American clients.

34. Outside the city, harbingers of the crisis were less newsworthy. Farmers had known nothing but depression since the Armistice boom burst, and even though their plight continued to worsen, they had the gloomy satisfaction of long conditioning. Smaller industrial cities and towns, however, were reluctant to admit the fact of hard times, which in many citizens' eyes was either a Manhattan gamblers' fiasco or else just a state of mind. They congratulated themselves upon a firmer foundation. Notwithstanding that every fourth factory worker in Muncie, Indiana—the Middletown of sociologists—had lost his job before the end of 1930, men of substance in that community kept insisting to the end of 1931 that the Depression was "mainly something we read about in the newspapers." Still feeding upon the gospel of keeping up appearances, a delegation of local business men in 1932 persuaded General Motors not to board up the windows of its abandoned Muncie plant, which stood in clear view of the passing trains. The philosophy of the peptomists died hard.

35. As the average citizen could see for himself, working capital and jobs were closely interlocked, and upon their joint scarcity the years of depression hinged. What happened to income may be shown briefly. National income dwindled from eighty-one billion dollars in 1929 to less than sixty-eight in 1930, then cascaded to fifty-three in 1931 and hit bottom in 1932 with forty-one. Correspondingly, the country's estimated wealth over this span shrank from three hundred and sixty-five billion to two hundred and thirty-nine, a loss representing diminished values in real property, capital and commodities. Much of the nation's physical plant, of course, rusted in idleness and disrepair. These three years took a toll of eighty-five thousand business failures with liabilities of four and a half billion dollars and the suspension of five thousand banks. Nine million savings accounts were wiped out, and wage losses upwards of twenty-six billion dollars sustained.

36. While the debt structure of the American economy remained little changed—only 3.5 per cent less money being paid out in interest in 1932 than in 1929—in other fields deflation proceeded furiously, making long-term debts more crushing than borrowers had anticipated when incurring them. The volume of money paid as salaries dwindled 40 per cent, dividends 56.6 per cent, and wages 60 per cent. Early in the crisis, at the Hoover administration's earnest request, major industries made few cuts in pay rates, but by drastic reduction of working hours and

days they contrived to slash pay rolls about 40 per cent between 1929 and September, 1931. Since a workingman's family had to live on the money he brought home, this procedure looked better in the headlines than in private.

[37.] For the country at large, per-capita realized income (adjusted to the cost of living) tumbled from $681 in 1929 to $495 in 1933. At the apex of the economic pyramid the number of persons reporting an annual income over a million dollars fell from seventy-five in 1931 to only twenty the next year. Despite repeated assurances from government circles and high finance that the recession had reached bedrock—the "terminal trough," forecasters liked to call it—the general course of business after the Wall Street crash plunged fitfully downward for more than three years.

[38.] Many industries and small businesses denied even lip service to the administration's plea for maintenance of wage rates. A growing backwater of unemployment led department stores to pay clerks as little as five or ten dollars weekly. Investigation of a group of working girls in Chicago showed the great majority toiling for less than twenty-five cents an hour, a fourth for less than ten cents. Makers of ready-to-wear dresses, confectionery employees and cannery workers were among the classes exploited most callously. First-class New York stenographers' salaries fell from $35 and $45 a week to $16; domestic servants were obliged to labor for room and board plus ten dollars a month. As usual, unskilled workers had been the shock troops, followed by white-collar workers and technicians. Professional classes felt the jar a little later, as teachers' and ministers' salaries were cut or fell into arrears, and the practice of other groups declined, with fees increasingly hard to collect. Even in 1936 physicians' incomes were still from eighteen to thirty per cent below their 1929 level, lawyers' between eighteen and thirty-eight per cent.

[39.] Turning from lowered income and diminished working capital to the other side of the coin, one comes upon the face of total unemployment. In April, 1930, President Hoover ordered a house-to-house survey of this situation, the first federal census of unemployment in the nation's history. In all, slightly more than three million employables were reported out of work, against forty-five million persons gainfully employed. But the tide was rising fast, and a special census by the department of commerce in January, 1931, based upon sampling, disclosed more than six million unemployed. Before the end of that year almost all appraisers agreed that the ten-million mark had been passed, and 1932 saw the addition of four or five million more. Thanks to seasonal factors and local flurries of advance or retreat, the national picture shifted constantly; unemployment tended also to propagate itself, with wives and older children of idle men now joining in the scramble for any crumbs of odd jobs. Exhaustion of savings and losses in modest investments drove aged folk to participate in the frantic search and be counted.

40. This cycle brought forth its changing tokens and symbols. If the still cheerful desperation of 1931 was crystallized in the song "Life Is Just a Bowl of Cherries," the grimmer abasement of 1932 was epitomized by "Brother, Can You Spare a Dime?" appealing on behalf of casualties like the jobless war veteran or the discarded builder of an industrial empire. The most memorable symbol of the great unemployment, and of pride in facing it, came to be the apple. In the autumn of 1930 the International Apple Shippers' Association devised a scheme to dispose of surpluses. It offered to sell the fruit on credit to the jobless, to retail at five cents apiece. By early November six thousand apple sellers had taken their stand on the sidewalks of New York, and the idea soon spread elsewhere. In this early phase of the Depression, the stubborn self-reliance of America—the poor as well as the rich—bridled at the notion of direct relief or a dole, as had been practised since the First World War in Britain. But this meager toll upon the passing throng soon lost its novelty. In 1931 Manhattan began to forbid apple selling upon certain streets. By 1932 people were reported to be "sick of apples."

41. Those who could lift their eyes from this bleak domestic picture to scan the international horizon could draw at least some solace from the proverbial fellowship of misery. President Hoover himself at first was inclined to lay the ultimate blame upon causes outside the United States. In the war of 1914-1918 and its aftermath he saw the wellspring of this bitter draught. Waste and destruction, loss of man power, war debts and taxes, inflation and subsequent devaluation, the greed and imperialism of others, together with the fears and new spending bred by rearmament, were the malign heritage of a struggle "for which our people had no blame." And so far as America was concerned, these complications sprang from the days of Woodrow Wilson, "this war having come on during a Democratic administration."[7]

42. If this analysis seemed overcomforting—presenting the American people in the classic rôle of innocents at home and abroad—at least none could deny that the Depression was fast spreading over an economically interdependent world. Nations were seen to be roped together like mountain climbers in the bonds of loans and debts, cartels and tariffs, and quick communication whether of hope or panic. The footing of

---

[7] Hoover, *State Papers*, II, 137, 437. "Without the war, we would have had no such depression," Hoover said flatly at Indianapolis in June, 1931. Myers and Newton, *Hoover Administration*, 90.

countries mainly agricultural tended to give way first, with the industrial powers slipping later but more spectacularly. By the spring of 1929 or slightly earlier, Australia, Brazil, the Orient, the Near East, Argentina, Canada and Poland were showing symptoms of decline, while Germany's chronic postwar depression deepened. Later than the United States to feel the shock were Great Britain, France, Czechoslovakia, Switzerland and the Scandinavian countries. A second wave, beginning about 1931 and more severe than the first, likewise affected all these lands, and did not begin to recede until around the spring of 1933.

43. In most places similar factors had been at work, although the shape and gravity of the crisis varied a good deal. A look at the global picture, however, showed that Americans had not been the only dupes of hit-or-miss prosperity, the Republicans not the sole villains of 1929, nor the Democrats the exclusive heroes of 1933.

44. Refusal to admit this fact of economic interdependence was never shown more clearly than by the Hawley-Smoot tariff of June, 1930, in itself an aggravation of the crisis. The armistice of 1918 found the United States for the first time in history a great creditor country. At the same time its citizens' private investments abroad were growing so rapidly that from a prewar total of three billion dollars they had swollen to fourteen by 1932. A mighty producing nation, America naïvely construed foreign commerce as the right to sell, with little or no obligation to buy in exchange. Indeed, the nightmare of foreign dumping led both farmers and industrialists to clamor for the highest protective rates yet known and to obtain them in 1930 at an average of forty per cent. President Hoover wished to limit the bill chiefly to a few agricultural commodities, but he was overborne.

45. Abroad the Hawley-Smoot act was interpreted as a declaration of economic war. It met such prompt retaliatory tariffs, quotas and anti-American embargoes that by 1932 twenty-five governments had joined in the reprisal, thus halving the volume of United States exports. The vicious spiral held another twist. To escape this threat of boycott, American manufacturers during the first two years of the Hawley-Smoot act set up two hundred and fifty-eight separate factories in foreign countries, including seventy-one across the Canadian line.

46. What the average American thought about these matters depended largely upon his region, politics and business. Southerners had always been taught to regard high tariffs as iniquitous, but in the industrial North and agricultural Midwest "protection" still exercised its charm. No doubt many solid citizens would have echoed an editorial in Middletown's press: "The difference between good times and bad times in the United States, so far as history indicates, is the difference between an adequate protective tariff for the products of our farms and our fac-

tories and an inadequate tariff." When regression rather than improvement followed, Middletown's editor stuck doggedly to his line, ridiculing the "mistaken" view that "conditions in Europe have something to do with America's coming out of the depression."

47. Within the United States the twenties had seen a remarkable increase in the number and influence of trade associations, by which rival producers pooled statistical information, credit standards, cost formulae, and the like, and sought to curb unfair marketing practices. To this extent they were beneficent, and so impressed Hoover as secretary of commerce and as president. But not infrequently they sought by their definition of "fair" and "unfair" price policies to achieve price control while sailing to the leeward of the Sherman antitrust act, and sometimes the effect was to eliminate the small independent operator. Their growth was further indulged by a series of Supreme Court decisions which an earlier progressivism would have eyed with suspicion as entering wedges for native cartels and capitalist syndicalism.[8]

48. Although domestic cartels remained illegal under federal law, in the international sphere certain American concerns benefiting by the concentration of economic power—Du Pont, United States Steel, General Electric, Westinghouse, Bendix Aviation, Diamond Match, Anaconda Copper, Standard Oil of New Jersey—entered into agreements in the twenties and the thirties with foreign producers often to restrict production in order to raise prices and increase profits, and still more commonly to divide world markets and exchange patents. In hampering free enterprise cartels tended to constrict the flow of supplies, retard foreign and domestic trade and prevent the introduction of new products and improvements (such, for example, as the "everlasting" match usable many times).

49. Their effect upon prices may be illustrated by the fact that in 1914 the cost of quinine sulfate was twenty-five cents an ounce, but after Merck joined the international cartel the price rose to seventy-five cents by 1941. The imposition of production quotas is suggested by the fact that, while in 1930 domestic aluminum production exceeded a hundred thousand metric tons and that of Germany was only thirty thousand, in 1934, three years after Alcoa entered the cartel, the American output had fallen to thirty-three thousand tons and the German had risen to thirty-seven.[9] In the Depression their effect apparently was to

---

[8] For example, the cracking patents pool in the oil industry (282 U. S., 163, 1931) and the organization of a joint sales agency among major producers in the Appalachian Coals case (288 U. S., 344, 1933).

[9] U. S. v. Aluminum Co. of America, 148 Fed. Rep., ser. 2, 416, an action which resulted on March 12, 1945, in a decision adverse to the aluminum interests, holding that they had violated the Sherman act.

aggravate unemployment and underconsumption. Later in the thirties cartels began to attract unfavorable notice from Senate investigating committees and the antitrust division of the justice department because of their alleged threat to the national security.[10] On the whole, the shapes assumed by the internationalism of Big Business seemed as futile as those of economic nationalism in promoting the greatest good for the greatest number.

50. Lurking in the background of the ordinary American's insularity remained the old issue of unpaid debts from the First World War. Here, he believed, was proof that in dealing with foreigners he and his compatriots always got trimmed. Isolation was best. Other persons saw the urgency of war debts and reparations as strangling the economy of Europe and ultimately harming the creditor as well. President Hoover's decision in June, 1931, to sponsor a moratorium on intergovernmental war debts was hailed in some circles as a great contribution to good will and recovery, by others as a ruse to help the bankers and holders of foreign bonds. By the time of Franklin D. Roosevelt's inauguration, practically all the war debts were in hopeless default. Popular grievance over these unpaid bills did much to feed the pacifism of the mid-thirties and impede the international education of Americans.

51. The period 1929-1941 began with a domestic débâcle which stemmed from many causes, but perhaps the most basic was selfish blindness to the bond between group welfare and the satisfactions of the individual. Disaster helped Americans to recollect that they were one nation and that only through coöperation could the cart be pulled from the mire. This period closed upon the eve of American participation in a global war which had been bred largely by the equally stubborn refusal of many nations to admit the tie between their security and the good estate of all—the concept of one world. About the commonalty of man and the commonweal of nations revolved the great debates, the most significant activity, of these dozen years. Even in his

---

[10] Most notably the cartel under which Standard Oil of New Jersey had promised the German firm, I. G. Farben, "the benefit of all its know-how in the oil and chemical fields." Special Committee Investigating the National Defense Program, *Hearings on Senate Resolution 71*, pt. xi, 4698 (77 Cong., 1 sess., March 1942). Wendell Berge, assistant attorney-general, declared in retrospect: "The good-neighbor policy, which is supposed to govern our relations with Latin America, the reciprocal trade treaties, our alien-property policy, and other basic principles of America's conduct of foreign affairs have in many instances been seriously weakened by the interference of cartel activities." Subcommittee of the Committee on the Judiciary, *U. S. Senate Hearings on S. 11*, 47 (79 Cong., 1 sess., May 1945). Cartels in the Great Depression are discussed by Louis Domeratzky, "Cartels and the Business Crisis," *Foreign Affairs*, X (1931), 34-53.

daily life the average American could not help being profoundly affected by the outcome.

Dixon Wecter wrote a number of books exploring American social and literary history. The selection here reprinted is the opening chapter in *The Age of the Great Depression 1929-1941*, which surveys the 1930's as Frederick Lewis Allen's *Only Yesterday* surveyed the 1920's. But although the two books have some overlap, and "From Riches to Rags" covers a portion of the same ground as "Crash!" the results are very different. Wecter's discussion has a different aim from Allen's, and he is writing for a different, more scholarly audience. (Thus he includes in an appendix additional, documentary footnotes, not here reprinted.) These facts alone account for a major portion of the contrast between the two selections.

1. Allen began his chapter with the statement of an incident; Wecter begins his with the statement of a situation. What does this suggest about the difference in purpose of the two? Allen reaches the beginning of the great stock market crash in his eleventh paragraph, Wecter in his twenty-third. What does this show about the relative emphasis of the two chapters? Allen's introductory material is largely concerned with the attitude of forecasters and financiers toward stock prices and business prospects. What do Wecter's first twenty-two paragraphs accomplish? Is his tone as well as his content different? Would you say that his emphasis was on financiers who made ludicrous forecasts or on small citizens already trapped in an unsound economy?

2. "Crash!" very naturally followed an essentially chronological pattern. Find time indications in pars. 1 and 23 which together show that the structure of this part of "From Riches to Rags" is not chronological. The chapter is divided by pars. 23 and 24 into a discussion of the situation before the crash and of the situation after. Pars. 25-31 have a certain chronological unity, built around the changing attitude of the public toward the crash and its aftermath. Par. 32 begins a new and non-chronological discussion. How is par. 32 linked to par. 31? Where in par. 32 is stated the subject of the whole group of paragraphs from 32 through 40? Where and how is the second half of this subject introduced? What is the central topic of pars. 41-50 and how is the transition made from the previous group (pars. 32-40)? Is par. 47 a digression from this topic? What is accomplished by par. 51? (Remember that this selection is the first chapter of a book about a whole decade.)

3. Wecter's style makes use of a number of skillful devices. How many other examples can you find of these: alliteration ("hysterias of hope or panic, or perhaps sun spots"; "guessing was garbed"; "priority over

planning"—par. 6); epigrammatic parallelism or contrast ("small fry with little cash but big hopes"—par. 7); the reversal or reworking of clichés ("From Riches to Rags"; "towers of Babel reaching to the skies and equally tremulous at the base"—par. 9). Wecter's style is full of allusions which he assumes the reader will recognize and enjoy. Is the sentence about the luxury liner in par. 25 an invented simile or does it refer in some detail to an actual event? What is the point of the irony in the phrase "heroes all" in par. 4? Guggenheim and Lamont have been noted as beneficent philanthropists as well as financiers. Who were Kreuger and Insull? Which differences in style between Allen and Wecter are the results of their writing for different audiences?

SUGGESTIONS FOR WRITING

1. What I have been told about the depression.
2. Pie in the sky on the installment plan.
3. The American frame of mind in the present year.

Who Are You?

by ALDOUS HUXLEY

I

THE MOST STRIKING FACT about human beings is that, in many respects, they are very unlike one another. Their bodies vary enormously in size and shape. Their modes of thought and speech and feeling are startlingly different. Startlingly different, too, are their reactions to even such basic things as food, sex, money, and power. Between the most highly gifted and those of least ability, and between persons endowed with one particular kind of talent or temperament and persons endowed with another kind, the gulfs are so wide as to be bridgeable only by the most enlightened charity.

2. These are facts which from time immemorial have been recognized,

described in plays and stories, commented on in proverbs, aphorisms, and poems. And yet, in spite of their obviousness and their enormous practical importance, these facts are still, to a very great extent, outside the pale of systematic thought.

³· The first and indispensable condition of systematic thought is classification. For the purposes of pure and applied science, the best classification is comprehensive, covering as many of the indefinitely numerous facts as it is possible for thought to cover without becoming confused, and yet is simple enough to be readily understood and used without being so simple as to be untrue to the essentially complex nature of reality. The categories under which it classifies things and events are easily recognizable, lend themselves to being expressed in quantitative terms, and can be shown experimentally to be meaningful for our specifically human purposes.

⁴· Up to the present, all the systems in terms of which men have attempted to think about human differences have been unsatisfactory. Some, for example, have conspicuously failed to cover more than a part of the relevant facts. This is especially true of psychology and sociology as commonly taught and practised at the present time. How many of even the best of our psychologists talk, write, think, and act as though the human body, with its innate constitution and its acquired habits, were something that, in an analysis of mental states, could safely be ignored! And even when they do admit, rather reluctantly, that the mind always trails its carcass behind it, they have little or nothing to tell us about the ways in which mental and physical characteristics are related.

⁵· Sociologists deal with abstractions even more phantasmally bodiless. For example, they will carry out laborious researches into the problems of marriage. But when we read the results, we are flabbergasted to find that the one factor never taken into account by the researchers is who the men and women under investigation actually *are*. We are told every detail about their social and economic background; nothing at all about their inherited psycho-physical constitution.

⁶· There are other classificatory systems which claim to be comprehensive, but in which the indispensable process of simplification has been carried so far that they are no longer true to the facts. The interpretation of all human activity in terms of economics is a case in point. Another type of oversimplification is to be found in such theories as those of Helvétius in the eighteenth century and of certain Behaviorists in the twentieth—theories which profess to account for everything that men do or are in terms of environment, education, or conditioned reflexes. At the

other extreme of oversimplification we find some of the more rabid Eugenists, who attribute all the observable differences between human beings to hereditary factors, and refuse to admit that environmental influences may also play a part.

7. It may be remarked in passing that most of the hypotheses and classification systems we use in our everyday thinking are grossly oversimplified and therefore grossly untrue to a reality which is intrinsically complex. Popular theories about such things as morals, politics, economics, and religion are generally of the either-or, A-causes-B variety. But in any real-life situation there are almost always more than two valid and workable alternatives and invariably more than one determining cause. That is why the utterances of speech-making politicians can never, in the very nature of things, be true. In half an hour's yelling from a platform it is intellectually impossible for even the most scrupulous man to tell the delicately complex truth about any of the major issues of political or economic life.

8. We come now to the classification systems which attempt to cover the whole ground, but which have proved scientifically unsatisfactory because (though founded, as they often are, upon profound insights into the nature of human reality) they have made use of categories which could not be expressed in quantitative terms. Thus, for several thousands of years, the Hindus have been classifying human beings within the framework of four main psycho-physico-social categories. Because the caste system in India has become petrified into a rigidity that is untrue to the facts of life and therefore often unjust, the whole idea of caste is repellent to Western minds. And yet that special branch of applied psychology which deals with vocational guidance is concerned precisely with assigning individuals to their proper place in the natural caste system. The work of the specialists in "human engineering" has made it quite clear that individuals belong congenitally to one kind of caste, and that they hurt themselves and their society if, by some mistake, they get enrolled in another caste. Some time in the next century or two the empirical findings of the vocational guidance experts will be linked up with a satisfactory method of analyzing the total psycho-physical organism. When that happens, society will be in a position to reorganize itself on the basis of a rejuvenated and thoroughly beneficent, because thoroughly realistic, caste system.

9. In the West, for more than two thousand years, men were content with a classification system devised by the Greek physician, Hippocrates. His theory was that one's innate psycho-physical constitution was determined by the relative predominance within one's body of one or other of the four "humors"—blood, phlegm, black bile, and yellow bile. (We still describe temperaments as "sanguine" or "phlegmatic"; we still talk

of "choler" and "melancholia.") Humoral pathology persisted into the nineteenth century. Diseases were attributed to a derangement of the normal balance of the individual's humors, and treatment was directed to restoring the equilibrium. This relating of disease to inherited constitution was essentially realistic, and one of the things that modern medicine most urgently needs is a new and sounder version of the Hippocratic hypothesis—a classification of human differences in terms of which the physician may interpret the merely mechanical findings of his diagnostic instruments.

10. Finally we come to those classification systems which are unsatisfactory because the categories they make use of, although susceptible of being expressed in quantitative terms, have not, in practice, turned out to be particularly meaningful. Thus the anthropometrists have measured innumerable skulls, determined the coloring of innumerable heads of hair and pairs of eyes, but have told us very little of genuinely scientific or practical value about human beings. Why? Because, as a matter of empirical fact, these records and measurements could not be related in any significant way to human behavior.

11. And, not content with telling us very little by means of a colossal volume of statistics, the anthropometrists proceeded to confuse the whole issue by trying to think about human differences in terms of fixed racial types—the Nordic, the Alpine, the Mediterranean, and so forth. But the most obvious fact about all the existing groups of human beings, at any rate in Europe and America, is that each one of them exhibits a large number of individual variations. In certain areas, it is true, a single closely related set of such variations may be more common than in other areas. It is upon this fact that the whole theory of racial types has been built up—a system of classification which has proved extremely unfruitful as an instrument of pure and applied science, and, in the hands of the Nazi ideologists, extremely fruitful as an instrument of discrimination and persecution.

II

12. So much, then, for the classification systems which have proved to be unsatisfactory. Does there exist a more adequate system? This is a question which it is now possible, I think, to answer with a decided yes. A classification system more adequate to the facts and more potentially fruitful than any other devised hitherto has been formulated by Dr. W. H. Sheldon in two recently published volumes, *The Varieties of Human Physique* and *The Varieties of Temperament*.

13. Sheldon's classification system is the fruit of nearly fifteen years

of research, during which he and his collaborators have made, measured, and arranged in order many thousands of standardized photographs of the male body, taken from in front, from behind, and in profile. A careful study of these photographs revealed that the most basic (first order) classification system in terms of which the continuous variations of human physique could adequately be described was based upon the discrimination of three factors, present to a varying degree in every individual. To these three factors Sheldon has given the names of *endomorphy, mesomorphy,* and *ectomorphy.*

14. Endomorphy is the factor which, when predominant, expresses itself in a tendency for anabolism to predominate over catabolism, which often results in soft and comfortable roundness of physique. At school the extreme endomorph is called Slob or Fatty. By middle life he or she may be so enormously heavy as to be practically incapable of walking. The endomorphic physique is dominated by its digestive tract. Autopsies show that the endomorphic gut is often more than twice as long and weighs more than twice as much as the intestine of a person in whom there is an extreme predominance of the ectomorphic constituent.

15. Predominant mesomorphy expresses itself in a physique that is hard and muscular. The body is built around strong heavy bones and is dominated by its extraordinarily powerful muscles. In youth, the extreme mesomorph tends to look older than his years, and his skin, instead of being soft, smooth, and unwrinkled, like that of the endomorph, is coarse and leathery, tans easily, and sets in deep folds and creases at a comparatively early age. It is from the ranks of extreme mesomorphs that successful boxers, football players, military leaders, and the central figures of the more heroic comic strips are drawn.

16. The extreme ectomorph is neither comfortably round nor compactly hard. His is a linear physique with slender bones, stringy unemphatic muscles, a short and thin-walled gut. The ectomorph is a lightweight, has little muscular strength, needs to eat at frequent intervals, is often quick and highly sensitive. The ratio of skin surface to body mass is higher than in endomorphs or mesomorphs, and he is thus more vulnerable to outside influences, because more extensively in contact with them. His body is built, not around the endomorph's massively efficient intestine, not around the mesomorph's big bones and muscles, but around a relatively predominant and unprotected nervous system.

17. Endomorphy, mesomorphy, and ectomorphy occur, as constituting components, in every human individual. In most persons the three com-

ponents are combined fairly evenly, or at least harmoniously. Extreme and unbalanced predominance of any one factor is relatively uncommon.

18. For example, less than ten boys out of every hundred are sufficiently mesomorphic to engage with even moderate success in the more strenuous forms of athletics, requiring great strength and physical endurance. Hence the almost criminal folly of encouraging all boys, whatever their hereditary make-up, to develop athletic ambitions. By doing this, educators condemn large numbers of their pupils to an unnecessary disappointment and frustration, plant the seed of neurosis among the unsuccessful, and foster a conspicuous bumptiousness and self-conceit in the extreme mesomorph. A rational policy with regard to athletics would be to tell all boys the simple truth, which is that very few of them can expect to excel in the more violent sports, that such excellence depends primarily on a particular inheritance of size and shape, and that persons of other shapes and sizes not suited to athletic proficiency have as good a right to realize their own *natural* capacities as the extreme mesomorph and can contribute at least as much to society.

19. In order to calculate the relative amounts of each component in the total individual mixture, Sheldon divides the body into five regions and proceeds to make a number of measurements in each zone. The records of these measurements are then subjected to certain mathematical procedures, which yield a three-digit formula. This formula expresses the amount of endomorphy, mesomorphy, and ectomorphy present within the organism, as measured on a seven-point scale of values. Thus the formula 7-1-1 indicates that the individual under consideration exhibits endomorphy in its highest possible degree, combined with the lowest degree of mesomorphy and ectomorphy. In practice, he would probably be extremely fat, gluttonous and comfort-loving, without drive or energy, almost sexless, and pathetically dependent on other people. How different from the well-balanced 4-4-4, the formidably powerful and aggressive 3-7-1, the thin, nervous, "introverted" 1-2-7!

20. The relationships between the components are such that only a certain number of the mathematically possible combinations can occur in nature. Thus it is obviously impossible for a human being to be a 7-1-7, or a 7-7-7, or a 1-7-7; for nobody can be simultaneously extremely round and soft and extremely hard and compact or extremely narrow, small-gutted, and stringy-muscled. Sheldon and his collaborators have found that, in terms of their seven-point scale of values for three components, seventy-six varieties of human physique can be clearly recognized. If a value scale of more than seven points were used, the number would of course be correspondingly greater. But they have found empirically that the seven-point scale provides an instrument of analysis sufficiently precise for most practical purposes.

21. The three-digit formula given by an analysis of the basic components tells some of the story, but not all. It needs to be supplemented by additional information in respect to three secondary components present in all individuals—the factor of *dysplasia* or disharmony; the factor of *gynandromorphy*, or the possession of characteristics typical of the opposite sex; and the factor of *texture*, whether fine or coarse, aesthetically pleasing or the reverse.

22. Dysplasia occurs when one region or feature of the body is more or less markedly in disharmony with the rest of the physique. We are all familiar, for example, with the big, barrel-chested man whose legs or arms taper off to an absurdly slender inefficiency. And who has not had to listen to the despairing complaints of the ladies to whom ironic nature has given an elegantly ectomorphic torso, with hips and thighs on the most amply endomorphic scale? Such disharmonies are significant and must be observed and measured, for they provide many clues to the explorers of human personality.

23. All persons exhibit characteristics of the opposite sex, some to a very slight degree, others more or less conspicuously. Again, the variations are significant. And the same is true of the factor of texture. Of two individuals having the same fundamental pattern one may be markedly fine-textured, the other markedly coarse-textured. The difference is one which cannot be neglected. That is why the basic formula is always supplemented by other descriptive qualifications expressing the amount of dysplasia, gynandromorphy, and fineness of texture observed in the individual under analysis.

III

24. So much for the varieties of physique and the methods by which they can be classified and measured. Inevitably two questions now propound themselves. First, is it possible for an individual to modify his basic physical pattern? Is there any system of dieting, hormone therapy, or exercise by means of which, say, a 1-1-7 can be transformed into a 7-1-1 or a 3-4-3? The answer would seem to be no. An individual's basic formula cannot be modified. True, an endomorph may be undernourished to the point of looking like a thing of skin and bones. But this particular thing of skin and bones will be measurably quite unlike the thing of skin and bones which is an undernourished, or even tolerably well nourished, ectomorph. Our fundamental physical pattern is something given and unalterable, something we can make the best of but can never hope to change.

25. The second question which naturally occurs to us is this: how closely is our fundamental psychological pattern related to our physical pattern? That such a relationship exists is a subject upon which every dramatist and story-teller, every observant student of men and women, has always been agreed. No writer in his senses would dream of associating the character of Pickwick with the body of Scrooge. And when the comic-strip artist wants to portray an athletic hero, he gives him the physique of Flash Gordon, not of Rosie's Beau. Further, men have always clearly recognized that individuals of one psycho-physical type tend to misunderstand and even dislike individuals whose basic psycho-physical pattern is different from their own. Here are the words which Shakespeare puts into the mouth of Julius Caesar:

> Let me have men about me that are fat;
> Sleek-headed men and such as sleep o' nights.
> Yond Cassius has a lean and hungry look;
> He thinks too much; such men are dangerous.

Translated into Sheldon's terminology, this means that the mesomorph is one kind of animal, the ectomorph another; and that their mutual incomprehension very often leads to suspicion and downright antipathy.

26. In a general way all this has been perfectly well known for the past several thousand years. But it has been known only in an intuitive, empirical way. No organized scientific thinking about the subject has been possible hitherto, because (in spite of some valuable work done in Europe and America) nobody had worked out a satisfactory classification system for describing temperamental differences.

27. Modern chemistry classifies matter in terms of a system of ninety-two first-order elements. In earlier times, men tried to do their thinking about matter in terms of only four elements—earth, air, fire, and water. But earth, air, and water are not first-order elements, but elaborate combinations of such elements; while fire is not an element at all, but something that happens to all kinds of matter under certain conditions of temperature. In terms of so inadequate a classification system it was impossible for scientific thought to go very far.

28. The problem of psychological analysis is identical in principle with that of the analysis of matter. The psychologist's business is to discover first-order elements, in terms of which the facts of human difference may be classified and measured. The failure of psychology—and it has conspicuously failed to become the fruitful Science of Man which ideally it should be—is due to the fact that it has done its analysis of human differences in terms of entities that were not first-order elements, but combinations of elements. Sheldon's great contribution to psychology

consists in this: that he has isolated a number of genuine first-order elements of the basic psychological pattern which we call temperament, and has demonstrated their close correlation with the individual's basic physical pattern.

29. What follows is a summing up—necessarily rather crude and oversimplified—of the conclusions to which his research has led.

30. Endomorphy, mesomorphy, and ectomorphy are correlated very closely with specific patterns of temperament—endomorphy with the temperamental pattern to which Sheldon gives the name of *viscerotonia*, mesomorphy with *somatotonia*, and ectomorphy with *cerebrotonia*. Close and prolonged observation of many subjects, combined with an adaptation of the technique known as factor-analysis, resulted in the isolation of sixty descriptive or determinative traits—twenty for each of the main, first-order components of temperament. From these sixty, I select a smaller number of the more striking and easily recognizable traits.

31. Conspicuous among the elements of the viscerotonic pattern of temperament are relaxation in posture and movement, slow reaction, profound sleep, love of physical comfort, and love of food. With this love of food for its own sake goes a great love of eating in company, an almost religious feeling for the social meal as a kind of sacrament. Another conspicuous viscerotonic trait is love of polite ceremony, with which goes a love of company, together with indiscriminate amiability and marked dependence on, and desire for, the affection and approval of other people. The viscerotonic does not inhibit his emotions, but tends to give expression to them as they arise, so that nobody is ever in doubt as to what he feels.

32. Somatotonia, the temperament associated with the hard and powerful mesomorphic physique, is a patterning of very different elements. The somatotonic individual stands and moves in an assertive way, loves physical adventure, enjoys risk and loves to take a chance. He feels a strong need for physical exercise, which he hugely enjoys and often makes a fetish of, just as the viscerotonic enjoys and makes a fetish of eating. When in trouble, he seeks relief in physical action, whereas the viscerotonic turns in the same circumstances to people and the cerebrotonic retires, like a wounded animal, into solitude. The somatotonic is essentially energetic and quick to action. Procrastination is unknown to him; for he is neither excessively relaxed and comfort-loving, like the viscerotonic, nor inhibited and 'sicklied o'er with the pale cast of thought,' like the cerebrotonic. The social manner of the somatotonic is uninhibited and direct. The voice is normally unrestrained, and he coughs, laughs, snores and, when passion breaks through his veneer of civilization, speaks

loudly. He is physically courageous in combat and enjoys every kind of competitive activity.

[33.] From a sociological point of view, the most significant of the somatotonic traits is the lust for power. The individual who is high in somatotonia loves to dominate, and since he is (when somatotonia is extreme) congenitally insensitive to other people's feelings, since he lacks the indiscriminate amiability and tolerance of viscerotonia and is devoid of cerebrotonic squeamishness, he can easily become a ruthless bully and tyrant. The somatotonic individual is always an extrovert in the sense that his attention is firmly fixed upon external reality, to such an extent that he is necessarily unaware of what is going on in the deeper levels of his own mind.

[34.] It should be noted that somatotonic extroversion is quite different from the extroversion of the viscerotonic; for while the latter is continually spilling the emotional beans and turning for support and affection to his fellows, the former tends to be insensitive to other people, feels little need to confide his emotions, and pursues his trampling course through external reality with an effortless callousness. For him the period of youth is the flower of life; he hates to grow old and often makes desperate efforts, even in advanced middle age, to live as actively as he did at twenty. The viscerotonic, on the other hand, is orientated toward childhood— his own and that of his offspring. He is the great family man. The cerebrotonic, on the other hand, looks forward, even in youth, to the tranquillity and the wisdom which, he hopes or imagines, are associated with old age.

[35.] With cerebrotonia we pass from the world of Flash Gordon to that of Hamlet. The cerebrotonic is the over-alert, over-sensitive introvert, who is more concerned with the inner universe of his own thoughts and feelings and imagination than with the external world to which, in their different ways, the viscerotonic and the somatotonic pay their primary attention and allegiance. In posture and movements, the cerebrotonic person is tense and restrained. His reactions may be unduly rapid and his physiological responses uncomfortably intense. It is the cerebrotonic who suffers from nervous indigestion, who gets stage fright and feels nauseated with mere shyness, who suffers from the various skin eruptions often associated with emotional disturbances.

[36.] Extreme cerebrotonics have none of the viscerotonic love of company; on the contrary, they have a passion for privacy, hate to make themselves conspicuous, and have none of the exhibitionistic tendencies displayed both by somatotonics and viscerotonics. In company they tend to be shy and unpredictably moody. When they are with strangers they fidget, their glances are shifting, sometimes furtive; their facial expression is apt to change frequently and rapidly. (For all these reasons no extreme cerebrotonic has ever been a good actor or actress.) Their normal manner is inhibited and restrained and when it comes to the expression of feelings they are outwardly so inhibited that viscerotonics suspect them of being heartless. (On their side, cerebrotonics tend to feel a strong repugnance for the viscerotonic's emotional gush and florid ceremoniousness.)

37. With self-conscious general restraint goes a marked restraint of voice and of all noise in general. To be compelled to raise the voice, as when speaking to the deaf, is, for the cerebrotonic, sheer torture. And it is also torture for him to have to endure noise made by other people. One of the best recipes for an unhappy marriage is to combine a high degree of noise-hating cerebrotonia with a high degree of loud-speaking, loud-laughing, loud-snoring and, in general, noise-making somatotonia. Cerebrotonics are extremely sensitive to pain, sleep poorly, and suffer from chronic fatigue; nevertheless they often live to a ripe old age—provided always that they do not permit themselves to be forced by the pressure of somatotonic public opinion into taking too much violent exercise. They do not easily form habits and are extremely bad at adapting themselves to an active routine, such as military life. They tend to look younger than their age and preserve a kind of youthful intensity of appearance far into middle life. Alcohol, which increases the relaxed amiability of viscerotonics and heightens the aggressiveness of the somatotonic, merely depresses the cerebrotonic and makes him feel thoroughly ill.

38. To determine the degree of viscerotonia, somatotonia, and cerebrotonia present in any given individual, Sheldon makes use of specially designed interviews, supplemented by a medical history and, where possible, by observation over a considerable period. The sixty traits are then assessed on a seven-point scale, in which *one* represents the minimum manifestation and *seven* the most extreme.

39. How do these temperamental assessments compare with the corresponding physical assessments of endomorphy, mesomorphy, and ectomorphy? The answer is that there is a high positive correlation. In some persons the correlation is complete, and the three-digit formula for temperament is identical with the three-digit formula for physique. More frequently, however, there is a slight deviation, as when a *four* in physical endomorphy is correlated with a *three* or a *five* in temperamental viscerotonia. Where there is a deviation, it is seldom of more than one point in any of the three components. Occasionally, however, the discrepancy

between physique and temperament may be as much as two points; when this happens, the individual is under very considerable strain and has much difficulty in adapting himself to life. Deviations of more than two points do not seem to occur in the normal population, but are not uncommon among the insane.

40. The discrepancies between physique and temperament are probably due, in the main, to what the French philosopher, Jules de Gaultier, has called "bovarism." Mme. Bovary, the heroine of Flaubert's novel, was a young woman who consistently tried to be what in fact she was not. To a greater or less degree we are all bovarists, engaged from earliest childhood in the process of building up what the psychologists call a *persona,* to suit the tastes of the society surrounding us. The sort of *persona* we try to build up depends very largely upon our environment, physical and mental. Thus, in pioneering days, every Westerner tried to bovarize himself into the likeness of an Indian fighter. This was necessary, partly because people had to be tough, wary, and extroverted if they were to survive under frontier conditions, partly because local public opinion condemned and despised the introverted, the tender-minded, the aesthetes, and the abstract thinkers. Sheldon's researches show exactly how far bovarism can go without risk of compromising the individual's sanity; and the highly significant fact is that the borderline between normal and abnormal is reached pretty quickly. Hence the enormous psychological dangers inherent in such dogmatic and intolerant philosophies of life as Puritanism or Militarism—philosophies which exert an unrelenting pressure on those subjected to their influence, forcing a majority to try to change their fundamental psycho-physical constitution, to become something other than what they basically are.

41. Here a word of warning is necessary. Knowledge of an individual's constitutional make-up is not the same as complete knowledge of his character. Persons with the same temperamental formula may behave in very different ways and exhibit very different characters. Temperamentally similar individuals can make dissimilar uses of their constitutional endowments. It all depends on circumstances, upbringing, and the exercise of free will. Of three men with the same high degree of somatotonia one may become a suavely efficient executive, another a professional soldier of the explosive, blood-and-guts variety, and the third a ruthless gangster. But each in his own way will be aggressive and power-loving, daring and energetic, extroverted and insensitive to other people's feelings. And no amount of training, no effort of the will, will serve to transform them into relaxed and indiscriminately amiable viscerotonics, or into inhibited, hyperattentional, and introverted cerebrotonics.

IV

⁴². We are now in a position to consider a few of the things that constitutional analysis and appraisal can do for us. First and most important, it makes it possible for us to know who we and other people really are—of what psychological and bodily elements we and they are composed. Having determined the statics of physique and the closely related dynamics of temperament, we can begin to think in a genuinely intelligent and fruitful way about the environment and the individual's reaction to it. Moreover, to understand is to forgive; and when we realize that the people who are different from us did not get that way out of wickedness or perversity, when we understand that many of the profoundest of such differences are constitutional and that constitution cannot be changed, only made the best of, we may perhaps learn to be more tolerant, more intelligently charitable than we are at present.

⁴³. Passing from the general to the particular, we find that constitutional appraisal has many important practical applications. In medicine, for example, the constitutional approach will undoubtedly prove helpful both in diagnosis and prognosis, in cure and prevention. To some extent, it is true, all physicians make use of the constitutional approach, and have been doing so for twenty-five centuries at least; but considering the importance of the subject, very little systematic research has been undertaken along these lines.

⁴⁴. Education can never in the nature of things be one hundred per cent efficient. Teaching is an art and, in every field, bad artists vastly outnumber good ones. Great educators are almost as rare as great painters and composers. The best we can hope to do is to improve the system within which teachers of average ability do their work. In this improvement of the system, constitutional analysis is likely to prove extremely helpful. Ideally, there should be several educational systems, one adapted to each of the main varieties of human beings. Of the progressive education which in recent years has largely ousted from our schools the formal, suppressive type of training that was at one time universal, Dr. Sheldon makes the following significant remark. "This vigorous progressive education is actually as suppressive as was Christian education at its darkest. It suppresses the third instead of the second component. It is as suppressive to a young cerebrotonic to press him to join in the dance or in the swim, and to make noise and mix and socialize, as it is suppressive to a young somatotonic to make him sit still."

⁴⁵. In the fields of history, sociology, and religion, the concepts of constitutional analysis may turn out to be extremely fruitful. From the

constitutional point of view, civilization may be defined as a complex of devices for restraining extreme somatotonics from destroying society by their reckless aggressiveness. Of the great world religions one, Confucianism, has been pre-eminently viscerotonic; it has sought to tame somatotonia by inculcating ceremonious good manners, general amiability, and the cult of the family. Most of the other world religions—Buddhism, the higher forms of Hinduism, and, until recent years, Christianity —have been predominantly cerebrotonic. (The figure of Christ in traditional Christian art is almost always that of a man with a high degree of ectomorphy and therefore of cerebrotonia.) These cerebrotonic religions have tried to keep somatotonics in order by teaching them the virtues of self-restraint, humility, and sensitiveness. At the same time they tried to sublimate somatotonic aggressiveness, or to direct it into channels thought to be desirable, such as crusades and wars of religion. On their side, the somatotonics have often succeeded in modifying the cerebrotonic philosophies and institutions of the prevailing religion. For example, no cerebrotonic or viscerotonic would ever have thought of talking about the Church Militant.

V

⁴⁶· In recent years there has been, in Sheldon's phrase, a great Somatotonic Revolution, directed against the dominance of cerebrotonic values as embodied in traditional Christianity. Thus, for traditional Christianity, it was axiomatic that the life of contemplation was superior to the life of action. Today the overwhelming majority even of Christians accept without question the primacy of action.

⁴⁷· For traditional Christianity the important thing was the development of the right state of mind about the environment. Today, the important thing is not the state of the mind, but the state of the environment. We believe that men and women will be happy when they are surrounded with the right kind of gadgets. Our forefathers believed that they would be happy if they achieved what one of the greatest of Christian saints called "a holy indifference" to their material surroundings. The change is from a cerebrotonic point of view to the point of view of a somatotonic extrovert.

⁴⁸· The Somatotonic Revolution has been greatly accelerated by technological advances. These have served to turn men's attention outward, and have encouraged the belief in a material apocalypse, a progress toward a mechanized New Jerusalem. Such beliefs have been carefully fostered by the writers of advertising copy—the most influential of all

authors because they are the only ones whose works are read every day by every member of the population. In a world peopled by cerebrotonics, living an inward-turning life in a state of holy, or even unholy, indifference to their material surroundings, mass production would be doomed. That is why advertisers consistently support the Somatotonic Revolution.

[49.] It is hardly necessary to add that total war is another potent factor in creating and sustaining the Somatotonic Revolution. Nazi education, which was specifically education for war, aimed at encouraging the manifestations of somatotonia in those most richly endowed with it, and making the rest of the population feel ashamed of its tendencies towards relaxed amiability or restrained and inward-looking sensitivity. During the war the enemies of Nazism have had to borrow from the Nazi educational philosophy. All over the world millions of young men and even young women are now being educated to be tough, and to admire toughness beyond every other moral quality. Never has somatotonia been so widely or so systematically encouraged as at the present time. Indeed, most societies in the past systematically discouraged somatotonia, because they did not wish to be destroyed by the unrestrained aggressiveness of their most active minority. What will be the result of the present worldwide reversal of what hitherto has been an almost universal social policy? Time alone will show.

COMMENTARY AND QUESTIONS

Aldous Huxley is best known as a very clever British novelist and essayist, now living in the United States. He is, by the way, the grandson of the Thomas Henry Huxley who wrote "The Method of Scientific Investigation" (the next selection); and his brother Julian is well known as a writer and scientist. In this article, Aldous Huxley departs from his usual subjects to explain for the more intelligent class of general reader a system of anthropological and psychological classification developed by Dr. W. H. Sheldon and to explain also the conclusions necessarily following from this classification. Since the system is accepted by some anthropologists but not by others, Huxley's article is to some extent persuasive or evaluative, for he thinks the system is fruitful and wishes to convince others into thinking so too. As, however, so much of the essay is devoted to explaining what the system is, why it is needed, and how it can be used, we may treat the article here as an example—and a very good one—of explanation of a moderately complex scientific subject.

1. What is the significance of Huxley's opening paragraph? What would have been the effect if the essay had begun with par. 3? The beginning of the article might be analyzed into several groups of paragraphs developing successively the following topics: the need for systematic

thought about human differences; the necessity of a system of classification in order to have systematic thought; the unsatisfactoriness of previous systems of classification for human differences; the system of Dr. Sheldon for classifying human differences in physique. What paragraphs compose each group? How does the author connect the groups? Could he have been equally effective with a different structure or order of topics? Par. 24 introduces two questions. Why is the one which requires the more space to answer put second?

2. In a good many of his paragraphs Huxley is setting down the characteristics of the various physical and mental types in Dr. Sheldon's system. These paragraphs might have turned into boresome lists; point out the ways in which Huxley has varied his sentences and means of introducing information to avoid monotony (for example, in par. 16). Note, on the other hand, his effective use of parallelism and balance. What is the effect of saying that "at school the extreme endomorph is called Slob or Fatty" (par. 14)? Find other places where the author has used concrete references or illustrations of this sort.

3. This essay necessarily introduces a good many strange words, most of them coined by Dr. Sheldon. Newly coined words are not uncommon in a scientific article dealing with new ideas and theories. You will understand and remember such terms more easily if you notice how they are put together. The fact that in this case their components are largely Greek should not be a great handicap to you, since these same components occur in other English words. Take *endomorph, mesomorph,* and *ectomorph* for examples. Look up in a good desk-size dictionary the root *morph* and find out how it is used in such words as *morphology* and *amorphous.* Do the same with *endo* as in *endocrine, meso* as in *Mesopotamia,* and *ecto* as in *ectoplasm.* What can you find in pars. 14-16 that might show why Dr. Sheldon uses these terms? Look up also the meanings and derivations of the words *tonic, viscera, somatic,* and *cerebral,* and see why Dr. Sheldon chose their roots to coin the terms introduced in par. 30.

SUGGESTIONS FOR WRITING

1. Which *morph* am I?
2. How to classify dogs.
3. In par. 18 Huxley speaks of the "almost criminal folly of encouraging all boys, whatever their hereditary make-up, to develop athletic ambitions." Explain why you agree or disagree with this statement.

The Method
of Scientific Investigation

by THOMAS HENRY HUXLEY

THE METHOD of scientific investigation is nothing but the expression of the necessary mode of working of the human mind. It is simply the mode at which all phenomena are reasoned about, rendered precise and exact. There is no more difference, but there is just the same kind of difference, between the mental operations of a man of science and those of an ordinary person, as there is between the operations and methods of a baker or of a butcher weighing out his goods in common scales, and the operations of a chemist in performing a difficult and complex analysis by means of his balance and finely-graduated weights. It is not that the action of the scales in the one case, and the balance in the other, differ in the principles of their construction or manner of working; but the beam of one is set on an infinitely finer axis than the other, and of course turns by the addition of a much smaller weight.

2. You will understand this better, perhaps, if I give you some familiar example. You have all heard it repeated, I dare say, that men of science work by means of induction and deduction, and that by the help of these operations, they, in a sort of sense, wring from Nature certain other things, which are called natural laws, and causes, and that out of these, by some cunning skill of their own, they build up hypotheses and theories. And it is imagined by many, that the operations of the common mind can be by no means compared with these processes, and that they have to be acquired by a sort of special apprenticeship to the craft. To hear all these large words, you would think that the mind of a man of science must be constituted differently from that of his fellow men; but if you will not be frightened by terms, you will discover that you are quite wrong, and that all these terrible apparatus are being used by yourselves every day and every hour of your lives.

3. There is a well known incident in one of Molière's plays, where the author makes the hero express unbounded delight on being told that he had been talking prose during the whole of his life. In the same way, I trust, that you will take comfort, and be delighted with yourselves, on the discovery that you have been acting on the principles of inductive

From *Darwiniana* (New York: D. Appleton and Company, 1896).

and deductive philosophy during the same period. Probably there is not one here who has not in the course of the day had occasion to set in motion a complex train of reasoning, of the very same kind, though differing of course in degree, as that which a scientific man goes through in tracing the causes of natural phenomena.

4. A very trivial circumstance will serve to exemplify this. Suppose you go into a fruiterer's shop, wanting an apple,—you take up one, and, on biting it, you find it sour; you look at it, and see that it is hard and green. You take up another one, and that too is hard, green, and sour. The shopman offers you a third; but, before biting it, you examine it, and find that it is hard and green, and you immediately say that you will not have it, as it must be sour, like those that you have already tried.

5. Nothing can be more simple than that, you think; but if you will take the trouble to analyse and trace out into its logical elements what has been done by the mind, you will be greatly surprised. In the first place, you have performed the operation of induction. You found that, in two experiences, hardness and greenness in apples went together with sourness. It was so in the first case, and it was confirmed by the second. True, it is a very small basis, but still it is enough to make an induction from; you generalise the facts, and you expect to find sourness in apples where you get hardness and greenness. You found upon that a general law, that all hard and green apples are sour; and that, so far as it goes, is a perfect induction. Well, having got your natural law in this way, when you are offered another apple which you find is hard and green, you say, "All hard and green apples are sour; this apple is hard and green, therefore this apple is sour." That train of reasoning is what logicians call a syllogism, and has all its various parts and terms,—its major premiss, its minor premiss, and its conclusion. And, by the help of further reasoning, which, if drawn out, would have to be exhibited in two or three other syllogisms, you arrive at your final determination, "I will not have that apple." So that, you see, you have, in the first place, established a law by induction, and upon that you have founded a deduction, and reasoned out the special conclusion of the particular case. Well now, suppose, having got your law, that at some time afterwards, you are discussing the qualities of apples with a friend: you will say to him, "It is a very curious thing,—but I find that all hard and green apples are sour!" Your friend says to you, "But how do you know that?" You at once reply, "Oh, because I have tried them over and over again, and have always found them to be so." Well, if we were talking science instead of common sense, we should call that an experimental verification. And, if still opposed, you go further, and say, "I have heard from the people in Somersetshire and Devonshire, where a large number of apples are grown, that they have observed

the same thing. It is also found to be the case in Normandy, and in North America. In short, I find it to be the universal experience of mankind wherever attention has been directed to the subject." Whereupon, your friend, unless he is a very unreasonable man, agrees with you, and is convinced that you are quite right in the conclusion you have drawn. He believes, although perhaps he does not know he believes it, that the more extensive verifications are,—that the more frequently experiments have been made, and results of the same kind arrived at,—that the more varied the conditions under which the same results are attained, the more certain is the ultimate conclusion, and he disputes the question no further. He sees that the experiment has been tried under all sorts of conditions, as to time, place, and people, with the same result; and he says with you, therefore, that the law you have laid down must be a good one, and he must believe it.

6. In science we do the same thing;—the philosopher exercises precisely the same faculties, though in a much more delicate manner. In scientific inquiry it becomes a matter of duty to expose a supposed law to every possible kind of verification, and to take care, moreover, that this is done intentionally, and not left to a mere accident, as in the case of the apples. And in science, as in common life, our confidence in a law is in exact proportion to the absence of variation in the result of our experimental verifications. For instance, if you let go your grasp of an article you may have in your hand, it will immediately fall to the ground. That is a very common verification of one of the best established laws of nature—that of gravitation. The method by which men of science establish the existence of that law is exactly the same as that by which we have established the trivial proposition about the sourness of hard and green apples. But we believe it in such an extensive, thorough, and unhesitating manner because the universal experience of mankind verifies it, and we can verify it ourselves at any time; and that is the strongest possible foundation on which any natural law can rest.

7. So much, then, by way of proof that the method of establishing laws in science is exactly the same as that pursued in common life. Let us now turn to another matter (though really it is but another phase of the same question), and that is, the method by which, from the relations of certain phenomena, we prove that some stand in the position of causes towards the others.

8. I want to put the case clearly before you, and I will therefore show you what I mean by another familiar example. I will suppose that one of you, on coming down in the morning to the parlour of your house, finds that a tea-pot and some spoons which had been left in the room on the previous evening are gone,—the window is open, and you observe

the mark of a dirty hand on the window-frame, and perhaps, in addition to that, you notice the impress of a hob-nailed shoe on the gravel outside. All these phenomena have struck your attention instantly, and before two seconds have passed you say, "Oh, somebody has broken open the window, entered the room, and run off with the spoons and the tea-pot!" That speech is out of your mouth in a moment. And you will probably add, "I know there has; I am quite sure of it!" You mean to say exactly what you know; but in reality you are giving expression to what is, in all essential particulars, an hypothesis. You do not *know* it at all; it is nothing but an hypothesis rapidly framed in your own mind. And it is an hypothesis founded on a long train of inductions and deductions.

⁹· What are those inductions and deductions, and how have you got at this hypothesis? You have observed, in the first place, that the window is open; but by a train of reasoning involving many inductions and deductions, you have probably arrived long before at the general law— and a very good one it is—that windows do not open of themselves; and you therefore conclude that something has opened the window. A second general law that you have arrived at in the same way is, that tea-pots and spoons do not go out of a window spontaneously, and you are satisfied that, as they are not now where you left them, they have been removed. In the third place, you look at the marks on the window-sill, and the shoe-marks outside, and you say that in all previous experience the former kind of mark has never been produced by anything else but the hand of a human being; and the same experience shows that no other animal but man at present wears shoes with hob-nails in them such as would produce the marks in the gravel. I do not know, even if we could discover any of those "missing links" that are talked about, that they would help us to any other conclusion! At any rate the law which states our present experience is strong enough for my present purpose. You next reach the conclusion, that as these kinds of marks have not been left by any other animals than men, or are liable to be formed in any other way than by a man's hand and shoe, the marks in question have been formed by a man in that way. You have, further, a general law, founded on observation and experience, and that, too, is, I am sorry to say, a very universal and unimpeachable one,—that some men are thieves; and you assume at once from all these premisses—and that is what constitutes your hypothesis—that the man who made the marks outside and on the window-sill, opened the window, got into the room, and stole your tea-pot and spoons. You have now arrived at a *vera causa;* —you have assumed a cause which, it is plain, is competent to produce all the phenomena you have observed. You can explain all these phenomena only by the hypothesis of a thief. But that is a hypothetical con-

clusion, of the justice of which you have no absolute proof at all; it is only rendered highly probable by a series of inductive and deductive reasonings.

10. I suppose your first action, assuming that you are a man of ordinary common sense, and that you have established this hypothesis to your own satisfaction, will very likely be to go off for the police, and set them on the track of the burglar, with the view to the recovery of your property. But just as you are starting with this object, some person comes in, and on learning what you are about, says, "My good friend, you are going on a great deal too fast. How do you know that the man who really made the marks took the spoons? It might have been a monkey that took them, and the man may have merely looked in afterwards." You would probably reply, "Well, that is all very well, but you see it is contrary to all experience of the way tea-pots and spoons are abstracted; so that, at any rate, your hypothesis is less probable than mine." While you are talking the thing over in this way, another friend arrives, one of that good kind of people that I was talking of a little while ago. And he might say, "Oh, my dear sir, you are certainly going on a great deal too fast. You are most presumptuous. You admit that all these occurrences took place when you were fast asleep, at a time when you could not possibly have known anything about what was taking place. How do you know that the laws of Nature are not suspended during the night? It may be that there has been some kind of supernatural interference in this case." In point of fact, he declares that your hypothesis is one of which you cannot at all demonstrate the truth, and that you are by no means sure that the laws of Nature are the same when you are asleep as when you are awake.

11. Well, now, you cannot at the moment answer that kind of reasoning. You feel that your worthy friend has you somewhat at a disadvantage. You will feel perfectly convinced in your own mind, however, that you are quite right, and you say to him, "My good friend, I can only be guided by the natural probabilities of the case, and if you will be kind enough to stand aside and permit me to pass, I will go and fetch the police." Well, we will suppose that your journey is successful, and that by good luck you meet with a policeman; that eventually the burglar is found with your property on his person, and the marks correspond to his hand and to his boots. Probably any jury would consider those facts a very good experimental verification of your hypothesis, touching the cause of the abnormal phenomena observed in your parlour, and would act accordingly.

12. Now, in this suppositious case, I have taken phenomena of a very common kind, in order that you might see what are the different steps

in an ordinary process of reasoning, if you will only take the trouble to analyse it carefully. All the operations I have described, you will see, are involved in the mind of any man of sense in leading him to a conclusion as to the course he should take in order to make good a robbery and punish the offender. I say that you are led, in that case, to your conclusion by exactly the same train of reasoning as that which a man of science pursues when he is endeavouring to discover the origin and laws of the most occult phenomena. The process is, and always must be, the same; and precisely the same mode of reasoning was employed by Newton and Laplace in their endeavours to discover and define the causes of the movements of the heavenly bodies, as you, with your own common sense, would employ to detect a burglar. The only difference is, that the nature of the inquiry being more abstruse, every step has to be most carefully watched, so that there may not be a single crack or flaw in your hypothesis. A flaw or crack in many of the hypotheses of daily life may be of little or no moment as affecting the general correctness of the conclusions at which we may arrive; but, in a scientific inquiry, a fallacy, great or small, is always of importance, and is sure to be in the long run constantly productive of mischievous, if not fatal results.

13. Do not allow yourselves to be misled by the common notion that an hypothesis is untrustworthy simply because it is an hypothesis. It is often urged, in respect to some scientific conclusion, that, after all, it is only an hypothesis. But what more have we to guide us in nine-tenths of the most important affairs of daily life than hypotheses, and often very ill-based ones? So that in science, where the evidence of an hypothesis is subjected to the most rigid examination, we may rightly pursue the same course. You may have hypotheses and hypotheses. A man may say, if he likes, that the moon is made of green cheese: that is an hypothesis. But another man, who has devoted a great deal of time and attention to the subject, and availed himself of the most powerful telescopes and the results of the observations of others, declares that in his opinion it is probably composed of materials very similar to those of which our own earth is made up: and that is also only an hypothesis. But I need not tell you that there is an enormous difference in the value of the two hypotheses. That one which is based on sound scientific knowledge is sure to have a corresponding value; and that which is a mere hasty random guess is likely to have but little value. Every great step in our progress in discovering causes has been made in exactly the same way as that which I have detailed to you. A person observing the occurrence of certain facts and phenomena asks, naturally enough, what process, what kind of operation known to occur in Nature applied to the particular case, will unravel and explain the mystery? Hence you have the scien-

tific hypothesis; and its value will be proportionate to the care and completeness with which its basis had been tested and verified. It is in these matters as in the commonest affairs of practical life: the guess of the fool will be folly, while the guess of the wise man will contain wisdom. In all cases, you see that the value of the result depends on the patience and faithfulness with which the investigator applies to his hypothesis every possible kind of verification.

COMMENTARY AND QUESTIONS

This little essay has been very often reprinted, because it is one of the simplest and clearest expositions of the basic principles of scientific discovery and rational thought. Written by the grandfather of the author of the preceding selection, it was originally given in 1862 as part of a series of *Six Lectures to Working Men on Our Knowledge of Causes of the Phenomena of Organic Nature.* Huxley, an excellent scientist himself, gained even more fame as the expounder and defender of biological science, particularly the theories of Charles Darwin, to the nineteenth-century British public. His success as writer and lecturer was due to his clarity of mind and more especially to his power of stating scientific facts and hypotheses in language easily understood by the technically untrained, such as the "working men" to whom this lecture was first addressed.

1. This essay achieves its purpose largely by stating abstract ideas in concrete terms. Point out several abstractions which are thus stated and comment on the appropriateness and effectiveness of the concrete illustrations.

2. Discuss the appropriateness and effectiveness of Huxley's style for the audience and purpose intended. Look up the dictionary definitions of *induction, deduction, syllogism,* and *hypothesis* and compare them to the definitions stated or implied in Huxley's essay. Which are you the more likely to remember?

SUGGESTIONS FOR WRITING

1. An induction made on my daily walk to class.
2. Hypotheses I have known.

The Universe
and Dr. Einstein

by LINCOLN BARNETT

I

IN HIS GREAT TREATISE *On Human Understanding* philosopher John Locke wrote three hundred years ago: "A company of chessmen standing on the same squares of the chessboard where we left them, we say, are all in the same place or unmoved: though perhaps the chessboard has been in the meantime carried out of one room into another. . . . The chessboard, we also say, is in the same place if it remain in the same part of the cabin, though perhaps the ship which it is in sails all the while; and the ship is said to be in the same place supposing it kept the same distance with the neighboring land, though perhaps the earth has turned around; and so chessmen and board and ship have every one changed place in respect to remoter bodies."

2. Embodied in this little picture of the moving but unmoved chessmen is one principle of relativity—relativity of position. But this suggests another idea—relativity of motion. Anyone who has ever ridden on a railroad train knows how rapidly another train flashes by when it is traveling in the opposite direction, and conversely how it may look almost motionless when it is moving in the same direction. A variation of this effect can be very deceptive in an enclosed station like Grand Central Terminal in New York. Once in a while a train gets under way so gently that passengers feel no recoil whatever. Then if they happen to look out the window and see another train slide past on the next track, they have no way of knowing which train is in motion and which is at rest; nor can they tell how fast either one is moving or in what direction. The only way they can judge their situation is by looking out the other side of the car for some fixed body of reference like the station platform or a signal light. Sir Isaac Newton was aware of these tricks of motion, only he thought in terms of ships. He knew that on a calm day at sea a sailor can shave himself or drink soup as comfortably as when his ship is lying motionless in harbor. The water in his basin, the soup in his bowl, will remain unruffled

From *The Universe and Dr. Einstein* (New York: William Sloane Associates, Inc., 1948). By permission of the publishers. Copyright 1948 by Harper & Row, Publishers, Incorporated; copyright 1948 by Lincoln Barnett.

201

whether the ship is making five knots, 15 knots, or 25 knots. So unless he peers out at the sea it will be impossible for him to know how fast his ship is moving or indeed if it is moving at all. Of course if the sea should get rough or the ship change course abruptly, then he will sense his state of motion. But granted the idealized conditions of a glass-calm sea and a silent ship, nothing that happens below decks—no amount of observation or mechanical experiment performed *inside* the ship—will disclose its velocity through the sea. The physical principle suggested by these considerations was formulated by Newton in 1687. "The motions of bodies included in a given space," he wrote, "are the same among themselves, whether that space is at rest or moves uniformly forward in a straight line." This is known as the Newtonian or Galilean Relativity Principle. It can also be phrased in more general terms: mechanical laws which are valid in one place are equally valid in any other place which moves uniformly relative to the first.

3. The philosophical importance of this principle lies in what it says about the universe. Since the aim of science is to explain the world we live in, as a whole and in all its parts, it is essential to the scientist that he have confidence in the harmony of nature. He must believe that physical laws revealed to him on earth are in truth universal laws. Thus in relating the fall of an apple to the wheeling of the planets around the sun Newton hit upon a universal law. And although he illustrated his principle of relative motion by a ship at sea, the ship he actually had in mind was the earth. For all ordinary purposes of science the earth can be regarded as a stationary system. We may say if we choose that mountains, trees, houses, are at rest, and animals, automobiles, and airplanes move. But to the astrophysicist, the earth, far from being at rest, is whirling through space in a giddy and highly complicated fashion. In addition to its daily rotation about its axis at the rate of 1000 miles an hour, and its annual revolution about the sun at the rate of 20 miles a second, the earth is also involved in a number of other less familiar gyrations. Contrary to popular belief the moon does not revolve around the earth; they revolve around each other—or more precisely, around a common center of gravity. The entire solar system, moreover, is moving within the local star system at the rate of 13 miles a second; the local star system is moving within the Milky Way at the rate of 200 miles a second; and the whole Milky Way is drifting with respect to the remote external galaxies at the rate of 100 miles a second—and all in different directions!

4. Although he could not then know the full complexity of the earth's movements, Newton was nevertheless troubled by the problem of distinguishing relative motion from true or "absolute" motion in a confusingly

busy universe. He suggested that "in the remote regions of the fixed stars or perhaps far beyond them, there may be some body absolutely at rest," but admitted there was no way of proving this by any celestial object within man's view. On the other hand it seemed to Newton that space itself might serve as a fixed frame of reference to which the wheeling of the stars and galaxies could be related in terms of absolute motion. He regarded space as a physical reality, stationary and immovable; and while he could not support this conviction by any scientific argument, he nevertheless clung to it on theological grounds. For to Newton space represented the divine omnipresence of God in nature.

5. In the next two centuries it appeared probable that Newton's view would prevail. For with the development of the wave theory of light scientists found it necessary to endow empty space with certain mechanical properties—to assume, indeed, that space was some kind of substance. Even before Newton's time the French philosopher, Descartes, had argued that the mere separation of bodies by distance proved the existence of a medium between them. And to eighteenth and nineteenth century physicists it was obvious that if light consisted of waves, there must be some medium to support them, just as water propagates the waves of the sea and air transmits the vibrations we call sound. Hence when experiments showed that light can travel in a vacuum, scientists evolved a hypothetical substance called "ether" which they decided must pervade all space and matter. Later on Faraday propounded another kind of ether as the carrier of electric and magnetic forces. When Maxwell finally identified light as an electromagnetic disturbance the case for the ether seemed assured.

6. A universe permeated with an invisible medium in which the stars wandered and through which light traveled like vibrations in a bowl of jelly was the end product of Newtonian physics. It provided a mechanical model for all known phenomena of nature, and it provided the fixed frame of reference, the absolute and immovable space, which Newton's cosmology required. Yet the ether presented certain problems, not the least of which was that its actual existence had never been proved. To discover once and for all whether there really was any such thing as ether, two American physicists, A. A. Michelson and E. W. Morley, performed a classic experiment in Cleveland in the year 1881.

7. The principle underlying their experiment was quite simple. They reasoned that if all space is simply a motionless sea of ether, then the earth's motion through the ether should be detectable and measurable in the same way that sailors measure the velocity of a ship through the sea. As Newton pointed out, it is impossible to detect the movement of a ship

through calm waters by any mechanical experiment performed *inside* the ship. Sailors ascertain a ship's speed by throwing a log overboard and watching the unreeling of the knots on the log line. Hence to detect the earth's motion through the ether sea, Michelson and Morley threw a "log" overboard, and the log was a beam of light. For if light really is propagated through the ether, then its velocity should be affected by the ether stream arising from the earth's movement. Specifically a light ray projected in the direction of the earth's movement should be slightly retarded by the ether flow, just as a swimmer is retarded by a current when going upstream. The difference would be slight, for the velocity of light (which was accurately determined in 1849) is 186,284 miles a second, while the velocity of the earth in its orbit around the sun is only 20 miles a second. Hence a light ray sent *against* the ether stream should travel at the rate of 186,264 miles a second, while one sent *with* the ether stream should be clocked at 186,304 miles a second. With these ideas in mind Michelson and Morley constructed an instrument of such great delicacy that it could detect a variation of even a fraction of a mile per second in the enormous velocity of light. This instrument, which they called an "interferometer," consisted of a group of mirrors so arranged that a light beam could be split in two and flashed in different directions at the same time. The whole experiment was planned and executed with such painstaking precision that the result could not be doubted. And the result was simply this: there was no difference whatsoever in the velocity of the light beams regardless of their direction.

8. The Michelson-Morley experiment confronted scientists with an embarrassing alternative. On the one hand they could scrap the ether theory which had explained so many things about electricity, magnetism, and light. Or if they insisted on retaining the ether they had to abandon the still more venerable Copernican theory that the earth is in motion. To many physicists it seemed almost easier to believe that the earth stood still than that waves—light waves, electromagnetic waves—could exist without a medium to sustain them. It was a serious dilemma and one that split scientific thought for a quarter century. Many new hypotheses were advanced and rejected. The experiment was tried again by Morley and by others, with the same conclusion; the apparent velocity of the earth through the ether was zero.

II

9. Among those who pondered the enigma of the Michelson-Morley experiment was a young patent office examiner in Berne, named Albert Einstein. In 1905, when he was just twenty-six years old, he published a

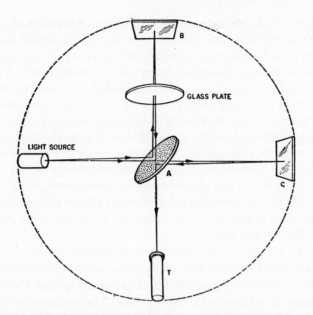

The Michelson-Morley interferometer consisted of an arrangement of mirrors, so designed that a beam transmitted from a light source (above left) was divided and sent in two directions at the same time. This was done by a mirror, A, the face of which was only thinly silvered, so that part of the beam was permitted to pass through to mirror C (right) and the remainder reflected at right angles toward mirror B. Mirrors B and C then reflected the rays back to mirror A where, reunited, they proceeded to an observing telescope T. Since the beam ACT had to pass three times through the thickness of glass behind the reflecting face of mirror A, a clear glass plate of equal thickness was placed between A and B to intercept beam ABT and compensate for this retardation. The whole apparatus was rotated in different directions so that the beams ABT and ACT could be sent with, against, and at right angles to the postulated ether stream. At first glance it might appear that a trip "downstream," for example from B to A, should compensate in time for an "upstream" trip from A to B. But this is not so. To row a boat one mile upstream and another mile downstream takes longer than rowing two miles in still water or across current, even with allowance for drift. Had there been any acceleration or retardation of either beam by the ether stream, the optical apparatus at T would have detected it.

short paper suggesting an answer to the riddle in terms that opened up a new world of physical thought. He began by rejecting the ether theory and with it the whole idea of space as a fixed system or framework, absolutely at rest, within which it is possible to distinguish absolute from relative motion. The one indisputable fact established by the Michelson-Morley experiment was that the velocity of light is unaffected by the motion of the earth. Einstein seized on this as a revelation of universal law. If the velocity of light is constant regardless of the earth's motion, he reasoned, it must be constant regardless of the motion of any sun, moon, star, meteor, or other system moving anywhere in the universe. From this he drew a broader generalization, and asserted that the laws of nature are the same for all uniformly moving systems. This simple statement is the essence of Einstein's Special Theory of Relativity. It incorporates the Galilean Relativity Principle which stated that mechanical laws are the same for all uniformly moving systems. But its phrasing is more comprehensive; for Einstein was thinking not only of mechanical laws but of the laws governing light and other electromagnetic phenomena. So he lumped them together in one fundamental postulate: all the phenomena of nature, all the laws of nature, are the same for all systems that move uniformly relative to one another.

10. On the surface there is nothing very startling in this declaration. It simply reiterates the scientist's faith in the universal harmony of natural law. It also advises the scientist to stop looking for any absolute, stationary frame of reference in the universe. The universe is a restless place: stars, nebulae, galaxies, and all the vast gravitational systems of outer space are incessantly in motion. But their movements can be described only with respect to each other, for in space there are no directions and no boundaries. It is futile moreover for the scientist to try to discover the "true" velocity of any system by using light as a measuring rod, for the velocity of light is constant throughout the universe and is unaffected either by the motion of its source or the motion of the receiver. Nature offers no absolute standards of comparison; and space is—as another great German mathematician, Leibnitz, clearly saw two centuries before Einstein—simply "the order or relation of things among themselves." Without things occupying it, it is nothing.

11. Along with absolute space, Einstein discarded the concept of absolute time—of a steady, unvarying, inexorable universal time flow, streaming from the infinite past to the infinite future. Much of the obscurity that has surrounded the Theory of Relativity stems from man's reluctance to recognize that sense of time, like sense of color, is a form of perception. Just as there is no such thing as color without an eye to discern it, so an instant or an hour or a day is nothing without an event to mark it. And just as space is simply a possible order of material objects, so time is simply a possible order of events. The subjectivity of time is best explained in Einstein's own words. "The experiences of an individual," he says, "appear to us arranged in a series of events; in this series the single events which we remember appear to be ordered according to the criterion of 'earlier' and 'later.' There exists, therefore, for the individual,

an I-time, or subjective time. This in itself is not measurable. I can, indeed, associate numbers with the events, in such a way that a greater number is associated with the later event than with an earlier one. This association I can define by means of a clock by comparing the order of events furnished by the clock with the order of the given series of events. We understand by a clock something which provides a series of events which can be counted."

¹². By referring our own experiences to a clock (or a calendar) we make time an objective concept. Yet the time intervals provided by a clock or a calendar are by no means absolute quantities imposed on the entire universe by divine edict. All the clocks ever used by man have been geared to our solar system. What we call an hour is actually a measurement in space—an arc of 15 degrees in the apparent daily rotation of the celestial sphere. And what we call a year is simply a measure of the earth's progress in its orbit around the sun. An inhabitant of Mercury, however, would have very different notions of time. For Mercury makes its trip around the sun in 88 of our days, and in that same period rotates just once on its axis. So on Mercury a year and a day amount to the same thing. But it is when science ranges beyond the neighborhood of the sun that all our terrestrial ideas of time become meaningless. For Relativity tells us there is no such thing as a fixed interval of time independent of the system to which it is referred. There is indeed no such thing as simultaneity, there is no such thing as "now," independent of a system of reference. For example a man in New York may telephone a friend in London, and although it is 7:00 P.M. in New York and midnight in London, we may say that they are talking "at the same time." But that is because they are both residents of the same planet, and their clocks are geared to the same astronomical system. A more complicated situation arises if we try to ascertain, for example, what is happening on the star Arcturus "right now." Arcturus is 38 light years away. A light year is the distance light travels in one year, or roughly six trillion miles. If we should try to communicate with Arcturus by radio "right now" it would take 38 years for our message to reach its destination and another 38 years for us to receive a reply.[1] And when we look at Arcturus and say that we see it "now," we are actually seeing a ghost—an image projected on our optic nerves by light rays that left their source in 1910. Whether Arcturus even exists "now" nature forbids us to know until 1986.

¹³. Despite such reflections it is difficult for earthbound man to accept the idea that *this very instant* which he calls "now" cannot apply to the

---

[1] Radio waves travel at the same speed as light waves.

universe as a whole. Yet in the Special Theory of Relativity Einstein proves by an unanswerable sequence of example and deduction that it is nonsense to think of events taking place simultaneously in unrelated systems. His argument unfolds along the following lines.

14. To begin with one must realize that the scientist, whose task it is to describe physical events in objective terms, cannot use subjective words like "this," "here," and "now." For him concepts of space and time take on physical significance only when the relations between events and systems are defined. And it is constantly necessary for him, in dealing with matters involving complex forms of motion (as in celestial mechanics, electrodynamics, etc.) to relate the magnitudes found in one system with those occurring in another. The mathematical laws which define these relationships are known as laws of transformation. The simplest transformation may be illustrated by a man promenading on the deck of a ship: if he walks forward along the deck at the rate of 3 miles an hour and the ship moves through the sea at the rate of 12 miles an hour, then the man's velocity with respect to the sea is 15 miles an hour; if he walks aft his velocity relative to the sea is of course 9 miles an hour. Or as a variation one may imagine an alarm bell ringing at a railway crossing. The sound waves produced by the bell spread away through the surrounding air at the rate of 400 yards a second. A railroad train speeds toward the crossing at the rate of 20 yards a second. Hence the velocity of the sound relative to the train is 420 yards a second so long as the train is approaching the alarm bell and 380 yards a second as soon as the train passes the bell. This simple addition of velocities rests on obvious common sense, and has indeed been applied to problems of compound motion since the time of Galileo. Serious difficulties arise, however, when it is used in connection with light.

15. In his original paper on Relativity Einstein emphasized these difficulties with another railway incident. Again there is a crossing, marked this time by a signal light which flashes its beam down the track at 186,284 miles a second—the constant velocity of light, denoted in physics by the symbol c. A train steams toward the signal light at a given velocity v. So by the addition of velocities one concludes that the velocity of the light beam relative to the train is c plus v when the train moves toward the signal light, and c minus v as soon as the train passes the light. But this result conflicts with the findings of the Michelson-Morley experiment which demonstrated that the velocity of light is unaffected either by the motion of the source or the motion of the receiver. This curious fact has also been confirmed by studies of double stars which revolve around a common center of gravity. Careful analysis of these moving systems has shown that the light from the approaching star in each pair reaches earth

at precisely the same velocity as the light from the receding star. Since the velocity of light is a universal constant it cannot in Einstein's railway problem be affected by the velocity of the train. Even if we imagine that the train is racing toward the signal light at a speed of 10,000 miles a second, the principle of the constancy of the velocity of light tells us that an observer aboard the train will still clock the speed of the oncoming light beam at precisely 186,284 miles a second, no more, no less.

16. The dilemma presented by this situation involves much more than a Sunday morning newspaper puzzle. On the contrary it poses a deep enigma of nature. Einstein saw that the problem lay in the irreconcilable conflict between his belief in (1) the constancy of the velocity of light, and (2) the principle of the addition of velocities. Although the latter appears to rest on the stern logic of mathematics (i.e., that two plus two makes four), Einstein recognized in the former a fundamental law of nature. He concluded, therefore, that a new transformation rule must be found to enable the scientist to describe the relations between moving systems in such a way that the results satisfy the known facts about light.

17. Einstein found what he wanted in a series of equations developed by the great Dutch physicist, H. A. Lorentz, in connection with a specific theory of his own. Although its original application is of interest now chiefly to scientific historians, the Lorentz transformation lives on as part of the mathematical framework of Relativity. To understand what it says, however, it is first necessary to perceive the flaws in the old principle of the addition of velocities. These flaws Einstein pointed out by means of still another railway anecdote. Once again he envisaged a straight length of track, this time with an observer sitting on an embankment beside it. A thunderstorm breaks, and two bolts of lightning strike the track simulta-

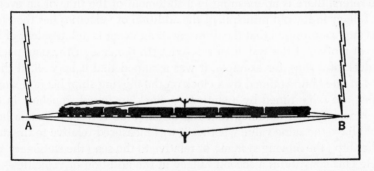

neously at separate points, A and B. Now, asks Einstein, what do we mean by "simultaneously"? To pin down this definition he assumes that the observer is sitting precisely half way between A and B, and that he is equipped with an arrangement of mirrors which enable him to see A and

B at the same time without moving his eyes. Then if the lightning flashes are reflected in the observer's mirrors at precisely the same instant, the two flashes may be regarded as simultaneous. Now a train roars down the track, and a second observer is sitting precariously perched atop one of the cars with a mirror apparatus just like the one on the embankment. It happens that this moving observer finds himself directly opposite the observer on the embankment at the precise instant the lightning bolts hit A and B. The question is: will the lightning flashes appear simultaneous to him? The answer is: they will not. For if his train is moving away from lightning bolt B and toward lightning bolt A, then it is obvious that B will be reflected in his mirrors a fraction of a second later than A. Lest there be any doubt about this, one may imagine temporarily that the train is moving at the impossible rate of 186,284 miles a second, the velocity of light. In that event flash B will never be reflected in the mirrors because it can never overtake the train, just as the sound from a gun can never overtake a bullet traveling with supersonic speed. So the observer on the train will assert that only one lightning bolt struck the track. And whatever the speed of the train may be the moving observer will always insist that the lightning flash ahead of him has struck the track first. Hence the lightning flashes which are simultaneous relative to the stationary observer are *not* simultaneous relative to the observer on the train.

18. The paradox of the lightning flashes thus dramatizes one of the subtlest and most difficult concepts in Einstein's philosophy: the relativity of simultaneity. It shows that man cannot assume that his subjective sense of "now" applies to all parts of the universe. For, Einstein points out, "every reference body (or coordinate system) has its own particular time; unless we are told the reference body to which the statement of time refers, there is no meaning in a statement of the time of an event." The fallacy in the old principle of the addition of velocities lies therefore in its tacit assumption that the duration of an event is independent of the state of motion of the system of reference. In the case of the man pacing the deck of a ship, for example, it was assumed that if he walked three miles in one hour as timed by a clock on the moving ship, his rate would be just the same timed by a stationary clock anchored somehow in the sea. It was further assumed that the distance he traversed in one hour would have the same value whether it was measured relative to the deck of the ship (the moving system) or relative to the sea (the stationary system). This constitutes a second fallacy in the addition of velocities—for distance, like time, is a relative concept, and there is no such thing as a space interval independent of the state of motion of the system of reference.

19. Einstein asserted, therefore, that the scientist who wishes to de-

scribe the phenomena of nature in terms that are consistent for all systems throughout the universe must regard measurements of time and distance as variable quantities. The equations comprising the Lorentz transformation do just that. They preserve the velocity of light as a universal constant, but modify all measurements of time and distance according to the velocity of each system of reference.[2]

20. So although Lorentz had originally developed his equations to meet a specific problem, Einstein made them the basis of a tremendous generalization, and to the edifice of Relativity added another axiom: the laws of nature preserve their uniformity in all systems when related by the Lorentz transformation. Stated thus, in the abstract language of mathematics, the significance of this axiom can scarcely be apparent to the layman. But in physics an equation is never a pure abstraction; it is simply a kind of shorthand expression which the scientist finds convenient to describe the phenomena of nature. Sometimes it is also a Rosetta Stone in which the theoretical physicist can decipher secret realms of

---

[2] The Lorentz transformation relates distances and times observed on moving systems with those observed on systems relatively at rest. Suppose, for example, that a system, or reference body, is moving in a certain direction, then *according to the old principle of the addition of velocities,* a distance or length x', measured with respect to the moving system along the direction of motion, is related to length x, measured with respect to a relatively stationary system, by the equation $x' = x \pm vt$, where v is the velocity of the moving system and t is the time. Dimensions y' and z', measured with respect to the moving system at right angles to x' and at right angles to each other (i.e., height and breadth), are related to dimensions y and z on the relatively stationary system by $y' = y$, and $z' = z$. And finally a time interval t', clocked with respect to the moving system, is related to time interval t, clocked with respect to the relatively stationary system, by $t' = t$. In other words, distances and times are not affected, *in classical physics,* by the velocity of the system in question. *But it is this presupposition which leads to the paradox of the lightning flashes.* The Lorentz transformation reduces the distances and times observed on moving systems to the conditions of the stationary observer, keeping the velocity of light c a constant for all observers. Here are the equations of the Lorentz transformation which have supplanted the older and evidently inadequate relationships cited above:

$$x' = \frac{x - vt}{\sqrt{1 - (v^2/c^2)}}$$
$$y' = y$$
$$z' = z$$
$$t' = \frac{t - (v/c^2)x}{\sqrt{1 - (v^2/c^2)}}$$

It will be noted that, as in the old transformation law, dimensions y' and z' are unaffected by motion. It will also be seen that if the velocity of the moving system v is small relative to the velocity of light c, then the equations of the Lorentz transformation reduce themselves to the relations of the old principle of the addition of velocities. But as the magnitude of v approaches that of c, then the values of x' and t' are radically changed.

knowledge. And so by deduction from the message written in the equations of the Lorentz transformation, Einstein discovered a number of new and extraordinary truths about the physical universe.

III

21. These truths can be described in very concrete terms. For once he had evolved the philosophical and mathematical bases of Relativity, Einstein had to bring them into the laboratory, where abstractions like time and space are harnessed by means of clocks and measuring rods. And so translating his basic ideas about time and space into the language of the laboratory, he pointed out some hitherto unsuspected properties of clocks and rods. For example: a clock attached to any moving system runs at a different rhythm from a stationary clock; and a measuring rod attached to any moving system changes its length according to the velocity of the system. Specifically the clock slows down as its velocity increases, and the measuring rod shrinks in the direction of its motion. These peculiar changes have nothing to do with the construction of the clock or the composition of the rod. The clock can be a pendulum clock, a spring clock, or an hour glass. The measuring rod can be a wooden ruler, a metal yardstick, or a ten-mile cable. The slowing of the clock and the contraction of the rod are not mechanical phenomena; an observer riding along with the clock and the measuring rod would not notice these changes. But a stationary observer, i.e., stationary relative to the moving system, would find that the moving clock has slowed down with respect to his stationary clock, and that the moving rod has contracted with respect to his stationary units of measurement.

22. This singular behavior of moving clocks and yardsticks accounts for the constant velocity of light. It explains why all observers in all systems everywhere, regardless of their state of motion, will always find that light strikes their instruments and departs from their instruments at precisely the same velocity. For as their own velocity approaches that of light, their clocks slow down, their yardsticks contract, and all their measurements are reduced to the values obtained by a relatively stationary observer. The laws governing these contractions are defined by the Lorentz transformation and they are very simple: the greater the speed, the greater the contraction. A yardstick moving with 90 per cent the velocity of light would shrink to about half its length; thereafter the rate of contraction becomes more rapid; and if the stick could attain the velocity of light, it would shrink away to nothing at all. Similarly a clock traveling with the velocity of light would stop completely. From this it follows that

nothing can ever move faster than light, no matter what forces are applied. Thus Relativity reveals another fundamental law of nature: *the velocity of light is the top limiting velocity in the universe.*

23. At first meeting these facts are difficult to digest but that is simply because classical physics assumed, unjustifiably, that an object preserves the same dimensions whether it is in motion or at rest and that a clock keeps the same rhythm in motion and at rest. Common sense dictates that this must be so. But as Einstein has pointed out, common sense is actually nothing more than a deposit of prejudices laid down in the mind prior to the age of eighteen. Every new idea one encounters in later years must combat this accretion of "self-evident" concepts. And it is because of Einstein's unwillingness ever to accept any unproven principle as self-evident that he was able to penetrate closer to the underlying realities of nature than any scientist before him. Why, he asked, is it any more strange to assume that moving clocks slow down and moving rods contract, than to assume that they don't? The reason classical physics took the latter view for granted is that man, in his everyday experience, never encounters velocities great enough to make these changes manifest. In an automobile, an airplane, even in a V-2 rocket, the slowing down of a watch is immeasurable. It is only when velocities approximate that of light that relativistic effects can be detected. The equations of the Lorentz transformation show very plainly that at ordinary speeds the modification of time and space intervals amounts practically to zero. Relativity does not therefore contradict classical physics. It simply regards the old concepts as limiting cases that apply solely to the familiar experiences of man.

24. Einstein thus surmounts the barrier reared by man's impulse to define reality solely as he perceives it through the screen of his senses. Just as the Quantum Theory demonstrated that elementary particles of matter do not behave like the larger particles we discern in the coarse-grained world of our perceptions, so Relativity shows that we cannot foretell the phenomena accompanying great velocities from the sluggish behavior of objects visible to man's indolent eye. Nor may we assume that the laws of Relativity deal with exceptional occurrences; on the contrary they provide a comprehensive picture of an incredibly complex universe in which the simple mechanical events of our earthly experience are the exceptions. The present-day scientist, coping with the tremendous velocities that prevail in the fast universe of the atom or with the immensities of sidereal space and time, finds the old Newtonian laws inadequate. But Relativity provides him in every instance with a complete and accurate description of nature.

25. Whenever Einstein's postulates have been put to test, their validity has been amply confirmed. Remarkable proof of the relativistic retarda-

tion of time intervals came out of an experiment performed by H. E. Ives of the Bell Telephone Laboratories in 1936. A radiating atom may be regarded as a kind of clock in that it emits light of a definite frequency and wavelength which can be measured with great precision by means of a spectroscope. Ives compared the light emitted by hydrogen atoms moving at high velocities with that emitted by hydrogen atoms at rest, and found that the frequency of vibration of the moving atoms was reduced in exact accordance with the predictions of Einstein's equations. Someday science may devise a far more interesting test of the same principle. Since any periodic motion serves to measure time, the human heart, Einstein has pointed out, is also a kind of clock. Hence, according to Relativity, the heartbeat of a person traveling with a velocity close to that of light would be relatively slowed, along with his respiration and all other physiological processes. He would not notice this retardation because his watch would slow down in the same degree. But judged by a stationary timekeeper he would "grow old" less rapidly. In a Buck Rogers realm of fantasy, it is possible to imagine some future cosmic explorer boarding an atom-propelled space ship, ranging the void at 167,000 miles per second, and returning to earth after ten terrestrial years to find himself physically only five years older.

COMMENTARY AND QUESTIONS

The name of Albert Einstein has long been a popular symbol for complicated theories and abstruse thought unintelligible to any but the most advanced scientist. While his theories often are necessarily complicated, many of the most significant of his conclusions, together with the line of reasoning upon which they are based, can nevertheless be at least partly explained in terms understandable to the non-scientist. To do just this was the task Lincoln Barnett set himself in *The Universe and Dr. Einstein*, from which this selection (Chapters 5, 6, and 7 in the book) was taken. His success is due largely to the combination of a thorough understanding of the concepts he is explaining with a more than ordinarily lucid expository style.

1. To work from the familiar to the unfamiliar (or the less familiar) is an old and indeed almost unavoidable rule in explaining complicated subjects. Find examples of this in pars. 1 and 2. Where else does the author use the ship illustration? Why does he use this illustration more than once?

2. For parts of his explanation, Barnett reverses the process suggested in question 1 by asking the reader to discard his sense of the familiar lest it be an obstacle to his grasping the new concepts being presented. What is the meaning of *subjective* and *objective* (pars. 11, 12, 14)?

Why is man called *earthbound* in par. 13? What irony is there in the use of the phrase *common sense* in par. 14 in the light of par. 23? Note how Barnett is careful in pars. 23 and 24 to re-unite in the reader his sense of the familiar and his awe at the unfamiliar by showing that the former is merely a special case of the latter. What is the effect of the peculiar combination of familiar and unfamiliar in the last half of par. 25?

3. Barnett in his book often achieves a certain dramatic quality by explaining a particular theory in some detail and then citing an exact experiment that either disproves or spectacularly confirms it. Why are the two such passages occurring in this selection placed near the ends of sections (that is, of chapters in the book)?

4. The publisher's jacket for this book asserts that it "can be understood by the high-school student of physics or chemistry and be read with admiration—as it has been—by Dr. Einstein." Defend or attack this statement.

5. Why is the moving observer in par. 17 said to be *precariously* perched atop the train? Why are the adjectives *sluggish* and *indolent* used (in par. 24)? Do they have more or less to do with the theory being explained than *precariously* in par. 17? Find examples of Barnett's phrasing or choice of illustrations that seem to you particularly helpful. Compare Barnett's style with that of Coates (pp. 101-110) and Langewiesche (pp. 122-134). Explain which likenesses and differences are due to variations in purpose and intended audience and which are due to variations in type of subject.

SUGGESTIONS FOR WRITING

1. Possible implications of a recent scientific theory.
2. Seeing ten years of sights in five years.
3. The limitations of man's senses.
4. "Common sense is actually nothing more than a deposit of prejudices laid down in the mind prior to the age of eighteen" (par. 23).

PART THREE

Evaluation

EVALUATION IS THAT TYPE OF WRITING WHICH IS CONCERNED
with judgment and interpretation, with criticism and appreciation. In
contrast to the material of explanation, which is objective, factual, and
provable, the material of evaluation is subjective and necessarily an expression of an individual point of view, which cannot be absolutely verified and must ultimately remain "a matter of opinion," but which does
impress the reader with its soundness and justice or with its lack of these
qualities.

This is not to say that the writer of evaluation does not use facts.
Facts must be offered in support of an opinion if the expression of that
opinion is to convince the reader, but in an evaluation the writer goes
beyond the facts because the facts in themselves are not as important to
him as the judgment or interpretation which he draws from them.

For example, E. B. White, in his evaluation of New York, gives his
reader a great many objective details, some of which would doubtless
be used by a geographer presenting a purely informative treatment of the
same subject; but White's essay is personal and individual. From it the
reader learns much about New York, but he also comes to know the author, his interests, his likes and dislikes, his opinions and his scale of
values.

Evaluation is not an abstruse art. The baby in his crib expressing
a preference for one rattle over another or the college student explaining to his roommate why he likes or dislikes a movie is evaluating. But
if one's evaluation is to be any more than an expression of a personal
whim it must be soundly based on facts; if it is not to seem a mere ex-

217

pression of prejudice it must give evidence that the writer has attempted to be fair, is not narrowly partisan, has considered the various significant qualities or characteristics of whatever he is discussing, and above all has not ignored evidence that would invalidate his appraisal or weaken the opinion that he is presenting.

The ability to make evaluations that are sound and just and are at the same time an individual expression of one's preference is surely one of the most important elements of intellectual maturity, regardless of the age of its fortunate possessor. "I trust his judgment" is praise indeed, and the writer who merits such praise has acquired a skill of the highest order.

Husbands: The New Servant Class

by RUSSELL LYNES

"I WISH I COULD," said my friend on the phone. "There's nothing I'd like better, but I'm up to my elbows in diapers." My friend is the father of two, the more recent one very recent indeed. I had asked him to play tennis, and when I hung up, my feeling was not one of surprise or pity; it was one of shame.

2. I didn't say to myself, "The poor henpecked fellow." I said, "Well, I guess I ought to be doing my household chores, too." The narrow-gauge train of thought that this set in motion, if you can call it thought, led me into elaborate speculation about the nature of husbands and the recent changes in their behavior around the house. How did it happen that my friend was diapering and I thought I ought to be waxing or dusting? What would my father have thought about this? I laughed out loud.

3. Then I was reminded of a remark that Bernard De Voto once made to a colleague of mine. "What every career woman needs," he said to her, "is a good wife." When he made this observation a number of years ago, the atmosphere of marriage was somewhat different from the atmosphere today. Only a woman with a career was then expected to have someone else assume the burdens of the household for her. It is only quite recently that (in cities and suburbs especially) every woman, regardless of her notions about a career, has adopted a different attitude. Now she takes it for granted that, when she marries, she is bound to get, almost as though it were a package deal, a husband who is also a part-time wife.

4. To call him a wife is, perhaps, to put it too bluntly. He is rather more servant than wife, though the distinction is sometimes a fine one. With a few interesting exceptions, the roles of the husband and wife are becoming less and less sharply differentiated. Whereas it was once a question of: "Who wears the pants in this family?" it is now a matter of pants all around, and the children are as likely to cling to Father's apron strings as Mother's. You may have noticed that, in recent years, women have come to refer to their husbands more and more often as their "mates"—a sexually indeterminate word and one that implies equal-

ity. Man, once known as "the head of the family," is now partner in the family firm, part-time man, part-time mother and part-time maid. He is the chief cook and bottle washer; the chauffeur, the gardener and the houseboy; the maid, the laundress and the charwoman.

5. If you are in any doubt that this is so, let me produce for you what are known as "the findings" of our favorite oracles, the pollsters. Crossley says that more than a third of the husbands in several of our northeastern states do the dishes, clean house and look after the children, and more than half of them do a lot of the shopping. The Gallup poll insists that 62 per cent of American husbands are intimate with dishwater and about 40 per cent help with the cooking. Kenneth Fink, director of the Princeton Research Service, has discovered that, in New York, 87 per cent of the young men from 21 to 29 help with the housework, but there seems to be some slight advantage in growing older. Only 70 per cent of men over 45 are part-time women. This suggests that patience and geriatrics may ultimately lick the husbands' domestic problem, but we shouldn't count on it.

6. How, I wondered as I put my tennis racket back in the closet, did women get into this frame of mind and men into this fix? What has happened to the shape and texture of family life in America? What has become of the servants of another day? What sort of men are we turning into with our aprons and safety pins and dishpan hands? If it is anybody's fault, whose fault is it? What drives this creature, the man who is part-time wife, and what keeps him in order? It is a puzzling lot of questions, but let's look.

7. The pollsters' findings suggest the first of our questions: How did men get in this fix? And that question cannot be answered without looking at how the position of women has changed and without finding out what has become of yesterday's servants.

8. It is doubtful that when men let women have the vote, back in 1920, they foresaw the sort of social revolution that they were letting loose on themselves. It is unlikely that they caught the slightest glimmer of a future in which they would share not only the political decisions of the nation with women, but also the dishpan and the oven and the mop. Actually, the revolution started long before the nineteenth amendment was adopted; it goes back to the time before the turn of the century when men discovered that they would rather have women run the typewriters in offices than run them themselves, and the business career woman, as we know her today, first got a finger hold in man's world. Imperceptibly at first, the distinctions between man's world and woman's world began to blur. Men stopped giving their seats to women on buses and subways and taking off their hats when women entered ele-

vators. "If they are going to compete in our world," men reasoned, "then they should be treated as men."

9. From the man's point of view, this was a major tactical blunder. He ought to have realized that he should preserve at all costs such distinctions as remained between men and women, and he should have kept the line clean as to what was expected of each. But once he had allowed the social differences of the sexes to be played down, it is only logical that he should ultimately have found himself assuming some of the functions of women. In this sense, the man in the apron has no one to blame but himself.

10. But it would be unfair to give the impression that the amount of housework performed by men is entirely the result of connivance by women or of their attempts to invade man's world. The gradual shrinking of the old servant class explains part of what has happened. Our changing ideas of what constitutes personal success explains another part, as does the shift in our notions about what makes the ideal family. What has happened is partly an economic phenomenon, partly an industrial and mechanical one and partly a social one.

11. The recent story of the servant class in America might be called "The Transformation of Bridie; or Who Stole the Upstairs Maid from Mrs. Cabot's Mansion?" Bridies and Maggies and Hildas by the hundreds of thousands arrived in America from many parts of Europe in the sixty years that followed the Civil War. Domestic service was the best employment they could find, and it was also the quickest way for them to learn the customs and manners of the new country. Households with six or seven Bridies, and their male counterparts, were not uncommon before World War I, and the "servant class" was a rigidly stratified society (within a much more fluid one) where everyone was supposed to "know his place."

12. It was World War I that took the duster out of Bridie's hand and replaced it with a wrench. War factories were hungry for workers, and they offered better wages and shorter hours than housewives could afford to give. After the war, in the frantic twenties, some of the Bridies went back to their old jobs; and in the depression years of the thirties, families that could afford servants found them in plentiful supply. It was war again in 1941 that emancipated the cooks and maids and butlers, and ever since that time, the number of women in domestic service has steadily dwindled. Before World War I, more women worked at domestic service than at any other kind of job; now, with more women employed than ever before in what we like to call peacetime, domestic service ranks fifth.

13. Something had to fill the undusted and unwashed gap between

the career woman and her home. As more and more married women took full-time and part-time jobs, more and more mechanical gadgets were invented to lighten the burdens of housework. Someone, however, had to help run the gadgets for the nine and a quarter million married women who worked. And now we begin to see the answer to the question of how men got themselves into their present domestic fix.

14. Henry Dreyfuss, the industrial designer, has called American women "gadget-conscious mammals." But it is well known that if you want to get an American male to do manual labor, he is a sucker for anything that whirs or hums or lights up. He is wafted aloft like the pilot of a jet; he becomes "the man at the controls," a Walter Mitty. He identifies himself far more easily with the flying saucer than with the saucer in the sink, and women know this.

15. With the war over and servants increasingly hard to come by, especially at prices that middle-class families could afford, washing machines, dishwashers, freezers, electric floor waxers and a multiplicity of other devices from mixers to mangles flooded the gadget shops (called appliance stores) which suddenly appeared on main streets of towns everywhere. Men, with their supposed superior knowledge of mechanical things, were consulted for the first time on the purchase of expensive pieces of domestic equipment, and before you could say "Change the water after each using," they were running them. As domestically unskilled labor, husbands came to pride themselves on being able to operate machines which manufacturers had so designed that they practically ran themselves.

16. But the scarcity of servants and the flood of gadgets that could be bought on time payments tell only part of the story of man's new captivity by women. World War II tore many families apart, and when they were put back together again, a strange new domestic pattern emerged that was quite unlike anything Americans had ever seen before. Millions of veterans went to college or to professional or trade schools on the GI bill. Many of these men were married and had small children, and in order to make ends meet, young wives went out and got jobs. Father, who had learned to make beds, darn socks and police up in the Army, was left with his books and his babies and his broom. He became not only a wife but a mother, and he was grateful for the chance to reestablish his life in this way, hopeful that the day would come when he might take off his apron and get out in the world. Those were the days when men used to gather in the self-service laundry and swap stories as they once had in the corner bar.

17. With our usual adaptability we have taken the shortage of servants, the influx of gadgets, the domestic skills that men learned as sol-

diers, the new role of women and the docility of men, and out of them have created a new mode of life. Our image of the ideal family has changed from one in which Father laid down the law while Mother made the wheels go round to something far more like a team roughly the size and character of a basketball team. The ball is passed from hand to hand and the responsibility is shared by everybody.

18. At the same time, we have become devoted to what Frederick Lewis Allen has called "the cult of informality." With nobody to cook and serve dinner at a given hour, we eat when we please and where we please—in the living room, in the back yard, in the kitchen. Not so long ago, most families, whether they could afford servants or not, used to observe many of the same formalities observed in families who were elaborately waited on. Now the families who can still afford servants affect many of the informalities of those who have none. The tables, you might say, have been turned into trays on the lap, the sit-down dinner has become a feast of squat-and-scramble. Some member of the family is always on his feet fetching something from the kitchen. Families, like toasters, have become pop-up, and Father no longer sits and is waited on.

19. My friend who couldn't play tennis because of the diapers is the servant-father in just such a family, and so, according to the poll takers, are a majority of the other husbands in America.

20. Briefly, then, this is how men have got themselves into what is not only a new role but a new frame of mind, and this brings us abruptly to the question of what sort of man is this member of the new servant class? How does he think of himself and what keeps him going? It will take him a long time to fight his way out of the cage that he has helped to build for himself. It has been men, we must remember, who have invented, promoted and sold the mechanical gadgets that now enslave them, though they did it in the name of making the little woman's burden lighter. Also, it is men who have fought for the shorter work week so that they might, as it has turned out, have longer week ends to clean out the cellar and paint the shutters and more hours in the evening to help with the dishes. They have made their own beds, and now they must lie in them. Furthermore, the chances are that they must get up in the morning and make them again.

21. It is too soon to divide husbands into neat categories within the new servant class. They are a higgledy-piggledy lot, self-assertive at the same time that many of them (but by no means all) are docile. There are those who complain bitterly that they have lost their freedom; there are as many others who take the new shape of the family for granted. But before housemaid's knee gets to be known as husband's knee, let us examine some of the motives that make the members of the new servant

class behave as they do. Some of these motives lie deep in the natures of men; others have to do with the nature of the times we live in.

22. In the first place, we must consider the part that vanity, as strong and timeless a motive as any, plays in the behavior of the husband-servant. It is no secret to women that female vanity is usually a means to an end, but that male vanity is an end in itself. It is also no secret that male vanity is easily played upon by sensible and clever women, even the nicest of women, and that its proper manipulation is the most reliable means of converting a husband into an adequate servant. There are two main techniques for applying the alchemy that turns the leaden mate into the golden slave. One is challenge and the other is flattery.

23. More often than not, the man with the hammer in his hand or with the waxer whirring at his feet is so employed because his wife has either suggested that he might not be clever enough or strong enough or skillful enough to do the job, or because she has implied that nobody could do it as well as he. ("Darling," she says, "I suppose it's too big a job for you, but . . ." or "Would you mind? Nobody can make it glisten the way you can.") In either case, something more than just family responsibility has spurred his efforts. It is vanity as surely as it is muscle that drives the nail or brings the floor to a gleam. But vanity goes further than merely sweetening the occasional chore; it plays its part in the performance of the routine job as well.

24. It is difficult to isolate vanity from any of the other deep-seated motives that cause men to assume their new share of household chores, for it runs through their performance of most of them. But we must make a distinction here between those chores that are traditionally the jobs of servants and those which have been regarded as what a man was expected "to do around the house."

25. Maintenance has, to a very great extent, always been Father's job. When he could afford not to do it himself, he ordered it done, but, in either case, it came within his domain and not his wife's. So it is in the maintenance jobs that the man feels at home with himself, for it is easier for him to picture himself with a hammer in his hand than with a dustpan and brush. He is happier when called upon to repair the screens or fix a drawer that sticks than he is when he is expected to make a bed. He likes those jobs that not only are traditionally man's work but also have a certain permanence about them. Beds never stay made nor dishes clean, but a new screen in the front door is good for years and a man can point to such a job with a pride of accomplishment.

26. "Do it yourself" is a byword of our day, and it is a slogan that applies to more than just maintenance and building—to fixing a faucet or adding a room on the house—it describes a frame of mind that typifies

the new husband better than anything else. Doing it ourselves is our answer to more than just the high cost of labor; it is our reply to the machine which has assumed so many of the functions that we have always considered to be our own. We are reclaiming in our small ways what technology has taken away from us in big ways. In performing our small chores, whether they are maintenance jobs or even servants' jobs, we are expressing our freedom from the bigness and impersonality of the world in which we earn our living and in which most of us are cogs and a few of us are wheels. But this is a large generality about a large motive. What does it mean in the communities in which we live?

27. It has come to pass that a man sharing the jobs of the household with his wife is an increasingly accepted part of the pattern of American family life. Indeed, in many communities, a man who doesn't help with the dishes and the dusting and the beds is regarded as only half a man. He is considered lazy or overbearing, or he is thought not to love his wife and children. Furthermore, he is selfish and he is failing to "fulfill" himself, and these epithets are not applied to him just by women but by other men in the community as well. Probably, however, none of them accurately describes him. It would be nearer the truth to say that he is out of date, living in a world that is gone and is not likely to return. He is the vestigial remnant of another age in which a man's position in the community was measured by the number of people who contributed to his creature comforts rather than by what he contributed to the community.

28. Whether we like it or not (and we apparently like it or we wouldn't put up with it on such a scale), the new pattern of life with the husband as a working member of the cast rather than as a spoiled financial backer has become the commonly accepted standard of urban and suburban life. We have allowed a social revolution to take place, not because of outside pressures on us but because we wanted it to. In a country with as vast wealth as ours, we could, if that were what we wanted, maintain a traditional servant class, but that did not suit us. We wanted everybody to have as much spiritual elbow room and as much chance to determine his own way of life as possible.

29. If not many people wanted to go on being servants, that was all right with most of the rest of us; we just moved over a little and took on some of their work while, quite literally, they took on some of ours. They moved into our corner of the labor market, and so we had to take on the chores that they used to perform for us. And we saw to it that we had time to do them. We cut down on our work week at the office and the factory, and we set about to produce the gadgets that would make being our own servants as painless as possible.

[30] But, further than that, we have made a game out of our new system. We have taken to the informal life, the life without the old and often suffocating airs and graces of formality, and moved it out of doors where it has become a picnic, or into the living room where it has become a party. We have divided up the chores so that every member of the family does his share, and the work is disposed of in concert. Mother is no longer the lonely slave in her kitchen or, as some pampered women used to say, a slave to her servants. She is now, at worst, a slave among slaves. Her sentence has been commuted from labor in solitary confinement to light housework, with the children gaily demolishing dishes at her elbow and her husband singing glees to the accompaniment of the humming refuse grinder.

[31] If you are in any doubt that husbands as a servant class are here to stay, let me point out to you a familiar but significant phenomenon. There are still a good many men in America who can well afford to have servants and do, indeed, have staffs of them. But these same men like to play at being servants themselves in much the same spirit that Marie Antoinette played at milkmaid at the Petit Trianon before the French Revolution. On their penthouse terraces or beside their swimming pools, they preside over a barbecue in chef's cap and apron, clutching long forks in asbestos-gloved hands. They are, in their quaint and self-conscious way, imitating the men who take their household chores as a matter of course.

[32] They are trying to be in the swim, for it has not only become necessary but it seems also to have become chic for husbands not only to stand and wait but also to serve.

COMMENTARY AND QUESTIONS

This essay, written for *Look* by the managing editor of *Harper's Magazine*, aims at interesting a wide variety of readers in a serious subject.

1. What is the function of par. 1? What would Lynes have lost by merely reporting the conversation instead of directly quoting it?
2. What is the function of par. 6? Explain the relationship of par. 7 to par. 6. At what point does Lynes complete his answer to the question in par. 7? Which of the questions asked in par. 6 is answered in pars. 20-27, and which in pars. 28-32? What purposes are served by the first five paragraphs of the essay? Notice that the first sentence of par. 6 refers to the author's tennis racket. In what other places is tennis referred to, and what is gained by these references? Notice the positions at which these references are found.

3. Par. 10 is a good example of a transitional paragraph. Which parts of it are more closely related to the immediately preceding paragraphs and which to the immediately following ones? Show that the paragraph is essentially well unified. Find at least one other transitional paragraph in this essay.

4. In this essay Lynes is presenting an evaluation not only of a group of people—modern husbands—but also of what he calls a social revolution. What attitude toward this revolution does he adopt initially: does he welcome or deplore it? Consider some of the ways in which he reveals this attitude. Why does he modify this attitude as he further develops the subject? In what circumstances is it appropriate to modify the tone one has initially adopted in an essay of evaluation?

5. Sometimes it is possible for two words to mean essentially the same thing but to convey entirely different impressions. For example, if you find a policeman about to put a parking ticket on your car, you may address him as "officer" when you are explaining that you left your car just a minute before to get a nickel for the meter, but later, among friends, you may refer to him as "flatfoot," especially if he has insisted on presenting you with the ticket. And the difference between "flatfoot" and "officer" will not be merely the difference between formal and informal diction. Rewrite each of the following passages in a way that retains the meaning of the original but alters the impression it makes on the reader:
   a. "Now she takes it for granted that, when she marries, she is bound to get, almost as though it were a package deal, a husband who is also a part-time wife" (par. 3).
   b. "How . . . did women get into this frame of mind and men into this fix?" (par. 6).
   c. "the man in the apron has no one to blame but himself" (par. 9).
   d. "flood of gadgets" (par. 16).
   e. "Briefly, then, this is how men have got themselves into what is . . . a new role" (par. 20).
   f. "the new pattern of life with the husband as a working member of the cast" (par. 28).

6. In this essay Lynes has the problem of gaining and holding the interest of his readers in the changed status of husbands. He does this largely by employing a specific, concrete, and often metaphorical style. Rephrase each of the following statements in more abstract and general terms, considering what is lost or gained in the rephrasing:
   a. "Whereas it was once a question of: 'Who wears the pants in this family?' it is now a matter of pants all around, and the children are as likely to cling to Father's apron strings as Mother's" (par. 4).
   b. "The Gallup poll insists that 62 per cent of American husbands are intimate with dishwater . . ." (par. 12).
   c. "It was World War I that took the duster out of Bridie's hand and replaced it with a wrench" (par. 12).

d. "Something had to be done to fill the undusted and unwashed gap between the career woman and her home" (par. 13).

7. Consider the appropriateness of the following metaphors: "Families, like toasters, have become pop-up" (par. 18); "the career business woman first got a finger hold in man's world" (par. 8). Note here Lynes's facility in turning a well-worn metaphor into something fresh and effective. Find an example of the same technique in par. 20 and another in par. 26.

8. This essay, like Ruth Benedict's "Are Families Passé?" (pp. 228-237), is a study of a sociological subject. Discuss the main differences in the ways in which the authors of these two essays handle their material. How do these differences reflect differences in the readers for whom each essay is intended?

SUGGESTIONS FOR WRITING

1. The American husband as I see him.
2. My experience with "Do It Yourself."
3. Junior's ideas about Father's new role.
4. The new status of women.

Are Families Passé?

by RUTH BENEDICT

A GREAT MANY PEOPLE today speak as if the family were in some special sort of danger in our times. We hear a great deal about "saving the family" and about "preserving the home." Authors and lecturers describe how the family is threatened by divorce, or by mothers who work outside of the home, or by unemployment, or by lack of religious training of children. Each of them, depending on his experience in his own home

Chapter IX, "The Family: *Genus Americanum*," by Ruth Benedict in *The Family: Its Function and Destiny*, edited by Ruth Nanda Anshen. Reprinted by permission of the Publishers. Copyright 1949 by Harper & Row, Publishers, Incorporated. Published in slightly condensed form under the title "Are Families Passé?" in *The Saturday Review of Literature*, December 25, 1948.

and on his observations in the families he knows, selects something which he thinks should be changed—or should be preserved—and says that, if this or that were done, the family would be "saved."

2. To an anthropologist such phrasings are dangerously misleading. He has studied the family among naked savages and in contemporary civilizations and he knows that it has survived in all human societies known in the record of mankind. Just as surely he knows that the family takes all kinds of different forms. It is not merely that unlettered primitive nomads have family arrangements different from Western industrial nations; even in Western nations around the Atlantic shores the family differs profoundly. The ethics of marriage, the specific close emotional ties which the family fosters, the disciplines and freedoms for the child, the nature of the dependency of the children upon the parents, even the personnel which makes up the family—all these differ in Western civilized nations. The anthropologist knows that the changes taking place in the home in any decade in any country do not mean that the family is now about to disintegrate under our eyes unless we do something about it. The problem as he states it is quite different: how do legal and customary arrangements in the family tally with the arrangements and premises of the whole way of life which is valued in any tribe or nation? If, for instance, the father has a heavy, authoritarian hand upon his children, the anthropologist asks: Is this in keeping with authoritarianism in the state and in industry? Or is it at odds with a society which values nonauthoritarianism and the pursuit of happiness? He asks the same kind of question about a nation's laws of inheritance from father to son, about the divorce laws, about the architectural layout of the house, about the reasons that are given to children when they are told to be good.

3. Customs enshrined in the family in any tribe or nation are likely to be sensitively adjusted to the values and customs of each particular people. This is no mystic correspondence; the persons who make up the family are the same people who are the citizens of that nation—the business men, the farmers, the churchgoers or non-churchgoers, the readers of newspapers, and the listeners to the radio. In all their roles they are molded more or less surely into a people with certain habits, certain hopes, and a certain *esprit de corps.* Americans come to share certain slogans, behavior, and judgments which differ from those of Frenchmen or Czechs. This is inevitable. And in the process the role of the family also becomes different. By the same token, just as economic and political changes occur over a period of time in the United States or in France or in Czechoslovakia, the family also changes.

4. An anthropologist, therefore, when he reads about the failure of the family, finds in such criticism a somewhat special meaning. He re-

members how often the family is made a convenient whipping boy among many peoples who disapprove of the way their world is going. He has seen it in Amazon jungles and on the islands of the Pacific. The author remembers an American Indian tribe which used to talk about the family in a most uncomplimentary fashion. They were a people who, not long before, had roamed over the great plains hunting buffalo and proving their courage by war exploits. Now they lived on a reservation, and tending crops was no adequate substitute for their old way of life. Their old economic arrangements of boastful gift giving, their political life, and their religious practices had either been destroyed by circumstances or had lost their old meaningfulness. Life had become pointless to them. These men talked with gusto about the failure of the family. They said that in the family the children no longer learned manners, or religion, or generosity, or whatever it was the individual Indian favored as a cure-all. The family, too, weighed a man down, they said; it was a burden to him.

5. To the anthropologist studying this tribe, however, the family was precisely the best arranged, most trustworthy institution in their whole culture. It was hard beset and it had not escaped the tragic effects of the general disintegration of tribal life, but it was what provided the warm, human ties and the dependable security which were left in that Indian tribe. The children were loved and cared for, the husbands and wives often had comfortable relations with each other, and family hospitality had a graciousness that was absent in more public life. At birth and marriage and death the family still functioned as an effective institution. And there seemed to be no man or woman of childbearing age who was not married or would not have preferred to be.

6. The writer thinks of this Indian tribe when she hears Americans talk about the decay of the family. Instead of viewing the family with such alarm, suppose we look at it as it exists in this decade in this country and see how it is arranged to fulfill its functions in American schemes of life. Let us leave aside for the moment the questions of whether conditions are provided that would keep it from preventable overstrain and of whether as human beings we are able to get all the satisfaction we might out of this institution; let us consider only the arrangements of the family as we know it and how these fit in with our values and with the way we should like to plan our lives.

7. Suppose we take marriage first. Marriage sets up the new family, and it seems to make a great deal of difference whether a society dictates that the new home shall be begun in tears and heartache or with rejoicing. Many human societies would not recognize a marriage without a wailing bride and a sullen groom. Often the bride has to be surrounded

by her mourning women, who lament her coming lifelong separation from her parents and her brothers and sisters, as well as her future misery as she goes to work for her mother-in-law. Often they cut her long hair and remove her jewelry as a sign that she is now a worker and no longer alluring. The groom's role, too, may be that of an unwilling victim. Often marriages are arranged by the parents without giving the two young people any chance to know each other.

8. All these circumstances are absent in marriage in the United States. The young people are hardly hampered in their choice of a mate; if occasionally parents deplore their choice, public opinion allows the young couple to outface them and expects the parents to accept the inevitable with as much decency as they can muster. We expect that the bride and groom will be in love or will have chosen each other for reasons known to themselves. Whether they marry for love or for money or to show they can win a sought-after mate from a rival, in any case they are making a personal choice and are not acting on command. Because in every field of life American culture puts such a high value on this kind of freedom and so bitterly resents its curtailment in peace time, the fact that young people do make their own choice of a mate is an important and auspicious arrangement. The arranged marriage which is traditional in France or the careful class restrictions which have been observed in Holland would be difficult to manage in the United States. The wide range of choice of a mate and the fact that the young people make their own selection are conditions which could hardly be made more satisfactory for Americans with their particular habits and demands.

9. After marriage, too, the new family has a wide range of choices about where to live, how the wife shall occupy herself, when to start a family, and a host of other important matters. Such freedom is extremely unusual in the world. Sometimes the couple must live with the husband's family, sometimes with the wife's. Often in other countries, until one or two children are born, the young man continues to work for his father and has no say about the farm or the flock and no money which he can control. But in the United States a young couple plans the family budget before the wedding and what they earn is theirs to spend.

10. The way the new family in this country sets up its own separate home makes possible a rare and delightful circumstance: the two of them can have an incomparable privacy. No matter how hard it has been to arrange for privacy before marriage, as soon as the wedding is over everybody expects them to have their own latch key and their own possessions around them. If they cannot manage this, they feel cheated and other people think something is wrong. It is the same if they have to give a home to a parent. In most civilized countries this is a duty to which as

a good son and good daughter they are bound, but if it is necessary in the United States their friends and neighbors will regard them as exceptionally burdened. Even the scarcity and high wages of domestic servants give the young family a greater privacy. Considering that they have chosen each other to their own liking, this privacy in the home is made to order to gratify them; the only problem is whether they can use it to their own happiness.

11. When they cannot, and when they find that their choice of a mate was not fool-proof just because they made it on their own, there is in the United States great freedom to get a divorce. Our growing divorce rate is the subject of much viewing-with-alarm; yet in a culture built as ours is on ever expanding personal choice, an important goal of which is the pursuit of happiness, the right to terminate an unhappy marriage is the other side of the coin of which the fair side is the right to choose one's spouse. Weak and stunted individuals will of course abuse both privileges, yet it is difficult to see how divorce could consistently be denied in a culture like ours. Certainly if we accepted it more honestly as a necessary phase of our way of life, however sorrowful, and put honest effort and sympathy into not penalizing the divorced, we should be acting more appropriately and in our own best interests. At any rate, the high divorce rate in the United States is no attack on marriage, for it is precisely the divorced—those who have failed in one or two attempts—who have the highest rate of marriage. Between the ages of twenty-five and thirty-five not even the unmarried or the widowed marry at so great a rate as the divorced.

12. Besides free choice and privacy, the American family has unusual potential leisure because of the labor-saving devices, prepared foods, and ready-made clothes available under modern conditions. The basic labor-saver is running water in the sink, and Americans have little idea how many millions of homes in civilized countries do not have it. Thus we are saved an endless round of drudgery that ties down women—and men also—in countries where homes have no running water, no gas and electricity, no farm tools but those which are driven into the earth by human hands or are swung in human arms, and no use of ready-made soaps and foods and clothes. Americans put high value on lessened drudgery, but they deprecate having free spaces of truly leisure time; the more time they save the more they fill up their days and nights with a round of engagements and complications. They are unwilling to admit that they have leisure, but the schedules of their lives prove clearly how much they have.

13. Universal schooling in the United States also frees the family of many duties when children have come. It is hard for Americans to imag-

ine the difference which regular school hours make in a mother's role. For a great part of the working day, American children are the responsibility of the teacher and not of the mother. As nursery schools spread over the country, younger and younger children get trained care outside the home and the mother's labors are correspondingly relieved. As the children grow older the mother's leisure increases, until finally she reaches that idle middle age with its round of card parties and clubs and window shopping and movies which engross and waste the energy of so many millions of American women. Her husband is earning more money now than when he was younger, and her children have flown; she has a plethora of privileges and freedom and leisure. In one sense she has everything.

14. It is obviously unfair to talk about the incomparable freedom from drudgery which the American home offers without emphasizing that interval of a few years when there is no leisure for the mother in the home —the years when the babies are little. In our great cities where each family is strange to all the others, a mother is likely to have to be baby tender every hour of the day, with no one to relieve her. Along with these duties she must do all her cooking and washing and cleaning. And, as all our magazines and women's pages reiterate, she must make efforts to keep her husband. She must keep herself looking attractive, must keep up social contacts, and be a companion to him. To European wives this program looks formidable. "I was always told that American women were so free," a Polish woman said to me, "but when I came here and saw how they had to manage with the babies and the house without any older women of the family to help, and then how they had to play around with their husbands in the evening to keep them happy, I decided I wouldn't change places with them for anything. In Poland a woman doesn't have to 'keep' her husband; it's all settled when they're married."

15. The striking fact about the nursery years in the United States is that in comparison with those in other countries they are so short and that nevertheless we do not really treat them as an interim. Mothers who are going through this period give remarkably little thought to the leisure that will come soon. They are often vocal enough about the turmoil of their present lives, and sometimes bitter, but the fact that the nursery years last so short a time in the United States and could be treated as an interim—like a professor's going into the government during war time— is all too seldom part of their thinking. No doubt this is due in part to a lag in our culture, since even with our grandparents conditions were different; but in part it is a result of the sentiment which selects this period, no matter how short, as the fulfillment of a woman's chief duty in life. A social engineer looking at the family, however, would certainly put his

major effort into better arrangements for the overburdened mother during these years and into thinking about effecting some transition from this period into that next one during which, in the United States, millions of women become idle parasites upon society—and dull and unhappy into the bargain.

16. Another notable feature of the American family is its peculiarly non-authoritarian character. The old rule that a child should be seen and not heard and the adage, "Spare the rod and spoil the child," are anachronistic in the United States; they are dispensed with even in immigrant groups which honored them in their native country. The rule of the father over the family is still a reality in some European nations, but in the United States the mother is the chief responsible agent in bringing up her children; here the father's opinions are something the children are more likely to play off against the mother's, to their own advantage, rather than a court of last authority from which there is no appeal. Children take the noisy center of the stage at the breakfast table and in the living room in a way that is quite impossible in European countries. The fact that they are expected to know right from wrong in their tenderest years and to act upon it on their own is often commented on by European mothers who have lived here. A Dutch mother once spoke to the author about how hard we are on our children because we expect this of them; she said, "I don't expect it of my children before they are seven; until then, I am there to see that they act correctly." But an American mother expects a child of three or four to be a responsible moral agent, and she gives him great latitude in which to prove that he can manage his little affairs by himself.

17. All this lack of strong authoritarianism in American families accords well with the values that are chiefly sought after in this country. No strong father image is compatible with our politics or our economics. We seek the opportunity to prove that we are as good as the next person, and we do not find comfort in following an authoritarian voice—in the state or in the home, from the landowner or the priest—which will issue a command from on high. We learn as children to measure ourselves against Johnny next door, or against Mildred whose mother our mother knows in church, and this prepares us for living in a society with strongly egalitarian ideals. We do not learn the necessity of submitting to unquestioned commands as the children of many countries do. The family in the United States has become democratic.

18. These free-choice and non-authoritarian aspects of the family, along with its privacy and potential leisure, evidence only a few of the many ways in which it has become consistent with major emphases in our national life. They seem, when one compares them with arrange-

ments in other civilized nations, to be quite well fitted to the role the family must play in a culture like the United States. This does not mean, however, that Americans capitalize to their own advantage upon all these consistently contrived arrangements which are institutionalized in the family as we know it. At the beginning of this essay two subjects were left for later discussion—how well our society protects the family from dangerous overstrain, and how well as human beings with special insights and blind spots we are able to get all the satisfactions we might out of our version of the home. These two subjects cannot be omitted.

19. In spite of all our American sentiment about the home and the family, we do not show great concern about buttressing it against catastrophe. Any well-considered national program must have regard for the children; if they are housed and fed below a certain minimum, if their health is not attended to, the nation suffers in the next generation. The lack of a tolerable economic floor under the family is especially crucial in a society like that of the United States, where competition is so thoroughly relied upon as an incentive and where so few families have anything but the weekly pay envelope to use for food and doctors' bills. When factories close, when inflation comes, the family gets little consideration in the United States. Especially in economic crises it gets the little end of the horn. Today the necessity of providing tens of thousands of new homes is of the greatest importance for healthy family life in the United States, but adequate housing programs are notoriously unsupported. Sickness insurance, too, which would provide preventive care as well as relieve the family budget of all expenses in a crisis, needs high priority in a national program. When one reads about families in trouble, it is clear that many of the reefs which are threatening shipwreck are avoidable by intelligent local, state, or national programs. Such programs have worked satisfactorily in non-communist countries—as, for instance, in the Scandinavian nations. But they cost money, and Americans have not been willing to be taxed for the sake of taking the excessive strain off the family and providing better circumstances for growing children. It could be done, and if it were done the incidental disadvantages of our highly competitive and unregulated economic system would be largely removed; it should be the surest way to ensure the successful continuance of what is known as the democratic way of life.

20. Besides this American political attitude toward the family, there is also a very different difficulty which threatens it. We have seen how as an institution it is particularly tailored to American ways of living. But the very best suit of clothes may be badly worn by a careless and irresponsible person. So, too, people may abuse a home well designed to suit them. It is no less true of marriage and the family. These exist as

institutions remarkably well adjusted to American life. But many Americans are miserably unable to achieve happiness within them.

21. It is of course easy to say that a culture like that of the United States, which allows individuals so much free choice among alternatives, is asking a great deal of human beings. In social life, as in literature, some of the finest human achievements have been within restrictions as rigid as those of the sonnet form. Our American culture is more like a sprawling novel where every page may deal with a new encounter and with a special choice. We ask a great deal of individuals when we give them such wide latitude and so little respected authority. But the United States is built on the premise that this is possible, and if ever we as a people decide otherwise our nation will change beyond recognition. We shall have lost the very thing we have been trying to build in this country.

22. It must not be imagined that this craving for individual freedom is what prevents Americans from enjoying the family as much as it might be enjoyed. In so far as the family is an overheavy economic burden on some wage earners, a more careful welfare program could take care of this complaint. Certainly women and children have a freedom in the American family which is hard to match elsewhere in the world, and from all portents this will probably increase rather than diminish.

23. The crucial difficulty in American happiness in marriage is, rather, a certain blind spot which is especially fostered in our privileged United States. An extreme instance of this was mentioned in connection with the millions of idle, middle-aged wives in this country. These are women who as a group are well set up and favored beyond any such great numbers of women in any other part of the world. But privilege to them is separate from responsibility. Comparatively few of them feel that it is compatible with their status to do responsible work in which they have had experience in their own households and which must now be done outside their homes, and few take the initiative in getting the training they would need in jobs which they can see need to be done—except in war time. In periods of peace they have a blind spot about what it takes to live happily. For that the motto is *noblesse oblige,* or, "Privilege obligates one to do something in return."

24. It is not only the middle-aged woman who accepts privilege without a sense of obligation. In marriage, the right of both men and women to choose their mates freely is a privilege which carries with it, if they are to live happily, an accompanying conviction that when things go wrong it is doubly their obligation—to themselves as well as to their spouses—to deal tolerantly. Perhaps a young man realizes that his wife is more petulant than he knew; exactly because he chose her, however, she is "a poor thing; but his own." Privileged as he was to choose her, he has a corresponding responsibility.

25. It is the same with children. In the United States the reason for having children is not, as it is in most of the world, the perpetuation of the family line down many generations. In most countries people have children because there must be someone to till the piece of land in the village where the family has lived for centuries, there must be an heir to inherit the *Hof*, or there must be a son to perform the ancestral rites. In our atomistic American families these motivations seldom arise. We have children, not because our parents are sitting in judgment, not because of the necessity of having an heir, but because we personally want them—whether as company in the home or to show our friends we can have them. It is a privileged phase of parenthood, and if it is to bring us happiness it implies an acceptance of responsibility. Nothing is all pleasure in this life, and bringing up two or three noisy children in our small urban apartments is no exception to the rule. But with us it is based on choice—far more than it is elsewhere in the world—and we can only make the most of a choice if we follow it through wholeheartedly in all its implications.

26. It is partly because of this blind spot in the American family, this walling off of privilege from responsibility and tolerance, that we so often ask of life an average happiness—as if it could be presented to us on a platter. Full normal happiness only comes to men and women who give as well as take—who, in this instance, give themselves warmly to their family life, and do not merely arrogate to themselves the rights they are so freely allowed in our society. In the United States, if happiness proves impossible they can get a divorce; but, until they have made this decision, they can capitalize on their privileges only if they bind around their arms the motto "Privilege has its obligations."

27. The family in the United States is an institution remarkably adapted to our treasured way of life. The changes that are occurring in it do not mean that it is decaying and needs to be saved. It offers a long array of privileges. It needs more consideration in political tax-supported programs, by means of which many difficulties that beset it could be eradicated. Finally, Americans, in order to get the maximum happiness out of such a free institution as the family in the United States, need to parallel their privileges with an awakening responsibility. It is hard to live up to being so privileged as we are in the United States, but it is not impossible.

COMMENTARY AND QUESTIONS

1. This essay was written by one of America's most distinguished anthropologists. The title of the selection, as it appears in a book of essays by various authorities on the family, is "The Family: *Genus Amer-*

icanum." Do you think that this is or is not a better title than the one we have used here, which is the title under which the essay appeared in *The Saturday Review of Literature?* Why?

2. In pars. 1-5 appears a contrast between two ways of looking at the same thing. How does this contrast serve as an introduction to the body of the essay?

3. Note other comparisons and contrasts in the first eighteen paragraphs of this essay. What purpose do they serve? How do they help to answer the question asked by the title?

4. What is the purpose of pars. 6 and 18?

5. Often an author, having presented an evaluation of a subject, wishes to persuade his readers that certain actions should be taken. Pars. 14 and 23 are on the same topic. Is there any difference in the way the author is handling her material in the two paragraphs? Why could the order of the two paragraphs not be reversed?

6. What purpose is served by the concluding paragraph?

7. How does the style of this essay differ from that described in "How to Write Like a Social Scientist" (pp. 519-523)?

SUGGESTIONS FOR WRITING

1. Is the small town passé?
2. Is the large city passé?
3. The family as I see it.
4. Democracy vs. authoritarianism in school and home.
5. The advantages and disadvantages of the American emphasis on individual, personal freedom.

English and American Education:

Depth versus Breadth

by SIR GEOFFREY CROWTHER

FOR THE PAST THREE YEARS I have been engaged, with my colleagues of the Central Advisory Council on Education in England, in a comprehensive study of the English educational system. I had some of my own education in the United States, and I have been a frequent visitor to America ever since. This double experience has bred in me a growing sense of astonishment that two countries which share the same language, so many of the same cultural traditions and ways of life, whose political, religious, and social aspirations are so largely identical, should have educational systems so utterly different as to provide almost no basis for a comparison between them.

2. That is a strong statement, and my present purpose is to try to justify it. Let me first say, however, that I have no intention whatever of trying to show that one national system is, on balance, better than the other; only that they are much more different than is usually realized.

3. The American and the English educational systems are different in purpose, structure, and method. Let us start with purpose. The two systems grew up in response to very different pressures and needs. In America, you have always been very conscious of the need to build up a new society. You have wanted to construct something bigger, richer, better than you have. This is said to arise from something in the American national character, but that seems to me to turn the logic upside down; it is the American national character that has arisen from the circumstances in which the American people have found themselves. From the start it was necessary to create a supply of ministers of religion, of lawyers, and of skilled artisans—I place them in the order of importance in which they were regarded at the time. Later on there came the obvious necessity of incorporating the great waves of immigrants into your society. Still later came the great task, in which you are still engaged, of knitting your varied economic, social, and racial groups into the harmonious and balanced society in which the principles of democratic government can work properly.

4. Consciously or unconsciously, American education has at all times been designed to serve these social purposes. It has been regarded as an instrument by which society can build its own future. From its nature, it has inescapably been concerned with the rank and file of the people. Its chief concern for many generations has been to do something to the masses—and I think the word is *to,* not *for*—in the interests of the American dream.

5. All this, of course, is platitude in America. What may not be quite so familiar is the contrast in the historical situation in England. We have never been very conscious of the necessity to build a new society. At all relevant times we have had a fully developed society already in being. And at all relevant times we have also, I am sorry to say, been on the whole pretty satisfied with the society we have. For most of the last two hundred years, American education has been designed to do a job of construction; English education has been designed primarily for maintenance, with improvement coming second. In the very latest period, perhaps, those attitudes have started to change. As with so many aspects of education, there seem to be the first signs of a tendency to change sides. Your education is becoming socially more conservative just when ours is becoming more consciously radical.

6. But that is a speculation for the future, on which I will not enlarge. I am talking of the influences of the past, which have shaped the structures of today. American education has always had to concern itself with the common man in his multitudes. The concern of English education has until very recently been with the maintenance of society, in the words of the old prayer which you will often hear in school and college chapels, "that there may never be wanting a succession of persons duly qualified to serve God in church and state." This is a conception which does not necessarily embrace the education of the great mass. There is a fine, rich, broad educational tradition in England. But it is not a tradition of education, above the minimum level, for the multitude. Postprimary education has always been thought of as a privilege in England; it was not until 1944 that the principle of secondary education for all was established, and it is hardly yet fully effective.

7. Let me pursue this contrast a little further. Let me give you two of the consequences, of which I would guess that one will shock you, while the other may perhaps surprise you more favorably.

8. I will start with the shocker. The consequence of our different attitude is that the sheer size, the volume or quantity, of English education is very much smaller than American. The age at which the legal

compulsion to attend school expires is still only fifteen. Moreover, that is an effective leaving age, and more than four children out of five in fact leave school before they are sixteen. Of the sixteen-year-old age group —those between their sixteenth and seventeenth birthdays—only 22 per cent are still in full-time education. In the seventeen-year-olds, the figure falls to 13 per cent of the boys and 11 per cent of the girls. Among eighteen-year-olds, it is 8 per cent of the boys and 5.5 per cent of the girls.

9. What strikes Americans, I find, as even odder than these figures is the fact that we are not, as a nation, greatly disturbed by them, although many of us think they ought to be larger. But we cannot assume that public opinion is on our side. I am very doubtful whether there would be any support in public opinion for a policy of keeping the majority of children in school after sixteen, and I am certain that you would find hardly anyone in England who believes, as you do, in keeping all children at school until eighteen. Our college students represent about 3 per cent of each age group, and there is an expansion program in hand that will raise it to about 5 per cent. Anybody who suggested that we needed any more than that would meet with the strongest resistance, and not least from the universities themselves.

10. This attitude does not arise from any lack of love for our children. It is not because we think we can't afford it. The proportion of our national income that we spend on general welfare services—social security, health, and the like—is about the highest in the world. It is not from lack of generosity or lack of means that we confine education after the middle teens to a minority. It is because we sincerely believe that it is the right thing to do, in the interests of the children themselves. After all, there can be no absolute rules about education. Nobody believes that any child should be allowed to leave school at twelve. I do not suppose a time will ever come when, even in America, it will become legal or compulsory for everyone to stay in full-time education until twenty-five. Where you fix the age between those limits is surely a matter of judgment. And why should it be the same age for all children? Our belief in England is that, balancing what can be got out of school against what can be got out of life, the average boy or girl has probably had the optimum dose after eleven years of schooling—and do not forget that we begin, by legal compulsion, at the age of five. Eleven years, after all, is one year out of every six or seven of the average lifetime.

11. Now let me give you the other side of the medal. Because education after fifteen or sixteen is confined to a minority, that minority gets every assistance that the state can provide. It is nowadays, to an overwhelming extent, a minority chosen for intelligence and attainment. There are, of course, still the independent schools, where very substan-

tial fees have to be paid. But the pressure of numbers upon them is such that a stupid boy or girl will have great difficulty getting in. And in the state schools, selection is by merit only. But once selected, a boy finds himself with his foot not so much on a ladder as an escalator. He will have the best resources of the best schools concentrated on him. If he can secure a place in a university, and that also is a matter of selection by merit, the state will pay his tuition fees and his living expenses, not only during the session but during the vacation as well. There is no such thing as working your way through college in England. We do not need a National Merit Scholarship scheme because we have one already. Nor is this a recent thing. It has been expanded in recent years, but it has always existed.

12. Let me move on to structure. The outstanding difference here lies in the fact that we have a very much smaller degree of local control than you do. There are about 50,000 school boards in the United States, each of them, I suppose, more or less free to run the schools as it thinks best. That gives a total population in the average school board area of about 3500 persons. In England there are about 130 local education authorities, which gives an average population per area of about 300,000. Moreover, there are two other differences, apart from this sharp difference in size. Your school boards consist, I believe, in most states, of persons specially elected for the purpose, with no other duties. In England the schools are run by the county council, or the borough council, which is the general-purpose government of the area.

13. Second, your school boards raise their own money by direct taxes, or at least the greater part of it. In England about 70 per cent of the expenditure of the local education authorities is met out of grants from the central government in London. There are advantages and disadvantages in this. It means that we do not have the enormous range in standards between rich areas and poor areas that you do. It means a much greater degree of standardization of conditions of employment among the teachers, and therefore of interchangeability between school and school and between area and area. But it also inevitably means a greater degree of uniformity imposed from the center. We think our system is decentralized, because it allows much more local freedom and variety than exist in the school systems of most Continental European countries. But there is no doubt that it is much more highly centralized than the American system.

14. The other great difference under the heading of structure is the principle of selection upon which our system is based. All children, ex-

cept the minority in fee-paying schools, go to undifferentiated schools from the age of five to the age of eleven. At eleven or thereabouts, a proportion of them, varying from area to area but averaging between 20 and 25 per cent, is selected for what we call grammar schools, which include children to the age of eighteen, though not all the pupils stay that long. The remainder go to what are called secondary modern schools, which include children to age fifteen and increasingly to sixteen, but no older.

15. You will see from this description that the crucial time for an English child is at the age of eleven or a little more. The selection test then applied—the famous or infamous eleven-plus examination—is supposed to be a classification purely by ability and aptitude, without any suspicion of being derogatory to those who are not selected. But, of course, everybody wants to be selected, and with the growing pressure of numbers as a result of the post-war bulge of population, the selection has been getting steadily more competitive. As the result of agitation, the Labor Party has adopted the policy of abolishing the eleven-plus examination by sending all children at that age to the same schools, the so-called comprehensive secondary schools. The Labor Party has moved toward this system in several of the areas where it controls the local council, and even in Conservative areas there is a distinct movement to experiment with systems that do not involve sending children to different schools at the age of eleven.

16. I have several times seen this movement quoted in America as evidence that English education is turning away from selection. I think this is a grave misunderstanding. The public objection to selection at eleven is social and political, not educational. It is an objection on the part of parents to having their children sent to different schools, not to their having different educations. And the remedies that are being applied are wholly in terms of institutions, not in terms of the education they provide. I know, for example, one large new comprehensive school built by a Labor council. Every child entering that school is tested and placed in one of fifteen "streams," differentiated by the children's intelligence and aptitude. This selection is done by the teachers; the parents have nothing to do with it; and the children are not even supposed to know which stream is which in intelligence grading. A child placed in one of the top streams will have an almost wholly different education from a child placed even in one of the middle streams. If this is not selection, I do not know the meaning of the term. But this is what we mean by a comprehensive school. Many people in England will tell you that the comprehensive school has been copied from the American comprehensive high school, some meaning it as a compliment, some as the reverse. I have often told them that they could hardly be more mistaken.

17. Nonselection—if that is the opposite of selection—as it is practiced in America is totally unknown in England. By nonselection I mean the principle of treating all children alike, allowing them to sort themselves out by their choice of courses, by what they find easy and difficult, or by their varying ambitions—with counseling assistance, no doubt, but without any compulsory segregations. I am sure that your system seems as odd to us as ours does to you. There is no retreat from selection in England; the only change is that a growing number of people—but still a minority—think that the selection should be within a common school, not between schools.

18. The differences between the two countries in educational method make an enormous subject, and I must restrict myself to four points out of many that it would be possible to make.

19. The first of these differences in method lies in the position of the teacher, in the relative positions of the teacher and the textbook. One of the things about American education that most strikes the English visitor is the importance you attach to textbooks. We have no parallel to that. To begin with, I do not think there are more than two or three, at most, of the local education authorities in England that tell their schools what textbooks to use. That is left to the teacher, occasionally the principal, or the head of department in a large school. And in the higher grades, more often than not, there is not a textbook at all. A teacher will often recommend a book as covering the subject pretty well and as being useful for reference but will not make any attempt to go through it chapter by chapter.

20. This system places a much greater responsibility on the individual teacher, and I have often been asked in America whether we do not have a lot of trouble with it. So far as the political and social responsibility of the teacher is concerned, I cannot recall having heard of a single case arising through a teacher's being accused of using a book which seems offensive or objectionable to somebody in authority. That is partly, perhaps mainly, because our system of large authorities and rather remote and indirect public control puts the individual teacher largely out of the reach of vigilance committees, whether of parents or of the local chamber of commerce. There is also a strong tradition against anything that smacks of political interference with the schools.

21. Educational responsibility, however, is another matter. Quite clearly, a system like ours, which places so much responsibility on the individual teacher, cannot work well unless the average standard of intelligence, knowledge, and teaching competence is high. Up to the pres-

ent, we have been able to maintain that standard. It is partly, of course, a matter of numbers. In the whole of England last year there were only some 260,000 schoolteachers. We were a little short, but 300,000 would have given us all we need. And this is in a country about one quarter the size of the United States. I do not know how many schoolteachers there are in the United States, but I am very sure it is many more than four times 300,000. I do not see how you could possibly have coped with the enormous increase in the American school population in the past forty years without being willing to take thousands of young men and women who needed close support from a textbook before they could teach. Indeed, under the pressure of rising numbers in the schools, I fear we shall find before long that we shall have to give the teacher more assistance, and that implies more external control on his teaching. This particular contrast is not, however, entirely a matter of numbers. It is partly also the result of a different tradition of teacher training, which, in England, has always laid a much greater emphasis on the content of what is to be taught than in America and much less on questions of pedagogic method.

22. The second difference in method is the absence in England of the course system which is so universal in your schools and colleges. Indeed, the word "course" has a wholly different meaning in the two countries. If you asked an English school child what courses he was taking, he wouldn't know what you meant. If you asked him what subjects he was taking, he would answer English, Latin, mathematics, history, and so forth. But that would not mean, as it would in America, that those were the subjects he had chosen to take. They would be the subjects that his form, or class, was taking, and therefore that he was taking with the rest of the class. Until the boy is about fifteen or sixteen, it is unlikely that he or his parents have had any say in the choice of form in which he is placed. And at no age does he have any say in deciding the curriculum of that form. At the higher ages, there is a choice between three or four different curriculums, but each curriculum has to be taken, within narrow limits, as it stands.

23. Here, indeed, is a contrast with the American system. Perhaps it is not quite so sharp a contrast in practice as it is in principle, as I observe that, more and more, those American boys and girls who have ambition to gain admittance to a good college find their choice of courses in high school made for them by the college entrance requirements. But there is one important consequence for teaching that is worth bringing out. In an English school, in any year but one (and that one is what we call the fifth form year, about the age of fourteen or fifteen), you can assume that the pupils who are taking a subject in one year will be taking the same subject next year. The study of a subject can therefore be

planned as a continuous process over a period of years. That is what we mean when we use the word "course." We mean a whole balanced curriculum of six or seven or eight subjects, planned to continue over three or four or five years. Once a boy or girl enters on such a course, he or she will normally pursue it to the end. And all the boys and girls in a course will take substantially the same subjects, with perhaps slight options, as between a second classical or a second modern language. You will therefore understand how bewildered we are when we contemplate one of your neat, packaged, self-contained, nine-month courses, such as high school physics. It is no good asking an English schoolboy when he enters college how many years of French he has had at school. Two boys might both truthfully answer nine years. But they might mean totally different things, and neither one would mean what you thought he meant.

24. How, then, do we measure what a student has accomplished, if we cannot count up the number of courses he has satisfactorily taken? The answer is that we rely, to an extent wholly unknown to you, on general examinations. Every year—sometimes every term—the pupil has to take a written examination in all the subjects of the curriculum, and his further progress depends, sometimes entirely, on his performance in that examination. Most of these examinations are set and assessed within the school itself, by his own teachers. But at three crucial points in his career the examination is set and assessed by an external body. The first of these is the eleven-plus examination, which determines to which sort of secondary school the child should go. The second comes at fifteen or sixteen and is called the Ordinary Level of the General Certificate of Education, set and assessed by one of nine examining boards closely associated with the universities. This examination can be taken in any number of subjects from one upwards, but the most usual practice is to take it in from five to nine subjects. Third, there is the Advanced Level of the General Certificate of Education, which is taken at eighteen or thereabouts and which plays a large part in university entrance.

25. I have been describing the practice of the grammar schools; that is, the schools for the brightest 20 to 25 per cent of the children. Examinations, especially written examinations, play a much smaller part in the life of the less intelligent children. Even in this case, however, they play a much larger part than they do in America; and there is a rising demand for public examinations, at lower standards of intelligence than those of the General Certificate of Education, for these less gifted children. I cannot honestly say that the children themselves clamor for examinations, but employers do, and therefore so do the parents. All the questions that Americans ask and answer in terms of the number and

variety of courses a student has taken we ask and answer in terms of the examinations he has passed.

26. I have left to the last what is the sharpest difference of all between our two systems. This is our system of specialization, in which England is, I think, unique in the world. A student will take the examination for the Ordinary Level of the General Certificate of Education at the age of fifteen or sixteen in a wide range of subjects drawn both from the humanities and from the natural sciences. But once he has passed that examination, he will specialize. That is to say, he will devote two thirds, or perhaps even more, of his time in school to a narrow range of subjects. In one boy's case it may be physics, chemistry, and mathematics; in another's it may be chemistry and biology, or it may be history or modern languages and literature, or classical languages and philosophy. But, whatever the choice, the greater part of the pupil's attention, in the classroom and in his private study time, is given to his specialty, and he will take the advanced level examination at eighteen in his special subjects only. When he gets to the university, the specialization is even more intense. The range of subjects does not usually get any narrower, but the student gives 100 per cent of his time to it.

27. I have found that to Americans, and indeed to educationalists from every country in the world except England, this seems a very strange system indeed. Perhaps you will have difficulty in believing that I really mean what I say. So let me cite my own case, though it is now more than thirty years old. I was a modern languages specialist. For my last three years at school, from the ages of fifteen to eighteen, I studied mostly French and German language and literature, perhaps three or four hours a week of history, and one hour of Scripture on Sundays. For another two years at Cambridge, even the history and the Scripture were cut out, and I studied French and German exclusively. Five years of my life were given to those languages. My experience was perhaps a little extreme; I think the admixture of general and contrasting subjects would nowadays, in a good school, be a little bigger. But the difference would not be great. The English boy or girl is a specialist from the age of fifteen or sixteen.

28. The advisory council of which I am chairman was specifically requested by the Minister of Education to review this system of specialization. We examined it most carefully and discussed it at great length, both with witnesses and among ourselves. In the end we came to the conclusion that we wanted to see it continued. We found that it was being pushed too far, and we have made a number of suggestions for removing what we think are abuses. But we have reported in favor of this system of specialization. And that is a unanimous conclusion reached by a council

made up of educators of all kinds. Perhaps you will find that fact as extraordinary as the system itself, and I must try to give you some of our reasons for thinking that, in this matter, we in England are in step and the whole of the rest of the world is out of step.

29. Let me begin by telling you of one argument that we reject. This is the argument that every intelligent citizen, or every educated man, ought to know something about each subject in a range so wide that it compels a balanced curriculum; that no one can afford to be ignorant of history, government, science, languages, and so forth. To this, we would give our answer in two parts. First, it is true that there are certain elementary skills and knowledges that everyone must have—reading, writing, arithmetic, and several more. But these essential elements can be, and should be, provided by the age of sixteen. If you go on with them after that age, you will be wasting your time, because the knowledge you instill will be forgotten unless it can be attached to the main intellectual interest of a boy's or girl's life, which begins to emerge at about that age.

30. The second part of the answer is that it is only when you have got these essential elementary skills and knowledges out of the way that you can confront the real task of education. The acquisition of factual knowledge is by itself a poor test of any education and a lamentably poor test of the education of boys and girls of seventeen and eighteen. It has been said that the process of education is not to be compared to that of filling up an empty pot, but rather to that of lighting a fire. The proper test of an education is whether it teaches the pupil to think and whether it awakens his interest in applying his brain to the various problems and opportunities that life presents. If these have once been done, then factual knowledge can easily be assimilated. If these have not been done, then no amount of nodding acquaintance with widely varying fields of human knowledge will equip a boy or girl with an educated mind. We in England argue the case for specialization not primarily on the score of the information it provides but because it awakens interest, teaches clear thinking, and induces self-discipline in study.

31. We believe that, if you can find which of the recognized intellectual disciplines most arouses a boy's interest—and we confine his choice to five or six recognized disciplines, chosen for their intellectual content, not for their vocational value—if you can let him spend his time on what interests him, but insist that he must work hard at it, go deep into it, follow it up in the library or the laboratory, get around behind the stage scenery that defines the formal academic subject, you will really be teaching him how to use the mind that God has given him. This sort of intensive study takes a great deal of time, and that is why it can only be applied, for any one student, to a restricted range of subjects.

No doubt you will say that the boy must be very narrow as a result. That may be. Are you sure that being narrow is worse than being shallow?

32. I find that English education has a high reputation among Americans. I am often asked, for example, whether it is not true that the eighteen-year-old boy in England is a year or two ahead of his American contemporary. I always answer that question, or assertion, by asking some others. What boy? If an English boy is still at school at eighteen, he is necessarily in the upper quartile in intelligence. Are you comparing him with the average American high school graduate, who is of average intelligence? And ahead in what? In the subjects to which he has been giving nearly all his time and attention for two years? It would be strange if he were not a long way ahead in those. Or over the whole range of a broad curriculum? He has been taught different things, by different methods, with a different purpose in view, in a different sort of school. There is no fair basis for a comparative judgment.

COMMENTARY AND QUESTIONS

From 1938 to 1950 Sir Geoffrey Crowther was the editor of *The Economist* (London), a journal highly respected in America as well as in Great Britain. The ideas contained in this essay were first presented by the author to the Conference of High School Principals and Supervisors in Baltimore, Maryland.

1. How early in the essay does it become obvious that Crowther is here writing for American readers?
2. As the author explains in par. 1, he has had the opportunity of becoming well acquainted with education in both America and England. Why is it desirable for him to give the reader this information early in the essay?
3. The author of an evaluation usually is not content merely to state his own preferences. Ordinarily he hopes also to get his readers to accept his appraisals. His success in doing this, however, depends somewhat on his making his readers believe that he is a fair-minded observer, and not a biased advocate of his own prejudices. On the whole, what is Crowther's opinion of English education? What evidence can you offer to support your answer? What tone is created by the second sentence of par. 2? by the final paragraph of the essay? Is there any special significance in the placement of these two passages?
4. Where in par. 5 does Crowther explicitly criticize the English? What effect does the inclusion of this criticism have on the reader? How does Crowther try in par. 21 to keep from antagonizing the American reader? In par. 28 the author obviously indicates his preference for the English system of specialization. What tone is created by the final

sentence in this paragraph? Is he a bit less conciliatory in the last sentence of par. 31?

5. Many contrasts and some comparisons are used in this essay. Do these serve any purpose other than that of explaining the unfamiliar by reference to the familiar? In this essay is the author more concerned with English education than with American? Justify your answer.

6. The first sentence in par. 3 indicates the main points of the essay. Where does the discussion of each of these begin? What is the function of par. 18?

7. Note the way in which par. 31 rounds out Crowther's discussion of specialization, presented in pars. 26-30, and also prepares for the conclusion of the essay in the next paragraph. Why is the topic of specialization considered near the end of the essay instead of earlier?

8. What use of metaphor does Crowther make in par. 11? Does Crowther make as extensive use of metaphor in this essay as Lynes makes in "Husbands: The New Servant Class," (pp. 219-226), and Highet makes in "The American Student as I See Him," (pp. 251-260)?

9. In "The American Student as I See Him," Highet, like Crowther here, is contrasting English and American education in a way that indicates he believes some changes should be made in the latter. Which essay do you consider to be the more effective in getting the American reader to accept this point of view? Why?

SUGGESTIONS FOR WRITING

1. By using the method of contrasting and comparing write an evaluation of two things, such as American and foreign automobiles; or a Volkswagen and some less familiar foreign automobile; or two localities, one of which is better known to the reader than the other.

2. My test of an education.

3. In defense of breadth rather than depth.

4. The disadvantages of comprehensive examinations.

The American Student
as I See Him

by GILBERT HIGHET

THE AMERICAN SCHOLAR I have long known and long respected. The American student I met first as an ambitious but depressed graduate working in the hard Scottish medical schools; then as an exotic graft on Oxford's gnarled trunk (like Vergil's tree, "admiring strange new leaves and fruit unlike her own"); and finally in several of the great universities of his own country. I like studying him, and he, by now inured to the fads of his preceptors, supports with surprising affability the endless process of being studied.

2. As far as I can judge, he is unlike any other student in the whole world. For one thing, he often works three or four hours a day at some job which is at least extra-curricular, if not extra-mural. My friends at St. Andrews and Glasgow were often poor—much poorer than the freshmen whom I see cheerfully filing clippings or toting luncheon trays—but in term-time they never worked at anything outside their studies. The vast mythology of Scottish education is full of stories about the crofter's son who lived all term in half a room on a barrel of oatmeal and a barrel of herrings brought from home, and then walked a hundred miles back to Inverquharity with the gold medal. And that ideal still persists. Occasionally British and French undergraduates do a little tutoring, and a dozen or two are bookshifters in the libraries or demonstrators in the labs; but they don't *work*. James Joyce's miserable Stephen Dedalus in Dublin, drinking watery tea and eating fried bread while he fingered his parents' pawn tickets, would have been far better for a decent meal earned by honest work.

3. But it is not, or seldom, done. The feeling is that it would interfere with real work and equally real play: that it would keep the undergraduate from having his full share in the life of the university. And there is some truth in this. To spend three or four hours a day on something wholly unacademic nearly always narrows the student's interest in his academic work. He is apt to feel that it too can be done in the same way: two lectures, four hours at his job, four hours' study, and then stop.

This therefore is one of the reasons why so few undergraduates in the universities here aspire to honors, compete for prizes, carry their interest in their courses further than the term paper. In France and Britain, on the other hand, it is common for lecturers to get notes from their under-graduate hearers questioning some statement, seeking a reference, asking for extended treatment of some difficulty. A not very intelligent pupil of my own at Oxford handed me a verse translation of six idylls of Theocritus, which he had made in his spare time during the two winter terms; in Jules Romains' *Les Hommes de Bonne Volonté* a student at the Ecole Normale Supérieure translates and annotates the choric odes of Sophocles, just for fun; and, at all the British universities, essay and poem competitions are nearly always burdensome to mark, there are so many competitors. But they would not have the energy, or even the interest, to do all that, if they had to manage a laundry agency for four hours a day.

4. The American student himself feels this; for when he becomes a graduate student, a radical change comes over him—a change far greater than the corresponding change in other countries. He will doggedly set himself to read and classify every Elizabethan sonnet, or memorize every decision arising out of the Snite Act; he will plunge into labyrinthine bibliographies, from whose depths he can be heard faintly crying, as if he battled with unseen monsters, and from which he emerges through the gate of ivory, pale but uplifted, like Aeneas from the world of the dead; and when you and I make jokes to him, he will copy them and write "laughter" in the margin. It is scarcely too much to say that he then feels himself for the first time to be a whole-time student; and the only thing to be regretted about this metamorphosis is that it often keeps him from being a whole-time member of the university, that he is so often debarred by it from games and societies and other junior academic activities. He feels, not without a certain justice, that he is paying for the comparative diffuseness of his undergraduate days. There is another way of putting this. No European country thinks that education is, or ought to be, wholly democratic. Not even the United States does, in the last resort—for, in awarding fellowships and scholarships, its universities base their distribution not on *need* but on *achievement*. The principle of competition, thus tacitly acknowledged, is carried much further in Europe. In France[1] the A. B. examination is a national contest, whose winners are rewarded not only with the civic tributes which the French know so well how to dispense, but with prizes, money, trips to Cambodia and certainty of a

---

[1] This refers of course to France before it was invaded by the Germans, and before its government determined to assist its conqueror in attaining his own ideal, *die Vernichtung Frankreichs,* "the destruction of France."

favorable start in their careers. The bad side of this is obvious—suicides are not at all uncommon among disappointed or overworked candidates, and a man's whole life can be darkened by a sense of his own inescapable inferiority, publicly and competitively demonstrated. But it makes the students read, and read hard. All scholarships in Britain (except a very few assigned to localities or family names) are awarded on the basis of a long and difficult competitive examination. And there are very many more scholarships there than there are in this country: scholarships are endowed and awarded by cities, counties, prep schools, "public" schools, colleges, universities, alumni societies, guilds and national associations. Besides those, there are hundreds upon hundreds of rich scholarships dependent on the wills of long-dead benefactors. I went through one university on money left by a thread manufacturer who died about 1850, and through another on the rentals of farms bequeathed for the purpose by a Court official of King James the First. It would not be too much to say that the rich man who, in the United States, gives $50,000 for cancer research, gives £10,000 in Britain to support "a student who desires to enter the medical profession, said student to be selected by an examination on the fundamentals of. . . ." The University of Oxford is thought to be full of the leisure class. Yet in 1937 60 per cent of its students were wholly or partially supported by scholarships; and all those scholarships had to be won by keen and difficult competition. From a certain Scots university there is one, and only one, scholarship which will take you to Oxford; and it is competed for by every student who wants it: pre-lawyers, chemists, historians, economists, mathematicians, philologists, they all sit there glowering at one another in the same examination room, and furiously laboring at the twelve three-hour papers on which their future depends. It is a painful ordeal; but it makes you study! Not only in France but in Britain too, enormous emphasis is laid on the exact position of a student in his class. Those who simply collect their grades and their clubs and leave are little regarded; must, practically speaking, have jobs waiting for them; find the higher careers closed. Those who try for honors find themselves arranged into a natural hierarchy, which, *ceteris paribus*, repesents their comparative chances of getting a good position when they graduate.

5. The American student, if I know him, would not care for this system. He would, I think, feel that it too highly rewarded the "grind" and undervalued the character-building and social qualities of college life; he would conclude it was unfair to boys who happened to attend schools which gave them less careful preparation for academic competition; ultimately he would think that, by subjecting him to a constant

implied pressure, it deprived him of a good deal of his liberty. And yet, it seems to me that it would do him good, and improve the service of schools and universities to individuals and to the state.

6. Take only one broad consideration. The development of government all over the world, in the democracies as well as in the despotisms, is towards a more numerous, more elaborate, and more highly trained bureaucracy. For good or bad, every national government now interests itself in the lives of its citizens far more closely than at any time since the Byzantine empire. Therefore it is necessary, year by year, for it to command a great supply of diverse and well-trained officials, mostly specialists of one kind or another. In the despotisms these officials are produced by the Party machine, selected and trained by a system which is at least methodically similar to education. In the democracies they are at present produced and trained by no system, except in a few fields like jurisprudence and public health. In Great Britain the diplomatic service, the higher branches of the civil service, and certain other administrative departments are recruited by rigorous competitive examinations for which, in practice, candidates prepare throughout the universities and even during their last years at school. That system is thought to work well, although it is limited in extent. But many educators feel that the bureaucracies, both local and national, ought to be wholly staffed by men and women trained *on purpose,* and that in the democracies the schools and universities ought to be the organizations which produce and train them. Many a large store will not engage salesmen and saleswomen unless they are college graduates with noticeably good records; it is ludicrous that states and colleges should be less careful about choosing their executives. If we are to have a mandarinate, let us be as sensible as the Chinese in selecting our mandarins. If we want intelligent officials let us train them and discipline them and sift them by competitive examination and reward them with good, appropriate jobs, instead of letting our universities annually pour out a huge undifferentiated mass of graduates, from which only luck or exceptional perseverance will direct the right man to the right place in the social machine.

7. However, at present that is not done; and the American student, except in a few eccentric universities, estimates his achievement by time spent, which is quantitative, rather than by competitive achievement, which is qualitative. And yet he is at heart emulous. If it is presented civilly and winningly to him, he will welcome authority. He would welcome it still more if it were organized: if he felt that in school and at college its consistent purpose was to make him fit for a career which depended not entirely on his own whim, but on a long series of tests of his abilities and a constructive estimate of his character and capacity.

8. Another unique attribute characterizes the American student: his huge numbers. Can four real universities exist in one city? Can it be possible that in one state fifty or sixty thousand youths and maidens are capable of the activity required to absorb a university education? Are the inhabitants of California (whose very name derives from a romance describing the Earthly Paradise) so talented that they can every year produce a myriad of university graduates? And what educators could be at once so inspiring and so industrious as to teach, effectively, this enormous horde? Or, finally, can the vast multitudes of adolescents in the United States all be so much more talented than their coevals in Canada, in France, in Sweden?

9. The paradox, of course, conceals a dichotomy. To put it bluntly and generally, the American student who is not preparing for a profession does not often go to the university in pursuit of higher education. He goes to complete the education which his school left incomplete. He has been badly schooled. It is not his fault, and not wholly the fault of the school. But it is a pity. It sometimes strikes me with a sense of pathos to read the grave works on education, ranging all the way from Mortimer Adler's *How to Read a Book* to the bulletins of the Carnegie Institute for Educational Research, which treat the American school system in total detachment from all others, as if it could learn nothing from Europe, and teach Europe nothing—still less other continents. Mr. Adler, in his efforts to teach his patients how to read books, makes one or two cursory references to the situation in Europe, and throughout the rest of his prescription treats the American students as a chimera bombinating in the void. But of course he finds it difficult to read Locke or Dante when he gets to college. He has seldom been compelled to read anything difficult in school. And a comparison, however invidious, would demonstrate that. I went to a perfectly ordinary school in Scotland, P.S. 93 as it were. In my last three years (ages 15-18) we were forced to read and understand *Hamlet, Macbeth, Henry IV,* Chaucer's *Prologue* and *Knight's Tale, Polyeucte, Le Cid, Le Misanthrope, Eugénie Grandet, Seven Against Thebes, The Persians, Iliad* XVI and XVIII, *Aeneid* II, IV, and VI, Livy IX and several other books. And we read them. (Dickens and Scott and Thackeray and so on, we had read long before.) We had to, under that stringent discipline. We could write a character of Macduff or Célimène, we could reproduce the various explanations and emendations of the "dram of eale" in *Hamlet,* we could compare the shields of Achilles and Aeneas, we could write little essays on Balzac's idea of realism. They were not very good; but they proved that we had read the books. And we were not alone. In Edinburgh they were doing the same. Bristol Grammar School was doing even more. Sheffield and Manchester and

London and Newcastle were doing at least as much. French schools are still more arduous, although they concentrate more closely on the classics of their own tongue; and so, in a more limited way, were Scandinavian and Dutch schools, and even German schools before the despotism.

10. Now why does the average American student need to learn how to read a book? Why does he approach *Hamlet* or *Crime and Punishment* with a mixture of awe and bravado, and usually look up from it with such puzzled delight and half-understood emotion? Manifestly because he has been ill taught at school. And, so far, that is nobody's fault: certainly not his; but there are two main reasons for the fact.

11. For one thing, the system of mass-education has nowhere else been applied to a population so huge and so various. Only a nation so gallant and so confident as the United States would have dreamt of administering approximately the same education to the children of long-settled western Europeans, recent central European immigrants, and many millions of emancipated Negroes, of whom Bigger Thomas with his revolt and his tragedy may well be partially symbolic. Whenever I ask my pupils about their schooling they invariably say, if they went to public school, that they were held back by the size of the classes or by lazy and recalcitrant classmates. One of the best students I have ever had praised the history master at his public school most highly, but added that he was forced to devote himself almost wholly to the upper one third of his class. In one of his more frankly autobiographical essays Mr. James Thurber describes a tough school in Columbus, Ohio, as it was a generation ago; and even if we allow for humorous exaggeration there is still the ring of truth in the sentence about his enormous Negro protector, Floyd: "I was one of the ten or fifteen male pupils in Sullivant School who always, or almost always, knew their lessons, and I believe Floyd admired the mental prowess of a youngster who knew how many continents there were and whether or not the sun was inhabited." And the problem is complicated by the almost inevitable rigidity of the school system. It is true that many high schools have recently endeavored to work out special courses of study for pupils who are more intelligent than the average; but such readjustments are not yet common, are nearly everywhere tentative, and often meet with opposition. It is a task of almost inconceivable difficulty to raise the educational standards of an entire population; for at least two thirds of the boys and girls now leaving American schools are much more highly educated than their parents were. This difficulty does not exist in western European countries, and it fills me with admiration to see the courage and tenacity with which it is being faced here. But, in education more than in other things, each generation stands on the shoulders of its predecessor, and in another decade or so a great part of this difficulty will have been removed.

¹²· The other reason is the comparatively lax discipline of schools in the United States. High school pupils spend appreciably less time in school here than they do in Britain, and much less than they do in France. In school they spend less time on actual study, because of the surprising amount of attention paid to extra-curricular activities. They spend far less time on preparation at home. And there is much less *drive* behind their learning than there is in western European schools. In the last two years at an ordinary British city school, corresponding to a good high school here, the ordinary pupil averages at least five and a half hours of actual classroom work in school and three hours' preparation at home, with a minimum of six hours' preparation at week ends. The working hours of two good provincial lycées in France, where friends of mine taught during the early '30s, are literally almost double those of an American high school.² Any extra-curricular occupation, like producing the school magazine, or football practice, or rehearsing in the school orchestra, takes place outside working hours. And there is a constant disciplinary pressure to keep the pupils at work, to keep them actively attentive, to pull up the laggards and push on the leaders. Attendances are rigidly kept: an incident such as that reported in the New York papers in 1940, when a squad of policemen and truant officers "combed" the cinemas on two different mornings and rounded up nearly two thousand school children A.W.O.L., is frankly inconceivable. If anything like it occurred in Europe it would be instantly followed by the discharge or demotion of dozens of school teachers. It may not be unfair to suggest that some of the laxity observable in American schools is due to the much higher proportion of women acting as teachers. Adolescent boys cannot be properly disciplined by women, and adolescent girls only with much difficulty. But there are other reasons, which are too well known or too controversial to be discussed here. The fact remains. The American high school student has a far better time, but he does far less work than his European counterpart.

¹³· Accordingly the American student, when he reaches college, is not so well prepared as the average European freshman. He has not read so much, and he does not know how to read and write so well. He does not buy nearly so many books for his own enjoyment, if indeed he buys any at all. One distinction seems to me particularly significant. English and French undergraduates are apt to publish little magazines in which they practise fine writing: the first sonnet, the first political manifesto, chapters from the first autobiographical novel and so on. The American

---

² The same system at an earlier date is admirably described by the Abbé Ernest Dimnet in his autobiography, *My Old World* (Simon and Schuster, New York: 1935). Arduous as it was, he has nothing but praise for it.

student hardly ever produces an imitation literary review. Instead, he produces an imitation of a daily newspaper, or occasionally an imitation of a comic weekly. Almost every distinguished contemporary French and British writer wrote his first publishable work when he was an undergraduate; almost no distinguished American writer wrote anything at college which in any way prefigured his later work.

14. If I have not misunderstood the fairly widespread movement towards establishing "junior colleges" and the frequently emphasized distinction between the first biennium of college work and the second, they are based on this same fact: that some fairly intensive work is required to make up the deficiencies of the schools. Viewed in this light, the multitudinousness of the American student becomes (although still a little bewildering) intelligible and sympathetic.

15. The third quality which forces itself on the observer of the American student is his freedom. He will, without great heart-searching, move from one university to another—a thing almost never done in France or Britain, and in Germany chiefly by very earnest undergraduates in search of a particular kind of specialized teaching or even of a particular professor. He will give up college altogether with a facility which still amazes me, although the dean's office usually knows exactly what proportion of the student body can be expected to drop out annually. He will in college drop subjects on which he spent four years in school; and he will take eccentric subjects or anomalous combinations of subjects with complete nonchalance. He is infinitely less cut to pattern (even allowing for his numbers) than the European student. In an English university it is often possible to tell what particular college an undergraduate attends, and even what school he came from, after five minutes' general conversation; but seldom in the United States.

16. This has its good side and its bad. It makes the American student far more self-reliant—one of my chief difficulties in Oxford was handling the timid, sheltered, hampered boy who might prove to be brilliant and might almost equally well be defeated and crushed; such difficulties hardly ever present themselves here. But, on the other hand, it makes him rather irresponsible, and even restless and discontented. Far too much is left to his own choice, at a time when he is scarcely capable of making a choice. Thanks to the kindly laxity initiated by President Eliot, he is free to take astronomy 17, comparative religion 1, government 33, Spanish drama in translation 21 and hygiene 2A (hygiene 2A is compulsory). A semester of that would, at best, produce a healthy cross between Sir Isaac Newton and the Duke of Plaza-Toro. It is no wonder that the

mixture sometimes fails to act, and discourages him that gives and him that takes. The opposite extreme is seen in the English "public" schools, where a schoolboy good at history will be tutored from the age of fifteen till the age of eighteen to win a history scholarship at a good college specializing in history, will spend three or four years reading history for a first class in the final examinations, and then take history at his examination for entrance to the home civil service. (Usually, he will spend most of his time on the same period of history—e.g. medieval history, with special emphasis on the 12th century.)[3] Both extremes are dangerous. The British extreme is often as narrowing as the other is bewildering: it needs, as an offset, the manifold external interests which only a great university and experienced tutors can give. But it has one merit in itself: it sets a premium on unremitting hard work and the long view. The other extreme broadens the student's mind; but it often broadens it without deepening it.

17. Thus it is that the American student in his last two years at school does not often know what he is going to be, and still less often knows what he will learn in his university; and in the first two years at the university (if he is not firmly steered by his parents into a profession) seldom knows how he will spend his junior and senior years, and how they will dovetail into his future. From one point of view, this shows a genuine, disinterested love of learning, a magnificent belief in the virtues of the university; but from another it means waste of good effort, waste of priceless time, waste of irreplaceable enthusiasm. The task of the university is to cast such a light on a man's youth as will illuminate him through his life, and yet to keep the light unblurred by the shadows of the temporary and the inessential. This task is always supremely difficult, but its difficulty is here enhanced by the inadequateness of the liaison between schools and universities and the lack of emphasis on the essentials of education. The schools have more than enough to do. They cannot tackle this job. It is for the American universities to look, like the wise man, before and after: to induce the student to surrender most of his freedom of choice for a more stable set of patterns in education. Wherever such compulsory patterns have been introduced he needs little persuasion to accept them; at Columbia he looks back on the arduous humanities course with feelings of pleasure and gratitude, not unmingled with surprise. He is a good fellow, the American student: he is energetic and ambitious; but he lacks direction, as the young do everywhere. "For,"

---

[3] An interesting document showing one boy's revolt against this system is Christopher Isherwood's autobiography, *Lions and Shadows,* Hogarth Press, London: 1938.

says Thomas Burton, "as he that plays for nothing will not heed his game; no more will voluntary employment so thoroughly affect a student, except he be very intent of himself." And, in these bad days, few of us are very intent of ourselves.

COMMENTARY AND QUESTIONS

In writing an evaluation there is some advantage in being apart from your subject, outside of it, where you can obtain an accurate perspective, undistorted by prejudice. Of course, when you are in this position you run the risk of making an evaluation that is thin or inaccurate because of its not being based on an adequate body of information, but this is a risk which can be avoided if you are willing to spend the time, energy, and thought necessary to obtain a real understanding of your subject.

1. Do you think that the author of this essay is sufficiently well acquainted with American students to write an evaluation of them? Justify your answer. How does Highet attempt in par. 1 to forestall the shallow criticism that he is not qualified to discuss his subject because he is a foreigner?

2. Highet writes at some length concerning educational practices in European countries. Is this material irrelevant to an evaluation of the American student? Justify your answer.

3. How and why does Highet attempt to make it clear that he is not prejudiced against the American system and that he is not blind to the faults of European education?

4. This essay originally appeared in *The American Scholar*, a quarterly journal published by Phi Beta Kappa. Do you think that Highet's style is more appropriate to such a magazine than is the style of Lynes's "Husbands: The New Servant Class" (pp. 219-226)? Consider such things as paragraph length, use of literary allusions, diction, figures of speech, and sentence construction.

5. Would you have broken par. 4 after the fourth sentence? Why or why not?

6. Highet discusses three characteristics of the American student in corresponding groups of paragraphs beginning respectively with pars. 2, 8, and 15. How has he marked the introduction of the second and third groups? Would you have found the discussion easier to follow if he had marked the beginning of the first group as clearly?

7. Par. 17 begins by considering the effect of what has been discussed in pars. 15-16. In the rest of the paragraph is the author merely summarizing the essay as a whole? What is the relation of the third sentence to the rest of the essay?

8. This essay was originally published in 1941. Would there be reason

for Highet to modify his evaluation if he were writing at the present time?

9. Define the following words as Highet has used them: *inured* (par. 1), *metamorphosis* (par. 4), *mandarinate* (par. 6), *eccentric* (par. 7), *emulous* (par. 7), *dichotomy* (par. 9), *invidious* (par. 9), *recalcitrant* (par. 11), *anomalous* (par. 15).

SUGGESTIONS FOR WRITING

1. The American student as I see him.
2. Students should (should not) have jobs.
3. Extra-curricular activities are (are not) an important part of one's education.
4. The deficiencies of my high-school education.

The Decline
of the Machine

by JOHN KENNETH GALBRAITH

THOSE WHO GUIDE our worries on large issues regularly ask us to ponder man's losing competition with the machine. On the assembly lines he is being replaced by automatic machinery which is regulated and instructed by electronic controls. If the resulting product is a consumer item it has almost certainly been designed to minimize both the effort and intelligence required of its user. Not even the question of whether people will want it has been left entirely to judgment. This has been ascertained by market surveys and insured by advertising and both, perhaps, were analyzed with the aid of an electronic computer, sometimes too ambitiously called an electronic brain.

The selection from John Kenneth Galbraith, *The Liberal Hour*, copyright © 1960 by John Kenneth Galbraith, is reprinted by permission of and arrangement with Houghton Mifflin Company, the authorized publishers.

2. The tendency to dispense with men and intelligence is held to go far beyond the consumer gadgets. The unmanned missile is about to replace the old-fashioned hand-operated bomber. In the near future, according to enthusiasts, unmanned missiles will take flight to intercept other unmanned missiles which will prevent these from intercepting other automated missiles. The operation will be handled under contract by IBM. If the globe were larger or the explosions smaller the prospect would be not unattractive. The machines having taken over, men would all be noncombatants. The charm of war has always been greatest for those whose role was to guide it from a certain distance.

3. These visions of the triumph of the machine can be multiplied endlessly. We do not take them quite seriously for we do not really believe that we are being replaced, and our instinct is sound. If there is a competition between man and machine, man is winning it—not for at least two centuries has his position been so strong as compared with the apparatus with which he works.

4. And the fact that this is the age of ascendant man, not triumphant machine, has practical consequences. If machines are the decisive thing, then the social arrangements by which we increase our physical plant and equipment will be of first importance. But if it is men that count, then our first concern must be with arrangements for conserving and developing personal talents. It will be these on which progress will depend. Should it happen, moreover, that for reasons of antiquated design our society does well in supplying itself with machines and badly in providing itself with highly improved manpower, there would be cause for concern. There is such cause, for that, precisely, is our situation.

5. But first, what is the evidence that men have been gaining on machines—that skill and intelligence have become more important in what we call economic progress than capital plant and equipment?

II

6. The change is most prominently reflected in the changed position of the owner or supplier of physical capital. For a half century he has been a man of steadily declining prestige and importance. Once it was taken for granted that ownership of an industrial enterprise—the ownership of the capital assets or a substantial share of them—gave a man a decisive voice in its direction. So it was with Ford, Carnegie, the elder Rockefeller, Commodore Vanderbilt, and John Jacob Astor. And to be a source of capital, as in the case of the elder Morgan, insured an almost equal power over the enterprise. It also insured a considerable position

in the community. Indeed, it was because the provision of capital conveyed such power that the system was called capitalism.

7. Now the ownership of capital, or the capacity to supply it, accords no such power. Few large corporations are now run by their owners; those like Du Pont where, for many generations, a talented family has had a decisive influence on the enterprise it owns, are becoming a rarity. Typically the power lies with the professional managers. These make elaborate obeisance to the stockholders. But they select the Board of Directors, which the stockholders then dutifully elect, and in equally solemn ritual the Board then selects the management that selected it. In some cases, for example the Standard Oil Company of New Jersey, once dominated by the first Rockefeller, the Board consists exclusively of managers selected by the managers who were selected by the Board.

8. There are a number of reasons for the rise of the professional manager, but by far the most important is that ownership of capital has come to count for much less than ownership of ability, knowledge, and brains. The man of ability could get the capital; the man who had capital and was devoid of other qualification had become pretty much a hopeless case. (Even to give away his money would eventually require the services of a professional.) The relatively impecunious but better-trained, more intelligent, more determined, or politically more adept managers have almost everywhere taken over. Once in office it is only rarely that the owners of capital can dislodge them.

9. Nor is this a misfortune for the companies in question. Some of the worst cases of corporate misfortune in recent times have been those in which the owners of the capital have managed to use their power to keep the professionals out. In the thirties and early forties the elder Henry Ford used his power as the sole owner of the Ford Motor Company to remain in command. It is now freely acknowledged that the company suffered severely as a result. Following his death the management was professionalized and much improved. The great merchandising house of Montgomery Ward under Sewell Avery provided a parallel example. Control and direction of a large company by a capitalist has become, indeed, a rather risky affair. He may try to do what can only be done well by a professionally qualified group of diverse and specialized talent.

III

10. But though it is most visible at the top, the shift in the comparative importance of men and capital is perceptible throughout the modern industrial enterprise. The procedures by which the large and successful

enterprise raises funds for new plant and equipment are orderly and pre-dictable. And, depending on circumstances, there is a considerable range of choice—earnings can be withheld, there can be resort to banks, or securities can be sold. A great deal of pompous ritual attends this process, but for the large and successful firm this signifies neither uncertainty nor difficulty but only that we have considerable respect for money and ex-pect large sums to be handled with decent ceremony.

11. There is no similar certainty in the procedures by which even the most successful concern supplies itself with talent. It must send its emis-saries to participate in the annual talent hunt, and if the most imposing men still go to the money markets, the most eloquent go to the colleges. The bag is always uncertain and frequently inadequate. If a sucessful firm is contemplating a considerable expansion it will almost certainly worry more about where to find the men than where to get the money.

12. And the change is reflected in the fears and apprehensions of the community at large. We wonder whether we are investing as much as we should in physical capital; we hear that the Soviets, who in our time have largely replaced conscience as the stern small voice of duty, are doing much more. But there is more everyday concern about the state of our schools and colleges. Are they doing properly by our children? Where can we find the resources to enable them to do better? Increas-ingly we are wondering about the adequacy of our output of highly trained and educated people.

13. This shows itself in a very practical way. Every family knows that the automobile industry is equipped to supply it with a new car almost on a moment's notice. Such is the admirable condition of our physical plant. But it cannot be at all sure there will be a place for all the chil-dren in a good college. Even the automobile executive may wonder where he can get his boy in. Such is the contrasting state of our facilities for human development.

IV

14. The forces back of the change in the relative position of man as compared with capital are not new. Some of them, curiously enough, are those which, at first glance, seem to suggest the ascendancy of the ma-chine.

15. The classical trinity of productive factors were land (including natural resources), labor (broadly defined to include both physical and intellectual effort), and capital. All production was seen as resulting from the combination of these factors in one form or another and in one

proportion or another. Some economists have questioned whether there was much difference between land and capital goods—both support man's efforts to produce things, and many economists have insisted on adding as a fourth factor of production entrepreneurship or the human effort which was devoted to organizing and managing the other three factors. Subject to these modifications and a few quibbles, the classical delineation of productive agents is still accepted and, indeed, is deeply imbedded in economic thought.

16. All production requires all three (or all four) factors and in this sense all are equally vital. But the importance attached to the different factors has changed remarkably in the last hundred and fifty years. At the beginning of the last century—the formative years of modern economics—land seemed peculiarly important. Population was growing. Europe and Asia seemed very crowded. The vast fertile spaces of the Americas, Australia, and Africa were but slightly appreciated. The effect of modern agricultural techniques on production per acre was, of course, beyond view. Both Ricardo and Malthus, two of the towering figures in the history of economic ideas, concluded that, in different ways, man's fate would be largely decided by the relentless pressure of population on limited land. Labor being abundant, perhaps excessively so, it seemed far less important than land. Capital, though important, also lacked the life-and-death significance of the land supply. Land was the factor of greatest prestige.

17. As the nineteenth century passed, capital gained rapidly to a position of dominance in the trinity. The new world added enormously to the supply of land. The decisive question was its development and for this ports, steamships, roads, railroads, farmsteads, and farm equipment were needed. The land was there; the labor came almost automatically; but the more capital the greater the pace of progress.

18. This emphasis on capital was reinforced by the nature of industrial advance during the last century. It consisted not of the invention of a great number of new techniques but the spread of a relatively small number of spectacularly important ones. Thus, textile manufacture became a factory industry. Steam power was applied to manufacturing, transport, and mining to replace power from men, animals, falling water, or wind. Iron and steel became plentiful and cheap and thus available for many new uses.

19. These inventions resulted, so far as anyone could tell, from a combination of accident, inspiration, and genius. Men like James Watt, Benjamin Franklin, and Eli Whitney could not be cultivated, and while they might under some circumstances be protected by the patent office, that was about all that could be done to foster technological progress.

20. But if little could be done to stimulate inventions, much could be done about putting them to use. Savings could be stimulated by exhortations to thrift—and even more by a system of ethics and religion which assured the diligent, abstemious, and self-denying man esteem in this world and salvation in the next. Investment could be encouraged by stable government and laws which assured investors that profits would be theirs to enjoy. Looking rationally at the thing that was subject to wise policy, economists came to measure progress by the proportion of the nation's income that, each year, was saved and invested.

V

21. Investment in physical capital is still a prime measure of progress but it is an obsolescent one. More and more progress is coming to depend on the quality rather than the quantity of the capital equipment in use and on the intelligence and skill of those who use it.

22. There are reasonably good figures to go on. Between the early seventies of the last century and the decade 1944-53, according to calculations made under the auspices of the National Bureau of Economic Research, the net output of the American economy increased by an average of 3.5 per cent a year. Less than half of this (1.7 per cent) is explained by increases in the supply of capital and labor.[1] The rest was the result of improvements in capital equipment—technological advance—and improvements in the working force, including, of course, its leadership and direction. The *share* in the advance attributable to technological improvement and to the improved skill and ability of workers, technicians, and managers has been increasing.

23. But both technological advance and improved skills and abilities are the product of personal development. Machines do not improve themselves; this is still the work of highly improved men. And most technological advance is now the result not of the accident of inspiration or genius but of highly purposeful effort. Once we had to wait for the accidental appearance of Edisons and Wrights. Now through education and organized effort in a laboratory or experimental shop we get something approaching the same results from much more common clay.

24. So it comes to this. We now get the larger part of our industrial growth not from more capital investment but from improvements in men and improvements brought about by highly improved men. And

---

[1] These figures have been most thoughtfully interpreted by Professor Theodore Schultz to whom all who discuss these matters are in debt. See his "Investment in Man: An Economist's View," *Social Service Review*, XXXIII, No. 2, June 1959.

this process of technological advance has become fairly predictable. We get from men pretty much what we invest in them. So now in its turn, after land and after capital, labor—highly improved labor to be sure—has come to the center of the stage. Investment in personal development is therefore at least as useful as an index of progress as investment in physical capital. It could be more valuable. This is the kind of change which solemn men of self-confessed soundness of judgment will continue to resist; the familiar is always defended with much more moral fervor just before it becomes foolish.

25. What then of our practical accommodation to this new urgency of investment in personal development?

VI

26. At first glance our position would seem to be quite good. We have been reaping large gains from the application of trained intelligence to our economic life. This is the fruit of one of the world's pioneer experiments in public education. Surely our advantage will continue.

27. We cannot be so optimistic. Until the last century learning and even literacy were the badges of privilege. They had always been reserved to the favored few. Accordingly learning was a symbol of equality—a symbol that our grandparents, determined to establish their claim to full equality, were not disposed to overlook. Hence the free elementary schools, high schools, the Land Grant College system, and the remarkable number and variety of other institutions of higher (and not excessively high) learning.

28. This system was adequate, even admirable, so long as education was a socially provided service designed to insure (though it had other purposes too) rough equality of opportunity. It has ceased to be sufficient as education has become a form of investment.

29. The test of what a community should spend on a social service is what it can afford—what it believes it can spare from other forms of consumption. The test of investment, by contrast, is what will pay for itself. We apply the investment test as a matter of course to physical capital and even the commonplace terminology reflects the different attitudes; while we "invest" in physical capital, we "spend" for education.

30. The investment test is far the more generous of the two—that is to say, it sanctions much larger outlays. It implies an aggressive canvass of all possible uses of funds to see what will pay off at a profit. To find new ways of investing at a profit is to prove one's enterprise. One of the most familiar theorems of accepted economics is that, subject to some

lags and irregularities, investment in physical capital will occur whenever marginal return exceeds the marginal cost; that is, whenever the return to additional investment is sufficient to cover the added cost including interest and some allowance for risk.

31. The test of what can be afforded, by contrast, invokes far more frugal attitudes. The outlay, even if it is for education, is vaguely self-indulgent. If we wish it—if we wish our children to have the prestige and satisfactions and opportunities from learning—we must measure the cost against other important alternatives. Virtue resides not in finding ways of investing more but in finding ways of spending less. The community honors the man who is identified with economy. These attitudes remain even though, as we have seen, the outlays economized may yield as large a return (perhaps larger) as those for physical capital.

32. Investment in personal development is also handicapped by the lack of a close relationship of outlay with the resulting benefit. A chemical company invests in a new plant because it knows it will get the higher earnings. If it invests in the education of a young chemist it has no similar assurance that it will get a return from its outlay. The fellow may decide to become an artist or a farmer, or he may go faithlessly to work for a competitor.

33. One can see by a simple illustration what the kind of firm relationship of cost to benefit that exists for physical capital would do for investment in personal development if it existed there. Imagine an arrangement by which promising youngsters, when halfway through high school, were indentured for life to a corporation. The corporation would then be responsible for all further education and would be assured of their services for life. Performance of the companies tomorrow, it would soon be evident, would depend on the quality of the postulant executives, scientists, and other specialists being selected and trained today. The quality of this group would become a matter of major concern. It would be under the eye of accomplished educators. Money would start flowing into it. Investment fund managers would send scouts to seek information on its quality. If one of the larger oil companies found that the schools and colleges available for training its oncoming geologists and engineers were inadequate, it would obviously have to take steps to remedy the situation—perhaps by establishing its own. Otherwise, in a few years, it would be outclassed by the companies with better talent. One can easily imagine bond issues by backward companies to develop stronger technical echelons. The result would be a substantial and possibly an astronomical increase in outlays for personal development—all justified by the resulting profit. All this would be the result of giving the corporation a firm lien on the individual's services and thus on the

return on the money it spends on him. It has such a lien on a machine; the example only makes human beings as privileged, for purposes of investment, as are machines.

³⁴· The final reason for thinking that our arrangements for investing in personal development are deficient is that the Soviets have, technically speaking, superior ones. They begin with all resources under public control; hence, there is no problem in transferring those to be devoted to personal development from private to public use. And outlays for physical capital and those for personal development are items in the same huge budget. The returns from one type of investment can be measured against the returns from the other. There is no inherent reason why physical capital should have a preference as in our case. The result is that the U.S.S.R., by our standards still a comparatively poor country, treats its schools, research and training institutes, universities, and adult and worker education with a generosity which impresses all Western visitors. These outlays, needless to say, not old-fashioned expansion of physical capital, were decisive for launching the Sputniks and for landing their successor on the moon.

VII

³⁵· We cannot solve the problem of personal investment by indenturing our youngsters at a tender age to a corporation. And we should not expect the kindly corporation to rise to the rescue with large voluntary grants for education. Time has already been wasted on this notion. The problem is far too serious to be left to the conscience of those with a particular willingness to spend the stockholder's money.

³⁶· Most likely we will solve the problem by making fuller and better use of the familiar instruments of public finance. We must see spending for personal development not as a cost but as an opportunity. Then we must make sure that we are taxing ourselves sufficiently to exploit this opportunity. That the Federal Government must play a role is elementary. It has access to fiscal resources that are inherently far greater than those of states and localities; now that education has become an investment rather than a social service, these resources are indispensable. It is also the unit of government with responsibility for national development and growth. There is at least a likelihood that investment in personal development is a better guarantee of national power than some of our military expenditures.[2]

---

[2] We must see too that waste, including that of the athletic circuses, is brought under control. It is not only indefensible in itself; it brings investment in human development into disrepute.

[37.] We need also to review our attitudes toward state and local taxation. In a poor country there are sound reasons for reluctance in taxing objects of everyday consumption in order to have more public services and amenities. But we are not a poor country and personal development has become not a service but an investment. So states and localities should no longer hesitate to use sales and excise taxes (as an addition to and not as a substitute for others) to pay for schools and universities. And liberals, in particular, should not be too indignant when this is proposed.

[38.] There is another way of putting provision for personal development on a par with capital development that we should consider. We assume that a corporation, either by withholding from earnings or by resort to the capital market, will take responsibility for improving and expanding its own physical plant. The pressure for voluntary contributions by corporations to education reflects, no doubt, a feeling that there is a similar responsibility for personal development. Corporations are the largest employers of trained talent. They reap the rewards from employing such people. Why shouldn't they pay a part of the cost of training this talent?

[39.] Perhaps they should. Voluntary contributions will always be inequitable as well as inadequate. Conscience can readily be assuaged by a small contribution and the levy falls only on those with a social view of the corporation. But a special tax for education and training would encounter no similar objection. Levied as a percentage of total payroll—executive, scientific, skilled and unskilled—it would be roughly proportioned to the quantity and quality of the people employed. Thus it would be related to benefit from past investment in personal development; and it would mean that the company was assuming its rough share of the cost of replacing with improved talent the skilled workers, technicians, scientists, and executives that it employs. Initially the tax would presumably be borne in the form of higher prices by the consumers of the product. Ultimately the better talent would bring better methods, improved efficiency, and hence lower prices. It would be self-liquidating for it supports a profitable investment.

[40.] Corporations are now at great pains to explain that their prices must include provision for earnings sufficient to replace and expand their physical capital. This, they regularly assure their public, means that production will continue and be more efficient in the future. But, as the National Bureau figures show, we have more to gain from improving the quality of people. So a levy for this purpose would be an even better bargain.

[41.] Maybe there are other ways of augmenting the flow of resources into personal development. In a society that is changing we dare not assume that we have thought the last thoughts on any such subject. For man has not retreated before the machine; rather the machine has become desperately dependent on the improvement of man. And our economy is still arranged to supply machines rather than to improve men.

COMMENTARY AND QUESTIONS

The author of this essay, a distinguished professor of economics who was appointed Ambassador to India, uses an evaluation of the relative importance of men and machines as the basis for his contention that the well-being of the nation requires an increasing emphasis on "conserving and developing personal talents." This contention is such a familiar one that a main problem of the author is to gain and hold the reader's attention; this he does in part by considering his topic primarily as an economist evaluating the return upon investment, and by relating his subject to our present fear that machines are becoming more important than men.

1. Why does the title get the reader's attention? What is the relation between the title and pars. 1-2? Why include pars. 1-2?

2. This essay has been divided into seven numbered sections and the author's strategy becomes apparent when one considers the arrangement of these. Summarize briefly the point of each.

3. What is the logical relationship between section II and section III? Is this relationship made clear by the first sentence in par. 10?

4. Sections IV and V are concerned with the history of economic developments, only part of which directly supports the author's contention that men are now more important than machines. How does this history contribute to the effectiveness of the essay?

5. What distinction between two tests for expenditures on education is made in par. 29? Is this merely a verbal distinction or is it basic to the point of the essay?

6. Pars. 33 and 34 offer illustrations in support of the same point. What is it? What is the basic difference between these two examples?

7. For what reasons does par. 41 provide a very effective conclusion? In arriving at your answer, don't ignore the first two sentences of the paragraph. How are they related to the general tone of the essay?

8. The sucess of this essay in holding the reader's attention is dependent to a considerable extent on skillful phrasing. What is distinctive about the diction of the following sentences:
   a. the first in par. 1
   b. the first in par. 4
   c. the last in par. 10
   d. the second in par. 12?

9. All too often we find that trite ideas are expressed in trite phrases. Justify the statement that in this essay independent thinking is given original expression. Note the success with which Galbraith, a social scientist, violates the ironic rules given by Williamson in "How to Write Like a Social Scientist" (pp. 519-523).

SUGGESTIONS FOR WRITING

1. The decline of man.
2. A new approach to an old subject.
3. The dangers of subsidization.
4. Can private enterprise do the job?
5. Contrast Galbraith's method and purpose in belittling the machine with Eiseley's in "The Bird and the Machine" (pp. 75-82).

The Natural History
of a Reluctant Suburb

by **WILLIAM M. DOBRINER**

ONE OF THE MOST PERSISTENT mistakes in the flood of literature about suburbia is the tendency to lump together under the label of "suburban" all sort of communities caught within the cultural and economic shadow of great cities. But in fact there is an enormous difference between an all-new suburb like a Levittown and an established rural village invaded by suburbanites and turned into a reluctant suburb.

2. The internal problems of the mass-produced suburb and the sacked village are quite different. A Levittown has to create its institutions—its schools, its churches, its civic organization, shopping centers, "culture" groups, and the like. The invaded village, on the other hand, is a going concern before the suburban assault begins. It has evolved a social system that works for a population of a certain size. There are

enough schools, churches, clubs, stores, streets, sewers, sidewalks, parking spaces, etc., to go around. But once the restless city discovers the
little village and pumps a stream of suburbanites into its institutions, the
social system soon develops a split personality. Where a Levittown is
faced with the problem of creating a community from scratch, the
sacked village has a community already, but it is soon divided between
the pushy, progressive, and plastic world of the newcomers on the one
hand, and the accustomed world of the oldtimers—"the villagers"—on
the other.

3. Wherever the suburban spearhead is pressing the rural village, the
village has little hope of surviving unchanged, because the forces behind
metropolitan expansion are irresistible. For a while the village may resist
by elaborate zoning requirements or other legal barriers to invasion, but
these are at best delaying actions. The tides of urbanism may be diverted
for a decade or so, but what direct assault has failed to do a fifth column
will accomplish. The city will seduce the young people of the village;
they will go to urban colleges, take jobs in the metropolis, extend their
range of contacts and eventually adopt an urban (suburban) way of life.

4. What it means for a long-established village to be suburbanized
can be seen from the recent history of a community called here, for reasons of tact, "Old Harbor." It is a real place, in the general New England
area, off the Atlantic Coast. Over 300 years old, Old Harbor lies at the
foot of a curving valley between two green necks of land stretching into
the sea. Its history resembles that of many another New England village.
In 1662, for example, a "morals committee" of six "respectable" citizens
and the minister carefully scrutinized all new settlers who arrived in the
community. If the newcomers failed to pass the committee's standards of
morality and respectability, they were asked to leave. So Old Harbor's
tradition of skepticism and caution as to the worth of recent arrivals is
anchored in over 300 years of experience.

5. In its early years, Old Harbor served as the local nexus of an
agrarian and colonial society. Its grist mills ground local grain into flour
through the power of the impounded waters of the tide ponds and mill
dams. The natural harbor drew shipping from all over the east coast.
Whaling ships worked out of the home port, and coastal shipping from
ports as far away as the West Indies unloaded hides, rum, cattle, cord-
wood, charcoal, etc., on Old Harbor's busy wharfs. Over the years the
farmers worked the land on the gently rolling slopes leading down to the
water. The wheelwrights turned their wheels, the metal smiths pounded
out their pewterware, the shipbuilders sent their vessels splashing into
the bay, and the carpenters built the "saltbox" cottages down near the

harbor. The village prospered but remained comparatively changeless in some fundamental ways—it continued to be a Yankee village of industrious merchants, seamen, farmers, and craftsmen. Certain family names appear again and again in its records: the Rodgerses, the Platts, the Tituses, the Woodses, the Brushes, the Conklins, the Wickses, the Scudders, the Sopers, the Skidmores. In time more land was cleared, more ships were built, and small but vigorously independent men set up industries and crafts, farms and homes. Yet the essential "ethos" of the village remained constant—Yankee, Protestant, independent, cautious, shrewd, calculating, hard working, and conservative.

6. Old Harbor figured in the American Revolution. One of its churches (still standing and functioning) served as headquarters for the local British forces. Eventually, George Washington came to Old Harbor and slept there. By the middle of the nineteenth century, in a society where so many persons, traditions, and things were new, Old Harbor had a lineage of 200 years to look back upon. But change was imminent. In 1867 the railroad came to the village and became a serious competitor with marine transportation, and thereafter the harbor declined as a vital force in the village's economy. Even more ominous was the fact that 36.6 miles from the village lay the borders of a city. By today's standards, it was an urban infant, but even then it was showing a capacity for incredible growth and its influence was extending beyond its borders. Though it was still an entity apart and a universe removed from Old Harbor, some of the more perceptive villagers looked to "the city" with something more than casual Yankee curiosity and superiority. In writing to a relative in 1872, one villager noted, "There has been a very curious thing this summer, I must have seen 15 or 20 strangers in town during July and August."

7. The first invaders of Old Harbor were members of the new industrial aristocracy who emerged in the decades after the Civil War. They were the first outsiders to discover the magical little coves and their verdant overcover, the unspoiled woodlands, the tiny village with so much history, and the green, gentle hills with the spectacular sweep of the sea. By the turn of the century, Old Harbor had become their carefully guarded preserve. They bought the old farms and cleared away acres for their summer playgrounds and gigantic estates. They fenced off two and three hundred acre parcels and created separate dukedoms populated by communities of servants and laborers.

8. On the surface things had not changed much. The rolling hills, the snug harbor, the Yankee village with its saltbox cottages and local crafts, the busy farms, all remained the same. The estates were secluded behind acres of greenery and the new leisure class strove to protect "the colonial

charm" of the village and its surroundings. The old inhabitants kept to themselves. They ran the village as they always had, but supplied the estates with provisions, ships, and such services as they were capable of providing. Though there was little basic understanding and compatibility between the "high society" of the nation and the "high society" of the village, the coming of the estates brought a new prosperity to Old Harbor and helped to take up the slack left by the decline of the fishing and whaling industries and the harbor in general. By the turn of the century, Old Harbor was passing into another stage of its life. By now the grist mills were great sway-backed structures rotting by the mill dams. The brickkilns, the tannery, and Ezra Prime's thimble factory were alive only in the memories of the very old. Children played sea games in the soft, pungent, peeling hulks of the whalers as they lay beached in the harbor marshes, their masts pointing like splayed fingers against the evening sky. And in the meantime, to the east, the urban goliath was yawning and stretching and looking fitfully about.

9. By the early 1920's, the township in which Old Harbor is located was undergoing rather intensive immigration from the metropolitan area. The city was going through one of its growth spasms, and the population was spilling over the city limits into the adjacent counties. Old Harbor was one county removed, but this was the decade in which the automobile drastically changed the character of American society and culture. Mass production had made Henry Ford's dream of a low-priced car for every family almost a reality. And a few miles to the south of the Village, in "Old Harbor Station," the railroad terminus, a new and rather singular figure stood on the platform waiting for the 8:05 to the city: the commuter, the classic suburbanite, with his freshly pressed tight trousers, starched white collar, and morning paper folded neatly under his arm.

10. Now the automobile and the new concrete highways were bringing transient strangers to Old Harbor. The strangers were noisily evident on hot summer nights when a two-hour drive would carry them from the heat and congestion of the city to the beaches and cool valleys of Old Harbor. The character of Old Harbor weekends rudely changed as streams of cranky autos on spindly wheels rattled through the center of town and jammed up at traffic lights. Not only was Main Street becoming a thoroughfare for the beach traffic on weekends, but the city people intruded into the private bathing places along the waterfront. "Private Property" and "No Admittance" signs began to obliterate "the view." The number of both permanent residents and weekend transients, or, as the villagers called them, "shoe boxers," increased.

11. By the 1930's, the age of the palatial estates, begun seventy-five

years earlier, was about over. The huge mansions in English Tudor, Renaissance, Baroque, Spanish, and various combinations had served their purpose. They had proclaimed the grandeur of American industrial growth and had bestowed calculated and lavish honor on those who built them. Now they were in the hands of the third generation or had been sold to second and third buyers, and each time a portion of the land had been sliced off in the transaction. In addition, government action unfriendly to the rich in the New Deal decade was making it difficult to maintain huge houses; income and inheritance taxes were forcing the estate holders to sell their property or simply to let the palaces go to seed. A few were given to educational institutions and one or two more were turned over to Old Harbor Township as museums or public parks. But there is little contemporary use for a decaying 30-room castle with its entourage of outbuildings, so they waste away in their crabgrass kingdoms, the gargantuan headstones of an excessive age.

¹². After the Second World War population that had been trapped in the city during the war years exploded into the county neighboring Old Harbor. In ten years, the number of people in this "rural" county passed a million and made it one of the most rapidly growing areas in the United States. Large numbers also spilled over into Old Harbor's county, whose sociological border by 1950 was well within the rural-urban fringe. In the ten years from 1945 to 1955, Old Harbor Township doubled its population, and the village itself has now absorbed between two and three times the numbers it had in 1940. In just ten years, a 300-year-old village, with many of the descendants of the original founders still living there, underwent a social shock that wrenched it from whatever remained of the patterns of the past.

¹³. As Old Harbor soaks up the steady stream of suburban migrants, it has taken on a physical pattern quite different from the community of twenty years ago. Toward the center of town is the "old village," the nucleus of the "oldtimer" community. There the streets are lined with aging oaks, elms, and maples. The houses are comparatively large and reflect the architectural trends of 150 years—authentic and carefully preserved saltboxes and Cape Cods, two-story clapboard or brick Colonials, straight and angular American Gothics, and prissy, frivolous Victorians. They stand fairly close to each other, but property lines are marked by mature hedges of privet, forsythia, and wygelia. Each house proclaims an identity of its own. In front of an occasional Colonial or cottage a small sign will read "1782" or "1712." In the old village, even on a sunny day, there is shade and the scent of many carefully tended flowers. The sunlight filters through the great overhead branches and throws delicately

filigreed shafts of yellow-green light on the clipped lawns, on the small barns and garages tucked behind backyard shrubbery, and on the hulls of old sailboats that will never again put to sea. The sidewalk slates are rippled by the massive roots below. Two elderly ladies, straight and thin, walk by with their market bags. There are few children. There is little noise. You sense that whatever these neighborhoods are now, the best in them has gone before.

14. Out along the periphery of the old village, up on what were farm-lands five years ago, out along the land necks reaching toward the bay, down in the cove valleys, and up among the woody ridges, range the dwellings of suburbia. Here among the asbestos shingle or "handsplit shakes," the plastic and stainless steel, the thermopane and picture win-dow, the two-car garages and pint-sized dining areas, the weathered wagon wheel and ersatz strawberry barrel, live the suburbanites in their multi-level reconstructions of Colonial America. It is impossible to avoid them. The signs strung along the highways point the way. "Butternut Hill—Turn Right." "This Way to Strawberry Farm Homes." This is no proletarian Levittown. "Peppermill Village" starts with a "minimum" house of "just" seven rooms and two baths for $22,500 and goes on up. But the architectural themes of all of the developments are the same— antiquity, early American, "good taste." The Limited Dream finds a con-cretized expression of the past's myth in "Authentic Farmhouse Recon-structions" and the "Modernized New England Village."

15. Where the villagers live in comparative quiet against the steady but increasing hum of Main Street, the suburbanites live in sun and din. The Suburban Sound is a blend of children, dogs, doors, machines, and mothers. The bedlam of children at play is a universal sound, but the constant clatter of small machines and the ever-present yapping of frus-trated dogs are uniquely suburban. In the summer months, the machines of suburbia are particularly vocal—the power lawn mowers (the grunt, click, and chug of the reel type serving as bass for the steady, high-powered whine of the rotary), the exhaust fans, the concrete mixers, the post-hole diggers, the tree cutters, the roto-tillers, the flooded-cellar pumpers, the hedge trimmers, and softly, in the distance, the growl and clink of the bulldozer steadily at work making more suburbs. Add to this the shouts of children, the cries of babies, the calls of mothers, and the muted tones of the dual tail pipes on the station wagon headed into the village, and the Suburban Sound is complete.

16. No longer is there enough space in Old Harbor. You can't park your car on Main Street any more, there may not be room in church if you arrive late on Sunday, classrooms are "overcrowded," and you have to wait your turn for telephones to be installed in your new house. But these are simply the unsurprising results of sudden growth, and the Old

Harborites are on their way to solving many of them. They have built schools and plan more. They are tearing down bits of the old village surrounding Main Street and are putting in parking lots. Some churches are adding wings or erecting entirely new buildings. They have added policemen and fire engines, and have widened the critical streets. The physical problems, in general, are understood and are being coped with realistically.

17. The fundamental schism between the world of the oldtimers and the world of the newcomers makes a problem that is less obvious but both more important and harder to cope with.

18. In their occupational characteristics, the old settlers range between the middle and upper-middle class. The majority are employed in Old Harbor as merchants, small manufacturers, and businessmen. They constitute the current rearguard of the entrepreneurs of the last century. The rest are mostly white collar people of various persuasions who are employed either in Old Harbor or the neighboring, highly suburbanized county. Less than 20 percent commute into the central city.

19. The average villager is middle-aged, married, and probably has two children either finishing high school or going to college. As a group the oldtimer's formal education did not go beyond high school, but they want their children to go to college and they will generally pick one of the better ones. About half of the oldtimers are Protestant, a third are Catholic, and seven percent are Jewish. The Catholic and Jewish populations represent the changes in Old Harbor's ethnic or religious character that began at the turn of the century. The median family income for the oldtimers in 1955 was about $6,700, roughly $2,300 over the national median for that year. Obviously not all oldtimers in Old Harbor are high-school educated, regular church attendants and securely anchored in the white collar occupations, but enough are to justify the image of the oldtimer as localistic, Protestant, economically "comfortable," conservative, and middle-class.

20. Some of the villagers trace their family lines back ten or twelve generations. Even those who arrived only fifteen or twenty years ago have spent enough time in Old Harbor to have become personally and deeply involved in the community. For them Old Harbor has become a "way of life" and an object of deep affection. When the oldtimer thinks of himself, of his identity as a person, he also thinks of Old Harbor. The community, the social system, the institutions, the organizations, the friendships have become a part of his character. Whatever is the fate of the village has also become each oldtimer's personal fate. An oldtimer merchant put the matter this way: "I have traveled a lot in this country and I've been to Europe a couple of times too. But the biggest thrill in

my life was when I got back from Europe and drove over Potter's Hill and saw the spire of Old First Church down in the valley. It was the most beautiful sight in the world. I really love this town—Old Harbor is the finest community in the United States."

21. The suburbanites are another story. They are a high-income group ($9,700 a year) of professional men and executives. Ninety-seven percent arrived in Old Harbor married and almost 94 percent bought houses there. They average about two grade-school children per family. Only a fourth are Roman Catholics; the great majority are Protestants, although a few more Jews have entered the community in recent years. Nearly four out of every ten of the newcomers were born outside the state. Two-thirds have been exposed to a college education. Close to half commute to the central city, and another third are employed in the county adjacent to the city.

22. Though the villagers are economically "comfortable," they are nonetheless rather stationary on the income ladder. They are pretty well frozen into an occupational *cul de sac*. The suburbanites, on the other hand, are upward bound—their jobs pay better and carry more prestige than the villagers'. For them the primary world is the metropolitan area. They work there, play there, and their most intimate friends live there. They tend to see in Old Harbor the familiar culture of the apartment house now spread into one-acre "country estates." To the villager, Old Harbor represents continuity between the generations, stability instead of the city's "chaos," and a place of permanence in a universe of bewildering change. The suburbanite sees in the village a weekend away from the advertising agency or the pilot's compartment. He experiences Old Harbor as a series of isolated, fragmented, unconnected social situations. Old Harbor is the family, a cocktail party, a bathing beach, a movie, a supermarket, a country club, a school, a church, a PTA meeting. It is a one-acre wooded retreat from all of the drive, bureaucracy, and anxiety of the city. But a weekend is enough for the necessary physical and psychological repairs; it's back to the city on Monday.

23. The temper of the suburbanite "community" may be summarized in the way the suburbanites talk about Old Harbor:

> I came to Old Harbor because there is still some green around here and yet I can still get to the airport in 45 minutes. It's a nice place to live— the schools are good, and I like being near the water. It is hard to say how long we'll be here. I would like to be based further south, but as a place to live Old Harbor is fine.

> I can't think of Old Harbor as my own town or anything like that. Most of my friends live closer to the city and I work there. I don't have any feeling of living in a small community or anything like that. I guess I

sleep more of my time here than anything else, but it's a good place for the kids. I've got a lot of contacts and interests outside.

I have to go pretty much where the company sends me. I was transferred up to the office over a year ago so we bought a place out here in Old Harbor. Probably be here for three or four years then most likely I'll be sent to South America. We like Old Harbor although the way it's building up it will be like the city in no time. Well, it doesn't bother me much; we won't be around here forever.

But an oldtimer says:

They (the suburbanites) don't know what's going on around here. They don't care. But I do; this is my town. I used to fish down at the tide basin. Now they're talking of tearing it down. I went to school here. All my friends live around here. It's crazy what's happening. I can look out of my shop window and can't recognize 49 out of 50 faces I see. There was a time I knew everybody. It used to be our town. I don't know whose it is any more.

24. For the villagers, Old Harbor is their community and they have a fierce sense of possession about it. It is a property that they share. And like any valuable property it is cared for and cherished. It must not be profanely or rudely used. This is the real issue that splits the suburbanite and villager communities apart. For the suburbanites, Old Harbor is another commodity; it is a product that can be rationally consumed; it is a means by which they hope to achieve a complex series of personal goals. For the villagers, on the other hand, Old Harbor is not a means to anything; it is simply an end in itself.

25. The two communities inevitably brush against each other in the course of everyday life. They flow together on the central streets, in the movie houses, on the beaches, at graduation exercises, and in the stores and shops of Main Street. In their economic relationships, villager and suburbanite have struck a symbiotic truce. They need each other, the villager to sell and the suburbanite to buy. Suburbia has brought new prosperity to the villager. Traffic and congestion on Main Street mean crowds of buyers. Parking lots may be expensive, but they also mean customers. On the other hand, there are signs that increasing suburbanization will threaten the retailers of Main Street. The shiny "super shopping centers" to the south of the village, where a couple of thousand cars can park with ease, make the village shops seem dingy and dull. The discount stores and mechanized supermarkets of the shopping centers out along the highway augur a bleaker future along Main Street.

26. Perhaps the greatest single issue separating villager from suburbanite has been "the school problem." With the tripling of the school population, Old Harbor has been faced with an intensive building program. Since they are essentially realists in their village microcosm, the oldtimers have reluctantly admitted the "need" for more schools. Enough of them have been eventually worn down in public meetings to cast an approving vote for new construction. For many a villager, however, it has seemed to mean money out of his pocket to pay for the schooling of other people's children. But the basic and decisive issue has not been whether to build more schools or not, but what kind of schools to build and what kind of education the children should have.

27. In their approach to this question, the villagers are traditionalists and conservative. They see a good education as including the basic skills taught by a dedicated but maidenly teacher in a plain school building. The suburbanites, on the other hand, are educational radicals; they are irrepressible spenders and cult-like in their dedication to the cause of modern education. It is an axiom among the oldtimers that the more costly a pending proposition is the more the newcomers will take to it, and they are not entirely wrong. The newcomers appear willing to sacrifice all else to their "children's education." At PTA gatherings and public meetings of the school board, an ecstatic speaker can bring tears to sophisticated suburbanite eyes and justify the most outlandish cause by reminding his audience that "no expense is too great when it comes to our children's welfare. It will just cost the price of a few cartons of cigarettes a year to give our children this new gymnasium. Isn't our children's education, and clean, wholesome recreational facilities worth a few cents more a year? Is there any parent here who can deny their children this? Is there anyone here who will deny their children what America can offer . . . ?"

28. Everyone will be on his feet applauding, for the side of "the children" has won again, and every villager who voted against the plastic gymnasium or marble swimming pool will have to face the terrible question: "Do I really hate children?"

29. For the newcomers, anything that is educationally worthwhile must also be very expensive. "After all, you get what you pay for." The villagers, on the other hand, will battle the "frills" and "extravagances" and will turn down "excessive" curricular and building proposals. Eventually a compromise is worked out. But in the suburbias of the upper-middle class, education is the cohesive issue around which a "consciousness of kind" develops for the newcomers. For many, education seems to have taken the place of religion.

30. While the newcomers have taken over the PTA's and infiltrated the

school board, the villagers continue to control the churches. Suburbanites usually join the PTA before they become members of a church, though they swell the numbers of those attending religious services. But even in the ranks of the devout, there have been indications of a schism.

31. The villagers tend to look upon their churches as something more than formal religious centers. Over the years they have served as rallying points for a good deal of coöperative community activity, and they tend to stand for a morality and a traditionalism highly compatible with villager perspectives. One villager remarked that you can hardly keep from feeling a little possessive about a church you have helped to build. The minister of one Protestant church who rather reluctantly admitted that all was not harmony within his flock, pointed out that the "older residents" had finished paying off the church mortgage sometime around 1947, and a few years later the church had almost doubled its congregation. As the minister saw it, the villagers were indignant over the invasion of "their" church by "outsiders." They were especially smarting over the fact that, because of the devoted work of the oldtimers, the newcomers had inherited a church free and clear of any financial encumbrance. The villagers felt that the solvency of their church had made it more attractive, and that the enthusiasm the suburbanites showed for it was not without crasser implications. As a consequence, the oldtimers began to champion all church causes that were particularly expensive. It has been the villagers who have stoutly called for a new Sunday School building and a finer parish house. The villagers have been on the side of free and easy spending by the church ever since the suburban influx began.

32. This is not the whole story. A few years back, one of the most fashionable churches of Old Harbor made some sympathetic overtures to a purely newcomer religious group—Jews of the "Reformed" group who were conducting their services in an empty store on Main Street. The minister of this old Protestant church, which traces its origins back to the American Revolution and whose membership consists of the elect of Old Harbor society, offered the facilities of his church to the Jewish newcomers. The Jews happily accepted the offer. This not only brought the two worlds together but the Protestant and localistic villagers and the Jewish, cosmopolitan suburbanites even sponsored joint "functions" together. The differences between the villagers and suburbanites are not insurmountable, nor are the two separated by an impenetrable curtain of prejudice and ignorance.

33. The newcomers have largely ignored the formal political organizations of Old Harbor. Traditionally the community has been solidly Republican, and the upper-middle-class suburbanites have not threatened the political balance. There are a few more egghead Democrats in Old

Harbor in recent years who write books or teach in a college, but they are regarded as odd and harmless, and no one pays much attention to them. This does not mean that the suburbanites are not politically active; they are, but they act outside political parties to do political things. Their means is the civic association. Each development or combination of developments has organized its own. As the Peppermill Village Civic Association, they lobby for sidewalks or against sidewalks, for street lights and sewers, or to keep out the sand and gravel contractor who wants to use the adjacent property for commercial purposes. Through the civic associations, the suburbanites engage in a series of running skirmishes with the villagers over local issues. Usually what they want costs more, so the villagers are against it.

34. The oldtimers fill almost all the political offices, where they serve to balance the limited and self-interested objectives of the civic associations against the "broader needs" of the village and the township. But in this capacity the oldtimers are more than oldtimers; they are also politicians. Having learned that the suburbanites are amazingly perceptive on the level of neighborhood self-interest, the politicians will throw an occasional sop to the militant civic associations with an eye to the coming elections. Though the suburbanites are circumscribed in their interests, they are nonetheless organized, and can marshal massive political displeasure at the polls. As a consequence, the villager politicians must somehow walk a tightrope, balancing the political expediency of pleasing the newcomers against their own desire to keep the village what it was.

35. One wonders how many towns like Old Harbor are currently fighting to keep their identities in the industrializing South or in the rapidly growing Far West. How many Old Harbors are there all together? No one can even chance a guess. Each of the 168 great metropolitan centers of the nation is at present consuming a whole series of villages now within its sociological borders. And each village has a different history, a geography of its own and a set of institutions practiced by a population that is the same as nowhere else. Yet beneath the idiosyncratic surface, the villagers look with universal anxiety as the crush of metropolitanization proceeds. Everywhere the spirit of the small village suffers with the encroachment of urban anonymity and transiency. The Levittowns are fresh and naked, yet of a single character. The Old Harbors are split by the struggles of two communities to shape the prevailing character of the whole.

36. Yet the future lies with the metropolis and not the village. You

can see it in the new super expressways that slice through Old Harbor's meadowlands. You sense the shift in internal balance in the village by the domination of the suburbanites at school board meetings. You know it on an autumn's evening, in the crisp sea air, and in the deepening twilight around the mill pond. The great shuddering bulk of the mill squats in the hollow, intimidated by the headlights of the commuters as they race down and through the valley, dreary from the city and hungry for home. Pencils of light search into the gaping slats and crudely intrude upon the embarrassment of the mill's decay—the rusting gears, the splintered shaft, the rotting timbers, and marsh slop heaped up by the last high tide. And then with a rush the auto is gone, driving a little eddy of defiant leaves against the listless doors, leaving the old mill momentarily in shadows, huddled against the lowering sky. Through the empty windows, across the tide basin, and over the harbor, you can see the new shopping center bathed in neon and fluorescent light. There is a busyness about it. Up along the darkening necks the lights are going on in the new split levels and "contemporaries" tucked into the ridges. The lights go on and off as the night rolls in. They seem to be winking at the senile mill as it sits and broods in the gathering darkness.

COMMENTARY AND QUESTIONS

The author of this essay, a professor of sociology and co-author of *The Suburban Community,* has given us here a case-study, a type of presentation frequently used by social scientists.

1. In which two points in his essay does Dobriner concentrate the generalizations that are illustrated by his case-study of Old Harbor? What advantage does he gain by devoting nearly all of his essay to a single illustration? Is extensive use of specific detail characteristic of the style of the whole essay? What effect is achieved by the use of the many details in, for example, par. 8?

2. Does the author seem to think that the change now taking place in Old Harbor is a good thing? Are his sympathies with the villagers or the suburbanites? How do you know? Can you find any evidence to support the opposite answer? If so, what effect does it have on the author's evaluation? Is the tone of the final paragraph the dominant tone of the essay as a whole?

3. Point out four words in par. 2 (excluding the final sentence) that clearly reveal the author's attitude toward the urbanization of once-independent villages. Substitute for the phrase "pushy, progressive, and plastic world" in the final sentence of par. 2 a phrase that has the same meaning but a more favorable connotation.

4. Pars. 4-12 give the history of Old Harbor. What purposes are served

by the inclusion of this material? Why is the particular detail from the early history of Old Harbor given in par. 4 especially appropriate?

5. Pars. 13-14 deal with Old Harbor as it is now. What method of development is predominant in this section? Why can pars. 25-34 be thought of as a unit? What order is followed in arranging the topics within this unit? What structural purpose is served by par. 29? What is the logical relationship between par. 32 and the two paragraphs preceding it?

6. Much of the effectiveness of this essay comes from Dobriner's skillful choice of words that do more than communicate the author's meaning. What is distinctive, for example, about the diction in the last sentence of par. 11, the last several sentences of par. 13, and the last two of par. 15? Which of the five senses is dominant in par. 15 and why is this sense emphasized here? How was this emphasis anticipated in par. 13?

7. Exactness as well as freshness is a virtue in diction. What is the meaning of *classic* in the last sentence of par. 9, *concretized* in the last of par. 14, and *symbiotic* in the third of par. 25? Note the etymology of *symbiotic*.

8. Contrast and compare the structure of the last five sentences of par. 13 with that of the first two of par. 14. What is the difference between the structure of the latter two and that of the fourth sentence in par. 15?

9. Is much use made of obvious exaggeration in this essay? How effective is the exaggeration in par. 28?

10. Much of the following essay, "Fluid Suburbia," particularly pars. 5-12 (pp. 287-288), also deals with the impact of the expanding city on near-by areas. What is the difference in point of view between the two treatments of this topic?

SUGGESTIONS FOR WRITING

1. By using an extensive illustration, present some situation that you are familiar with, such as the destruction of a wilderness area, the clash of two groups of people, or of two cultures.

2. All suburbs aren't reluctant.

3. That's progress!

4. You wouldn't recognize the old place (such as university, town, summer resort).

Fluid Suburbia

by WILLIAM ZECKENDORF

EVERY DAY of the week, hundreds of people travel by air between Boston and Washington. During this 400-mile journey the city is always below them; only the name changes. They could extend their trip north to Portland, Maine, and south to Norfolk, Virginia, with the same result: between those two places urban areas merge imperceptibly to form, in effect, a single city.

2. This is the megalopolis, the supercity, sometimes known as the linear city or interurbia. It is a shapeless mass of fluid city and suburb which results when the city's outlying districts flow together and intermingle seemingly without plan or logic into one urban sprawl. The fluid city of the East Coast contains more than thirty million people, almost one-fifth of the nation's total population crammed into one-twenty-fifth of its area, and beset by a staggering array of problems.

3. They have trouble getting to work. They have trouble finding adequate places to live. Recreation is often denied them. To see green grass and trees they often are forced to travel great distances. They are oppressed by heavy traffic and overcrowded schools, by noise and fumes, by dreary and monotonous surroundings, by high taxes and municipal problems. They suffer from the actions of their neighbors: one town's refuse pollutes the next town's water, or its air, or its beaches. Meanwhile, the central city which supports the suburb is haunted by the specter of bankruptcy.

4. Although I am speaking now primarily of the East Coast supercity, a study of this area has meaning for people all over the United States. Fluid suburbia, as I call it, is a national phenomenon. On the West Coast, Los Angeles and San Diego are growing together, and the resultant urban area is slowly advancing northward toward Santa Barbara. Another tangle of cities and suburbs is developing around San Francisco. Farther north, a similar growth is occurring in the Puget Sound area, encompassing the cities of Seattle and Tacoma and many smaller communities. At least three such regions are growing up in the Midwest: Pittsburgh-Cleveland, Detroit-Toledo, and Chicago-Milwaukee. Eventually, if the expansion of these three sections continues, they will all merge into one vast city, the nation's largest in area.

kee. Eventually, if the expansion of these three sections continues, they will all merge into one vast city, the nation's largest in area.

5. Thus has man's urge to escape been frustrated by his own short-sighted planning. He has tried to get out of the city, and in so doing he has taken the city with him. This problem, second only to that of national defense, is the most pressing, vexing, provocative, and yet important enigma that faces the country today. The psychologist tells us that change of pace is essential to the well-being of man. If we are to avoid a nation of psychotics, this natural urge must be appeased.

6. What has happened in the Los Angeles area is fairly typical. There the population seems to jump and bypass each new community as it goes out into the mountains, the wilderness, and on to the plains. As soon as people escape to a new section, they are bypassed again, and find themselves looking at somebody else's rear light. They have urbanized the mountains, the plains, the valleys. In their urge to escape they have created a condition from which there is no escape. It has finally reached the point where it is impossible to say, "Let's get in the car and go out of town to dinner tonight." There is no out of town in Los Angeles. No matter where you go, no matter how fast and how far and in what direction you drive, you arrive where you have just left.

7. In every part of the United States, the outlying areas of our metropolitan centers have grown with astonishing rapidity. The flight from the city to the suburbs commenced slowly following the first decade of this century and has reached full tide in the years since the Second World War. The reasons for it are many and complex. Foremost among them is the fantastic increase in the population.

8. We are now experiencing what scientists appropriately call a population "explosion." In 1850 there were about one billion people on the earth. One hundred years later there were two billion. The third billion will be here in only 25 years, by 1975. The influence of this population increase on the United States has been staggering. The 1940 census counted 131,669,275 Americans; in 1950 there were 150,697,361; 1960 will show an estimated 179,358,000; 1970, 209,380,000. One expert has predicted that less than 100 years from now there will be nine billion people in the world—600 million of them in the United States.

9. All the people added to our population since the war have needed some place to live. Coinciding with the population growth has come a vast improvement in automobile transportation and a great increase in the income of the average American. The urge for green spaces, better school facilities, and modern, efficient housing did the rest. The suburbs seemed to be the obvious solution.

10. The means of turning this desire into a practicality were already

restimulate business activity and prime the economic pump with new housing construction. Under the Act, easy term mortgages were insured by the government to lighten the risk for the money lenders. The GI Bill of the 'forties made home financing even easier; houses could be bought with little or no down payment and with low-interest mortgages. To meet the demand for housing stimulated by these measures, mass construction techniques were worked out by builders. The only space available for mass building was outside the cities, and subdivisions began to spring up in the suburbs. Eventually they extended far beyond the traditional suburban areas, covering farm and estate lands with countless rows of boxlike houses which from the air look like loaves of bread fresh from the baker's oven. Without plan or pattern the larger cities in ever widening ranges absorbed towns, hamlets, and rural areas.

11. Potent sociological and economic factors are also at work in the expansion of the suburbs. There is snob appeal—the desire of the rich or the newly rich or the aspiring rich to disassociate themselves from those in a more modest economic category. The established families tend to hold themselves above the Johnny-come-latelies. The Johnny-come-latelies soon reach the same category as their former "superiors," when their income improves and their education or their children's education brings them up to acceptable country club standards. The tracks can be crossed either way, and the crosscurrents soon get mixed after the third generation.

12. Formerly the downtown areas of most cities were the best residential sections because of their convenience. But as new arrivals encroached on the established communities, the old residents often moved farther out. As this process went on, the suburbs filled up and the downtown areas were abandoned, to be occupied by those of the lowest economic level.

13. The result is that all over the United States we have some of our worst slums within the shadow of City Hall. The same pattern is to be found in almost every community over a hundred years old. First, the older generation built a residence and settled. Second, the younger people moved to the new green belt areas. Third, the house was rented to a more ambitious, large family of lesser social and economic standing. Fourth, the building, now outmoded and lacking in modern conveniences, was leased as a rooming house. Finally, it was allowed to deteriorate with the general neighborhood. Consequently many of our cities rot at the core while the continued migration to the periphery creates a stronger and stronger vacuum at the center.

14. In many cases, industry has stimulated this outward movement.

Factories found it harder and harder—and increasingly more expensive —to expand and to operate inside the cities. The growth of trucking made them less dependent on rail and ship transportation; they moved out to the surrounding countryside where there was plenty of space and where operating costs were often lower. An industry, for example, would much prefer 100,000 square feet in a one-story horizontal building serviced by a rail siding and truck docks and surrounded by green areas and plenty of parking to ten floors of 10,000 square feet in a vertical operation. Sometimes hundreds of workers followed them out.

15. All this movement away from the city had concomitant effects. Department stores opened branches in the new, heavily populated suburbs and soon discovered that the branches were taking the trade away from the original downtown locations. A number of old stores have even left the cities entirely and are operating only in the suburbs, luring still more people out of the cities. Two examples are John Wanamaker's in New York and R. H. White in Boston.

16. The same cycle occurred with automobile transportation. As the suburbs grew, new roads had to be built to accommodate the increased auto traffic. The new roads made it easier than ever to reach the suburbs, and more people moved out. Now the new roads are often jammed, and more must be built.

17. A good example of a city's being injured by its own suburbs is New York, which has seen its metropolitan area grow until the population of the outlying districts almost equals that of the central city, big as it is. The result has been almost disastrous for both the city-dweller and the suburbanite.

18. Today the western half of Long Island, northeastern New Jersey, large areas of Westchester and Rockland counties in New York State, and the southwestern tip of Connecticut are, in effect, part of New York City, a "bedroom area" for those who work in the central metropolis. There are hundreds of thousands of these suburbanites, many of whom must take a one-hour—or in some cases even a two-hour—train or automobile trip to get to work.

19. And the commuting life lines are steadily deteriorating. Railroads, struggling to minimize losses in the unprofitable commuter service, are forced to cut quality. They are seeking to abandon some lines entirely, to provide fewer trains on others, to avoid heavy new expenditures on modern rolling stock that may never be able to pay for itself.

20. The decline in rail service compels many commuters to travel by automobile, and traffic on the feeder highways grows progressively worse. On Long Island, a strip of land 120 miles long but only ten to twenty miles wide, no less than seven major highways—including three

big expressways—funnel commuter traffic into the city from suburban communities. It is not likely that another road could be fitted into this pattern, yet more are certainly needed. During the rush hours all present highways are jammed, sometimes to a standstill.

21. Besides creating transit problems the New York commuter is responsible for difficulties of another kind. He is a man of divided loyalties, and the city that supports him almost always runs a poor second in his sense of responsibility to the community where he lives. Moreover, there is a tremendous duplication of expense with much of the extra cost borne by those who can least afford it.

22. Scores of residential towns around New York City maintain their own fire and police departments, each with its own equipment—far more equipment than would be required if the communities all came under a central government. Water and sewage disposal systems, instead of being integrated, tend to compete with each other. Town roads end at the town line and maintenance varies from one community to another.

23. The suburbanite earns his salary in the city and spends it outside. As a result, while the city's problems and expenses multiply, its money-raising ability grows ever less. When New York City instituted a sales tax to help pay for, among other things, services required by nonresidents, shoppers began to travel in large numbers to outlying communities, and business in New York was hurt. Meanwhile, New York City is expected to provide—and does provide—the cultural facilities that have always been recognized as a responsibility of urban government: museums, sports arenas, auditoriums, libraries, zoos, aquariums, and the like. They all cost money. They all comprise an additional burden on the city taxpayer.

24. To summarize, satellite towns, the product of decentralization, are parasitic. The high cost of maintenance of the central core that supports the whole metropolitan area is borne by the city, but the revenue and benefits go to the towns at the periphery—each having its own separate fire and police departments, water supply, mayor, and councilmen: all a duplication of the cost of the city's core.

25. Every satellite town saps off the buying power, the taxing power, and the vital factors that make for a cohesive, comprehensive, healthy city. This is just as though the United States lost the taxing power in California and New York through their setting up independent operation, but continued to have the cost of maintaining the central bureaucracy, the army and navy, and so on. It wouldn't take very long for the United States to go broke on such a basis; and as long as this sort of thing can be done by the satellite towns around the mother city, we are jeopardizing the entire fiscal and political future of our great municipalities.

26. However, all is not lost. Decentralization has been going on for a long time. There is not a person in this country who is not either a decentralizee or the progeny of a decentralizee. We have all come from somewhere else—either this generation, our fathers', grandfathers', or our great-grandfathers'.

27. Yet the timeless metropolis, the great historic communities of the world, which are able to define what they have to offer to their nation and to world commerce, have a virility that seems to be able to withstand all the departures of their sons and daughters. Even though we have come from France, from Greece, from Germany, from Ireland, there are more of us who return to visit Paris or Rome or Athens or Dublin or London than there are of those who live there and who come to visit us. We come home at times with the impression of terrific and unhappy decadence in the midst of great splendor and beauty in those capitals and principal cities of Europe. But we are all impressed by one thing: that notwithstanding the vagaries of war, the misfortunes of economic debacle, the problems that have arisen from revolution, the vitality of certain cities of the world seems to be invulnerable.

28. This is not an invariable thing, of course, but it is well to bear it in mind when one thinks of decentralization. There are many cities of antiquity that have died on the vine, and there are many in our own country that are dying and will die on the vine.

29. What is going to happen to the central city as a result of decentralized activities? It depends entirely, in my opinion, on what action the city takes. Whatever has happened to the cities, they have been asking for it. Certainly there is no across-the-board answer for all cities: each must analyze its own potential and draw its plans accordingly. Many, of course, have neglected rapid transit, adequate parking, and adequate zoning. But the highway to the periphery runs both ways. The automobile has no sense of direction. It has no memory. It goes where it is pointed. It is possible, therefore, for the city to recentralize at the core.

30. There is one determining principle by which every city and town and community can be guided in its self-analysis. Each must ask itself: What am I really like? What have I to offer? What are my resources? How can I fit into the economy of the region? Where do I stand in the national orbit? Each city without regard to any other, and casting aside all delusions, must determine where its strength and its weaknesses lie, and then go ahead and make plans for its own development.

31. This brings us to the heart of the matter—the problem of over-all planning. I am a great believer in planning but a great disbeliever in spot planning. Planning must be of two types: regional and city-wide. Coöperation is the key in both. First let us take a look at a situation

which calls for regional planning. New York City once again gives us an example.

$^{32.}$ The importance of New York harbor to its city and to the nation is hard to overestimate. Yet not for a long time has New York had complete control of the port and its piers. On the harbor's west banks, seven New Jersey communities control the waterfront, each with its own rules and tax structures. My own firm, Webb & Knapp, Inc., owns Pier 16 in Hoboken but is about to give it up: although it would cost $1,500,000 today to build a pier like it, real estate taxes are so unrealistic that they cost us half again as much as the maximum rental we could hope to collect on it.

$^{33.}$ Bad as it is now—and it is bad for various reasons—the situation in New York harbor was far worse years ago. During the First World War the New York-New Jersey port facilities proved so inadequate that at one time more than 200,000 freight cars were in the yards waiting to be unloaded while in the nation as a whole there was a severe shortage of cars to move essential war materials. This intolerable situation could be remedied during wartime, as it was, by exercise of the President's broad powers. After the war the states of New York and New Jersey moved to make sure that such a situation would never arise again. In 1921 one of the nation's first regional governmental agencies, the Port of New York Authority, was established to do what the individual cities and states alone could not do.

$^{34.}$ The Port Authority is charged with coördinating and controlling terminals and other transportation facilities which affect the commerce within a 25-mile radius of the Statue of Liberty. It is a nonpolitical, self-supporting agency, six of whose twelve members are appointed by the governor of New York, the others by the governor of New Jersey. The Authority today is a mighty business. Its investments total more than $600,000,000 and it engages in such far-flung operations that it is virtually impossible to enter New York City, or to ship in any product, without making use of one of its facilities. The Authority operates four marine terminals, five air terminals including LaGuardia and Idlewild airports and a midtown Manhattan helicopter landing site, a bus terminal, two truck terminals, and a rail freight terminal. Great interstate spans like the George Washington Bridge are within its domain, as are New York's famous Hudson River automobile tubes, the Lincoln and Holland tunnels.

$^{35.}$ In fact, there may be some reason to believe that the Port Authority's activities are too wide in scope. In its efforts to maintain its self-supporting status, the agency has ventured into fields (I am thinking specifically of my own field, real estate) where it is competing with private enterprise. The special authority, with its own taxing powers and functions, can be an efficient governmental entity; it can also be an autocratic and unresponsive agency. I feel it is only fair to say that I believe the Port of New York Authority has on occasion been both.

36. Nevertheless, the establishment of the Authority was a magnificent forward step toward the solution of the fluid city's problems, and its operations should be closely examined by experts in municipal affairs who will objectively study its operations in the light of economic efficiency and the democratic process.

37. In an effort to deal with its commuter problems, New York has joined with New Jersey and Connecticut in an interstate body, the Metropolitan Transit Authority, to give the matter intensive study on a regional basis. It was even suggested recently that the Port Authority itself take over responsibility for New York's traffic headaches, a suggestion which the Authority, having plenty of headaches of its own, quickly rebuffed. It may be that some form of subsidy for rail transportation will be required. After all, Federal participation in road building provides subsidies at present for automobile transportation.

38. The Tri-Borough Bridge and Tunnel Authority, although not an interstate body, under the guidance of Robert Moses has made a tremendous contribution toward improving vehicular ingress and egress in New York. Its expanded highways have resulted in interstate as well as intrastate benefits. Its Tri-Borough and Whitestone bridges and Brooklyn-Battery Tunnel, the contemplated bridge across the Narrows to Staten Island, the planned 30th Street Expressway in Manhattan, are examples of what is being done to coördinate and expedite traffic patterns.

39. Swift, convenient, attractive mass transportation must be provided into our cities if they are not to wither. The problem is being widely studied—in San Francisco and Washington, D. C., for example, as well as New York—and perhaps these studies will produce additional solutions. Mass transportation, in my opinion, is more effective by rail than by rubber.

40. But solving the allied transit-and-traffic difficulties will not go to the heart of the problem of fluid suburbia. I believe there is only one solution and that a drastic one. The parasite towns and the central city must be brought together into one urban organism so that the suburb will be governed by the city off which it lives. Only those communities which are truly independent should not be incorporated into the large city. The test of independence is simple: can this community survive— socially and economically—without the benefits it derives from the mother city? Take employment, for example. Do the bulk of the town's

workers travel to jobs in the city, or can they find employment near home? If they can't—and they can't in 90 percent of the satellite towns in the immediate vicinity of large cities—then the city should have the right to incorporate the town.

41. That there will be widespread opposition to such a move I am well aware. Small towns value their independence. They like doing things their own way. Often they tend to look down on their larger neighbor. Sometimes they can truly boast more honest and more efficient governments than the nearby cities. Nevertheless, the advantages of incorporation—or at least, concerted action under an overall authority—are so great as to outweigh all other considerations.

42. Take a look at Toronto. After the Second World War, tremendous growth hit this Canadian city and its neighboring communities. The effort to duplicate city facilities and services was too much for many of the suburbs. Two of them nearly went broke in the attempt. Yet the small municipalities jealously guarded their independence.

43. The solution arrived at was a compromise which went into effect about four years ago. Under it, Toronto and eleven neighboring towns joined together in an incorporated federation called the Municipality of Metropolitan Toronto, locally known as Metro. Metro has assumed responsibility for construction of schools, sewage plants, expressways, and even homes for the aged. It operates one police department for the entire area and will shortly take over fire-fighting services as well. In its first full year of operation it brought about total savings of more than $3,000,000 for the communities involved (although it must be added that some towns, better off than their neighbors to begin with, found life under Metro a trifle more expensive than complete independence had been).

44. The Metro plan has not been without flaws. It is a compromise involving the imposition of an additional government above those of the city and its surrounding suburbs, and consequently its operation has been burdened with red tape. Nevertheless, it has solved the problems it was created to meet, and some people believe that it will ultimately lead to real annexation under the Toronto city government—which probably would have been the best solution all along.

45. As things are now in many metropolitan areas of the United States, a kind of municipal anarchy exists which does no one any good. So long as we continue growing in this unrelated pattern—where each community imposes its own zoning and controls its own street system, does its own taxing and wastes its own money, meanwhile disregarding what happens to the central core—just so long we shall have more and more taxes by the central city and less and less control of central

city politics by the general citizenry who will have abandoned the mother city to ward politics of the lower order. The eventual result will be catastrophe.

46. Another approach to the problems of the city has never been given adequate consideration, I believe, and deserves mention in passing. Cities should devote more thought to the lighter side of life for the people who live and work in them. Pittsburgh is doing it by developing a new recreation park in what was once a railroad yard. But few other cities pay enough attention to recreation facilities. To most people the cities are, consequently, just a place to get away from.

47. We have the trend towards shorter hours and more leisure time. Almost every town has a blighted area which could be redeveloped as a play area—a place for fun. I visualize a tremendous recreation hall, bowling alleys, skating rinks, merry-go-rounds for the children, swimming pools for both children and adults—in short, a happy place for exercise and entertainment. In addition to lifting morale, such a center would attract residents back to the city. People would say, "Let's go to town. Let's have some fun tonight!" They would feel that their city is a great place to live in, not a great place to get away from. Moreover, such an area would pay for itself; no other type of investment pays a higher return in relation to the invested capital.

48. Finally, and most important of all from the point of view of private enterprise, we can solve the problem of the exodus to the suburbs by making the city a better place to live in. This is a solution in which I believe devoutly. I know it can be done, because my firm is doing it. The real estate economist and developer with his team of architects and city planners, his more than passing knowledge of land values and land uses, his capacity to finance and build, is performing his most useful function in this field of urban reconstruction.

49. Two forces are at work which will make the cities more desirable as living areas. One is a volunteer citizens group called ACTION—American Council To Improve Our Neighborhoods. This group functions through local organizations with a view to stopping the growth of slums by house-to-house improvement. It is doing superb work.

50. The other force is Title I of the National Housing Act of 1949—surely one of the most creative pieces of legislation passed by Congress in our time. The intent of this Act is to regenerate cities by a partnership between private and public enterprise. Under it, the city designates slum areas as suitable for clearance. With a loan from the Federal Government it then buys such areas, relocates the families (except in New York City), and demolishes the substandard structures. This cleared land is then sold at a somewhat lower price to a private developer who agrees

to develop it in accordance with a plan approved by the city. Two-thirds of the cost to the city is met by Federal grant. The city itself pays the rest—but since it is credited with its investment in utilities, streets, schools, etc., it actually pays relatively little cash. Moreover, it recaptures its outlay within a few years and thereafter enjoys a higher tax return based on new construction as well as the better social conditions brought into being.

51. So far as I am concerned, modern urban redevelopment is based on the principle that man has achieved his highest cultural development in the urban area and that there is nothing wrong with the city that cannot be cured by eliminating its sick areas and importing something of the countryside. To achieve this, cities of the future will be generally more vertical, with most buildings made taller and more slender to let in the weather, the snow and the sun, to bring to urban man the great rotation of the seasons. These new buildings will retain the same cubic footage, block by block, as those that now occupy the land, but they will be higher, more functional, gracious spires surrounded by quiet green areas.

52. Among these sky-rise apartments, as they might be called, will be interspersed single family houses of two or three stories and row houses designed specifically for urban living. These town houses will have private gardens and garages; in some places they will be built around a central park. This city of the future will be a place where families can raise children in a quiet and safe atmosphere. The major highways, conveniently served by mechanized parking, will bound the development rather than traverse it, serving as buffers between residential and non-residential areas. Living accommodations will be tailored for all needs—for the family with children, for the couple whose children have married and left home, for the single person, for the elderly. This pattern of urban living will offer many of the amenities of suburbia without its drawbacks.

53. This is almost a description, admittedly in glowing terms, of a project already in the works under the sponsorship of my company, Webb & Knapp. The Southwest quadrant of Washington, D. C. has been a residential and commercial slum for more than a hundred years. In cooperation with the National Capital Planning Commission we have drawn up a master plan for 446 acres of this area in the heart of the capital and will develop there a residential community of 20,000, in addition to a government-business complex containing Federal and commercial office buildings, a shopping center, parking area, restaurants, and public and private waterfront facilities, all in a park-like setting.

54. Washington's slums have long been a local and national embar-

rassment. In addition, Washington has suffered from fluid suburbia in the same way other American cities have. By simultaneously replacing at least one of its major slum areas and providing new housing that will attract people back from the suburbs, Washington is coming boldly to grips with two of the major problems of the megalopolis.

55. One additional word. A factor of unknown but tremendous potential is the further acceleration of the speed of travel through the introduction of the jet plane. The day is upon us when travel from the greater to the lesser metropolis and back between breakfast and dinner is possible. Why should not the strong magnets (New York, Chicago, San Francisco, Los Angeles, Dallas, Toronto, Montreal) attract back to themselves all of their departing ambassadors by nightfall, like so many birds coming home to roost? This may mean that those cities of the world and of the nation that have the most to offer will become cumulatively greater at the expence of the less potent communities. As the flame draws the moths so will the most brilliant beacons of art, finance, commerce, dining, and fun gradually absorb and monopolize the most powerful buying element from everywhere.

56. The problem of designing a city to be able to capture its share may become an increasingly vexing one. The plane, like the automobile, has no sense of direction: it goes where it is directed and it is pointed to the place where one gets the most for the least trouble and expense. Thus a new pattern and a new threat that might create additional vacuums in localities which now presumably sit smugly secure arise as an apparition difficult to conjure with.

57. Let no one in the more populated American cities take solace from all this because they too will become vulnerable to the attractions of the cities everywhere else in the world—particularly Europe. Now Vienna, Paris, and Rome are more accessible to New Yorkers than New York City was to Chicagoans a generation ago. And so the horizon of a new form of decentralization already begins to take shape.

COMMENTARY AND QUESTIONS

In this essay William Zeckendorf, a well-known builder and developer interested in urban renewal, presents an evaluation of our modern cities—their faults, the causes of these faults, and what needs to be done about them. Basic to this evaluation is the author's appraisal of the past contribution of cities to civilized living and of their potential in the future.

1. In par. 51 Zeckendorf states his basic assumption concerning cities. Does this assumption become apparent before par. 51? In par. 24 and again in par. 40 the author uses two derogatory terms in referring to

towns that are dependent on near-by cities. What are these terms? Does their use indicate that he lacks appreciation of the values of living outside a city? Consider particularly par. 5. Where else can you find evidence on this point?

2. The impression of a megalopolis presented in par. 1 is deliberately neutral, but quite a different impression is given by pars. 2-6. Is the physical point of view the same in par. 1 as in pars. 3-6? How does this give the author an opportunity to achieve a contrast through change in tone? In par. 2 the transition from a neutral to an unfavorable impression is achieved by the use of such terms as *shapeless mass, without plan or logic, sprawl, crammed,* and *beset.* Find terms in pars. 3-6 which maintain this unfavorable impression.

3. Pars. 1-7 comprise the introduction of this essay. What purposes are served by this introduction? What is the function of the next-to-last sentence of par. 7? of the following one? Is a similar function performed by the final sentence of par. 2?

4. In pars. 7-14 Zeckendorf explains the reasons for the recent very rapid development of the areas surrounding our cities. What is the topic of pars. 15-25? Why do you think the author put his discussion of slums in par. 13 instead of including it in the section to which he devotes pars. 15-25?

5. What purpose is served by par. 24? How does this paragraph prepare us for par. 40?

6. In par. 25 the author uses an analogy. Why is it effective? If an analogy is to serve its purpose fully what requirements must it meet?

7. What is the logical relationship between pars. 42-44 and the final sentence of par. 41? If the author could have used an area within the United States for his example here would he have strengthened his point by doing so? What does this tell you about the characteristics of the most effective examples? In pars. 17-23 and again in pars. 32-38 New York is used as an example. What is it an example of in each place? What advantage is gained here by using the same city as example of two different points?

8. Do pars. 55-57 serve as a conclusion? If not, what is their function? Did the author's metaphorical momentum perhaps carry him a bit too far in the last sentence of par. 55?

9. In "The Natural History of a Reluctant Suburb" (pp. 272-284) Dobriner also is concerned with what Zeckendorf calls "megalopolis, the supercity." Contrast the two essays in style, scope, tone, and purpose.

SUGGESTIONS FOR WRITING

1. Write an appraisal of a situation you are familiar with, indicating both its favorable and unfavorable elements, the causes of the unfavorable ones, and what should be done about them.

2. In "Here is New York" (pp. 299-314) E. B. White's subject is the same city that Zeckendorf is concerned with in much of his article. Do these two authors seem to be describing the same place? Write an essay in which you defend your answer. Alternatively, write an essay in which you discuss Zeckendorf's treatment of New York in relation to E. B. White's treatment. Consider such topics as the following (the paragraph identification refers to "Here is New York"):
   a. the commuter (pars. 9-10)
   b. the mixture of slums and skyscrapers (par. 12)
   c. slum life (par. 29)
   d. housing developments (par. 38)
   e. the complexities of urban life (par. 15)
   f. New York's "dedication to the arts" (pars. 9, 21).
3. My evaluation of megalopolis.
4. Urban renewal as I see it.

Here Is New York

by E. B. WHITE

ON ANY PERSON who desires such queer prizes, New York will bestow the gift of loneliness and the gift of privacy. It is this largess that accounts for the presence within the city's walls of a considerable section of the population; for the residents of Manhattan are to a large extent strangers who have pulled up stakes somewhere and come to town, seeking sanctuary or fulfillment or some greater or lesser grail. The capacity to make such dubious gifts is a mysterious quality of New York. It can destroy an individual, or it can fulfill him, depending a good deal on luck. No one should come to New York to live unless he is willing to be lucky.

2. New York is the concentrate of art and commerce and sport and religion and entertainment and finance, bringing to a single compact arena the gladiator, the evangelist, the promoter, the actor, the trader

From *Here Is New York* by E. B. White. Reprinted by permission of Harper & Row, Publishers, Incorporated. Copyright 1949 by The Curtis Publishing Company. Originally published in *Holiday*, April, 1949.

and the merchant. It carries on its lapel the unexpungeable odor of the long past, so that no matter where you sit in New York you feel the vibrations of great times and tall deeds, of queer people and events and undertakings. I am sitting at the moment in a stifling hotel room in 90-degree heat, halfway down an air shaft, in midtown. No air moves in or out of the room, yet I am curiously affected by emanations from the immediate surroundings. I am twenty-two blocks from where Rudolph Valentino lay in state, eight blocks from where Nathan Hale was executed, five blocks from the publisher's office where Ernest Hemingway hit Max Eastman on the nose, four miles from where Walt Whitman sat sweating out editorials for the Brooklyn Eagle, thirty-four blocks from the street Willa Cather lived in when she came to New York to write books about Nebraska, one block from where Marceline used to clown on the boards of the Hippodrome, thirty-six blocks from the spot where the historian Joe Gould kicked a radio to pieces in full view of the public, thirteen blocks from where Harry Thaw shot Stanford White, five blocks from where I used to usher at the Metropolitan Opera and only a hundred and twelve blocks from the spot where Clarence Day the Elder was washed of his sins in the Church of the Epiphany (I could continue this list indefinitely); and for that matter I am probably occupying the very room that any number of exalted and somewise memorable characters sat in, some of them on hot, breathless afternoons, lonely and private and full of their own sense of emanations from without.

3. When I went down to lunch a few minutes ago I noticed that the man sitting next to me (about eighteen inches away along the wall) was Fred Stone. The eighteen inches were both the connection and the separation that New York provides for its inhabitants. My only connection with Fred Stone was that I saw him in *The Wizard of Oz* around the beginning of the century. But our waiter felt the same stimulus from being close to a man from Oz, and after Mr. Stone left the room the waiter told me that when he (the waiter) was a young man just arrived in this country and before he could understand a word of English, he had taken his girl for their first theater date to *The Wizard of Oz*. It was a wonderful show, the waiter recalled—a man of straw, a man of tin. Wonderful! (And still only eighteen inches away.) "Mr. Stone is a very hearty eater," said the waiter thoughtfully, content with this fragile participation in destiny, this link with Oz.

4. New York blends the gift of privacy with the excitement of participation; and better than most dense communities it succeeds in insulating the individual (if he wants it, and almost everybody wants or needs it) against all enormous and violent and wonderful events that are taking place every minute. Since I have been sitting in this miasmic

air shaft, a good many rather splashy events have occurred in town. A man shot and killed his wife in a fit of jealousy. It caused no stir outside his block and got only small mention in the papers. I did not attend. Since my arrival, the greatest air show ever staged in all the world took place in town. I didn't attend and neither did most of the eight million other inhabitants, although they say there was quite a crowd. I didn't even hear any planes except a couple of westbound commercial airliners that habitually use this air shaft to fly over. The biggest ocean-going ships on the North Atlantic arrived and departed. I didn't notice them and neither did most other New Yorkers. I am told this is the greatest seaport in the world, with six hundred and fifty miles of water front, and ships calling here from many exotic lands, but the only boat I've happened to notice since my arrival was a small sloop tacking out of the East River night before last on the ebb tide when I was walking across the Brooklyn Bridge. I heard the *Queen Mary* blow one midnight, though, and the sound carried the whole history of departure and longing and loss. The Lions have been in convention. I've seen not one Lion. A friend of mine saw one and told me about him. (He was lame, and was wearing a bolero.) At the ballgrounds and horse parks the greatest sporting spectacles have been enacted. I saw no ballplayer, no race horse. The governor came to town. I heard the siren scream, but that was all there was to that—an eighteen-inch margin again. A man was killed by a falling cornice. I was not a party to the tragedy, and again the inches counted heavily.

⁵· I mention these merely to show that New York is peculiarly constructed to absorb almost anything that comes along (whether a thousand-foot liner out of the East or a twenty-thousand-man convention out of the West) without inflicting the event on its inhabitants; so that every event is, in a sense, optional, and the inhabitant is in the happy position of being able to choose his spectacle and so conserve his soul. In most metropolises, small and large, the choice is often not with the individual at all. He is thrown to the Lions. The Lions are overwhelming; the event is unavoidable. A cornice falls, and it hits every citizen on the head, every last man in town. I sometimes think that the only event that hits every New Yorker on the head is the annual St. Patrick's Day parade, which is fairly penetrating—the Irish are a hard race to tune out, there are 500,000 of them in residence, and they have the police force right in the family.

⁶· The quality in New York that insulates its inhabitants from life may simply weaken them as individuals. Perhaps it is healthier to live in a community where, when a cornice falls, you feel the blow; where, when the governor passes, you see at any rate his hat.

⁷· I am not defending New York in this regard. Many of its settlers

are probably here merely to escape, not face, reality. But whatever it means, it is a rather rare gift, and I believe it has a positive effect on the creative capacities of New Yorkers—for creation is in part merely the business of foregoing the great and small distractions.

8. Although New York often imparts a feeling of great forlornness or forsakenness, it seldom seems dead or unresourceful; and you always feel that either by shifting your location ten blocks or by reducing your fortune by five dollars you can experience rejuvenation. Many people who have no real independence of spirit depend on the city's tremendous variety and sources of excitement for spiritual sustenance and maintenance of morale. In the country there are a few chances of sudden rejuvenation—a shift in weather, perhaps, or something arriving in the mail. But in New York the chances are endless. I think that although many persons are here from some excess of spirit (which caused them to break away from their small town), some, too, are here from a deficiency of spirit, who find in New York a protection, or an easy substitution.

9. There are roughly three New Yorks. There is, first, the New York of the man or woman who was born here, who takes the city for granted and accepts its size and its turbulence as natural and inevitable. Second, there is the New York of the commuter—the city that is devoured by locusts each day and spat out each night. Third, there is the New York of the person who was born somewhere else and came to New York in quest of something. Of these three trembling cities the greatest is the last—the city of final destination, the city that is a goal. It is this third city that accounts for New York's highstrung disposition, its poetical deportment, its dedication to the arts, and its incomparable achievements. Commuters give the city its tidal restlessness; natives give it solidity and continuity; but the settlers give it passion. And whether it is a farmer arriving from Italy to set up a small grocery store in a slum, or a young girl arriving from a small town in Mississippi to escape the indignity of being observed by her neighbors, or a boy arriving from the Corn Belt with a manuscript in his suitcase and a pain in his heart, it makes no difference: each embraces New York with the intense excitement of first love, each absorbs New York with the fresh eyes of an adventurer, each generates heat and light to dwarf the Consolidated Edison Company.

10. The commuter is the queerest bird of all. The suburb he inhabits has no essential vitality of its own and is a mere roost where he comes at day's end to go to sleep. Except in rare cases, the man who lives in Mamaroneck or Little Neck or Teaneck, and works in New York, discovers nothing much about the city except the time of arrival and departure

of trains and buses, and the path to a quick lunch. He is desk-bound, and has never, idly roaming in the gloaming, stumbled suddenly on Belvedere Tower in the Park, seen the ramparts rise sheer from the water of the pond, and the boys along the shore fishing for minnows, girls stretched out negligently on the shelves of the rocks; he has never come suddenly on anything at all in New York as a loiterer, because he has had no time between trains. He has fished in Manhattan's wallet and dug out coins, but has never listened to Manhattan's breathing, never awakened to its morning, never dropped off to sleep in its night. About 400,000 men and women come charging onto the Island each week-day morning, out of the mouths of tubes and tunnels. Not many among them have ever spent a drowsy afternoon in the great rustling oaken silence of the reading room of the Public Library, with the book elevator (like an old water wheel) spewing out books onto the trays. They tend their furnaces in Westchester and in Jersey, but have never seen the furnaces of the Bowery, the fires that burn in oil drums on zero winter nights. They may work in the financial district downtown and never see the extravagant plantings of Rockefeller Center—the daffodils and grape hyacinths and birches and the flags trimmed to the wind on a fine morning in spring. Or they may work in a midtown office and may let a whole year swing round without sighting Governors Island from the sea wall. The commuter dies with tremendous mileage to his credit, but he is no rover. His entrances and exits are more devious than those in a prairie-dog village; and he calmly plays bridge while buried in the mud at the bottom of the East River. The Long Island Rail Road alone carried forty million commuters last year; but many of them were the same fellow retracing his steps.

11. The terrain of New York is such that a resident sometimes travels farther, in the end, than a commuter. Irving Berlin's journey from Cherry Street in the lower East Side to an apartment uptown was through an alley and was only three or four miles in length; but it was like going three times around the world.

12. A poem compresses much in a small space and adds music, thus heightening its meaning. The city is like poetry: it compresses all life, all races and breeds, into a small island and adds music and the accompaniment of internal engines. The island of Manhattan is without any doubt the greatest human concentrate on earth, the poem whose magic is comprehensible to millions of permanent residents but whose full meaning will always remain illusive. At the feet of the tallest and plushiest offices lie the crummiest slums. The genteel mysteries housed in the Riverside Church are only a few blocks from the voodoo charms of Harlem. The merchant princes, riding to Wall Street in their limousines

down the East River Drive, pass within a few hundred yards of the gypsy kings; but the princes do not know they are passing kings, and the kings are not up yet anyway—they live a more leisurely life than the princes and get drunk more consistently.

[13.] New York is nothing like Paris; it is nothing like London; and it is not Spokane multiplied by sixty, or Detroit multiplied by four. It is by all odds the loftiest of cities. It even managed to reach the highest point in the sky at the lowest moment of the depression. The Empire State Building shot 1250 feet into the air when it was madness to put out as much as six inches of new growth. (The building has a mooring mast that no dirigible has ever tied to; it employs a man to flush toilets in slack times; it has been hit by an airplane in a fog, struck countless times by lightning, and been jumped off of by so many unhappy people that pedestrians instinctively quicken step when passing Fifth Avenue and 34th Street.)

[14.] Manhattan has been compelled to expand skyward because of the absence of any other direction in which to grow. This, more than any other thing, is responsible for its physical majesty. It is to the nation what the white church spire is to the village—the visible symbol of aspiration and faith, the white plume saying that the way is up. The summer traveler swings in over Hell Gate Bridge and from the window of his sleeping car as it glides above the pigeon lofts and back yards of Queens looks southwest to where the morning light first strikes the steel peaks of midtown, and he sees its upward thrust unmistakable: the great walls and towers rising, the smoke rising, the heat not yet rising, the hopes and ferments of so many awakening millions rising—this vigorous spear that presses heaven hard.

[15.] It is a miracle that New York works at all. The whole thing is implausible. Every time the residents brush their teeth, millions of gallons of water must be drawn from the Catskills and the hills of Westchester. When a young man in Manhattan writes a letter to his girl in Brooklyn, the love message gets blown to her through a pneumatic tube—*pfft*—just like that. The subterranean system of telephone cables, power lines, steam pipes, gas mains and sewer pipes is reason enough to abandon the island to the gods and the weevils. Every time an incision is made in the pavement, the noisy surgeons expose ganglia that are tangled beyond belief. By rights New York should have destroyed itself long ago, from panic or fire or rioting or failure of some vital supply line in its circulatory system or from some deep labyrinthine short circuit. Long ago the city should have experienced an insoluble traffic snarl at some impossible bottleneck. It should have perished of hunger when food lines failed for a few days. It should have been wiped out by a plague starting in its slums or carried in by ships' rats. It should have been overwhelmed by the sea that licks at it on every side. The workers in its myriad cells should have succumbed to nerves, from the fearful pall of smoke-fog that drifts over every few days from Jersey, blotting out all light at noon, and leaving the high offices suspended, men groping and depressed, and the sense of world's end. It should have been touched in the head by the August heat and gone off its rocker.

16. Mass hysteria is a terrible force, yet New Yorkers seem always to escape it by some tiny margin: they sit in stalled subways without claustrophobia, they extricate themselves from panic situations by some lucky wisecrack, they meet confusion and congestion with patience and grit— a sort of perpetual muddling through. Every facility is inadequate—the hospitals and schools and playgrounds are overcrowded, the express highways are feverish, the unimproved highways and bridges are bottlenecks; there is not enough air and not enough light, and there is usually either too much heat or too little. But the city makes up for its hazards and its deficiencies by supplying its citizens with massive doses of a supplementary vitamin—the sense of belonging to something unique, cosmopolitan, mighty and unparalleled.

17. To an outlander a stay in New York can be and often is a series of small embarrassments and discomforts and disappointments: not understanding the waiter, not being able to distinguish between a sucker joint and a friendly saloon, riding the wrong subway, being slapped down by a bus driver for asking an innocent question, enduring sleepless nights when the street noises fill the bedroom. Tourists make for New York, particularly in summertime—they swarm all over the Statue of Liberty (where many a resident of the town has never set foot), they invade the Automat, visit radio studios, St. Patrick's Cathedral, and they window shop. Mostly they have a pretty good time. But sometimes in New York you run across the disillusioned—a young couple who are obviously visitors, newlyweds perhaps, for whom the bright dream has vanished. The place has been too much for them; they sit languishing in a cheap restaurant over a speechless meal.

18. The oft-quoted thumbnail sketch of New York is, of course: "It's a wonderful place, but I'd hate to live there." I have an idea that people from villages and small towns, people accustomed to the convenience and the friendliness of neighborhood over-the-fence living, are unaware that life in New York follows the neighborhood pattern. The city is literally a composite of tens of thousands of tiny neighborhood units. There are, of course, the big districts and big units: Chelsea and Murray Hill and Gramercy (which are residential units), Harlem (a racial unit), Greenwich Village (a unit dedicated to the arts and other matters), and

there is Radio City (a commercial development), Peter Cooper Village (a housing unit), the Medical Center (a sickness unit) and many other sections each of which has some distinguishing characteristic. But the curious thing about New York is that each large geographical unit is composed of countless small neighborhoods. Each neighborhood is virtually self-sufficient. Usually it is no more than two or three blocks long and a couple of blocks wide. Each area is a city within a city within a city. Thus, no matter where you live in New York, you will find within a block or two a grocery store, a barbershop, a newsstand and shoeshine shack, an ice-coal-and-wood cellar (where you write your order on a pad outside as you walk by), a dry cleaner, a laundry, a delicatessen (beer and sandwiches delivered at any hour to your door), a flower shop, an undertaker's parlor, a movie house, a radio-repair shop, a stationer, a haberdasher, a tailor, a drugstore, a garage, a tearoom, a saloon, a hardware store, a liquor store, a shoe-repair shop. Every block or two, in most residential sections of New York, is a little main street. A man starts for work in the morning and before he has gone two hundred yards he has completed half a dozen missions: bought a paper, left a pair of shoes to be soled, picked up a pack of cigarettes, ordered a bottle of whisky to be dispatched in the opposite direction against his homecoming, written a message to the unseen forces of the wood cellar, and notified the dry cleaner that a pair of trousers awaits call. Homeward bound eight hours later, he buys a bunch of pussy willows, a Mazda bulb, a drink, a shine—all between the corner where he steps off the bus and his apartment. So complete is each neighborhood, and so strong the sense of neighborhood, that many a New Yorker spends a lifetime within the confines of an area smaller than a country village. Let him walk two blocks from his corner and he is in a strange land and will feel uneasy till he gets back.

19. Storekeepers are particularly conscious of neighborhood boundary lines. A woman friend of mine moved recently from one apartment to another, a distance of three blocks. When she turned up, the day after the move, at the same grocer's that she had patronized for years, the proprietor was in ecstasy—almost in tears—at seeing her. "I was afraid," he said, "now that you've moved away I wouldn't be seeing you any more." To him, *away* was three blocks, or about seven hundred and fifty feet.

20. I am, at the moment of writing this, living not as a neighborhood man in New York but as a transient, or vagrant, in from the country for a few days. Summertime is a good time to re-examine New York and to receive again the gift of privacy, the jewel of loneliness. In summer the city contains (except for tourists) only die-hards and authentic charac-

ters. No casual, spotty dwellers are around, only the real article. And the town has a somewhat relaxed air, and one can lie in a loincloth, gasping and remembering things.

21. I've been remembering what it felt like as a young man to live in the same town with giants. When I first arrived in New York my personal giants were a dozen or so columnists and critics and poets whose names appeared regularly in the papers. I burned with a low steady fever just because I was on the same island with Don Marquis, Heywood Broun, Christopher Morley, Franklin P. Adams, Robert C. Benchley, Frank Sullivan, Dorothy Parker, Alexander Woollcott, Ring Lardner and Stephen Vincent Benét. I would hang around the corner of Chambers Street and Broadway, thinking: "Somewhere in that building is the typewriter that Archy the cockroach jumps on at night." New York hardly gave me a living at that period, but it sustained me. I used to walk quickly past the house in West 13th Street between Sixth and Seventh where F.P.A. lived, and the block seemed to tremble under my feet— the way Park Avenue trembles when a train leaves Grand Central. This excitation (nearness of giants) is a continuing thing. The city is always full of young worshipful beginners—young actors, young aspiring poets, ballerinas, painters, reporters, singers—each depending on his own brand of tonic to stay alive, each with his own stable of giants.

22. New York provides not only a continuing excitation but also a spectacle that is continuing. I wander around, re-examining this spectacle, hoping that I can put it on paper. It is Saturday, toward the end of the afternoon. I turn through West 48th Street. From the open windows of the drum and saxophone parlors come the listless sounds of musical instruction, monstrous insect noises in the brooding field of summer. The Cort Theater is disgorging its matinee audience. Suddenly the whole block is filled with the mighty voice of a street singer. He approaches, looking for an audience, a large, cheerful Negro with grand-opera contours, strolling with head thrown back, filling the canyon with uninhibited song. He carries a long cane as his sole prop, and is tidily but casually dressed—slacks, seersucker jacket, a book showing in his pocket.

23. This is perfect artistic timing; the audience from the Cort, where *The Respectful Prostitute* is playing, has just received a lesson in race relations and is in a mood to improve the condition of the black race as speedily as possible. Coins (mostly quarters) rattle to the street, and a few minutes of minstrelsy improves the condition of one Negro by about eight dollars. If he does as well as this at every performance, he has a living right there. New York is the city of opportunity, they say. Even the mounted cop, clumping along on his nag a few minutes later, scans

the gutter carefully for dropped silver, like a bird watching for spilt grain.

24. It is seven o'clock and I re-examine an ex-speakeasy in East 53rd Street, with dinner in mind. A thin crowd, a summer-night buzz of fans interrupted by an occasional drink being shaken at the small bar. It is dark in here (the proprietor sees no reason for boosting his light bill just because liquor laws have changed). How dark, how pleasing; and how miraculously beautiful the murals showing Italian lake scenes—probably executed by a cousin of the owner. The owner himself mixes. The fans intone the prayer for cool salvation. From the next booth drifts the conversation of radio executives; from the green salad comes the little taste of garlic. Behind me (eighteen inches again) a young intellectual is trying to persuade a girl to come live with him and be his love. She has her guard up, but he is extremely reasonable, careful not to overplay his hand. A combination of intellectual companionship and sexuality is what they have to offer each other, he feels. In the mirror over the bar I can see the ritual of the second drink. Then he has to go to the men's room and she has to go to the ladies' room, and when they return, the argument has lost its tone. And the fan takes over again, and the heat and the relaxed air and the memory of so many good little dinners in so many good little illegal places, with the theme of love, the sound of ventilation, the brief medicinal illusion of gin.

25. Another hot night I stop off at the Goldman Band concert in the Mall in Central Park. The people seated on the benches fanned out in front of the band shell are attentive, appreciative. In the trees the night wind stirs, bringing the leaves to life, endowing them with speech; the electric lights illuminate the green branches from the under side, translating them into a new language. Overhead a plane passes dreamily, its running lights winking. On the bench directly in front of me, a boy sits with his arm around his girl; they are proud of each other and are swathed in music. The cornetist steps forward for a solo, begins, "Drink to me only with thine eyes. . . ." In the wide, warm night the horn is startlingly pure and magical. Then from the North River another horn solo begins—the *Queen Mary* announcing her intentions. She is not on key; she is a half tone off. The trumpeter in the bandstand never flinches. The horns quarrel savagely, but no one minds having the intimation of travel injected into the pledge of love, "I leave," sobs Mary. "And I will pledge with mine," sighs the trumpeter. Along the asphalt paths strollers pass to and fro; they behave considerately, respecting the musical atmosphere. Popsicles are moving well. In the warm grass beyond the fence, forms wriggle in the shadows, and the skirts of the girls approaching on the Mall are ballooned by the breeze, and their bare shoulders catch

the lamplight. "Drink to me only with thine eyes." It is a magical occasion, and it's all free.

26. On week ends in summer the town empties. I visit my office on a Saturday afternoon. No phone rings, no one feeds the hungry IN-baskets, no one disturbs the papers; it is a building of the dead, a time of awesome suspension. The whole city is honeycombed with abandoned cells —a jail that has been effectively broken. Occasionally from somewhere in the building a night bell rings, summoning the elevator—a special fire-alarm ring. This is the pit of loneliness, in an office on a summer Saturday. I stand at the window and look down at the batteries and batteries of offices across the way, recalling how the thing looks in winter twilight when everything is going full blast, every cell lighted, and how you can see in pantomime the puppets fumbling with their slips of paper (but you don't hear the rustle), see them pick up their phone (but you don't hear the ring), see the noiseless, ceaseless moving about of so many passers of pieces of paper: New York, the capital of memoranda, in touch with Calcutta, in touch with Reykjavik, and always fooling with something.

27. In the café of the Lafayette, the regulars sit and talk. It is busy yet peaceful. Nursing a drink, I stare through the west windows at the Manufacturers Trust Company and at the red brick fronts on the north side of Ninth Street, watching the red turning slowly to purple as the light dwindles. Brick buildings have a way of turning color at the end of the day, the way a red rose turns bluish as it wilts. The café is a sanctuary. The waiters are ageless and they change not. Nothing has been modernized. Notre Dame stands guard in its travel poster. The coffee is strong and full of chicory, and good.

28. Walk the Bowery under the El at night and all you feel is a sort of cold guilt. Touched for a dime, you try to drop the coin and not touch the hand, because the hand is dirty; you try to avoid the glance, because the glance accuses. This is not so much personal menace as universal— the cold menace of unresolved human suffering and poverty and the advanced stages of the disease alcoholism. On a summer night the drunks sleep in the open. The sidewalk is a free bed, and there are no lice. Pedestrians step along and over and around the still forms as though walking on a battlefield among the dead. In doorways, on the steps of the savings bank, the bums lie sleeping it off. Standing sentinel at each sleeper's head is the empty bottle from which he drained his release. Wedged in the crook of his arm is the paper bag containing his things. The glib barker on the sight-seeing bus tells his passengers that this is the "street of lost souls," but the Bowery does not think of itself as lost; it meets its peculiar problem in its own way—plenty of gin mills, plenty

of flophouses, plenty of indifference, and always, at the end of the line, Bellevue.

29. A block or two east and the atmosphere changes sharply. In the slums are poverty and bad housing, but with them the reassuring sobriety and safety of family life. I head east along Rivington. All is cheerful and filthy and crowded. Small shops overflow onto the sidewalk, leaving only half the normal width for passers-by. In the unshaded lights gleam watermelons and lingerie. Families have fled the hot rooms upstairs and have found relief on the pavement. They sit on orange crates, smoking, relaxed, congenial. This is the nightly garden party of the vast Lower East Side—and on the whole they are more agreeable-looking hot-weather groups than some you see in bright canvas deck chairs on green lawns in country circumstances. It is folksy here with the smell of warm flesh and squashed fruit and fly-bitten filth in the gutter, and cooking.

30. At the corner of Lewis, in the playground behind the wire fence, an open-air dance is going on—some sort of neighborhood affair, probably designed to combat delinquency. Women push baby carriages in and out among the dancers, as though to exhibit what dancing leads to at last. Overhead, like banners decorating a cotillion hall, stream the pants and bras from the pulley lines. The music stops, and a beautiful Italian girl takes a brush from her handbag and stands under the street light brushing her long blue-black hair till it shines. The cop in the patrol car watches sullenly.

31. The Consolidated Edison Company says there are eight million people in the five boroughs of New York, and the company is in a position to know. Of these eight million, two million are Jews—or one person in every four. Among this two million who are Jewish are, of course, a great many nationalities—Russian, German, Rumanian, Austrian, and so forth. The Urban League of Greater New York estimates that the number of Negroes in New York is about 700,000. Of these, about 500,000 live in Harlem, a district that extends northward from 110th Street. The Negro population has increased rapidly in the last few years. There are half again as many Negroes in New York today as there were in 1940. There are about 230,000 Puerto Ricans living in New York. There are half a million Irish, half a million Germans. There are 900,000 Russians, 150,000 English, 400,000 Poles, and there are quantities of Finns and Czechs and Swedes and Danes and Norwegians and Latvians and Belgians and Welsh and Greeks, and even Dutch, who have been here from away back. It is very hard to say how many Chinese there are. Officially there are 12,000, but there are many Chinese who are in New York illegally and who don't like census takers.

32. The collision and the intermingling of these millions of foreign-

born people representing so many races and creeds make New York a permanent exhibit of the phenomenon of one world. The citizens of New York are tolerant not only from disposition but from necessity. The city has to be tolerant, otherwise it would explode in a radioactive cloud of hate and rancor and bigotry. If the people were to depart even briefly from the peace of cosmopolitan intercourse, the town would blow up higher than a kite. In New York smolders every race problem there is, but the noticeable thing is not the problem but the inviolate truce. Harlem is a city in itself, and being a city Harlem symbolizes segregation; yet Negro life in New York lacks the more conspicuous elements of Jim Crowism. Negroes ride subways and buses on terms of equality with whites, but they have not yet found that same equality in hotels and restaurants. Professionally, Negroes get on well in the theater, in music, in art and in literature; but in many fields of employment the going is tough. The Jim Crow principle lives chiefly in the housing rules and customs. Private owners of dwellings legally can, and do, exclude Negroes. Under a recent city ordinance, however, apartment buildings that are financed with public moneys or that receive any tax exemption must accept tenants without regard to race, color or religion.

33. To a New Yorker the city is both changeless and changing. In many respects it neither looks nor feels the way it did twenty-five years ago. The elevated railways have been pulled down, all but the Third Avenue. An old-timer walking up Sixth past the Jefferson Market jail misses the railroad, misses its sound, its spotted shade, its little aerial stations, and the tremor of the thing. Broadway has changed in aspect. It used to have a discernible bony structure beneath its loud bright surface; but the signs are so enormous now, the buildings and shops and hotels have largely disappeared under the neon lights and letters and the frozen-custard façade. Broadway is a custard street with no frame supporting it. In Greenwich Village the light is thinning: big apartments have come in, bordering the Square, and the bars are mirrored and chromed. But there are still in the Village the lingering traces of poesy, Mexican glass, hammered brass, batik, lamps made of whisky bottles, first novels made of fresh memories—the old Village with its alleys and ratty one-room rents catering to the erratic needs of those whose hearts are young and gay.

34. Grand Central has become honky-tonk, with its extradimensional advertising displays and its tendency to adopt the tactics of a travel broker. I practically lived in Grand Central Terminal at one period (it has all the conveniences and I had no other place to stay) and the great hall always seemed to me one of the more inspiring interiors in New York, until Lastex and Coca-Cola got into the temple.

35. All over town the great mansions are in decline. Schwab's house facing the Hudson on Riverside is gone. Gould's house on Fifth Avenue is an antique shop. Morgan's house on Madison Avenue is a church administration office. What was once the Fahnestock house is now Random House. Rich men nowadays don't live in houses; they live in the attics of big apartment buildings and plant trees on the setbacks, hundreds of feet above the street.

36. There are fewer newspapers than there used to be, thanks somewhat to the late Frank Munsey. One misses the *Globe,* the *Mail*, the *Herald;* and to many a New Yorker life has never seemed the same since the *World* took the count.

37. Police now ride in radio prowl cars instead of gumshoeing around the block swinging their sticks. A ride in the subway costs ten cents, and the seats are apt to be dark green instead of straw yellow. Men go to saloons to gaze at televised events instead of to think long thoughts. It is all very disconcerting. Even parades have changed some. The last triumphal military procession in Manhattan simply filled the city with an ominous and terrible rumble of heavy tanks.

38. The slums are gradually giving way to the lofty housing projects —high in stature, high in purpose, low in rent. There are a couple of dozen of these new developments scattered around; each is a city in itself (one of them in the Bronx accommodates 12,000 families), sky acreage hitherto untilled, lifting people far above the street, standardizing their sanitary life, giving them some place to sit other than an orange crate. Federal money, state money, city money and private money have flowed into these projects. Banks and insurance companies are in back of some of them. Architects have turned the buildings slightly on their bases, to catch more light. In some of them, rents are as low as eight dollars a room. Thousands of new units are still needed and will eventually be built, but New York never quite catches up with itself, is never in equilibrium. In flush times the population mushrooms and the new dwellings sprout from the rock. Come bad times and the population scatters and the lofts are abandoned and the landlord withers and dies.

39. New York has changed in tempo and in temper during the years I have known it. There is greater tension, increased irritability. You encounter it in many places, in many faces. The normal frustrations of modern life are here multiplied and amplified—a single run of a crosstown bus contains, for the driver, enough frustration and annoyance to carry him over the edge of sanity: the light that changes always an instant too soon, the passenger that bangs on the shut door, the truck that blocks the only opening, the coin that slips to the floor, the question asked at the wrong moment. There is greater tension and there is greater

speed. Taxis roll faster than they rolled ten years ago—and they were rolling fast then. Hackmen used to drive with verve; now they sometimes seem to drive with desperation, toward the ultimate tip. On the West Side Highway, approaching the city, the motorist is swept along in a trance—a sort of fever of inescapable motion, goaded from behind, hemmed in on either side, a mere chip in a millrace.

[40.] The city has never been so uncomfortable, so crowded, so tense. Money has been plentiful and New York has responded. Restaurants are hard to get into; businessmen stand in line for a Schrafft's luncheon as meekly as idle men used to stand in soup lines. (Prosperity creates its bread lines, the same as depression.) The lunch hour in Manhattan has been shoved ahead half an hour, to 12:00 or 12:30, in the hopes of beating the crowd to a table. Everyone is a little emptier at quitting time than he used to be. Apartments are festooned with No Vacancy signs. There is standing-room-only in Fifth Avenue buses, which once reserved a seat for every paying guest. The old double-deckers are disappearing—people don't ride just for the fun of it any more.

[41.] At certain hours on certain days it is almost impossible to find an empty taxi and there is a great deal of chasing around after them. You grab a handle and open the door, and find that some other citizen is entering from the other side. Doormen grow rich blowing their whistles for cabs; and some doormen belong to no door at all—merely wander about through the streets, opening cabs for people as they happen to find them. By comparison with other less hectic days, the city is uncomfortable and inconvenient; but New Yorkers temperamentally do not crave comfort and convenience—if they did they would live elsewhere.

[42.] The subtlest change in New York is something people don't speak much about but that is in everyone's mind. The city, for the first time in its long history, is destructible. A single flight of planes no bigger than a wedge of geese can quickly end this island fantasy, burn the towers, crumble the bridges, turn the underground passages into lethal chambers, cremate the millions. The intimation of mortality is part of New York now: in the sound of jets overhead, in the black headlines of the latest edition.

[43.] All dwellers in cities must live with the stubborn fact of annihilation; in New York the fact is somewhat more concentrated because of the concentration of the city itself, and because, of all targets, New York has a certain clear priority. In the mind of whatever perverted dreamer might loose the lightning, New York must hold a steady, irresistible charm.

[44.] It used to be that the Statue of Liberty was the signpost that proclaimed New York and translated it for all the world. Today Liberty shares the role with Death. Along the East River, from the razed slaughterhouses of Turtle Bay, as though in a race with the spectral flight of planes, men are carving out the permanent headquarters of the United Nations—the greatest housing project of them all. In its stride, New York takes on one more interior city, to shelter, this time, all governments, and to clear the slum called war. New York is not a capital city— it is not a national capital or a state capital. But it is by way of becoming the capital of the world. The buildings, as conceived by architects, will be cigar boxes set on end. Traffic will flow in a new tunnel under First Avenue. Forty-seventh Street will be widened (and if my guess is any good, trucks will appear late at night to plant tall trees surreptitiously, their roots to mingle with the intestines of the town). Once again the city will absorb, almost without showing any sign of it, a congress of visitors. It has already shown itself capable of stashing away the United Nations—a great many of the delegates have been around town during the past couple of years, and the citizenry has hardly caught a glimpse of their coattails or their black Homburgs.

45. This race—this race between the destroying planes and the struggling Parliament of Man—it sticks in all our heads. The city at last perfectly illustrates both the universal dilemma and the general solution, this riddle in steel and stone is at once the perfect target and the perfect demonstration of nonviolence, of racial brotherhood, this lofty target scraping the skies and meeting the destroying planes halfway, home of all people and all nations, capital of everything, housing the deliberations by which the planes are to be stayed and their errand forestalled.

46. A block or two west of the new City of Man in Turtle Bay there is an old willow tree that presides over an interior garden. It is a battered tree, long suffering and much climbed, held together by strands of wire but beloved of those who know it. In a way it symbolizes the city: life under difficulties, growth against odds, sap-rise in the midst of concrete, and the steady reaching for the sun. Whenever I look at it nowadays, and feel the cold shadow of the planes, I think: "This must be saved, this particular thing, this very tree." If it were to go, all would go—this city, this mischievous and marvelous monument which not to look upon would be like death.

COMMENTARY AND QUESTIONS

For many years E. B. White wrote a weekly commentary for *The New Yorker* called "The Talk of the Town," in which he not only reported odd facts and amusing incidents with wit, humor, and an extraordinary felicity of expression, but also managed often to make his apparently lighthearted jottings the means of communicating profound insights into human experience. "Here Is New York" has a similar and characteristic blend of facts, humor, and insight. For White not only reports with a superbly pungent accuracy the unique and particular flavor of New York; he sees it also as a symbol of concentrated human experience, endeavor, and aspiration—"this mischievous and marvelous monument which not to look upon would be like death."

1. Pars. 1-19 of this essay are successive parts of a general answer to the reader's unspoken query, "But what is New York really *like*, if it is not just 'Spokane multiplied by sixty, or Detroit multiplied by four'?" How do such phrases in par. 1 as *queer prizes* and *dubious gifts* set the tone for the essay? Notice that *gift of loneliness* and *gift of privacy* are echoed in the last sentence of par. 2, the first of par. 4, and the second of par. 20. What use does White make in succeeding paragraphs of *eighteen inches* (par. 3) and *cornice* (par. 4)? Pars. 1-8 interpret the interaction of New York with the individual; pars. 9-19 describe the physical and social characteristics of the city. What is the function of par. 20, and how is this function carried out? How is par. 22 connected with par. 21?

2. Pars. 22-30 give a series of glimpses of particular scenes and places in New York at various hours and seasons. What devices of connection and contrast does White use to weave these separate paragraphs into a smooth and satisfying pattern?

3. Pars. 31-32 present significant statistics and facts about the people of New York. Why did White not begin his essay with these? Pars. 33-46 describe the many ways in which the city has been changing. How does White use this topic to lead into his climax? Discuss the appropriateness and effectiveness of White's use in the final paragraph of the willow tree as a symbol of New York (and of human life itself). Would this symbol have been equally effective if it had been used at the beginning of the essay?

4. One source of White's pungency of style is his use of ironic contrasts and his ability to mingle different moods in the same passage. For example, are the people named in par. 2 of the same degree and kind of importance? In par. 25 White tells us how the horns of the cornetist and the *Queen Mary* "quarrel savagely," yet complement each other; show how he himself has here (as elsewhere) mingled imaginative warmth with a faintly satiric humor so that they do not clash but blend. Trace the contrasts of mood in pars. 10, 12, and 26.

5. Another source of White's stylistic effectiveness is his apt use of figures of speech. Discuss the appropriateness of the figures in the third sentence of par. 9, the fifth of par. 10, the second of par. 11, the sixth of par. 15, the fifth of par. 22, the last of par. 39. How many details in par. 14 emphasize *upwardness*? Is the suggestion merely physical? Show how material which has been introduced in pars. 5, 18, 38, and 42 is used in the third, fourth, and tenth sentences of par. 44.

"Here Is New York" is a lively answer to anyone who thinks that it is impossible to write about a time-worn subject without being trite and dull. Write an evaluation of some community or region that you are familiar with, including plenty of information but making your essay a reflection of your own sense of values and your own point of view. The following are some suitable topics:

1. Here is my home town.
2. The Midwest as I see it.
3. The personality of a place I have known.
4. A college or university community.

The Big Change

by FREDERICK LEWIS ALLEN

IN AN UPPER HALLWAY of the New York Public Library there have been hanging, this year, a series of prints of American cities dating from about 1850. To the eye of today these pictures show what look like overgrown villages and small towns—clusters of red brick and white wooden houses, here and there crowded closely along narrow streets, elsewhere set comfortably apart from one another, with clumps of trees about them and green gardens sloping down to the inevitable river. In a few of these towns one will see a factory chimney or two rising above the roof-tops; but the striking thing, to the eye of 1950, is that in most of the pictures —whether they are of Davenport, Iowa, or Hartford, Connecticut, or even New York City—the skyline is broken only by church spires. Hence the village effect; for today it is only a village which is dominated by its steeples.

2. If we should wish to see where we have come from in a hundred years—how the everyday life of American men and women and children

From *Harper's Magazine*, Centennial Issue, October, 1950. By permission of the publishers. Copyright 1950 by Frederick Lewis Allen.

has changed since 1850, what people lacked then that we take for granted now, what people possessed then that is only a memory now, and whether the gap between rich and poor has narrowed or widened since industrialism began to transform American life—I suggest that we begin by trying to look through those pictures to the reality that lay behind them, a full century ago.

3. To begin with, are those engravings fair portraits of the America of 1850? Well, we must remember that American life was vastly more varied geographically then than now. At that moment in the mid-nineteenth century when the United States had only just reached out to its present continental boundaries (as a result of the Mexican War), and when California had only just become, abruptly, a land of bright American opportunity (as a result of the discovery of gold at Sutter's Mill), America was still a land of violent contrasts. A silk-waistcoated merchant prince of Boston or New York or Philadelphia lived in a wholly different world from a family of homespun pioneers setting out by covered wagon from the bleak and muddy streets of Independence to cross the "Great American Desert." The high-thinking Transcendentalists of Concord, strolling about Walden Pond to note the blooming of the arbutus and to discuss natural aristocracy, were continents apart, in their way of life, from Brigham Young's Mormons building their new city beside the Great Salt Lake, or from the black slaves of a Georgia plantation, or from the gold-hungry prospectors in the town of tents and shacks that was San Francisco, or from the farmer trying out a new McCormick reaper on a quarter-section of scraggly Illinois prairie.

4. If America was so varied geographically, this was largely because it took so much time and effort for either people or goods to get about. When young Joseph Jefferson, the actor, traveled from New Orleans to New York in 1846, what he had to do was to take a Mississippi River steamboat to Wheeling, in what is now West Virginia (being delayed for days by ice, for it was winter); then bump for twenty-four hours in a chilly stagecoach over rutted roads to Cumberland, Maryland, stopping every few hours for a meal while the horses were changed; then proceed by primitive train to his destination. Early in the eighteen-fifties Ralph Waldo Emerson, taking a lecture trip in Michigan, had to make a forty-eight-mile journey through the woods from town to town by horse and buggy. And the fastest time anybody could make from New York to San Francisco was eighty-nine days by swift clipper ship around the Horn.

5. We must remember, too, when we look at those engravings of American cities in 1850, that the men who made them did not show us the grimier streets, or the citizens eating with their knives or blowing

their noses with their fingers. They could not show us the smell of household privies. Yet those pictures of red and white and green towns clinging to the banks of sailboat-studded rivers do reflect the central fact of the United States of 1850; that as a whole it was still a land of farmers, shopkeepers, merchants, and artisans—above all, farmers. Today, among "gainfully employed" Americans, only about one in five works on a farm; at that time, over half of them did. And the cities were small. New York, then as now the biggest of them, had about one-tenth of its present population.

6. To be sure, industrialism had long since begun its smoky invasion of the land. Along the banks of the Merrimac and other New England rivers, big textile mills were turning out cotton and woolen cloth, and there were a few scattered factories even west of the Alleghenies. But the basic units of American life were still the village and the farm; and the great majority of the American people—the lively, sociable, irritable, dyspeptic, boastful, uncouth, energetic, disorderly, wasteful, and hospitable American people—were villagers at heart.

7. How well did they live? It is easy today to forget that many comforts and conveniences which we now take for granted were then available to nobody, or almost nobody. For one thing, cities were just beginning to install water-supply and drainage systems. Philadelphia had been an early innovator with its Fairmount Water Works, which long had been pumping water from the Schuylkill River, but New York did not have Croton water till 1842, and Boston did not introduce Cochituate water till 1848. Before public water supplies became general, you either subscribed for water provided by a private company such as the Jamaica Pond Corporation in Boston, or, if you were not within reach of its piping system or could not pay the price, you relied on a well of your own. In Boston, for instance, a census taken in 1845 showed that the 10,370 houses in the city got their water from no less than 5,287 separate wells, and supplemented this supply with rain water collected (for washing purposes) in 4,445 cisterns. (As the city gradually became smokier, cistern water naturally became sootier.)

8. Even after public reservoirs and aqueducts had been built, it took a long time to lay the water mains to take this new blessing to people's houses. All through the late eighteen-forties, for example, New York was busily constructing mains along the streets of the city, and the authorities were discovering to their dismay how much water people used when all they needed to do to get it was to turn a tap. In 1853 the head of the Croton Aqueduct Department, in his annual report, remarking that a modern hotel on Broadway had installed "more than four hundred openings through which water is delivered, and discharged into public

sewers," said in tones of despair, "With such arrangements for the consumption of water, under the control of a little army of careless servants,
and irresponsible guests, how is any reasonable economy in its use to
be expected?"

9. The sewers that this official mentioned were brand new; for as late
as 1845 even the biggest city in the country had had no public sewerage
system at all. And although the modern hotel which he described had had
a number of suites equipped with bath and water closet, and had installed in the basement six water closets for domestics, and had provided,
adjacent to the barroom, nine public water closets and three wash basins
with hot and cold water, these were innovations connoting extreme luxury. In all or almost all private houses there was still no such thing as a
water closet; people relied upon chamber pots or upon a drafty expedition to the privy; or—in the case of the prosperous—upon commodes
which the servants would periodically empty. And except along the chief
streets of the chief cities, they relied too upon cesspits and culverts and
the gutters of the streets to dispose of their sewage.

10. No wonder their well water was widely contaminated; and no
wonder the term of life was so short, particularly in the cities. Today the
average expectation of life in the United States is over 67, and rising; in
1850 it was under 40. A health report published in Boston in 1850 disclosed that the average age of all who died in the city was 21.43 years,
and that among the Catholic population—who were, of course, mostly
poor immigrants from Ireland—it was less than 14 years. Those grim figures reflect not only a general ignorance of antisepsis and sanitation, but
also the result of living, in fast-growing cities, under conditions which
were still those of primitive village life.

11. Nor were private houses centrally heated. Even the wealthy depended on kitchen stoves, Franklin stoves, and open fireplaces for warmth
in winter. Mark Twain describing in *Life on the Mississippi* the typical
big house of any town along the river in about 1850—"a big, square, two-
story frame house painted white and porticoed like a Grecian temple behind a white paling fence," noted that there was no bathroom and added
that there might be, but wouldn't certainly be, a pitcher and washbowl in
each of the square bedrooms upstairs. The first duty of the average
American householder, in the morning, was to light the fires and empty
the slops; until the fires really took hold, the chill of the house made any
but the most cursory washing an ordeal. And the German writer, Ole
Munch Raeder, describing a trip which he took in 1847 through what we
now call the Middle West, remarked on the lamentable but general custom of spitting at the stove, not always accurately, adding with evident
relief that there were cuspidors in some of the better homes in Madison,

Elkhorn, and Janesville. All in all, it is likely that if we of 1950 were to visit the United States of 1850, we should find it a dirty place inhabited by dirty people.

12. Ready-made clothing was limited in amount and kind, ill-fitting, and hand-sewn. Accordingly, shirts and underwear were generally stitched at home by the housewife, from materials spun by the textile mills and bought by the yard at the store; shoes were made by shoemakers, suits by tailors (or sometimes by the housewife), dresses by the housewife or by seamstresses and dressmakers. The well-to-do imported their suits from London, their dresses from Paris, or else employed tailors and dressmakers versed in the foreign modes to fashion them out of fine imported materials. Naturally a new article of clothing represented a considerable expense, in either money or toil; the people in any gathering were far more varied in costume than today; and the women of the family were perpetually sewing.

13. Against these and other lacks and inconveniences must be set certain advantages. First of all, space and air. The shopkeeper or blacksmith in an Ohio town was likely to have a house with more room in it than can be found today in the New York or Chicago apartment of a $30,000-a-year executive. In Philadelphia, my grandfather as a young man could take his wife skating in winter, or sailing in summer, on a Schuylkill River as yet undarkened by commerce or industry. Not yet was there any need for week-end escape from the cities, or for summer places, or for elaborately organized sports; the vast majority of the people found chances to walk, ride, drive, skate, swim, fish, or shoot, within ready reach on almost any day when the weather suited—if their long labors left them time enough. Although the American public school system was only partly established, although great numbers of children could not get even elementary schooling, and few went on to high school, and far fewer yet to college, at least the average American boy and girl had a countryside close at hand to run wild in when the chores that were their share in the work of family life were done. And one final advantage was possessed by nine families out of ten: when the crops failed, when the family store went broke, when their jobs folded up, they could tighten their belts and go on working—if not in their home communities, then at least in the beckoning West. In a land still dominated by small-scale and individual enterprise, a self-reliant man could be far more independent than could his son or grandson in later years.

14. The gulf between rich and poor was great, both in income and in the nature of their clothing, equipment, and pattern of life. At a time when the dollar was so big that $5,000 a year was an inviting salary to offer to the head of an insurance company, there were merchants in the

seaboard cities who were making hundreds of thousands a year; one Boston merchant is said to have cleared $100,000 from one voyage of one of his ships. Not only was such a man rich—with of course no income tax to pay—and not only did he have fine carriages, and a splendid house with satin-covered furniture and a paneled library and a cellar full of Madeira and other imported wines, and a staff of dutiful servants, but his wealth was instantly apparent to anybody who saw him and his lady on the street. You could tell at a distance of fifty paces that their clothes were quite different in material and cut from those of ordinary folk.

15. By contrast, not only the slaves of the South (who were looked after well or ill according to the whim of their slaveholder) but also the poorer people of the Northern cities and towns, were in miserable plight. For the floor of wages had been dropping. Years of famine in Ireland had brought into the country a horde of newcomers willing to work for next to nothing. In earlier years the rising textile mills of Lawrence and Lowell and Fall River had largely employed farmers' daughters; but as Irish labor became available a change was taking place. Wages fell— even when profits were booming—until whole families labored at the machines for three or four dollars a week per worker; a twelve-hour day was average, and a fourteen-hour day was not unusual. Stop for a moment and reflect upon what it would be like to work a fourteen-hour day —say from five o'clock in the morning till eight at night, with half an hour off for breakfast and half an hour for dinner—six days a week, in an ill-lighted, ill-ventilated factory; and ask yourself how much recreation, how much sunshine, how much education for children of fourteen or less, such an appalling routine permitted.

16. Meanwhile the wages of seamen, which in the early years of the century had been as high as $18 a month, had fallen to $8 or $10 or $12 a month, and the adventurous farmer boys who had formerly yearned for two years before the mast had been supplanted by foreign deck-hands, until the slim and beautiful clipper ships of the eighteen-fifties were manned by the drifting scum of many continents. When, for example, the *Reindeer* sailed from Canton to Boston in 1851 she had as her crew 2 French, 1 Portuguese, 1 Cape Verde Islander, 1 Azores man, 1 Italian, 1 Dutchman, 1 Mulatto, 2 Kanakas, 1 Welshman, 1 Swede, 2 Chinese, and 2 Americans.

17. One catches a glimpse of the labor market in the mid-century in an article in *Harper's* for October 1866, outlining a reasonable budget for a young couple living in the outskirts of New York on $2,000 a year— roughly equivalent to perhaps $6,000 or $7,000 now—with one servant. At a time when roast beef cost 35 cents a pound, corned beef 23½ cents a pound, fish 12 cents a pound, bread 10 cents a loaf, milk 10 cents a

quart, and sugar 15 cents a pound—prices which were mostly, though not all, a fraction of what they are today—this family was allowed $114.75 a year for coal (for the kitchen range and a "portable furnace" in the cellar), and a mere $96 a year for the servant's wages—*at the rate of $8 a month!*

18. What did people think of these contrasts? Most people apparently regarded them as part of the order of nature. That men and women of the favored class approved of them is of course not surprising; the striking fact is that the tailor, the farmer, and the mill-hand on the whole agreed. For the reigning idea in America was that every individual should have a fair chance in the contest of life, and that he should be on his own, beholden to no man; to work for somebody else was spineless unless one were a young apprentice, or a girl waiting for marriage, or an immigrant who didn't know any better; and if such people chose to work for very little, this was their own affair. Couldn't they break away and get better jobs if they had the ability and the will? Meanwhile employers had a virtually unquestioned right to make all the money they could lay their hands on. For America was a young country with a future, in which it was considered every man's duty to play a constructive part; and if he made money—a lot of it—this was a good sign that he was contributing to the common weal. If he made a million while paying his workers a pittance, that was mighty smart. If he outwitted his neighbor in a slick trade, that was mighty smart. Disapprove of him? People admired him, and hoped to be as fortunate themselves one day.

19. For the tide of industrialism was only beginning to run strong, and opportunity still seemed to be within the reach of all. Americans felt this in their bones, and held their heads high. Said Oliver Wendell Holmes to Edward Dicey, an English visitor, "We should find it hard to match five thousand American gentlemen with five thousand English, but we could match five million ordinary Americans against the same number of your countrymen, without fear of the result." If there were almost 25,000 paupers in Massachusetts, were not 91 per cent of them foreigners, and were they not therefore simply people who had not yet got off to a start in the free-for-all race? Even the ill-clad immigrants felt the breezes of hope in the air. Said a poor Irishwoman to Dicey, "This is a blessed country, sir; I think God made it for the poor."

II

20. As the second half of the nineteenth century began, industrialism took a new lease on life. Samuel Colt, making revolvers at Hartford, had pushed to a new perfection Eli Whitney's principle of the use of inter-

changeable parts; Colt had completely mechanized his factory, so that presently, with the aid of some 400 machines, his men were turning out over 24,000 revolvers a year. Such a performance was an eye-opener to inventors, manufacturers, investors: couldn't you make almost anything cheaply and swiftly, provided you had the right machines to do it with? And now the most essential tools for the making of such machines were ready; for the stocking lathe, the universal miller, and the turret lathe had all been invented. Elias Howe, Jr., had conceived the sewing machine, and now Isaac Singer was producing this new contrivance in quantity. Telegraph lines were being extended from town to town. In 1858 the first cable was laid across the Atlantic Ocean. The next year oil was discovered in Pennsylvania—an event destined to end the era of the whale-oil lamp. Meanwhile thousands of miles of railroad track were being laid; and as the fat-funneled locomotives wound their way through the wooded Alleghenies and chugged across the vast flatlands of the central basin, they brought town after town into new and exciting contact with the news and ideas of the outside world.

21. Each new miracle of invention seized the public imagination. When Joseph Jefferson received the first telegram of his life in Cumberland, Maryland, he could hardly believe that he was actually hearing from the partner in Baltimore to whom he had written only the day before. "I called at the office to inquire if it were really so; yes, there could be no doubt of it. A small group of people had collected about the operator . . . all wearing a look of surprise and incredulity. We began showing one another our dispatches. . . . People were rushing to and fro with little messages in their hands, and stopping one another in the street to talk and wonder over the new event." Just so, in scores of American towns, the new instruments and gadgets set boys and men to dreaming fantastic dreams—of getting a scientific training, devising some new wonder which would simplify the long labor of manufacturing, setting up a company to produce it, selling it by the thousands, and making a fabulous fortune. The future seemed full of wild promise.

22. The Civil War, though it left the South prostrate, did not halt the march of industrialism in the North, but rather accelerated it, bringing as it did outsize demands for weapons and equipment and quicker communication, and especially for uniforms in quantity. By the war's end industrialism was in full flood, irresistible and tremendous.

23. It brought with it both wonders and abominations. The wonders have become so familiar to us that it is hard for us to imagine a world in which they did not exist. Yet even a short list of the changes that came between 1850 and 1900 is staggering. Here are some of them:

A vast growth of steel production, resulting from the Bessemer process, the multiplication of steel mills, and the coming of the open-hearth furnace. (This meant more and better steel for rails, wires, bridges, ships, steel-skeleton buildings, and a host of other uses; steel became the basic material out of which the new industrial era was built.)

An equally vast boom in railroad-building, till the rails not only crossed the Rockies to unite East with West, but made a network tying the whole country together into one economic unit.

The installation of improved water and sewerage systems for cities and towns, making possible—for those who could afford it—the immense convenience of modern plumbing.

The lighting of homes, as well as city streets, by gas light and then by the magic of electric light.

Electrical transportation: the coming of the cable car, the trolley car, the elevated railroad (powered at first by steam, then by electricity), and the subway.

The development of electric motors and dynamos to do more and more of the work of the country; the introduction of the electric-power plant and of modern hydro-electric systems, so that the virtue of electricity could be on tap miles—or hundreds of miles—away from its source.

That incredible annihilator of distance, both between friends and between business offices, the telephone.

The revolutionizing of business life by the invention of the typewriter—which incidentally began to bring women into business life— and by the electric elevator, which, along with the development of steel-skeleton construction, made possible the skyscraper.

And, finally, the beginnings of that prime revolutionizer, the automobile, which had been introduced abroad as early as 1884 but did not begin to take its American forms until the early nineties.

24. To these wonders one might add the introduction of seaworthy ocean-going steamships; the opening of the Great Plains to settlement with the aid of the invention of barbed wire; the simplification and improvement of photography, and the coming of the half-tone process which accommodated it to publication; the invention of the linotype, to the great benefit of printing; and the contriving of all the machines which supplemented Elias Howe's sewing machine to facilitate the growth of the clothing and shoe industries. Yet even if we extended this list of new marvels indefinitely, we could hardly begin to convey a sense of the magnitude of the change which was wrought between 1850 and 1900. A land of formerly separate communities had been linked together. A land mostly of farmers and villagers had become a land mostly of cities and roaring industrial towns. Comforts, conveniences, and wealth had so piled up as to make possible a great extension of education on every

level and a general widening of horizons. It was almost as if a whole new world had been invented for people to work and play in.

25. But industrialism in those days of its raw growth brought abominations too. To begin with, wherever it advanced, ugliness came with it —smoke, soot, grime, the darkening of skies once clear, the withering of foliage once green, the pollution of rivers once clean. Indeed, so completely did men assume that money-making and beauty lived in separate compartments—beauty being something which you could buy after you made the money, or must run away to, from the city or the factory where the money was produced—that even the profitable building of houses, except for the rich, was undertaken as if by blind men. It should come as no surprise that the grimmest sections of most of our cities today date from between 1850 and 1900.

26. Not only did industrialism uglify the land wherever it moved; it also, while subduing it, despoiled it. Forests were hacked to pieces, farm land misused and overused, natural resources plundered right and left as if the bounties of America would be forever inexhaustible.

27. Morally, too, industrialism proved at first to be a destroyer of standards. So thoroughly had the idea sunk into men's minds that it was smart to make money in any way, straight or crooked, that the third quarter of the nineteenth century brought a contagion of fraudulence. It brought, too, a trend toward monopoly that if unchecked would have drawn all the economic power of the country into the hands of a few men. But the most disturbing thing about industrialism, in those days of its spring blooming, was the way in which it distributed the wealth it produced.

28. In the early days of the factory system in England, David Ricardo had enunciated the grim principle which he called the Iron Law of Wages: the principle that all wages tend to fall to the level which the most unskillful or most desperate man will accept. In pre-industrial times this Iron Law had not often operated unchecked. The prince, or the baron, or the squire, or the neighbors had tended to look after those who by reason of incompetence or illness or adversity were in want. And in the pre-industrial United States, as we have seen, men and women who were in want could at least go on working, for whatever pittance they could command, or could move on elsewhere to try again. But the new industrial community brought a change. For when a man built a mill or factory surrounded by a mill village or factory town, those who came to work for him were in great degree imprisoned by their choice. They did not own the tools with which they worked, and therefore were dependent on what employment the mill offered; and anyhow there was not enough other work in such a community for all who would be looking

for it if the mill shut down. And if their wages were low they could not afford to look elsewhere for jobs. So they ceased to be free agents. They were at their employer's mercy. And the Iron Law really went into action.

29. One great advantage the American workingman had—if he could raise the cash. He could still go West. But as the discards of industrialism, along with the men of most adventurous ambition, became Western pioneers, their places were taken by an imported proletariat—the incoming immigrants. First it was the Irish, who in the eighteen-fifties were the diggers of ditches, the builders of levees, the new class of mill-workers; then, as the Irish bettered themselves, it was the Italians, and then the Slavs of Eastern Europe. Each group tended to form a proletarian layer under the previous one. (At the bottom, in the most menial and ill-paid jobs of all, remained our own Negro population, slaves no longer, but remaining largely in a servitude of ignorance and exclusion from opportunity.) Thus the very hope that was symbolized by the Goddess of Liberty brought immigrants in such vast numbers as to glut the labor markets and delay the modification of the Iron Law.

30. As time went on there were to be other mitigating factors. One was the slow and uneven growth of labor unions. Another was the belated recognition, by a gradually aroused public conscience, of the horrors of American poverty; little by little the law began to prescribe more decent conditions of work. And another, of course, was the fact that the abounding flow of wealth from hugely increased productivity *did* tend to percolate down through the ranks of society and lift the living standard for the great majority. By 1891 wages in twenty-two industries had increased since 1860 on the average over 68 per cent, while wholesale prices had declined over 5 per cent. Yes, the *average* well-being, even in industry, was rising fast.

31. But there were sub-average areas where the terms of life were miserable. As late as 1887 a writer for *Harper's* found a coal-yard laborer in an Eastern mill town who earned seven dollars a week, while his wife earned five dollars, their elder daughter four dollars, and their fourteen-year-old daughter three dollars and a quarter, working from 6:30 in the morning till 6:30 at night in the mill. Total per year for *four* money-earners—$924. Not much improvement there over the conditions of the mid-century. The status of the anthracite workers in the Pennsylvania coal fields was sharply worse: there the workers who slaved grimly and dangerously underground were kept in a state of perpetual debt to the company on which they were dependent for their meager housing, their food, everything. And worse still were the conditions on New York's Lower East Side, where 290,000 people were packed into one square mile of tenements; where, in the filth and stench of Mulberry Bend, Jacob Riis found twelve men and women sleeping for "five cents a spot"

in one room not thirteen feet square; where the wife of an incapacitated invalid earned an income of $1.20 a week making shirts, while her oldest daughter cut out Hamburg edging for the noble wage of 2½ cents per hour for ten hours of steady labor. Here, at the very bottom of the pit of poverty, the Iron Law was iron indeed.

32. Meanwhile at the other end of the scale there was magnificence unstinted. Consider, for example, the mansion which Samuel Colt had built near Hartford out of the profits of his industrial pioneering. In 1876, reported a rapt chronicler in the *Art Journal,* the Colt lawn was daily rolled, cut, and trimmed to perfection by thirty men; while the green-houses, 2,634 feet in length, produced yearly at least a ton of grapes, to say nothing of 8,000 figs, peaches, and other fruits, and 400 quarts of strawberries. By the early eighteen-eighties American millionaires, led by the Vanderbilts, had become possessed with the idea that a successful man should build himself a mansion suitable for a European prince. They hired accomplished architects to produce for them Renaissance palaces, monumental Italian villas, or turreted French châteaux, with authen-tically princely bronze doors, grilled iron gates, ancient fireplaces, tap-estries, and paintings imported from abroad; and in these feudal edifices, staffed in many cases by thirty or more servants, they lived in marble grandeur. Nor was the luxury of the rich limited to their palaces. Pier-pont Morgan, whose house in New York was comparatively unassuming, as were his house in London, his country estate outside London, his American country estate on the Hudson, his Adirondack estate, his fish-ing box at Newport, and his suite at Jekyll Island, satisfied his desire for big things by building in 1898 a steam yacht 302 feet long, and by amassing an art collection worth at least fifty million dollars. Those were the days when private yachts, private art galleries, and racing stables were multiplying; when dinner parties included up to twenty courses; and when one young blood would be heard remarking to another, "Never ask the old man for less than fifty thousand."

33. It was on contrasts like these, at an early stage of European indus-trialism, that Karl Marx had predicated his theory of revolution. But one did not have to have a radical bias to be dismayed at the gulf one saw widening between rich and poor. In the year 1882—just a few months before the Vanderbilt fancy-dress ball on which was spent an estimated quarter of a million dollars (equivalent to much more than half a million today)—Junius Henry Browne wrote in *Harper's:* "Year after year New York seems to justify the painful, dispiriting averment that it is a city of paupers and millionaires. Are not the rich growing richer and the poor poorer as time moves on? Will there ever be a period when the distance between them will be less? Hope answers, 'Yes'; Reason answers, 'No.'"

34. The answer was still "No" at the turn of the century. At about

that time—a period of relative prosperity—the mass of unskilled workers were receiving less than $460 a year in wages in the North, less than $300 in the South; while Andrew Carnegie's *personal* share of the profits of his steel company was a little over six and a half million dollars for the year 1898, a little over twelve million dollars for 1899, and more than twenty-three million dollars for 1900. With no income taxes whatever to pay.

III

35. It could not go on without making a mockery of democracy. It did not go on. The story of American progress during the first half of the twentieth century has been the story of the repeal of the Iron Law, and of the slow disciplining of an industrialism still expandingly and excitingly productive.

36. A vehement rebellion against the way things were going had begun during the latter decades of the nineteenth century, chiefly among the farmers and small business men of the Midwest and the Great Plains, where the old Jeffersonian idea of a nation of self-reliant free men had been reinforced, within living memory, by frontier experience. It was the indignation of these people against the greedy and arbitrary power of the big railroad and manufacturing companies that was chiefly responsible for the passage of the Interstate Commerce Act of 1887 and the Sherman Anti-Trust Act of 1890, and for the fervor of the Populist movement of the early nineties. This grass-roots rebellion was reinforced by the anger of industrial workers, who were making grim and often bloody attempts to unionize. And as time went on it was still further reinforced by what might be called the revolt of the American conscience: a widespread and rising disapproval, among citizens by the millions, of what looked to them like the coming of a new feudalism. When they read the eye-opening reports of men like Jacob Riis on slum life, when the muckraking journalists uncovered for them the sordid business deals and political corruption of the day, their dismay had a moral basis: the way things had been going was not right.

37. And so the center of gravity of American opinion began to shift. In all walks of life, during the first fifteen years or so of the twentieth century, people began to think of society at large as an entity for which they were partly responsible. This feeling lent strength to political progressives and liberals like Theodore Roosevelt, the elder LaFollette, and Woodrow Wilson. In the churches there was a new emphasis on the "social gospel"; social service began to be recognized as a profession;

economists for the first time produced the concept of the "national income"; the two richest Americans, Carnegie and Rockefeller, converted great parts of their fortunes into foundations for the public weal; and Henry Ford, by voluntarily raising wages and cutting prices, dramatized a concept of industrialism as different from that of the nineteenth-century mill-owners as his assembly line was different from their crude mechanization. The Iron Law was on its way out.

38. Meanwhile invention continued at a breathless pace. We are all familiar with what it has brought us in the half century since 1900: such marvels as the airplane, the movies, the radio, television, a bewildering array of plastics and synthetics, and electronics. If we broaden the term "invention" to include a wider range of research, it has brought us a greatly increased knowledge of nutrition, a new battery of useful drugs, and—along with innumerable other wonders—the certainty of the future boon of atomic power, a certainty which only the misuse of atomic knowledge for purposes of mutual human destruction can long forestall. Likewise our increase in technological efficiency has been steady and formidable; during World War II our rate of production astonished the world. But along with this furious advance of industrialism has gone the disciplining of industrialism: its transformation from a force which made the rich richer and the poor poorer into a force which has narrowed the gulf between rich and poor.

39. For this great change there has been a surprising variety of causes. We need not detail here the long series of events through which they have manifested themselves—World War I, with its demand for high production at high wages; the confident competition of the nineteen-twenties; the crisis of the Great Depression, which dramatized the helplessness of the unemployed; the resulting spate of New Deal laws; World War II, with its unprecedented need for goods in quantity and its unprecedented government controls; and the post-1945 boom. Let us forget chronology and look at the tamers of industrialism group by group, in all their wild variety. We can lump them into five general classes:

(1) *Legislation*—including not only all manner of laws to protect the health and safety of the worker, to grant him a minimum wage, to permit him to organize, and to protect him as tenant and consumer, but also laws for the regulation of business practices, and—immensely important—the graduated income tax, first adopted in 1913, which has increasingly redistributed the national prosperity.

(2) *Public services*—including the vast expansion of public school systems, state universities, highway systems, park systems, and government aids and benefits of innumerable kinds. Municipal, state, and federal governments have all grown colossally; for instance, the federal

government now spends *eighty* times as much money annually as in 1900. Most of the expansion of the public services has been attributable, not to any conscious trend toward socialism, but to recognition of the simple fact that in a complex urbanized society, people cannot live decently unless the organized community provides them with services and opportunities which in earlier days the self-reliant man could get for himself.

(3) *Union action*—which, especially during the past fifteen years, has helped to lift wage-rates and standards of employment far above the level they would have remained at under the Iron Law.

(4) *A change in the attitude of business managements*—a growing realization that good working conditions, handsome factories, acceptable housing for workers, and an intelligent concern with worker relations, and also with public relations, can be business assets. This change has been gradual and in some degree forced by public hostility, as well as by government regulations which have placed big business in the bright glare of publicity: a goldfish has got to be good. But the change has been pervasive and salutary.

And (5) *the logic of mass production*—which is that the more goods you can produce, the less it costs to produce them; and that the more people are well off, the more they can buy, thus making this lavish and economical production possible. The continuing discovery and demonstration of this logic has been, in some ways, the most powerful force for change of the lot. For it has had its corollaries: that a nation of men and women secure against exploitation and acute poverty is a nation of delighted buyers of goods, to everybody's profit; that it pays better to produce the same sort of food, clothing, and equipment for everybody, of all income levels, than to produce luxury goods for a few, and second- and third-rate goods for the rest; and that therefore one can make money by lowering class barriers. Thus is Marxism confounded—not by dogma, but by the logic of advanced industrialism itself; or, to put it another way, by capitalism turned to democratic ends.

40. So much for generalization. Now let us glance at a few of the specific things that this modernized and disciplined industrial order has brought us during the past half century.

41. In fifty years, the amount of goods consumed per person in America has gone up 2½ times, while the average work week has dropped from about 58 hours to about 40.

42. The telephone dates from 1876, but in 1900 there were only a little over a million and a third telephones in America. At the end of 1949 there were over forty and a half million—just about thirty times as many.

43. The automobile, too, dates from the late nineteenth century, but

in 1900 there were still only a few thousand of them in the country. They were a rich man's luxury (and a mechanic's despair). Now there are over forty million—with paved roads everywhere to drive on.

44. And not only has the radio, which as a distributor of entertainment dates only from 1920, become a possession of almost every family in the country, but its new-come rival, television, has not even begun its career in the old-time way, as a plaything of the rich: from the beginning of the television boom in 1947, sales of sets have been distributed fairly evenly among all income groups. The logic of mass production has dictated for them a falling price and a mass appeal; and the purchase of a set has been, accordingly, an index less of wealth than of gadget-mindedness.

45. Or, to move into another field, take a look at education. In 1900 less than one American boy or girl out of ten of high school age was actually at high school; now over four out of five are. Meanwhile the number of students in American universities, colleges, and teacher-training institutions has increased eightfold. If we have a crisis in education today, this is because our training and paying of teachers has not yet caught up with the spread of American opportunity.

46. What has been taking place has been both a narrowing of the gap *in income* between rich and poor—though there are still islands of deep poverty in America, and there are also families and individuals by the millions who, through illness or adversity, live on the ragged edge of want—and, even more impressively, *a narrowing of the difference between rich and poor in their ways of living.*

47. For instance, consider the matter of personal appearance, remembering that in 1850 the merchant prince and his wife, or in 1900 the frock-coated, silk-hatted banker and his Paris-gowned wife were recognizable at a distance, if they ventured among the common herd, as beings apart. Forty or fifty years ago the countryman in a metropolis was visibly a "hayseed"; the purchaser of inexpensive men's clothing was betrayed by his tight-waisted jackets and bulbous-toed shoes. Today the difference in appearance between a steelworker (or a clerk) and a high executive is noticeable only to the attentive eye. And as for women, the difference in appearance between the one who spends $5,000 a year on clothes and the one who spends $250 is by no means as conspicuous as the difference between the woman who has good taste and the woman who lacks it. The fact that the wealthy woman has thirty dresses to the poor woman's three is not visible on the street, and the fact that her dresses are made of better materials and are better cut is observable only by the expert eye at close range. Fashion used to be decreed by Paris, imported by the most expensive dress shops, then modified by the more expensive Amer-

ican dress manufacturers, and finally—after an interval of six months to a year—modified still further, almost beyond recognition, by the manufacturers of cheap dresses. The process is now quicker and the differences much less sharp. Women of every income group wear nylon stockings (which offer the perfect illustration of the democratic logic of mass production). Unless the poor woman is exceptionally poor—or indifferent—she like the rich woman has had her hair recently shampooed and set. It could almost be said that the only easily visible mark of wealth which a woman can put on is a mink coat. A generation ago the great mail-order houses produced different clothes for the Western farmer's wife and for the city woman in the East; today there is no such distinction, and a friend of mine whose train stopped recently at a small Oklahoma town remarked that the girls on the railroad platform there were virtually indistinguishable in appearance from girls on Madison Avenue or Michigan Boulevard.

48. Let us proceed from clothes to the equipment of daily living. As Professor H. Gordon Hayes pointed out in *Harper's* in 1947, the rich man smokes the same sort of cigarettes as the poor man, shaves with the same sort of razor, uses the same sort of telephone, vacuum cleaner, and radio, has the same sort of lighting and heating equipment in his house, and so on indefinitely. The differences between his automobile and the poor man's are minor. Essentially they have similar engines, similar fittings. In the early years of the century there was a hierarchy of automobiles. At the top, as marks of dashing wealth, were such imported cars as the Rolls-Royce, Mercedes-Benz, and Isotta Fraschini. There was also an American aristocracy of the Pierce Arrow, Peerless, and Packard. Then came group after group, in descending scale, till you reached the homely Model-T Ford. Today, except for a few survivals such as the obstinately rectangular Rolls-Royces of the old school, and a few oddities such as the new British sports cars, there is a comparative uniformity; and although the owner of a big, brand-new car probably has a large income, he may merely, like the purchaser of a television set, be someone who adjusts a slender budget to cover the machines that entrance him.

49. In the matter of running water and plumbing, uniformity has approached much more slowly but nevertheless steadily. Throughout the latter part of the nineteenth century the rich and the middle-income group in the cities and towns were progressively installing running water, bathrooms, and water closets in their houses; but at the turn of the century not only did factory workers and farmers (except for a few owners of big farms) hardly dream of enjoying such luxuries, but even in the houses of well-to-do people beyond the reach of city water and sewerage lines, there was likely to be no bathroom. Not until 1908 did Ellsworth M. Statler build in Buffalo the first hotel which offered every guest a

room and private bath at a moderate price. Not until 1916 did the double-shell enameled bathtub go into mass production, replacing the painted cast-iron tub with roll-rim and claw feet. Today only the older and poorer tenements and dwellings in American cities and towns lack bathtubs or showers and water closets, and these conveniences are fast being installed in farmhouses.

50. Meanwhile the electrification of American farms has reached a point which would have been unimaginable in 1900, when even the prosperous city-dweller had only just begun to install electricity in his new house without adding gas, too, lest the current fail suddenly. The coming of the electric refrigerator and also, increasingly, the deep-freeze unit have not only made for domestic convenience but also—along with our expanding knowledge of nutrition—have improved the year-round diet of millions. (Where, today, is the once-famous American dyspepsia?) Meanwhile the servant class has almost vanished, although servants' wages have a purchasing power today from five to ten times bigger than in 1900; its virtual disappearance—which has imposed upon all but a tiny percentage of American families the chores of cooking and cleaning and washing (with, increasingly, the aid of a dishwasher and a washing machine)—marks the virtual absorption of the immigrant proletariat of yore into general American society, in which domestic service has always been regarded as humiliating.

51. One of the most striking effects of the logic of mass production has been the way in which the mass circulation magazines, the movies, and the radio have tended to impose upon Americans of all income levels the same patterns of emulation: in other words, to make them all want to be the same sort of people. This has been a purely twentieth-century phenomenon, for the big magazines were just beginning to push their circulations over the million mark in 1900, while the first nickelodeon theaters did not begin to show movies till about 1905, and radio broadcasting dates only from 1920.

52. In the movies, popular stars like Clark Gable, Cary Grant, Gary Cooper, Humphrey Bogart, and Gregory Peck may play the parts of people who are supposed to be rich and stylish, or of people who are at the end of their economic rope; but whatever role any one of them assumes, his popularity depends upon his representing a kind of charm that any young American male can appreciate and at least approach; in other words, upon his conforming to what old-fashioned people would call middle-class standards of speech and behavior—standards which might more properly be called classless or all-American. Whether he is cast as a millionaire's son or as a truck driver, he remains essentially the same. In radio Jack Benny, for all his big income, plays the part of a Jack Benny who lives in a modest house, owns a wheezy old car, watches the

pennies, and has for his sole servant a jack-of-all-trades helper with whom he is on the breeziest of terms. Thus the logic of mass production pushes the idols of Hollywood into roles which represent general American behavior.

53. And what is the result? Both the rich man's fourteen-year-old son, who dismays his conservative parents by trying to talk like Humphrey Bogart, and the truck-driver's son, who longs to be as funny as Bob Hope, will grow up to behave more like their idols—and thus, more like one another—than they would have otherwise. And something else happens too. Half a century ago a coal-miner who found himself at a fashionable restaurant would not have the faintest notion of how to behave; nowadays he has only to ask himself, "How would Gregory Peck do it?" In short, the social distance between the extremes of American society is shrinking.

54. Whenever I think of this change, I think of something I saw the other day in New York City. A street was being torn up for repairs, and while the workmen were standing waiting for the arrival of new equipment, one of them, who had in his hands an iron rod presumably used for prying off manhole covers, was enjoying a little relaxation. I looked twice to see what he was doing with that rod. He was practising a graceful golf stroke.

IV

55. So much for the change since 1850. And where are we headed now —during the next half century, or century, if you will?

56. I believe that we have hardly started; that the expansion of industrialism is still in its early stages, and its civilizing is in a still earlier stage. Professor Sumner H. Slichter says that by such an early date as 1980 the annual output of goods and services in the United States should rise from about $4,065 per worker to at least $5,744 per worker (at present prices), and probably more, while the labor week is being reduced from an average of 40 hours today to an average of 30 hours. That seems to me a modest estimate—if we can surmount certain dangers which threaten us.

57. The first danger is, of course, that total war may smash the whole system. But in this particular context, even this danger can be exaggerated. It is quite true that the existence of atom bombs, and the possibility of hydrogen bombs, threaten millions of us with annihilation. But it is useful to recall that in the twenties and thirties many people predicted that another world war would "end civilization"; but that when the war came, on a lethal scale, it was accompanied and followed by an unex-

pected *increase* in population, not only in the United States but in other warring nations; and that although international trade has since then been hobbled, production has more or less recovered in Europe and has been given a new boost in the United States. The danger of extinction for whole communities is real; the danger to the progress of industrialism is not necessarily final.

58. The second danger is that we may defeat our great experiment in the negating of the Iron Law by applying the lessons of that defeat on too rapid a scale. We may get the fatal notion that benefits to various sections of the population can be brought about by government handouts and guarantees larger than the increase in our national productivity can support. This is not primarily a danger of socialism, which in its doctrinaire form is almost as outdated a concept as communism; among the guarantees and handouts that could most endanger our national solvency are the kind that even the most conservative citizens (such as potatogrowers) delight in—when they are the beneficiaries. The balance between economic liberty and political intervention offers a delicate problem in adjustment.

59. There is a third danger: that the trend toward American uniformity may reach the point where we are standardized into universal acceptance of the second-rate—or, even worse, into complete susceptibility to mass emotion, which in turn could be manipulated to turn the United States into a police state. Well, possibly. Every wave of hysteria which crosses the country—like that which today fills many people with a preposterous terror of American communism—reminds us once more that eternal vigilance is the price of liberty. But if American flexibility, horse sense, and humor carried us through the dark days of 1933, they ought to be able to do it again.

60. If these dangers can be surmounted, the prospects are exciting. The remaining islands of real poverty in America are a challenge; so are our congested and debt-laden cities, which become more expensive to run, and offer their inhabitants a more unnatural and nerve-racking life, as they lure more and more people to enjoy their glitter; so is the failure, thus far, of most Americans to get any chance to savor the joy of work done under agreeable conditions for a satisfying purpose. The best of our factories, today, are things of a new and lively beauty; the worst— which include most of the older ones—are still in essence "dark, Satanic mills." More satisfaction and enjoyment on the job might prove even more desirable for the general well-being than more pay for less work. But in all these directions progress can be made, with luck, if we can keep wide open the roads along which scientific research and technology are taking us—and can steer around those other dangers that I have mentioned. The technicians were never more active than today; science,

like industrialism, is still in its youth; a single new discovery, like that of atomic power, if harnessed for peaceable use, could by the year 2000 help to make 1950 seem as primitive a time as 1900, to say nothing of 1850, seems to us today.

⁶¹· Those villages of 1850 were mighty pretty, with their lawns reaching to the river. I see no reason why—if we keep our wits about us— American communities of 2000 and 2050 should not be just as satisfying to the eye; far cleaner, more convenient, more comfortable; far prouder as residences for even the least fortunate man, woman, and child who live in them; and more favorable as seed-beds of the human spirit.

COMMENTARY AND QUESTIONS

Frederick Lewis Allen wrote "The Big Change" for the Centennial Issue of *Harper's Magazine,* of which he was for many years the editor-in-chief. He later developed this essay into a book published under the same title.

1. A consideration of all the significant changes that took place in America between 1850 and 1950 is a subject much too broad and general to be treated effectively in an essay of this length. What is the central theme that Allen has selected for development here? Explain the title. Does it cover the essay as a whole? Does par. 2 provide the reader with an accurate indication of the main topics to be treated? What do you think was Allen's reason for not placing it at the very beginning of the essay?

2. This essay is divided into four main sections, indicated by roman numerals. Give a title to each of these sections. What principle of organization determines the order in which these sections are presented, and why is this principle especially suitable here? What principle is followed in the arrangement of the three main parts (pars. 20-22, 23-24, 25-34) of section II? Sections I, II, and III conclude with a discussion of the same specific subject. What is it? Why do you think Allen concluded each of these sections with a discussion of this subject? Is it also discussed in section IV?

3. What purposes are served by section IV? Why is par. 61 an effective conclusion to the essay as a whole as well as to section IV?

4. What is the function of the first sentence in par. 7? Of the first in par. 13, the last in par. 27, the first in par. 33?

5. The key sentence of section II is the first one in par. 23: "It brought with it both wonders and abominations." In what way is the sense of balance suggested by this sentence characteristic of the essay as a whole?

6. To a marked extent the effectiveness of this essay is the result of Allen's careful use of exact and appropriate words. Consider, for example, the

series of adjectives he uses in the final sentence of par. 6 to describe the American people. Which are the most effective words in the concluding sentence of par. 20, and what special quality other than exactness and appropriateness makes them effective? In the same paragraph, why is *contrivance* particularly appropriate? What is the reason for Allen's use, near the end of par. 18, of the phrase *mighty smart?* Which words and phrases make the last two sentences of par. 25 especially effective?

7. Par. 2 is composed of only one sentence. What special feature of its structure makes it relatively easy for the reader to follow Allen's thought here?

SUGGESTIONS FOR WRITING

1. This essay shows how effectively examples can be used to develop contrasts in writing about a change that has taken place. Select a change with which you are familiar (such as a change in your home town, in a person you know, or in yourself) and write an essay about it, using examples to develop contrasts.
2. The future of America.
3. I prefer the old days (or today).

The Character
of the American Polity

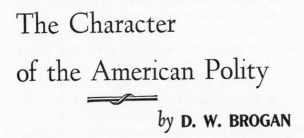

by D. W. BROGAN

THE AMERICAN CONSTITUTION is the oldest written constitution in existence. It can claim, indeed, to be the first constitution in the modern world, and that it has survived so long is a tribute to the sagacity, moderation, and sense of the possible shown by its makers. When it went into effect in 1789, the French monarchy still stood; there was a Holy

From *Politics in America* by D. W. Brogan. By permission of Harper & Row, Publishers. Copyright 1954 by D. W. Brogan.

Roman Emperor, a Venetian Republic and a Dutch Republic, an Autocrat in St. Petersburg, a Sultan-Caliph in Constantinople, an Emperor vested with the 'mandate of Heaven' in Pekin and a Shogun ruling the hermit empire of Japan in the name of a secluded, impotent and almost unknown Mikado.

2. Even in countries where formal political continuity has been preserved, it can plausibly be maintained that far greater changes have taken place in the political realities, if not in the forms, than have taken place in the United States. Queen Elizabeth II and King Gustaf Adolf VI hold offices far less like those of their predecessors of 1789, than the office held by General Eisenhower is like the office held by General Washington. Forms and realities have changed less in the United States than in any other political organization, even than in Tibet.[1]

3. Duration is not the only political virtue, but it is a virtue. Constitutions, by their name and function, can be deemed successes only if they last long enough to give stability to the political life of the society they are supposed to serve. The American Constitution passes that test. But a constitution can survive in a form that makes it less and less adequate for the needs of the society it purports to serve, and either that society is cribbed, cabined and confined, held within an armour that forbids adaptation or growth, or the constitution is disregarded and the true political forces grow up beside it, paying only lip service to the antique and obsolete forms, as Prussia grew up in the carapace of the constitution of the Holy Roman Empire of the German People. That has not happened in the United States. The Constitution is still at the centre of American government and politics. It must be reckoned with every day by the President, by the Congress, by the Courts, by labour, by business. It has proved sufficiently adaptable to permit the expansion of the thin line of newly emancipated colonies along the Atlantic seaboard to the Pacific, the multiplication of the population fifty-fold and the extension of the armed power of the United States almost round the globe. It has permitted the growth of these remote and, in 1789, impoverished colonies to an economic power and a material wealth unprecedented in human history. And it has done all this without distorting its fundamental character or denying the political theories and system of values on which it was based.

4. The American Constitution has been a success; so Americans think, so the reflective portion of non-American mankind must concede. But because the Constitution has been a success, it has acquired in the

---

[1] General Eisenhower took, in 1953, exactly the same oath as did General Washington in 1789.

eyes of those who have best reason to know how successful it has been, 'The People of the United States', a claim to reverence, to uncritical acceptance, that has no parallel in the world. For it should be remembered that the United States is based on this written document, that the shrine in which it and the Declaration of Independence are housed, has the same claim on American religious awe as Westminster Abbey and the Stone of Destiny have for the English, that the sacred *ampoule* of Reims had for the French before the cutting of the thread of French history in 1789.[2]

5. There are other constitutions and other constitutional documents. But they are not foundation documents as is the Constitution of the United States. Magna Charta is not the birth certificate of England. The British North America Act is not the birth certificate of Canada; it is the record of the terms on which other colonies joined themselves to Canada. The name of Australia, to some degree the fact of Australia, existed before the Commonwealth of Australia was called into existence by an act of the British Parliament. But 'We the People of the United States' came into existence either in 1776 or 1789, not before and not otherwise than in these two documents.[3]

6. The consequences of an identifiable birth of the United States not merely certified by, but caused by, the issuance and acceptance of these documents are great and permanent. Even if the Declaration of Independence has no legal effect in America, its declaration of truths held to be self-evident—'That all men are created equal, that they are endowed by their Creator with certain unalienable rights, that among these are Life, Liberty and the Pursuit of Happiness' has been and is of incalculable importance. It is this declaration of purposes and principles that creates what Gunnar Myrdal has called 'the American dilemma', the contrast between promise and performance. That contrast, in the American

---

[2] Until 1952, these two documents were kept in an illuminated shrine in the Library of Congress. They are now housed in the National Archives building in a stronghold believed adequate to protect not only against the moth, the rust, the thieves, but the atom bomb.

[3] It has been plausibly held that the phrase with which the Constitution opens, 'We the People of the United States', did not describe and was not meant to describe any 'people' existing in 1787 when the Constitution was drafted, but was shorthand for the names of the peoples of the states then existing who might, by accepting the Constitution, create 'The People of the United States'. It might be held by the pedantic that the Articles of Confederation in 1781 are the first constitution, the present operative document being an elaborate amendment of the earlier. That, if true, would merely show that there were three, not two, fundamental documents to consider. But the Articles of Confederation, in life or in death, never evoked any of the admiration or adoration given, after a time, to the Constitution, and that is the political fact which we are considering.

political religion, as in the religion of St. Paul, produces tensions, repentance and better performance. The preamble to the Constitution has no legal force either. Yet the phrases 'We the People of the United States, in order to form a more perfect Union, establish Justice, insure domestic Tranquility, provide for the common Defense, promote the general Welfare, and secure the Blessings of Liberty to ourselves and our Posterity, do ordain and establish this Constitution for the United States of America', have made history and effective law. 'The People of the United States', in part at least, exists because it was so named in the bond. The Union is more perfect because the People was called on to form a more perfect Union and the general welfare has been sought and in great degree promoted, because that was laid down in 1787 as one main duty of the new polity.[4]

7. One result of this concentration of attention and of reverence on a document which is a formal law has been to give to the political life of 'the People of the United States' a peculiarly legal, often a pedantically legal character. There, in this known document, is the sole source of the power of the government of the United States. Behind that document may lie the unlimited power of 'the People of the United States', but since 1789, that People has seen itself embodied, has seen its will expressed only through this document.

8. The importance of this legal way of looking at political problems was never made more manifest than in the period when the Constitution was most manifestly failing to promote or preserve a 'more perfect Union'. For both sides in the Civil War appealed to the Constitution. Jefferson Davis did not claim to act on the unalienable right of 'the People to alter or abolish ... any government destructive of the ends for which it was formed', which the Declaration of Independence had declared to be one of the bases of free government. He claimed to be acting on a true interpretation of the Constitution of the United States and on the authority of its makers, the Peoples of the States. And Lincoln did not retort, even after the Emancipation Proclamation, that he was waging war for the establishment of the unalienable rights of man, of which liberty was one. He, too, was concerned with the rights and duties given him and imposed on him by the Constitution which he had sworn 'faith-

---

[4] The 'general Welfare' referred to in the preamble is often confused by the man in the street (and by at least one President, Franklin D. Roosevelt) with the 'general Welfare' referred to in Article I, Section 8 of the Constitution. 'The Congress shall have power to lay and collect, Taxes, Duties, Imposts and Excises, to pay the Debts and provide for the common Defence and general Welfare of the United States.' Courts and most lawyers distinguish between the pious aspiration of the Preamble and the specific and more limited power granted in this section, but the average American has confused the two, with important political consequences.

fully [to] execute'. He might, in the Second Inaugural, when both slavery and secession were visibly doomed, see in this terrible war the due punishment of national sin. But divine vengeance on national sin is not a doctrine to be found in the Constitution of the United States, nor, we may assume, did many Americans, North or South, accept it even as a religious doctrine, as Lincoln well knew.

9. More instances could be given to show the permanence of this legal-constitutional approach and more will be given in their proper place. All that it is needful to insist on here, is that the American people, after more than a century and a half of experience, is as much as ever convinced that, within the framework of that Constitution and in no other way, lies political salvation for them. This may be a foolish doctrine but it is the doctrine, the living political faith of the American people. That faith is shown in another way, in the acceptance of the idea that the normal extension of the territorial authority of the United States is by the accession or creation of new states, with the same powers, the same duties, the same general political character as the original thirteen founders. There was no absolute necessity for the application of this doctrine. The remoter territories could have been kept in a tutelary condition for long periods. They could have been admitted on inferior terms; discrimination could have been made between state and state (and more power or less accorded to the various states in consequence). But with a deep and justified confidence in the adequacy and powers of expansion of the American system, the thirteen states have been increased to forty-eight, despite the fears and ambitions of spokesmen for states and sections. The system is not yet complete; outlying territories like Alaska, Hawaii and Puerto Rico are not yet admitted to the sisterhood, but if they remain in the Union, their day will come and come soon, for the system has its own logic and its own power of compelling action.[5] This unity has been dearly bought and has, in its practical effects, often been resented. Even in a small, homogeneous, easily defined society, there are local interests and there are stresses and strains arising from them. How much more is this true of a country the size of all Europe (including European Russia), with a population of 160,000,000 scattered, in very differing degrees of density, over 3,000,000 square miles, over an area

---

[5] There is a marked difference in British and American 'imperial' theory. British theory accepts, even rejoices in, differences, in anomalies, in the tax autonomy of the Isle of Man, in the indescribable relation to the Commonwealth of the Republic of India (or the even more indescribable relationship of the Republic of Ireland to Great Britain). American theory and practice, like French imperial theory, prefer assimilation, uniformity of powers and institutions. Of course there is a further difference between the French and American theories of expansion; the French is mainly theory, the American is a theory put into practice.

with climate and resources ranging from those of Finland to those of Andalusia, even of Egypt! It is not surprising that the Union still needs perfecting; what is surprising is the degree of union attained. And the great emotional tragedy of American history, the war that stirs the deepest emotions, is still the Civil War that came when other ends than unity were preferred.

10. The memory of the breakdown of political sagacity and political discipline that resulted in the Civil War is not the only reason for the formal conservatism of much of American political life, for an antiquarianism which may be harmless, but often is not. Like all great political peoples, like the Romans and the English, the Americans understand the need for maintaining forms. The political augurs may smile as they meet each other in the cloakrooms of Congress or in hotel rooms at national conventions, but it is a rash man who abolishes a ritual merely because it is obsolete and serves no immediately visible 'practical' function (as if the maintenance of political habits of loyalty and cooperation were not practical in the highest degree).

11. The phrase 'the People of the United States' is a phrase that, at any given moment, is not free from ambiguity. The Constitution was framed, among other reasons, to 'secure the Blessings of Liberty to ourselves and our Posterity', but it has extended these blessings to many millions who are not the posterity of the Founders or of their contemporaries. Probably more than half of the American people, in 1954, are descended from immigrants who have entered the United States since 1789. Nearly a tenth of the present inhabitants of the United States were born outside its boundaries (in the not remote past, the proportion was higher); nearly a third of the present population are only one or, at most, two generations deep in the United States.

12. It is natural and right, then, that such a political society should rely on verbal affirmations, on formal organization of loyalty, of national feeling, should see allegiance, not as an accident of birth, but as an exercise of will, should preach, out of necessity as well as taste, a political religion, set up a political church outside which there is, in America, no salvation. The United States did not just come into existence over a long period of time. It was made in what is, historically, a brief period of time and by conscious will. The Americans (even before they existed as a body politic) willed to exist as an independent group of republics, of 'cities' in the antique sense, before becoming the United States created by the Constitution.[6]

---

[6] The Latin title of the United States brings out this antique view of the constituting states, 'Civitates Americae Foederatae'.

¹³· And not only is there present the element of will, there is absent the element of the traditional, the time-hallowed, the charismatic. The United States has a birthday, so there is a pre-United States yet American past. But 1776 is a very different date from 1066 or 1789. King Alfred and St. Joan both antedate the two great years of English and French history. A society expanding so rapidly in area and in numbers, accepting new states and new peoples, was and is in danger of internal dissolution, as the Roman Republic and the Roman hegemony in Italy were weakened and finally destroyed. Yet more strange streams have flowed into the Hudson and Mississippi, from Europe, from Africa, from other parts of America, than ever flowed from Orontes into Tiber. The making of Americans has been a continuous task. And as Augustus tried to give the deliquescent Roman society of his time a basis in the habits and traditions of an older and healthier age, so the Americans have continually borne in mind the precept of Ennius, given long before Augustus:

> *Moribus antiquis res stat Romana verisque.*

Yet the maintenance of the ancient ways is attempted under special difficulties. There is no hereditary monarchy to canalize emotion, especially female emotion; there is no established church; there is no naturally accepted hierarchy; there is no real national capital, concentrating within itself the leaders in politics, the arts, business, conspicuous consumption. Although, as will be shown, the American people are today far more 'religious' than are most of the peoples of western Europe, their government is formally 'Godless'.⁷ Nor has the United States, until very recent times, known the solidifying pressure of outside danger or rivalry. Its exterior history has been a series of happy solutions (from the American point of view) of exterior problems, none of them, except the acquisition of both sides of the Mississippi by the Louisiana Purchase and the extension to the Pacific by the Mexican War and the Oregon settlement with Britain, of any great importance. No amount of patriotic oratory about the iniquities of Britain, Germany or, today, Russia, has ever been as effectual, politically speaking, as the evocation of the memories of the

---

⁷ The inscription 'In God We Trust' was put on the coins during the Civil War by the Secretary of the Treasury, that eminent Episcopalian layman, Salmon P. Chase. Before the Civil War and after there were many attempts to 'put God into the Constitution', but they have all failed. The United States in theory is 'laïc'. It might be noted that in the Constitution of the Confederate States, one of the few changes made on the original constitution was the insertion of the name of God. In that preamble 'the People of the Confederate States, each State acting in its sovereign and independent character' invoked 'the favor and guidance of Almighty God'. This was not accorded.

Civil War, the 'waving of the bloody shirt' in the North and in the South alike. And that evocation of the past made for disunity, not unity.

14. Moreover, the United States was founded by a Revolution and based on a revolutionary theory. It is easy to forget that today, when the word 'revolution' is no longer blessed like Mesopotamia, or has been taken over by revolutionaries who dismiss the principles of the Declaration of Independence and the practices of the Constitution as bourgeois confidence tricks played on a gullible proletariat. So much that was new, daring, and dangerous in 1776 is commonplace or repudiated today. But the fact remains that it was new then.[8] That 'all Governments derive their just powers from the consent of the governed' is not, in 1954, a self-evident truth. But old-fashioned Americans like Senator Hoar who held to the Jeffersonian dogma against innovators like Senator Beveridge, knew the temper of the American people better than did the imperialists who found 'manifest destiny' in the Philippines. The ancestral voices (and other causes) were enough, in the not very long run, to end the American dream of empire. Nor has the basic premise of the equality of man been ineffectual in the long run. It was the Jeffersonian dogma that Lincoln appealed to, at Gettysburg, when he asked himself and the world whether a 'nation conceived in liberty and dedicated to the proposition that all men are created equal . . . could long endure'. It did endure, but at a terrible cost, and the equality dogma of the Declaration is still (like the more perfect Union) in the making, not made. Americans know that their freedom was bought at a great price, even though

---

[8] 'The story of the revolted colonies impresses us first and most distinctly as the supreme manifestation of the law of resistance, as the abstract revolution in its purest and most perfect shape. No people was so free as the insurgents; no government less oppressive than the government which they overthrew. Those who deem Washington and Hamilton honest can apply the term to few European statesmen. Their example presents a thorn, not a cushion, and threatens all existing political forms, with the doubtful exception of the federal constitution of 1787. It teaches that men ought to be in arms even against a remote and constructive danger to their freedom; that even if the cloud is no bigger than a man's hand, it is their right and duty to stake the national existence, to sacrifice lives and fortunes, to cover the country with a lake of blood, to shatter crowns and sceptres and fling parliaments into the sea. On this principle of subversion they erected their commonwealth, and by its virtue lifted the world out of its orbit and assigned a new course to history. Here or nowhere we have the broken chain, the rejected past, precedent and statute superseded by unwritten law, sons wiser than their fathers, ideas rooted in the future, reason cutting as clean as Atropos.' Lord Acton's review, in 1889, of Bryce's *American Commonwealth*, reprinted in *Bryce's American Commonwealth Fiftieth Anniversary* (1939), edited by Robert C. Brooks, p. 201. These are not the views of all Americans today about their Revolution, but Jefferson, even Washington, would be as much out of place at a meeting of the 'Daughters of the American Revolution' as any accidentally surviving old Bolshevik in the Kremlin of 1954.

they were formally born free and equal. They still think, with Emerson, that it was not mere provincial vanity to elevate the skirmish at Concord bridge in 1775 to one of the great events of human history.[9] They think that the July days of 1776, like the July days of 1789 and the October days of 1917, are 'days that shook the world'. They are conscious that their history, their destiny, has set them a little apart from the rest of the world, even from that part of it with which they have the closest spiritual and blood ties. They are unmoved, then, when it is pointed out to them that much of their life, much of their attitude to social and political problems, is different from that of Europe. They remember, emotionally, if not intellectually, that the Founders chose as a motto for the new political society, 'novus ordo seculorum', a new order of the ages. They are not surprised that this vaulting ambition should have been justified, creating a new political order, not to be judged by some ideal pattern laid up in Heaven or Westminster. 1776 was a new order and, inevitably, it had new and original political consequences.[10]

15. It follows from this, that the study of American political organization and method imposes on the European student a humility before the facts that may not come easily. Even if his admiration for the British Constitution is as warm and uncritical as that of Burke, Macaulay or Woodrow Wilson, he must remember that he is inspecting a system based on different principles and formed by a different experience. He must be willing to learn, to assess, to judge, by human standards, indeed, but human standards that have a new embodiment. He must be willing to notice the extraordinary phenomena he is studying, without reacting like the farmer who saw the giraffe and said 'impossible'. *Sic fortis Etruria crevit*. Thus and not otherwise did America grow. No one can deny the growth or should refuse to the study of the political conditions of that growth at least the courtesy of a suspended judgment.

COMMENTARY AND QUESTIONS

It is often difficult for one nation to understand another, even when the two speak what appears to be the same language. D. W. Brogan, an Englishman, has written a number of thoughtful and perceptive

---

[9] By the rude bridge that arched the flood,
Their flag to April's breeze unfurled,
Here once the embattled farmers stood,
And fired the shot heard round the world.

[10] Anticipating the first French Republic and outdaring the Bolsheviks, the Americans date all important official documents by the 'Year of Our Lord and of the Independence of the United States'. (Thus 1954 A.D. 'and of the Independence of the United States, the one hundred and seventy-seventh'.)

books for the purpose of explaining America to his countrymen. These books have been well received in Great Britain because they were so successful in showing the British what Americans are like and why they are as they are. Brogan's writing has been equally popular in the United States, perhaps because, as an observant and watchful outsider, he has pointed out to us the significance of many things about ourselves that we might otherwise overlook or take for granted.

An earlier volume by Brogan, *The American Character*, entertainingly discussed American habits and personality. *Politics in America*, a more formal and elaborate book about the American system of government as it works out in actual practice, discusses such phenomena as the American party system, political machines and bosses, national party conventions, and the relationships between the President and Congress. The selection here reprinted, which constitutes the first section of the book's opening chapter, interprets the American concept of the foundation stone of our political system—the Constitution itself.

1. In his preface to the book which contains this essay, Brogan wrote:

> The purpose of this book is simply to make the American political system intelligible. It has no thesis except that the system has its own logic, its own justification, and is, in general, a success. It cannot be easily altered (despite the adoption since the end of the first world war of five constitutional amendments). This system, too, should be studied in its own terms; its successes and failures seen in their American context.

What evidence do you find in Brogan's method of approach in this selection that he is following his own injunction to study the American political system in its own terms?

2. Significantly, the book in which this essay appears was published in England under the title of *An Introduction to American Politics*. When introducing readers to new information or new concepts, a writer often finds it advantageous to relate this new material to facts or concepts that are already well known to his readers. Note Brogan's use of this technique in pars. 4, 5, and 13, and in the footnote referring to par. 9. How do Brogan's references to aspects of British political history help the American reader to gain greater understanding of the government of his own country?

3. In par. 1, what means does Brogan use to make his readers realize the full significance of his statement that "the American Constitution is the oldest written constitution in existence"? Does he employ the same means in par. 2?

4. State in unmetaphorical language the point of the sixth sentence in par. 13. What is gained and what is lost in the restatement?

5. Brogan has an exceptionally large and exact vocabulary from which to choose precisely the right word to express his thought. In some places

this has led him to use terms that may not already be part of your own vocabulary. Give the derivation and meaning of each of the following as Brogan has used it: *carapace* (par. 3), *tutelary* (par. 9), *augurs* (par. 10), *charismatic* (par. 13), *hegemony* (par. 13), *deliquescent* (par. 13), and *hierarchy* (par. 13). What does Brogan suggest by his use of *antiquarianism* in par. 10?

6. Alistair Cooke, like Brogan, is an Englishman who has written about America for the benefit of his countrymen. What differences do you find between the vocabulary of this essay and that of Cooke's (pp. 63-67)? How can you account for these differences?

7. In this selection Brogan uses a highly allusive style. The careful and inquiring reader may find explanations of many of Brogan's allusions in reference works that are generally available. For example, in *Webster's New International Dictionary, Second Edition,* he will find that the Stone of Destiny (par. 4) is the Stone of Scone, or the British Coronation Stone, which, according to legend, was used by Jacob as a pillow. And from *The Columbia Encyclopedia* he will learn that "the sacred *ampoule* of Reims" (par. 4), which was long used in the coronation of French monarchs, was destroyed in the French Revolution. Does your dictionary explain the phrase *manifest destiny* (par. 14)?

8. *The Oxford Dictionary of Quotations* contains the following translation of the precept of Ennius cited in par. 13: "The Roman state and manhood stands by ancient customs." The Latin quotation in par. 15, *Sic fortis Etruria crevit* (Thus strong Etruria grew), is from Virgil's *Georgics* (Book II, l. 533). Explain the relationship of this quotation to the context in which Brogan uses it. Name an English word derived from *fortis.*

9. For what purpose does Brogan use most of the many footnotes in this selection? Why did he not incorporate into the body of his essay the material contained in them?

SUGGESTIONS FOR WRITING

1. An example of "the American dilemma" (par. 6).
2. Outmoded conventions.
3. The electoral college.
4. The practical value of political rituals.
5. The blessings of diversity.

The Place of Thought
in American Life

by DANIEL J. BOORSTIN

No ONE CAN STUDY the history of thought in Europe without taking account, at the outset, of two basic facts. First, there is the separation of the thought of the community into two streams: the stream of "high culture"—the thought, art and vocabulary of the aristocrats, priests, and all members of the privileged and ruling classes; and the stream of "popular culture"—the thought, art, customs, lore and folkways of the great mass of the people. The gulf is so deep and the separation so wide between the two in most European countries, and has been for most of their history, that the definition of what is being talked about offers no problem to the historian of European thought. He is talking about either the "thinking class" or the "working class." It is a truism that in many periods the aristocracy of France felt a closer fellowship with the aristocrats of Germany than with the peasants of their own country. The folk culture of the English people is at least as remote from that of its aristocratic and educated classes as the culture of England is different from that of France or Italy. When, for example, Sir Leslie Stephen wrote his *History of English Thought in the Eighteenth Century*, it was perfectly obvious that he was writing about the ideas which filled the heads of that small fraction of the English population who were literate, educated and close to the seats of power.

2. Second—and this feature is closely connected with the first—the history of European thought (by which is usually meant the thought of the only "thinking" people, that is the aristocratic classes) is on the whole reducible to the history of systems and schools of thought. It is the history of "Thomism," "Rationalism," "Transcendentalism," et cetera— terms which to most of the people of those days were as foreign as another language. It is the history of the specialized architecture of philosophies, rather than of the general physiology of thinking. The grander, the more filigreed and intricate a system, supposedly the greater its claim to treatment in the history of thought. Those elegant intellectual

From *The American Scholar*, Spring, 1956. By permission of the author. Copyright © 1956 by the United Chapters of Phi Beta Kappa. This essay appears with slight modifications in *America and the Image of Europe* (New York: Meridian Books, 1960).

chapels built by Thomas Aquinas and Immanuel Kant thus have become the destinations of the historians' pilgrimage. Scholars find them a welcome refuge from the confusion of the market place.

3. But it is misleading to take these characteristics of European thought as the starting points for an American history. Our society, unlike most other modern nations, has not been marked by the separation into high culture and popular culture; nor has our thinking been dominated by systems and schools. On the contrary, there have been a number of other large and persistent characteristics of the place of thought in American life. There are those which concern the *form* of American intellectual life, and those which concern the *substance* of our way of thinking.

I

4. Beginning with the form of our intellectual life, we find two important and apparently contradictory characteristics: first, its unity or homogeneity; and second, its diffuseness.

A. The unity of American culture

5. From one point of view the history of culture in the most developed European countries in modern times has been rather uniform. For the growth of their liberal institutions has not removed their basic distinction between aristocratic culture and folk culture. What has happened is either that their aristocratic culture has been watered down piecemeal to make it more accessible and more palatable to the half-educated masses, or that a few places have been made available within the aristocracy for more talented and ambitious members of the lower classes ("the career open to talent"). A typical example of the first of these was the translation of the Greek and Latin classics into the vernacular languages, which was one of the major intellectual events of the European Renaissance. An example of the second was the growth of a system of scholarships which brought to Oxford and Cambridge some young men whose wealth and ancestry had not entitled them to that advantage. But the basic fact is that the modern intellectual and cultural life of the European community is still simply a modification and adaptation of the old aristocratic (high) culture to the sporadic demands

of members of the rising classes. How little progress has yet been made is illustrated by the fact that throughout Western Europe (where alone true universities remain), with insignificant exceptions, a higher education is still the prerogative of the rich and the well-born; but the student population in American colleges and universities is currently over two million. To say the very least, the culture of modern Europe bears the birthmark of its aristocratic origin: it was made by and for the very few, though it may gradually, in some places and to some extent, have become available to a few more.

6. American culture is basically different from all this. In this, as in so many other ways, here is something new under the sun. With due allowance for the influence of the European doctrine and example, one must not fail to see the vast importance of the peculiar American situation. For ours is a modern culture which skipped the aristocratic phase. While having the literary and vernacular resources of the European Renaissance and the Reformation behind us, we started our culture with some semblance of wholeness and homogeneity. We have been without that deep bifurcation into high and low, which was the starting point of the national cultures of Western Europe.

7. The student body of Harvard College in the seventeenth century was probably already more representative of the community at large than the universities of many European countries today. As Samuel Eliot Morison points out, in the earliest years of the College almost every Harvard student was the child of parents who actually farmed the soil, in addition to whatever else they did, and "it does seem that the College was fairly successful, after 1654, in recruiting boys of scholarly ambition from the plain people of New England." Part of the explanation of this phenomenon is found, for Massachusetts Bay at least, in the extraordinarily high proportion of university graduates to the whole population in those earliest years. But this was only one factor which happened to be important in that part of America. The more universal and characteristically American phenomenon was a homogeneity of thought and culture quite alien to the European experience. This was what Governor Thomas Hutchinson described, in the late eighteenth century, as the fact of "the generality of the colony being very near upon a level."

8. In Europe the progress of liberal and democratic movements has been measured by the extent to which they have broken down the barriers of the old aristocratic culture; anything which made the language and thought of the aristocracy available to more people was considered progressive. But in America the starting point has been the opposite: the unity of our society has been taken for granted. It is, rather, any failure to make culture available to all the people that has required justification.

9. While European liberals have tried to put the luxury of a classical education within the reach of members of the underprivileged classes, American democrats have attacked the very idea of a classical education because of its aristocratic overtones. Before the end of the eighteenth century, Benjamin Rush opposed the inclusion of Latin and Greek within the standard curriculum of a liberal education for the simple reason that these languages might be difficult for women to learn; and, he urged, nothing should be part of an American education which was not within the reach of all citizens. From the time of Rush and Jefferson to that of John Dewey, our educators have been primarily interested in what Rush called "the mode of education proper in a Republic." Thus, foreign travel and study in a foreign university, basic to the European aristocratic ideal of culture and congenial to the cosmopolitan and international allegiances of their educated classes, were urged by the arbiters of European culture, at least from the seventeenth century. But in 1798, Benjamin Rush asked (in words with which Jefferson would have agreed) that Americans be educated at home rather than in a foreign country. Only in the New World could the unique republican principles of American life be properly reinforced in the young, and only so could the equality of men and the unity of American culture be encouraged. "I conceive the education of our youth in this country to be particularly necessary in Pennsylvania," he wrote, "while our citizens are composed of the natives of so many different kingdoms in Europe. Our schools of learning, by producing one general, and uniform system of education, will render the mass of the people more homogeneous, and thereby fit them more easily for uniform and peaceable government." This desire for uniformity and homogeneity has had, of course, a profound effect on our conception of higher education, particularly in supporting movements to water it down and flatten its flavor to suit everybody's palate. Thus, a profound truth about our culture lurks in Bliss Perry's facetious suggestion that the ideal of American education could most easily be attained by awarding every American citizen the degree of bachelor of arts at birth. There is no denying that we started with the assumption that a society should have a single culture whose highest thoughts should be accessible to most men.

10. Even our geographic vastness and variety have contributed to this. Because differences of region and climate are so overwhelming, the differences of social classes in the several parts of the country have actually seemed less important. The American who goes to England, France or Italy cannot but note linguistic versatility as a mark of social caste; the upper classes not only speak their national language with an aristocratic accent, they actually speak several languages. In contrast to this, in the United States, of course, accent is a sign not of class but of

regional origin. Even the regional dialects have been much less marked here than in other countries of comparable size. English travelers and American lexicographers noted this in the eighteenth and early nineteenth centuries. "It is agreed," John Pickering observed in 1816, "that there is greater uniformity of dialect throughout the United States (in consequence of the frequent removals of people from one part of our country to another) than is to be found throughout England." On the whole, it is the members of our lower classes who tend to know another language—such as German or Italian or Yiddish—in addition to English. It is partly by losing their cosmopolitan character, by forgetting all languages other than English that people become homogenized into American culture. In the United States we all try to speak the same language, and only a few know more than one.

11. Our ideal of equality has carried with it the fact of universal literacy, and in this and other ways has contributed to the ideal of cultural unity. The Protestant tradition, our lack of ancient institutions and the absence of a professional class of articulators—a "learned" or "cultured" class—all these have played their part. Unprecedented technological development, taken together with natural wealth, a high standard of living and a domestic mass-market for all kinds of products, has produced a uniformity of standards of consumption and a homogeneity in the particular articles consumed. In America, brand names (with all they imply of universal familiarity with a single product, of homogeneity of product, and of potentially universal consumption of the same product) are symbols of the unity of our culture. A Ford car and a Bendix washer are owned by the chairman of the board of directors as well as by the night watchman. Finally, our yen for orthodoxy has encouraged people both to wish for and to believe in a unity in our ways of thinking and acting.

B. The diffuseness of American intellectual life

12. A feature complementary to the aristocratic starting point of European culture is the sharpness with which it is focused on one or a few centers. In modern Europe, the intellectual capital is almost as universal a phenomenon as the aristocracy. Almost every country has had its Paris, its mecca of culture, where one could sit and be at the center of things. One of Europe's main appeals to the American intellectual who has had even a taste of it is the ease with which the focus of intellectual influence and power can be discovered. The young American who goes to Oxford or Cambridge has the comfortable feeling of knowing—or being in a position to get to know—everybody who is anybody in English culture.

The other day I talked with a young American student who had just returned from a couple of years in one of the English universities. Having been only another student in America, required to show what he could do in order to acquire a status, he had found himself suddenly offered a position of status and privilege simply because he was a student at Cambridge, England. "It's awfully comfortable," he said, "to be one of the ruling class." After such an experience, the young American cannot but feel a loss of privilege as well as a loss of bearings when, on return to the United States, he discovers that there is no such center.

13. Looking at our history as a whole, one sees a diffuseness and a shifting of intellectual life quite alien to the modes of culture in the great nations of Europe. True, different cities have had their days of glory: Boston, Philadelphia, Williamsburg, New York, Chicago and others. But none has had much more than a day. Our cultural center has been nowhere because it has been everywhere. We are almost alone among nations in having found it necessary and possible to create, *ad hoc*, a special city to serve as the national political capital; that city has never been our cultural capital. From time to time we have had something like an elite, a group which took to itself the privileges—and claimed the immunities—of the intellectual ruling classes of Europe. The most recent and most striking (and the most difficult for our intellectuals to forget) was the New Deal, when American intellectuals had a taste of that sense of power and of sitting at the center which has been familiar to those of Europe. But as Bernard De Voto has described under the useful title of "The Literary Fallacy," American history and American culture, even more than those of other countries, are imperfectly and partially estimated if literature is confused with life, if our society is judged by its literary product. For many reasons, then, American intellectual history can be neither the history of our intellectuals nor the story of our philosophies.

II

14. Turning from the form of American intellectual life to the substance of our way of thinking, we find a number of equally striking characteristics. They describe the peculiar vitality and formlessness of our culture. The more rigid and dead the thought of a people, the more easily it is described and reduced to the systems which delight and comfort the academic mind. The more alive a culture and its ways of thought, the more elusive it is and the harder to capture it in systems and categories. The following characteristics are actually ways of describing the elusiveness of American culture.

A. Interest in institutions rather than ideologies, in process rather than product

15. Our most important and most representative thinkers have been more interested in institutions than in ideologies. For an ideology is something fixed and rigid: it is a posture of the truth which some men see in one age and which they seek to get other men to accept as the whole truth. But institutions live and grow and change. They have a life of their own as a philosophy cannot; and our major accomplishments have been in the realm of institutions rather than of thought.

16. At least since the eighteenth century, observers of our society have noted equality as a characteristic of American life. But it is the *fact* rather than the *theory* of equality which has flourished here. If European countries have been strong in theories of equality, as in other political theories, they have been feeble in developing equalitarian institutions. In the United States, on the contrary, where we have had unprecedented success in developing the institution of social equality, we have never been able to produce a pretty or an important theory about it. This is but an example, if one of the more spectacular, of how our talent for improving life has excelled our capacity for perfecting thought.

17. We have shown very little interest in producing things which would endure: monuments have not been in our line. We have been more concerned with whether an idea or a thing actually serves its purpose than whether it will continue to serve that purpose for a day or a century. We have been anxious not to freeze the categories of thought, for we are ready to believe that old purposes and old needs will be supplanted by new. In exhibiting his plant, an Italian businessman will show with pride the original workshop where his great-great-grandfather started and which is still in use; an American businessman points out with pride that not a brick of his original plant remains, that the old has been thoroughly replaced by superior modern materials.

18. Our lack of interest in systems of thought, in ideologies and philosophies, is but a particular illustration of our general lack of interest in perfecting the *product*. This goes with our special interest in improving the *process*. We have been more interested in how and whether things work than in how beautiful they can be in themselves. Our architecture has been concerned less with houses than with housing; our engineers, less with producing sturdy automobiles than with developing satisfactory transportation. We have been interested less in good food than in satisfactory diet. We have been worried less over the content of an education, the meaning of truth, knowledge and culture, than over understanding and improving the learning process. Our dramatic artists

have been less anxious to produce rounded and enduring works of dramatic art than to provide moments and experiences of entertainment and amusement. The "movies"—from this point of view appropriately and significantly named—is the most characteristic of American art forms. It is an artistic object which from its very nature can never be grasped as a whole; the form is elusiveness itself. It cannot be held in the hand and examined for its perfection, like a play of Shakespeare or an oil painting. It can *only* be experienced; and its "meaning" is the accumulated sensation of many separate moments.

19. About a century ago, Sir Henry Maine made his famous suggestion that "the movement of the progressive societies has hitherto been a movement from Status to Contract." There is a great deal of truth in his observation, even when applied to American as contrasted with European society. But a more general principle, of which Maine's maxim is in this case but a corollary, is that the transit of civilization from Europe to America has been a movement from product to process, from art to institutions, from an interest in things to an interest in ways. The great wealth of America has actually had much to do with this. The abundance of our material resources has encouraged a wholesome unconcern for material things in themselves. We have been able to afford to experiment with the ways of doing a job without worrying about preserving any of the particular physical devices perfected for the purpose. If they no longer do, we throw them away and try others. Thus, our domestic architecture, unlike that of Europe, is not the production of inheritable estates, but the perfection of housing; our automobiles are not heirlooms (as they have become in England or in Italy), but transportation; our dress manufacturers, instead of producing garments which are beautiful and durable, aim to offer the wearer the sensation of being modish for a season.

20. Never has a people been more wasteful of the things of the earth, and never has that waste expressed greater contempt for the things of this world. America and Asia, as W. H. Auden observes, have in common the fact that they are built on waste: Asia on the waste of human life, America on the waste of material wealth. While scarcity has tempted people in Europe to treat physical means as if they were ends, to give them the reverence and the loving care which the objects of this world may not deserve, the people of the United States have tended to treat all means as expendable and have become preoccupied with getting the job done. In the secondhand-automobile market in Turin, Italy, when I went to sell a car which I had used for a year, the dealers felt its pulse, listened to its cough, and pityingly, almost tenderly, remarked that it was *stanca*—"tired." When in Chicago I took my used car to such a market, the dealer looked hastily at his handbook, rather than the car, told

me what a machine of that vintage was worth, and turned quickly to persuade me of the superior operating advantages of a new model. The printed word, in the form in which it reaches most people here, aims less to be a rounded literary product than a means of entertainment, of topical and relevant instruction, of information on the qualities and prices of all the other available means of living.

21. In this sense—contrary to current clichés about us—our willingness to waste things has expressed our unconcern for the things of life and our greater interest in the ways of life. Our distinctive interest in process has been expressed in myriad aspects of American culture which have enabled us to see through the object to the objective; to view art not as the perfection of artistic objects, but as a kind of experience; to see religiosity expressed not in the construction of religious monuments and churches, but in a "religious experience" for which the church building is only a more or less effective instrument.

22. In the realm of material things, all this has been encouraged basically by our great material wealth with all it has meant in the way of an indefinitely expandable market and a continuing demand for better ways of doing all sorts of things. The distinction here is crucial. We must not consider the growing demand for air conditioners in middle-class homes as just a simple expression of materialism and greed for more things of this world. It is more precise to recognize this as but another illustration of our passionate preference for the experience of being cool in summer and for being comfortable in many other ways.

23. In the realm of ideas, this frame of mind has carried a distinctive lack of interest in the form of thought, a cavalier indifference to whether our thought is consistent and systematic. We are immensely interested in ideas when they wear work clothes, when they are embodied in institutions. Even then we are less interested in how they look than in how they work. We are less interested in how they sound in the salon or from the lecture platform than in how they function in the market place.

B. The success criterion

24. The intellectual landscape of contemporary Europe is haunted by the ghosts of lost causes. There is hardly a movement in the checkered history of a European nation which does not have its active partisans today. A catalogue of living philosophies in Italy now is an index to Italian history. In those more metaphysically minded countries, which have possessed dominant intellectual classes, political parties are ideological. Philosophers classify themselves as disciples of dead centuries. And all intellectual life becomes a museum of past ideologies. Where

ways of thought are judged by their intellectual consistency and by their aesthetic appeal, by their appeal to a distinctively intellectual ruling class rather than by their ability to become embodied in institutions, the intellectual life of the community becomes one with the speculations of its visionaries and the vagaries of its metaphysicians. And this is true in most of the countries of Europe.

25. But in the United States, almost from the beginning, our ideas have been tested by their ability to become embodied in institutions. Puritanism was to prove itself in Zion; Quakerism in a City of Brotherly Love. Where success is a test of truth, men lose interest in lost causes. They cannot be excited by ideas or philosophic systems (however symmetrical or well constructed or well argued) which do not still give promise of being put into practice. The feasibility of a philosophy becomes one with its validity. The intellectual vision of the community becomes confined by the limits of the practical. This may bound the speculative life, but it has its advantages.

26. Defeat and oblivion become a single fate. Somehow, systems of thought seem to lose their immortality; if only once proved unworkable, they die. Thus, intellectual life in the United States at any moment is both more and less cumulative than elsewhere. For our history is a process of elimination which has disposed of irrelevant ideas; and the living ideas at any particular time are all those remaining ideas with some reasonable prospect of adoption. If our intellectual life is a less rich museum for philosophers, it may be a richer tool house for cultivating our garden.

C. The importance of context: the implicitness of ideas

27. Never before was a culture so much nourished on the belief that values grow from the context, that the appropriate way of thinking grows out of the particular style of living. "We ever held it certain," declared Cabeza de Vaca in 1535, "that going toward the sunset we would find what we desired." The Puritans, too, believed that Westward the course of the Gospel would have its way: following Jesus' prophecy in Matthew 24:27, they were confident that, as the light of the Gospel had formerly shone out of the East, so now it would shine out of the West. Through the eighteenth and nineteenth centuries—from Crèvecoeur's notion that America had produced a new man, through Jefferson's belief in the wealth, promise and magnificence of the continent, and Turner's faith in a frontier-born culture and frontier-nourished institutions—runs the refrain that American values spring from the circumstances of the New World, that these are the secret of the "American Way of Life."

This has been both an example of our special way of dealing with ideas and an encouragement to it. For lack of a better word, we may call this a leaning toward *implicitness*, a tendency to leave ideas embodied in experience and a belief that the truth somehow arises out of the experience.

28. This carries with it a preference for the relevance of ideas as against their form and a surprising unconcern for the separability of ideas. We have seldom believed that the validity of an idea was tested by its capacity for being expressed in words. The beliefs that values come out of the context and that truth is part of the matrix of experience (and hardly separable from it) become themselves part of the way of American thinking—hence, the formlessness of American thought, its lack of treatises, schools and systems.

D. The nirvana of success: self-annihilation through mastery and adaptation

29. All this has produced a quaint inversion of the Buddhist approach to life, or rather something like an American notion of Nirvana. For the Buddhist, bliss is attained by the loss of personal identity, by being absorbed into the universal oneness and nothingness. His self-annihilation is arrived at by transcending the physical environment, by rising above wind and rain, hunger, life and death. The characteristic notion of bliss developed on the American continent involves a comparable process of absorption and loss of identity. But here that oneness is attained by a complete adaptation to the environment which involves seizing the opportunities which it offers, by "fitting in." The objective is an almost mystic and naïvely sensed accord with everything about one. The oblivion of Nirvana and the oblivion of success have much in common. In both, the individual transcends his own personality to become part of what surrounds him. The desire to master the forces of nature, to wrest from the environment all the wealth it holds, to find all possible uses of every material—this has carried with it a willingness to adapt to the social situation, to make the social norm not the fulfillment of some preconceived, philosophy-sharpened ideal, but the fulfillment of the possibilities in the situation, the attainment of compromise. So, for the American, it is not Nirvana, but Rotariana.

E. Continuity and conservatism of ways of thought

30. Perhaps never before has there been a society with such remarkable continuity in its ways of thought even from the time of its first settlement. The success criterion, the implicitness, the concern for institutions—all these have prevented abrupt breaks in the direction of our

thought. For the chain of circumstances is not casually broken as the chain of ideas can be. A philosopher in his study can think up a new and sometimes attractive frame of ideas; he can propose an anarchy, a revolution or a new beginning; he is free as the air. But circumstances hold within them certain limits; every event somehow grows out of its predecessors. And American empiricism has tied our thinking to the slow, organic growth of institutions. By rejecting ideologies, we reject the sharp angles, the sudden turns, the steep up-and-down grades, which mark political life in many parts of the world, in favor of the slow curves, the imperceptible slopes of institutional life. If ever the circumstances of a culture have suited a people to think "institutionally," American history has done so. For us, fortunately, it is impossible to distinguish the history of our thought from the history of our institutions.

COMMENTARY AND QUESTIONS

In "English and American Education: Depth versus Breadth" (pp. 239-249) and in "The American Student as I See Him" (pp. 251-260) two British writers appraise American education by considering it in relation to English education. In this essay, Daniel J. Boorstin, an American professor of history who has taken degrees at both English and American universities and been admitted to the English bar, develops an evaluation of American thought by contrasting it with European.

1. What is Boorstin's basic attitude toward his subject? Is he adversely criticizing America in pars. 20-21, in par. 28, in par. 29? Does the qualifying adverb in the last sentence of par. 30 express the basic attitude presented by the essay as a whole?

2. In many parts of this essay the author identifies himself with the aspects of American thought and life that he is discussing. Does his doing so have any effect on your acceptance of his adverse criticisms of America? Consider particularly the last three sentences of par. 9 and pars. 18-20.

3. When reading the parenthetical statement in the next-to-last sentence of par. 5, note that Boorstin presumably is distinguishing Western European universities from those in Eastern Europe. Why is it wise for him to do this before moving on to his discussion of the difference between American and European culture and education in the following paragraphs?

4. This essay is composed of two main sections, to which Boorstin has given no titles. What sentences in his text serve as titles? The author devotes almost twice as much space to Section II as he does to Section I. Does this suggest which aspect of his subject he wishes to emphasize here?

5. Is the title of the essay an accurate indication of its subject? Why does Boorstin devote nearly all of the introduction of the essay to European thought? What is the basic structural pattern of both Part A and Part B of Section I?

6. In par. 16 a generalization is made clear by use of example. Is the same technique used in pars. 17 and 18? Why is this technique particularly appropriate for this essay?

7. What is the logical relationship connecting pars. 23, 24, and 25? How are various topics of Section II tied together in par. 30?

8. This essay often makes effective use of concrete metaphors to express abstract ideas. Explain the meaning of the third sentence of par. 2. What words continue the architecture metaphor in the rest of the paragraph?

9. How are the metaphors in par. 24 related to each other? What metaphors in pars. 23 and 24 are picked up and continued by the metaphors in the last sentence of par. 26?

10. What is the basic structural pattern of sentences 2, 3, and 4 of par. 11? Is it likely that this paragraph would have been more or less effective if the sentences composing it had been cast in a similar pattern?

SUGGESTIONS FOR WRITING

1. Evaluate an individual who is well known to you (through experience or reading) by comparing or contrasting him to an individual who is well known to your readers.

2. Discuss the following statement from par. 11: "This desire for uniformity and homogeneity has had, of course, a profound effect on our conception of higher education, particularly in supporting movements to water it down and flatten its flavor to suit everybody's palate."

3. In relation to the ideas in pars. 18-23 discuss the following line from Emerson: "Beauty is its own excuse for being."

4. The place of thought in college life.

The Essence of Tragedy

by MAXWELL ANDERSON

ANYBODY WHO DARES to discuss the making of tragedy lays himself open
to critical assault and general barrage, for the theorists have been hunting for the essence of tragedy since Aristotle without entire success.
There is no doubt that playwrights have occasionally written tragedy
successfully, from Aeschylus on, and there is no doubt that Aristotle came
very close to a definition of what tragedy is in his famous passage on
catharsis. But why the performance of tragedy should have a cleansing
effect on the audience, why an audience is willing to listen to tragedy,
why tragedy has a place in the education of men, has never, to my
knowledge, been convincingly stated. I must begin by saying that I have
not solved the Sphinx's riddle which fifty generations of skillful brains
have left in shadow. But I have one suggestion which I think might lead
to a solution if it were put to laboratory tests by those who know something about philosophical analysis and dialectic.

2. There seems no way to get at this suggestion except through a reference to my own adventures in playwriting, so I ask your tolerance
while I use myself as an instance. A man who has written successful
plays is usually supposed to know something about the theory of playwriting, and perhaps he usually does. In my own case, however, I must
confess that I came into the theater unexpectedly, without preparation,
and stayed in it because I had a certain amount of rather accidental success. It was not until after I had fumbled my way through a good many
successes and an appalling number of failures that I began to doubt the
sufficiency of dramatic instinct and to wonder whether or not there were
general laws governing dramatic structure which so poor a head for
theory as my own might grasp and use. I had read the *Poetics* long
before I tried playwriting, and I had looked doubtfully into a few well-
known handbooks on dramatic structure, but the maxims and theories
propounded always drifted by me in a luminous haze—brilliant, true,
profound in context, yet quite without meaning for me when I consid-

ered the plan for a play or tried to clarify an emotion in dialogue. So far as I could make out every play was a new problem, and the old rules were inapplicable. There were so many rules, so many landmarks, so many pitfalls, so many essential reckonings, that it seemed impossible to find your way through the jungle except by plunging ahead, trusting to your sense of direction and keeping your wits about you as you went.

3. But as the seasons went by and my failures fell as regularly as the leaves in autumn I began to search again among the theorists of the past for a word of wisdom that might take some of the gamble out of playwriting. What I needed most of all, I felt, was a working definition of what a play is, or perhaps a formula which would include all the elements necessary to a play structure. A play is almost always, probably, an attempt to recapture a vision for the stage. But when you are working in the theater it's most unsatisfactory to follow the gleam without a compass, quite risky to trust "the light that never was on sea or land" without making sure beforehand that you are not being led straight into a slough of despond. In other words you must make a choice among visions, and you must check your chosen vision carefully before assuming that it will make a play. But by what rules, what maps, what fields of reference can you check so intangible a substance as a revelation, a dream, an inspiration, or any similar nudge from the subconscious mind?

4. I shan't trouble you with the details of my search for a criterion, partly because I can't remember it in detail. But I reread Aristotle's *Poetics* in the light of some bitter experience, and one of his observations led me to a comparison of ancient and modern playwriting methods. In discussing construction he made a point of the recognition scene as essential to tragedy. The recognition scene, as Aristotle isolated it in the tragedies of the Greeks, was generally an artificial device, a central scene in which the leading character saw through a disguise, recognized as a friend or as an enemy, perhaps as a lover or a member of his own family, some person whose identity had been hidden. Iphigeneia, for example, acting as priestess in an alien country, receives a victim for sacrifice and then recognizes her own brother in this victim. There is an instant and profound emotional reaction, instantly her direction in the play is altered. But occasionally, in the greatest of the plays, the recognition turned on a situation far more convincing, though no less contrived. Oedipus, hunting savagely for the criminal who has brought the plague upon Thebes, discovers that he is himself that criminal—and since this is a discovery that affects not only the physical well-being and happiness of the hero, but the whole structure of his life, the effect on

THE ESSENCE OF TRAGEDY

him and on the direction of the story is incalculably greater than could result from the more superficial revelation made to Iphigeneia.

5. Now scenes of exactly this sort are rare in the modern drama except in detective stories adapted for the stage. But when I probed a little more deeply into the memorable pieces of Shakespeare's theater and our own I began to see that though modern recognition scenes are subtler and harder to find, they are none the less present in the plays we choose to remember. They seldom have to do with anything so naïve as disguise or the unveiling of a personal identity. But the element of discovery is just as important as ever. For the mainspring in the mechanism of a modern play is almost invariably a discovery by the hero of some element in his environment or in his own soul of which he has not been aware—or which he has not taken sufficiently into account. Moreover, nearly every teacher of playwriting has had some inkling of this, though it was not until after I had worked out my own theory that what they said on this point took on accurate meaning for me. I still think that the rule which I formulated for my own guidance is more concise than any other, and so I give it here: A play should lead up to and away from a central crisis, and this crisis should consist in a discovery by the leading character which has an indelible effect on his thought and emotion and completely alters his course of action. The leading character, let me say again, must make the discovery; it must affect him emotionally; and it must alter his direction in the play.

6. Try that formula on any play you think worthy of study, and you will find that, with few exceptions, it follows this pattern or some variation of this pattern. The turning point of *The Green Pastures*, for example, is the discovery by God, who is the leading character, that a God who is to endure must conform to the laws of change. The turning point of *Hamlet* is Hamlet's discovery, in the play scene, that his uncle was unquestionably the murderer of his father. In *Abe Lincoln in Illinois* Lincoln's discovery is that he has been a coward, that he has stayed out of the fight for the Union because he was afraid. In each case, you will note, the discovery has a profound emotional effect on the hero, and gives an entirely new direction to his action in the play.

7. I'm not writing a disquisition on playwriting and wouldn't be competent to write one, but I do want to make a point of the superlative usefulness of this one touchstone for play structure. When a man sets out to write a play his first problem is his subject and the possibilities of that subject as a story to be projected from the stage. His choice of subject matter is his personal problem, and one that takes its answer from his personal relation to his times. But if he wants to know a possible play subject when he finds it, if he wants to know how to mold the subject

into play form after he has found it, I doubt that he'll ever discover another standard as satisfactory as the modern version of Aristotle which I have suggested. If the plot he has in mind does not contain a playable episode in which the hero or heroine makes an emotional discovery, a discovery that practically dictates the end of the story, then such an episode must be inserted—and if no place can be found for it the subject is almost certainly a poor one for the theater. If this emotional discovery is contained in the story, but is not central, then it must be made central, and the whole action must revolve around it. In a three-act play it should fall near the end of the second act, though it may be delayed till the last; in a five-act play it will usually be found near the end of the third, though here also it can be delayed. Everything else in the play should be subordinated to this one episode—should lead up to or away from it.

8. Now this prime rule has a corollary which is just as important as the rule itself. The hero who is to make the central discovery in a play must not be a perfect man. He must have some variation of what Aristotle calls a tragic fault; and the reason he must have it is that when he makes his discovery he must change both in himself and in his action—and he must change for the better. The fault can be a very simple one—a mere unawareness, for example—but if he has no fault he cannot change for the better, but only for the worse, and for a reason which I shall discuss later, it is necessary that he must become more admirable, and not less so, at the end of the play. In other words, a hero must pass through an experience which opens his eyes to an error of his own. He must learn through suffering. In a tragedy he suffers death itself as a consequence of his fault or his attempt to correct it, but before he dies he has become a nobler person because of his recognition of his fault and the consequent alteration of his course of action. In a serious play which does not end in death he suffers a lesser punishment, but the pattern remains the same. In both forms he has a fault to begin with, he discovers that fault during the course of the action, and he does what he can to rectify it at the end. In *The Green Pastures* God's fault was that he believed himself perfect. He discovered that he was not perfect, that he had been in error and must make amends. Hamlet's fault was that he could not make up his mind to act. He offers many excuses for his indecision until he discovers that there is no real reason for hesitation and that he has delayed out of cowardice. Lincoln, in *Abe Lincoln in Illinois*, has exactly the same difficulty. In the climactic scene it is revealed to him that he had hesitated to take sides through fear of the consequences to himself, and he then chooses to go ahead without regard for what may be in store for him. From the point of view of the playwright, then, the essence of a tragedy, or even of a serious play, is the spiritual awakening, or regeneration, of his hero.

9. When a playwright attempts to reverse the formula, when his hero makes a discovery which has an evil effect, or one which the audience interprets as evil, on his character, the play is inevitably a failure on the stage. In *Troilus and Cressida* Troilus discovers that Cressida is a light woman. He draws from her defection the inference that all women are faithless—that faith in woman is the possession of fools. As a consequence he turns away from life and seeks death in a cause as empty as the love he has given up, the cause of the strumpet Helen. All the glory of Shakespeare's verse cannot rescue the play for an audience, and save in *Macbeth* Shakespeare nowhere wrote so richly, so wisely, or with such a flow of brilliant metaphor.

10. For the audience will always insist that the alteration in the hero be for the better—or for what it believes to be the better. As audiences change the standards of good and evil change, though slowly and unpredictably, and the meanings of plays change with the centuries. One thing only is certain: that an audience watching a play will go along with it only when the leading character responds in the end to what it considers a higher moral impulse than moved him at the beginning of the story, though the audience will of course define morality as it pleases and in the terms of its own day. It may be that there is no absolute up or down in this world, but the race believes that there is, and will not hear of any denial.

11. And now at last I come to the point toward which I've been struggling so laboriously. Why does the audience come to the theater to look on while an imaginary hero is put to an imaginary trial and comes out of it with credit to the race and to himself? It was this question that prompted my essay, and unless I've been led astray by my own predilections there is a very possible answer in the rules for playwriting which I have just cited. The theater originated in two complementary religious ceremonies, one celebrating the animal in man and one celebrating the god. Old Greek Comedy was dedicated to the spirits of lust and riot and earth, spirits which are certainly necessary to the health and continuance of the race. Greek tragedy was dedicated to man's aspiration, to his kinship with the gods, to his unending, blind attempt to lift himself above his lusts and his pure animalism into a world where there are other values than pleasure and survival. However unaware of it we may be, our theater has followed the Greek patterns with no change in essence, from Aristophanes and Euripides to our own day. Our more ribald musical comedies are simply our approximation of the Bacchic rites of Old Comedy. In the rest of our theater we sometimes follow Sophocles, whose tragedy is always an exaltation of the human spirit, sometimes Euripides, whose tragicomedy follows the same pattern of an excellence achieved through suffering. The forms of both tragedy and comedy have

changed a good deal in nonessentials, but in essentials—and especially in the core of meaning which they must have for audiences—they are in the main the same religious rites which grew up around the altars of Attica long ago.

¹². It is for this reason that when you write for the theater you must choose between your version of a phallic revel and your vision of what mankind may or should become. Your vision may be faulty, or shallow, or sentimental, but it must conform to some aspiration in the audience, or the audience will reject it. Old Comedy, the celebration of the animal in us, still has a place in our theater, as it had in Athens, but here, as there, that part of the theater which celebrated man's virtue and his regeneration in hours of crisis is accepted as having the more important function. Our comedy is largely the Greek New Comedy, which grew out of Euripides' tragicomedy, and is separated from tragedy only in that it presents a happier scene and puts its protagonist through an ordeal which is less than lethal.

¹³. And since our plays, aside from those which are basically Old Comedy, are exaltations of the human spirit, since that is what an audience expects when it comes to the theater, the playwright gradually discovers, as he puts plays before audiences, that he must follow the ancient Aristotelian rule: he must build his plot around a scene wherein his hero discovers some mortal frailty or stupidity in himself and faces life armed with a new wisdom. He must so arrange his story that it will prove to the audience that men pass through suffering purified, that, animal though we are, despicable though we are in many ways, there is in us all some divine, incalculable fire that urges us to be better than we are.

¹⁴. It could be argued that what the audience demands of a hero is only conformity to race morality, to the code which seems to the spectators most likely to make for race survival. In many cases, especially in comedy, and obviously in the comedy of Molière, this is true. But in the majority of ancient and modern plays it seems to me that what the audience wants to believe is that men have a desire to break the molds of earth which encase them and claim a kinship with a higher morality than that which hems them in. The rebellion of Antigone, who breaks the laws of men through adherence to a higher law of affection, the rebellion of Prometheus, who breaks the law of the gods to bring fire to men, the rebellion of God in *The Green Pastures* against the rigid doctrine of the Old Testament, the rebellion of Tony in *They Knew What They Wanted* against the convention that called on him to repudiate his cuckold child, the rebellion of Liliom against the heavenly law which asked him to betray his own integrity and make a hypocrisy of his affection, even the repudiation of the old forms and the affirmation of new by

the heroes of Ibsen and Shaw, these are all instances to me of the groping of men toward an excellence dimly apprehended, seldom possible
of definition. They are evidence to me that the theater at its best is a
religious affirmation, an age-old rite restating and reassuring man's belief
in his own destiny and his ultimate hope. The theater is much older than
the doctrine of evolution, but its one faith, asseverated again and again
for every age and every year, is a faith in evolution, in the reaching and
the climb of men toward distant goals, glimpsed but never seen, perhaps
never achieved, or achieved only to be passed impatiently on the way to
a more distant horizon.

COMMENTARY AND QUESTIONS

"The Essence of Tragedy" is an essay of evaluation on a large scale
in that it assesses the worth of tragedy itself rather than being concerned
with one drama or the work of one author. It is also an essay in interpretation, as is indicated by the title. The author of this interpretative evaluation, a Pulitzer Prize winner, wrote more than twenty-five plays,
including *Anne of the Thousand Days* and *Winterset*. "The Essence of
Tragedy" was written to be read at a session of the Modern Language Association, an organization whose membership is composed chiefly of college and university professors of language and literature.

1. What is the tone of the first paragraph of this essay? Does the tone of
   this paragraph indicate to you that the author had his audience in
   mind?
2. Why is it appropriate that Anderson should discuss his own experiences in an essay of this sort? Notice the tactful ways in which he mentions himself and his writing experiences in pars. 1-5.
3. Note that par. 6 develops the final sentence of the preceding paragraph by discussing three examples. Do you think that these examples
   are well chosen? Why?
4. Why is par. 9 important to the development of the author's point of
   view?
5. The fourth sentence of par. 14 is periodic in structure, in that the main
   idea is expressed at the end. Why is this sentence effective? What
   other structural pattern gives the sentence added effectiveness and
   keeps it from confusing the reader?
6. Do the best plays and films that you have seen support Anderson's
   statement in par. 8 that the hero of a tragedy must not be a perfect
   man? Do Anderson's statements about the "recognition scene" and
   "the tragic flaw" apply to any novels or short stories that you have
   read?

SUGGESTIONS FOR WRITING

1. Drawing on your knowledge of contemporary and earlier drama, attack or defend Anderson's statement (par. 13) that "our plays, aside from those which are basically Old Comedy, are exaltations of the human spirit."
2. Analyze a drama or motion picture from the standpoint of the "recognition scene."
3. Explain why you read tragic literature or see tragic plays and films.

PART FOUR

Persuasion

THOUGH A MAN BE A SOURCE OF WISDOM AND A FOUNTAINHEAD of truth, he does no good thereby to the rest of mankind unless he can somehow convey the truth and wisdom from his mind to theirs. And since the rest of mankind are notoriously slow about changing their minds, except under strong urging, it is often not enough for him merely to *convey* his ideas; he must actively push them, present them in their best light, forge unbreakable chains of logic, and pile up impregnable mountains of evidence in their behalf. He may also have to admonish, exhort, and plead in order to impress his audience. In short, he may have to use all the resources of what we call persuasion.

Meanwhile his fellowmen, many of them equally certain that it is they who have truth and wisdom on their side and not he, are mustering counter-arguments and gathering evidence in opposition. They too are attempting persuasion.

Fortunately the world is not quite such a turmoil of controversy as this picture implies; for there *are* large areas of agreement, and men do convince one another. If they did not, persuasion would be a futile occupation. But it is also true, as John Stuart Mill pointed out long ago and as Walter Lippmann so ably reminded us eighty years later, that this clash of opinion is a necessary part of finding truth and wisdom. From the collision of opposing ideas and methods come better ideas and methods. And in a democracy this is the only acceptable way of proceeding; for a democracy assumes, not that all ideas have equal value, but that all ideas have a right to be heard, and that no one man or group has a monopoly on wisdom. If, then, we are to have a selective competition of

369

opinions, a market place of ideas, it behooves those who have ideas which they value at great price to commend them to others as forcefully as possible. Herein lie the reason and the justification for the art of persuasion.

Not all persuasion, of course, is concerned with problems of great moment. It is proper to debate about small things as well as large. Many people have become excited over the commercialization of college football—though few so wittily as Morris Bishop; but this is not an issue on which the nation will stand or fall. On the other hand, Winston Churchill in his "Dunkirk" speech was exhorting his countrymen to stand firm in a back-to-the-wall struggle that proved to be every bit as crucial for Britain as he said it was. Persuasion, then, may be used for many ends, from the trivial to the most profound. Men differ from each other in taste, in opinion, in standards of values; they hold conflicting views on art, morals, and politics; they argue about how to bring up a son and where to build the new waterworks. But it is always their privilege, and sometimes their duty, to try to persuade others to their way of thinking.

The means of persuasion are as various as its ends. Sometimes persuasion draws its conclusions inductively from an accumulation of evidence. Sometimes it starts with certain premises and shows what must be their inescapable inference. More often it combines the two methods. Though assertion unsupported by evidence or logical reasoning is often said to be an improper method of argument, it may be highly and justly effective if the assertion reminds the readers or hearers of real truths which they have overlooked or forgotten. Sometimes persuasion achieves its ends by indirection: in demolishing the argument of the opposition, it suggests the strength of its own. There are, in fact, almost as many successful kinds of persuasion as of persuaders.

The one essential ingredient in persuasion is sincerity. In the market place of ideas, the man who does not know how to make his opinions pass at their true value is sorry enough, but he who cannot even believe in his own wares is eventually found out as a fraud and a cheat. Whatever the strength of idea and soundness of argument in the following thirteen selections, it is certain that the author of each believed he had truth on his side, and sought to commend it to others as strongly as he knew how.

Letter to a Seventeen-Year-Old Son

ANONYMOUS

I

Dear Greg:

In one sense I have been planning to write this letter for several years in order to pull together for what they may be worth some notions on your choice of an occupation and how to train yourself for it. In another sense the letter is occasioned by the recent news story about Pearlstein, the Brooklyn College basketballer, who carried a couple of books but never went to class. . . . So you see you're in for a large dose of the Old Man's ideas. . . .

2. In a novel by Bulwer-Lytton, whose books you would not like (which is just as well), a character says: "What a terrible and unfair advantage merely living longer gives a man!" It is both a wise and sad remark, one that can serve as a warning to members of different generations when dealing with each other. The older always know that they know more; the young always know that the old don't know enough to keep from messing up the world. Both, of course, are quite right. Progress would occur if each generation could pass on what it learned to the next and if the next picked up from there and went on. This hardly ever happens. In our day we try to hand over to specialists in schools the responsibility for telling the next generation what preceding generations have learned. On the whole this probably works better than if we tried it ourselves. But it doesn't work very well; there is a machine-like quality about it which lacks the individual touch. What follows in this letter is just an attempt to apply the advantage I have, because I have lived longer, to you, because I know you better than a teacher does, or a college catalogue, or a newspaper, or a recruiting poster.

3. I have not only lived longer, but have had unusual advantages for seeing what's going on in the world. The average man gets a chance to look at the world only when his work is over. My full-time job for almost twenty years has been to try to figure it out. I get paid for the privilege

of talking to almost anybody on earth, asking questions about the things they are supposed to know, and I have been given plenty of time to figure out the answers. What's more, I have carried to extremes the habit of reading books (where more answers are to be found than in the heads of one's contemporaries). I'm not sure I know many answers, and anyhow I couldn't expect you to accept the ones I think I know. But now that you are up against decisions that involve very general questions of what kind of a world it is and how to act in it, it would be wrong and lazy of me, I think, if I didn't try to pass on my ideas. . . .

II

⁴· I go wholeheartedly along with you in judging that your general bent and aptitude are along the line of the physical sciences. That's true of most American boys. Americans as a people have outstanding mechanical aptitude and a tremendous number of them want to work with things rather than with words and ideas. For every American boy who wants to be a lawyer there must be a hundred who want to be aviation and automotive engineers. As a result, most male students in American schools learn the physical sciences a lot better than they learn the word sciences. You are an example of this. The word subjects like history, English, and other languages seem irrelevant nuisances that you'll never use. Partly for this reason and partly because schools and parents do an incredibly bad job of explaining the purpose of the word subjects to boys, American education is sadly off base in terms of future citizenship and in terms of what people need to lead happy, useful lives.

⁵· Men a lot better than I am have tried to make the points I'm going to make now, but instead of referring you to their writings I'm going to try my own version. People like Hutchins of Chicago go to ridiculous lengths in making claims for the kind of education that stresses the word subjects. They give the impression that just reading Virgil and Homer and studying dead civilizations unlocks the understanding of life. They reduce the "utilitarian subjects" to the level of cooking. But the other extreme is just as bad, and has made a lot more headway in forming the actual attitude of American youth toward education.

⁶· To listen to the utilitarians you would think that human progress began with the development of the scientific method about three hundred years ago and that the outstanding achievements of man have been the invention of radio, the harnessing of electricity, and the development of modern medicine. As a matter of fact, the greatest invention of the human race is language (and thought: thinking is just talking to yourself, not out loud. You think with words, and you can't think without words).

7. To realize the relative importance of language suppose first of all that all the doctors in Washington suddenly died. The death rate would go up, maybe epidemics would result, work would be performed less efficiently. Within a month you would probably notice some difference in your daily life. But now suppose everybody in Washington suddenly forgot language. Work, all work, would stop. Transit would stop. All food distribution would stop. People unable to organize their food supply would kill each other to get at what food was available. Within a week most of the population would be dead and the rest would be in Rock Creek Park grubbing for roots to eat. It's a far-fetched example, but you need one like that to point out the obvious.

8. It's a bad thing that there should be people like me around who don't know a volt from a velocity; bad for me and bad for the society of which I'm a part. My education was one-sided, I must admit. But it's a thousand times worse that the world is full of people who can't make a clear statement of a thought, which is another way of saying they can't think straight. Talking (either to yourself or somebody else) is a technique like building dynamos or growing turnips or removing tonsils. Centuries upon centuries went into developing the technique of talking. The finest men who ever lived gave their lives to it—and their contribution is, even in a strictly utilitarian sense, the most important. The radio is useful only because of the words and music that come over it. Radio is a marvel, of course, but compared to a symphony or a poem or a news broadcast it's just a mechanical gadget, a detail that helps us get the all-important sounds faster and more conveniently.

9. Not everybody has to work in words (although there are calculations indicating that in a really advanced civilization like ours about 40 per cent of the people work in, or in support of, the word occupations, as distinguished from the thing occupations). But everybody has to know a lot about words and how to use them. I can get by without being able to build a dynamo; but the dynamo builder can't get by without words.

10. The next most important human developments are the sciences of politics and economics. They are particular branches of the word sciences. They are the techniques by which people organize their relations with one another. A herd of sheep follows a set of rules that are different from the behavior of an individual sheep and which can't be figured out even if you know all about an individual sheep. Sheep pick leaders, make herd decisions as to where they will graze, whether they will run or walk, and so on. Those rules and decisions, which nobody understands, are sheep politics.

11. Even with the tenderest care by shepherds and dogs, sheep couldn't survive without their politics. Men are their own shepherds and dogs. They don't get any help in working out their politics of how

to organize themselves to survive and progress. They have to figure out every hard decision in the light of factors whose interrelation is as much more complex than radar as radar is more complex than a simple lever. Fortunately, each generation doesn't have to start from scratch. The record of politics, economics, and sociology—and of technological development for that matter—is contained in history and in art. (Art, including music, is really a highly intensified kind of history. You may not believe this; sometime if you're interested I'll try to prove it to you. Give me a month's notice to get the evidence together.)

12. Sheep have a herd instinct that tells them to get under a sheltering bank when they smell a blizzard coming. Men have no political instinct to protect them. Instead, we have history, which takes the place of instinct. A people which doesn't know history is like a sheep which can't smell a wolf in the wind. In a democracy a citizen cannot entirely delegate to experts his duty of thinking (language) and his share in exercising the herd instinct for self-preservation (history).

13. Not all history (as I indicated in that crack about art) is contained in history books. Some of the best history is in novels: Lord Wavell, who is a damned good soldier, as Marshal Rommel found out, told the graduating class at Sandhurst, the British West Point, to learn something about history and humanity and to do it by reading good historical and other novels. One of the most important questions of our day, for instance, is what the Russian people are like. If anybody ever wrote a decent history of Russia, I haven't been able to find it. But there was a crop of magnificent Russian novelists and story-tellers who told the Russians and the rest of the world about the Russian character. Almost all that the world really knows of Russian temperament, personality, and development comes from Tolstoy (try *War and Peace*), Dostoievski (too gloomy for you), Chekhov (you might like him since you like Saroyan: Saroyan is phony Chekhov).

14. Whether our chances of getting on with the Russians are good or bad, they are a lot better than they would be if there had been no Russian novelists, who made Russians into real, understandable people. Russian temperament has undoubtedly been changing since the Russian revolution; there have been no great writers handling the post-revolutionary period. Russian development and foreign relations in the next fifty years will be partly determined by whether novelists and playwrights arise in Russia who can explain the Russians to themselves and the rest of the world.

15. The ultra-materialists and the utilitarians tend to interpret all history in terms of things. They will explain the British Empire, for instance, by talking about the British coal and iron deposits. Undoubtedly, the

British Empire would have been unlikely without the coal and iron. But the Chinese had more coal and iron than the British yet they went downhill during all the period in which coal and iron were most important. If you look for reasons for the difference, one thing worth noticing is that the English language kept getting better and better, more flexible, clearer, better able to express complicated things, during all the period of Britain's growth, while the Chinese language ceased to grow, tended to break up into dialects and to be a less and less useful instrument. A good case can be made for saying that Shakespeare (responsible for the greatest single advance in the English language) had more to do with the growth of the British Empire than his contemporary, Queen Elizabeth (who was a first-rate practitioner of politics), and that either of them was considerably more important than all the scientists and inventors put together.

III

16. I want to repeat for emphasis that this is *not* said to pooh-pooh the physical scientists or to try to talk you out of a field of work where I agree you belong. It is said to redress a balance in present-day American thinking, especially among people of your age. Ultra-materialism, which concentrates on things, bears a large part of the responsibility for the war and for the mess the peace is quite likely to be. On every side people say the Germans are the way they are because their standard of living was so low. The Germans themselves believe they went to war in order to better a subnormal and unjust living standard imposed on them. Actually their living standard was one of the highest in the world. What ailed them was bad thinking, bad understanding of human nature, including their own, and an inability to present such case as they had in language that would induce other people to listen to them.

17. The German and American educational systems seem to be more alike than a lot of Americans realize. It's one of the things that worry me most about this country. Both our educational systems turn out enormous quantities of people sufficiently educated to be intelligent soldiers, skilled laborers, foremen, engineers, and third-rate lawyers and journalists. But as *people,* as human beings, it is doubtful if these expensively educated Germans and Americans are as wise, as happy, as mentally healthy as a French peasant or a German peasant or an American pioneer of a century ago. Obviously, the answer isn't to go back to illiterate peasantry. An industrialized world requires more education, not less. But —and this is the important thing—it requires an education that gives to

a man of our time the simple human understanding that the peasant and the pioneer used to get naturally out of the lives they led and the surroundings in which they grew up.

18. Medicine, for instance, is a pretty good profession, especially for one of your temperament which combines a better-than-average knack of getting along with people and a mechanical and scientific bent. But too many of our American physicians, though expensively trained and full of medical information, are dull fellows and unenlightened citizens because their knowledge of people is limited to their specialty. This fact shouldn't discourage you from being a doctor; it should simply discourage you from being the kind of doctor who thinks human beings are just digestive machines with pocketbooks, or that the circulation of the blood is more important than the Constitution of the United States.

19. That goes for all the other fields open to you. Take farming: in your time that is going to be a far better profession than it has been for three generations. Why? Partly because of scientific advances; but these were making considerable headway in the seventy-five years ending about 1930, during which farming as a way of life kept getting more and more unattractive and insecure. The main reason is because around 1930 some smart people dealing with words and ideas (including a lot of smart dirt farmers) began to figure out what was wrong with farming and began to make some headway in doing something about it. The things that were wrong weren't on the farm itself, they weren't physical things; they were ideas embodied in tariff laws; they were complicated matters like the relation of interest rates to farm prices and the relation of the price of what the farmer sold and what he bought. Farming is a physical science, but it was politics, economics, and the language which finally expressed clearly and effectively what was wrong, that saved the American farmer, and promises to make farming a decent life again. This doesn't mean that you must be an agricultural economist or a farm lobbyist. It means that a farmer has to know enough politics, economics, history, language, and human nature to be a good farmer-citizen. You can apply this to engineering or anything else.

20. This world is full of wonderful technicians making $40 a week and eating their hearts out because the profits of their work and the direction of their work are in the hands of lawyers, bankers, politicians, and other word-artists and organizers. The world, say the technicians, ought not to be like that. So it oughtn't, but the reason why it is lies in the technicians and the way they were trained. Organization—which is done with thoughts, with words—will always be more important, more difficult than any technique in the physical field. The organizers will always get the power because they perform the hardest job. The technicians will

always be slaves to the word-artists until the technicians learn how to handle people, how to think logically outside their own narrow fields, how to talk, and how to live.

21. It's worth noticing that in this highly scientific war almost every important leader has been conspicuously a non-scientist. Roosevelt organized the greatest industrial war effort ever seen, yet there are few Americans who know as little about the technical side of industry as F.D.R. did. Churchill is strictly a poet. He looks very deeply into his country's history, into its soul, and puts what he sees in words that make people act. His speech "we will fight in the streets . . . on the hills" is worth more in purely military terms than all the secret weapons that ever came out of German laboratories. Churchill got that way from reading Shakespeare. . . .

IV

22. What does this add up to in terms of the decisions that you must soon make? In the first place, it is an argument against over-specialization at an early age in engineering or any other physical science. It is a plea that in choosing a college, picking courses, and above all in your general reading and interests, you try to develop that side of you which needs most development—namely, what the colleges call liberal arts or the humanities. These are the really practically important achievements of the human race; the ones which determine whether we go ahead or back. An engineer or a farmer, as well as a lawyer or a journalist, who doesn't know a little of them is likely to be frustrated as a person and not very useful as a citizen. . . .

23. What college you go to is important but not as important as the attitude with which you go. I assume you read the Pearlstein story. We all got a laugh at this guy walking around a campus and never attending a class or cracking a book. Probably his Polish ancestors would have given their eye-teeth for his chance to get into a college. Yet in one generation, so bad is our system of explaining education to the young, the Pearlsteins produce an offspring without enough curiosity to sit through a lecture. I think about half our high school and college students are Pearlsteins. Let me say again that it is not the fault of the Pearlsteins but of the schools that the Pearlstein attitude develops. But every individual Pearlstein must accept the responsibility for not learning. Bad as they are, the schools have the stuff on tap. You can get it if you look for it.

[24.] It may take you quite a while to digest this. Don't try to accept or reject it right away. Let it rattle around a little and jot down some comments or points on which you might like further examples or argument. Above all don't worry about yourself. You're doing fine. If you weren't I wouldn't bother to write such a long letter to you.

Love,

C. B.

COMMENTARY AND QUESTIONS

"What profession should I follow, and how should I train for it?" These questions, so often asked by students, lead to the immediate and practical question, "What courses should I take?" To one student asking these queries as he was about to reach college age, his father offered a tentative answer in the actual letter partly reprinted here. In 1945, when the letter was written, the choice of a career for a seventeen-year-old was complicated by the imminence of various possible forms of military service, actual or proposed. The parts of the letter dealing with this problem have been omitted. What remains, however, is an informal but wise and forceful argument against too narrow an education.

1. The immediate retort to a man busy persuading others to take his advice is the query, "What do you know about the matter, anyhow? What are your qualifications to speak on the subject?" How does the author of this letter forestall this objection, and how does he do it tactfully? What is the main purpose of pars. 1-3? Do you find other examples of tact in pars. 4 and 5? In par. 24?

2. A wise controversialist makes clear to his readers just which opinions, attitudes, or courses of action he is upholding and which he is not. In par. 5 this author first makes clear what he is not arguing for. Can you find a later place where he restates this careful limitation? Why is he so emphatic about it?

3. Since the author believes to be false and pernicious the theory of human values which he finds to be widely prevalent in America, the course of his argument is determined by his need to refute the prevailing theory and suggest wherein it needs mending. The ideas he is attacking are stated first at the beginning of par. 6. How does he go about demolishing them and the assumptions underlying them? How is par. 15 linked in idea to pars. 6-9?

4. Pars. 6-15 develop the author's central conclusion about the relative importance of the "word occupations" and the "thing occupations." Pars. 16-21 reinforce this conclusion by applying it to groups of people, some of whom have suffered by lack of word skills and others of whom have profited by the use of word skills. Which are which?

5. Note how the author in par. 22 makes the specific application of his general argument and at the same time sums up that argument. What is the function of par. 23? Does it connect with anything in par. 1?
6. Discuss the appropriateness of the language of this letter to its purpose. Consider on the one hand such expressions as *off base* (par. 4) and *phony* (par. 13), and on the other hand words like *ultra-materialists* and *utilitarians* (par. 15).

SUGGESTIONS FOR WRITING

1. A letter to my parents.
2. An answer from the seventeen-year-old son.
3. In par. 6 the author specifies one attitude toward human progress. What is your definition of progress?
4. In par. 11 the author parenthetically remarks that art "is really a highly intensified kind of history." Interpret this statement, drawing examples from your acquaintance with the arts.

Moonlight and
Poison Ivy

by DAVID L. COHN

I

THERE IS LITTLE DOUBT that our attitudes toward marriage, stemming as they must from our attitudes toward life and living, are crippling, if not fatal, to the central relationship in men's lives. If we tell the young that life is easy, when it is hard; that it is kind, when it is replete with cruel ironies; that all is to be had for the asking, when every blessing must be paid for singly or doubly; that it is a succession of high moments, when

From *The Atlantic Monthly*, January, 1949. By permission of the publishers and the author. Copyright 1948 by The Atlantic Monthly Company.

most of it is pedestrian; that it is "romantic," in the sense of affording high adventure, when its glory lies in man's struggle against forces he cannot even comprehend; that bigness is greatness and success is achievement— if we teach all these things, then not only is youth corroded, corrupted, and misled, while its wellsprings are poisoned at the source, but the revulsion when it comes is, and must be, shattering.

2. Yet this is what we do tell the young; what they are told every day by many magazines, the movies, the radio, and national advertisers. It is, apparently, what we believe, or affect to believe. It is also false, it does not square with human experience, and it is disastrous to marriage.

3. More and more, American marriage is coming to be a detour to divorce. The divorce rate alone does not fully illuminate the whole shabby matrimonial scene since it reflects only those cases of discord that are made public, but it is an index to private failure become national failure on a huge scale.

4. Of what significance are miracles of production, our hard work and ingenious gadgets, our cluttered catalogue of things sensible and nonsensical that make up our so-called high standard of living, if millions of men and women take little or no joy in each other; if the house vanishes, the family breaks up, the home is transient? For what does the ordinary man strive if not for a wife, a home, children, permanence of tenure and affection under one roof? And if these prove to be but an illusion, if the husband becomes an alimony payer, the father a stranger to his children, the seeker for permanency a wanderer, is not ours a matrimonial anarchy?

5. Why should such anarchy prevail? There is no easy answer to this question. Investigators attribute it to sexual maladjustments, money troubles, friction with in-laws, poor housing, the increasing financial independence of women. These play their part, but some of its causes lie in our national character and attitudes. Marriage and divorce are what they are, to a large degree, because we are what we have become.

6. American marriage is dangerously weakened at its inception because of our preference for moonlight and poison ivy—the lies elders tell the young about marriage, and the hourly elaboration of these lies, cunningly persuasive, by many magazines, the radio, the movies, national advertisers. It is rarely portrayed for what it is: a difficult and demanding exercise in human relationships; a partnership, not without austerity, in which losses as well as profits are shared; an undertaking dynastic as well as individual. More commonly—vulgarly and infantilely—marriage is portrayed as a gumdrop heaven: soft, gooey, chewy, and oh, so sweet.

7. It is, of course, a heaven of huge dimensions—not for us a one-room, walk-up Nirvana—so that the couple attaining it must move about

in a Cadillac with a sliding top, and are showered with completely furnished cottages, tickets for trips to Bermuda, whole wardrobes by Christian Dior, television sets, memberships in a country club, and two foam rubber clouds; all delicately scented with Elizabeth Arden's Blue Grass perfume. The country that invented the airplane and the drive-in movie, where you neck while you look, is certainly not going to cling to yesterday's antiquated model of marriage.

8. We are not content, therefore, to marry for reasons that have always moved most people elsewhere. It is not enough that marriage is desirable as a division of labor; that a man wants a woman to run his house and the woman wants a house to run. We scorn the fact that monogamic marriage was born of race experience, the trial-and-error method of centuries having demonstrated that, for most of us, it is the best way for a man and woman to live together and to transmit property through inheritance. We find it repulsive that marriage is no "It must be fate" relationship dreamed up by a bored faun who missed his train at Indianapolis.

9. Nor are we content, even, that marriage should proceed from love as other men have known it, for this would be to recognize the emotion for what it, in part, is: bitter-sweet, subtly demanding, frequently tempestuous, and capable of vanishing for no apparent reason. It is intolerable to us who dread the tenuous as primitive men dread the evil eye, that love's life might hang upon threads so gossamer as the cadence of a voice, the clasp of hands, the looks of eyes, the word said, the word unsaid. We find it unbearable that love demands constant replenishing and care; as much care indeed as one gives to one's car. But we do not, for these reasons, reject romantic love in marriage. Allegedly we marry for no other reason. We have created our own moonlight and poison ivy image of love and marriage: a handsome couple, forever fair and young, perpetually embracing on the moon-misty shores of a Cytherea that the map reveals to be Deaf Smith County, Texas.

10. So, too, we say "Love is blind." We mean thereby that the lover sees no imperfections or incompatibilities in the beloved, and love's blindness, therefore, will ensure forever love and marriage. Since this is palpably false, and is indeed anti-romantic, lending to the one or the other a wooden perfection suitable for a department store dummy but not for flesh and blood, whose living wonder is its mixture of elements, it follows that when, some morning at the breakfast table, the shuttered eye sees once more, all is disillusion.

11. Other peoples, wiser perhaps than we, if less "romantic," give another interpretation to the same phrase. Love is blind, they say, because the lover consciously closes his eyes to the beloved's failings, content that

the good outweighs the bad. These are not our optics, however, since in love we prefer the straight line irresolute, the rounded curve wavy. It is, moreover, a mature point of view that we find shocking because we invariably associate love with immaturity. Hence Hollywood grandmothers are condemned to go on playing ingénue roles, and Hollywood lovers, with arteries of '98, are forever Princeton '41.

12. We do not want to look at life steadily and whole, seeing that it is noble and ignoble, generous and mean, beautiful and ugly, cleanly and filthy, melancholy and joyous; compounded of pain as well as happiness; its gold inextricably mingled with baser metals. Not for us the concept that symmetry derives from asymmetry; or that, in the words of William Blake, "There is a strange disproportion in beauty."

13. Powerful agencies disseminate our deadly notion of marriage as a tinsel heaven on earth, often to the muted music of woodwinds blown by those quaint people known as parents. For every dealer in reality who languishes for lack of trade, there are a thousand dealers in illusion besieged by anxious customers. Yet they did not invent the moonlight and poison ivy concept of love and marriage. They merely exploit what is in our minds.

II

14. High among our illusions affecting love, marriage, and much else —a natural child of moonlight and poison ivy—is the installment plan mentality. It dictates that you do not have to do anything, or become anything, if you can wangle the small down payment on what you want; the rest "just a few cents a day."

15. Do you want to marry a rich, handsome young man with (as the magazines put it) "lean flanks" and "strong teeth," the better to eat you, mah chile? It's easy. Simply use Princess Mafou's Face Powder. At your next dinner party three men, dead ringers for Winthrop Rockefeller, will trample one another in the rush to marry you.

16. Suppose you have no face. Do not be discouraged. Hands will do the trick as well; or eyelashes, fingernails, hair. There was the girl who could not bring her man to gaff until she discovered Beautress (pronounced Bow-tress). "My date with Bill that night," runs the ad, "found me confident in the new-found glamour of my sparkling Beautress lovely hair . . . His cheek touched its new alluring softness while we danced . . . My heart stood still when he murmured: 'Dream Girl, that gorgeous hair rates a bridal veil.'"

17. They were married in a rented submarine, spent their honeymoon at the Stork Club, ocasionally left their Martinis to pick up a peck of emeralds at Cartier's, and because of the housing shortage are now roughing it in a twenty-room hut at Palm Springs. They are deliriously happy and will always be in a state of delirium. For when Bill occasionally looks grumpy, his Dream Girl orders a "festive walnut cake," chockful of genuine Shasta Brand Walnuts. "Imagine getting kissed for your cake!" says the ad.

18. This being the case, why should any woman burden herself with such old-fashioned backbreaking loads as brains, charm, literacy, efficiency, or resemblance to the human race? She can get her man with a shampoo and keep him with walnuts. Go to your favorite drugstore tomorrow, buy yourself a bottle of the American Dream in the new economy size, shake well before using, and live luxuriously ever afterward.

19. If you can read the ads, it is not unlikely that you can read a book, although the strain will be greater. There are dozens of books telling you how to handle every question of love and marriage in this happy world rapidly becoming free of dandruff. It is as simple as finding the recipe for lemon pie in Fannie Farmer. Why, then, be concerned with understanding and patience? Why listen to the shy counsel of the shy heart when the ready-made answer to your perplexities is at hand just as the biscuit mix is on your pantry shelf, leaving little to do except heat and serve?

20. Whence our feverish search for the easy way; our obsession with the opiate dream? Is it that we have no faith except in the infallibility of machinery and so stand incredulous and shaken when the airplane falls? Has ours become a culture from the periphery of the eyelids outward, lacking inner content? Are we, despite our physical energy, an intellectually lazy people, satisfied to take shadow for substance, package for contents, and black or white for truth because we are too lethargic to search out the nuances where truth, ever elusive, lies? Has some malign enchantment unfitted us to face life as it is, so that its essence escapes us and we face eventual destruction from within or from without? Is the high point of our civilization reached when a radio announcer screams to a nation enthralled, "That's right, Mrs. Deffenbaugh!" while $20,000 worth of things, including a houseboat and a wall can-opener, drop into the lap of the lucky winner?

21. Better marriage relations in this country await an extensive revaluation of our attitude towards life and living. If our values are shabby and our attitudes adolescent, how can American marriage, made in our image, be anything but a monumental failure?

COMMENTARY AND QUESTIONS

Many observers of American society have attacked its attitude toward marriage and its exploitation of material pleasures through advertising. Few have suggested so clearly and so concisely as David L. Cohn the connection of both attitude and exploitation with a fundamental error in values. In this article he urges his readers to recognize a truer standard of human life than that which we seem bent on upholding.

1. Although the first sentence of par. 1 and the last of par. 2 mention marriage, which is the immediate subject of the essay, the rest of pars. 1 and 2 are not directly concerned with marriage at all. Why? Show that this is fundamental to the author's whole treatment of the subject. Note that he reminds us at intervals throughout the essay of his belief that the trouble lies deeper than mere maladjustment in marriage. How are pars. 5, 12, 13, 20, and 21 related to pars. 1 and 2?

2. Pars. 6-11 mingle and alternate the author's description of marriage as a wiser people would view it and his picture of marriage as we seem to regard it. What does he gain from setting details of the two pictures side by side? Why is the bitterly satiric sketch of marriage as it appears in American advertising delayed until pars. 14-19?

3. An often effective method of argument is that which is known as *reductio ad absurdum*—reduction to an absurdity. By this method a debater pushes his opponent's principles and line of reasoning to their logical extreme, hoping thereby to convince his audience that if the extreme is absurd, the principles and reasoning must be false at every level. In demonstrating the nightmarish results of the bottled American dream of happiness, Cohn uses a subtle version of this *reductio ad absurdum* strategy. Here the logic and the characteristics of the system of values Cohn is opposing are only slightly exaggerated—just enough to show up their essential ridiculousness, not enough to let the reader feel that the picture is so overdrawn as to be inapplicable. Point out a few of these conscious exaggerations. Point out details that can be almost exactly paralleled in real life. Cohn means the reader to be amused by his exaggerations; what other feelings does he intend the reader to have?

4. Cohn's style is unusually rich in wit, well-turned sentences, and apt phrasing. What makes the second sentence in par. 1 so effective? Pars. 4, 19, and 20 make extensive use of searching questions. Why? Note how in the last two sentences of par. 11 Cohn translates a general statement into highly pungent concrete illustrations. Find other good examples of this technique. In par. 12 he echoes a well known phrase of Matthew Arnold ("to see life steadily and see it whole"); "forever fair and young" in par. 9 is probably an oblique allusion to Keats' "Ode on a Grecian Urn." Why are these allusions appropriate to the

context? What does Cohn mean in talking about a "one-room, walk-up Nirvana" (par. 7) and "the shores of a Cytherea" (par. 9)? Why "moonlight and poison ivy"?

SUGGESTIONS FOR WRITING

1. Mother love on the nation's billboards.
2. Hollywooden romance.
3. Marriage as a career.
4. History as seen through historical novels.

Give the Games Back
to the Students

by HENRY STEELE COMMAGER

ALMOST EVERY YEAR the public is startled by revelations of some new scandal in college athletics—the bribery of basketball players, the open purchase of football players, the flagrant violation of rules by the college authorities themselves.

2. It is regrettable that these scandals should excite so much attention, for, by dramatizing the ostentatious immoralities of college athletics, they tend to distract attention from the more permanent and pervasive immoralities.

3. Indignation at the more overt manifestations of corruption is thus a kind of moral catharsis; having expressed it, we then can contemplate with apathy the conditions which almost inevitably produce the corruption.

4. Thirty years ago a report of the Carnegie Foundation on College Athletics concluded as follows:

5. "The paid coach, the special training tables, the costly sweaters

From *The New York Times Magazine*, April 16, 1961. By permission of the publishers and the author. Copyright © 1961 by The New York Times Company.

and extensive journeys in special Pullman cars, the recruiting from the high schools, the demoralizing publicity showered on players, the devotion of an undue proportion of time to training, the devices for putting a desirable athlete, but a weak scholar, across the hurdles of the examinations, these ought to stop and the intramural sports be brought back to a stage in which they can be enjoyed by a large number of students and where they do not involve an expenditure of time and money wholly at variance with any ideal of honest study."

⁶· "These ought to stop!" Instead, they have become all but universally accepted and legalized—nay, the malpractices themselves have become respectable, and we can look back upon our old view of them with a certain nostalgia.

⁷· For today's malpractices are more extreme and more widespread. Worse yet, they have percolated down to the high school and they have corrupted large segments of our society.

⁸· For almost half a century now, educators have talked hopefully about de-emphasizing college athletics. And every year the emphasis has grown greater, not weaker.

⁹· The problem is not one of overemphasis. It is not even one of emphasis. The problem is the enterprise itself—intercollegiate athletics.

¹⁰· If we are going to solve that problem, we must begin by restating principles so elementary and so obvious that they should not have to be stated at all:

¹¹· The function of colleges and universities is to advance education.

¹²· Whatever contributes to education is legitimate. Whatever does not contribute to education is illegitimate.

¹³· The only justification, therefore, for games, sports, athletics, is that these do in some way contribute to education.

¹⁴· By education we mean nothing narrow. Clearly, it involves physical and moral as well as intellectual well-being. But these are by-products of education. There are a number of institutions that have responsibility for the physical and moral well-being of the young, but the schools and colleges are the only institutions that have primary responsibility for their intellectual well-being.

¹⁵· Does our current system of intercollegiate or interschool athletics contribute either to the central function of education, or to its by-products?

¹⁶· Clearly, it does not. As now organized and directed in most colleges and in a good many, if not most, high schools as well, athletics contribute nothing whatsoever to education. They simply distract the time, the energy and the attention of the whole community from the main business of education—and from its legitimate by-products.

17. Our system of athletics does not contribute to the physical fitness of the young. On the contrary, it concentrates on physical training for a mere handful of students—whom it often harms by overtraining—and reduces the great majority of students to the role of passive spectators, or television viewers. Even the facilities provided for physical training are often monopolized by the "teams," to the detriment of most of the student body.

18. It does not contribute to sportsmanship—which was one of its original purposes. On the contrary, the tremendous emphasis on winning the game has largely destroyed sportsmanship and has corrupted both players and spectators.

19. It does not contribute to initiative, independence, alertness and other desirable qualities. Instead, by centering authority in paid coaches whose primary interest is winning games, it has gone far to destroy initiative and independence on the part of players.

20. No impartial student of college and high-school athletics today can doubt that, on balance, these sports—far from making any contribution—actually do immense and irreparable harm. It is not only physical training and sports that are corrupted by the current malpractices; it is the whole educational enterprise. And since the whole community is involved in the educational enterprise, it is the whole community.

21. Educational institutions themselves are corrupted. They publicly confess that their athletic functions are more important than their academic, and acquiesce in malpractices that they would not tolerate in any other branch of their activities.

22. Colleges that spend more money on athletics than on the library, that excite more interest in basketball than in music, that cater to the demand for "winning teams" rather than for sportsmanship are faithless to their moral and intellectual obligations.

23. The community itself is corrupted by being bribed with athletic spectacles to support educational programs which should be supported on their merits.

24. Perhaps worst of all, the boys and girls of the country are corrupted: here is the real corruption of the innocent. Almost every newspaper, every weekly magazine, every television network makes clear to them that what is most important in education is athletics, and what is most important in athletics is winning.

25. No newspaper ever celebrates the scholarly achievements of local students in its biggest headlines. Why, then, should we expect the young to believe us when we tell them, on ceremonial occasions, that it is the scholarly achievements that are important? Alumni demand a winning team, and so does the community. Not long ago, a North Carolina coach

was quoted as asking, "How can I be proud of a losing team?" Can we, then, expect young people to take us seriously when we tell them that it is the game that counts—not the victory?

26. What is the explanation of this deep and pervasive corruption of games and sports? What has happened to us?

27. What has happened is that we have taken games away from the students, to whom they belong, and given them to adults, to whom they do not belong.

28. We now require of high school and college boys—and, sometimes, girls—that they provide entertainment for the community and bring money to local shopkeepers and restaurants and other business men. (Recently a New York official said of an Army-Syracuse game that "the restaurants reported business to be fabulous . . . the Transit Authority reported 28,000 extra riders that day . . . immensely increased hotel business.") They are expected to provide copy for the local newspapers, for magazines, and for TV and radio.

29. We do not permit children to work in shops or factories for our profit. Why should they be expected to make money for business interests in the community?

30. We do not permit our daughters to put on performances in burlesque shows or night clubs for our entertainment. Why should we require our sons to put on gladiatorial spectacles in stadia for our entertainment?

31. We do not expect the young to pay school taxes, or to support the chemistry department of a university. Why should we expect them to earn money for the athletic programs of the local high school, or to support the athletic departments of our colleges and universities?

32. The problem is deep and pervasive, but fortunately not complex. The solution is drastic, but fortunately not difficult; all that is needed is the will to apply it. The solution is threefold:

33. First, give games back to the students.

34. Second, eliminate all outside pressures to win games.

35. Third, take the dollar sign entirely out of school and college athletics.

36. First: Let students manage their own games, as they do at English universities. Let them play their games for the fun of it, not to entertain adults, or make money for the community or win glory for old Pugwash.

37. An end to games as spectacles. An end to bands in uniforms and drum majorettes and well-trained cheering sections, all of them artificial and all giving a fantastically exaggerated importance to the games. An end to the recruiting of players by coaches or alumni, to coaches who

play the games from the side lines and, for that matter, to formal coaching. If there must be coaches, let them depart on the day of the game and permit the players to play their own games. After all, professors do not help the students pass examinations!

38. Second: Eliminate all outside pressures. Alumni letters about the football team should go into the waste basket, where they belong. An end to pressure from coaches; their jobs should not depend on victories. An end to pressure from newspapers; let them report professional games, and leave students alone to play as well or as badly as they please. An end to pressure from public relations offices of colleges; let them report academic activities or go out of business. An end to pressure from townspeople; they can get their entertainment, find emotional safety valves and get rid of their vicarious sadism elsewhere.

39. Third: Eliminate money—all the way. No more paid coaches. Let students do their own coaching, or let school teams draw on "old boys," or get such aid as they need from members of the teaching staff who are primarily and legitimately teachers. After all, paid coaches are both new and singular in history: they did not exist until this century, and they do not now exist in England or Europe.

40. An end to all athletic subsidies, direct and indirect; to athletic "scholarships," a contradiction in terms. No student should be encouraged, in high school, to subordinate studies to athletic prowess. No student should be admitted to college on any grounds but those of academic competence; no student should be allowed to stay in college unless he is intellectually competent.

41. An end to separate athletic budgets; to admission charges for games; to the expectation that football or basketball will somehow "pay for" other parts of physical training. Games should be as much a normal part of school or college as music or drama or the college newspaper, and should no more expect to be self-sustaining.

42. An end to the building or maintenance of costly stadia. Let us make drastic reductions in expenditures for athletic equipment, for uniforms, for other superfluities. No more travel expenditures for spring training camps, for fall training camps, for airplane junkets to the other end of the country. Let schools play their neighbors in the same town or —at an extreme—in the same state.

43. Adopt these policies and nine-tenths of the evils that plague intercollegiate athletics would evaporate overnight.

44. Of course, if they *were* adopted, the games would deteriorate—as spectacles. Those who want to see brilliant performances in football or basketball can then go to professional games, as even now they go to professional rather than to college baseball games.

^{45.} Let the fans—the subway alumni of Notre Dame or the vicarious old grads of Michigan—organize city or state football and basketball teams, just as the English have city or county soccer teams.

^{46.} Naturally, student interest in organized athletics will decline; it should. Sensible students already know that if they are going to get on with their education—if they are going to get into a law school or a medical school—they have no time for organized athletics.

^{47.} European universities have managed to survive for centuries without the benefit of "teams," and doubtless American colleges and universities can learn to do so.

^{48.} Of course, there will be a falling-off in enthusiasm for old Siwash among certain kinds of alumni. Perhaps, in time, colleges can produce alumni whose interest is in intellectual rather than in athletic programs. In any event, there seems to be a pretty close correlation between high-powered athletics and low-powered finances. It is a sardonic commentary on the current scene that public pressure for winning teams rarely finds expression in lavish gifts or in generous appropriations. Institutions such as M. I. T. and Amherst, at any rate, seem to manage pretty well without the exploitation of athletics, and institutions such as Ohio State, which has yielded to pressure for winning teams, are treated with niggardliness by an ungrateful Legislature.

^{49.} These are negative consequences which we may anticipate from the elimination of money and of pressures from college athletics and the return of games to the students. The positive consequences which we may confidently anticipate are exhilarating:

^{50.} This simple program will restore integrity to athletics, making clear once more the blurred distinction between the amateur and the professional. And it will enormously improve programs for physical education for the young people in schools and colleges, an improvement desperately needed.

^{51.} It will release the energies of educators and students for the primary job of education. The colleges will be freed from improper pressures and influences and permitted to do what they are best equipped to do and what they have a moral responsibility to do: educate the young.

^{52.} But is all this a counsel of perfection? Can this program of cleansing and restoration be achieved? Well, it has been achieved at Johns Hopkins, at the University of Chicago, and at M. I. T. It has been achieved at Swarthmore and Oberlin and Reed. Somehow, all continue to flourish.

^{53.} No halfway measures will do. As long as nonacademic organizations have an interest in athletics, as long as games belong to coaches or alumni or townspeople or the business community instead of to the

young people who play them, all the evils which have afflicted school and college athletics in the past will continue.

⁵⁴· Radical surgery is needed. But it is radical surgery from which the patient is sure to recover and which guarantees good health and good spirits.

COMMENTARY AND QUESTIONS

One of the functions of the press is to provide a channel through which responsible citizens may attempt to persuade their fellow citizens to certain policies or courses of action. In this essay, written for the Sunday magazine section of a widely influential New York newspaper, an educator and noted American historian argues for total abolition of present-day intercollegiate athletics. While there is no one "correct" pattern for the structure of an argumentative essay, Professor Commager's article employs so logical and effective an arrangement of material that it will serve as a useful model for this kind of persuasion.

1. Public debate on any controversial issue is likely to generate confusion unless the debaters carefully define what the issue is. In which paragraphs does Commager identify the problem he is discussing? How does he manage at the same time to make the reader feel that this problem is important, and needs action?

2. Debate is also likely to be confused unless the debaters state clearly the assumptions or premises underlying their arguments. In which paragraphs does Commager state his fundamental assumptions? Note that in par. 13 he suggests the application of his assumptions to the particular problem under discussion; in par. 14 he clarifies the significance of a key term (*education*) used in par. 13; and in par. 15 he again connects his assumptions with the problem by asking what may be called "the crucial question"—an effective debating device. Par. 16 states Commager's answer to his own question. In pars. 17-25 he presents evidence in support of his answer. Into what two sorts of evidence may this material be divided?

3. When a controversialist asserts that there is a serious problem, he is likely to meet the query, perhaps especially from his more skeptical listeners, "If the problem is as bad as you say it is, how did we ever get into such a mess anyhow?" Commager anticipates such a question by raising it himself in par. 26. How does he simultaneously answer this question and put his opponents (those who favor continuation of intercollegiate athletics) on the defensive?

4. After stating briefly in pars. 32-35 his proposed solution to the problem, Commager elaborates each part of it in pars. 36-42. What is the function of par. 43? A controversialist who has proposed a course of action must usually dispose of possible objections to, or disadvantages

of, such action; and he usually finds it effective to suggest possible advantages to the policy he has recommended. In which paragraphs does Commager do each of these things, and how does he relate his arguments to the fundamental assumptions he has earlier stated?

5. Skeptics commonly greet any proposal for a course of action with the question "But is it practical?" How does Commager meet this question? Why does he divide the institutions named in par. 52 into two groups? This kind of argument, used also in par. 48, may be called the appeal to examples. What are the possible strengths and weaknesses of this particular argumentative device?

6. Pars. 29-31 contain examples of argument by analogy. Can you find other examples in this essay? What are the possible strengths and weaknesses of this particular argumentative device?

7. Why does Commager begin pars. 40-42 with the same three words? Find other examples of parallelism in the essay.

8. It is common to find newspaper material divided into very short paragraphs: partly because paragraphs printed in the narrow columns of a newspaper look much longer than they really are, and partly, perhaps, because many editors feel that the attention span of their readers is not sufficient to sustain interest through a long paragraph. It is probable that Commager's essay would have been divided differently had it originally appeared in a different format. Suggest possible revisions of the paragraph structure.

SUGGESTIONS FOR WRITING

1. Give education back to the students.
2. In defense of spectator sports.
3. Using approximately the same structure and argumentative method as Commager, define a different public problem and defend your proposed solution.

The Last Days
of Football

by MORRIS BISHOP

THE TRANSFORMATION of football may be traced back to the season of 1947, when Pasty Post, coach of South Dakota Wesleyan, first equipped his quarterback with a radio receiver. The device was merely an aviator's headset, surplus property from the war, which fitted neatly under the quarterback's helmet. Pasty Post claimed that this innovation was necessitated by the inability of his quarterback, Yegg Olsen, to remember, ratiocinate, or even count.

2. Pasty Post's little idea accounted, at least in part, for the brilliant success of South Dakota Wesleyan that year. It defeated, successively, New Jersey Christian, Weinberg Secretarial, and Our Lady of Sorrows in post-season games that extended the football season almost to Commencement Day.

3. At the annual coaches' convention, Post's device was bitterly denounced, especially by the coaches of New Jersey Christian, Weinberg Secretarial, and Our Lady of Sorrows. It was, however, upheld by the representatives of the great gas-and-oil companies that owned the football radio rights. For the gas-and-oil companies saw in it an answer to their own problem, one of profound seriousness. They had paid enormous sums for the privilege of broadcasting the games, and a number of the big classics had turned out to be downright dull. One of them, indeed (Death Valley Teachers vs. Dismal Swamp A. and M.), had been nothing but an endless series of ineffectual charges in mid-field for two mortal hours. The broadcast of this encounter had so bored the great radio audience that a number of listeners had actually turned their radios off.

4. The gas-and-oil companies were, therefore, warmly in favor of an innovation which, they felt, would ensure excitement to their listeners. They pointed out that they had too much money invested in football to leave the games entirely to chance. While they would not dream of interfering with the legitimate goals of sport, they had, after all, the right

to insist that the performances should have that pace which the great radio audience demands, and which, gentlemen, it has a right to demand. They asked only a little friendly consideration of their problem. They argued that a coach who didn't use Post's device had to communicate with his performers by sending in a substitute with a message. Then, gentlemen, what happens? The timekeeper's whistle blows, the substitute runs out, slaps a player on the back. The slapped player runs off, the whistle blows, the team goes into a new huddle. Meanwhile, the announcer ad-libs about the cheerleaders or the lovely day. These delays are wearisome to the listener, are deplorable from the point of view of dramatic structure, and are contrary to all common sense. In these days of instantaneous communication, etc.

5. The coaches' convention accepted the courteous recommendations of the gas-and-oil companies as, in fact, orders. The system of coach-to-team radio communication was legalized in the rules for 1948. Meanwhile, to improve American football, the gas-and-oil companies retained some of the most brilliant radio producers and directors to lay out the strategy of the important games. Carefully refraining from prearranging the outcomes, these men labored to make the contests continuously interesting to the millions of listeners whose pleasure they had at heart. They insisted, for instance, that a big game should have a genuine dramatic structure, that it should not, as it too often had in the past, concentrate its interest in the first half and then trail off in a long, dull anticlimax. They made sure that stars who had captured the public affection should have a proper role in the field, and not be allowed to languish on the sidelines through some caprice of the coach. It was arranged that a radio man, in white knickers, should be constantly on the field, ready, after each sensational play, to broadcast a few words by the player involved.

6. The improvement in broadcast football was immediately noticeable. The season of 1948 was certainly the greatest in football history. But even at that time, it now appears, the seeds of disintegration were being sown.

7. On New Year's Day, 1949, the greatest game of the season was to be played in the Rose Bowl. The contestants were the Alaska Aggies and Panama Tech. The game was the property of Git-There Gas.

8. But just an hour before the game was scheduled to begin, both teams were laid low by food poisoning. A pretty problem was thus put up to Git-There Gas. Some fifty million people were sitting at their radios, demanding a play-by-play account of the classic. Git-There Gas could not fail its public. In a hasty conference, it was decided that the game must go on—in a New York radio studio.

9. Two of the most eminent football strategists in the world were placed opposite each other at a large table, with charts and lists of players before them. An umpire sat at mid-table. By turns, the strategists called their plays and defensive measures. The umpire decided between them—awarded yardage gained or lost, ruled passes complete or incomplete, and from time to time granted a touchdown. The conversation of all three was piped to a second studio, where a famous sports announcer sat before the microphone. The announcer, modulating his celebrated voice to broad amusement, quiet appreciation, agony, exultation, and hysteria, told the world. The sound-effects man used his most effective recordings of college bands, roars of the crowd, comic drunks, screams and moans of ladies epileptic with loyalty.

10. Never had there been such a football game. The strategists, snarling and sweating, produced plays of astounding subtlety and complication, and defenses that were marvels of brilliant improvisation. The deceptions and devices that long ago they had conceived in moments of midnight clairvoyance were now bodied forth. The umpire imperturbably ruled them successful or unsuccessful. Every now and then, he would maim one of the leading players, and half America would groan in unison. At the end, he ruled the game a tie.

11. It was obvious from the fan mail that this was the most successful football broadcast of all time, and the directors of Git-There Gas drew the logical conclusion. As far as radio was concerned, there was no reason why college football games—clumsy, amateurish, inartistic, unstructural —should be played at all. On every count, studio football was an improvement. It was decided that for the season of 1949 the enormous bother of reporting actual college games would be eliminated and that all football would originate in the radio studios.

12. During the 1949 season, most of the football fans stayed at home on Saturday afternoons to listen to the great Git-There Gas series. The colleges, deprived of radio revenue, and with their stadia occupied only by pitiful little bands of college students, were obliged to curtail or abolish their sports programs. A number of the smaller colleges went bankrupt and were forced to close.

13. When, eventually, all the college athletic associations were disbanded and there were no regularly scheduled football games, the students invented a new game, which came to be called "soft football." It was played everywhere—in abandoned stadia and on vacant lots, and on campus quadrangles between classes—by students dressed in old clothes. Sometimes there were twenty or twenty-five on a side. It was great fun. It was, in fact, the same football that had been played in American colleges in 1870.

COMMENTARY AND QUESTIONS

Morris Bishop has written many witty satires for *The New Yorker.* Here he attacks one prevalent attitude toward college football by imaginatively carrying out to their logical conclusion the assumptions underlying that attitude.

1. For each of the following passages show what assumption is implied by it and what opposite assumption (presumably favored by the author) is contradicted by it:
   a. "a number of the big classics had turned out to be downright dull" (par. 3).
   b. "they had too much money invested in football to leave the games entirely to chance" (par. 4).
   c. "his performers" (par. 4).
   d. "The game was the property of Git-There Gas" (par. 7).
   e. "college football games—clumsy, amateurish, inartistic, unstructural" (par. 11).
   f. "their stadia occupied only by pitiful little bands of college students" (par. 12).

2. Is there any connection between the various assumptions satirized by details such as those quoted in question 1? Since Bishop's title is "The Last Days of Football," why doesn't he end with par. 12?

3. This selection was originally published in 1946, but the three football seasons described in it are specified as those of 1947, 1948, and 1949. Why did Bishop use the past tense in narrating these "events"? Placing the time of a story or satiric sketch in the future is a very old device in writing. That it is still useful may be seen, for example, in the "science fiction" so popular in recent years. What advantages does this device offer to a writer bent on satirizing or at least critically examining the social values and customs of his own day?

4. What rhetorical device is common to the following phrases:
   a. "the inability of his quarterback, Yegg Olsen, to remember, ratiocinate, or even count" (par. 1).
   b. "post-season games that extended the football season almost to Commencement Day" (par. 2).
   c. "ladies epileptic with loyalty" (par. 9).
   Why did Bishop not use this device more often?

SUGGESTIONS FOR WRITING

1. Mr. Bishop is unfair to colleges.
2. College football *vs.* professional football.
3. The role of audience imagination in radio and television.

4. The psychology of "college spirit."
5. The last days of television (when someone invented a machine that could make you laugh or cry at the touch of a button).

Time on Our Hands

by RUSSELL LYNES

RECENTLY I DISCOVERED among some papers that my mother had stowed away in a deserted file a clipping from a magazine of the 1920s. It was headed "Schedule for a One-Maid House." The house, it said, "has seven rooms: a living-room, dining-room, porch, kitchen, maid's room and bath, three bedrooms, and two baths." The schedule starts with:

> 6:45 A.M. *Wash and Dress*

and ends with:

> 8:00 P.M. *Plans for the evening will be adapted to the household convenience.*

2. Bridget, if that was her name, was busy in the intervening hours with cleaning, cooking, bed-making, baking, and polishing silver and brass. Her respite came sometime between 1:30 and 3:00 P.M. when, according to the schedule, she was to "clear table, wash dishes, go to own room to rest, bathe, and change dress." At 3:00 she was back in the kitchen, "ready to answer door, etc."

3. Leisure was not much of a problem for Bridget at work in a one-maid house. Her schedule covers six days (on Saturday it says: "Bake cake for Sunday") and like everyone else she had Sunday as her only day off. (She doesn't seem to have had "maid's night out" on the customary Thursday.)

4. The familiar picture of the maid on her day off was of a girl dressed "fit to kill" on her way to meet her friends at church. The equally familiar picture of the man of the house was father asleep in a hammock

buried under the Sunday paper. Leisure in those days was merely a restorative for work. Now leisure has become work in its own right . . . and a worry to lots of earnest Americans.

5. Last year at the commencement exercises at New York University a clergyman said to the graduating class: "America can be undone by her misuse of leisure. Life is getting easier physically, and this makes life harder morally."

6. There are, of course, a great many professional and business men who wonder what all this talk about leisure is; somehow it is no problem to them—or so they think. There are also a good many women, es-pecially young married women, who would give their heirlooms for a few minutes to themselves. They have only to wait.

7. But leisure is making some thoughtful people uneasy. In January the American Council of Churches met in Columbus to discuss the spare time of our increasingly urbanized populace. The Twentieth Century Fund is deep in an investigation of leisure and the University of Chicago is (with the help of Ford Foundation funds) making a study of the na-ture of leisure and how people use it. Corporations not only worry about the leisure of their employees; they do something about it. Schoolteachers and social workers and local politicians worry about it, about footloose youngsters, about long summer vacations for teen-agers, and about ju-venile delinquency. City planners, safety experts, highway engineers watch the growing number of hours when families are not at work and feel they have to go somewhere. Where? To what extent is the boredom of leisure responsible for young drug addicts, for the common cold, for muggings on city streets?

8. Every new scientific development, whether it is aimed at saving our skins or washing our dishes, leads in one way or another to reducing still further the sweat of the public brow. The four-day week which looms on the immediate horizon (and which causes such consternation in the corporate breast) is, of course, less the product of labor's demands than of manufacturing genius. Machines not men have created the three-day weekend, and men are worried about what to do with it. Not long ago the Oil, Chemical, and Atomic Workers Union made a survey of its membership. It asked them: ". . . if and when the Union enters a bargain-ing program for shorter hours" how would they like this additional leisure to be distributed? Would a housewife, for example, "want her husband at home three consecutive days?" Good question.

9. The attitude of many large corporations has been somewhat differ-ent. They have attacked the problem of employee leisure head on. They have provided all sorts of sports facilities, music clubs, theater groups, and bowling leagues. IBM has its own golf courses for its employees. Bell

and Howell has baseball fields lighted for night games. Ford's River Rouge plant has an indoor shooting range, tennis courts, baseball diamonds (nine of them), and horseshoe pits. Corning Glass has its own museum, visiting repertory theater, and changing exhibitions, in addition to automatic bowling alleys, basketball courts, and dancing classes.

10. Business is not sentimental about the new leisure. "Many of these off-the-job or after-hours activities," the head of employee relations for General Motors has said, "have not only a therapeutic value, but can actually sharpen or increase employees' skills." And the President of Bell and Howell has said, "Everyone in the organization gains from a well-planned recreational program."

11. But these efforts to sponge up the ocean of the so-called leisure time which has engulfed us can only put a few drops in the bucket. The truth is that while the new leisure has come on us fairly gradually, it has found us not at all prepared. If we are to cope agreeably with it, we are going to have to change our minds about some shibboleths and even some rather basic beliefs. To do this, we need to understand what has happened to the pattern of our leisure and where it is likely to lead.

12. Leisure is not a new problem born of automation, but it is a new problem for a great many kinds of people who were never much concerned with it when Bridget was working her seventy- or eighty-hour week in the one-maid house. America has had a leisure class since the industrialization of our country began, and in the 1850s the art critic James Jackson Jarves complained in shocked tones of the number of scions of wealthy families who threw themselves into rivers because they were so bored that life seemed not worth living. (Mr. Jarves wanted to interest such young men in the arts as a suitable outlet for their energies and money.) These young men, whom we would call the idle rich, had on a large scale the same problem that nearly everybody in America has today on a small scale. In its simplest terms, the primary problem of leisure is how to avoid boredom.

13. We used to be more accomplished at being bored than we are today, or at least we seem to have taken boredom with better grace in the days of party calls and decorous parlor games. We assumed a high moral tone toward leisure, and in some respects this tone persists. "The devil finds work for idle hands," our parents said and shook their heads; and when they said, "All work and no play makes Jack a dull boy," they meant, of course, that Jack should work most of the time but not quite all of it. Primarily leisure was thought of as a way to get a man back on his feet so that after Sunday he could put in sixty or so productive hours

from Monday through Saturday. Leisure for women (few women in those days had jobs) was something quite else—it was the custody of culture and good works. Women in their spare time were expected to cultivate the arts, foster the education of their children, and play the role of Lady Bountiful in the community.

14. It was a neat division of family functions and a tidy way of life. Father's leisure was restorative; mother's was extremely productive. But more has changed than just the roles of men and women; the whole complex machinery of leisure has changed.

15. Briefly the changes are these:

16. In the last few decades what had started about a century ago as a trickle of people from the country and small towns to the cities became a torrent. Cities filled like cisterns and overflowed into suburbs, and as we shifted from a predominantly agricultural economy to a predominantly industrial one, we changed the nature of much of our leisure from what might be called a natural one to an artificial one, from pleasures provided by nature to pleasures concocted by man. Ways of using leisure began to come in packages—in cars, in movies, in radios, and most recently in television sets, and what was once the sauce only for the city goose became the sauce for the country gander as well. City culture is now within easy reach of everyone everywhere and everyone has the same access to talent that only a few decades ago used to be reserved for the rich and the urbane.

17. During the time when we were changing from a rural to an urban culture, the length of the work-week fell from sixty hours or more to forty or thirty-five. Gradually the five-day week became an almost universal reality, and the four-day week is on the immediate horizon. With more leisure time, men have, quite naturally, taken on some of the household chores that only a short while ago they wouldn't have been caught dead at, and have assumed some of the cultural responsibilities which were once the domain of their wives. They have also, with time on their hands and cars at their disposal, turned again to many kinds of rural recreation . . . to fishing and hunting, especially, but also to sailing and skiing. The most solitary of all sports, fishing, is also the most popular of all sports with American men.

18. But the greatest assault on old patterns of leisure and on the shibboleths about devil's work for idle hands, has been industry's discovery that it needs the consuming time of workers as much as it needs their producing time. In an economy, geared as ours is to making life comfortable for everyone, it is essential to business that people have time to enjoy their comfort and to use up the things that make life comfortable.

19. A tremendous part of our production plant is committed to promoting leisure—to automobiles, to television sets, to time-saving gadgets, to sports equipment, and to hundreds of services which are unnecessary to life but which contribute to relaxed living. Our economy, in other words, is more and more involved with Time Off. Think of the industries, the purveyors of pleasure, that would collapse if we were to go back to the sixty-hour week. It looks as though we were far more likely (and not because of pressures from labor but the demands of technology and automation) to go to a twenty-eight hour week.

20. Urbanization, the shorter working day and week, and the changing roles of the sexes have, heaven knows, produced tremendous changes in the ways Americans live. But the premium put on the consuming time of the worker by our economic system presents us with a tidily packaged moral dilemma. When idleness is a public virtue, what becomes of the moral value of work? What are we going to substitute for the old adages on which we were brought up? What are we going to tell our children? What will happen to the economy if we go on saying that virtue is its own reward, that work is good for the soul, and that leisure is only a reward for toil? What happens to the Calvinist ethic?

21. This is a problem I would rather refer to a dilettante than to an economist or a clergyman or certainly to an engineer. The economist would consider it from the point of view of wealth, the clergyman of the after life, and the engineer of production. The dilettante can be counted on to look at it from the point of view of life, liberty, and especially the pursuit of happiness.

22. I would like to contend in all seriousness, at this moment when there is such a cry for engineers and when our theological seminaries are bursting at the doors, that what we need is more dilettantes. Compared with good dilettantes, good engineers and good clergymen are a dime a dozen. Every newspaper account of the engineering shortage is contradicted by another story of how big corporations are hoarding engineers the way people hoarded butter during the war. Recently, Dr. Robert J. Havighurst of the University of Chicago made it quite clear that the number of engineers and technologists being trained in our technical schools is more than adequate to our needs: the shortage, he said, is in good teachers. In the long run our civilization will be measured more accurately by our know-why than by our know-how.

23. It is probably because in the triumvirate of our ideals—life, liberty, and the pursuit of happiness—the last of these has always seemed to our Calvinist society rather naughty, that we have come to look down our noses at the dilettante. We have dismissed him as a trifler; we have

despised him as a parasite on other people's work, the fritterer, the gad-fly. But there was a time when the word dilettante was by no means the term of opprobrium it has become.

24. Originally *dilettante* meant a lover of the fine arts (it comes from the Latin word for delight) and it was used to distinguish the consumer from the producer. Its application spread beyond the arts in England, and in the eighteenth century the Society of the Dilettanti was a club of influential men interested not only in the arts but in the sciences and in archaeology. It meant the man of intellectual curiosity who devoted part of his time to the intelligent cultivation of the arts and sciences, to the resources of leisure and the satisfactions of the mind.

25. If you transplant the idea of the eighteenth-century dilettante from England to America, you discover that he was Thomas Jefferson and Benjamin Franklin—one a farmer who dabbled in architecture and introduced a new style to America, the other a printer who dabbled in natural science and flew a kite into a thunderstorm. You discover several others who got together and started a talkfest that became the Philosoph-ical Society of Philadelphia, and others who, dabbling in the arts, some-how founded a string of distinguished museums across the nation and filled them with masterpieces, and, of course, a good many bad guesses. These men were dilettantes. There is no other word that fits them.

26. In the nineteenth century the word came on hard times. "The con-noisseur is 'one who knows,' as opposed to the dilettante who 'only thinks he knows,'" said F. W. Fairholt in the 1850s. Fairholt, an antiquary who wrote among other things *A Dictionary of Terms in Art,* was, there is no question, a connoisseur, and like all experts he was impatient of non-scholars who pretended to the delights he reserved for himself and his kind. A connoisseur, he said, "is cognisant of the true principles of Art, and can fully appreciate them. He is of a higher grade than the ama-teur, and more nearly approaches the artist." In his definition of an amateur he puts the emphasis on his "skill" as a performer and his non-professionalism, just as we do today, and in his definition of the dilettante, while he acknowledges the seriousness of the original meaning of the word, he bemoans the dilettante's pretentiousness and his use of the arts for purposes of social climbing. He admits (as people who consider themselves connoisseurs today rarely admit, however far they may go in buttering up the dilettante for their own purposes) that the arts need the enthusiasm that the dilettante's support brings to them.

27. The trouble (and it is a trouble) is that, with the decline of the word *dilettante,* there is no word left to describe the enthusiast who is more serious than the fan, less knowledgeable than the connoisseur, and hasn't the skill that makes an amateur. (The amateur is, after all, basic-ally a performer.) What we need in our society, I contend again, is more

real dilettantes, and we need to extend the meaning of the word to many delights besides the arts and sciences.

28. The dilettante is just a consumer. He is a man who takes the pursuit of happiness seriously, not frivolously, and he works at it. He is part sensualist, part intellectual, and part enthusiast. He is also likely to be a proselytizer for those causes in which his interests are involved, and to be rather scornful of those people who do not take their pleasures seriously and who are passive instead of active in the cultivation of them. But whatever else he may be he is not lazy. He may or may not have a job that he finds interesting, but he does not use his leisure in a miscellaneous and undirected fashion. He knows what he wants out of life and will go to a lot of trouble to get it. Primarily, in Voltaire's sense, he wants to cultivate his own garden.

29. You will find dilettantes everywhere and in every aspect of our culture. I found one a few weeks ago driving a taxi in New York. He was a man in his early sixties.

30. "I only drive this hack three days a week," he said. "The other four days I go fishing. I like to fish and I'm pretty good at it."

31. By the time he had delivered me home I knew what he fished for at what times of year, what bait he used and where and in what weather, and which were the best fishing boats and captains going out of New York harbor. I asked him what he did with all the fish he caught.

32. "I got a son-in-law runs a saloon," he said. "I give them to his customers."

33. Probably the most common and in some ways the most accomplished of American dilettantes is the baseball fan, though the national pastime is being crowded out of its position as top banana of entertainment these days by serious music. The baseball fan knows his subject with something very close to genuine scholarship. He is an expert in the minutiae of its history and understands the nuances and subtleties of its performace. He takes as much pleasure from the refinements of its details as from the outcome of any single game, and he enjoys the company of others with whom he can argue the relative virtues of performance and make comparisons with other similar situations. He demands skill on the field of a truly professional caliber, and he lets his displeasure with anything less be known in the most direct and uncompromising manner. He is, by and large, a less tolerant dilettante than the one whose interest is devoted to art, for his expert eye is less subject to changes in fashion. Unquestionably without him the standards of baseball would long since have gone to pot.

34. The simple fact is that the dilettante is the ideal consumer, not

ideal, perhaps, from the point of view of those producers who would like their customers to accept their products with blind confidence, but ideal from the point of view of maintaining standards of quality . . . whether material or cultural. He takes his functions as a consumer seriously. He takes the trouble to know what he likes and to sort out the shoddy and the meretricious from the sound and reasonable. If he is a dilettante of music, for example, he demands the best performance from his record-player. He is unimpressed by an imitation mahogany cabinet in the Chippendale manner, but he knows that the components of his hi-fi equipment are the very best that he can afford. (He can, in fact, be credited with the very great improvement in mass-produced sound equipment; it was his interest in high-fidelity that spread the word to the general public and raised the level of public acceptance.)

³⁵· We are likely to associate the dilettante only with the arts, which is one reason why he has such a bad name in America. In the rambunctious and expansive days of the nineteenth century when America was growing and fighting its way across the continent, toil was man's business; culture was left to women. So were most other refinements of life, and the arts were thought of as sissy and men who showed any interest in them as something less than virile. A man who didn't sleep through a concert or an opera was regarded with suspicion. It was only when a man retired from business that it was considered suitable for him to spend his money on art—not necessarily because he liked it or knew anything about it but because it gave him social prestige. Except in a few Eastern Seaboard cities, the arts were women's work, and there was no time and place for the dilettante.

³⁶· The nature of our new-found leisure is rapidly changing the old stereotypes. The businessman who doesn't make some pretense at an interest in culture, who doesn't support the local symphony and museum, who isn't on the library board or out raising money for his college is looked upon as not doing his duty, much less serving his own interests. Babbitt isn't Babbitt any more. Babbitt is by way of becoming a dilettante. A lot worse things could happen to him. In no time at all being a dilettante will not be considered un-American.

³⁷· The point at which the dilettante becomes an "expert" but not a "professional" is an indistinct one. Two successful business men who have, in their leisure time, become naturalists of considerable reputation are an officer of J. P. Morgan & Co., R. Gordon Wasson, who has recently produced an important book of original research on mushrooms, and Boughton Cobb, a textile manufacturer who is one of the world's leading

authorities on ferns. A few years ago an ancient language known to scholars as "Minoan Linear B" that had had scholars completely at sea for years was "broken" by an English architect, Michael Ventris, for whom cryptanalysis was a leisure activity. These three men became experts, not professionals, dilettantes in the best sense, not amateurs.

38. Obviously not many men in any generation are going to be able to extend their leisure activities to such levels of distinction. But leisure without direction, without the satisfaction of accomplishment of some sort is debilitating to anyone brought up in an atmosphere, like ours, in which the virtues of work have been so long extolled and are so deeply imbedded in our mythology. The greatest satisfaction of the dilettante is not in doing but in discovering, in discriminating, and in enjoying the fruits of his knowledge and his taste.

39. There will, of course, always be those who can only find satisfaction in making something, the eternal do-it-yourselfers, the cabinetmakers, and needlepointers, and gardeners, and model builders, and rug hookers. These are the amateur craftsmen who often achieve professional competence. There are also those who will find their only satisfactions apart from work in sensuous pleasures, in sports, and food and drink, and love. The dilettante finds his satisfactions primarily in the mind. He is the ideal traveler, the perfect audience, the coveted reader, and the perceptive collector.

40. But he is not by any means necessarily a highbrow. Indeed the ideal dilettante is not. He may be a professional intellectual or he may not, but he does not pose as what he isn't. His tastes and his knowledge may well run to abstruse and esoteric things, to the dances of Tibet or the jewelry of pre-Columbian Mexico, but they may just as well run to the square dance and baseball cards. The dilettante of jazz, the man who knows the names of the instrumentalists in all of the great bands of the last thirty years, is as important a dilettante as the man who knows his Mozart by Koechel numbers. It is genuine, not simulated, enthusiasm that counts. The function of the dilettante is to encourage a high degree of performance in whatever field of interest happens to be his, to be an informed, but by no means conventional, critic, and to be a watchdog. He must be both an enthusiast and an irritant who will praise what measures up to his standards and needle producers into doing as well as they know how, and better. He is an incorrigible asker of hard questions. He keeps controversy in our culture alive, and if he is sometimes proved to be dead wrong, he is at least never dead on his feet. He is the want-to-know-why man and the traditional anathema of the know-how man.

41. Several months ago I found myself in an argument, or the beginnings of one, in a radio interview with a well-known broadcaster. "Our colleges need to produce more and better trained men," he said, and I countered with the suggestion that they needed to produce better educated men. "We need experts," he said.

42. "We need dilettantes," I replied, and the word so surprised him that he gingerly changed the subject to safer ground.

43. I would like to change my position, but only slightly. What we need are trained men with the capacity for being dilettantes. There can be no argument with the fact that an industrialized society must have a great many highly trained men and women with specialized knowledge and skills. But in this country the consumers and the producers are the same people; all of us work both sides of the economic street. We are, the great majority of us, the part-time idle rich, and no nation, so far as I know, has ever found itself in such a position before. Ours is a society in which no man's nose need be permanently to the grindstone, and where every man is a potential dilettante.

44. We have thought of our know-how as our most exportable commodity, and when somebody else demonstrated, moon-fashion, a superior know-how, we took it as a blow to our "national prestige." In fact our most exportable commodity has been a cultural one, a way of life that balances work and leisure for almost everyone and distributes the fruits of labor with astonishing, if not complete, evenness. Our most effective know-how has been in the production of leisure, a commodity filled with promise and booby traps. It is the engineer with his slide rule who knows how to produce leisure, but it is the dilettante who knows how to use it and make it productive.

45. It will be as dilettantes and consumers that we will, in the long run, determine the quality of our culture. We will determine not only the gadgets of our civilization but the fate of its arts as well. We will determine whether the pursuit of happiness has, after all, been worth it.

COMMENTARY AND QUESTIONS

Since many citizens shy away from serious discussions of serious subjects, there is a place for the clever persuader who, by his briskly colloquial tone, charms his restive audience into listening just long enough to grasp a few solid thoughts. In writing this essay, Russell Lynes may well have anticipated an audience likely to be even more restive than usual. The use of leisure time is a subject already much discussed, often with forbidding solemnity; and, as he points out, many readers have also been led to associate leisure with either long hair or laziness.

It was essential, therefore, that Mr. Lynes catch and hold the attention of his readers, and divert their suspicions. He chose to do so by a combination of slightly tongue-in-cheek sophistication with an informal and relaxed style. Direct imitation of such a style has its dangers for beginners; it is perhaps best left to professionals or to those serious dilettantes of whom Mr. Lynes speaks; but even the beginner can learn much from the deceptive simplicity of these easy-flowing sentences.

1. Why does Lynes begin with an account of the duties of a maid of the 1920's? Why does he give her a name?

2. What is the function of par. 4 and how does it achieve its purpose? Why is the tone of pars. 5-10 somewhat different from that of pars. 1-3? Find at least two short phrases in pars. 5-10 that slyly relieve the prevailing sobriety of tone.

3. Pars. 11-17 furnish a historical explanation of the growth of leisure time in the United States. Presumably the apparent inexorability of history might reassure those readers inclined to disapprove of the growth of leisure. How does Lynes use pars. 18-20 to make a further defense of leisure? Note the echo of these paragraphs in the word *consumer* in pars. 28, 43, and 45.

4. What is the effect of introducing the term *dilettante* in connection with the words *life, liberty, and especially the pursuit of happiness* (par. 21)? Note that the latter is echoed in pars. 23, 28, and 45. Why do you think Lynes chose to mention the particular people cited in par. 25?

5. Can you suggest a reason for the order of the illustrative examples of dilettantism presented in pars. 29-34? Can you suggest, in view of what is said in pars. 35 and 36, the reasons for choosing the particular examples given in par. 37 of dilettantes who became "experts"? Why is Lynes so anxious in par. 40 to dissociate the dilettante from the highbrow?

6. Lynes speaks in par. 13 of the "high moral tone toward leisure" assumed by our ancestors, and mentions that "in some respects this tone persists." In par. 20 he refers to the "moral value of work," in par. 38 to "the virtues of work." Show how the wording of par. 28 seems to be so chosen as to associate the American emphasis on work with the dilettante's cultivation of leisure. Is there anything in the essay, especially in pars. 44-45, to suggest that Lynes sees moral values in dilettantism (as he defines it) as well as in work?

SUGGESTIONS FOR WRITING

1. The hardest working dilettante I ever knew.
2. Dilettantism and the arts.
3. How high is a dilettante's brow?
4. Leisure—what's that?
5. Fewer dilettantes, not more.

The Tyranny
of Democratic Manners

by MORTON CRONIN

I MAINTAIN that democratic manners—typified by the practice of calling the boss by his first name—have reached the point in our country where they conduce not to the preservation of personal dignity but to the abject submission of one man to another. These manners, gradually developed in colonial and post-revolutionary days, worked well in a society largely of self-sufficient farmers. But circumstances have changed, with the usual ironical result.

2. What happens on the job at the present time? An employee greets the boss by his first name, sits down in his presence, wears the same kind of clothes the boss wears, avoids the use of *sir*, and ostensibly comports himself in general as if he and the boss were as equal as two farmers. But of course he and the boss are not equal, and this inequality must be signalized. It must be signalized, first, because the employee is anxious to please the boss, who can advance or impede his fortunes; and, secondly, because the boss is anxious that his authority receive recognition, without which he cannot function with any confidence.

3. In the absence of overt and conventional methods of expressing deference, how then does the American employee acknowledge the boss's superior status? He does so by perfecting a subtle repertoire of body movements and vocal expressions. This repertoire includes the boyish grin, the deprecatory cough, the unfinished sentence, the appreciative giggle, the drooping shoulders, the head-scratch and the bottom-waggle. But there are employees, the truly gifted ones—as actors, they would adorn the Stanislavski school—who can dispense with these definable maneuvers and simply *live* the part, their whole being radiating a kind of sweet eloquence of submission.

4. Now this body language, in both its definable and indefinable forms, is almost impossible to fake successfully, at least in any long-continued relationship. If it is not accompanied quite genuinely by the emotions appropriate to it, it will be contradicted and rendered sinister

by involuntary movements and expressions which accord with the individual's true feelings. It is easy to execute a military salute, regardless of one's private thoughts, but the deprecatory cough—to say nothing of the Stanislavski method—requires great sincerity, else they appear villainous.

5. American manners, in short, decree egalitarian behavior in a hierarchical society. The result is that a subordinate, compelled to behave formally and superficially in a democratic way, is forced in making his adjustments to the facts of life to behave informally and profoundly in a hierarchical way. It should be just the opposite—the system of etiquette ought to furnish him with formal gestures of respect for his superiors and let his informal self work out its own salvation. It should be easier to render the boss what is the boss's without throwing in one's soul too.

6. Out of a doctrinaire devotion to palsy-walsy manners has sprung that misshapen, anomalous growth, the despotism of the nice guy. It is a truism that success on the job depends less on competence in performing one's duties than it does on ability to Get Along With People. But what is left out of this statement—it is not sporting to mention it—is that the word *People* refers to just one person—the boss. And the boss, barred from receiving any obvious obeisance, is commonly in a chronic state of insecurity—what he craves most of all is the assurance that he is really and truly the boss. The nice guy, with his fine talent for the right body language, provides this assurance better than the man who is merely efficient, is rewarded accordingly, and thus sets the pace for his clumsy fellows.

7. But the despotism of the nice guy reaches its fully convoluted luxuriance when, as happens, he himself is made the boss. He has not been soft-spoken, unassertive, accommodating and eager to please out of sheer masochism. However various the motives which explain his personality, ambition is one of them. Good Old Charlie likes the idea of being a boss. And if his underlings could give him a snappy salaam every day, all might be well. But Charlie would recoil from anything so Oriental in its disrespect for human dignity. All that he expects is that his subordinates will make the same sensitive, informal adjustments to his person which he used to make for the boss, a process which practically requires that they exchange their personalities for his. Only a few of them are capable of such virtuosity—Charlie's word for it is *loyalty*—but most of them do well enough to demonstrate that it is really the nice guy in authority, more than the rambunctious one, who has made America the natural habitat of the yes-man. Of course the situation is complicated by the fact that Charlie soon becomes pitifully dependent on his loyal supporters, one of whom usually emerges as a split-personality and, like a skillful wife, sweetly dominates Charlie in all things.

8. Everybody complains that life is too competitive, but our national imagination is so limited that the principal remedies proposed for this or any other social disease are economic remedies—better jobs, better houses, and more social security. However justified on other grounds, these remedies, beyond a certain point, just hot up this particular fire, for life becomes not less competitive but decidedly more so as one moves up the ladder. Naturally. There is more to compete for. But still the fever could be brought down a few points by a modification of manners. Once men acquire everything they need—a condition soon reached in this country—they struggle primarily for recognition. But with manners as frustratingly egalitarian as they are, who knows when he has it made? Under present circumstances the ambitious can discern no resting place short of a crushing superiority of popular fame or material wealth. Hence, the devotion of many originally fine minds to Hollywood, Broadway and the medical profession.

9. Consider, for instance, the folly of our disparagement of honorific titles. If a mayor were regularly addressed as *Your Honor*, and could count on this distinction after leaving office, he would be heartened in his efforts to remain honest. As it is, he must play it democratic, pooh-pooh his title, and prepare against the day when, defeated for re-election, he must face the indifference of the public at large. Mayors are commonly corrupt, judges rarely. But judges are unfailingly objects of formal homage in office, and keep their titles for life.

10. The sobriquets which used to attach to politicians—*Old Hickory, Tennessee Johnson, The Little Giant, The Plumed Knight*—conferred distinction. They were titles of a sort and reflected a popular disposition to honor character, individuality and superior force in public men. But now the popular taste, encouraged by gee-whiz politicians who tutoyer one another in public, is for first names and demure diminutives—*Ike, Dick, Stu, Bob, Estes* and *Foster*. What makes these familiarities characteristic of our time is precisely that they ignore what is distinctive in either the personalities or the duties of the men they designate and thus suggest that government is best which is managed by Good Joes recently graduated from a basketball team. If Woodrow Wilson were in politics today, he would probably have to submit to *Woody*—if not *Willie*—and wipe that purposeful and responsible look off his face.

11. But the avoidance of titles of respect is equally the fashion among highbrows. Professors in famous universities, for instance, make fun of their fellows in teachers' colleges because the latter often call one another *professor* or *doctor*, instead of plain *mister*, and are notorious for responding benignly when their students use these terms. But on this point it is the prominent professors whose perception is defective, for an ex-

amination of their total behavior reveals that they are much less democratic than those they smile at for putting on airs. Occupying positions in institutions of outstanding prestige—positions for which they have scrambled ferociously—they can afford to underemphasize their status, like wealthy men who insist that their limousines be inconspicuously black. The fact is that they maintain great distance between town and gown and also between their students and themselves.

12. Many of them deplore their remoteness, but without an improvement of manners there is little they can do about it. Since they discourage formal acknowledgments of their status, any meeting between them and townfolk, or even between them and their own students, imposes on both sides such a strain on their respective capacities for the appropriate body language that it is almost unbearable. The man at Lower South Central Normal suffers his students to call him professor—doctor—sir— but he can often be observed chatting loftily and genially among them, snapping his suspenders the while, undisturbed by their politely impudent questions.

13. But the deprecation of titles and of formal manners in general characterizes all sorts of highbrows, not just those in universities. Yet no group in America complains so clamorously that it is not sufficiently respected and appreciated. And those among them who complain most bitterly are the ones who embrace the mucker pose passionately, not only in their speech and manners but even in their dress. This furious contradiction necessitates a furious resolution. Men who will not permit their attainments to be recognized conventionally and symbolically will seek such recognition radically and violently.

14. But democratic manners have not only promoted unnatural relations among men in their economic and professional careers. They have also corrupted relations between men and women in their romantic and domestic lives. Here, however, the democratization of manners has been one-sided. Many suitable formalities still govern the man's behavior—he follows a woman through a door, sashays around to the gutter-side of the street, etc., etc., in all of which he pays decorous tribute to her as a woman. But our culture has relieved her almost entirely of any reciprocal gestures of conventional tribute to him as a man. She does not curtsy, nor use respectful forms of address, nor stand at his shoulder when he has his picture taken. Her grandmother practiced a sweet, conventional smile. She grins, laughs uproariously, and talks in a loud voice. For her the emphasis is now completely on body language—but, unlike that used by men with their bosses, hers is *challenging* rather than deferential.

15. Since he does not receive from women any standard courtesies, courtesies which, besides telling him that just being a man is a thing of

some consequence, would remind him of his responsibilities, the American male gravitates in his dealings with women toward one of two roles —that of a little boy or that of a predator. Frequently he ricochets between the two. In the first role he simply abandons the effort to command respect as a male and, oddly enough, often becomes an abstract enthusiast for women, like a dull student whose every humiliation in class somehow increases his school spirit. In the role of predator he compels specific respect for himself as a man in the one decisive way that is still open. And, fortunately or unfortunately, such consolation has grown steadily more available. Women as well as men are symbolic creatures, and the radical elimination of ceremony reduces the human element in them and increases the animal part. Frustrated in her naturally human desire to express her feelings formally and stylistically, the American woman must express them directly and elementally.

16. But the inhuman effects of democratic manners afflict another fundamental relationship, that between parents and children. They spawn the ultimate in absurdity in those instances where parents, assuming the character of domestic politicians, encourage their youngsters to abjure the use of *mother* and *father* in favor of their parents' first names. The trouble with *mother* and *father* of course is that they suggest authority (as well as love), and thus strike an undemocratic note in the family. Often the parents' real motives, like those of tail-wagging politicians, are more complicated, for people who shun authoritative titles commonly shrink from responsibility too. But they could not persevere in this self-deception if our dedication to democratic manners did not furnish them with an exalted rationale.

17. Fortunately, this first-name business for parents is as yet limited. But manners generally are primitive enough in American homes, as anyone knows who accepts invitations from his friends to dine *en famille*. It is undemocratic to set up a children's table. It is also undemocratic to encourage children to listen to adult conversation. Parents and guests, consequently, listen to children's conversation. During intervals—when little mouths happen simultaneously to be stuffed up with food, for instance—the parents inevitably discuss the subject of children. Children, they tell you, are *people*. The children express themselves. The parents preen themselves. The only person who does not get a piece of this democracy is the guest. This lopsided egalitarianism even favors dogs and cats, with whom a guest must often cope with no assistance whatever from his host. They too, it seems, are *people*.

18. I have nearly finished. But I know that some fool—most likely, one with a Ph.D.—will read this article and forever after assert as a well-known fact that I yearn for a restoration of Tsardom, for a reinvigora-

tion of the Hindu caste system and for a truly Chinese subjugation of women and children. So let me recapitulate, in the course of which I shall add one or two points that I forgot to mention earlier.

19. A sensible system of manners, sensibly formal, performs various services. Besides acting as a constant reminder of some important facts of life, it affords human beings the distinctly human satisfactions of symbolic expression. Besides making collective living possible, it provides a person, thanks to its formalities, with protective armor against collective pressures. For these formalities allow the individual to acquiesce in the social order while reserving his final judgment of it. They enable him to pledge his loyalty to men in authority without making those fine adjustments whose long-term results are the same as those of brainwashing.

20. Democratic manners in America are eating the heart out of American democracy. With no impressive way of saluting the system, and the position which a given official occupies in it, one must prostrate himself before the man. There is a country where such prostration is even more prostrate than in America. There the humblest citizen calls his mighty ruler *comrade*.

21. I suggest a prudent reform in American manners, not a revolution. If the only alternative to egalitarian manners is a nerveless society exhausted by protocol and ceremony, then this discussion is futile. But that is not the only alternative, except in the minds of latter-day Jacobins for whom the stratifications of the *ancien regime* are more real than the proletarianizations of their own time. There are in-between solutions, attuned to reality, however they resist simple and consistent formulation, as the English know, and as America, in her own fashion, can discover. Pedantic democrats presume to speak for wisdom, creative ability and service, as against mere money in the bank. But without a rectification of manners most men would rather achieve a Cadillac than such virtues, for these virtues, unacknowledged in any regular way, do not show on a man, at least not conspicuously, whereas a Cadillac shows on anyone, conspicuously.

COMMENTARY AND QUESTIONS

Confusion between ends and means, between inner reality and outer show, is a common phenomenon. To disentangle them—to demonstrate that the latter may not automatically produce the former—often requires careful analysis and, in order to convince others of the correctness of the analysis, even more careful attention to the arts of persuasion. In this essay Morton Cronin sets out to persuade his readers that our present "democracy" of everyday etiquette does not lead to, and in fact leads away from, a true democracy of the human spirit.

1. Cronin states his proposition in the opening sentence of the essay. Though it is stated in general terms, he immediately translates one of these general phrases—*democratic manners*—into a specific example —*the practice of calling the boss by his first name.* Suggest possible reasons for choosing this particular example.

2. Many persuasive arguments rest on some fundamental assumption; Cronin states his in the third sentence of par. 2 and in the second half of the fourth sentence. In which sentences of pars. 6, 7, and 8 is this assumption echoed or restated? Find other echoes of it in the essay. What evidence does Cronin offer in support of this assumption? Under what circumstances may a controversialist be justified in not providing evidence in support of a fundamental assumption on which his argument depends?

3. Par. 2 asserts that those in authority crave recognition of their status; par. 3 reports that only one outward form of such recognition is considered acceptable in present-day American life; par. 4 makes a subsidiary assertion that this form of behavior cannot be faked. Par. 5 summarizes the situation arising from these facts, describes it in terminology which relates it to inward and outward democracy, and asserts that a reversal of the present situation is desirable. What is the function of pars. 6-17? Into what five main groups can these paragraphs be divided? Point out the means used by Cronin to provide clearly marked transitions from one group to the next. Does each of these groups use a different argumentative approach or is a similar point made by similar means in all of them?

4. A skillful controversialist anticipates the objections likely to be raised by his opponents. It is particularly important that he prevent his opponents from attacking him for holding beliefs which may seem to be implied by what he has said but which he does not in fact hold. In which paragraph does Cronin attempt to forestall this kind of attack? What is the function of each of pars. 19-21?

5. Cronin contrasts inward and outward democracy and asserts that the latter can endanger the former. This is suggested by his title; find other phrases which imply a contrast between democracy and tyranny, especially in pars. 1, 7, 8, 19, and 20. What is the point of the last sentence of par. 5?

6. Can you explain the allusions to *Old Hickory, Tennessee Johnson, The Little Giant, The Plumed Knight* (par. 10)? Remembering that this essay first appeared in 1958, during the second Eisenhower administration, can you explain the choice of nicknames in par. 10? What characteristics of Woodrow Wilson might have made *Woody* or *Willie* an inappropriate nickname? Is Cronin's illustration invalidated by the fact that President Calvin Coolidge was often referred to as "Silent Cal"?

7. The vocabulary of this essay ranges from the sophisticated to the col-

loquial, from *obeisance* (par. 6) to *bottom-waggle* (par. 3). What effect does Cronin achieve, in context, by his use of the following expressions: *palsy-walsy manners* (par. 6), *play it democratic* (par. 9), *gee-whiz politicians* (par. 10), *snapping his suspenders* (par. 12), *sashays around to the gutter-side of the street* (par. 14)? What does Cronin mean to imply about the academic standing of the hypothetical institution he refers to in par. 12 as *Lower South Central Normal?*

SUGGESTIONS FOR WRITING

1. Mr. Cronin is undemocratic.
2. The need for socially acceptable ways of recognizing and rewarding talent, status, or authority.
3. Are children people?
4. I'd rather be right than a nice guy.

The Decline of Heroes

by ARTHUR M. SCHLESINGER, JR.

OURS IS AN AGE without heroes—and, when we say this, we suddenly realize how spectacularly the world has changed in a generation. Most of us grew up in a time of towering personalities. For better or for worse, great men seemed to dominate our lives and shape our destiny. In the United States we had Theodore Roosevelt, Woodrow Wilson, Franklin Roosevelt. In Great Britain, there were Lloyd George and Winston Churchill. In other lands, there were Lenin, Stalin, Hitler, Mussolini, Clemenceau, Gandhi, Kemal, Sun Yat-sen. Outside of politics there were Einstein, Freud, Keynes. Some of these great men influenced the world for good, others for evil; but, whether for good or for evil, the fact that each had not died at birth made a difference, one believed, to everyone who lived after them.

From *Adventures of the Mind* (New York: Vintage Books, 1960). Originally published as "The Decline of Greatness" in *The Saturday Evening Post*, November 1, 1958. By permission of the author. Copyright © 1958 The Curtis Publishing Company.

2. Today no one bestrides our narrow world like a colossus; we have no giants who play roles which one can imagine no one else playing in their stead. There are a few figures on the margin of uniqueness, perhaps: Adenauer, Nehru, Tito, De Gaulle, Chiang Kai-shek, Mao Tse-tung. But there seem to be none in the epic style of those mighty figures of our recent past who seized history with both hands and gave it an imprint, even a direction, which it otherwise might not have had. As De Gaulle himself remarked on hearing of Stalin's death, "The age of giants is over." Whatever one thought, whether one admired or detested Roosevelt or Churchill, Stalin or Hitler, one nevertheless felt the sheer weight of such personalities on one's own existence. We feel no comparable pressures today. Our own President, with all his pleasant qualities, has more or less explicitly renounced any desire to impress his own views on history. The Macmillans, Khrushchevs and Gronchis have measurably less specific gravity than their predecessors. Other men could be in their places as leaders of America or Britain or Russia or Italy without any change in the course of history. Why ours should thus be an age without heroes, and whether this condition is good or bad for us and for civilization, are topics worthy of investigation.

3. Why have giants vanished from our midst? One must never neglect the role of accident in history; and accident no doubt plays a part here. But too many accidents of the same sort cease to be wholly accidental. One must inquire further. Why should our age not only be without great men but even seem actively hostile to them? Surely one reason we have so few heroes now is precisely that we had so many a generation ago. Greatness is hard for common humanity to bear. As Emerson said, "Heroism means difficulty, postponement of praise, postponement of ease, introduction of the world into the private apartment, introduction of eternity into the hours measured by the sitting-room clock." A world of heroes keeps people from living their own private lives.

4. Moreover, great men live dangerously. They introduce extremes into existence—extremes of good, extremes of evil—and ordinary men after a time flinch from the ultimates and yearn for undemanding security. The Second World War was the climax of an epoch of living dangerously. It is no surprise that it precipitated a universal revulsion against greatness. The war itself destroyed Hitler and Mussolini. And the architects of victory were hardly longer-lived. After the war, the British repudiated Churchill, and the Americans (with the adoption of the 22nd Amendment), Roosevelt. In due course, the French repudiated De Gaulle (they later repented, but it took the threat of civil war to bring him back); the Chinese, Chiang Kai-shek; and the Russians, Stalin.

Khrushchev, in toppling Stalin from his pedestal, pronounced the general verdict against the uncommon man: the modern world, he said, had no use for the "cult of the individual." And, indeed, carried to the excesses to which the worshipers of Hitler and Stalin carried it, even to the much milder degree to which admirers of Roosevelt and Churchill sometimes carried it, the cult of the individual was dangerous. No man is infallible, and every man needs to be reminded of this on occasion. Still, our age has gone further than this—it objects not just to hero worship but to heroes. The century of the common man has come into its own.

5. This term, "common man," suggests the deeper problem. There is more involved than simply a dismissal of those colossi whom the world identified with a season of blood and agony. The common man has always regarded the great man with mixed feelings—resentment as well as admiration, hatred as well as love. The Athenian who refused to vote for Aristides because he was so tired of hearing him called "the Just" expressed a natural reaction. Great men make small men aware of their smallness. Rancor is one of the unavowed but potent emotions of politics; and one must never forget that the envy of the have-nots can be quite as consuming when the haves have character or intelligence as it is when they have merely material possessions.

6. Modern democracy inadvertently gave envy new scope. While the purpose of democracy was to give everyone a fair chance to rise, its method enabled rancorous men to invoke "equality" as an excuse for keeping all down to their own level. "I attribute the small number of distinguished men in political life," wrote Alexis de Tocqueville after visiting the United States in the 1830's, "to the ever-increasing despotism of the majority. . . . The power of the majority is so absolute and irresistible that one must give up one's rights as a citizen and almost abjure one's qualities as a human being, if one intends to stray from the track which it prescribes." James Bryce even titled a chapter in his American Commonwealth, Why Great Men Are Not Chosen President.

7. History has shown these prophets unduly pessimistic. Distinguished men do enter American politics; great men have been chosen President. Democracy demonstrates a capability for heroic leadership quite as much as it does a tendency toward mediocrity. Yet Tocqueville and the others were correct enough in detecting the dislike of great men as a permanent potentiality in a democracy. And the evolution of industrial society appears to have given this sentiment new force. More and more of us live and work within great organizations; an influential book has already singled out the organization man as the American of the future. The bureaucratization of American life, the decline of the working class, the growth of the white-collar class, the rise of suburbia—all

this has meant the increasing homogeneity of American society. Though we continue to speak of ourselves as rugged individualists, our actual life has grown more and more collective and anonymous. As a Monsanto Chemical film put it, showing a group of technicians at work in a laboratory: "No geniuses here; just a bunch of average Americans working together." Our ideal is increasingly smooth absorption into the group rather than self-realization in the old-fashioned, strong-minded, don't-give-a-damn sense. Where does the great man fit into our homogenized society?

8. "The greatness of England is now all collective," John Stuart Mill wrote a century ago: "individually small, we only appear capable of anything great by our habit of combining." He might have been writing about contemporary America; but where we Americans are inclined to rejoice over the superiority of the "team," Mill added somberly, "It was men of another stamp than this that made England what it has been; and men of another stamp will be needed to prevent its decline."

9. But was Mill right? Do individuals really have impact on history? A powerful school of philosophers has denied any importance at all to great men. Such thinkers reject heroes as a childish hangover from the days when men ascribed everything to the action of gods. History, they assert, is not made by men, but by inexorable forces or irrevocable laws: if these forces or laws do not manifest themselves through one individual, they will do so through another. What has happened already has comprehensively and absolutely decided what will happen in the future. "If there is a single human action due to free will," wrote Tolstoi, "no historical law exists, and no conception of historical events can be formed." If all this is so, obviously the presence or absence of any particular "hero" at any particular time cannot make the slightest difference.

10. This view of history is a form of fatalistic determinism; and Tolstoi's War and Peace offers one of its most eloquent statements. Why, Tolstoi asked, did millions of men in the time of Napoleon, repudiating their common sense and their human feelings, move from west to east, slaughtering their fellows? The answers provided by historians seemed to him hopelessly superficial. His own answer was: "The war was bound to happen simply because it was bound to happen"; all previous history predetermined it. Where did this leave the great men? In Tolstoi's view, they were the most deluded figures of all. Great men, he said, "are but the labels that serve to give a name to an event and, like labels, they have the least possible connection with the event itself." The greater the man, "the more conspicuous is the inevitability and predestination of every act he commits." The hero, said Tolstoi, "is the slave of history."

11. There are many forms of historical fatalism. Toynbee and Spen-

gler, with their theory of the inexorable growth and decay of civilizations, represent one form. The Marxists, with their theory that changes in the modes of production control the course of history, represent another. When Khrushchev denounced the practice of making "a hero" out of "a particular leader" and condemned the cult of the individual as "alien to the spirit of Marxism-Leninism," he was speaking the true spirit of his faith. And Marxism is not the only form of economic determinism; there are also, for example, economic determinists of the laissez-faire school who believe that all civilization is dependent on rigid adherence to a certain theory of the sacredness of private property.

12. Fatalists differ greatly among themselves. But, however much they differ, they unite in the conclusion that the individual plays no role of his own in history. If they are right, then nothing could matter less whether or not this is an age without heroes.

13. But they are not right. The philosophy of historical fatalism rests on serious fallacies. For one thing, it supposes that, because a thing happens, it had to happen. But causation is one matter; predestination another. The construction of a causal explanation after an event merely renders that event in some sense intelligible. It does not in the least show that this particular event, and no other, had to take place; that nothing else could possibly have occurred in its stead. The serious test of the fatalist case must be applied before the event. The only conclusive proof of fatalism would lie in the accurate prediction of events that have not yet happened. And to say, with Tolstoi, that all prior history predetermines everything that follows is to say nothing at all. It is to produce an explanation which applies equally to everything—and thus becomes so vague and limitless as to explain nothing.

14. Fatalism raises other difficulties. Thus it imputes reality to mystical historical "forces"—class, race, nation, the will of the people, the spirit of the times, history itself. But there are no such forces. They are merely abstractions or metaphors with no existence except in the mind of the beholder. The only evidence for them is deduction from the behavior of individuals. It is therefore the individual who constitutes the basic unit of history. And, while no individual can be wholly free—and, indeed, recent discoveries of the manifold ways in which we are unconsciously conditioned should constitute a salutary check on human vanity—one must assume the reality of an area of free choice until that assumption is challenged, not by metaphysical affirmation, but by verifiable proof—that is, consistently accurate prediction of the future.

15. Fatalism, moreover, is incompatible with human psychology and human morality. Anyone who rigorously accepted a deterministic view of life, for example, would have to abandon all notions of human respon-

sibility, since it is manifestly unfair to praise or punish people for acts which are by definition beyond their control. But such fatalism is belied by the assumption of free choice which underlies every move we make, every word we utter, every thought we think. As Sir Isaiah Berlin observes of determinism, "If we begin to take it seriously, then, indeed, the changes in our language, our moral notions, our attitudes toward one another, our views of history, of society and of everything else will be too profound to be even adumbrated." We can no more imagine what the universe of the consistent determinist would be like than we can imagine what it would be like to live in a world without time or one with seventeen-dimensional space.

16. For the historian concerned with concrete interpretation of actual events, he can easily demonstrate the futility of fatalism by trying to apply it to specific historical episodes. According to the extreme determinist view, no particular individual can make the slightest difference. As slaves of history, all individuals are, so to speak, interchangeable parts. If Napoleon had not led his armies across Europe, Tolstoi implies, someone else would have. William James, combating this philosophic fatalism, once asked the determinists whether they really believed "the convergence of sociological pressures to have so impinged on Stratford on Avon about April 23, 1564, that a W. Shakespeare, with all his mental peculiarities, had to be born there." And did they further believe, James continued, that "if the aforesaid W. Shakespeare had died of cholera infantum, another mother at Stratford on Avon would needs have engendered a duplicate copy of him to restore the sociologic equilibrium?" Who could believe such stuff? Yet, if the determinists do not mean exactly this, how can they read the individual out of history?

17. In December, 1931, a British politician, crossing Fifth Avenue in New York between 76th and 77th streets around ten-thirty at night, was knocked down and gravely injured by an automobile. Fourteen months later an American politician, sitting in an open car in Miami, Florida, was fired on by an assassin; a man standing beside him was killed. Would the next two decades of history have been the same had Contasini's car killed Winston Churchill in 1931 and Zangara's bullets killed Franklin Roosevelt in 1933? Suppose, in addition, that Adolf Hitler had been killed in the street fighting during the Munich *Putsch* of 1923, and that Lenin and Mussolini had died at birth. Where would our century be now?

18. Individuals, of course, must operate within limits. They cannot do everything. They cannot, for example, propel history into directions for which the environment and the human material are not prepared: no genius, however heroic, could have brought television to ancient

Troy. Yet, as Sidney Hook has convincingly argued in his thoughtful book, The Hero in History, great men can count decisively "where the historical situation permits of major alternative paths of development."

19. This argument between fatalism and heroism is not one on which there is a lot to be said on both sides. The issue is far too sharp to be straddled. Either history is rigidly determined and foreordained, in which case individual striving does not matter; or it is not, in which case there is an essential role for the hero. Analysis of concrete episodes suggests that history is, within limits, open and unfinished; that men have lived who did what no substitute could ever have done; that their intervention set history on one path rather than another. If this is so, the old maxim, "There are no indispensable men," would seem another amiable fallacy. There is, then, a case for heroes.

20. To say that there is a case for heroes is not to say that there is a case for hero worship. The surrender of decision, the unquestioning submission to leadership, the prostration of the average man before the Great Man—these are the diseases of heroism, and they are fatal to human dignity. But, if carried too far, hero worship generates its own antidote. "Every hero," said Emerson, "becomes a bore at last." And we need not go too far. History amply shows that it is possible to have heroes without turning them into gods.

21. And history shows, too, that when a society, in flight from hero worship, decides to do without great men at all, it gets into troubles of its own. Our contemporary American society, for example, has little use for the individualist. Individualism implies dissent from the group; dissent implies conflict; and conflict suddenly seems divisive, un-American and generally unbearable. Our greatest new industry is evidently the production of techniques to eliminate conflict, from positive thoughts through public relations to psychoanalysis, applied everywhere from the couch to the pulpit. Our national aspiration has become peace of mind, peace of soul. The symptomatic drug of our age is the tranquilizer. "Togetherness" is the banner under which we march into the brave new world.

22. Obviously society has had to evolve collective institutions to cope with problems that have grown increasingly complex and concentrated. But the collective approach can be overdone. If Khrushchev worried because his collectivist society developed a cult of the individual, maybe we Americans should start worrying as our so-called individualist society develops a cult of the group. We instinctively suppose that the tough questions will be solved by an interfaith conference or an interdisciplinary research team or an interdepartmental committee or an assembly of wise men meeting at Arden House. But are not these group tactics essen-

tially means by which individuals hedge their bets and distribute their responsibilities? And do they not nearly always result in the dilution of insight and the triumph of mish-mash? If we are to survive, we must have ideas, vision, courage. These things are rarely produced by committees. Everything that matters in our intellectual and moral life begins with an individual confronting his own mind and conscience in a room by himself.

23. A bland society will never be creative. "The amount of eccentricity in a society," said John Stuart Mill, "has generally been proportional to the amount of genius, mental vigor and moral courage it contained. That so few now dare to be eccentric marks the chief danger of the time." If this condition frightened Mill in Victorian England, it should frighten us much more. For our national apotheosis of the group means that we systematically lop off the eccentrics, the originals, the proud, imaginative, lonely people from whom new ideas come. What began as a recoil from hero worship ends as a conspiracy against creativity. If worship of great men brings us to perdition by one path, flight from great men brings us there just as surely by another. When we do not admire great men, then our instinct for admiration is likely to end by settling on ourselves. The one thing worse for democracy than hero worship is self-worship.

24. A free society cannot get along without heroes, because they are the most vivid means of exhibiting the power of free men. The hero exposes to all mankind unsuspected possibilities of conception, unimagined resources of strength. "The appearance of a great man," wrote Emerson, "draws a new circle outside of our largest orbit and surprises and commands us." Carlyle likened ordinary, lethargic times, with their unbelief and perplexity, to dry, dead fuel, waiting for the lightning out of heaven to kindle it. "The great man, with his free force direct out of God's own hand, is the lightning. . . . The rest of men waited for him like fuel, and then they too would flame."

25. Great men enable us to rise to our own highest potentialities. They nerve lesser men to disregard the world and trust to their own deepest instinct. "In picking out from history our heroes," said William James, "each one of us may best fortify and inspire what creative energy may lie in his own soul. This is the last justification of hero worship." Which one of us has not gained fortitude and faith from the incarnation of ideals in men, from the wisdom of Socrates, from the wondrous creativity of Shakespeare, from the strength of Washington, from the compassion of Lincoln, and above all, perhaps, from the life and the death of Jesus? "We feed on genius," said Emerson. "Great men exist that there may be greater men."

26. Yet this may be only the smaller part of their service. Great men have another and larger role—to affirm human freedom against the supposed inevitabilities of history. The first hero was Prometheus, who defied the gods and thus asserted the independence and autonomy of man against all determinism. Zeus punished Prometheus, chaining him to a rock and encouraging a vulture to pluck at his vitals.

27. Ever since, man, like Prometheus, has warred against history. It has always been a bitter and remorseless fight; for the heavy weight of human inertia lies with fatalism. It takes a man of exceptional vision and strength and will—it takes, in short, a hero—to try to wrench history from what lesser men consider its preconceived path. And often history tortures the hero in the process, chains him to a rock and exposes him to the vulture. Yet, in the model of Prometheus, man can still hold his own against the gods. Brave men earn the right to shape their own destiny.

28. An age without great men is one which acquiesces in the drift of history. Such acquiescence is easy and seductive; the great appeal of fatalism, indeed, is as a refuge from the terror of responsibility. Where a belief in great men insistently reminds us that individuals can make a difference, fatalism reassures us that they can't. It thereby blesses our weakness and extenuates our failure. Fatalism, in Berlin's phrase, is "one of the great alibis" of history.

29. Let us not be complacent about our supposed capacity to get along without great men. If our society has lost its wish for heroes and its ability to produce them, it may well turn out to have lost everything else as well.

COMMENTARY AND QUESTIONS

As an American historian, essayist, and political activist, Arthur M. Schlesinger, Jr., has been in an excellent position to use his knowledge of the past as a means of judging the present. The essay here reprinted was written as part of a series published during 1958 and following years in a mass-circulation magazine; a series in which a large number of contemporary writers and scholars were invited to discuss matters such as art, religion, and society which interested them and which presumably might also be of interest to those readers who had minds to think with and the urge to use them. In other words, these were intellectual discussions aimed at the more intellectual fraction of a national audience.

Persuasive essays are often intended to move readers to a particular course of action: to study foreign languages, abolish athletics, or revive honorific titles. Others, like this one, are designed simply to

change attitudes. Since present attitudes shape future action, both types
of persuasion may be equally important.

1. In his first eight paragraphs, Schlesinger not only tells us that heroes
   have disappeared from today's world but suggests possible reasons
   for the disappearance. Most of the rest of the essay is a refutation
   of two notions with which Schlesinger strongly disagrees: that heroes
   can have no effect on history (the doctrine of historical fatalism), and
   that heroes today are not really needed. In which paragraphs does
   he refute the first notion? Why does he take the trouble to point out
   four or five alleged fallacies in the doctrine of fatalism, all more or
   less independent of each other? How does he provide a transition from
   his refutation of fatalism to his assertion of the need for heroes? What
   is the function of par. 20?

2. In pars. 7-8 Schlesinger notes the tendency of American society to
   grow "more and more collective and anonymous." In view of the fact
   that these paragraphs follow immediately on the discussion in pars.
   5-6 of the common man's envy of the great man and the pessimistic
   interpretations of Tocqueville and Bryce, how do you think Schlesinger means his readers to view the tendency analyzed in pars. 7-8?
   Does the phrase *homogenized society* in the last sentence of par. 7
   have quite the same flavor as *the increasing homogeneity of society*
   in the seventh sentence? What effect does Schlesinger gain from this
   earlier discussion when he returns to a consideration of the "collective approach" in pars. 21-23?

3. Having disposed of the doctrine of historical fatalism (since there is
   obviously no point in discussing the need for heroes if heroes can have
   no effect on history), Schlesinger then attacks the belief that we do
   not need heroes by a common variety of twofold argumentative strategy. In pars. 21-23 he discusses the effect on society of not having
   heroes; in pars. 24-27 he discusses the effect of having them. Why did
   he not reverse the order of these two halves of his argument? Pars.
   21-23 contain a number of mildly satiric expressions, such as *Our
   greatest new industry* (par. 21), *the triumph of mish-mash* (par. 22),
   a conspiracy against creativity (par. 23). Point out other phrases and
   sentences in these three paragraphs that have a similar flavor. Why
   is the flavor of the language in pars. 24-27 quite different?

4. The heroes of an earlier generation mentioned in par. 1 have obviously been chosen so as to be probably recognizable to any reasonably
   well informed citizen of middle age or older; and the modern "figures
   on the margin of uniqueness" listed in par. 2 are pretty sure to be familiar to any reasonably well informed contemporary adult. Later
   on in the essay Schlesinger refers to, or quotes, such men as Tocqueville, Bryce, J. S. Mill, Tolstoi, Toynbee, Spengler, Sir Isaiah Berlin,
   William James, Sidney Hook, Emerson, and Carlyle. Discuss the appropriateness, considering the nature of the essay and the audience

for which it was intended, of such references. How far do Schlesinger's arguments depend on recognition by his readers of any one of these names? Why, although he gives no hint that the first sentence of par. 2 echoes a pair of lines from *Julius Caesar*, does he take the trouble in par. 26 to mention all the pertinent details of the legend of Prometheus, which is at least as well known as this particular quotation from Shakespeare?

5. Schlesinger begins his essay with the pithy and attention-catching statement, "Ours is an age without heroes"; and, although he avoids here the more showy pyrotechnics of style, much of the essay's cogency comes from the precision and force of such epigrammatic statements as "Great men make small men aware of their smallness" (par. 5) or ". . . the great appeal of fatalism, indeed, is as a refuge from the terror of responsibility" (par. 28). Find other felicities of phrasing. Why did Schlesinger say that "The Macmillans, Krushchevs and Gronchis have measurably less specific gravity than their predecessors" (par. 2) rather than "The statesmen of today are of lighter weight than those of an earlier age"?

SUGGESTIONS FOR WRITING

1. How can heroes arise in an unheroic world?
2. Second thoughts on the team approach.
3. The century of the common man.
4. "Every hero becomes a bore at last."

Dunkirk

by SIR WINSTON CHURCHILL

FROM THE MOMENT that the French defenses at Sedan and on the Meuse were broken at the end of the second week of May, only a rapid retreat to Amiens and the south could have saved the British and French Armies who had entered Belgium at the appeal of the Belgian King;

Reprinted by permission of G. P. Putnam's Sons from *Blood, Sweat and Tears* by Winston S. Churchill. Copyright 1941 by Winston S. Churchill. Permission also granted by McClelland and Stewart, Limited, Publishers.

but this strategic fact was not immediately realized. The French High Command hoped they would be able to close the gap, and the Armies of the north were under their orders. Moreover, a retirement of this kind would have involved almost certainly the destruction of the fine Belgian Army of over 20 divisions and the abandonment of the whole of Belgium. Therefore, when the force and scope of the German penetration were realized and when a new French Generalissimo, General Weygand, assumed command in place of General Gamelin, an effort was made by the French and British Armies in Belgium to keep on holding the right hand of the Belgians and to give their own right hand to a newly created French Army which was to have advanced across the Somme in great strength to grasp it.

2. However, the German eruption swept like a sharp scythe around the right and rear of the Armies of the north. Eight or nine armored divisions, each of about four hundred armored vehicles of different kinds, but carefully assorted to be complementary and divisible into small self-contained units, cut off all communications between us and the main French Armies. It severed our own communications for food and ammunition, which ran first to Amiens and afterwards through Abbeville, and it shore its way up the coast to Boulogne and Calais, and almost to Dunkirk. Behind this armored and mechanized onslaught came a number of German divisions in lorries, and behind them again there plodded comparatively slowly the dull brute mass of the ordinary German Army and German people, always so ready to be led to the trampling down in other lands of liberties and comforts which they have never known in their own.

3. I have said this armored scythe-stroke almost reached Dunkirk—almost but not quite. Boulogne and Calais were the scenes of desperate fighting. The Guards defended Boulogne for a while and were then withdrawn by orders from this country. The Rifle Brigade, the 60th Rifles, and the Queen Victoria's Rifles, with a battalion of British tanks and 1,000 Frenchmen, in all about four thousand strong, defended Calais to the last. The British Brigadier was given an hour to surrender. He spurned the offer, and four days of intense street fighting passed before silence reigned over Calais, which marked the end of a memorable resistance. Only 30 unwounded survivors were brought off by the Navy, and we do not know the fate of their comrades. Their sacrifice, however, was not in vain. At least two armored divisions, which otherwise would have been turned against the British Expeditionary Force, had to be sent to overcome them. They have added another page to the glories of the light divisions, and the time gained enabled the Graveline water lines to be flooded and to be held by the French troops.

4. Thus it was that the port of Dunkirk was kept open. When it was found impossible for the Armies of the north to reopen their communications to Amiens with the main French Armies, only one choice remained. It seemed, indeed, forlorn. The Belgian, British and French Armies were almost surrounded. Their sole line of retreat was to a single port and to its neighboring beaches. They were pressed on every side by heavy attacks and far outnumbered in the air.

5. When, a week ago today, I asked the House to fix this afternoon as the occasion for a statement, I feared it would be my hard lot to announce the greatest military disaster in our long history. I thought— and some good judges agreed with me—that perhaps 20,000 or 30,000 men might be re-embarked. But it certainly seemed that the whole of the French First Army and the whole of the British Expeditionary Force north of the Amiens-Abbeville gap would be broken up in the open field or else would have to capitulate for lack of food and ammunition. These were the hard and heavy tidings for which I called upon the House and the nation to prepare themselves a week ago. The whole root and core and brain of the British Army, on which and around which we were to build, and are to build, the great British Armies in the later years of the war, seemed about to perish upon the field or to be led into an ignominious and starving captivity.

6. That was the prospect a week ago. But another blow which might well have proved final was yet to fall upon us. The King of the Belgians had called upon us to come to his aid. Had not this Ruler and his Government severed themselves from the Allies, who rescued their country from extinction in the late war, and had they not sought refuge in what has proved to be a fatal neutrality, the French and British Armies might well at the outset have saved not only Belgium but perhaps even Poland. Yet at the last moment, when Belgium was already invaded, King Leopold called upon us to come to his aid, and even at the last moment we came. He and his brave, efficient Army, nearly half a million strong, guarded our left flank and thus kept open our only line of retreat to the sea. Suddenly, without prior consultation, with the least possible notice, without the advice of his Ministers and upon his own personal act, he sent a plenipotentiary to the German Command, surrendered his Army, and exposed our whole flank and means of retreat.

7. I asked the House a week ago to suspend its judgment because the facts were not clear, but I do not feel that any reason now exists why we should not form our own opinions upon this pitiful episode. The surrender of the Belgian Army compelled the British at the shortest notice to cover a flank to the sea more than 30 miles in length. Otherwise all would have been cut off, and all would have shared the fate to which King Leo-

pold had condemned the finest Army his country had ever formed. So in doing this and in exposing this flank, as anyone who followed the operations on the map will see, contact was lost between the British and two out of the three corps forming the First French Army, who were still farther from the coast than we were, and it seemed impossible that any large number of Allied troops could reach the coast.

8. The enemy attacked on all sides with great strength and fierceness, and their main power, the power of their far more numerous Air Force, was thrown into the battle or else concentrated upon Dunkirk and the beaches. Pressing in upon the narrow exit, both from the east and from the west, the enemy began to fire with cannon upon the beaches by which alone the shipping could approach or depart. They sowed magnetic mines in the channels and seas; they sent repeated waves of hostile aircraft, sometimes more than a hundred strong in one formation, to cast their bombs upon the single pier that remained, and upon the sand dunes upon which the troops had their eyes for shelter. Their U-boats, one of which was sunk, and their motor launches took their toll of the vast traffic which now began. For four or five days an intense struggle reigned. All their armored divisions—or what was left of them—together with great masses of infantry and artillery, hurled themselves in vain upon the ever-narrowing, ever-contracting appendix within which the British and French Armies fought.

9. Meanwhile, the Royal Navy, with the willing help of countless merchant seamen, strained every nerve to embark the British and Allied troops; 220 light warships and 650 other vessels were engaged. They had to operate upon the difficult coast, often in adverse weather, under an almost ceaseless hail of bombs and an increasing concentration of artillery fire. Nor were the seas, as I have said, themselves free from mines and torpedoes. It was in conditions such as these that our men carried on, with little or no rest, for days and nights on end, making trip after trip across the dangerous waters, bringing with them always men whom they had rescued. The numbers they have brought back are the measure of their devotion and their courage. The hospital ships, which brought off many thousands of British and French wounded, being so plainly marked were a special target for Nazi bombs; but the men and women on board them never faltered in their duty.

10. Meanwhile, the Royal Air Force, which had already been intervening in the battle, so far as its range would allow, from home bases, now used part of its main metropolitan fighter strength, and struck at the German bombers and at the fighters which in large numbers protected them. This struggle was protracted and fierce. Suddenly, the scene has cleared, the crash and thunder has for the moment—but only for the

moment—died away. A miracle of deliverance, achieved by valor, by perseverance, by perfect discipline, by faultless service, by resource, by skill, by unconquerable fidelity, is manifest to us all. The enemy was hurled back by the retreating British and French troops. He was so roughly handled that he did not hurry their departure seriously. The Royal Air Force engaged the main strength of the German Air Force, and inflicted upon them losses of at least four to one; and the Navy, using nearly 1,000 ships of all kinds, carried over 335,000 men, French and British, out of the jaws of death and shame, to their native land and to the tasks which lie immediately ahead. We must be very careful not to assign to this deliverance the attributes of a victory. Wars are not won by evacuations. But there was a victory inside this deliverance, which should be noted. It was gained by the Air Force. Many of our soldiers coming back have not seen the Air Force at work; they saw only the bombers which escaped its protective attack. They underrate its achievements. I have heard much talk of this; that is why I go out of my way to say this. I will tell you about it.

11. This was a great trial of strength between the British and German Air Forces. Can you conceive a greater objective for the Germans in the air than to make evacuation from these beaches impossible, and to sink all these ships which were displayed, almost to the extent of thousands? Could there have been an objective of greater military importance and significance for the whole purpose of the war than this? They tried hard, and they were beaten back; they were frustrated in their task. We got the Army away; and they have paid fourfold for any losses which they have inflicted. Very large formations of German aeroplanes—and we know that they are a very brave race—have turned on several occasions from the attack of one-quarter of their number of the Royal Air Force, and have dispersed in different directions. Twelve aeroplanes have been hunted by two. One aeroplane was driven into the water and cast away by the mere charge of a British aeroplane, which had no more ammunition. All of our types—the Hurricane, the Spitfire and the new Defiant— and all our pilots have been vindicated as superior to what they have at present to face.

12. When we consider how much greater would be our advantage in defending the air above this Island against an overseas attack, I must say that I find in these facts a sure basis upon which practical and reassuring thoughts may rest. I will pay my tribute to these young airmen. The great French Army was very largely, for the time being, cast back and disturbed by the onrush of a few thousands of armored vehicles. May it not also be that the cause of civilization itself will be defended by the skill and devotion of a few thousand airmen? There never has been, I sup-

pose, in all the world, in all the history of war, such an opportunity for youth. The Knights of the Round Table, the Crusaders, all fall back into the past—not only distant but prosaic; these young men, going forth every morn to guard their native land and all that we stand for, holding in their hands these instruments of colossal and shattering power, of whom it may be said that

> "Every morn brought forth a noble chance
> And every chance brought forth a noble knight,"*

deserve our gratitude, as do all of the brave men who, in so many ways and on so many occasions, are ready, and continue ready, to give life and all for their native land.

13. I return to the Army. In the long series of very fierce battles, now on this front, now on that, fighting on three fronts at once, battles fought by two or three divisions against an equal or somewhat larger number of the enemy, and fought fiercely on some of the old grounds that so many of us knew so well—in these battles our losses in men have exceeded 30,000 killed, wounded and missing. I take occasion to express the sympathy of the House to all who have suffered bereavement or who are still anxious. The President of the Board of Trade[1] is not here today. His son has been killed, and many in the House have felt the pangs of affliction in the sharpest form. But I will say this about the missing: We have had a large number of wounded come home safely to this country, but I would say about the missing that there may be very many reported missing who will come back home, some day, in one way or another. In the confusion of this fight it is inevitable that many have been left in positions where honor required no further resistance from them.

14. Against this loss of over 30,000 men, we can set a far heavier loss certainly inflicted upon the enemy. But our losses in material are enormous. We have perhaps lost one-third of the men we lost in the opening days of the battle of 21st March, 1918, but we have lost nearly as many guns—nearly one thousand—and all our transport, all the armored vehicles that were with the Army in the north. This loss will impose a further delay on the expansion of our military strength. That expansion had not been proceeding as fast as we had hoped. The best of all we had to give had gone to the British Expeditionary Force, and although they had not the numbers of tanks and some articles of equipment which were desirable, they were a very well and finely equipped army. They had the first-fruits of all that our industry had to give, and that is gone. And now here is this further delay. How long it will be, how long it will last, depends upon the exertions which we make in this Island. An effort the like of

---

* See Tennyson's *Morte d'Arthur*, ll. 230-231.
[1] Sir Andrew Duncan, now [1941] Minister of Supply.

which has never been seen in our records is now being made. Work is proceeding everywhere, night and day, Sundays and week days. Capital and Labor have cast aside their interests, rights, and customs and put them into the common stock. Already the flow of munitions has leaped forward. There is no reason why we should not in a few months overtake the sudden and serious loss that has come upon us, without retarding the development of our general program.

15. Nevertheless, our thankfulness at the escape of our Army and so many men, whose loved ones have passed through an agonizing week, must not blind us to the fact that what has happened in France and Belgium is a colossal military disaster. The French Army has been weakened, the Belgian Army has been lost, a large part of those fortified lines upon which so much faith had been reposed is gone, many valuable mining districts and factories have passed into the enemy's possession, the whole of the Channel ports are in his hands, with all the tragic consequences that follow from that, and we must expect another blow to be struck almost immediately at us or at France. We are told that Herr Hitler has a plan for invading the British Isles. This has often been thought of before. When Napoleon lay at Boulogne for a year with his flat-bottomed boats and his Grand Army, he was told by someone, "There are bitter weeds in England." There are certainly a great many more of them since the British Expeditionary Force returned.

16. The whole question of home defense against invasion is, of course, powerfully affected by the fact that we have for the time being in this Island incomparably more powerful military forces than we have ever had at any moment in this war or the last. But this will not continue. We shall not be content with a defensive war. We have our duty to our Ally. We have to reconstitute and build up the British Expeditionary Force once again, under its gallant Commander-in-Chief, Lord Gort. All this is in train; but in the interval we must put our defenses in this Island into such a high state of organization that the fewest possible numbers will be required to give effective security and that the largest possible potential of offensive effort may be realized. On this we are now engaged. It will be very convenient, if it be the desire of the House, to enter upon this subject in a secret Session. Not that the Government would necessarily be able to reveal in very great detail military secrets, but we like to have our discussions free, without the restraint imposed by the fact that they will be read the next day by the enemy; and the Government would benefit by views freely expressed in all parts of the House by Members with their knowledge of so many different parts of the country. I understand that some request is to be made upon this subject, which will be readily acceded to by His Majesty's Government.

17. We have found it necessary to take measures of increasing strin-

gency, not only against enemy aliens and suspicious characters of other nationalities, but also against British subjects who may become a danger or a nuisance should the war be transported to the United Kingdom. I know there are a great many people affected by the orders which we have made who are the passionate enemies of Nazi Germany. I am very sorry for them, but we cannot, at the present time and under the present stress, draw all the distinctions which we should like to do. If parachute landings were attempted and fierce fighting attendant upon them followed, these unfortunate people would be far better out of the way, for their own sakes as well as for ours. There is, however, another class, for which I feel not the slightest sympathy. Parliament has given us the powers to put down Fifth Column activities with a strong hand, and we shall use those powers, subject to the supervision and correction of the House, without the slightest hesitation until we are satisfied, and more than satisfied, that this malignancy in our midst has been effectively stamped out.

^{18.} Turning once again, and this time more generally, to the question of invasion, I would observe that there has never been a period in all these long centuries of which we boast when an absolute guarantee against invasion, still less against serious raids, could have been given to our people. In the days of Napoleon the same wind which would have carried his transports across the Channel might have driven away the blockading fleet. There was always the chance, and it is that chance which has excited and befooled the imaginations of many Continental tyrants. Many are the tales that are told. We are assured that novel methods will be adopted, and when we see the originality of malice, the ingenuity of aggression, which our enemy displays, we may certainly prepare ourselves for every kind of novel strategem and every kind of brutal and treacherous maneuver. I think that no idea is so outlandish that it should not be considered and viewed with a searching, but at the same time, I hope, with a steady eye. We must never forget the solid assurances of sea power and those which belong to air power if it can be locally exercised.

^{19.} I have, myself, full confidence that if all do their duty, if nothing is neglected, and if the best arrangements are made, as they are being made, we shall prove ourselves once again able to defend our Island home, to ride out the storm of war, and to outlive the menace of tyranny, if necessary for years, if necessary alone. At any rate, that is what we are going to try to do. That is the resolve of His Majesty's Government—every man of them. That is the will of Parliament and the nation. The British Empire and the French Republic, linked together in their cause and in their need, will defend to the death their native soil, aiding each

other like good comrades to the utmost of their strength. Even though large tracts of Europe and many old and famous States have fallen or may fall into the grip of the Gestapo and all the odious apparatus of Nazi rule, we shall not flag or fail. We shall go on to the end, we shall fight in France, we shall fight on the seas and oceans, we shall fight with growing confidence and growing strength in the air, we shall defend our Island, whatever the cost may be, we shall fight on the beaches, we shall fight on the landing grounds, we shall fight in the fields and in the streets, we shall fight in the hills; we shall never surrender, and even if, which I do not for a moment believe, this Island or a large part of it were subjugated and starving, then our Empire beyond the seas, armed and guarded by the British Fleet, would carry on the struggle, until, in God's good time, the New World, with all its power and might, steps forth to the rescue and the liberation of the old.

COMMENTARY AND QUESTIONS

On June 4, 1940, the Right Honorable Winston S. Churchill, prime minister of Great Britain, gave to the House of Commons his report on the evacuation of French and British troops from the coast of France. For days, as the German forces attacked on all sides with all weapons, hundreds of boats, from small private motor cruisers and fishing smacks to warships of the British Navy, had dodged back and forth across the English Channel, plucking the remnants of the Allied armies off the Dunkirk beaches. They had finished their work early on the day when Churchill made his speech to Commons. Although the prime minister warned his hearers that "wars are not won by evacuations," the rescue from Dunkirk has become a memorable symbol of defeat turning into a kind of victory.

Most of Churchill's speech is expository narrative, couched in his usual vigorous and eloquent prose. His purpose, however, was not merely to report what had happened, but to draw for his countrymen fresh inspiration from the terrible task just accomplished, to stir up in them courage for the bitter and lonely days to come. As Dunkirk itself grew to be a symbol of desperate courage, so Churchill's final paragraph came to be a symbol for a tenacity that would not admit defeat. Of all Churchill's rhetoric, few sentences have been more quoted than his famous and defiant promise: "We shall fight on the beaches, we shall fight on the landing grounds, we shall fight in the fields and in the streets, and we shall fight in the hills; we shall never surrender."

1. Churchill is one of the few modern masters of the grand oratorical style. It is not a good style for the college student to imitate directly, but from it he can learn a great deal about the resources of the English language. The sentence which concludes par. 12 shows the

Churchillian rhetoric at its most magniloquent—too flowery, perhaps, for ordinary use, but entirely appropriate to the extraordinary occasion which it marked. A quieter strength, used for dramatic emphasis, appears in the final sentence of par. 6. The whole of pars. 2 and 8 are marked by a particularly efficient and sustained narrative force. Look carefully at this style to see whether you can discover what qualities of diction, cadence, and sentence structure produce its effect.

2. After you have read Churchill's speech, turn back to p. 377 to read what the author of the "Letter to a Seventeen-Year-Old Son" had to say about the importance of Churchill's mastery of language in making him a great leader of a nation at war. Do you agree?

SUGGESTION FOR WRITING

"Dunkirk," delivered as a speech in Parliament, reported and interpreted events which had only just happened. After the war Churchill published in six volumes a considered history of the whole conflict. Look up in the second volume of this history (*Their Finest Hour*, Book I, Chaps. 4-5) Churchill's postwar account of these events. Compare the two versions and write a discussion of some of the reasons for the differences between them.

The Indispensable

Opposition

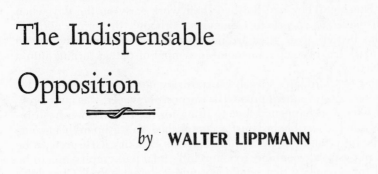

by WALTER LIPPMANN

I

WERE THEY PRESSED HARD ENOUGH, most men would probably confess that political freedom—that is to say, the right to speak freely and to act in opposition—is a noble ideal rather than a practical necessity. As the case for freedom is generally put to-day, the argument lends itself to this

From *The Atlantic Monthly*, August, 1939. By permission of the publishers and the author. Copyright 1939 by The Atlantic Monthly Company.

feeling. It is made to appear that, whereas each man claims his freedom as a matter of right, the freedom he accords to other men is a matter of toleration. Thus, the defense of freedom of opinion tends to rest not on its substantial, beneficial, and indispensable consequences, but on a somewhat eccentric, a rather vaguely benevolent, attachment to an abstraction.

2. It is all very well to say with Voltaire, 'I wholly disapprove of what you say, but will defend to the death your right to say it,' but as a matter of fact most men will not defend to the death the rights of other men: if they disapprove sufficiently what other men say, they will somehow suppress those men if they can.

3. So, if this is the best that can be said for liberty of opinion, that a man must tolerate his opponents because everyone has a 'right' to say what he pleases, then we shall find that liberty of opinion is a luxury, safe only in pleasant times when men can be tolerant because they are not deeply and vitally concerned.

4. Yet actually, as a matter of historic fact, there is a much stronger foundation for the great constitutional right of freedom of speech, and as a matter of practical human experience there is a much more compelling reason for cultivating the habits of free men. We take, it seems to me, a naïvely self-righteous view when we argue as if the right of our opponents to speak were something that we protect because we are magnanimous, noble, and unselfish. The compelling reason why, if liberty of opinion did not exist, we should have to invent it, why it will eventually have to be restored in all civilized countries where it is now suppressed, is that we must protect the right of our opponents to speak because we must hear what they have to say.

5. We miss the whole point when we imagine that we tolerate the freedom of our political opponents as we tolerate a howling baby next door, as we put up with the blasts from our neighbor's radio because we are too peaceable to heave a brick through the window. If this were all there is to freedom of opinion, that we are too good-natured or too timid to do anything about our opponents and our critics except to let them talk, it would be difficult to say whether we are tolerant because we are magnanimous or because we are lazy, because we have strong principles or because we lack serious convictions, whether we have the hospitality of an inquiring mind or the indifference of an empty mind. And so, if we truly wish to understand why freedom is necessary in a civilized society, we must begin by realizing that, because freedom of discussion improves our own opinions, the liberties of other men are our own vital necessity.

6. We are much closer to the essence of the matter, not when we quote Voltaire, but when we go to the doctor and pay him to ask us the

most embarrassing questions and to prescribe the most disagreeable diet. When we pay the doctor to exercise complete freedom of speech about the cause and cure of our stomachache, we do not look upon ourselves as tolerant and magnanimous, and worthy to be admired by ourselves. We have enough common sense to know that if we threaten to put the doctor in jail because we do not like the diagnosis and the prescription it will be unpleasant for the doctor, to be sure, but equally unpleasant for our own stomachache. That is why even the most ferocious dictator would rather be treated by a doctor who was free to think and speak the truth than by his own Minister of Propaganda. For there is a point, the point at which things really matter, where the freedom of others is no longer a question of their right but of our own need.

7. The point at which we recognize this need is much higher in some men than in others. The totalitarian rulers think they do not need the freedom of an opposition: they exile, imprison, or shoot their opponents. We have concluded on the basis of practical experience, which goes back to Magna Carta and beyond, that we need the opposition. We pay the opposition salaries out of the public treasury.

8. In so far as the usual apology for freedom of speech ignores this experience, it becomes abstract and eccentric rather than concrete and human. The emphasis is generally put on the right to speak, as if all that mattered were that the doctor should be free to go out into the park and explain to the vacant air why I have a stomachache. Surely that is a miserable caricature of the great civic right which men have bled and died for. What really matters is that the doctor should tell *me* what ails me, that I should listen to him; that if I do not like what he says I should be free to call in another doctor; and that then the first doctor should have to listen to the second doctor; and that out of all the speaking and listening, the give-and-take of opinions, the truth should be arrived at.

9. This is the creative principle of freedom of speech, not that it is a system for the tolerating of error, but that it is a system for finding the truth. It may not produce the truth, or the whole truth all the time, or often, or in some cases ever. But if the truth can be found, there is no other system which will normally and habitually find so much truth. Until we have thoroughly understood this principle, we shall not know why we must value our liberty, or how we can protect and develop it.

II

10. Let us apply this principle to the system of public speech in a totalitarian state. We may, without any serious falsification, picture a condition of affairs in which the mass of the people are being addressed

through one broadcasting system by one man and his chosen subordinates. The orators speak. The audience listens but cannot and dare not speak back. It is a system of one-way communication; the opinions of the rulers are broadcast outwardly to the mass of the people. But nothing comes back to the rulers from the people except the cheers; nothing returns in the way of knowledge of forgotten facts, hidden feelings, neglected truths, and practical suggestions.

11. But even a dictator cannot govern by his own one-way inspiration alone. In practice, therefore, the totalitarian rulers get back the reports of the secret police and of their party henchmen down among the crowd. If these reports are competent, the rulers may manage to remain in touch with public sentiment. Yet that is not enough to know what the audience feels. The rulers have also to make great decisions that have enormous consequences, and here their system provides virtually no help from the give-and-take of opinion in the nation. So they must either rely on their own intuition, which cannot be permanently and continually inspired, or, if they are intelligent despots, encourage their trusted advisers and their technicians to speak and debate freely in their presence.

12. On the walls of the houses of Italian peasants one may see inscribed in large letters the legend, 'Mussolini is always right.' But if that legend is taken seriously by Italian ambassadors, by the Italian General Staff, and by the Ministry of Finance, then all one can say is heaven help Mussolini, heaven help Italy, and the new Emperor of Ethiopia.

13. For at some point, even in a totalitarian state, it is indispensable that there should exist the freedom of opinion which causes opposing opinions to be debated. As time goes on, that is less and less easy under a despotism; critical discussion disappears as the internal opposition is liquidated in favor of men who think and feel alike. That is why the early successes of despots, of Napoleon I and of Napoleon III, have usually been followed by an irreparable mistake. For in listening only to his yes men—the others being in exile or in concentration camps, or terrified—the despot shuts himself off from the truth that no man can dispense with.

14. We know all this well enough when we contemplate the dictatorships. But when we try to picture our own system, by way of contrast, what picture do we have in our minds? It is, is it not, that anyone may stand up on his own soapbox and say anything he pleases, like the individuals in Kipling's poem who sit each in his separate star and draw the Thing as they see it for the God of Things as they are. Kipling, perhaps, could do this, since he was a poet. But the ordinary mortal isolated on his separate star will have an hallucination, and a citizenry declaiming from separate soapboxes will poison the air with hot and nonsensical confusion.

15. If the democratic alternative to the totalitarian one-way broadcasts

is a row of separate soapboxes, then I submit that the alternative is unworkable, is unreasonable, and is humanly unattractive. It is above all a false alternative. It is not true that liberty has developed among civilized men when anyone is free to set up a soapbox, is free to hire a hall where he may expound his opinions to those who are willing to listen. On the contrary, freedom of speech is established to achieve its essential purpose only when different opinions are expounded in the same hall to the same audience.

16. For, while the right to talk may be the beginning of freedom, the necessity of listening is what makes the right important. Even in Russia and Germany a man may still stand in an open field and speak his mind. What matters is not the utterance of opinions. What matters is the confrontation of opinions in debate. No man can care profoundly that every fool should say what he likes. Nothing has been accomplished if the wisest man proclaims his wisdom in the middle of the Sahara Desert. This is the shadow. We have the substance of liberty when the fool is compelled to listen to the wise man and learn; when the wise man is compelled to take account of the fool, and to instruct him; when the wise man can increase his wisdom by hearing the judgment of his peers.

17. That is why civilized men must cherish liberty—as a means of promoting the discovery of truth. So we must not fix our whole attention on the right of anyone to hire his own hall, to rent his own broadcasting station, to distribute his own pamphlets. These rights are incidental; and though they must be preserved, they can be preserved only by regarding them as incidental, as auxiliary to the substance of liberty that must be cherished and cultivated.

18. Freedom of speech is best conceived, therefore, by having in mind the picture of a place like the American Congress, an assembly where opposing views are represented, where ideas are not merely uttered but debated, or the British Parliament, where men who are free to speak are also compelled to answer. We may picture the true condition of freedom as existing in a place like a court of law, where witnesses testify and are cross-examined, where the lawyer argues against the opposing lawyer before the same judge and in the presence of one jury. We may picture freedom as existing in a forum where the speaker must respond to questions; in a gathering of scientists where the data, the hypothesis, and the conclusion are submitted to men competent to judge them; in a reputable newspaper which not only will publish the opinions of those who disagree but will reëxamine its own opinion in the light of what they say.

19. Thus the essence of freedom of opinion is not in mere toleration as such, but in the debate which toleration provides: it is not in the vent-

ing of opinion, but in the confrontation of opinion. That this is the practical substance can readily be understood when we remember how differently we feel and act about the censorship and regulation of opinion purveyed by different media of communication. We find then that, in so far as the medium makes difficult the confrontation of opinion in debate, we are driven towards censorship and regulation.

20. There is, for example, the whispering campaign, the circulation of anonymous rumors by men who cannot be compelled to prove what they say. They put the utmost strain on our tolerance, and there are few who do not rejoice when the anonymous slanderer is caught, exposed, and punished. At a higher level there is the moving picture, a most powerful medium for conveying ideas, but a medium which does not permit debate. A moving picture cannot be answered effectively by another moving picture; in all free countries there is some censorship of the movies, and there would be more if the producers did not recognize their limitations by avoiding political controversy. There is then the radio. Here debate is difficult: it is not easy to make sure that the speaker is being answered in the presence of the same audience. Inevitably, there is some regulation of the radio.

21. When we reach the newspaper press, the opportunity for debate is so considerable that discontent cannot grow to the point where under normal conditions there is any disposition to regulate the press. But when newspapers abuse their power by injuring people who have no means of replying, a disposition to regulate the press appears. When we arrive at Congress we find that, because the membership of the House is so large, full debate is impracticable. So there are restrictive rules. On the other hand, in the Senate, where the conditions of full debate exist, there is almost absolute freedom of speech.

22. This shows us that the preservation and development of freedom of opinion are not only a matter of adhering to abstract legal rights, but also, and very urgently, a matter of organizing and arranging sufficient debate. Once we have a firm hold on the central principle, there are many practical conclusions to be drawn. We then realize that the defense of freedom of opinion consists primarily in perfecting the opportunity for an adequate give-and-take of opinion; it consists also in regulating the freedom of those revolutionists who cannot or will not permit or maintain debate when it does not suit their purposes.

23. We must insist that free oratory is only the beginning of free speech; it is not the end, but a means to an end. The end is to find the truth. The practical justification of civil liberty is not that self-expression is one of the rights of man. It is that the examination of opinion is one of the necessities of man. For experience tells us that it is only when free-

dom of opinion becomes the compulsion to debate that the seed which our fathers planted has produced its fruit. When that is understood, freedom will be cherished not because it is a vent for our opinions but because it is the surest method of correcting them.

24. The unexamined life, said Socrates, is unfit to be lived by man. This is the virtue of liberty, and the ground on which we may best justify our belief in it, that it tolerates error in order to serve the truth. When men are brought face to face with their opponents, forced to listen and learn and mend their ideas, they cease to be children and savages and begin to live like civilized men. Then only is freedom a reality, when men may voice their opinions because they must examine their opinions.

III

25. The only reason for dwelling on all this is that if we are to preserve democracy we must understand its principles. And the principle which distinguishes it from all other forms of government is that in a democracy the opposition not only is tolerated as constitutional but must be maintained because it is in fact indispensable.

26. The democratic system cannot be operated without effective opposition. For, in making the great experiment of governing people by consent rather than by coercion, it is not sufficient that the party in power should have a majority. It is just as necessary that the party in power should never outrage the minority. That means that it must listen to the minority and be moved by the criticisms of the minority. That means that its measures must take account of the minority's objections, and that in administering measures it must remember that the minority may become the majority.

27. The opposition is indispensable. A good statesman, like any other sensible human being, always learns more from his opponents than from his fervent supporters. For his supporters will push him to disaster unless his opponents show him where the dangers are. So if he is wise he will often pray to be delivered from his friends, because they will ruin him. But, though it hurts, he ought also to pray never to be left without opponents; for they keep him on the path of reason and good sense.

28. The national unity of a free people depends upon a sufficiently even balance of political power to make it impracticable for the administration to be arbitrary and for the opposition to be revolutionary and irreconcilable. Where that balance no longer exists, democracy perishes. For unless all the citizens of a state are forced by circumstances to com-

promise, unless they feel that they can affect policy but that no one can wholly dominate it, unless by habit and necessity they have to give and take, freedom cannot be maintained.

COMMENTARY AND QUESTIONS

In 1859, in his great essay *On Liberty,* John Stuart Mill pointed out that "all silencing of discussion is an assumption of infallibility." "Not the violent conflict between parts of the truth," he continued, "but the quiet suppression of half of it is the formidable evil; there is always hope when people are forced to listen to both sides; it is when they attend only to one that errors harden into prejudices, and truth itself ceases to have the effect of truth, by being exaggerated into falsehood."

Much of the world since then has forgotten or ignored Mill's warning. Even in the United States the freedom of discussion has sometimes been thought an expensive luxury. But in 1939, when dictators strutted on almost every horizon, Walter Lippmann reminded us that freedom of speech is no luxury but an absolute necessity.

1. Why does Lippmann begin by discussing the interpretation of political freedom with which he disagrees? Where does he first state his own interpretation? In par. 5 he takes pains to demolish the assumption of noble-mindedness in the usual view of freedom; what sentence in par. 4 does this passage pick up and develop? Why is he so anxious to demonstrate that the argument for freedom must not rest on a sort of tired magnanimity?

2. Having cleared the ground of illusions, Lippmann proceeds to set forth his own view. What is the advantage of doing this by means of the analogy of doctor and stomachache in par. 6? Notice how in par. 8 the analogy is continued to discredit further the attitude Lippmann is attacking. What is the purpose of par. 9?

3. Pars. 10-13 make the first specific application of the general principles already expounded. Why does Lippmann choose first an application that shows what happens when his interpretation of freedom is *not* followed?

4. The key sentence in the next group of paragraphs is the last of par. 15. Show how the criterion of freedom set forth in this sentence is applied in a slightly different way in each one of pars. 18-24. Notice the progression of application in pars. 20 and 21. Is there any reason other than convenience of length for printing these as two separate paragraphs instead of one?

5. What is the function of pars. 25-28? There is a great deal of repetition of idea in these paragraphs as well as in the whole essay. When a writer has to present an idea which rests on fairly simple reasoning but is still hard to grasp or likely to encounter much disbelief, what

is the advantage of repeating it with different illustrations and applications? What are the possible dangers?

6. What does Lippmann gain by using commonplace and earthy expressions such as these: *a howling baby next door, heave a brick through
the window* (par. 5), *stomachache* (par. 6)? Wherein lies the force
of the last sentence in par. 16?

SUGGESTIONS FOR WRITING

1. Lippmann says that "the defense of freedom of opinion consists primarily in perfecting the opportunity for an adequate give-and-take of
opinion; it consists also in regulating the freedom of those revolutionists who cannot or will not permit or maintain debate when it does
not suit their purposes" (par. 22). Discuss the practical application
of this principle to suppressing so-called subversive groups. What
kind of "regulation" is in order?

2. Lippmann suggests in par. 19 and following paragraphs that in the
modern world of organized and monopolistic communication, it is
difficult to arrange "sufficient debate." Discuss ways of overcoming
this difficulty.

Life, Liberty and the Pursuit of Welfare

by JOSEPH WOOD KRUTCH

"Welfare" is one of the key words of our time. What too many men now
seem to desire is not virtue or knowledge or justice, but welfare. To the
majority the word sums up the principal object of government and, indeed, of all social institutions.

2. Had you asked a Greek philosopher what the purpose of govern-

ment should be, he would have said something about the maintenance of justice. And had you pressed him to say in what justice consists, he would have replied—not very satisfactorily—"In assuring to every man that which is rightfully his."

3. A medieval theologian would have added something about the City of God and the extent to which a community of mortals might approximate it. On the other hand that brutal seventeenth-century realist, Thomas Hobbes, would have gone to the other extreme. To him the principal aim of government is simply the maintenance of order, the taming of that state of nature which is anarchy of war. And the state of anarchy, he would have added, is so terrible that any government is better than no government.

4. Finally, had you posed the same question to an eighteenth-century philosopher, he would have said something to the effect that the chief purpose of government is not simply the maintenance of order, but the assurance to each man of his inalienable rights. And if you had asked him what these inalienable rights are, he would have answered in some form not too different from that of the Declaration—"Life, liberty and the pursuit of happiness."

5. In any event, it is obvious that none of these formulas is entirely satisfactory to most people today. They do not explicitly reject life, liberty and the pursuit of happiness, but they obviously consider them something less than enough. The invention of the term "welfare state" to describe something more than the democratic state is an expression of this dissatisfaction. It is intended to define a new ideal, which its proponents would call an extension of the ideal of a merely democratic state.

6. If it be objected that the philosophers, theologians and social critics cited above did not actually speak for the masses and that the great majority of the people would always have preferred "welfare" to the less easily understood goods proposed to them, the answer is that even if this be granted, it is not crucial to the argument which follows. The fact remains that the power of the masses is now for the first time decisive and that the sociologists and political scientists most influential today tend both to accept this fact and to concur in regarding "welfare" as the chief legitimate aim of government.

7. In a broad, general way we all know what welfare so used implies, what specific laws and institutions are called welfare measures, and what are the premises upon which they are advocated. No one would object very much if I said that the welfare state assumes, not only that men should be protected against those who would deprive them of their right to life, liberty and the pursuit of happiness, but that it should go beyond mere protection to something more positive. All men not only

must be guaranteed their liberties but also, to a very considerable extent, "looked after." Many of the arguments both for and against the policy of looking after people are too familiar to need mentioning. But certain fundamental questions are seldom asked. What is the ultimate definition of welfare—in what does it consist, and who decides what it is? Or, to put the question in a simpler form: Does the promotion of welfare mean giving people what they want or seem to want or think they want, or does it consist in giving them what they ought to have?

8. The answer implied in various specific welfare proposals is sometimes the one and sometimes the other. But few have ever dared to put the question boldly and to give a positive answer one way or another. If welfare means that people get what they want, then which wants of which people come first? If welfare means giving them what they ought to have, then who decides what they ought to have, and on the basis of what criteria is the decision made?

9. This last is a very tough question indeed for an age which has rejected absolutes and enthusiastically embraced both cultural and moral relativism. One of the few bold answers I have ever encountered was given by David Thompson, a lecturer in history at Cambridge University. "The welfare state," said he, "exists to promote whatever the community regards as beneficial and good. If the community regards automobiles, TV sets and football pools as of greater value than better schools, more generous care for old people, and a creative use of leisure, then the democratic state will provide more automobiles, TV sets and football pools."

10. In the course of the article Mr. Thompson gives the impression that he has preferences of his own and that they are not what he believes to be those of most people. But he does not appear to have his tongue in his cheek when he yields to the only definition of democracy and the only definition of welfare which his relativistic philosophy will permit. Like most of our contemporaries, he is unwilling to consider the possibility that what the community regards as valuable is not the only possible standard by which values may be judged. Nor, as a matter of fact, can anyone escape such a conviction unless he is willing to assume what most today refuse to assume, namely, that some basis for calling one thing intrinsically and absolutely better or righter or higher than another can be found somewhere: In nature, in reason or in the law of God—all of which are independent of either custom or majority opinion.

11. Refuse, as most sociologists, psychologists and anthropologists do refuse, to make such an assumption, and you are driven to the conclusion which Mr. Thompson accepts: That nothing is better or more desirable than anything else except insofar as more people want it. Thus he comes

to defend democracy not because of any conviction that its decisions are wiser by some independent standards than those arrived at by other forms of government, but simply because any decision which has majority sanction is wise and right by the only possible definition of those terms.

12. If, as most people seem to assume, the normal is merely the average, if the good life is whatever the majority thinks or has been persuaded to think it is, if what men should do is whatever they do do, then it must follow that the desirable is whatever is most widely desired, and that democracy means that what the majority admires is necessarily to be called excellent. Mr. Thompson himself may prefer what he calls "the creative use of leisure" to TV sets and football pools, but he is too broad-minded—as we now call it—to suppose that such a preference is anything more than just another one of those tastes about which there is no disputing.

13. *Laissez faire* is generally supposed to describe the social theory diametrically opposed to that of the welfare state, but here one sort of *laissez faire* is exchanged for another. Though the economy is to be planned, society is to be allowed to drift intellectually and culturally with whatever economic, technological or other currents may vary in this direction or that.

14. Under democracy of the older sort the most fundamental right of the citizen was assumed to be the pursuit of happiness. The welfare state substitutes welfare—usually defined in material terms—for happiness. But by way of compensation it assures the citizen that his right is not merely to pursue happiness but to attain welfare; and under this arrangement we lose something as well as, perhaps, gain something. Though we may pursue whatever kind of happiness seems to us most worth pursuing, the welfare which is going to be assured us must be mass-produced, whether it is defined, under a dictatorship, as what the dictator thinks we ought to have, or, as in our society, by what the majority wants or has been persuaded to want.

15. If I object that to define welfare as whatever most people seem to want tends to mean more things and fewer ideas and, in general, tends toward the vulgarest possible conception of what constitutes the good life, I will be told that the answer is education—that, given enough schools, and schools that are good enough, the community will want what is truly most desirable; and that, if properly educated, it will provide for itself and ultimately reach a truly acceptable definition of welfare.

16. But despite all the schooling which Americans get, many of them do not seem to be very effectively learning any ideals or cultivating any interests other than those which seem to prevail among the uneducated.

High-school graduates and college graduates also very frequently prefer television and shinier automobiles to any of the more intellectual and less material forms of welfare.

17. This fact brings us again up against the unanswered question and it suggests that education is failing to help people to achieve an acceptable definition of welfare for the same reason that the ideal of welfare itself is failing—because, in other words, we are unable to give any definition of education except the same kind of definition we give of welfare.

18. If students do not want classical literature, philosophy or science, if they do want sports, courses in movie appreciation and in the accepted social conventions, then, just as the other things constitute welfare, so these things must constitute education. Once the school, like the church, tended to embody a protest, or at least a countervailing influence, against what the other forces in society tended to make of that society and of man himself. The church held that man undisciplined by religion was wicked. The school held that unless he was educated, he would be ignorant and crass. But both the church and the school seem now to have fallen in love with the world as it is. They talk more and more about adjustment—and by that to mean "adjustment to things as they are."

19. The church halfheartedly, the school with real enthusiasm, gives up the attempt to direct society and is content to follow it, like the political leader who watches where the mob is going, puts himself at the head of it and says, "Follow me." Educators so-called have said, "Don't teach literary English; teach acceptable English." If, as a New York commission recently has proposed, children are not interested in the classics, don't waste time trying to arouse their interests; give them something they are interested in—teach them how to drive automobiles, how lipstick is best applied or, and this is part of one actual course in a Midwestern institution of learning, how to order groceries over the telephone.

20. These are the things many of the students will be doing; this is what their lives will be made up of. And if the business of education is to prepare for life, then these are the things that they ought to be taught. But the statement so commonly made, that education should be a preparation for life, is meaningless unless the kind of life it is supposed to prepare for is specified. If education is properly defined as hardly more than what anthropologists call "acculturation," then it is worth taking account of the fact that most children get much more of their education in this sense from advertisements, moving pictures, television, popular songs and so on, than they do from school. Preparation for life as the schools are tending to define it is much better accomplished by those institutions outside the school system than by those within it.

21. It would, of course, be inaccurate as well as unfair to leave the impression that there is no protest against the ideals and practices of the schools as typified by the examples just given. During the past few years such protests have grown from a whisper to an outcry. Various organizations, notably the Council for Basic Education, have been formed to combat the prevailing tendencies. The latter especially has conducted a vigorous campaign of propaganda, buttressed by news bulletins, which report both outrageous examples of denatured education and reforms in the directions of which it approves.

22. Such protests have had their effect. In California, for instance, the recent report of a state-appointed commission puts itself squarely on record as finding the prevailing aims and methods of the school system to be in many instances radically undesirable. Even more important perhaps is the fact that many parents have expressed their dissatisfaction and called for reform. The National Education Association, a very powerful and well entrenched group, has bitterly resented most such criticisms, but if the tide has not actually turned, it looks as though it might be on the point of turning.

23. Nevertheless, it is not enough merely to ridicule current extravagances, to call for a return to the three R's and to insist that education does not consist in miscellaneous instruction in such varied specific subjects as safety rules for automobilists, the use of consumer credit and the current conventions governing "dating." Neither is it enough to say only that schools should be concerned primarily with the intellect and that those who talk about "educating the whole child" seem to forget that his head is part of him. Any rational theory must be based upon some conviction that the man of whom the child is the father ought to be in mind, in taste and in convictions something more than what he will be if he is allowed to follow only his simplest inclinations and whatever happens to be the current conventions of his group. In other words, what is necessary is a standard of values. Education is simply not changing people as much as it should.

24. Many critics of our society have said that we lack standards. This has been said so often by preachers and by the makers of commencement addresses that we have almost stopped asking what, if anything, it means to say that our society "lacks standards." But that we do lack standards for welfare and standards for education is obvious. Welfare turns into vulgar materialism because we have no standard by which to measure it. Education fails because it also refuses to face the responsibility of saying in what education consists. Both tend to become merely what people seem to want.

25. To any such complaint most sociologists, psychologists and edu-

cators will shrug and say, "Perhaps. But where can you find standards other than those which are set by society itself? Who is arrogant enough to set them up? Where can the authority for such standards be found?"

²⁶· Most periods of human history have believed that they could be found somewhere outside mere custom. They have usually been sought in one or all of three places: (1) In the revealed will of God; (2) in the operation of right reason, supposedly capable of defining good and evil; (3) in something permanent in human nature itself.

²⁷· If I say this to the modern relativist, he replies that none of these things will any longer do. (1) God no longer exists. (2) Though man is capable of thinking instrumentally—that is to say, capable of scheming to get what he wants—there is no such thing as pure reason capable of reaching an absolute; and whenever men have thought they were doing so, they were, in fact, only rationalizing their desires or the customs of their particular country. (3) What we call "human nature" is merely the result of the conditioning of the individual, either by the society in which he lives or by the peculiar experiences which have happened to be his. Since neither God nor pure reason exists, and since human nature is infinitely variable, it is evident that morals are merely mores, or custom; that right reason is merely a rationalization of the prejudices of the individual or his society; and that human nature is merely what social circumstances have made it.

²⁸· If all these characteristic modern convictions—or lack of convictions—are sound, then we must agree that whatever most people want is welfare, and that whatever pupils think they would least dislike doing in school is education. It is then useless to ask whether society is going in the right direction or whether men today are leading a good life. Nothing is absolutely better than anything else; things are what they are and will be what they will be, and we cannot control or direct. We must follow where events may lead us.

²⁹· Before accepting this counsel of despair once and for all, it would be worth while to ask again if it really is certain that all three of the conceivable bases upon which some standard might be founded really are merely illusory. Each of them might be taken up in turn. One might ask again does God exist; one might ask again is right reason a mere figment of the imagination? Does human nature exist?

³⁰· I here raise only what is perhaps the least difficult of all these questions—the last one. Granted that man may be conditioned in various ways, is it nevertheless true that there are limits to the extent to which he can be conditioned? Is it true that human nature tends to return to some norm, that it is not limitlessly conditionable? And is it possible that to some extent one thing is better or higher or more valuable than an-

other because human nature tends persistently to think that it is? Or, to put the question in its most general form, is there a good life which might be loosely defined as "that which is in accord with the most fundamental and persistent wants, desires and needs of human nature"?

31. If ours is the richest and most powerful civilization that has ever existed, but if it is also the most anxious and ill at ease, is that in part because human nature needs something more than the wealth and power it has acquired? Is it possibly because human nature needs to believe just what modern thought has forbidden it to believe—that is, that morals are more than mores and that value judgments are more than merely rationalized prejudices? Once you insist that human nature as such does not exist, all the relativisms of our time—cultural, moral and social—inevitably follow. So, almost in desperation, let us ask again, "How good is the evidence that there is no such thing as human nature, that it is nothing but what experience or culture has made it?"

32. We must begin by remembering that the theory that human nature is nothing in itself is not actually new. In that enormously influential seventeenth-century book, *Leviathan* by Thomas Hobbes, the theory is already implicit. Hobbes attempts to account for all the phenomena of human life by assuming that there is nothing innate in man except the ability to receive stimuli, the ability to react to them and the desire to experience pleasure. There is, accordingly, nothing in the mind which has not been first in the senses. There are no such things as innate ideas or desires other than the simple desire to experience pleasure or to exercise power, which latter is said to be the same thing. Hence man becomes whatever experience makes him and, to use the phrase which became popular later, he is born with a blank slate upon which anything may be written.

33. We have enormously complicated this theory. We have drawn from it many deductions. But we have added little if anything essentially new. The whole of modern relativism seems to follow logically from Hobbes. If the human mind begins as a blank slate upon which anything may be written, then morals are only mores, our ideas of what is good or evil, just or unjust, beautiful or ugly, seemly or unseemly, are simply learned from the society in which we grow up. Nothing is eternally or inherently better than anything else—cultures vary from time to time and from place to place, but there is no external standard by which one may be judged as better than another. Incidentally, this complete abandonment of the right to judge we now commonly call "getting rid of our prejudices."

34. Contemporary anthropologists are fond of pointing out that what was considered right and desirable in one society was not so considered

in another. Already by the end of the nineteenth century the historian Lecky could assert in his *History of European Morals* that there is no act which has not at one time or place been commanded as a duty and at another time or place forbidden as a sin—which is to say again that morals are only mores. Or, as a contemporary college textbook on psychology, written by a professor at the University of Southern California, puts it in a very short chapter on morals, "We call a man moral when he acts in accord with the laws and customs of his society"—by which definition, no doubt, a Nazi who took part in the persecution of the Jews would be a moral man, and one who did not would be an immoral one.

35. In a world which has so definitely rejected transcendental sanctions for either codes of morals or standards of value, the question whether human nature itself might supply them becomes enormously important. Is the usual negative answer really justifiable? Shall we one day swing again in a different direction and discover evidence now neglected that human nature is something in itself and does provide certain absolutes, valid at least within the human realm?

36. Have the anthropologists, for instance, been so preoccupied with the collection of materials to demonstrate the enormous differences between cultures that they have overlooked some things which are common to all? Have the experimental psychologists been so busy conditioning both men and animals that they have paid little attention to the resistance to conditioning which both can put up?

37. One little breeze in psychological doctrine might seem to point in this direction. Some skeptical psychologists have begun to wonder whether instinct on the one hand and the conditioned reflex on the other really can account for all of the behavior of living organisms. Certain sufficiently obvious facts have recently been re-emphasized.

38. Consider three of them which seem ludicrously simple. (1) Birds know by instinct how to fly and do not have to be taught, though mother birds sometimes seem to be teaching them. This is an example of instinct. (2) Seals do not instinctively know how to swim, but they learn very easily how to swim when they are taught by their parents. (3) You would have a very hard time indeed teaching most songbirds to swim. In other words, there are not just two classes of animal behavior—that which is inborn and that which is learned. There is also a third and possibly an enormously important one—namely, that behavior which is not inborn, though the ability to learn it easily is.

39. Considering such facts, some have begun to wonder whether the same might be true not only of skills but throughout the whole psychic realm of beliefs, tastes, motives, desires and needs. The thesis of the moral relativist is—to take an extreme case—that since no one is born

with an innate idea that dishonesty and treachery are evil, then the conviction that they are evil can be nothing but the result of social education, and the opposite could just as easily have been taught, since value judgments are merely the rationalized prejudices of a given culture. May it not be true on the contrary that certain ideas are much more easily learned than others, and that what the eighteenth century called natural law, natural taste and the rest, is real—consisting in those beliefs and tastes which are most readily learned and most productive of health and happiness?

40. Perhaps you can condition an individual or a society to think and behave unnaturally just as you might possibly teach a robin to swim, but men who have been conditioned to think or behave unnaturally are unhappy—as unhappy and as inefficient as swimming robins. Perhaps Hobbes was right to the extent that no ideas are innate; but if the capacity to entertain readily some ideas and not others is innate, then it comes down to much the same thing. As Alexander Pope wrote nearly two and a half centuries ago, "Nature affords at least a glimmering light; the lines, though touched but faintly, are drawn right"—which is to say that the faint lines on the not quite blank slate constitute the reality behind the idea of a normal human being.

41. What Pope thought of as a metaphor may be an accurate biological statement. On the not quite blank slate the lines are touched too faintly to constitute an automatic instinct—they may even be destroyed by resolute conditioning and education—but they are rather like a latent image on a photographic plate, imperceptible until developed, though development will reveal only what already exists. If this is true, then there is such a thing as human nature. What we are born with is not a blank slate, but a film bearing already a latent image.

42. No doubt, as Pope himself said elsewhere, as experimental psychologists prove in the laboratory and as dictators as well as educators have too often demonstrated, the lines may be overlaid, and the unnatural may cease to seem a creature of hideous mien. But the conditioners have to work hard. Men, I suspect, believe much more readily in the reality of good and evil than they accept cultural relativism. Perhaps that means that belief in the reality of good and evil is according to nature and the modern tendency to dismiss them as mere prejudices of culture is fundamentally unnatural.

43. Such an assumption is at least one which no valid science forbids, and if we make even such a minimum assumption, we can be saved from the nihilism of the present-day social, cultural and moral relativism. We have again some point of reference now lacking in every inquiry which sets out to determine what kind of society or education or culture would

be best for us. One thing is no longer as good as another provided only it can be shown or made to exist. We would no longer need to talk only about what can be done to men or what we might possibly be able to make them into, for we would be able to talk again about what men are in themselves.

44. We would have the beginning of a basis for a definition of welfare and a definition of education such as we now totally lack. We could say, for example, that welfare is not merely what people at a given moment believe they want, but that which experience has proved to be conducive to health and happiness.

45. We could say that education is not whatever a pupil thinks he wants in school, but that it is that which experience has shown will lead to a true understanding of his own nature, his own needs and his own wants. We could say the ideal of education is not conformity, not acculturation, but the full development of human nature's potentialities.

46. We could say that the normal is not the same as the average, but rather that the normal is normative—that is to say, that by which a thing is to be judged. And we could add that the normal human being is not the average human being, but the thing to which human nature aspires.

47. To attempt to determine what is part of permanent human nature is to undertake no easy task. To distinguish between what is truly natural and what is merely conditioned is extremely difficult. But to conclude that the question is actually a meaningful one is already to have concluded something vastly important. We talk much today about the extent to which we can control nature and our destiny, of how we have taken the future of the human race into our hands. But control implies some idea of the direction in which you want to go. We have the power, perhaps, but what good is the power unless we know what we want to do with it? "Give me a fulcrum for my lever, and I will move the world," said Archimedes. But a fulcrum for a lever is exactly what we lack. It implies a point of support which is necessary if you are going to move the world. We are trying to lever society without having any fulcrum on which to rest the lever and, in the absence of any other, we might possibly find it in some understanding of fundamental human nature.

48. However much there may be still to learn about human nature, certain of its characteristics seem to me obvious enough to suggest some of the ways in which our society has been going wrong.

49. The first of these permanent characteristics seems to me to be that man is inveterately a maker of value judgments. His idea of what constitutes right and wrong conduct, of what is just or unjust, has been—perhaps will continue to be—extremely diverse. But he has nearly always believed that good and evil, justice and injustice, are realities which

it is of the first importance to define and to cherish, while moral and cultural relativism—the idea that morals are nothing but mores and that one society is not absolutely better than another—is so profoundly unnatural a conviction that it has seldom been entertained for long and is destructive of human welfare when it is.

50. Closely related to the value judgment is the idea of justice. Men have varied enormously, irreconcilably, over the question of what constitutes justice. But they have nearly always believed that there is some such thing and that they should adhere to it. Part of that feeling is, I believe, the conviction that acts should have consequences, and that the way you are treated should be in some degree affected by the way in which you behave. A spoiled child, one who never pays any penalty for his follies or misdeeds, one who is given what some of the modern educators call "uncritical love," is usually an unhappy child because something fundamental in his human nature tells him that acts should have consequences and makes him profoundly uneasy in a world where they do not.

51. Similarly I believe that a society is unhappy if it holds—as so many sociologists now profess to hold—that no man should be held responsible for his imprudences or his crimes. He may be glad to escape those consequences, but he is finding himself in a world without justice, in a world where the way in which you act has no effect upon the way in which you are treated. And I believe that, like the spoiled child, he is profoundly uneasy in that unnatural situation.

52. I believe that it is also in accord with fundamental human nature to want some goods other than the material, that a society which defines the good life as merely a high standard of living and then defines the high standard of living in terms of material things alone is one which, in that respect, is denying expression to a fundamental characteristic of man. Few societies, whether primitive or not, have ever accepted the belief that welfare thus narrowly defined is the one and only supreme good. Men have sought all sorts of other things—they have sought God, they have sought beauty, they have sought truth or they have sought glory, militarily or otherwise. They have sought adventure; they have even—so anthropologists tell us—sometimes believed that a large collection of dried human heads was the thing in all the world most worth having. But seldom if ever, so it seems to me, have they confessedly sought only what is now called "welfare."

53. This is a mere beginning. You may dispute, if you like, even the few general statements I have made about permanent human nature. But if you admit that some things are and some things are not in accord with human nature, then you have grasped an instrument capable of doing something which few men today seem able to do, namely, attempt a rational criticism of things as they are.

COMMENTARY AND QUESTIONS

Joseph Wood Krutch (whose name, by the way, rhymes not with *Dutch* but with *brooch*) has written and lectured on many subjects: among them, English literature, drama both ancient and modern, natural history, and the ills of modern society. Like Arthur M. Schlesinger, Jr. (see "The Decline of Heroes," pp. 415-423), he was invited by the editors of a well-known popular magazine to write one of an extensive series of thoughtful articles appearing under the general title *Adventures of the Mind.*

Krutch's thoughts in this article no doubt did indeed seem adventuresome to his readers, at least to some of them, because he was attempting to refute certain widely held current views on the purpose (and justifying values) of government, of education, and of life itself, and yet to do so without relying on certain traditional religious and philosophical assumptions which he felt had already been discarded or downgraded by many of those whose minds he wished to change. He could, of course, count on some readers to agree with his point of view at once. He could also be sure that some others would be immediately and firmly unpersuadable. His appeal was perhaps chiefly to a sizable fraction of the public in between these two extremes: a group ranging from would-be dissenters who yet might just stop to listen if the arguments offered were sufficiently cogent, to would-be sympathizers who were eager to agree with Krutch but had previously been unable to find for themselves sufficient intellectual grounds for adopting his views. In addition to the fractions of his audience who agreed, who disagreed, and who hadn't yet made up their minds, no doubt a great many of his readers were inclined to be simply bored or indifferent about the whole subject.

As many controversialists face audiences of precisely this kind, Krutch's essay is worth examining to see how he goes about his task of reinforcing agreement, minimizing dissent, and winning over the uncommitted and the indifferent.

1. Why does Krutch's title command attention and suggest his point of view? How does the wording of the first paragraph achieve a similar effect? Does the quick historical survey of previous concepts of the purpose of government given in pars. 2-4 contradict or reinforce the effect of the title and first paragraph?

2. Par. 5 restates and enlarges the proposition set forth so succinctly in par. 1; par. 6 disposes of a possible objection to the implication of the historical survey of pars. 2-4; par. 7 states a question; and par. 8 states two corollary questions. In various forms these questions recur throughout the essay. What is the implication of the following sentences: the fifth in par. 7; the second in par. 8; the first in par. 9? Krutch evidently respects the unequivocal forthrightness of the "bold

answer" he quotes in par. 9; is there anything in the wording of pars. 10 and 11 to suggest that Krutch himself does not find this particular answer quite satisfactory? Why does he devote pars. 12-14 to elaborating the implications of this answer?

3. The last clause of par. 14 looks backward, especially to key words in pars. 7, 8, and 10, as well as forward to par. 15 and the new subject it introduces. What advantage does Krutch gain by this wording? What is the effect of par. 17? What is the function of pars. 18-20?

4. Par. 10 spoke of a "possible standard by which values may be judged." Where in par. 23 is there an echo of this earlier expression? How does Krutch further exploit this echo in pars. 24 and 25 and use it to lead into par. 26?

5. Par. 27 elaborates the refusal noted in par. 11 of some modern social scientists to make the assumption stated at the end of par. 10 and repeated in par. 26. Par. 28 restates the rest of par. 11. Why has Krutch come back to these particular topics at this point in the essay? Remembering the nature of his audience, suggest possible reasons for asking the same question in different form in pars. 29, 30, and 31, and again in pars. 35 and 36. Why does he sandwich his discussion of Hobbes's theory of the mind and the deductions later drawn from it between pars. 29-31 and 35-36? What is the function of par. 37?

6. The key sentence of par. 38 is the last. What metaphors and similes does Krutch use in pars. 40-41 to illustrate this concept?

7. Comment on the argumentative tactics used in par. 43. What is the effect of the parallel construction used in pars. 43-46? What is the logical and rhetorical effect of the final example of a "good other than the material" given in the fourth sentence of par. 52?

8. Par. 10 contained the words *In nature, in reason or in the law of God.* Suggest possible reasons for the particular order of these words. Par. 26 repeats these words in a different form; suggest a possible reason for the fact that the key words now appear in a different order. Why are they repeated in par. 29? Discuss the order in which Krutch takes up in pars. 49-52 the "permanent characteristics" he detects in human nature.

9. The word *custom* appears in par. 10; it reappears in par. 27, coupled with the statement *morals are merely mores;* this statement is repeated, in various modifications, in pars. 31, 33, 34, and 49. Discuss the effect of this repetition. Discuss similar effects achieved by the use of *blank slate* in pars. 32, 33, 40, and 41 (twice); of *normal* in pars. 12, 40, and 46; of *things as they are* in pars. 18, 28, and 53. Find other skillful repetitions of key words and their derivatives: for example, *welfare, relativism, material,* and *nature.*

10. Krutch is very careful in this essay to found his main arguments as

far as possible on what seems to him valid evidence and sound logic, not on mere rhetorical assertion. In a quiet way, however, he constantly makes clear through the flavor of his sentences where he himself stands; by his choice of words, he needles foes and comforts friends. Comment on the implications of the following expressions: *too broad-minded—as we now call it* (par. 12), *drift* (par. 13), *denatured education* (par. 21), *no longer* (par. 27), *a very short chapter on morals* (par. 34). What principle seems to govern the choice of examples of school subjects cited in pars. 19 and 23? From the strategic point of view, are there dangers as well as advantages in such weapons of controversy?

SUGGESTIONS FOR WRITING

1. Education is not acculturation.
2. Are there any absolutes in aesthetics (or the arts)?
3. The permanent and the transient in human nature.
4. Read Russell Lynes's defense of the dilettante in "Time on Our Hands" (pp. 397-406) and then write a discussion of dilettantism in the light of what Krutch says about "goods other than material" in par. 52 of this essay.

The Sentimentalists

by PHYLLIS McGINLEY

WITH MY BREAKFAST ORANGE JUICE I like to read the morning paper.

2. In more peaceable times I used to turn first to the front page, eager to learn what had happened overnight to the world. Recently, though, for the sake of my digestion (which is easily upset by news that Armageddon is just around the corner) I have been starting with Books. After all, in books, bombs destroy only paper planets. How long, however, even that department will help me down my toast and egg I can't

From *Ladies' Home Journal*, July, 1961. Reprinted by permission of the author.

say; for the furies pursue me there. The page is explosive with double-column advertisements which run pretty much like this:

^{3.} *Did you think you were shockproof? That you had explored in literature every avenue of sadism, vice, perversion? Then read* SEX IS A MANY-COLORED COAT, *the thrilling new novel by Delbert de Sade, and see how wrong you were. A tenderly brutal examination of love and lust in this decadent decade.*

^{4.} "*A must for every thinking citizen. Leaves no stone unturned.*"—The HoHoKus Bulletin.

^{5.} "Explicit, daring, violent," cries the blurb for THE TWO-LEGGED INSECT, another five-hundred-page dissertation on "The manners and morals of Exurbia" by "the most daring of our younger writers, Casanova Stubbs."

^{6.} "Nothing you have ever read before could have prepared you for the frankness of NAKED IN THE LABYRINTH," shouts another, if there are still type and newsprint left to assault my shrinking spirit.

^{7.} It is with relief that I pick up a pencil to solve the daily crossword puzzle over a final cup of coffee. Like the novels advertised, it will also abound in four-letter words, but of a less picturesque sort. If this trend in Books continues I may have to fall back on Sports. It is not only that I lack stamina. I also lack patience. For—and now I am going to be as frank and explicit as any novelist about to come to grips with an unsuccessful marriage—I am as bored with the books as I am with the advertisements. I am weary of immorality in fiction. I am sick to death of shock. Particularly I tire of sentimentality, the great wave which washes over literature in these self-indulgent years and which the ads are exploiting. Not since the nineteenth century has the public been so deluged with treacle.

^{8.} "Ridiculous!" you may say if you have read thus far. "The stamp of the age is violence. How can you call sentimental a body of writing which leans so heavily on sin and suffering, vice and despair?"

^{9.} I refer such dissenters to the dictionary definition of the word.

^{10.} "Sentimental" it states: "Indulging the sensibilities for their own sake; artificially tender; mawkishly or superficially emotional."

^{11.} Exactly. Except that the uses of the adjective have been reversed. For the sentimentality of virtue we have substituted the sentimentality of wickedness, weakness, self-pity. Instead of long-suffering wives, barefoot match girls, gallant gentlemen making speeches from a gallows they have elected for love's sake, we have different but equally trite stock figures. We have the prostitute with the golden heart, the suburban Casanova at odds with his environment, the subnormal protagonist who compulsively murders his poor old grandmother because nobody gave

him a toy dump truck when he was five. We have sex as the only goad to human behavior. Thus we have dispensed with one sort of sugary syrup and now immoderately pour out the sauce of horror. *Yet to overstress evil is as banal as to overemphasize goodness.* If *Little Lord Fauntleroy* seems ludicrous to us now, so—on thinking it over—does William Styron's *Set This House on Fire* and John O'Hara's *From the Terrace*—and for the same reason. Each puts more burden on a single emotion than it is able to carry.

12. In Dickens's day, the Victorians wept over the misfortunes of orphans, child brides and underfed chimney sweeps. It took an Oscar Wilde to dry their tears with his famous quip: "He must have a heart of stone who can read of the death of Little Nell without smiling." We need a new satirist to laugh away our novelists' preoccupation with what is merely sordid. For fashion's wheels has swung full circle and we are back to the maudlin.

13. Three highly praised novels, all by men of talent, I have read in the last month occur to me as tangible proof of this charge. All three are so laced and larded with sentimentality that *Black Beauty* seems astringent.

14. In one we meet as chief characters a psychopath, and a man devoured by that stylish modern device, the death wish. Both bring the house of life down about their ears, but only after pages of such self-pitying dialogue as has not been heard since Elsie Dinsmore defied her cruel father by refusing to play worldly songs on the Sabbath.

15. In another story, exquisitely told, a famous scholar wrecks the lives of his three mistresses who are respectively a middle-aged beauty, her daughter by another man, and her granddaughter, with all three affairs going on simultaneously. After such an avalanche of horrors, the double suicide at the end of the book seems wholesome if unaffecting.

16. The third is at once the least emotional yet the most overwrought. For in lieu of a hero we are presented with an ex-basketball player without mind, heart or will. We are spared no detail of his feeble nastiness; of his grubby sex life, his self-indulgent miseries. And the story might have a kind of grim validity were we not supposed to regard him as Everyman. "There," one can hear the author murmuring, "but for the grace of Fate and a college education, go you and I and the next-door neighbor." Everyman is *not* a man, however, but a human rabbit, running from one desperate warren to another, pursued not by remorse but by accidental evil and toward nothing dignified enough to call tragedy. Our rabbit is not trying to outwit the furies or save his soul. He runs because it is all he knows how to do. One can agree that such people exist. But to expect

them to carry on their shoulders the whole destiny of man is, once more, outrageously sentimental.

17. It is as false as *The Girl of the Limberlost,* as determined to see only one side of the picture as Pollyanna, the Glad Girl. Its landscape is not a true canvas. For the world, no matter how full of threat, is more various than current novelists are willing to admit.

18. Certainly it is a world heavy with peril, peopled by many sick minds and disordered spirits. Savagery and wickedness, rape and murder, cruelty and perversion occur as they have occurred in every age and at every step in human history—in Chaucer's time, and in Jane Austen's, and in any era since Cain did Abel in, or David took his general's wife to bed and sent her husband off to be killed at the head of his army. But it is at the same time a place inhabited by many good and unselfish men, by many virtuous women, and by human beings who have not abdicated their right to the title. Not all husbands hate their wives. Not all children dislike their parents. There are commuters who come home happy and sober from a day's work and a job which does not disgust them. There are housewives who sleep with their own husbands. There are businessmen with principles and priests who have kept their faith and adolescent girls who do not get pregnant at Fort Lauderdale over Easter vacation. There are, I persistently contend, people on this planet who still own consciences, decency, courage, kindness and free will. Leave them out altogether and we have a literature contrived and unenduring.

19. What is worse, we have a boring one. For affectation breeds tedium. With violence become a cliché, with sexual descriptions losing power to impress, where shall we go for novelty? Writers reach farther and farther into Freud, Krafft-Ebing, and the files of police courts for a new vice, a corruption which has not already been over used as pivot for a plot. We remain stolid. Even a *Lolita* we take in stride. (Although in defense of that brilliant perversity, I must add that it is not really sentimental; only wicked.) We have put up with *Peyton Place* and its myriad imitations; with historical novels where the aberrations of the protagonists keep getting in the way of the scenery. And we have watched the last gates go down as sex and pathos clutter up what used to be purely a mathematical delight, the detective story. (Now we are called on to feel compassion for the murderer.) Still the boredom grows. Unless someone of sizable gifts finds out how to fuse all this material into a believable corpus of literature, the tide may menacingly turn. We'll have Victorian swoons again, and deathbed conversions. We'll have Tiny Tim and The Virginian. For sheer shock there seems nowhere to go except back to morality.

20. What is dangerous is that this return may be forced on writers

from outside. More and more often one hears the mutter of "There ought to be a law!" Pressure groups grow restive. Even avant-garde critics begin to deplore our nihilistic art. Some bleak day censorship may descend upon us officially, with the same stultifying results as in Russia or Ireland or any other country which tries to sift the "good" from the "bad" by palpable tests. We will then be rid of the original along with the unworthy; have not free growth but totalitarian restriction. Sweetness and light will reign, but by state proclamation. Then writers and critics and even readers will be able to put the blame neatly—on themselves.

21. For we are today afflicted by a further sentimentality to which most of the literate world has blindly subscribed. It is as untrue as any other catchword. We have cried over and over, "Artists must be free." And we have added, parroting the adage, "Nobody was ever seduced by a book."

22. What nonsense! Nobody ever seduced by books? Since the invention of writing, people have been seduced by the power of the word into all kinds of virtues, follies, conspiracies and gallantries. They have been converted to religions, incited to revolutions, inspired to patriotism, urged into sin and lured into salvation. It was with a book that Luther sparked the Reformation; and by another book that St. Ignatius was won from the life of a Basque cavalier to that of God's soldier. Not all the tea dumped into Boston Harbor was as influential in bringing about the American Revolution as was Thomas Paine, busy with his tracts. Soviet Russia was bred in the brain of Karl Marx, scribbling grimly away at *Das Kapital* in the British Museum. St. Augustine came to Christianity by way of a book he picked up and read "in a garden." We are all swayed, whether we know it or not, by what we read. A people drenched, drowned, suffocated by what is sick is bound to be infected.

23. Consider the generation now growing up. No matter how solid the environment of their homes, no matter how strong their early training in ethics, morals or religion, the constant rain of literary ugliness which pours on them must to some extent erode their characters. Also it is not only what they read but what they do *not* find in their reading that seduces them. The young are romantic. They long for a test of their caliber, for a hero to whom they may respond. They hunger for the bread of bravery, sacrifice, great deeds. They receive the stone of self-pity. I think it a minor miracle that we have young people of any worth at all left in the country when I consider the stuff on which their minds are fed. I can only conclude that half of them do not read.

24. "But remember," says the unreasoning commentator, "an artist can only hold a mirror up to nature. This is a violent age. We have had two wars. Over us hangs a half-promise of annihilation. We have known Hit-

ler and Stalin, Dachau and Korea. How is a writer to put down anything but the horror to which he is living witness?"

25. Sentimentality again! There were heroes as well as dupes and victims in those wars. There was an Anne Frank in the concentration camps as well as an Eichmann. There were tens of thousands of plain men and women who gave their lives and their wits toward fighting the evil at their doors. Slums breed saints as well as switchblade killers. Cities spawn scholars as often as profiteers. Small towns are not all sinks of iniquity. Relentlessly to insist the world is all black is as inartistic as to show it all shining white. The mirror held up to nature must not wholly distort.

26. What is more, it is entirely possible to write a serene and truthful book in a time of great trouble. When Jane Austen worked out her six perfect novels Napoleon was beating at England's gates and invasion might have come at any time. The Roman Empire was falling apart when Vergil wrote *The Georgics* and he is credited with holding it together for a while by virtue of those pastoral masterpieces. St. Augustine finished *The City of God* as the barbarians were literally bursting into the city of Man. As for the Stuart dramatists who next to our own writers were probably most skillful at picturing contemporary nastiness—who reads them now except graduate students? And one must also recall that Stuart villains at least understood their own acts. One was not expected to admire them.

27. The Stuart emphasis on what was shocking ended in Puritan severity. So did the cynicism of Restoration writers end in Victorian primness. There is some lesson here if I read it right. Since we have nowhere to travel nowadays for further shock, we must take one of three roads left to us. One path is most probable as well as most dangerous—official censorship which pleases nobody except the censors. Another is toward unofficial reaction, with a new era of sugared propriety as the only novelty to be seized.

28. The third is the hardest but the only one worth following. Writers must turn away from sentimental preoccupation with evil only and examine the whole of life. Then we may have our Tolstoys. We'll have our Balzacs. We'll even have our Dickenses. (For Dickens, one remembers, invented not Nell Trents alone. He also imagined his Fagins and his Uriah Heeps and his Mr. Micawbers.) Then we will have black and white, sin and suffering, good and bad, all on the same canvas, translated from life freely but faithfully. Out of what seems an exhausted literature we may create, if not an age of gold, at least one of some sound metal. We'll have heroes again. We'll have aspirers again.

29. And I shall have a little peace in the morning with my coffee.

COMMENTARY AND QUESTIONS

Serious arguments can sometimes be effectively conveyed in very lighthearted tones. This is especially true when the object of attack lends itself to ridicule. Part of the problem in writing this kind of polemic, however, is to know how far to be lighthearted, how far to be sober. In this essay Phyllis McGinley skillfully catches her readers' attention and smiles them into a receptive expectancy with her judiciously satirical exaggerations; then, without any jarring discontinuity of tone, she leads them through a concisely reasoned argument.

1. The opening section of this essay draws a humorous contrast between the peaceable and the upsetting. What is the effect of such words as *Armageddon, bombs, furies,* and *explosive* in par. 2, of *cries, shouts,* and *assault* in pars. 5 and 6? Comment on the preservation of balance in pars. 3-6 between verisimilitude and deliberate exaggeration.

2. Par. 7 is quieter in tone than the preceding passages and introduces a new idea. Why is the statement *It is not only that I lack stamina* followed immediately by *I also lack patience?* In the sixth, seventh, eighth, and ninth sentences of this paragraph the verbal phrases *am bored with, am weary of, am sick to death of,* and *tire of* at first deliberately increase the degree of emphasis and then (with the fourth verb) destroy emphasis so as to devaluate or disparage the term *sentimentality.* In the sixth sentence, what is the point of the phrase *frank and explicit?* Why is the metaphor in the last sentence particularly appropriate after the metaphor of the preceding sentence?

3. Turning a definition against one's opponents can be a useful polemical device. If *sentimentality* is something which modern sophisticates have come to think of as both reprehensible and old-fashioned, what is the effect of demonstrating that today's hard-boiled fiction may properly be called *sentimental?* In the fifth sentence of par. 11, the first two examples of "trite stock figures" are presented in comparatively neutral terms. What is the effect of the third example?

4. After the first seven paragraphs, the essay is relatively serious in tone, yet the style of the latter part does not seem inconsistent with that of the beginning. Point out some of the means by which the author achieves this sense of consistency; consider, for example, the quotation in par. 12, the example concluding par. 14, the last sentence of par. 15. Does the part of the essay beginning with par. 8 become more or less serious in tone as it progresses? What is the function of par 29?

5. What is the relation to par. 11 of par. 12? of pars. 13-16? of par. 17? With what much earlier paragraph is par. 19 connected by content as well as by verbal echo? The last sentence of par. 19 is connected both with the opening of the essay (through the phrase *For sheer shock*) and with the new topic introduced in par. 20 (*this return* echoes *no-*

where to go except back to morality). How are pars. 21 and 25 tied to the earlier portions of the essay? How is par. 27 related by verbal echoes to both par. 19 and par. 20? Why, of the "three roads left to us" (par. 27), is the third given a whole paragraph to itself?

6. This essay makes highly effective use of concrete detail to illustrate or support general statements. Par. 18 might be called documentation by example; pars. 22 and 25, refutation by example. What are some of the advantages—and dangers—of this particular weapon of controversy?

7. Is it merely accidental that the sound of *s* is prominent in the words *sin and suffering, vice and despair* (par. 8)? in *sugary syrup* and *sauce of horror* (par. 11)? What is the connection between the metaphors embodied in these latter phrases and the mention of *treacle* in par. 7, and *sugared propriety* in par. 27?

8. In "The Bird and the Machine" (pp. 75-82) Loren Eiseley also pictures himself as reading a newspaper at the breakfast table. Both he and Phyllis McGinley use this structural device to provide settings for their respective essays, but the effect of these settings is rather different. Characterize the tone of each, and discuss the reasons for the difference.

SUGGESTIONS FOR WRITING

1. The sentimentality of violence on TV (or in the movies).
2. Indecency and dullness.
3. The follies of censorship.
4. Armageddon at the breakfast table.

The Poet and
the Press

by ARCHIBALD MacLEISH

IT IS AN AXIOM of our civilization, if that is the proper name for the chaos of ideas in which we live, that poetry is the opposite of journalism and that journalism is the opposite of poetry. The two are about as likely to meet in an evening's conversation as John Keats and Arthur Krock, and each becomes, when applied to the other, a pejorative term. If you want to insult Scotty Reston, as a number of people in Washington now do, you will refer to those superb pieces of diplomatic correspondence of his as "poetry"—meaning piffle. If you want to insult Thomas Stearns Eliot, as nobody in Washington or anywhere else would now dream of doing, you will call *The Waste Land* "journalism"—meaning journalism. Elder writers addressing younger writers in those invaluable interviews in the *Paris Review* advise them to avoid the practice of journalism as they would wet socks and gin before breakfast, and the New York *Mirror* returns the compliment by announcing in an editorial as solemn as a sermon that anyone who does not regard Robert W. Service as a great poet is a fancy pants, and may even be an intellectual. In short, the two limits of the typewriter keyboard in our time, the two extremes which will never meet, the East and West of our fractured world, are poetry and journalism. But why, if you really stop to think of it, should poetry and journalism be the two poles of the world of words in our time? Why should they appear to us as each other's opposites? There are manifest differences between the two—differences which any of us could tick off—but are they really as manifest as all that? Poetry is an art, yes; or should be. But is journalism the opposite of art?

2. No one would claim that the usual news story in the, let us say, Chicago *Tribune* is a work of art, at least in the ordinary sense of that term. But no one would deny either that great works of journalism exist and that when they exist they exist within a discipline of their own—a discipline which reveals itself, as the disciplines of art always reveal

From *The Atlantic Monthly*, March, 1959. Copyright © 1959 The Atlantic Monthly Company. Reprinted by permission of the author. Delivered as a speech at the University of Minnesota, October 12, 1958.

themselves, in form. The style of a great work of journalism is not, as the glib phrase goes, the man. The style of a great work of journalism is the man in terms of the purpose: a man working at the utmost intensity of which he is capable toward an end to which he is wholly committed. But this, of course, is precisely the characteristic of the style of any work of art—the precise characteristic which distinguishes a work of art from a mere indulgence of personality on the one hand or an impersonal "job" on the other.

3. You cannot, in other words, distinguish journalism from poetry, to the extreme degree in which we distinguish them, merely by saying that one is an art and the other is not. And neither, I think, can you justify their antipodal relationship by the device used in most college catalogues, where courses in expository writing are courses in expository writing, but courses in the writing of poems are courses in creative writing. The theory would be, I imagine, that the poet is supposed to create a world in his poems, whereas the journalist is supposed not to create one but stick as closely as he can to the world he's got. This means that the poet makes something new, but the journalist describes something old, or in any case something that has already happened, for if it has not already happened he is no journalist. More precisely, this means that the journalist selects from among things that already are: events that have in fact befallen, actions actually acted, objects seen, sounds heard; whereas the poet must spin his chronicle out of himself like a spider. But if we leave the theory and look at the practice—specific poems, specific journalisms—will this distinction as between creative and selective hold?

4. Take the first poem that walks into your mind; for of course all of us have such visitors. "Old favorites" we call them because they are free of the house and enter without knocking. Some of you—quite a few, I should guess—will find yourselves thinking of Herrick's "Daffodils," not only because it is one of the finest of English lyrics and one of the poems most frequently taught to children, but because its tune, once echoed in the corridors of the ear, will never stop:

> Fair daffodils, we weep to see
> You haste away so soon:
> As yet the early-rising sun
> Has not attain'd his noon.
> Stay, stay,
> Until the hasting day
> Has run
> But to the even-song;

> And, having pray'd together, we
>   Will go with you along.
>
> We have short time to stay, as you.
>   We have as short a Spring;
> As quick a growth to meet decay,
>   As you, or any thing.
>   We die,
>   As your hours do, and dry
>   Away,
>   Like to the Summer's rain;
> Or as the pearls of morning's dew
>   Ne'er to be found again.

Or some of you will fish up Keats's murex because those five long "I" sounds at the beginning of the "Ode on a Grecian Urn" have held an instant of your mind motionless since the day in your childhood when you first heard them:

> Thou still unravished bride of quietness!
>   Thou foster-child of Silence and slow Time,
> Sylvan historian.

5. For myself, I always think, when I look for touchstones such as these, of a poem I cannot read, written in a tongue no man living can now pronounce—the poem the Emperor Wu Ti wrote in the second century B.C. for his dead mistress, Li Fu Jen. Arthur Waley's translation goes like this:

> The sound of her silk skirt has stopped
> On the marble pavement dust grows
> Her empty room is cold and still
> Fallen leaves are piled against the door
>   Longing for that lovely lady
> How can I bring my aching heart to rest?

6. But whatever poem you call back to mind, the question I would put to you would be the same: Does your poem seem to you, as you contemplate it in your imagination, to be "created" in the sense in which we use that word of the events described in the book of Genesis? Is there not rather a selection and ordering, as there is a selection and ordering in the art of history and in the practice of journalism? The selection is of a different kind, yes: things are chosen which history would find too trivial to touch and which journalism, in its passionate haste to get on with the story, would have no time for. The organization of the fragments selected is also different. Things are put together in poetry which history would never put together because of its addiction to the logic of cause

and effect and which journalism would never put together because of its commitment to the lucidities of common sense. Men do not pray with daffodils in history if they care for the opinion in which posterity will contemplate them, and grief in journalism is sobs, not dead leaves at a door sill or the silence of the sound of silk—the silence after the ceasing of the sound. But granted all this—granted, too, that the structure of words in poetry is very different, far more orderly, immeasurably more strict, than the structure of words in the prose of journalism or of history —does it really follow that the enormous gulf we have dug between the conception of journalism and the conception of poetry is explained away by calling poetry a creative art?

7. I should not say so. I should say that an examination of actual poems and actual journalisms would lead any reader to the conclusion that the difference between them, wide though it is, cannot be stated in terms of creation. Both are re-creations, different in degree but not different in kind, for the material in each case is our human experience of the world and of ourselves; and not fundamentally different in method or even in purpose, since the method of poetry like the method of journalism is selection from the chaotic formlessness of experience, and the purpose of both is the recording of the fragments selected in a sequence that makes sense.

8. It is perfectly true that the sense which poetry makes of its fragments is not the sense which journalism makes. No reporter in America or anywhere else would organize fragments of the experience of a divorce case to read: "love is not love which alters when it alteration finds or bends with the remover to remove. O, no! it is an ever-fixed mark that looks on tempests and is never shaken; it is the star to every wand'ring bark, whose worth's unknown, although his height be taken." In journalism this summation of experience is not sensible at all. It is not even true. Love, in journalism, does not bear "it out even to the edge of doom."

9. And the opposite is also obvious. The sense which journalism makes of the life of a man and the life of a woman, or the life of a man and the lives of two women, is not sensible or even true in poetry. But the fact remains that both Shakespeare's sonnet and the news story of the broken marriage are re-creations of fragments selected from the confusion of human experience in an effort to give them order and make them comprehensible. The purpose in one case may merely be to make them comprehensible to human curiosity, whereas the purpose in the other is very evidently to reach the human intelligence at its most perceptive and most alive: Shakespeare's sonnet has undertones of irony which only a most subtly listening ear can hear. But in both cases and however different their levels, the end is comprehension, understanding.

10. Poetry, despite the almost magical powers of the greatest poets, is a human labor, and what humanity most desperately needs is not the creation of new worlds but the re-creation, in terms of human comprehension, of the world we have, and it is to this task that all the arts are committed. Indeed, it is for this reason that the arts go on from generation to generation in spite of the fact that Phidias has already carved and Homer has already sung. The Creation, we are informed, was accomplished in seven days with Sunday off, but the re-creation will never be accomplished because it is always to be accomplished anew for each new generation of living men. To hold the vast, whirling, humming, buzzing, boggling confusion of the Greek world still long enough to see it is not to hold the vast, whirling, humming, buzzing, boggling confusion of our world still. New charms are necessary, new spells, new artifices. Whether they know it or not, the young men forgather in Paris in one generation, in San Francisco in another, because the world goes round, the light changes, and the old jugs will not carry living water. New jugs must be devised which the generation past will reject as monstrosities and the generation to come will, when it arrives, reject for other reasons: as banalities and bores.

11. But the essential point is that this labor does not differ in kind from the continuing labor of generations of journalists and historians who also face a new and turning world and who must also find new ways to speak of it. The materials of poetry, whatever the miracles accomplished with them, are gathered where the materials of history, present and past, are gathered, in what Keats called the arable field of events. Poetry transforms these materials by a faculty the use of which is discouraged in journalism, the faculty of imagination, but the product of the metamorphosis is not an opposite thing from the product of the process known in journalism as reporting. It is not what our grandfathers used to say it was: a "fancy" as opposed to the sober "facts" of practical men. For one thing, the constructions of the imagination are not fancies and never were. For another, facts are not what our grandfathers supposed them to be in those happy far-off Victorian generations when science picked facts out of life like grits out of porridge and marshaled them in patterns on a page.

12. The re-creations of the imagination do correspond to the experience of the real physical world. Poetry may take liberties with the materials of that experience which history and journalism are not free to take. It may translate them into unexpected and even improbable forms. But it neither will nor can disguise their origins in experience, for the moment it did so it would cease to be an art. It would become a sorcery, a magic. Those Grecian centaurs, half man, half horse, those Oriental mother goddesses all arms and breasts—these derive from nature. It is only the

arrangement of the parts which is unnatural! The parts themselves—the horse, the man, the arms, the breasts—have been discovered in the world the senses know. Even what we call "abstraction" in the art of our own day is not new creation in the sense in which the world of Genesis is new. Vision reduced to line, balance, color, proportion is still vision and still belongs in a world in which line, balance, color, and proportion exist.

13. Indeed, this dependence of poetry, of all art, on human experience of the actual world is only made the more obvious by the attempts of art, which have been frequent in our time, to escape from the actual world. Poems, for example, which derive from the subconscious mind as the poems of the early Surrealists did, or purported to do, are still poems of experience and still poems composed by a process of selection from among the moments of experience. The only difference is that the selecting sieve is set up somewhere outside the conscious mind. But the poem does not become, in consequence, a parentless, pristine creation. On the contrary, it is even more obviously and immediately derived from the common human reality than a poem made, as the Greeks made poems, under the selective direction of a conscious intelligence. The proof lies in the experiments of those contemporary psychiatrists who have attempted to work their way back through completed poems to their roots in experience. They have made very little of the poems of, say, John Donne, but they have had a harvest home with the works of the Surrealists. A Surrealist poem is a direct recording of the experiencing mind on the tape of speech, and all that need be done to make one's way to the unhappy childhood or the illicit love is to play the recording back. John Donne is another matter. The conscious act of art is there to make a mechanical playback impossible. All you will get if you try is that series of garbled screams and whinnies with which the amateurs of tape recordings are familiar.

14. But one need not go to the Surrealists or their successors to make the point. The most apparently fanciful of all familiar poems will testify, if you will truly read them, that their fancies are no less substantial, no less true, no less (if the word is still permitted) real—at least no less authenticated by experience—than the most substantial facts. Consider Prospero's great trope in *The Tempest:* those cloud-capped towers, gorgeous palaces, solemn temples, the great globe itself, which "like this insubstantial pageant faded" dissolve, "leave not a rack behind." Consider Rimbaud's pianos in the Alps, his hares praying to the rainbow through the spider's web, his little boy waving his arms to the weather vanes "Après le Déluge," after the Deluge had subsided, in the *Illuminations.* Compare these extravagant fancies with the hard facts of history and journalism. You will find it difficult, I think, to say just what the substantial difference is. You may even find yourself concluding that, if any-

thing, the fancies are harder than the facts. We are, we are indeed, "such stuff as dreams are made on," and any man who has not yet learned that "our little life is rounded with a sleep" has not yet begun to live that little life. We do, after every Deluge which drowns the world, whether for one man or for many, come upon that moment when everything is new again and possible, even the impossible; when little boys and weather vanes salute each other. There can scarcely be a man or a woman in my generation, if he has really shared that generation's life, who has not known that moment—and then lost it, as Rimbaud's poem loses it. Are these fancies not as substantial as our facts? Are they not as real as murder or the World Series or Governor Faubus, to say nothing of our China policy or a Dow-Jones average? Has anyone ever met a Dow-Jones average on a Sunday afternoon, or bathing, or anywhere else in the world? And as for our China policy, would anyone know its face if it walked onto this platform and sat down and arranged its smile?

15. I am not suggesting that the facts of journalism are insubstantial. I am merely suggesting that there is no such difference between the facts of journalism and the fancies of poetry as we assume when we turn them into each other's opposites. You can prove it to yourself in either way: by reading poems or by reading newspapers. What do you remember about the recent revolution in Iraq—in some ways the most important news story of the year, though not the best reported? What I remember is the account of the assassination of the old Premier, the famous desert fox and the most powerful man in the valley of the two rivers, who was shot in the dress of an old woman. Why do I remember that? Because the fact becomes something more than fact in that telling. Because I understand something of the man—and of those who killed him. Because the political event becomes a human event and casts a shadow far beyond Baghdad, far beyond the desert, far beyond the Middle East. It is only when the scattered and illegible fragments in which we pick up our experience of the world are recomposed in such a way that they make sense *as* human experience that great journalism can result. And the same thing is true in the same words of poetry. What poetry composes of its fragments is more lasting than what journalism composes. It is larger. It goes deeper. It is more meaningful. It has beauty. But it is not contrary in kind. Poetry and journalism—to put it in more inclusive terms, poetry and history— are not opposites and cannot be opposites, and the notion that they are is a delusion.

16. Something more than error is involved in this respectable and sanctified confusion. There are popular errors of various kinds. Some are

harmful. Some are merely silly. This one is harmful. It has hurt poetry. It has altered journalism. And its effect, or the effect of the deeper delusions which have fathered it, on our unhappy civilization has been and continues to be disastrous. What really distinguishes poetry from journalism, aside from the obvious distinctions of form—uses of words, patterns of words, sequences of words—is not a difference in kind but a difference in focus. Journalism is concerned with events, poetry with feelings. Journalism is concerned with the look of the world; poetry with the feel of the world. Journalism wishes to tell what it is that has happened everywhere as though the same things had happened for every man. Poetry wishes to say what it is like for any man to be himself in the presence of a particular occurrence as though only he were alone there.

17. The best definition of journalism appears daily in the New York *Times:* "All the News That's Fit to Print." The best definition of poetry is spelled out in Coleridge's *Biographia Literaria:* "the balance or reconcilement of discordant qualities . . . a more than usual state of emotion with more than usual order." To separate journalism and poetry, therefore—history and poetry—to set them up at opposite ends of the world of discourse, is to separate seeing from the feel of seeing, emotion from the acting of emotion, knowledge from the realization of knowledge.

18. The poet, with us, stops his horse at twilight at the wood's edge in falling snow and yields for a moment to that longing for sleep in the cold, white, drifting stillness which is also another and deeper longing all reflective men have known, but the journalist permits himself to see only a man in a buggy stopping in inclement weather at a remote and unlikely spot; since nothing has "happened," he publishes nothing. And the same thing is true in reverse. The journalist dodges hand grenades in the bazaar of a hot, dusty, dirty, flea-bitten desert city to report an obscure war which may be the beginning of the ultimate war, but the poet, because all this is merely happening, does not write at all; because nothing is felt, he has nothing to say.

19. I exaggerate, of course. There have been journalists of our generation, men like Elmer Davis as well as men like Ernie Pyle, who would not have separated the feel of things from the look of them if they could, and there are contemporary poets who not only felt but saw the war in Spain —saw it, in fact, far more clearly than the journalists or the foreign offices or the professional observers of world affairs. Indeed, the greatest of contemporary poets was also one of the most exact and penetrating observers of the history of his time, if not always the most intelligent interpreter of that history.

> Turning and turning in the widening gyre
> The falcon cannot hear the falconer;

Things fall apart; the centre cannot hold;
Mere anarchy is loosed upon the world,
The blood-dimmed tide is loosed, and everywhere
The ceremony of innocence is drowned;
The best lack all conviction, while the worst
Are full of passionate intensity.

[20.] No journalist writing of the tragic events with which the name of the late Senator McCarthy is associated ever defined that aspect of contemporary life as precisely as Yeats had defined it some thirty years before:

The best lack all conviction, while the worst
Are full of passionate intensity.

[21.] But Yeats is an exception in this as in many other things. And not even Yeats was able to bring the event and the feel of the event together as they were brought in Homer's time and Dante's and Shakespeare's. Journalism, with us, tends more and more toward an admirably dispassionate objectivity which presents the event in the colorless air of intellectual detachment at the cost of its emotional significance, and poetry, reacting to the same divisive influence but in an opposite direction, turns more and more to the emotional significance divorced from the event. I do not know that it is possible to say that this fracture of the word is bad for journalism as such, for the great modern newspapers are, as newspapers, far superior to their predecessors. They collect more news faster and present it more accurately. It is only too possible to say, however, that it is bad for poetry and bad for the civilization.

[22.] Great poems are instruments of knowledge—a knowledge carried alive into the heart by passion, but knowledge nevertheless. Feeling without knowing never made a work of art and never will. And the attempt which contemporary poetry increasingly makes to detach feelings from their occasions—to pursue feelings as themselves and for their own sakes, resolutely ignoring the events from which they derive—can only be harmful to the art. Poems so composed are like kites without strings. They cannot bear up against the carrying away of time, because they have no attachment to a point in time.

[23.] The consequences to poetry itself of its increasing inwardness are of concern, unhappily, only to poets. What the rest of us might wish to think of is the effect of all this on our civilization. It is not difficult to define. Some time ago, Lewis Mumford, certainly one of the most intelligent of living Americans, wrote a letter to the New York *Times* expressing his horror at the apathy of his countrymen in the face of the dangers inherent in our policy and conduct in the Straits of Formosa. Here we were, he said, on a brink from which we might at any moment be shoved by the Chinese Nationalists or dragged by the Chinese Communists, with a war yawning before us which could only be fought by the horrible weapons of genocide and with the end of human life on the earth as a very possible consequence. And yet we neither protested nor objected. We merely sat there in numb indifference, leaving the decision of life or death to a Secretary of State whose previous decisions or indecisions were responsible for our predicament.

24. It was an angry letter, and one with which men of certain opinions might differ. But what struck me about it was not its statement of the facts, which seemed to me only too painfully correct, but its explanation of the reason for our national indifference to the facts. Our apathy, Mr. Mumford suggested—I do not know how seriously—could only be the consequence of our enormous consumption of tranquilizers and sedatives. Only a nation doped into unreality could possibly contemplate in silence a series of events and declarations which might at any moment lead to the extermination of enormous numbers of peaceful human beings, first in Asia and then throughout the world, including the part of the world in which we live ourselves.

25. I say I was struck by this explanation. I was struck by it because I found myself wishing the real explanation might be as simple and ironic. For the truth is, of course, that our apathy with regard to the incredible and terrifying events in Amoy Harbor and the disastrous consequences which might at any moment follow was the result not of our habits in the taking of pills but of our habits in the thinking of thoughts. And the further truth is that this strange dislocation in the thinking of thoughts by which we can "know" what we cannot feel—by which we can know that the consequence of a merely diplomatic maneuver may be the atomizing of the city of Peiping and then Tokyo and then Moscow and then New York, but cannot imagine in our live emotions what this knowing would feel like—this dislocation is the consequence of a deeper dislocation not only in ourselves but in our civilization.

26. For this divorce between knowing and feeling is not anything we Americans can claim as our own peculiar prerogative. The Germans have exhibited the same curious capacity: the "good Germans" who knew about the gas ovens of the concentration camps but were nevertheless able to live with their knowledge in tranquillity and good conscience until they began to go in crowded, silent audiences to performances of *The Diary of Anne Frank.* And we ourselves—shall we call ourselves the "good Americans"?—are guilty of the same peace of mind. We know what happened at Hiroshima. We have read, or read about, John Hersey's account of the results of the atomic bombing of that city. Most of us

are at least aware of the specters which crawl through Dr. Hachiya's book: "Their faces and hands were burnt and swollen and great sheets of skin had peeled away from their tissues to hang down like rags on a scarecrow. They moved like a line of ants. All through the night they went past our house, but this morning they had stopped. I found them lying on both sides of the road so thick that it was impossible to pass without stepping on them." We know all this. But do we feel our knowledge? Could we even *think* about risking the possibility of a world-wide atomic war as a matter of face or official vanity if we did?

27. I am not going to discuss foreign policy—if that is the right term for our recent behavior off the China coast. But nothing could better illustrate the flaw at the heart of our civilization than this strange chapter of our history. Nothing could more convincingly demonstrate that knowledge without feeling is not knowledge and can lead only to public irresponsibility and indifference, and conceivably to ruin. Nothing could more clearly prove that when the fact is disassociated from the feel of the fact in the minds of an entire people—in the common mind of a civilization—that people, that civilization, is in danger.

28. Some of you, I have no doubt, will think the terms I have been using throughout this discussion are inadequate to so serious an indictment. Journalism seems, to most of us, a profession like another, and poetry seems remote indeed from matters of such moment as the survival of the world. But the fact is, of course, that the survival of the world—at least the survival of a world which has prepared as ingeniously for its own suicide as the world we live in—depends, madmen and accidents aside, solely on the knowledge of the men and women who inhabit it. And that knowledge is composed precisely of the two increments which journalism and poetry provide. Information is essential to the kind of knowledge on which an opinion relevant to the situation on Quemoy can be based. But the feel of the facts which that information communicates is also essential if the knowledge and the opinions it fathers are to be trustworthy and reliable. What has happened with us is that the first has outrun the second. We are, as we are constantly and justly being reminded, the best informed people on an earth which is better informed now than it ever was before in its history. But though we are provided with more facts than any previous generation, we are not necessarily possessed of more knowledge of those facts.

29. On the contrary, we seem to be less and less capable of receiving our facts into our imaginations, where they can come alive with feeling. Benjamin Franklin's contemporaries were not told within a few hours that some hundreds of coal miners had been trapped in a mine in what is now Yugoslavia, but when, after many months, the news of such a disas-

ter at last came through, it would have come as a human tragedy with its human significance about it. The news of Napoleon's retreat from Moscow would be broadcast today minute-by-minute, photographed, columnized, interpreted, recorded to the last detail. When Napoleon actually turned back, the news was brought to New York in a brig commanded by my great-grandfather months after the event and in an individual witness's report, but it loomed in the New York newspapers of the next morning like news from Troy, which, in a sense, it was. What the Greeks knew about Troy, they knew through a man's slow telling.

30. I am not deploring the advances of journalism. They are miraculous. No man who has grown used to the news coverage of an expertly managed paper could live without it. But every improvement, and particularly every improvement made possible by mechanical invention, exacts its price, as we are discovering in our increasingly mechanized country. Often the price is exacted at the cost of nature and sometimes even at the cost of human nature. We are deluged with facts, but we have lost, or are losing, our human ability to feel them. Poetry still survives with us, survives with vigor and inventiveness, throwing up new masters capable of standing with the old. But the poem itself has lost its power in men's minds. We have not discarded the art as Herbert Spencer thought men would when the machine had come to flower, but we have impaired the practice of the skill the art can give, the skill of feeling truly and so truly knowing. We know with the head now, by the facts, by the abstractions. We seem unable to know as Shakespeare knew, who makes King Lear cry out to blinded Gloucester on the heath, "you see how this world goes," and Gloucester answers, "I see it feelingly."

31. Why we are thus impotent, I do not know. I know only that this impotence exists and that it is dangerous, increasingly dangerous. I know, too, or think I know, that whatever the underlying cause of the divorce of feeling from knowing, that divorce reveals itself most vividly in the strange and ignorant belief that the life of the imagination lies at an opposite pole from the life of the inquiring mind—that men can live and know and master their experience of this darkling earth by accumulating information and no more.

32. Men who believe that have, in effect, surrendered their responsibilities as men. They have gone over to the enemy, to those unhappy hordes, victims of the new and terrible tyranny of our time, who are not meant to know for themselves and with their whole beings but only to accept the daily ration of news and hates which Peiping or Moscow issues to them. Slavery begins when men give up the human need to

know with the whole heart, to know for themselves, to bear the burden for themselves—the "burden," as Wordsworth called it, "of the mystery." To acquiesce, as the Russians and the Chinese and the Poles—even the Hungarians—have had to acquiesce in someone else's knowing is to acquiesce in someone else's deciding, and at that point, whatever the society is called, it is not free.

33. The real defense of freedom is imagination, that feeling life of the mind which actually knows because it involves itself in its knowing, puts itself in the place where its thought goes, walks in the body of the little Negro girl who feels the spittle dribbling on her cheek, follows in that line of ants whose skin is ragged tatters. The man who knows with his heart knows himself to be a man, feels as himself, cannot be silenced. He is free no matter where he lives, as Boris Pasternak has shown that he is free even in Russia. The man who knows with his mind only, who will not commit himself beyond his wits, who will not feel the thing he knows, or know the thing he feels—that man has no freedom anywhere. He is tugged by the string of whatever is told him, maneuvered by slogans. Sooner or later his life will seem indifferent to him, something managed by others, and he will acquiesce in the management, think about it as little as possible, occupy himself with the only things near enough to seem real—his car, his front lawn, those shadows on the television screen —symbolic shadows.

34. To me—not many others think so—the real crisis in the life of our society is the crisis of the life of the imagination. Far more than we need an intercontinental missile or a moral rearmament or a religious revival, we need to come alive again, to recover the virility of the imagination on which all earlier civilizations have been based: Coleridge's "synthetic and magical power" by which "the whole soul of man" may be brought to activity and knowledge may be *known*. It is for this reason that I have permitted myself to speak of my concern in a great university. I do not mean that I think education is wholly responsible for the flaw which has split knowledge of heart from knowledge of head, though it has surely its fair share of the blame. I mean rather that it is principally by the process of education that the flaw can be healed. The need for a review of the relation between education and the arts was never greater than at this moment, when our whole attention is fixed on the relation between education and the sciences. A society which has so lost the capacity to see the world feelingly that it can watch in silence while the possibility of nuclear extermination is employed as a diplomatic maneuver may stand in need of thousands of young manufacturing scientists sooner than it thinks. But even sooner, it will need to learn to know.

COMMENTARY AND QUESTIONS

Archibald MacLeish has had experience of law, of war, of journalism, of librarianship, of teaching, and of government service. He has also been, throughout his career, a practising and publishing poet. That poetry, in the widest sense of the word—the power of feeling, the power of the re-creating imagination—must enter into all men's lives, lest their present be perilous and their future lost, is the argument of this essay.

1. "The Poet and the Press" was originally delivered as a special lecture at the University of Minnesota. It is useful for a lecturer not personally known to most of his hearers to establish as quickly as possible a rapport with his audience. Point out words, phrases, and allusions in the first paragraph which, in addition to introducing the subject of discussion, would be likely to put MacLeish's audience in a receptive state of mind.

2. In a speech or essay aimed at a more or less uniformly educated audience, it is appropriate to use frequent allusions to authors and events and to leave some of them—not too many—unexplained, as a possible source of pleasure for the hearers or readers who succeed in recognizing them. If you did not recognize it, you can go fishing for "Keats's murex" (par. 4) in a poem by Robert Browning called "Popularity"; the reference to the spider at the end of par. 3 is probably a consciously ironic echo of the image of the spider and the bee used by Jonathan Swift in *The Battle of the Books*. MacLeish identifies for us the authors of the poems quoted in pars. 4-5, 8, and 19-20; why might he have felt it unnecessary to name the author of the play cited near the beginning of par. 14 or to mention either author or title of the poem referred to at the beginning of par. 18? What principles would you say ought to govern the choice and handling of illustrative allusions in a speech or essay? Compare the frequency and nature of the allusions used here by MacLeish with those used by Joseph Wood Krutch in "Life, Liberty and the Pursuit of Welfare" (pp. 442-453); how far may the differences be attributed to differences in the audiences for which the two authors were writing?

3. In his opening paragraph MacLeish introduces, as supposed opposites, the terms *poetry* and *journalism*. In par. 6 he speaks of *the art of history* as parallel to *the practice of journalism*, and in several succeeding passages uses sometimes *journalism*, sometimes *history*, as the opposite of *poetry*. After looking at the final sentence of par. 15 and considering the tenor of the whole essay, suggest why, on the one hand, MacLeish introduces the term *history* as an alternate to *journalism*, and why, on the other hand, *journalism* is the term receiving greatest emphasis. Can you generalize about the method of argumentation prevailingly used in this essay?

4. After the initial confrontation of poetry and journalism, MacLeish devotes a number of paragraphs to showing that each is an art, and that each is characteristically a re-creation "of fragments selected from the confusion of human experience in an effort to give them order and make them comprehensible" (par. 9). In par. 11 he introduces the term *imagination.* How is his discussion of imagination connected with his use of the term *re-creation?* with his use of the term *experience?* Why is his discussion of experience essential to his thesis that "poetry and journalism . . . are not opposites and cannot be opposites, and the notion that they are is a delusion" (par. 15)?

5. Par. 15 concludes the first of the two main divisions of the essay with the summary assertion of its final sentence. A skeptical hearer might have said at this point, "I agree that poetry and journalism are not opposites. So what?" How does MacLeish go about meeting this possible challenge? Would you say that the latter half of the essay is less important than the first? If not, why is the material of the first half given so much emphasis? *Poetry* and *journalism* are the two seemingly opposed terms around which MacLeish structures the first half of his essay; around what parallel pair does he build much of the second half? Why is it so appropriate to reintroduce the term *imagination* into the concluding portion of the essay (pars. 29, 31, 33, 34)?

6. As might be expected in the work of a writer who is both a practising poet and a successful journalist and man of affairs, MacLeish's essay embodies a precise and graceful style. Consider, for example, both the sound and the sense of such sentences as the sixth of par. 6 ("Men do not pray . . ."), the last of par. 18, the second of par. 26, or the second of par. 32. Except perhaps in the tongue-in-cheek persiflage of the opening paragraph, MacLeish permits himself little showiness of style, yet such easy lucidity, such rightness of rhythms, come only from having a practised hand and a superb ear. Comment on the particular flavor of the following expressions: history's *addiction to the logic of cause and effect* (par. 6), *the old jugs will not carry living water* (par. 10), *sat down and arranged its smile* (par. 14).

SUGGESTIONS FOR WRITING

1. The emotional callouses of headline readers.
2. The poet and the laboratory.
3. Painting as experience.
4. Objectivity and feeling—a journalist's dilemma.

Mr. Bennett
and Mrs. Brown

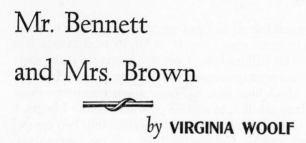

by VIRGINIA WOOLF

It SEEMS TO ME POSSIBLE, perhaps desirable, that I may be the only person in this room who has committed the folly of writing, trying to write, or failing to write, a novel. And when I asked myself, as your invitation to speak to you about modern fiction made me ask myself, what demon whispered in my ear and urged me to my doom, a little figure rose before me—the figure of a man, or of a woman, who said, "My name is Brown. Catch me if you can."

2. Most novelists have the same experience. Some Brown, Smith, or Jones comes before them and says in the most seductive and charming way in the world, "Come and catch me if you can." And so, led on by this will-o'-the-wisp, they flounder through volume after volume, spending the best years of their lives in the pursuit, and receiving for the most part very little cash in exchange. Few catch the phantom; most have to be content with a scrap of her dress or a wisp of her hair.

3. My belief that men and women write novels because they are lured on to create some character which has thus imposed itself upon them has the sanction of Mr. Arnold Bennett. In an article from which I will quote he says: "The foundation of good fiction is character-creating and nothing else. . . . Style counts; plot counts; originality of outlook counts. But none of these counts anything like so much as the convincingness of the characters. If the characters are real the novel will have a chance; if they are not, oblivion will be its portion. . . ." And he goes on to draw the conclusion that we have no young novelists of first-rate importance at the present moment, because they are unable to create characters that are real, true, and convincing.

4. These are the questions that I want with greater boldness than discretion to discuss to-night. I want to make out what we mean when we talk about "character" in fiction; to say something about the question of

reality which Mr. Bennett raises; and to suggest some reasons why the younger novelists fail to create characters, if, as Mr. Bennett asserts, it is true that fail they do. This will lead me, I am well aware, to make some very sweeping and some very vague assertions. For the question is an extremely difficult one. Think how little we know about character—think how little we know about art. But, to make a clearance before I begin, I will suggest that we range Edwardians and Georgians into two camps; Mr. Wells, Mr. Bennett, and Mr. Galsworthy I will call the Edwardians; Mr. Forster, Mr. Lawrence, Mr. Strachey, Mr. Joyce, and Mr. Eliot I will call the Georgians. And if I speak in the first person, with intolerable egotism, I will ask you to excuse me. I do not want to attribute to the world at large the opinions of one solitary, ill-informed, and misguided individual.

5. My first assertion is one that I think you will grant—that every one in this room is a judge of character. Indeed it would be impossible to live for a year without disaster unless one practised character-reading and had some skill in the art. Our marriages, our friendships depend on it; our business largely depends on it; every day questions arise which can only be solved by its help. And now I will hazard a second assertion, which is more disputable perhaps, to the effect that on or about December, 1910, human character changed.

6. I am not saying that one went out, as one might into a garden, and there saw that a rose had flowered, or that a hen had laid an egg. The change was not sudden and definite like that. But a change there was, nevertheless; and, since one must be arbitrary, let us date it about the year 1910. The first signs of it are recorded in the books of Samuel Butler, in *The Way of All Flesh* in particular; the plays of Bernard Shaw continued to record it. In life one can see the change, if I may use a homely illustration, in the character of one's cook. The Victorian cook lived like a leviathan in the lower depths, formidable, silent, obscure, inscrutable; the Georgian cook is a creature of sunshine and fresh air; in and out of the drawing-room, now to borrow *The Daily Herald,* now to ask advice about a hat. Do you ask for more solemn instances of the power of the human race to change? Read the *Agamemnon,* and see whether, in process of time, your sympathies are not almost entirely with Clytemnestra. Or consider the married life of the Carlyles, and bewail the waste, the futility, for him and for her, of the horrible domestic tradition which made it seemly for a woman of genius to spend her time chasing beetles, scouring saucepans, instead of writing books. All human relations have shifted—those between masters and servants, husbands and wives, parents and children. And when human relations change there is at the same time a change in religion, conduct, politics, and literature. Let us agree to place one of these changes about the year 1910.

7. I have said that people have to acquire a good deal of skill in character-reading if they are to live a single year of life without disaster. But it is the art of the young. In middle age and in old age the art is practised mostly for its uses, and friendships and other adventures and experiments in the art of reading character are seldom made. But novelists differ from the rest of the world because they do not cease to be interested in character when they have learnt enough about it for practical purposes. They go a step further; they feel that there is something permanently interesting in character in itself. When all the practical business of life has been discharged, there is something about people which continues to seem to them of overwhelming importance, in spite of the fact that it has no bearing whatever upon their happiness, comfort, or income. The study of character becomes to them an absorbing pursuit; to impart character an obsession. And this I find it very difficult to explain: what novelists mean when they talk about character, what the impulse is that urges them so powerfully every now and then to embody their view in writing.

8. So, if you will allow me, instead of analyzing and abstracting, I will tell you a simple story which, however pointless, has the merit of being true, of a journey from Richmond to Waterloo, in the hope that I may show you what I mean by character in itself; that you may realize the different aspects it can wear; and the hideous perils that beset you directly you try to describe it in words.

9. One night some weeks ago, then, I was late for the train and jumped into the first carriage I came to. As I sat down I had the strange and uncomfortable feeling that I was interrupting a conversation between two people who were already sitting there. Not that they were young or happy. Far from it. They were both elderly, the woman over sixty, the man well over forty. They were sitting opposite each other, and the man, who had been leaning over and talking emphatically to judge by his attitude and the flush on his face, sat back and became silent. I had disturbed him, and he was annoyed. The elderly lady, however, whom I will call Mrs. Brown, seemed rather relieved. She was one of those clean, threadbare old ladies whose extreme tidiness—everything buttoned, fastened, tied together, mended and brushed up—suggests more extreme poverty than rags and dirt. There was something pinched about her—a look of suffering, of apprehension, and, in addition, she was extremely small. Her feet, in their clean little boots, scarcely touched the floor. I felt that she had nobody to support her; that she had to make up her mind for herself; that, having been deserted, or left a widow, years ago, she had led an anxious, harried life, bringing up an only son, perhaps, who, as likely as not, was by this time beginning to go to the bad. All this shot through my mind as I sat down, being uncomfortable, like most people, at travelling with fellow passengers unless I have somehow or other ac-

counted for them. Then I looked at the man. He was no relation of Mrs. Brown's I felt sure; he was of a bigger, burlier, less refined type. He was a man of business I imagined, very likely a respectable corn-chandler from the North, dressed in good blue serge with a pocket-knife and a silk handkerchief, and a stout leather bag. Obviously, however, he had an unpleasant business to settle with Mrs. Brown; a secret, perhaps sinister business, which they did not intend to discuss in my presence.

10. "Yes, the Crofts have had very bad luck with their servants," Mr. Smith (as I will call him) said in a considering way, going back to some earlier topic, with a view to keeping up appearances.

11. "Ah, poor people," said Mrs. Brown, a trifle condescendingly. "My grandmother had a maid who came when she was fifteen and stayed till she was eighty" (this was said with a kind of hurt and aggressive pride to impress us both perhaps).

12. "One doesn't often come across that sort of thing nowadays," said Mr. Smith in conciliatory tones.

13. Then they were silent.

14. "It's odd they don't start a golf club there—I should have thought one of the young fellows would," said Mr. Smith, for the silence obviously made him uneasy.

15. Mrs. Brown hardly took the trouble to answer.

16. "What changes they're making in this part of the world," said Mr. Smith looking out of the window, and looking furtively at me as he did so.

17. It was plain, from Mrs. Brown's silence, from the uneasy affability with which Mr. Smith spoke, that he had some power over her which he was exerting disagreeably. It might have been her son's downfall, or some painful episode in her past life, or her daughter's. Perhaps she was going to London to sign some document to make over some property. Obviously against her will she was in Mr. Smith's hands. I was beginning to feel a great deal of pity for her, when she said, suddenly and inconsequently,

18. "Can you tell me if an oak-tree dies when the leaves have been eaten for two years in succession by caterpillars?"

19. She spoke quite brightly, and rather precisely, in a cultivated, inquisitive voice.

20. Mr. Smith was startled, but relieved to have a safe topic of conversation given him. He told her a great deal very quickly about plagues of insects. He told her that he had a brother who kept a fruit farm in Kent. He told her what fruit farmers do every year in Kent, and so on, and so on. While he talked a very odd thing happened. Mrs. Brown took out her little white handkerchief and began to dab her eyes. She was crying. But she went on listening quite composedly to what he was saying, and he

went on talking, a little louder, a little angrily, as if he had seen her cry often before; as if it were a painful habit. At last it got on his nerves. He stopped abruptly, looked out of the window, then leant towards her as he had been doing when I got in, and said in a bullying, menacing way, as if he would not stand any more nonsense,

21. "So about that matter we were discussing. It'll be all right? George will be there on Tuesday?"

22. "We sha'n't be late," said Mrs. Brown, gathering herself together with superb dignity.

23. Mr. Smith said nothing. He got up, buttoned his coat, reached his bag down, and jumped out of the train before it had stopped at Clapham Junction. He had got what he wanted, but he was ashamed of himself; he was glad to get out of the old lady's sight.

24. Mrs. Brown and I were left alone together. She sat in her corner opposite, very clean, very small, rather queer, and suffering intensely. The impression she made was overwhelming. It came pouring out like a draught, like a smell of burning. What was it composed of—that overwhelming and peculiar impression? Myriads of irrelevant and incongruous ideas crowd into one's head on such occasions; one sees the person, one sees Mrs. Brown, in the centre of all sorts of different scenes. I thought of her in a seaside house, among queer ornaments: sea-urchins, models of ships in glass cases. Her husband's medals were on the mantelpiece. She popped in and out of the room, perching on the edges of chairs, picking meals out of saucers, indulging in long, silent stares. The caterpillars and the oak-trees seemed to imply all that. And then, into this fantastic and secluded life, broke Mr. Smith. I saw him blowing in, so to speak, on a windy day. He banged, he slammed. His dripping umbrella made a pool in the hall. They sat closeted together.

25. And then Mrs. Brown faced the dreadful revelation. She took her heroic decision. Early, before dawn, she packed her bag and carried it herself to the station. She would not let Smith touch it. She was wounded in her pride, unmoored from her anchorage; she came of gentlefolks who kept servants—but details could wait. The important thing was to realize her character, to steep oneself in her atmosphere. I had no time to explain why I felt it somewhat tragic, heroic, yet with a dash of the flighty, and fantastic, before the train stopped, and I watched her disappear, carrying her bag, into the vast blazing station. She looked very small, very tenacious; at once very frail and very heroic. And I have never seen her again, and I shall never know what became of her.

26. The story ends without any point to it. But I have not told you this anecdote to illustrate either my own ingenuity or the pleasure of travelling from Richmond to Waterloo. What I want you to see in it is this.

Here is a character imposing itself upon another person. Here is Mrs. Brown making someone begin almost automatically to write a novel about her. I believe that all novels begin with an old lady in the corner opposite. I believe that all novels, that is to say, deal with character, and that it is to express character—not to preach doctrines, sing songs, or celebrate the glories of the British Empire, that the form of the novel, so clumsy, verbose, and undramatic, so rich, elastic, and alive, has been evolved. To express character, I have said; but you will at once reflect that the very widest interpretation can be put upon those words. For example, old Mrs. Brown's character will strike you very differently according to the age and country in which you happen to be born. It would be easy enough to write three different versions of that incident in the train, an English, a French, and a Russian. The English writer would make the old lady into a "character"; he would bring out her oddities and mannerisms; her buttons and wrinkles; her ribbons and warts. Her personality would dominate the book. A French writer would rub out all that; he would sacrifice the individual Mrs. Brown to give a more general view of human nature; to make a more abstract, proportioned, and harmonious whole. The Russian would pierce through the flesh; would reveal the soul—the soul alone, wandering out into the Waterloo Road, asking of life some tremendous question which would sound on and on in our ears after the book was finished. And then besides age and country there is the writer's temperament to be considered. You see one thing in character, and I another. You say it means this, and I that. And when it comes to writing each makes a further selection on principles of his own. Thus Mrs. Brown can be treated in an infinite variety of ways, according to the age, country, and temperament of the writer.

27. But now I must recall what Mr. Arnold Bennett says. He says that it is only if the characters are real that the novel has any chance of surviving. Otherwise, die it must. But, I ask myself, what is reality? And who are the judges of reality? A character may be real to Mr. Bennett and quite unreal to me. For instance, in this article he says that Dr. Watson in *Sherlock Holmes* is real to him: to me Dr. Watson is a sack stuffed with straw, a dummy, a figure of fun. And so it is with character after character—in book after book. There is nothing that people differ about more than the reality of characters, especially in contemporary books. But if you take a larger view I think that Mr. Bennett is perfectly right. If, that is, you think of the novels which seem to you great novels—*War and Peace, Vanity Fair, Tristram Shandy, Madame Bovary, Pride and Prejudice, The Mayor of Casterbridge, Villette*—if you think of these books, you do at once think of some character who has seemed to you so real (I do not by that mean so lifelike) that it has the power to make you think

not merely of it itself, but of all sorts of things through its eyes—of religion, of love, of war, of peace, of family life, of balls in county towns, of sunsets, moonrises, the immortality of the soul. There is hardly any subject of human experience that is left out of *War and Peace* it seems to me. And in all these novels all these great novelists have brought us to see whatever they wish us to see through some character. Otherwise, they would not be novelists; but poets, historians, or pamphleteers.

28. But now let us examine what Mr. Bennett went on to say—he said that there was no great novelist among the Georgian writers because they cannot create characters who are real, true, and convincing. And there I cannot agree. There are reasons, excuses, possibilities which I think put a different colour upon the case. It seems so to me at least, but I am well aware that this is a matter about which I am likely to be prejudiced, sanguine, and near-sighted. I will put my view before you in the hope that you will make it impartial, judicial, and broad-minded. Why, then, is it so hard for novelists at present to create characters which seem real, not only to Mr. Bennett, but to the world at large? Why, when October comes round, do the publishers always fail to supply us with a masterpiece?

29. Surely one reason is that the men and women who began writing novels in 1910 or thereabouts had this great difficulty to face—that there was no English novelist living from whom they could learn their business. Mr. Conrad is a Pole; which sets him apart, and makes him, however admirable, not very helpful. Mr. Hardy has written no novel since 1895. The most prominent and successful novelists in the year 1910 were, I suppose, Mr. Wells, Mr. Bennett, and Mr. Galsworthy. Now it seems to me that to go to these men and ask them to teach you how to write a novel—how to create characters that are real—is precisely like going to a bootmaker and asking him to teach you how to make a watch. Do not let me give you the impression that I do not admire and enjoy their books. They seem to me of great value, and indeed of great necessity. There are seasons when it is more important to have boots than to have watches. To drop metaphor, I think that after the creative activity of the Victorian age it was quite necessary, not only for literature but for life, that someone should write the books that Mr. Wells, Mr. Bennett, and Mr. Galsworthy have written. Yet what odd books they are! Sometimes I wonder if we are right to call them books at all. For they leave one with so strange a feeling of incompleteness and dissatisfaction. In order to complete them it seems necessary to do something—to join a society, or, more desperately, to write a cheque. That done, the restlessness is laid, the book finished; it can be put upon the shelf, and need never be read again. But with the work of other novelists it is different.

Tristram Shandy or *Pride and Prejudice* is complete in itself; it is self-contained; it leaves one with no desire to do anything, except indeed to read the book again, and to understand it better. The difference perhaps is that both Sterne and Jane Austen were interested in things in themselves; in character in itself; in the book in itself. Therefore everything was inside the book, nothing outside. But the Edwardians were never interested in character in itself; or in the book in itself. They were interested in something outside. Their books, then, were incomplete as books, and required that the reader should finish them, actively and practically, for himself.

30. Perhaps we can make this clearer if we take the liberty of imagining a little party in the railway carriage—Mr. Wells, Mr. Galsworthy, Mr. Bennett are travelling to Waterloo with Mrs. Brown. Mrs. Brown, I have said, was poorly dressed and very small. She had an anxious, harassed look. I doubt whether she was what you call an educated woman. Seizing upon all these symptoms of the unsatisfactory condition of our primary schools with a rapidity to which I can do no justice, Mr. Wells would instantly project upon the windowpane a vision of a better, breezier, jollier, happier, more adventurous and gallant world, where these musty railway carriages and fusty old women do not exist; where miraculous barges bring tropical fruit to Camberwell by eight o'clock in the morning; where there are public nurseries, fountains, and libraries, dining-rooms, drawing-rooms, and marriages; where every citizen is generous and candid, manly and magnificent, and rather like Mr. Wells himself. But nobody is in the least like Mrs. Brown. There are no Mrs. Browns in Utopia. Indeed I do not think that Mr. Wells, in his passion to make her what she ought to be, would waste a thought upon her as she is. And what would Mr. Galsworthy see? Can we doubt that the walls of Doulton's factory would take his fancy? There are women in that factory who make twenty-five dozen earthenware pots every day. There are mothers in the Mile End Road who depend upon the farthings which those women earn. But there are employers in Surrey who are even now smoking rich cigars while the nightingale sings. Burning with indignation, stuffed with information, arraigning civilization, Mr. Galsworthy would only see in Mrs. Brown a pot broken on the wheel and thrown into the corner. Mr. Bennett, alone of the Edwardians, would keep his eyes in the carriage. He, indeed, would observe every detail with immense care. He would notice the advertisements; the pictures of Swanage and Portsmouth; the way in which the cushion bulged between the buttons; how Mrs. Brown wore a brooch which had cost three-and-ten-three at Whitworth's bazaar; and had mended both gloves —indeed the thumb of the left-hand glove had been replaced. And he

would observe, at length, how this was the non-stop train from Windsor which calls at Richmond for the convenience of middle-class residents, who can afford to go to the theatre but have not reached the social rank which can afford motor-cars, though it is true, there are occasions (he would tell us what), when they hire them from a company (he would tell us which). And so he would gradually sidle sedately towards Mrs. Brown, and would remark how she had been left a little copyhold, not freehold, property at Datchet, which, however, was mortgaged to Mr. Bungay the solicitor—but why should I presume to invent Mr. Bennett? Does not Mr. Bennett write novels himself? I will open the first book that chance puts in my way—*Hilda Lessways*. Let us see how he makes us feel that Hilda is real, true, and convincing, as a novelist should. She shut the door in a soft, controlled way, which showed the constraint of her relations with her mother. She was fond of reading *Maud;* she was endowed with the power to feel intensely. So far, so good; in his leisurely, sure-footed way Mr. Bennett is trying in these first pages, where every touch is important, to show us the kind of girl she was.

³¹· But then he begins to describe, not Hilda Lessways, but the view from her bedroom window, the excuse being that Mr. Skellorn, the man who collects rents, is coming along that way. Mr. Bennett proceeds:

³²· "The bailiwick of Turnhill lay behind her; and all the murky district of the Five Towns, of which Turnhill is the northern outpost, lay to the south. At the foot of Chatterley Wood the canal wound in large curves on its way towards the undefiled plains of Cheshire and the sea. On the canal-side, exactly opposite to Hilda's window, was a flour-mill, that sometimes made nearly as much smoke as the kilns and the chimneys closing the prospect on either hand. From the flour-mill a bricked path, which separated a considerable row of new cottages from their appurtenant gardens, led straight into Lessways Street, in front of Mrs. Lessways' house. By this path Mr. Skellorn should have arrived, for he inhabited the farthest of the cottages."

³³· One line of insight would have done more than all those lines of description; but let them pass as the necessary drudgery of the novelist. And now—where is Hilda? Alas. Hilda is still looking out of the window. Passionate and dissatisfied as she was, she was a girl with an eye for houses. She often compared this old Mr. Skellorn with the villas she saw from her bedroom window. Therefore the villas must be described. Mr. Bennett proceeds:

³⁴· "The row was called Freehold Villas: a consciously proud name in a district where much of the land was copyhold and could only change owners subject to the payment of 'fines,' and to the feudal consent of a 'court' presided over by the agent of a lord of the manor. Most of the

dwellings were owned by their occupiers, who, each an absolute monarch of the soil, niggled in his sooty garden of an evening amid the flutter of drying shirts and towels. Freehold Villas symbolized the final triumph of Victorian economics, the apotheosis of the prudent and industrious artisan. It corresponded with a Building Society Secretary's dream of paradise. And indeed it was a very real achievement. Nevertheless, Hilda's irrational contempt would not admit this."

35. Heaven be praised, we cry! At last we are coming to Hilda herself. But not so fast. Hilda may have been this, that, and the other; but Hilda not only looked at houses, and thought of houses; Hilda lived in a house. And what sort of a house did Hilda live in? Mr. Bennett proceeds:

36. "It was one of the two middle houses of a detached terrace of four houses built by her grandfather Lessways, the tea-pot manufacturer; it was the chief of the four, obviously the habitation of the proprietor of the terrace. One of the corner houses comprised a grocer's shop, and this house had been robbed of its just proportion of garden so that the seigneurial garden-plot might be triflingly larger than the other. The terrace was not a terrace of cottages, but of houses rated at from twenty-six to thirty-six pounds a year; beyond the means of artisans and petty insurance agents and rent-collectors. And further, it was well built, generously built; and its architecture, though debased, showed some faint traces of Georgian amenity. It was admittedly the best row of houses in that newly settled quarter of the town. In coming to it out of Freehold Villas Mr. Skellorn obviously came to something superior, wider, more liberal. Suddenly Hilda heard her mother's voice. . . ."

37. But we cannot hear her mother's voice, or Hilda's voice; we can only hear Mr. Bennett's voice telling us facts about rents and freeholds and copyholds and fines. What can Mr. Bennett be about? I have formed my own opinion of what Mr. Bennett is about—he is trying to make us imagine for him; he is trying to hypnotize us into the belief that, because he has made a house, there must be a person living there. With all his powers of observation, which are marvellous, with all his sympathy and humanity, which are great, Mr. Bennett has never once looked at Mrs. Brown in her corner. There she sits in the corner of the carriage—that carriage which is travelling, not from Richmond to Waterloo, but from one age of English literature to the next, for Mrs. Brown is eternal, Mrs. Brown is human nature, Mrs. Brown changes only on the surface, it is the novelists who get in and out—there she sits and not one of the Edwardian writers had so much as looked at her. They have looked very powerfully, searchingly, and sympathetically out of the window; at factories, at Utopias, even at the decoration and upholstery of the carriage; but never at her, never at life, never at human nature. And so they have

developed a technique of novel-writing which suits their purpose; they have made tools and established conventions which do their business. But those tools are not our tools, and that business is not our business. For us those conventions are ruin, those tools are death.

38. You may well complain of the vagueness of my language. What is a convention, a tool, you may ask, and what do you mean by saying that Mr. Bennett's and Mr. Wells's and Mr. Galsworthy's conventions are the wrong conventions for the Georgians? The question is difficult: I will attempt a short cut. A convention in writing is not much different from a convention in manners. Both in life and in literature it is necessary to have some means of bridging the gulf between the hostess and her unknown guest on the one hand, the writer and his unknown reader on the other. The hostess bethinks her of the weather, for generations of hostesses have established the fact that this is a subject of universal interest in which we all believe. She begins by saying that we are having a wretched May, and, having thus got into touch with her unknown guest, proceeds to matters of greater interest. So it is in literature. The writer must get into touch with his reader by putting before him something which he recognizes, which therefore stimulates his imagination, and makes him willing to coöperate in the far more difficult business of intimacy. And it is of the highest importance that this common meeting-place should be reached easily, almost instinctively, in the dark, with one's eyes shut. Here is Mr. Bennett making use of this common ground in the passage which I have quoted. The problem before him was to make us believe in the reality of Hilda Lessways. So he began, being an Edwardian, by describing accurately and minutely the sort of house Hilda lived in, and the sort of house she saw from the window. House property was the common ground from which the Edwardians found it easy to proceed to intimacy. Indirect as it seems to us, the convention worked admirably, and thousands of Hilda Lessways were launched upon the world by this means. For that age and generation, the convention was a good one.

39. But now, if you will allow me to pull my own anecdote to pieces, you will see how keenly I felt the lack of a convention, and how serious a matter it is when the tools of one generation are useless for the next. The incident had made a great impression on me. But how was I to transmit it to you? All I could do was to report as accurately as I could what was said, to describe in detail what was worn, to say, despairingly, that all sorts of scenes rushed into my mind, to proceed to tumble them out pell-mell, and to describe this vivid, this overmastering impression by likening it to a draught or a smell of burning. To tell you the truth, I was also strongly tempted to manufacture a three-volume novel about the

old lady's son, and his adventures crossing the Atlantic, and her daughter, and how she kept a milliner's shop in Westminster, the past life of Smith himself, and his house at Sheffield, though such stories seem to me the most dreary, irrelevant, and humbugging affairs in the world.

40. But if I had done that I should have escaped the appalling effort of saying what I meant. And to have got at what I meant I should have had to go back and back and back; to experiment with one thing and another; to try this sentence and that, referring each word to my vision, matching it as exactly as possible, and knowing that somehow I had to find a common ground between us, a convention which would not seem to you too odd, unreal, and far-fetched to believe in. I admit that I shirked that arduous undertaking. I let my Mrs. Brown slip through my fingers. I have told you nothing whatever about her. But that is partly the great Edwardians' fault. I asked them—they are my elders and betters—How shall I begin to describe this woman's character? And they said, "Begin by saying that her father kept a shop in Harrogate. Ascertain the rent. Ascertain the wages of shop assistants in the year 1878. Discover what her mother died of. Describe cancer. Describe calico. Describe—" But I cried, "Stop! Stop!" And I regret to say that I threw that ugly, that clumsy, that incongruous tool out of the window, for I knew that if I began describing the cancer and the calico, my Mrs. Brown, that vision to which I cling though I know no way of imparting it to you, would have been dulled and tarnished and vanished for ever.

41. That is what I meant by saying that the Edwardian tools are the wrong ones for us to use. They have laid an enormous stress upon the fabric of things. They have given us a house in the hope that we may be able to deduce the human beings who live there. To give them their due, they have made that house much better worth living in. But if you hold that novels are in the first place about people, and only in the second about the houses they live in, that is the wrong way to set about it. Therefore, you see, the Georgian writer had to begin by throwing away the method that was in use at the moment. He was left alone there facing Mrs. Brown without any method of conveying her to the reader. But that is inaccurate. A writer is never alone. There is always the public with him—if not on the same seat, at least in the compartment next door. Now the public is a strange travelling companion. In England it is a very suggestive and docile creature, which, once you get it to attend, will believe implicitly what it is told for a certain number of years. If you say to the public with sufficient conviction, "All women have tails, and all men humps," it will actually learn to see women with tails and men with humps, and will think it very revolutionary and probably improper if you say "Nonsense. Monkeys have tails and camels humps. But men and

women have brains, and they have hearts; they think and they feel,"—that will seem to it a bad joke, and an improper one into the bargain.

42. But to return. Here is the British public sitting by the writer's side and saying in its vast and unanimous way, "Old women have houses. They have fathers. They have incomes. They have servants. They have hot water bottles. That is how we know that they are old women. Mr. Wells and Mr. Bennett and Mr. Galsworthy have always taught us that this is the way to recognize them. But now with your Mrs. Brown—how are we to believe in her? We do not even know whether her villa was called Albert or Balmoral; what she paid for her gloves; or whether her mother died of cancer or of consumption. How can she be alive? No; she is a mere figment of your imagination."

43. And old women of course ought to be made of freehold villas and copyhold estates, not of imagination.

44. The Georgian novelist, therefore, was in an awkward predicament. There was Mrs. Brown protesting that she was different, quite different, from what people made out, and luring the novelist to her rescue by the most fascinating if fleeting glimpse of her charms; there were the Edwardians handing out tools appropriate to house building and house breaking; and there was the British public asseverating that they must see the hot water bottle first. Meanwhile the train was rushing to that station where we must all get out.

45. Such, I think, was the predicament in which the young Georgians found themselves about the year 1910. Many of them—I am thinking of Mr. Forster and Mr. Lawrence in particular—spoilt their early work because, instead of throwing away those tools, they tried to use them. They tried to compromise. They tried to combine their own direct sense of the oddity and significance of some character with Mr. Galsworthy's knowledge of the Factory Acts, and Mr. Bennett's knowledge of the Five Towns. They tried it, but they had too keen, too overpowering a sense of Mrs. Brown and her peculiarities to go on trying it much longer. Something had to be done. At whatever cost of life, limb, and damage to valuable property Mrs. Brown must be rescued, expressed, and set in her high relations to the world before the train stopped and she disappeared for ever. And so the smashing and the crashing began. Thus it is that we hear all round us, in poems and novels and biographies, even in newspaper articles and essays, the sound of breaking and falling, crashing and destruction. It is the prevailing sound of the Georgian age—rather a melancholy one if you think what melodious days there have been in the past, if you think of Shakespeare and Milton and Keats or even of Jane Austen and Thackeray and Dickens; if you think of the language, and the heights to which it can soar when free, and see the same eagle captive, bald, and croaking.

⁴⁶· In view of these facts—with these sounds in my ears and these fancies in my brain—I am not going to deny that Mr. Bennett has some reason when he complains that our Georgian writers are unable to make us believe that our characters are real. I am forced to agree that they do not pour out three immortal masterpieces with Victorian regularity every autumn. But instead of being gloomy, I am sanguine. For this state of things is, I think, inevitable whenever from hoar old age or callow youth the convention ceases to be a means of communication between writer and reader, and becomes instead an obstacle and an impediment. At the present moment we are suffering, not from decay, but from having no code of manners which writers and readers accept as a prelude to the more exciting intercourse of friendship. The literary convention of the time is so artificial—you have to talk about the weather and nothing but the weather throughout the entire visit—that, naturally, the feeble are tempted to outrage, and the strong are led to destroy the very foundations and rules of literary society. Signs of this are everywhere apparent. Grammar is violated; syntax disintegrated; as a boy staying with an aunt for the week-end rolls in the geranium bed out of sheer desperation as the solemnities of the Sabbath wear on. The more adult writers do not, of course, indulge in such wanton exhibitions of spleen. Their sincerity is desperate, and their courage tremendous; it is only that they do not know which to use, a fork or their fingers. Thus, if you read Mr. Joyce and Mr. Eliot you will be struck by the indecency of the one, and the obscurity of the other. Mr. Joyce's indecency in *Ulysses* seems to me the conscious and calculated indecency of a desperate man who feels that in order to breathe he must break the windows. At moments, when the window is broken, he is magnificent. But what a waste of energy! And, after all, how dull indecency is, when it is not the overflowing of a super-abundant energy or savagery, but the determined and public-spirited act of a man who needs fresh air! Again, with the obscurity of Mr. Eliot. I think that Mr. Eliot has written some of the loveliest single lines in modern poetry. But how intolerant he is of the old usages and politenesses of society— respect for the weak, consideration for the dull! As I sun myself upon the intense and ravishing beauty of one of his lines, and reflect that I must make a dizzy and dangerous leap to the next, and so on from line to line, like an acrobat flying precariously from bar to bar, I cry out, I confess, for the old decorums, and envy the indolence of my ancestors who, instead of spinning madly through mid-air, dreamt quietly in the shade with a book. Again, in Mr. Strachey's books, *Eminent Victorians* and *Queen Victoria*, the effort and strain of writing against the grain and current of the times is visible too. It is much less visible, of course, for not only is he dealing with facts, which are stubborn things, but he has

fabricated, chiefly from eighteenth-century material, a very discreet code of manners of his own, which allows him to sit at table with the highest in the land and to say a great many things under cover of that exquisite apparel which, had they gone naked, would have been chased by the men-servants from the room. Still, if you compare *Eminent Victorians* with some of Lord Macaulay's essays, though you will feel that Lord Macaulay is always wrong, and Mr. Strachey always right, you will also feel a body, a sweep, a richness in Lord Macaulay's essays which show that his age was behind him; all his strength went straight into his work; none was used for purposes of concealment or of conversion. But Mr. Strachey has had to open our eyes before he made us see; he has had to search out and sew together a very artful manner of speech; and the effort, beautifully though it is concealed, has robbed his work of some of the force that should have gone into it, and limited his scope.

47. For these reasons, then, we must reconcile ourselves to a season of failures and fragments. We must reflect that where so much strength is spent on finding a way of telling the truth the truth itself is bound to reach us in rather an exhausted and chaotic condition. Ulysses, Queen Victoria, Mr. Prufrock—to give Mrs. Brown some of the names she has made famous lately—is a little pale and dishevelled by the time her rescuers reach her. And it is the sound of their axes that we hear—a vigorous and stimulating sound in my ears—unless of course you wish to sleep, when, in the bounty of his concern, Providence has provided a host of writers anxious and able to satisfy your needs.

48. Thus I have tried, at tedious length, I fear, to answer some of the questions which I began by asking. I have given an account of some of the difficulties which in my view beset the Georgian writer in all his forms. I have sought to excuse him. May I end by venturing to remind you of the duties and responsibilities that are yours as partners in this business of writing books, as companions in the railway carriage, as fellow-travellers with Mrs. Brown? For she is just as visible to you who remain silent as to us who tell stories about her. In the course of your daily life this past week you have had far stranger and more interesting experiences than the one I have tried to describe. You have overheard scraps of talk that filled you with amazement. You have gone to bed at night bewildered by the complexity of your feelings. In one day thousands of ideas have coursed through your brains; thousands of emotions have met, collided, and disappeared in astonishing disorder. Nevertheless, you allow the writers to palm off upon you a version of all this, an image of Mrs. Brown, which has no likeness to that surprising apparition whatsoever. In your modesty you seem to consider that writers are of different blood and bone from yourselves; that they know more of Mrs.

Brown than you do. Never was there a more fatal mistake. It is this division between reader and writer, this humility on your part, these professional airs and graces on ours, that corrupt and emasculate the books which should be the healthy offspring of a close and equal alliance between us. Hence spring those sleek, smooth novels, those portentous and ridiculous biographies, that milk-and-watery criticism, those poems melodiously celebrating the innocence of roses and sheep which pass so plausibly for literature at the present time.

49. Your part is to insist that writers shall come down off their plinths and pedestals, and describe beautifully if possible, truthfully at any rate, our Mrs. Brown. You should insist that she is an old lady of unlimited capacity and infinite variety; capable of appearing in any place; wearing any dress; saying anything and doing heaven knows what. But the things she says and the things she does and her eyes and her nose and her speech and her silence have an overwhelming fascination, for she is, of course, the spirit we live by, life itself.

50. But do not expect just at present a complete and satisfactory presentment of her. Tolerate the spasmodic, the obscure, the fragmentary, the failure. Your help is invoked in a good cause. For I will make one final and surpassingly rash prediction—we are trembling on the verge of one of the great ages of English literature. But it can only be reached if we are determined never, never to desert Mrs. Brown.

COMMENTARY AND QUESTIONS

The members of nearly every new literary movement, or followers of a new literary fashion, must sooner or later explain why they write as they do, and defend themselves against charges that they are abandoning true standards, ignoring proper precept, producing trash instead of art. The older literary generation is often skeptical and sometimes contemptuous of the younger, while the young are apt to be defiant toward their elders.

Virginia Woolf, herself one of the most gifted writers of the 1920's and 1930's, here sets forth, urbanely, wittily, and persuasively, her own conception of the aim and function of a novelist. In so doing she is simultaneously defending the experimental and not always successful attempts of the younger "Georgians" (that is, those beginning their serious writing during the reign of King George V, who came to the throne in 1910) to carry out this and other literary concepts; and she is also clearly and sometimes a little tartly suggesting the limitations of a trio of older "Edwardians" (those first reaching fame during the reign of Edward VII, who died in 1910). As a statement and defense of a literary ideal, and a rebuttal to its detractors, what she has written here is a remarkably persuasive document.

Most of her own novels (*Mrs. Dalloway* and *To the Lighthouse*, for example) were a series of powerful experiments in techniques very different from the highly detailed realism of Arnold Bennett which she here seeks to discredit. Whether or not the "crashing and destruction" of the experimental Georgians led or will lead to "one of the great ages of English literature" which Mrs. Woolf in 1924 felt trembling on the verge of, their work and her own caused a stir and excitement that has not yet died down.

By way of information, the American reader may like to know that Richmond is an outer suburb of London, that Waterloo is the name of one of the largest London railway terminals, and that British railway coaches are divided into separate compartments for six or eight. But these are perhaps facts as irrelevant as Mr. Bennett's copyhold and freehold. The important thing, as Virginia Woolf tells us, is not to lose sight of Mrs. Brown.

1. By what stylistic device does Mrs. Woolf tie her essay together and enforce her central argument? Note the mention of Brown in par. 1; the imaginative application of the railway train anecdote in par. 30; the renewed echo in par. 37; and the fact that of the last twelve paragraphs, Mrs. Brown is referred to in ten—in nine of them by name. Just what does the author symbolize by Mrs. Brown and why is the symbol so apt?

2. Mrs. Woolf's essay suggests how important is character to a novelist, points out that his problem is to convey character to his readers, explains why the Edwardians' method of doing this is no longer satisfactory, and offers a defense of the Georgians for not immediately finding a new method that is. Analyze the structure of the essay to show how its different parts carry on the course of the argument and how they are connected to each other. What is the function of the last three paragraphs and how are they related to the rest of the essay?

3. Part of the piquancy of Mrs. Woolf's style lies in her gift for little jabs of irony and satire—sometimes merely merry, sometimes distinctly edged. Look, for example, at the sentence in par. 6 about the Georgian cook; the remark in par. 30 about the imaginary citizens being "rather like Mr. Wells himself"; the statement comprising par. 43; the final sentence of par. 47. Can you find other examples? Notice that the author is, though sometimes ironic, always urbane: that is, smoothly polite, even-tempered, good-humored. What evidence does the essay contain that Mrs. Woolf has sympathy and understanding as well as wit and urbanity?

4. Another part of the piquancy of Mrs. Woolf's style, and much of its power also, lies in her extraordinarily apt use of metaphor and illustration. What are the implications of the figure about boots and watches in par. 29? The word *tool* is a rather common and well-worn metaphor; how does Mrs. Woolf give it new life and a touch of humor in pars.

37-41 and 44? Notice how in par. 44 the phrases about tools, houses, and the hot water bottle, used symbolically in previous paragraphs, are all powerfully combined in one sentence, while in the next sentence is an effective echo of the train metaphor developed in par. 41 and used as an extension of the original anecdote of the railway carriage. Par. 46 is particularly full of striking and amusing figures; is their main function merely to surprise and amuse the reader?

5. "I let my Mrs. Brown slip through my fingers. I have told you nothing whatever about her," says the author in par. 40, speaking of her own anecdote. Is she being too modest?

SUGGESTIONS FOR WRITING

1. The failure or success of the author of a recent piece of fiction in keeping sight of Mrs. Brown.

2. Defend or attack a literary movement or a group of authors using closely related literary techniques, on the ground that they do or do not (or, for authors in the past, did or did not) meet the needs of their own day.

3. Read one of Mrs. Woolf's own novels and discuss the means by which she conveys to her readers the character of Mrs. Brown.

PART FIVE

Research

RESEARCH IS THE ORGANIZED AND SYSTEMATIC ATTEMPT TO discover new knowledge or to uncover new meanings in old knowledge. It seeks out facts—not facts merely in isolation and by themselves, but facts as they fit into some pattern and are thus capable of yielding new theories, new generalizations, new conclusions: in short, new ways of understanding man and nature.

The raw material for research and the methods of examining it are of almost limitless variety. Laboratory research, for example, is conducted by the biologist with his microscope, the physicist with his spectrograph. Field research is what the geologist does when he explores rock strata and upthrusts, and also what the sociologist does when he asks questions and makes surveys to find out why certain neighborhoods breed crime. Library research is the ready tool of the historian, the biographer, and the literary scholar, whose raw material is in books, magazines, newspapers, manuscripts—anything printed or written. No one of these methods is used exclusively by one set of researchers: the scientist, for example, can almost never discover *all* the facts he needs in his own laboratory, but must build on a foundation of facts already discovered and interpreted by other scientists; and to learn and use these he employs the tool of library research.

To discover new knowledge by these methods is a fascinating pursuit in itself, but knowledge does not become useful to others until it is made available for them to learn, to test, and to build upon in seeking out more knowledge. The results of discovery must therefore be set forth in writing, and not until this is done can the research process be

497

called complete. Such writing, according to its length and form, is called a research book, a research article, or a research paper.

Research, then, is fundamentally the same, whether it is based on work in the field, the laboratory, or the library. In its complete cycle, from the initial discoveries to the completion of publication, we may distinguish three essential parts: the collection of facts; the organization and synthesis of these facts; and the publication of the results in documented form. Let us look again at each of these briefly.

Collection must be systematic, thorough, and unbiased. The researcher ought not to overlook or ignore pertinent facts, and he ought to have some idea of what he is looking for. Once he has collected his facts, if they are to be of any use, he must see what they prove or demonstrate, and draw from them inductive conclusions that will answer a question, solve a problem, or provide new understanding. Finally, when the facts and conclusions are written down systematically for publication, the researcher must include for his readers some form of documentation which will show them where he got his raw material. For laboratory or field research, he may do this through a description of experiments or surveys and his tabulations of the results. For library research, which is what we are mainly concerned with here, documentation means telling the reader what printed or written material the facts were found in. The usual way of doing this is by means of footnotes, a bibliography of sources, or both. Such documentation is important; it helps the reader to judge the completeness and reliability of the researcher's collection of facts, and it also enables the reader to go to the sources himself, either for verification or to carry out further research on his own part.

The following selection is an example of a documented research publication, written by a professional scholar. In it the author is concerned not only with uncovering new facts but also with putting together facts already published elsewhere, in order to arrive at a new conclusion or to reinforce an old one never before so well authenticated (in this case, that Lincoln was a great military strategist and was largely responsible for the development of the first modern military command system in America). The research technique is also illustrated by the selection reprinted in Part II (pp. 159-177) from Dixon Wecter's *The Age of the Great Depression* (though not all of Wecter's footnotes and sources are there included). For that selection Wecter searched out the manifold and apparently chaotic details of social history and wove them into an understandable pattern of narrative and interpretation.

Most of you, in your everyday lives, will not be doing exactly this kind of formal research; and the type of writing frequently assigned to students under the name of "research paper" is necessarily a compromise with the practical limitations of the classroom and the campus. But whether you are going to do formal research or not, you can profit by studying, and to some extent practising, the three essentials of research technique: making an orderly search for facts, combining these facts inductively to form general conclusions, and communicating the results to others with an exact and useful disclosure of sources. Even in everyday life outside the library and laboratory, this is in essence the way in which knowledge is discovered and made fruitful.

Lincoln and His Generals:
The Pattern of Command

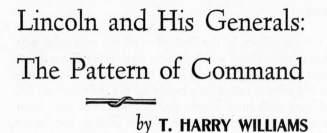

by T. HARRY WILLIAMS

THE CIVIL WAR was the first of the modern total wars, and the American democracy was almost totally unready to fight it. The United States had in 1861 almost no army, few good weapons, no officers trained in the higher art of war, and an inadequate and archaic system of command. Armies could be raised and weapons manufactured quickly, but it took time and battles to train generals. And it took time and blunders and bitter experiences to develop a modern command system. Not until 1864 did the generals and the system emerge.

2. In 1861 the general in chief of the army, which at the beginning of the war numbered about 16,000 men, was Winfield Scott. He was a veteran of two wars and the finest soldier in America. But he had been born in 1786, and he was physically incapable of commanding an army in the field. He could not ride, he could not walk more than a few steps without pain, and he had dropsy and vertigo.[1] The old General dreamed wistfully of taking the field. "If I could only mount a horse, I—" he would say sadly and pause, "but I am past that."[2] He was one of two officers in the army as the war started who had ever commanded troops in numbers large enough to be called an army. The other was John E. Wool, who was two years older than Scott. Wool had been a good soldier in his time, but he too showed the effects of age. He repeated things he had said a few minutes before, his hands shook, and he had to ask his aides if he had put his hat on straight.[3] Besides Scott and Wool, not an officer in the North had directed the evolutions of as large a unit as a brigade.[4] The largest single army that most of the younger officers had ever seen was Scott's force of 14,000 in the Mexican War.

[1] Winfield Scott to Simon Cameron, October 31, 1861, *War of the Rebellion . . . the Official Records of the Union and Confederate Armies,* Ser. 3, I, 611. Hereafter cited as *Official Records;* unless otherwise noted, all citations are to Ser. 1.

[2] Frederick W. Seward, *Reminiscences of a War-Time Statesman and Diplomat, 1830-1915,* 167-168.

[3] Henry M. Flint to Frederic Hudson, September 10, 1862, James Gordon Bennett MSS.

[4] Charles W. Elliott, *Winfield Scott: The Soldier and the Man,* 718.

[3.] There was not an officer in the first year of the war who was capable of efficiently administering and fighting a large army. Even Scott, had he been younger and stronger, would have had difficulty commanding any one of the big armies called into being by the government. All his experience had been with small forces, and he might not have been able to adjust his thinking to the organization of mass armies. The young officers who would be called to lead the new hosts lacked even his experience. Not only had they never handled troops in numbers, but they knew almost nothing about the history and theory of war or of strategy. They did not know the higher art of war, because there was no school in the country that taught it. West Point, which had educated the great majority of the officers, crammed its students full of knowledge of engineering, fortifications, and mathematics. Only a minor part of its curriculum was devoted to strategy, and its graduates learned little about how to lead and fight troops in the field. They were equally innocent of any knowledge of staff work: the administrative problems of operating an army or the formulation of war plans. Most of them never learned anything of it in the army, except for those few who could read French or who went abroad.[5] They spent most of their army careers fighting Indians or building forts, and there was not much of a staff organization in America for them to get any experience with.

[4.] The staff of the army, such as it was, consisted of Scott and the heads of the important departments and bureaus in the military organization—the adjutant general, the quartermaster general, the chief of engineers, the chief of ordnance, and others. Some of these officers were men of ability and would do good work in the war. Their agencies were going concerns with years of experience behind them when hostilities started and needed only to be expanded to meet the larger needs of a larger army. None of the staff chiefs had made any plans for war, and none of them was accustomed to thinking in terms of supplying the needs of mass armies. Some of the departments, notably the quartermaster general's, made the shift from peace to war with efficiency; others never got completely adjusted. All of them were unready for war in 1861, and in that year and even later were not able to furnish field commanders with the technical information or advice or supplies which they were suddenly called on to provide. One of the most ironic examples of American military unreadiness was the spectacle of Northern—and Southern—generals fighting in their own country and not knowing where they were going or how to get there. Before the war the government had collected

---

[5] Arthur Latham Conger, "President Lincoln as War Statesman," *Wisconsin Historical Publications, Proceedings,* 1916, 12; Jacob Dolson Cox, *Military Reminiscences of the Civil War,* I, 177-180.

no topographical information about neighboring countries or even the United States, except for the West. No accurate military maps existed. General Henry W. Halleck was running a campaign in the western theater in 1862 with maps he got from a book store. With frenetic haste, the general set topographical officers and civilian experts to work making maps, but the resulting charts were generally incorrect. Benjamin H. Latrobe, the civil engineer, drew a map for a general going into western Virginia, but the best he could promise was that it would not *mislead* the expedition. General George B. McClellan had elaborate maps prepared for his Virginia campaign of 1862 and found to his dismay when he arrived on the scene that they were unreliable; "the roads are wrong . . . ," he wailed. Not until 1863 did the Army of the Potomac have an accurate map of northern Virginia, its theater of operations.[6] Poor staff work continued in some departments until the end of the war. As late as 1864 there was not an office in Washington that could tell a general organizing a campaign what railroads were under military control, what the condition of their equipment was, or how many men and supplies they could transport.[7]

5. In no section of the staff organization was there any person or division charged with the function of studying strategy or formulating war plans for even a theoretical war. The work of the staff was completely technical and routine. Scott, the general in chief, had done no thinking before the war about what strategy should be adopted if war came. He had busied himself chiefly with devising political schemes to avert civil conflict. When the shooting started, he had no strategic design in mind to subdue the South. No other officer had one. Nobody in the army had thought it was important to think of war in strategic terms.

6. At the head of the American military organization was the president, the commander in chief of all the armed forces of the nation. The man who was president when the war began had been a civilian all his life, had had no military experience except as a militia soldier in a pygmy Indian war, and in 1861 probably did not even know how to frame a military order. The president of the rival nation, the Confederate States, was a graduate of West Point; he had been in the regular army and had seen battle service in the Mexican War. Abraham Lincoln was a great war

---

[6] Henry W. Halleck to D. C. Buell, February 13, 1862, *Official Records,* VII, 609; B. H. Latrobe to Frederick W. Lander, January 4, 1862, Lander MSS.; George B. McClellan, *McClellan's Own Story,* 253, 264; Emerson Gifford Taylor, *Gouverneur Kemble Warren . . . ,* 106-107.

[7] Herman Haupt to Lincoln, January 16, 1864, the Robert Todd Lincoln Collection of the Papers of Abraham Lincoln, vol. 138. Hereafter cited as Lincoln MSS.

president; Jefferson Davis was a mediocre one. Nowhere in the history of war is there a better illustration of Clausewitz's dictum that an acquaintance with military affairs is not the principal qualification for a director of war but that "a remarkable, superior mind and strength of character" are better qualifications.[8]

7. With no knowledge of the theory of war, no experience in war, and no technical training, Lincoln, by the power of his mind, became a fine strategist. He was a better natural strategist than were most of the trained soldiers. He saw the big picture of the war from the start. The policy of the government was to restore the Union by force; the strategy perforce had to be offensive. Lincoln knew that numbers, material resources, and sea power were on his side, so he called for 400,000 troops and proclaimed a naval blockade of the Confederacy. These were bold and imaginative moves for a man dealing with military questions for the first time. He grasped immediately the advantage that numbers gave the North and urged his generals to keep up a constant pressure on the whole strategic line of the Confederacy until a weak spot was found—and a breakthrough could be made. And he soon realized, if he did not know it at the beginning, that the proper objective of his armies was the destruction of the Confederate armies and not the occupation of Southern territory. His strategic thinking was sound and for a rank amateur astonishingly good.[9]

8. During the first three years of the war, Lincoln performed many of the functions that in a modern command system would be given to the chief of the general staff or to the joint chiefs of staff. He formulated policy, drew up strategic plans, and even devised and directed tactical movements. Judged by modern standards, he did some things that a civilian director of war should not do. Modern critics say that he "interfered" too much with military operations. He and his contemporaries did not think that he interfered improperly. In the American command system it was traditional for the civilian authority to direct strategy and tactics. The Continental Congress in the Revolution and the president and cabinet in the War of 1812 and the Mexican War had planned extensive and detailed campaigns. Lincoln was acting only as the civil authority had acted in every previous war. He was doing what he and most people thought the commander in chief ought to do in war.

9. Sometimes Lincoln made excellent plans and decisions; sometimes he made bad mistakes. Some of his mistakes resulted from his initial ignorance in 1861-62 of how to translate his strategical concepts into work-

---

[8] Karl von Clausewitz, *On War*, 599, Modern Library Edition.

[9] Colin R. Ballard, *The Military Genius of Abraham Lincoln: An Essay*, 2-3, 6, 28-29, 239; John C. Ropes, *The Story of the Civil War*, I, 111.

able instructions for his generals. His first generals, especially McClellan, were equally ignorant of how to establish relations with the head of the government so that they could find out his ideas about strategy and counsel him. When Lincoln asked them for advice, he usually got *ipse dixit* opinions. McClellan, who succeeded Scott as general in chief, did not seem to know that he ought to offer guidance to his political chief.[10] If McClellan and other generals had known how to talk to Lincoln or had wanted to talk with him about the military situation, the President would have interfered in military affairs less than he sometimes did. On several occasions, he intervened because the generals had not frankly told him what they were going to do or had not explained their purposes to him in terms that he could understand. Sometimes Lincoln "interfered" without meaning to. He had the type of mind that delighted to frame a plan of military operations. He loved to work up a plan and spring it on a general. The mental exercise gave him pleasure, and he liked to get the reactions of soldiers to his schemes. He did not mean for the generals to adopt his designs, but they did not always understand this. What he intended as a presentation of his ideas or a suggestion to be considered sometimes came through to the military mind as an order from the commander in chief.[11]

[10] Much of Lincoln's so-called interfering with the conduct of the war occurred in the first years of the conflict, when he believed, with some reason, that he was more capable of managing operations than were most of the generals. When the war started, he was inclined to defer to the judgments of trained soldiers. He soon came to doubt and even scorn the capabilities of the military mind. He asked of the generals decision, action, fighting, victory. They replied with indecision, inaction, delay, excuses. He became oppressed by the spectacle, so familiar in war, of generals who were superb in preparing for battle but who shrank from seeking its awful decision. "Tell him," he wrote in preparing instructions for one general, "to put it through—not to be writing or telegraphing back here, but put it through."[12] He wanted victories, but he got more letters than victories, letters from generals who wrote back that they could not put it through unless Lincoln provided them with more men and more guns . . . and still more.

[11] One of the most important functions Commander in Chief Lincoln had to perform was choosing generals to manage the armies. He

---

[10] Sir Frederick Maurice, "Lincoln as a Strategist," *Forum*, LXXV, 1926, 164.

[11] Sir Frederick Maurice, *Statesmen and Soldiers of the Civil War*, 95-96.

[12] Lincoln to Simon Cameron, June 20, 1861, John G. Nicolay and John Hay (eds.), *The Complete Works of Abraham Lincoln*, VI, 294. Hereafter cited as *Works of Lincoln*.

never had to worry that too few would apply for commissions. At the beginning of the war especially, he was showered with requests and demands for appointments from would-be generals and their political and military supporters: from officers who had spent weary years in the regular army in junior rank and now saw a chance to get their stars; from former officers who had resigned from the army to take lucrative civilian jobs and now wanted to return as generals; from politicians who thought military heroes would be popular after the war; from men who were ambitious, patriotic, able, mediocre, and incompetent. The rush for rank impressed, amused, and irritated the President. A popular jest of the war, one with a bitter undertone, was his reported remark about a brigadier general who got himself captured along with some horses and mules: "I don't care so much for brigadiers; I can make them. But horses and mules cost money."[13]

12. Lincoln handed out many commissions at the start of the war for reasons that were completely political but completely sound in a military sense. He used the military patronage to unite discordant groups in support of the war and to keep down divisions in the North. Creating and maintaining national unity was a necessary and vital phase of warmaking in 1861, and Lincoln performed brilliantly with his appointments. He had to satisfy his own Republicans, who thought he gave too many commissions to Democrats, and he had to soothe the Democrats, who thought he was letting Republicans run the war.[14] He dispensed commissions to ambitious political chieftains with large personal followings, especially if they were Democrats, like Nathaniel P. Banks, John A. McClernand, and Ben Butler. These selections saddled the army with some prize incompetents in high places, but they were good investments in national cohesion.[15] Some of Lincoln's appointments went to men who were leaders of important nationality groups like the German-Americans. Lincoln realized the importance of enlisting the Germans in support of the war, but he was amused by their eagerness to get their prominent men on the list of generals. Once a staff officer heard a conversation between the President and Secretary of War Edwin M. Stanton about some appointments of brigadier generals. Lincoln said he agreed with most of Stanton's recommendations, but, continued the President, "there has got

---

[13] James Harrison Wilson, *Under the Old Flag*, I, 349.

[14] George W. Julian, *Speeches on Political Questions, 1850-1868*, 202-204; Senator Henry Wilson in *Congressional Globe*, 2 Sess., 38 Cong., pt. 1, 164; P. A. Ladue to Lincoln, January 6, 1862, Lincoln MSS.; Joseph Medill to Lincoln, February 17, 1864, *ibid*.

[15] Fred Harvey Harrington, *Fighting Politician, Major General N. P. Banks*, 54-56.

to be something done unquestionably in the interest of the Dutch, and to that end I want Schimmelfennig appointed." Lincoln uttered the name with great enjoyment. Stanton said there were German officers who were better recommended. "No matter about that," said Lincoln; "his name will make up for any difference there may be." It had to be Schimmelfennig, and he went off repeating the name.[16]

13. With Schimmelfennig, Lincoln was getting a saving laugh out of a serious situation. He was escaping momentarily from the grimness of war in the same way he did when he told one of his stories to a pompous senator or read Artemus Ward in a Cabinet meeting. Selecting generals was a galling, dull business, and he seized every chance he had to get some fun out of it. He liked to have attractive wives of officers besiege him for promotions for their husbands. In the Lincoln Papers is a list he made in 1861 of officers he wanted to remember when he made appointments. After the name of Lieutenant Slemmer is the notation: "His pretty wife says a Major, or first Captain."[17] Of another wife who wanted him to make her husband a brigadier general, he wrote: "She is a saucy woman and I am afraid she will keep tormenting me until I may have to do it."[18]

14. In dealing with the applicants for appointments and promotions, Lincoln demonstrated his most skilled techniques in managing men and situations. Once the Pennsylvania Congressional delegation came buzzing angrily at Lincoln to get a promotion for the state's son, General Samuel P. Heintzelman. They extolled him, said he was a fine general, a good man. Seizing on the last claim, the President agreed that Heintzelman certainly was a good man; in fact he was "a good egg," and therefore he would keep. "You must trust me," he said, "to see that the General has justice done him." There was a pause, and then one of the delegation said: "We have trusted you a long time on this." "Gentlemen, you must do so longer," said Lincoln, and bowed them out.[19]

15. Lincoln probably enjoyed his exchange with the Pennsylvanians. But sometimes he got terribly angry when people criticized his military appointments. Once General Carl Schurz, the ebullient and incompetent German-American officer, wrote Lincoln that the administration was failing politically because the war was failing and that Lincoln was to blame for it all because he had entrusted the important commands to

---

[16] Allen Thorndike Rice (ed.), *Reminiscences of Abraham Lincoln by Distinguished Men of His Time*, 391-392.

[17] Memorandum, April, 1861, Lincoln MSS., vol. 44.

[18] Memorandum, August 23, 1862, *ibid.*, vol. 85.

[19] MS. Journal of Samuel P. Heintzelman, entry of June 22, 1862. There are no quotation marks around the spoken statements in Heintzelman's account.

men whose hearts were not in the war. By men without hearts, Schurz meant Democrats. With a dramatic reference to his brave boys dying in an aimless war, he concluded: "I do not know whether you have ever seen a battlefield. I assure you, Mr. President, it is a terrible sight."[20] Lincoln liked Schurz, but he was angered by the General's letter. And he had no intention of letting Schurz patronize him. In a cutting reply, one of the best of his war letters, he read Schurz a lecture on how to pick generals. Who is to decide who shall be generals? he asked. "If I must discard my own judgment and take yours, I must also take that of others; and by the time I should reject all I should be advised to reject, I should have none left, Republicans or others—not even yourself. For be assured, my dear sir, there are men who . . . think you are performing your part as poorly as you think I am performing mine." Republican and Democratic generals had been about equally successful, continued Lincoln, naming some officers from each party who had performed well. Then came the crusher: "I will not perform the ungrateful task of comparing failures."[21] Anybody else but Schurz would have been demolished. He kept on writing letters.

[16.] Lincoln never discarded his judgment to others in choosing generals. But he was willing to discard his judgment of what was good strategy and take the opinion of any general whom he considered to be able. He was willing to yield the power to direct strategic operations to any general who could demonstrate that he was competent to frame and execute strategy. Lincoln sensed that there was something wrong in the command system. Somewhere, he thought, there ought to be a division of function between him and the military. But where should the line be drawn? And who was the general to whom he could confide the power to control? Lincoln was to go through some bitter and agonizing experiences before he got the answers to these questions. In the process, he and the army and the nation were to learn a lot about command. By 1864 the United States would have a modern command system. Lincoln did not know it in 1861, but he was going to make a large and permanent contribution to the organization of the American military system.

BIBLIOGRAPHY*

Ballard, Colin R.: *The Military Genius of Abraham Lincoln: An Essay* (London, 1926).
Bennett, James Gordon: Manuscripts (Library of Congress).

---

[20] Carl Schurz to Lincoln, November 8, 1862, Lincoln MSS., vol. 92.

[21] Lincoln to Schurz, November 24, 1862, *Works of Lincoln*, VIII, 84-87.

* Items in the bibliography of *Lincoln and His Generals* which are cited in the footnotes for this chapter.

Conger, Arthur L.: "President Lincoln as War Statesman," *Wisconsin Historical Publications, Proceedings,* 1916, 106-140 (Madison, 1917).

Cox, Jacob Dolson: *Military Reminiscences of the Civil War* (2 vols., New York, 1900).

Elliott, Charles W.: *Winfield Scott: The Soldier and the Man* (New York, 1937).

Harrington, Fred Harvey: *Fighting Politician, Major General N. P. Banks* (Philadelphia, 1948).

Heintzelman, Samuel P.: Manuscript Journal (Library of Congress).

Lander, Frederick W.: Manuscripts (Library of Congress).

Lincoln, Robert Todd: Manuscripts (Library of Congress).

McClellan, George B.: *McClellan's Own Story* (New York, 1887).

Maurice, Sir Frederick: "Lincoln as a Strategist," *Forum,* LXXV, 161-169 (February, 1926).

————: *Statesmen and Soldiers of the Civil War: A Study of the Conduct of War* (Boston, 1926).

Nicolay, John G. and John Hay (eds.): *Complete Works of Abraham Lincoln* (12 vols., New York, 1905).

Rice, Allen Thorndike (ed.): *Reminiscences of Abraham Lincoln by Distinguished Men of His Time* (New York, 1888).

Ropes, John Codman: *The Story of the Civil War* (2 vols., New York, 1933).

Seward, Frederick W.: *Reminiscences of a War-Time Statesman and Diplomat, 1830-1915* (New York, 1916).

Taylor, Emerson Gifford: *Gouverneur Kemble Warren . . .* (Boston, 1932).

War of the Rebellion: A Compilation of the Official Records of the Union and Confederate Armies (128 vols., Washington, 1880-1901).

Wilson, James Harrison: *Under the Old Flag* (2 vols., New York, 1912).

COMMENTARY AND QUESTIONS

This essay is the first chapter of *Lincoln and His Generals,* a work based solidly on research. That the book has been of interest to the general reader as well as to the scholar is indicated by the fact that it was a Book-of-the-Month Club selection.

1. In the preface to *Lincoln and His Generals,* Williams defines the area of his study as follows:

> I have written in this book the story of Abraham Lincoln the commander in chief. I have not written a military history of the Civil War or a group biography of the principal Union generals or a description of the military organization of the North, although there is something of these in the book. My theme is Lincoln as a director of war and his

place in the high command and his influence in developing a modern command system for the nation.

To what phase of this subject does Williams devote the first chapter of his book? What are the two main divisions of the chapter, and what is the importance of par. 6 in relation to its structure?

2. Often the writer of a research paper is able to bring together in one paragraph material from several sources and to fuse this material into a coherent whole that develops a central point, his own point, which, in turn, has its own special place in the development of his work as a whole. Par. 2 uses material from four sources. Show how Williams succeeded in making a unified, coherent whole of this material. What is the central point of the paragraph? Is it presented in a topic sentence?

3. What is the purpose of footnote 7? of footnote 8? of footnote 9? Why is it desirable to support a point with material from several different sources when such material is available?

4. Williams does not use any footnotes to document par. 8. If he himself had not already established a reputation as a research scholar in American history, which of the statements in this paragraph would probably have been supported by references to sources?

SUGGESTION FOR WRITING

Select a significant historical event, or an individual who had an influential part in such an event. Consult the available sources of information about the subject that you have selected and draw your own conclusions about the significance of the event or the influence of the individual. Embody your conclusions in a well-organized essay which includes documentation of sources.

PART SIX

The Craft of Writing

WE HAVE INCLUDED THE FOLLOWING ESSAYS NOT ONLY FOR THE way they are written but also for what they say about writing and thinking. Like any other craft, writing makes severe demands on the individual who respects his work. Words are the writer's tools. He must use them exactly and economically if his work is to have precision. He must use them boldly if his work is to have strength. He must use them knowingly and honestly if his work is to have character. By being clear and interesting, he will win his reader's attention; by being sincere, reasonable, and logical, he will deserve his reader's approval.

If you are avoiding the pitfalls of grammar and style uncovered by James Thurber and Samuel T. Williamson in their essays, you will appreciate John Mason Brown's description of writing as a "pleasant agony." If you are a bold user of words, you will enjoy H. L. Mencken as he unmasks trades and professions which would hide the elemental nature of their work. If you are a knowing and honest user of words, you will listen to Sir Ernest Gowers as he suggests a test for new words and to Wilson Follett and Bergen Evans as they discuss the decisions of the lexicographers. If you recognize the power of writing, you will understand and approve Robert Gorham Davis's plea for rigorous thinking.

Ladies' and Gentlemen's Guide
to Modern English Usage

by JAMES THURBER

I *Which*

THE RELATIVE PRONOUN "WHICH" can cause more trouble than any other word, if recklessly used. Foolhardy persons sometimes get lost in which-clauses and are never heard of again. My distinguished contemporary, Fowler, cites several tragic cases, of which the following is one: "It was rumoured that Beaconsfield intended opening the Conference with a speech in French, his pronunciation of which language leaving everything to be desired . . ." That's as much as Mr. Fowler quotes because, at his age, he was afraid to go any farther. The young man who originally got into that sentence was never found. His fate, however, was not as terrible as that of another adventurer who became involved in a remarkable which-mire. Fowler has followed his devious course as far as he safely could on foot: "Surely what applies to games should also apply to racing, the leaders of which being the very people from whom an example might well be looked for . . ." Not even Henry James could have successfully emerged from a sentence with "which," "whom," and "being" in it. The safest way to avoid such things is to follow in the path of the American author, Ernest Hemingway. In his youth he was trapped in a which-clause one time and barely escaped with his mind. He was going along on solid ground until he got into this: "It was the one thing of which, being very much afraid—for whom has not been warned to fear such things—he . . ." Being a young and powerfully built man, Hemingway was able to fight his way back to where he had started, and begin again. This time he skirted the treacherous morass in this way: "He was afraid of one thing. This was the one thing. He had been warned to fear such things. Everybody has been warned to fear such things." Today Hemingway is alive and well, and many happy writers are following along the trail he blazed.

2. What most people don't realize is that one "which" leads to another. Trying to cross a paragraph by leaping from "which" to "which" is

like Eliza crossing the ice. The danger is in missing a "which" and falling in. A case in point is this: "He went up to a pew which was in the gallery, which brought him under a colored window which he loved and always quieted his spirit." The writer, worn out, missed the last "which" —the one that should come just before "always" in that sentence. But supposing he had got it in! We would have: "He went up to a pew which was in the gallery, which brought him under a colored window which he loved and which always quieted his spirit." Your inveterate whicher in this way gives the effect of tweeting like a bird or walking with a crutch, and is not welcome in the best company.

3. It is well to remember that one "which" leads to two and that two "whiches" multiply like rabbits. You should never start out with the idea that you can get by with one "which." Suddenly they are all around you. Take a sentence like this: "It imposes a problem which we either solve, or perish." On a hot night, or after a hard day's work, a man often lets himself get by with a monstrosity like that, but suppose he dictates that sentence bright and early in the morning. It comes to him typed out by his stenographer and he instantly senses that something is the matter with it. He tries to reconstruct the sentence, still clinging to the "which," and gets something like this: "It imposes a problem which we either solve, or which, failing to solve, we must perish on account of." He goes to the water-cooler, gets a drink, sharpens his pencil, and grimly tries again. "It imposes a problem which we either solve or which we don't solve and . . ." He begins once more: "It imposes a problem which we either solve, or which we do not solve, and from which . . ." The more times he does it the more "whiches" he gets. The way out is simple: "We must either solve this problem, or perish." Never monkey with "which." Nothing except getting tangled up in a typewriter ribbon is worse.

II *The Perfect Infinitive*

4. It is easy enough to say that a person should live in such a way as to avoid the perfect infinitive after the past conditional, but it is another matter to do it. The observance of the commonest amenities of life constantly leads us into that usage. Let us take a typical case. A gentleman and his wife, calling on friends, find them not at home. The gentleman decides to leave a note of regret couched in a few well-chosen words, and the first thing he knows he is involved in this: "We would have liked to have found you in." Reading it over, the gentleman is assailed by the suspicion that he has too many "haves," and that the whole business has somehow been put too far into the past. His first reaction is to remedy this by dating the note: "9 p.m. Wednesday, Jan. 21, 1931." This at once

seems too formal, and with a sigh he starts in again on the sentence itself. That is where he makes a fatal mistake. The simplest way out, as always, is to seek some other method of expressing the thought. In this case the gentleman should simply dash off, "Called. You were out. Sorry," and go home to bed. What he does, however, is to lapse into a profound study of this particular grammatical situation, than which there is no more hazardous mental occupation. His wife should, above all things, not choose this time to nag at him, or hurry him. His condition now calls for the utmost kindness and consideration.

⁵· First the victim will change the sentence to: "We would have liked to find you in." Now as a matter of fact, this is correct (barring the use of "would" instead of "should"), but, alas, the gentleman does not realize it. Few people ever do realize it. This is because the present infinitive, "to find," seems to imply success. They therefore fall back on the perfect infinitive, "to have found," because it implies that the thing hoped for did not come to pass. They have fallen back on it so often that, after the ordinary past tenses, its use has come to be counted as idiomatic, even though it is incorrect. After past conditionals, however—such as our gentleman caller has got into—the use of the perfect infinitive is not even idiomatic. It is just dangerous.

⁶· The gentleman, with two variants on his hands, takes to mumbling them to himself, first one and then the other—"We would have liked to have found you in," "We would have liked to find you in." After he does this several times, both expressions begin to sound meaningless. They don't make any sense at all, let alone make precise sense. His mental feeling is analogous to the terror that strikes into children's minds when they get to repeating some common word, like "saucer," over and over again, until it sounds idiotic and legendary. At this point it would be infinitely better not to leave any note at all, but the gentleman's education and his strength of mind have been challenged. He takes an envelope out of his pocket and grimly makes a list of all the possible combinations, thus getting: "We would have liked to have found," "We would have liked to find," "We would like to have found," and "We would like to find." A dull pain takes him back of the ears. This is the danger sign, and his wife should have the presence of mind to summon assistance, for he is now out of hand and uncontrollable. What she does, however, is to say, "Here, let me write it." He instantly snarls, "I'm no child" or "Get away" or some such thing, and his difficulties are added to by the quarrel which follows. At length he has the bright inspiration of going into the hope clauses and turns out: "We had hoped to have been able to have found." If he has married the right kind of woman, she will hastily scratch a brief word on a calling card, shove it under the door, and drag her husband away.

Otherwise he will sink rapidly into a serious mental state, from which it may take him weeks to emerge.

7. There is a simple rule about past conditionals which will prevent a lapse into that deep contemplation which is so often fatal. After "would have liked," "would have hoped," "would have feared," etc., use the present infinitive. The implication of non-fulfillment is inherent in the governing verb itself, that is, in the "would have liked," etc. You don't have to shade the infinitive to get a nice note of frustration. Let it alone. Dr. Fowler himself says: "Sometimes a writer, dimly aware that 'would have liked to have done' is wrong, is yet so fascinated by the perfect infinitive that he clings to that at all costs." That's what it is—a fascination—like a cobra's for a bird. Avoid the perfect infinitive after the past conditional as you would a cobra.

III   *The Subjunctive Mood*

8. The importance of correct grammar in the home can not be over-estimated. Two young people should make sure that each is rhetorically sound before they get married, because grammatical precision, particularly in mood, is just as important as anything else. Rhetoric and sex, in fact, are so closely related that when one becomes confused they both become confused. Take the subjunctive. Fowler, in his book on modern English usage, says the subjunctive is dying, but adds that there are still a few truly living uses, which he groups under "Alives, Revivals, Survivals, and Arrivals." Curiously enough, he leaves out Departures, which it seems to me are just as important as Arrivals. Let us examine the all too common domestic situation where the husband arrives just after another gentleman has departed—or just after he thinks another gentleman has departed (Suppositional Departures lead to just as much bitterness, and even more subjunctives, than Actual Departures).

9. The wife, in either case, is almost sure to go into the subjunctive—very likely before any accusation is made. Among the most common subjunctives which she will be inclined to use are those of indignation and hauteur, such as "Be that as it may," "Far be it from me," etc. For the moment, she is safe enough in the subjunctive, because her husband has probably gone into it, too, using "Would God I were," "If there be justice," and so on. Wives select the subjunctive usually because it is the best mood in which to spar for time, husbands because it lends itself most easily to ranting and posturing. As long as they both stay in it they are safe. Misunderstandings are almost certain to arise, however, when the husband goes into the indicative, as he is pretty sure to do. He usually does this preparatory to dismissing his suspicions, a step toward which

every husband is impelled by his natural egotism. First he will begin with a plain past-tense indicative if-clause—just to show that he knows who the man is—prior to dismissing him.

10. "If George Spangrell was here," the husband will begin, lighting a cigarette, "I . . ."

11. "Well, what would you do if he *were*?" demands the wife.

12. The confusion, which begins at this point, is pretty intricate. The husband has gone into the indicative, but his wife has stayed in the sub-junctive and, furthermore, she thinks that he is still there, too. Thus she thinks he intended to say: "If George Spangrell was here [that is, now] I would tell him what I think of him, the low scoundrel." There is no excuse for a wife prematurely imputing such a suspicion or such a rhetor-ical monstrosity to her husband. What he probably intended to say was merely something like this: "If George Spangrell was here, I wouldn't like it, but of course I know he wasn't, dear." However, misunderstand-ings now begin to pile up. The husband is instantly made suspicious by her "What would you do if he *were*?" He considers her "were" tanta-mount to "is." (This quick-tempered construction, of course, makes the "would" in his wife's sentence ridiculous, for, had she meant "is" instead of "were," she would have substituted "will" for "would.") The situation is much too involved now, however, for the husband to make an effort to parse anything. He instantly abandons all grammatical analysis, and be-gins to look about, peering into the wardrobe, swishing under beds with a cane or umbrella.

13. His wife now has the advantage of him, not only in mood, but in posture. A woman must naturally view with disdain and contempt any man who is down on all fours unless he has taken that position for the purpose of playing horse with some children—an extenuation which we need not discuss here. To meet her on even terms, the husband should walk, not crawl, from wardrobe to chaise-longue, using the mandatory subjunctive in a firm voice, as follows: "If anyone be in (or under) there, let him come out!" ["Come out" is better here than "emerge" because stronger, but a husband should not fall into the colloquial "Come on out of that!" He may, however, if he so wishes, address the gentleman, whether he be present or not, as "Spangrell" but never "Mr. Spangrell" (Hypocritical Dignification) and certainly never as "George"—the use of the given name being in extreme bad taste where no endearment is intended.]

14. The wife of course will resent all these goings-on, and the quarrel that results will probably last late into the night.

15. There are several ways to prevent a situation like this. In the first place, when a husband says "was" a wife should instantly respond with "wasn't." Most husbands will take a "wasn't" at its face value, because

it preserves their egotism and self-respect. On the other hand, "if . . . were" is always dangerous. Husbands have come to know that a wife's "if . . . were" usually means that what she is presenting as purely hypothetical is, in reality, a matter of fact. Thus, if a wife begins, one evening after an excellent dinner, "Dear, what would you do, if I were the sort of woman who had, etc.," her husband knows full well that it is going to turn out that she is the sort of woman who has. Husbands are suspicious of all subjunctives. Wives should avoid them. Once a woman has "if . . . were'd" a Mr. Spangrell, her husband is, nine times out of ten, going to swish under the chaise-longue. Even if he finds no one, the situation becomes extremely awkward, and there is of course always the plaguey hundredth chance that he may discover a strange cane or pair of gloves.

16. The best of all ways out is for the husband to go instantly into the future indicative and say, with great dignity, "I shall go down to the drugstore." Ordinarily, his wife would reply, "Oh, no you won't," but with all the doubt and suspicion in the air, she will be inclined to humor him and let him have his way. She is certain to, if Spangrell is in the clothes hamper.

COMMENTARY AND QUESTIONS

These three sections are taken from a group of essays published under the general title we have used here: *Ladies' and Gentlemen's Guide to Modern English Usage.* The man and book frequently referred to by Thurber are H. W. Fowler and his *Dictionary of Modern English Usage.*

1. In the first two sections Thurber does not merely have his tongue in his cheek when he offers a way out for the tired "whicher" and for the man having trouble with the perfect infinitive. In section I the solution comes near the end (par. 3). Is the solution in section II given at an equally effective spot?

2. In a sentence enclosed in parentheses near the end of par. 12, Thurber explains why the husband's misunderstanding of his wife's subjunctive cannot be defended. But Thurber leaves it for the reader to judge the wife's misunderstanding (earlier in the paragraph) when she fails to realize that her husband has shifted from the subjunctive to the indicative. Is she merely being tactful?

SUGGESTIONS FOR WRITING

1. Ladies' and gentlemen's guide to campus usage.

2. Are you a "whicher"? Analyze one of your recent pieces of writing: can you defend each *which*?

How to Write

Like a Social Scientist

by SAMUEL T. WILLIAMSON

DURING MY YEARS as an editor, I have seen probably hundreds of job applicants who were either just out of college or in their senior years. All wanted "to write." Many brought letters from their teachers. But I do not recall one letter announcing that its bearer could write what he wished to say with clarity and directness, with economy of words, and with pleasing variety of sentence structure.

2. Most of these young men and women could not write plain English. Apparently their noses had not been rubbed in the drudgery of putting one simple, well-chosen word behind the other. If this was true of teachers' pets, what about the rest? What about those going into business and industry? Or those going into professions? What about those who remain at college—first for a Master of Arts degree, then an instructorship combined with work for a Ph.D., then perhaps an assistant professorship, next a full professorship and finally, as an academic crown of laurel, appointment as head of a department or as dean of a faculty?

3. Certainly, faculty members of a front-rank university should be better able to express themselves than those they teach. Assume that those in the English department have this ability: Can the same be said of the social scientists—economists, sociologists, and authorities on government? We need today as we never needed so urgently before all the understanding they can give us of problems of earning a living, caring for our fellows, and governing ourselves. Too many of them, I find, can't write as well as their students.

4. I am still convalescing from overexposure some time ago to products of the academic mind. One of the foundations engaged me to edit the manuscripts of a socio-economic research report designed for the thoughtful citizen as well as for the specialist. My expectations were not high—no deathless prose, merely a sturdy, no-nonsense report of explorers into the wilderness of statistics and half-known fact. I knew from experience that economic necessity compels many a professional writer

to be a cream-skimmer and a gatherer of easily obtainable material; for unless his publisher will stand the extra cost, he cannot afford the exhaustive investigation which endowed research makes possible. Although I did not expect fine writing from a trained, professional researcher, I did assume that a careful fact-finder would write carefully.

5. And so, anticipating no literary treat, I plunged into the forest of words of my first manuscript. My weapons were a sturdy eraser and several batteries of sharpened pencils. My armor was a thesaurus. And if I should become lost, a near-by public library was a landmark, and the Encyclopedia of Social Sciences on its reference shelves was an ever-ready guide.

6. Instead of big trees, I found underbrush. Cutting through involved, lumbering sentences was bad enough, but the real chore was removal of the burdocks of excess verbiage which clung to the manuscript. Nothing was big or large; in my author's lexicon, it was "substantial." When he meant "much," he wrote "to a substantially high degree." If some event took place in the early 1920's, he put it "in the early part of the decade of the twenties." And instead of "that depends," my author wrote, "any answer to this question must bear in mind certain peculiar characteristics of the industry."

7. So it went for 30,000 words. The pile of verbal burdocks grew— sometimes twelve words from a twenty-word sentence. The shortened version of 20,000 words was perhaps no more thrilling than the original report; but it was terser and crisper. It took less time to read and it could be understood quicker. That was all I could do. As S. S. McClure once said to me, "An editor can improve a manuscript, but he cannot put in what isn't there."

8. I did not know the author I was editing; after what I did to his copy, it may be just as well that we have not met. Aside from his cat-chasing-its-own-tail verbosity, he was a competent enough workman. Apparently he is well thought of. He has his doctorate, he is a trained researcher and a pupil of an eminent professor. He has held a number of fellowships and he has performed competently several jobs of economic research. But, after this long academic preparation for what was to be a life work, it is a mystery why so little attention was given to acquiring use of simple English.

9. Later, when I encountered other manuscripts, I found I had been too hard on this promising Ph.D. Tone-deaf as he was to words, his report was a lighthouse of clarity among the chapters turned in by his so-called academic betters. These brethren—and sister'n—who contributed the remainder of the foundation's study were professors and assistant professors in our foremost colleges and universities. The names of

one or two are occasionally in newspaper headlines. All of them had, as the professorial term has it, "published."

10. Anyone who edits copy, regardless of whether it is good or bad, discovers in a manuscript certain pet phrases, little quirks of style and other individual traits of its author. But in the series I edited, all twenty reports read alike. Their words would be found in any English dictionary, grammar was beyond criticism, but long passages in these reports demanded not editing but actual translation. For hours at a time, I floundered in brier patches like this: "In eliminating wage changes due to purely transitory conditions, collective bargaining has eliminated one of the important causes of industrial conflict, for changes under such conditions are almost always followed by a reaction when normal conditions appear."

11. I am not picking on my little group of social scientists. They are merely members of a caste; they are so used to taking in each other's literary washing that it has become a habit for them to clothe their thoughts in the same smothering verbal garments. Nor are they any worse than most of their colleagues, for example:

> In the long run, developments in transportation, housing, optimum size of plant, etc., might tend to induce an industrial and demographic pattern similar to the one that consciousness of vulnerability would dictate. Such a tendency might be advanced by public persuasion and governmental inducement, and advanced more effectively if the causes of urbanization had been carefully studied.

12. Such pedantic Choctaw may be all right as a sort of code language or shorthand of social science to circulate among initiates, but its perpetrators have no right to impose it on others. The tragedy is that its users appear to be under the impression that it is good English usage.

13. Father, forgive them; for they know not what they do! There once was a time when everyday folk spoke one language, and learned men wrote another. It was called the Dark Ages. The world is in such a state that we may return to the Dark Ages if we do not acquire wisdom. If social scientists have answers to our problems yet feel under no obligation to make themselves understood, then we laymen must learn their language. This may take some practice, but practice should become perfect by following six simple rules of the guild of social science writers. Examples which I give are sound and well tested; they come from manuscripts I edited.

14. RULE 1. *Never use a short word when you can think of a long one.* Never say "now" but "currently." It is not "soon" but "presently." You did not have "enough" but a "sufficiency." Never do you come to the "end" but to the "termination." This rule is basic.

15. RULE 2. *Never use one word when you can use two or more.* Eschew "probably." Write, "it is probable," and raise this to "it is not improbable." Then you'll be able to parlay "probably" into "available evidence would tend to indicate that it is not unreasonable to suppose."

16. RULE 3. *Put one-syllable thought into polysyllabic terms.* Instead of observing that a work force might be bigger and better, write, "In addition to quantitative enlargement, it is not improbable that there is need also for qualitative improvement in the personnel of the service." If you have discovered that musicians out of practice can't hold jobs, report that "the fact of rapid deterioriation of musical skill when not in use soon converts the unemployed into the unemployable." Resist the impulse to say that much men's clothing is machine made. Put it thus: "Nearly all operations in the industry lend themselves to performance by machine, and all grades of men's clothing sold in significant quantity involve a very substantial amount of machine work."

17. RULE 4. *Put the obvious in terms of the unintelligible.* When you write that "the product of the activity of janitors is expended in the identical locality in which that activity takes place," your lay reader is in for a time of it. After an hour's puzzlement, he may conclude that janitors' sweepings are thrown on the town dump. See what you can do with this: "Each article sent to the cleaner is handled separately." You become a member of the guild in good standing if you put it like this: "Within the cleaning plant proper the business of the industry involves several well-defined processes, which, from the economic point of view, may be characterized simply by saying that most of them require separate handling of each individual garment or piece of material to be cleaned."

18. RULE 5. *Announce what you are going to say before you say it.* This pitcher's wind-up technique before hurling towards—not at—home plate has two varieties. First is the quick wind-up: "In the following sections the policies of the administration will be considered." Then you become strong enough for the contortionist wind-up: "Perhaps more important, therefore, than the question of what standards are in a particular case, there are the questions of the extent of observance of these standards and the methods of their enforcement." Also, you can play with reversing Rule 5 and *say what you have said after you have said it.*

19. RULE 6. *Defend your style as "scientific."* Look down on—not up to—clear, simple English. Sneer at it as "popular." Scorn it as "journalistic." Explain your failure to put more mental sweat into your writing on the ground that "the social scientists who want to be scientific believe that we can have scientific description of human behavior and trust-

worthy predictions in the scientific sense only as we build adequate taxonomic systems for observable phenomena and symbolic systems for the manipulation of ideal and abstract entities."

20. For this explanation I am indebted to Lyman Bryson in an *SRL* article (Oct. 13, 1945) "Writers: Enemies of Social Science." Standing on ground considerably of his own choosing, Mr. Bryson argued against judging social science writing by literary standards.

21. Social scientists are not criticized because they are not literary artists. The trouble with social science does not lie in its special vocabulary. Those words are doubtless chosen with great care. The trouble is that too few social scientists take enough care with words outside their special vocabularies.

22. It is not too much to expect that teachers should be more competent in the art of explanation than those they teach. Teachers of social sciences diligently try to acquire knowledge; too few of them exert themselves enough to impart it intelligently.

23. Too long has this been excused as "the academic mind." It should be called by what it is: intellectual laziness and grubby-mindedness.

COMMENTARY AND QUESTIONS

1. Do you think Williamson substantiates his attack? Is he attacking social scientists for their ideas?
2. What is the relationship of these three groups of paragraphs: 1-3, 4-9, 10-12? What is the function of par. 13? Does par. 20 include information that might have been put in a footnote?
3. Do the concluding paragraphs (21-23) involve too great a shift from ironic to direct attack? Does the conclusion harmonize with the tone in pars. 1-3?
4. In addition to avoiding in his own essay the faults of writing he singles out for censure, does Williamson possess any positive virtues of style?
5. Would the statement of his six rules have been as effective if it had not been made ironically?

SUGGESTIONS FOR WRITING

1. Jargons I have known.
2. How to write like a sports writer.
3. A defense of specialized language.
4. Can you suggest any situations in which more words rather than fewer words might be excusable? Consider, for example, the conversation of someone who is trying to be tactful in an embarrassing moment.

Pleasant Agony

by JOHN MASON BROWN

AT A SEASON'S END, when the country is calling, it may be permissible to talk shop before shutting it up, however temporarily. For four and a half years now, mine has been the privilege, hence the pleasant agony, of filling these pages each week, or almost every week. I say pleasant agony because I know of no other words with which to describe what writing is to me.

2. I claim no singularity in this. There may be, there must be, writers to whom writing comes as effortlessly as breathing. There may even be (though I doubt it) writers whose happiness is complete while they are actually writing. But most of us who live by putting words together are not so fortunate. We are tortured while we write and would be tortured were we not allowed to do so. Although when we are done we feel "delivered," as Sainte-Beuve put it, this delirium of delivery is not accomplished without labor pains for which medicine has, as yet, provided no soothing drugs. If all attempts to coerce words into doing what we would have them do are at best painful pleasures, the pains and pleasures of summoning the right words to meet a weekly deadline are of a special kind.

3. A cook faced with getting dinner when lunch is over knows something of the routine, if not all the anguishes, of a columnist. No mortals, however, have appetites as insatiable as a column's. A column is an omnivorous beast. Its hunger is never appeased. Feed it, and almost at once it demands to be fed again.

4. Though he used a different image to express this same idea, even Shaw, seemingly the most easeful of writers, knew this. When he abandoned the job of drama critic on London's *Saturday Review*, he protested against the weekly deadlines which had confronted him for nearly four years. He likened himself to a man fighting a windmill. "I have hardly time," wrote he, "to stagger to my feet from the knock-down blow of one sail, when the next strikes me down."

5. His successor in the same job on that same fortunate magazine shared an identical dislike of deadlines. For twelve years, Max Beerbohm admitted in his valedictory article, Thursdays had been for him the least

pleasant day of the week. Why Thursday? Because that was the day, the latest possible one, he set aside each week to get his writing done. On every Wednesday, therefore, he would be engulfed by "a certain sense of oppression, of misgiving, even of dread." It was only on Friday, when once the danger was passed, that the sun would shine again. Then he would move on dancing feet.

6. I quote my betters to console myself by the reminder that they, too, knew the pangs of weekly columnizing. Yet the consolation I seek is denied me when I discover, for example, that it took Beerbohm one, and only one, short day of pain to turn out the delectable copy which he could write. Shaw, I am certain, was also a one-day man. I wish I were. I wish even more ardently that I could claim any of the merits which glorify their reviews for what it takes me two, three, or sometimes five days of ceaseless sweating to produce as fodder for these columns.

7. Beerbohm ascribed his disrelish for the act of writing to "the acute literary conscience" with which he had been cursed. It was this conscience, he maintained, which kept his pen from ever running away with him. I know what he means. Unblessed with any of his gifts, I am none the less cursed with something of his conscience. Beerbohm insisted that "to seem to write with ease and delight is one of the duties which a writer owes to his readers." If he worked hard at his sentences, it was because Beerbohm hoped they would read easily. In other words, he was in complete agreement with Sheridan's "easy writing's vile hard reading." One statement of Beerbohm's I could truthfully apply to my own efforts for the *SRL*. It runs, "I may often have failed in my articles here, to disguise labor. But the effort to disguise it has always been loyally made."

8. There is a passage in "The Goncourt Journals" which has haunted me since I read it. Envy has kept it green for me, and wonder (or is it disbelief?) has kept it alive. I have in mind Gautier's boast that he never thought about what he was going to write. "I take up my pen," he explained, "and write. I am a man of letters and am presumed to know my job. . . . I throw my sentences into the air and I can be sure that they will come down on their feet, like cats. . . . Look here: here's my script: not a word blotted."

9. When I think of the one-legged kittens that land on my pages; when I remember the false starts, illegible scribblings, unfinished sentences, discarded drafts, changed constructions, and altered words which mark my beginnings, my continuings, and my endings, I blush with shame and, like the voyagers in Dante's realm, abandon all hope.

10. In these journalistic days the first word that pops into an author's mind is held to be the acceptable, if not the best, word. We are supposed to smile because Wordsworth, at a day's end, was wearied from his quest for the exact word. But where Wordsworth the man may win a smile, Wordsworth the writer, fatiguing himself by doing what is a writer's duty, is far from laughable. The *mot juste* is not just any word. Even if it eludes its pursuer, the search for it seems to me to remain among the obligations of authorship. Indeed, the true hope of anyone who loves the language and respects it is to stumble upon, not the correct word or phrase, but the word or phrase which is so right that it seems inevitable.

11. The word and the phrase are not the only hurdles—and joys—of authorship. The sentence and the paragraph, by means of which points are made, thoughts communicated, emotions transferred, pictures painted, personalities caught, rhythms established, and cadences varied, offer other challenges and should supply their own sources of delight and pride. When so much hurried writing is done for hurried reading, I find it comforting to have Shaw, a veritable geyser with words and ideas, admit in his "Sixteen Self Sketches" how depleting he found his labors as a weekly feuilletonist for ten years. Why? Because, says he, of "taking all the pains I was capable of to get to the bottom of every sentence I wrote."

12. One of the modern world's luckier occurrences was what happened at Harrow when a boy named Winston Churchill was being "menaced with Education." Three times, he tells us in "A Roving Commission," his backwardness as a classical scholar forced him to remain in the same form and hence repeat the same elementary course in English. "Thus," writes he (and who can question him?), "I got into my bones the essential structure of the ordinary British sentence—which is a noble thing. . . . Naturally I am biased in favor of boys learning English. I would make them all learn English: and then I would let the clever ones learn Latin as an honor, and Greek as a treat. But the only thing I would whip them for would be for not knowing English. I would whip them hard for that." One trembles to think how many of us whose profession is writing would be flogged today if lapses in English, or American, were whippable offenses.

13. Later on in that same grand book, Churchill has his more precise say on the subtleties, intricacies, and possibilities of the writer's craft. It is his opinion, and one worth heeding, that, "just as the sentence contains one idea in all its fulness, so the paragraph should embrace a distinct episode; and as sentences should follow one another in harmonious sequence, so the paragraphs must fit on to one another like the automatic couplings of railway carriages."

14. I quote Churchill and these others belonging to the peerage of prose-writers because, for any author with a memory, one of the disheartening and humbling aspects of writing is the recollection, as his own pen moves, of how those whom he admires have faced and solved identical problems. This recollection of what has been done, this sensing of what could and should be done, this awareness of what one hopes to do regardless of whether one can or cannot do it—these are parts of that literary conscience, mentioned by Beerbohm, which keeps a writer's pen from running away with him. I know they are factors in retarding my own pen (meaning my typewriter, pencil, or dictation) even on those happy days when a subject seems to write itself, when sentences come easily, and one paragraph gives way to another.

15. Style is a strange and mysterious thing. Some contemporary writers appear to get along without it and to want to do so, and most of us rightly disparage it when it shows the effort that has gone into it. Few of us, for example, can read Pater today without being irritated and put off by the deliberate intricacies and involutions of his sentences. His style, once held to be a model, remains a model, although as we see it it is one to be avoided rather than followed. Pater could not bring himself to say a simple thing simply. His orchestration is so elaborate that the melody of his thought is lost.

16. Hazlitt comes closer to present-day tastes. More than being the enemy of the gaudy and "Occult" schools of writing, Hazlitt was not only a champion but at his best a matchless practitioner of "The Familiar Style." Although he had the art to make a long sentence seem short, he knew the value of short sentences. "I hate anything," wrote he, "that occupies more space than it is worth. I hate to see a load of band-boxes go along the street, and I hate to see a parcel of big words without any meaning in them."

17. The perpetual challenge of writing, the challenge presented by each new sentence is to say exactly what one wants to say exactly as one wants to say it. This is where the anguish of composition mixes with the delights. This is where, too, style, as I see it, comes into the picture. Style is merely the means, chosen or instinctive (doubtless both), by which a writer has his precise say.

18. Certainly, style is not affectation. Conscious though it may be, when self-conscious it is an obstruction. Its purpose, to my way of thinking, is to give the reader pleasure by sparing him the work which the writer is duty-bound to have done for him. Writers, notwithstanding their hopes or ambitions, may or may not be artists. But there is no excuse for their not being artisans. The style is the man, we are told. True in the final and spiritual sense as this is, style is more than that. It is the writing

man *in print*. It is, so to speak, his written voice and, if it is truly his voice, even in print it should be his and his alone. The closer it comes to the illusion of speech, perhaps the better. Yet the closeness of the written word to the spoken can, and in fact should, never be more than an illusion. For the point of the written word is planning, as surely as the charm of the spoken one is its lack of it.

19. Without shame I confess that, regardless of how unsatisfactory the results may be, I labor when writing these weekly pieces to lighten the labor of those who may read them. That I fail again and again I know to my own chagrin, but I can honestly say I try. I not only rewrite; I often rewrite and rewrite again. I do this though I am well aware that the result is sentences and paragraphs which do not bear rereading. I rewrite partly in longhand, partly by dictation, occasionally sitting down, sometimes walking, but most often snaking my way across the floor on my stomach. My desk, a migratory one, is the small piece of beaverboard I push before me. On it are sheets of typewriter paper darkened with hieroglyphics which must be deciphered immediately to be read at all.

20. Endeavoring to square my writing with my writing conscience, and having to live with the difference between what I would like to have done and am able to do, is one of the reasons why writing is to me an agony, however pleasant. There are other contributors to the pleasures and the agonies of trying to keep these columns fed. Upon these I shall touch next time. Since there is no earthly reason why anyone should be interested, this can be taken as a threat, not a promise. I can delve into these personal problems of authorship only at a season's end. What is more, I find I want to do so. Surely this is as good a reason for writing as any, and a better one than so regular an offender as the conductor of a weekly column can always claim.

COMMENTARY AND QUESTIONS

When this essay was published, John Mason Brown faced almost weekly the "pleasant agony" of writing an article for *The Saturday Review of Literature*. This one appeared in a June issue, as the author was about to leave on a summer vacation, and is the first of a pair of articles on the subject of writing. In the second he speaks, as he indicates in par. 20 here, of other "pleasures and agonies" of writing, especially those of a drama critic.

1. Part of the last paragraph furnishes a transition to "Pleasant Agony— II." How much of the paragraph could be omitted? Would the new conclusion be effective?

2. In par. 3 the routine of the columnist is compared to that of a cook. Find other direct or implied comparisons that make the writing concrete (don't omit quoted passages).
3. What is the subject of pars. 15-18? What is the justification for including these paragraphs in this essay?

SUGGESTION FOR WRITING

The pleasant agony of my hobby.

Scented Words

by H. L. MENCKEN

OFT IN THE STILLY NIGHT, ere slumber's chain has bound me, I find myself sweating over a problem both philological and psychological; to wit, why in hell have the used-car dealers of this great republic never devised a better term to designate their profession? What could be more soaring than their idealism—I always think of them, in fact, as one of the great glories of the Rotarian metaphysic—and yet what could be more prosaic and forbidding than the name by which they call themselves? The realtors, if they were of like backwardness, would still be *real-estate agents* and brothers to the ox, and the morticians would still be *undertakers* and brothers to the buzzard. Are the used-car boys, then, too dumb to invent a match for *realtor* and *mortician*? Hardly, for haven't they already got rid of the vulgar and sordid *second-hand* by substituting the tasty *used,* and do not some of them proceed from *used* to *nearly new* and *experienced*? No, it can't be that. They are smart enough to excogitate something as far beyond *realtor* and *mortician* as either is beyond *mixologist,* for bartender, or *commissionnaire,* for door opener. They have simply fumbled their chance and neglected their duty. They suffer from a form of aphasia, and every lover of beauteous words must hope that it will be as evanescent as it is deplorable.

2. If my talent for constructive onomatology were as lively as it used to be, I'd throw myself into the breach without further ado and offer them something nifty. There was a time when this gift of mine was so powerful that I tossed off *ecdysiast* for the strip-tease gals and *bootician* for the more recherché bootleggers without blowing a vein, but that, alas, was some years ago, before morticians began to send me Christmas cards. As things stand, the best I can do is lament that all terms based upon the obvious word *service* are barred out, for the keepers of gas stations and roadside feed troughs have already hogged them, including even the verb *to service*, which Robert Louis Stevenson invented in 1893 and then abandoned. It would be hard to imagine any group of Americans more devoted to the dream of Service than the used-car dealers, for even the most earthy of them, when he ropes a prospect, serves him by saving him from the others, but words of the *service* class, as I say, are out, since such forms as *service station, tire service, curb service,* and so on, not only are already hogged but have become banal. For a couple of weeks, I toyed with terms, chiefly from foreign languages, that plausibly adumbrated the used-car dealers' stern and, indeed, almost suicidal ideal of rectitude, but I had to give it up when I found no better sources than the French *probité* and *confidence,* one of which suggests prying grand juries and the other of which has been preempted by the confidence men. That the problem will be solved soon or late, and in a poetic and dashing manner, I am sure; at the time, unhappily, I am unequal to it.

3. Pondering it, I have been led to cast my eye over some of the more recent bedfellows of *realtor* and *mortician,* and find that several very nobby ones have been invented within the past few years. Perhaps the nobbiest of all is *zymurgeon,* to designate one who serves humanity by working in a brewery. This was thrown to the winds in 1947 by the St. Louis *Star-Times,* which maybe got the idea from a book by the English wordmonger Ivor Brown, who discovered several years ago that the tony word for brewing is *zymurgy. Zymurgy,* at that time, was certainly not new. It had been listed in all the dictionaries, in fact, for nearly a century, but inasmuch as it always appeared near the bottom of the last page, it was overlooked by all previous connoisseurs of verbal delicatessen. It had an analogue, the adjective *zymotic,* which was quite as old, and probably even older. *Zymotic,* however, has nothing to do with the confection of malt liquor. It was used by medical men, in the days before the germ theory of disease, to designate such contagious maladies as smallpox, measles, and typhoid fever, for they were then thought to be produced by a process resembling fermentation. That process, in truth, *did* resemble fermentation more or less, but when Pasteur, Koch, and company began proving that not ferments but bacilli were to blame,

zymotic disappeared from the medical books, and any doctor who used it today would be dismissed as paleolithic. Both *zymurgy* and *zymotic*, the former suggested by *metallurgy*, were derived originally from a Greek word, *zyme*, meaning a ferment or leaven. The *Star-Times*, starting with *zymurgy*, arrived at *zymurgeon* by thinking of *surgeon*, just as the undertakers arrived at *mortician* by thinking of *physician*, their immemorial pal, and the real-estate boys at *realtor* by thinking of such elegant words as *senator* and *ambassador*. I should add that the *Star-Times* is not indissolubly wedded to *zymurgeon*; it is also flirting with *zymeotechnician*, and may hatch even gaudier ones later on. So far, the brewworkers of St. Louis have not indicated their preference, if, indeed, they have ever heard of the matter at all. My own choice is *zymurgeon*, though I am still willing to hear argument in favor of *zymeotechnician*, and even *zymor*, *zymologist*, *zymiast*, *zymician*, and *zymurgic engineer*. When a brewmaster, fearing the return of prohibition, takes a header into one of his vats and is not found until the next morning, he is obviously a *zymocide*. So is a boozer who makes a bet that he can drink thirty kegs of beer in thirty days.

4. The year 1947 also saw the birth of *sanitor* for janitor, a crown and climax to the process that, some time previously, had worked through *superintendent*, *custodian*, *custodian-engineer*, *custodial engineer*, and, finally, *building engineer*. The new term was born in Louisville and has since made its way to most other cultural centers, though the janitors in the New York public schools are still *custodian-engineers* and those in the warrens of job-holders at Washington are officially *custodian-personnel*. There seems to be a powerful pull, probably inspired by the roaring success of *realtor*, toward the suffix *-or*, and it is thus not surprising that the janitors have come back to it. Many neighborhood butchers and greengrocers are now calling themselves *purveyors*, and virtually all house painters of any tone have become *decorators*. (Meanwhile, not a few interior decorators, disgusted by this invasion from below, have taken to calling themselves *interiorists*.) In many ambitious crafts *-or* is reached by simply turning a traditional *e* into *o*. In 1941, for example, a faction of welders, having seceded in a huff from the American Federation of Labor, changed their name to the more genteel *weldor*, and have since operated a Brotherhood of *Weldors*, Cutters and Helpers of America. The possibilities along this line are manifest. The bartenders, who have scored a failure with *mixologist*, might very well turn to *bartendor*, and the plumbers, who have done almost as badly with *sanitarian* and *sanitary engineer*, might try *plumbor*. Also, there are *truckor*, *roofor*, *jewellor*, *waitor*, *gardenor* and *bouncor*. Each of these would borrow some of the fragrance of *realtor*.

⁵· The pull of *-or* is so strong that the pedagogues, who began to call themselves *educationists* a decade or so ago, have now gone back to *educator,* which appeared as a rival for the homely *teacher* in Shakespeare's time. I myself once proposed *autor* for dealers in new cars (not used, nearly new, or experienced), but it did not take, maybe because it was too close to *author,* which designates a generally insolvent and contemptible class of men. Nearly all bookkeepers are now *auditors,* and those that are not are *accountants. Operator* is used often, as in *rodent operator* or *pest-control operator* (abbreviated to *P.C.O.*), for rat-catcher. The keeper of a necktie shoppe in New York calls himself a *cravateur,* which has a family resemblance to the French *cravatier* and may be only a way stop on the road to *cravator.* In other directions, there is the same steady progress toward euphemism. Some of the sweller jewellers, having muffed *jewellor,* have resorted to *jewellist,* and every rubber in a Turkish bath is now a *physiotherapist.* The regular doctors who specialize in muscle bending formerly used that term, but in 1946 they began to look for something more polished, and now they vacillate between *physiatrist, physiatrician,* and *physicologist,* with the medical journals reporting that *physiatrist* is winning out, though it is hard on the tongue. I add a few more: *home aide,* for servant girl (apparently invented in Canada); *dietician* or *nutritionist,* for cook; *insurance consultant,* for insurance agent (vice *insuror,* which was a flop); and *wedding manager* or *director,* for *shadchen.* The goons who chase small boys playing hooky are no longer *truant officers,* as aforetime, but *attendance officers.* The maids who mop up in hospitals have ceased to be maids and become *nurses' orderlies.* Garbage men are now *sanitary officers,* or, in some towns, *sanitation expediters.* The boys who wrap up packages in stores are *packageers,* builders are *constructioneers,* soda jerks are *fountaineers,* cleaners of cesspools are *septicians,* chimney sweeps (who survive in England) are *fluonomists,* disc jockeys are *transcription directors,* junkmen are *salvagers* or *waste-material dealers,* window dressers are *directors of visual presentation,* washwomen are *clothing refreshers,* and the girls in the ten-cent stores, in certain ultra-progressive communities, have become *counter clerks, sales assistants,* or *service women.*

⁶· The hairdressers, as everyone knows, long ago abandoned their ancient designation, traced to 1771, for *beautician, cosmetician, cosmetologist, hair stylist,* and *beauty engineer.* The name *cosmetologist* has been recognized in many states, and also in the District of Columbia, where, in 1938, Congress set up a board to examine practitioners and defined their art as that of doing "arranging, dressing, styling, curling, waving, cleansing, cutting, removing, singeing, bleaching, coloring, or similar work upon the hair of any person by any means, and with hands or me-

chanical or electrical apparatus or appliances, or by the use of cosmetic preparations, antiseptics, tonics, lotions, or creams, massaging, cleansing, stimulating, exercising, beautifying, or similar work, the scalp, face, neck, arms, bust, or upper part of the body, or manicuring the nails of any person." In their first days of glory, the gals called their dens *parlors, shops, shoppes* (including *beauté shoppés*), and *salons,* but of late they have taken to *center, bar, clinic, laboratory, studio,* and even *villa* and *château.* Like the *chirotonsors,* or barbers, they have pushed their prices so high that they now suffer from a buyers' strike, and have laid in large lines of unguents to be used at home, in the hope of squeezing a few more dollars out of their patrons, who are not customers but *clients* or *patients.*

7. The morticians also are now using *patient* to designate a customer, though some prefer *case* and a few of the less progressive, at least in their clinical conferences, cling to *body, remains,* and even *stiff* and *meat.* But *corpse,* according to a manual issued by the National Selected Morticians in 1941, "is an offensive word." Just why it is offensive is not explained. It dates from the early fourteenth century, was used with no thought of gaucherie by Chaucer, Shakespeare, Milton, Bacon, and Ruskin, and occurs four times in the King James Bible. Some of the ultra- or super-morticians of Hollywood are now toying with *loved one* for the deceased, as readers of Evelyn Waugh's novel of that name well know. The same dreamers call the place where he is on show the *slumber room,* though I gather that the Selected Morticians prefer *reposing room.* So far as I can make out, no one, even in Hollywood, has ever invented a euphemism for *embalmer,* but the atelier in which he works is no longer his *morgue* but his *preparation room, operating room,* or *laboratory.* In circles of any refinement, the term *coffin* has given way to *casket,* though the latter was derided by Nathaniel Hawthorne in 1863 as "a vile modern phrase" (*sic*) that takes all the poetry out of death. *Coffin* came into English from the French centuries ago, but has been under fire since the rise of elegance in Early Victorian days. During the Civil War era, it had a formidable rival in *case,* but *casket* knocked out both soon afterward, Hawthorne to the contrary notwithstanding. The Selected Morticians say that *coffin* now means only "a special wedge-shaped receptacle," like those still in use both in the British Isles and on the Continent of Europe. But the War Department, perhaps remembering that George Washington is buried in one at Mt. Vernon, sticks to the term.

8. I know an undertaker in Baltimore, of the highest chop, who continues to call his establishment a *funeral parlor,* but most of the others have now substituted *chapel, drawing room,* or *funeral home.* Back in the nineties of the last century, as I am informed by a stenographic report

of the Carlyle W. Harris murder trial, there was at least one undertaker in New York who called his place a *store*. The Selected Morticians warn their members that the can or jar in which clean dirt is carried to the loved one's last resting place ("ashes to ashes, dust to dust") is under no circumstances to be called the *sandbox*, even *sotto voce*. In Hollywood, incidentally, burial is going out, at least among Class A movie folk. They are now disposed of by *inhumement, entombment, inurnment, immurement*, or *insarcophagusment*. A spot close enough to Valentino to be in his glare of immortality costs something on the order of twenty-five thousand dollars.

⁹· Who invented *mortician* is not known, but the records show that it was first used in the *Embalmer's Monthly* early in 1895. It was not, however, until September 17, 1917, that the Selected Morticians launched their very exclusive organization, which is confined to one practitioner in a town and is almost as snobbish as the Porcellian Club, at Harvard. I am told, indeed, by one of its stars that even a former fellow of the Porcellian Club is occasionally blackballed, not to mention a member of Phi Beta Kappa or the Union League of Philadelphia. Dr. Louise Pound reported in *Dialect Notes* in 1918 that there were already country undertakers in both central Iowa and western Washington who had grabbed *mortician*, and even debased it to *morticianer*, and since then it has come into such widespread use in all parts of the country that even the *Journal of the American Medical Association*, the bible of the doctors, has formally recognized it. On July 19, 1897, the *Journal* printed a learned article in which morticians and pathologists were jointly given some good advice about the use of rubber gloves in their procedures.

¹⁰· In 1940, the cobblers of the United States suddenly decided to call themselves *shoetricians*, apparently in imitation of *mortician* and *physician*, and on February 25th of that year those of Texas and the adjacent states formed the Texas-Southwestern Association of *Shoetricians*, at Fort Worth. But the New York *Times* poked such vicious sport at the new name on March 13th, and so many other newspapers joined in reviling it, that it quickly died the death. The cobblers then went back to *shoe rebuilder*, which had been invented in 1935, and it still survives. Their trade journal is the *Master Shoe Rebuilder*, of Boston, which has a large circulation and has absorbed the archaic *Shoe Repairer*. So far, not many of them have followed the beauticians and morticians in inventing fancy names for their studios, though I have heard of a *shuchâteau* in Denver. The morticians themselves have set up a monthly *Mid-Continent Mortician*, in Minneapolis, but their principal organ is the poetically named *Casket and Sunny Side*, which was founded in 1871 and is still flourishing lushly. Its runner-up, only ten years younger, bears the old-fashioned title of the *American Funeral Director*.

11. The morticians made one capital mistake at the start of their distinguished career: they neglected to register their new name as a trademark. As a result, it is in the public domain, and anyone who chooses to do so may use it. The realtors were a good deal smarter. *Realtor* is their private property, and whenever any unauthorized person cabbages it, their lawyers clamp down on him hard. Indeed, they even pursue and afflict newspapers and magazines that apply it inadvertently to a heathen and a stranger. This, I suppose, accounts for the fact that Negro real-estate agents have had to invent a name of their own; to wit, *realtist*. But Negro undertakers are free to use *mortician* in a wide and lavish way, and they do so everywhere in the United States.

COMMENTARY AND QUESTIONS

H. L. Mencken became famous in the 1920's for his debunking of the shams and hypocrisy of American life as he saw it. He is also well known for *The American Language*—published in 1919, later revised and supplemented by separate publications—in which he stresses the individuality of our language as distinct from that spoken in England. "Scented Words" is one of a series of supplementary articles having the general heading "Postscripts to the American Language."

1. On what principle did Mencken choose the first eleven words in this article? Does this principle have any relation to the rest of the article?
2. Do you think this selection would be more effective if an explicit definition of the phrase *scented words* were given at the beginning?
3. If you have read "Pleasant Agony" (pp. 524-528), do you think John Mason Brown would agree with Mencken's attitude toward scented words?
4. Can you add to Mencken's list?
5. How has Mencken managed to write an article containing dozens of separate examples of words and phrases without letting the article become a mere series of monotonous lists?

Correctness

by SIR ERNEST GOWERS

ENGLISH IS NOT STATIC—neither in vocabulary nor in grammar, nor yet in that elusive quality called style. The fashion in prose alternates between the ornate and the plain, the periodic and the colloquial. Grammar and punctuation defy all the efforts of grammarians to force them into the mould of a permanent code of rules. Old words drop out or change their meanings; new words are admitted. What was stigmatised by the purists of one generation as a corruption of the language may a few generations later be accepted as an enrichment, and what was then common currency may have become a pompous archaism or acquired a new significance.

2. Eminent men with a care for the language, from Dean Swift[1] to Lord Wavell,[2] have from time to time proposed that an Authority should be set up to preserve what is good and resist what is bad. "They will find", said Swift, "many words that deserve to be utterly thrown out of the language, many more to be corrected, and perhaps not a few long since antiquated, which ought to be restored on account of their energy and sound." "They should issue", said Lord Wavell, "a monthly journal of words that required protection and a pillory of misused words, and so on." Swift's plea, which was made in the form of a letter to the Lord Treasurer, came to nothing. This, Lord Chesterfield drily observed, was not surprising, "precision and perspicuity not being in general the favourite objects of Ministers". Dr. Johnson thought the task hopeless:

> Academies have been instituted to guard the avenues of the languages, to retain fugitives and to repulse invaders; but their vigilance and activity have been vain; sounds are too volatile and subtile for legal restraints, to enchain syllables and to lash the wind are equally the undertakings of pride, unwilling to measure its desires by its strength.

[1] *Proposal for correcting, improving and ascertaining the English Tongue.*
[2] Letter from Lord Wavell to Mr. Ivor Brown quoted in *Ivor Brown's Book of Words.*

3. In our own day we have seen a Society for Pure English, with leaders as eminent as Henry Bradley, Robert Bridges and Logan Pearsall Smith, inviting the support of all those who "would preserve all the richness of differentiation in our vocabulary, its nice grammatical usages and its traditional idioms, but would oppose whatever is slipshod and careless and all blurring of hard-won distinctions, and oppose no less the tyranny of schoolmasters and grammarians, both in their pedantic conservatism and in their enforcing of new-fangled rules". But it is now defunct.

4. Dr. Johnson was right, as usual. One has only to look at the words proposed by Swift for inclusion in his *Index Expurgatorius* to realise how difficult, delicate and disappointing it is to resist new words and new meanings. He condemns, for instance, *sham, banter, mob, bully* and *bamboozle*. A generation later Dr. Johnson called *clever* a "low word" and *fun* and *stingy* "low cant". Should we not have been poorer if Swift and Johnson had had their way with these? There is no saying how things will go. The fight for admission to the language is quickly won by some assailants and long resistance is maintained against others. The word that excited Swift to greatest fury was *mob*, a contraction of *mobile vulgus*. Its victory was rapid and complete. So was that of *banter* and *bamboozle*, which he found hardly less offensive. And if *rep* for *reputation* proved ephemeral, and *phiz* for *physiognomy* never emerged from slang status, and is now dead, that is not because Swift denounced them, but because public opinion disliked them or got tired of them. *Nice* in the sense in which it is ordinarily used today in conversation has not yet established itself in literary English, though we know from the rather priggish lecture that Henry Tilney gave to Catherine Morland about it in *Northanger Abbey* that it was trying to get over the barrier nearly a hundred and fifty years ago. *Reliable* was long opposed on the curious ground that it was an impossible construction; an adjective formed from *rely* could only be *reli-on-able*. I remember noticing as a junior in the India Office many years ago that John Morley as Secretary of State struck it out of a draft dispatch and wrote in *trustworthy*. That must have been almost the last shot fired at it. The objection to it was a survival of the curious theory, widely held in pre-Fowler days, and not yet wholly exorcised, that no sentence could be "good grammar", and no word a respectable word, if its construction violated logic or reason. (I shall have more to say about this reign of pedantry when we consider grammar in Chapter IX.) It is not the habit of the English to refrain from doing anything merely because it is illogical; in any case it was less illogical to accept *reliable* than to strain at it after swallowing *available* and *objectionable*.

⁵· Some words gatecrash irresistibly because their sound is so appropriate to the meaning they are trying to acquire. *Spiv* is a recent example. *Blurb*, Professor Weekley tells us, was described by Robert Bridges as "an admirable word, quite indispensable". *Haver* does not mean *vacillate* (it means *blather*), but almost everyone south of the Border thinks it does: there is no withstanding its suggestion of simultaneous hovering and wavering. The dictionaries do not yet recognise this, but doubtless they will soon bow to the inevitable; for, as Sir Alan Herbert has reminded us, "modern dictionaries are pusillanimous works, preferring feebly to record what has been done than to say what ought to be done".[3] Vidkun Quisling won instant admission to the company of the immortals who, like the Earl of Sandwich, Mr. Joseph Aloysius Hansom, General Shrapnel and Captain Boycott, have given their names to enrich the language. There has been stout resistance against certain words that attacked the barrier in the nineteenth century with powerful encouragement from Dickens—*mutual, individual, phenomenal* and *aggravate*. *Mutual* in the sense of *common*, pertaining to both parties, as in *Our Mutual Friend*, goes back to the sixteenth century, according to the O.E.D., but is "now regarded as incorrect". Perhaps the reason why it is so difficult to restrain the word to its "correct" meaning is the ambiguity of *common*. "Our common friend" might be taken as a reflection on the friend's manners or birth. The use of *individual* that is unquestionably correct is to distinguish a single person from a collective body, as it is used in the Income Tax Acts to distinguish between a personal taxpayer and a corporate one. But its use as a facetious term of disparagement (like the French *individu*) used to be common and still lingers. That was how Mr. Jorrocks understood it when Mr. Martin Moonface described him as an "unfortunate individual", and provoked the retort "You are another indiwidual". *Phenomenal* to the purists means nothing more than "perceptible to the sense", and a *phenomenon* is an occurrence so perceptible; they would say that Mr. Vincent Crummles ought to have called his daughter not "the infant phenomenon" but "the juvenile prodigy". Over *aggravate* the long-drawn-out struggle still continues between those who, like Dickens, use it in the sense of *annoy* and those who would confine it to its original sense of *make worse*. About all these words the issue is still in the balance, but as *aggravating* for *annoying* and *phenomenal* for *prodigious* have unimpeachable contemporary au-

---

[3] When this book was first published a Scottish friend wrote to me: "As a Scot I wept bitter tears over your defeatist attitude in the matter of *haver*. I think it is utterly damnable that a perfectly honest word with a clearly defined meaning should be taken by 'havering bodies' and given a meaning, quite arbitrarily, which violates all its past history. . . . I deplore your weak-kneed acquiescence."

thority—the one of Professor Trevelyan and the other of Professor Week-ley—these two at least may claim victory to be in sight.[4]

6. Today the newcomers are mostly from the inventive and colourful minds of the Americans. The gates have been opened wide for them by film, radio and comic. We have changed our outlook since Dean Alford declared eighty years ago that the way the Americans corrupted our language was all of a piece with the character of that nation "with its blunted sense of moral obligation and duty to men". Yet we still have defenders of our tongue who scrutinise these immigrants very closely. That is as it should be, for some of them are certainly undesirables. But we ought not to forget how greatly our language has been enriched by the vigorous word-making habit of the Americans. Bridges' tribute to *blurb* might be applied to other more recent acquisitions, *gatecrasher, debunk, cold war, baby-sitter, stockpile, bulldoze, commuter* and many others. Nor do I see why anyone should turn up his nose at *teenager,* for it fills a gap usefully. We have no word that covers both sexes in what it is fashionable to call that "age-bracket", except *adolescents,* which vaguely suggests what I believe the psychologists call "imbalance", *juveniles,* which has been tainted by its association with delinquency, and *young persons,* which, though adopted by the law, retains a flavour of primness inappropriate to the young person of today: we are no longer in danger of feeling, as Mr. Podsnap did, that "the question about everything was, would it bring a blush to the cheek of the young person?" But these things are matters of taste, and one's own taste is of no importance unless it happens to reflect the general.

7. It is around new verbs that the battle now rages most hotly. New verbs are ordinarily formed in one of three ways, all of which have in the past been employed to create useful additions to our vocabulary. The first is the simple method of treating a noun as a verb; it is one of the beauties of our language that nouns can be so readily converted into adjectives or verbs. This was the origin, for instance, of the verb *question.* The second is what is called "back-formation", that is to say, forming from a noun the sort of verb from which the noun might have been formed if the verb had come first. In this way the verb *diagnose* was formed from *diagnosis.* The third is to add *ise*[5] to an adjective, as *sterilise* has been formed from *sterile.* All these methods are being used today

---

[4] "But Archbishop Tenison, though much out of favour with the Queen, outlived her in a most aggravating manner, so that Lambeth was never available for a Tory or a High Churchman." *Blenheim,* p. 171.

"English finds itself in possession of a phenomenal number of unrelated words identical in form and sound." *Something about Words* (New York: Dutton), p. 5.

[5] On the question whether this should be *ise* or *ize* see Chapter XI.

with no little zest. New verbs for something that is itself new (like *pressurise*) cannot be gainsaid. *Service* is a natural and useful newcomer in an age when almost everyone keeps a machine of some sort that needs periodical attention. But it provides an interesting example of the way these new verbs take an ell, once you give them an inch. *Service* is already trying to oust *serve*, as in

> A large number of depots of one sort or another will be required to service the town,

and

> To enable a Local Authority to take advantage of this provision it is essential that sites should be available, ready serviced with roads and sewers.

8. The credentials of *to contact* are still in dispute between those who, like Sir Alan Herbert, think it a "loathsome" word and those who hold, with Ivor Brown, that it can claim indulgence on the ground that "there is no word which covers approach by telephone, letter and speech, and *contact* is self-explanatory and concise". If I were to hazard a prophecy, it would be that *contact* will win, but for the present it still excites in some people the same feeling as used to be aroused by split infinitives, *very pleased's* and *those kind of things* in the days when the observance of grammarians' shibboleths was regarded as the test of good writing. So do *feature, glimpse, position, sense* and *signature* when used as verbs, though all have long since found their way into the dictionaries. So do the verbs *loan, gift* and *author*, though these were verbs centuries ago, and are only trying to come back again after a long holiday, spent by *loan* in America, by *gift* in Scotland and by *author* in oblivion. Whatever may be the fate of these, we shall not be disposed to welcome such a word as *reaccessioned*, used by a librarian of a book once more available to subscribers. To *underground* (of electric cables) seems at first sight an unnecessary addition to our vocabulary of verbs when *bury* is available, but an editor to whom a protest was made retorted that *bury* would not have done because the cables were "live".

9. But these words are merely skirmishers. The main body of the invasion consists of verbs ending in *ise*. "There seems to be a notion", says Sir Alan Herbert, "that any British or American subject is entitled to take any noun or adjective, add *ise* to it, and say, 'I have made a new verb. What a good boy am I.'" Among those now nosing their way into the language are *casualise* (employ casual labour), *civilianise* (replace military staff by civil), *diarise* (enter in a diary), *editorialise* (make editorial comments on), *finalise* (put into final form), *hospitalise* (send to hospital), *publicise* (give publicity to). All these except *diarise* are new

enough not to have been included in the Shorter Oxford English Dictionary, published in 1933, or (except *hospitalise*) in the 1928 edition of Webster's International Dictionary. The reason for inventing them seems to be to enable us to say in one word what would otherwise need several. Whether that will prove a valid passport time alone can show.[6] If the words I have listed were all, they might eventually be swallowed, though with many wry faces. But they are by no means all; a glut of this diet is being offered to us (*trialise, itinerise* and *reliableise* are among the specimens sent to me), and we are showing signs of nausea. It is perhaps significant that at the Coronation of Queen Elizabeth II the word *Inthroning* was substituted for the first time for the word *Inthronisation,* used in all previous Coronations. This may be symptomatic of a revolt against the ugliness of *ise* and still more of *isation,* which Sir Alan Herbert has compared to lavatory fittings, useful in their proper place but not to be multiplied beyond what is necessary for practical purposes.

10. Another popular way of making new words is to put *de, dis* or *non* at the beginning of a word in order to create one with an opposite meaning. *De* and *dis* are termed by the O.E.D. "living prefixes with privative forces". "Living" is the right word; they have been living riotously of late. Anyone, it seems, can make a new verb by prefixing *de* to an existing one. Some years ago Sir Alan Herbert made a collection of some remarkable creations of this sort, and included them in his *index expurgatorius* of "septic verbs". Among them were *debureaucratise, decontaminate, dedirt, dehumidify, deinsectize, deratizate, derestrict, dewater, dezincify.* The Ministry of Food, I am told, once fixed maximum prices for *defeathered* geese.

11. Some of these, it is to be hoped, may prove to be freaks of an occasion and will be seen no more. But there is a class which has come to stay, whether we like it or not. This comprises *decontaminate, derestrict* and *derequisition.* Their origin is the same: they all denote the undoing of something the doing of which called for—or at any rate was given—a special term. If to affect with gas is to *contaminate,* to enforce a speed limit is to *restrict,* and to commandeer a house is to *requisition,* then the cancellation of those things will inevitably be *decontaminate, derestrict* and *derequisition,* whether we like it or not, and it is no use saying that they ought to be *cleanse, exempt* and *release,* or any other words that are not directly linked with their opposites. But some people will still wince on reading that the Ministry of Transport have decided to detrunk a road, as though it were an elephant, and on hearing that witnesses in a postponed trial have been dewarned.

---

[6] A remarkable experiment in this direction is the American verb to *nolle prosse,* meaning to enter a writ of *nolle prosequi.*

¹²· Most of the new *dis*-words since the war have been invented by economists (several by *The Economist* itself). *Disincentive* and *disinflation*, received at first with surprised disapproval, seem to have quite settled down. It is recognised that the old-fashioned opposites of *incentive* and *inflation*—*deterrent* and *deflation*—will not do: we need special words for that particular form of deterrent that discourages men from working hard, and for that process of checking inflation which is something less than deflation. On the heels of these new arrivals come *diseconomy* and *dissaving*.

> It would yield economies that would far outweigh the diseconomies that are the inevitable price of public ownership and giant size.
>
> Some 13.4 million of the 22 million income earners . . . kept their spending in such exact step with their incomes that they saved or dissaved less than £ 25 in that year.

¹³· Will these be accepted also on the ground that in the first no positive word—neither *extravagance* nor *waste* nor *wastefulness*—would express the writer's meaning so well as *diseconomies*, and that in the second *dissaved* is the only way of expressing the opposite of *saved* without a clumsy periphrasis that would destroy the nice balance of the sentence? Perhaps; it is at least certain that these words spring from deliberate and provocative choice and not from mental indolence. What is deplorable is that so many of those who go in for the invention of opposites by means of "living prefixes with privative force" do not know when to stop. It becomes a disease. *Disincentive* replaces *deterrent*; then *undisincentive* ousts *incentive*, and then *disincentive* itself has to yield to *nonundisincentive*. No wonder Mr. G. V. Carey is moved to write to *The Times*:

> I have long been waiting for somebody to dispel my growing bewilderment at the modern expression of affirmative and negative (or should I say "disaffirmative"?) in English. I had always imagined that the opposite of "harmony" was "discord", not "disharmony"; of "incentive", "deterrent", and so on. But at the present rate of distortion of our language it looks as though we shall soon be talking about "black and disblack", "good and disgood".

¹⁴· In the "newspeak" which George Orwell pictured as the language of 1984 *very bad* has become *doubleplusungood*.

¹⁵· The same warning is needed about the prefix *non*. To put *non* in front of a word is a well-established way of creating a word with the opposite meaning. *Non-appearance, non-combatant, nonconformist* and *non-existent* are common examples. But the lazy habit of using *non* to turn any word upside-down, so as not to have the trouble of thinking of

its opposite, is becoming sadly common. "Institutions for the care of the *non-sick*" presumably means something different from "institutions for the care of the healthy", but the difference is not apparent. Sir Alan Herbert remarked some years ago that no one would think of saying *non-sober* when he meant drunk. I cannot feel sure that that is still true. I should have said that this trick was of recent origin if Mr. G. M. Young had not sent me an eighty-year-old example of it that would hold its own against any modern rival. Sir John Simon, F.R.S., the eminent surgeon who later became a Government official, giving evidence before the Royal Commission on the Sanitary Laws in 1869, referred to "a disease hereditarily transmissible and spreading among the non-fornicative part of the population". Mr. Young says he was surprised to come across this, because Simon was a man of culture and a friend of Ruskin. "It just shows", he added unkindly, "what Whitehall can do."

16. Yet another favourite device for making new words is the suffix *ee*. This is an erratic suffix, not conforming wholly to any rule. But in its main type it serves to denote the object of a verb, generally the indirect object, as in *assignee, referee* and *trustee*, but sometimes the direct object, as in *examinee, trainee* and *evacuee*. It therefore makes for confusion of language if the suffix is used to form a word meaning the subject of the verb. *Escapee* is worse than useless; we already have *escaper*. When unskilled labour is used to "dilute" skilled labour, the unskilled ought to be called not *dilutees,* as they are officially termed, but *dilutors.* The skilled are the *dilutees.* Apart from misuse such as this, we are getting too many *ee* words; they are springing up like weeds. Their purpose seems to be the same as that of many of our new verbs: to enable us to use one word instead of several. But we have got on very well for quite a long time without such words as *expellee, persecutee* and *amputee.*

17. While the age-long practice of creating new words has quickened its tempo, so has the no less ancient habit of extending the meaning of established words. Here again we ought to examine the novelties on merits, without bias. The main test for both is whether the new word, or the new meaning, fills a need in the vocabulary. If it is trying to take a seat already occupied—as the new verbs *decision* and *suspicion* are squatting in the places of *decide* and *suspect,* and the enlarged meanings of *anticipate* and *claim* in those of *expect* and *assert*—they are clearly harming the language by "blurring hard-won distinctions". Still more are words like *overall* and *involve* open to that charge: they are claiming the seats of half a dozen or more honest words. But those that claim seats hitherto empty may deserve admittance. *Stagger,* for example, has recently enlarged its meaning both logically and usefully in such a phrase as *staggered holidays. Deadline* (originally a line around a military

prison beyond which a prisoner might be shot) has done the same in taking over the task of signifying a limit of any sort beyond which it is not permissible to go. Nor do I see why purists should condemn the use of *nostalgic* not only for a feeling of homesickness but also for the emotion aroused by thinking of the days that are no more. An appeal to etymology is not conclusive. When a word starts straying from its derivative meaning it may often be proper, and sometimes even useful, to try to restrain it; there are many now who would like to restrain the wanderlust of *alibi* and *shambles*. The ignorant misuse of technical terms excites violent reactions in those who know their true meanings. The popular use of *to the nth degree* in the sense of *to the utmost* exasperates the mathematician, who knows that strictly the notion of largeness is not inherent in *to the nth* at all. The use of *by and large* in the sense of *broadly speaking* exasperates the sailor, who knows that the true meaning of the phrase—alternately close to the wind and with the wind abeam or aft—has not the faintest relation to the meaning given to it by current usage. But there is a point where it becomes idle pedantry to try to put back into their etymological cages words and phrases that escaped from them many years ago and have settled down firmly elsewhere. To do that is to start on a path on which there is no logical stopping-point short of such absurdities as insisting that the word *anecdote* can only be applied to a story never told before, whereas we all know that it generally means one told too often. As Sir Clifford Allbutt used to remind his students, "the word *apostate* means for us far more than an *absentee* or a *dissenter*, and a *muscle* more than a *little mouse; monks* rarely live alone; *rivals* contend for more than water rights, and *hypocrites* are no longer confined to the theatre."

18. Sometimes words appear to have changed their meanings when the real change is in the popular estimate of the value of the ideas they stand for. *Imperialism,* which Lord Rosebery defined as "a greater pride in Empire, a larger patriotism", has fallen from its pedestal. *Academic* is suffering a similar debasement owing to the waning of love of learning for its own sake and the growth of mistrust of intellectual activities that have no immediate utilitarian results. In music, according to the music critic of *The Times,* the word "has descended from the imputation of high esteem to being a withering term of polite abuse", in spite of Stanford's attempt to stop the rot by defining the word as "a term of opprobrium applied by those who do not know their business to those who do". A change in popular sentiment may also account for a confusing enlargement of the meaning of *afford.* "Can we afford to do it?" asks one of our legislators in a debate on some expensive project, meaning "have we the financial resources to do it?" "Can we afford not to do it?" retorts

another, meaning "can we face the consequences of not doing it?" Unless this means "Shall we not have to spend more money in some other way if we do not do it?" the arguments are not in the same plane, and will never meet.

19. Public opinion decides all these questions in the long run; there is little that individuals can do about them. Our national vocabulary is a democratic institution, and what is generally accepted will ultimately be correct. I have no doubt that if anyone should read this book in fifty years' time he would find current objections to the use of certain words in certain senses as curious as we now find Swift's denunciation of *mob*. Lexicographers soon find this out. I have quoted Dr. Johnson; seventy years later Noah Webster said the same thing in different words:

> It is quite impossible to stop the progress of language—it is like the course of the Mississippi, the motion of which at times is scarcely perceptible yet even then it possesses a momentum quite irresistible. Words and expressions will be forced into use in spite of all the exertions of all the writers in the world.

COMMENTARY AND QUESTIONS

This selection is taken from Chapter IV of *Plain Words: Their ABC*, which is a revision and combination of two books written earlier by Sir Ernest Gowers at the request of the British government as part of its attempt to improve the English used by officials. (Gowers himself was in the British civil service for thirty-five years.) In Chapter III Gowers urges writers of official documents to remember three fundamental precepts: "Be simple. Be short. Be human." The fourth precept, "Be correct," is the burden of Chapter IV. But "correctness"—and here Gowers is applying the term to vocabulary—is determined ultimately by general usage over a long period of time, not by the wishes of a few individuals at any particular moment. Gowers concludes his discussion in Chapter IV by counseling civil servants to follow general usage: "It is the duty of the official in his use of English neither to perpetuate what is obsolescent nor to give currency to what is novel, but, like a good servant, to follow what is generally regarded by his masters as the best practice for the time being."

1. In par. 17 Gowers states that the main test for a new word or a new meaning is whether "it fills a need in the vocabulary." How is this test related to the ideas discussed in pars. 1-6?

2. Gowers quotes approvingly passages by Dr. Johnson (end of par. 2) and Noah Webster (end of par. 19). How might Gowers defend himself from a charge of inconsistency in also making such a statement as this (end of par. 16): "But we have got on very well for quite a long time without such words as *expellee, persecutee* and *amputee*"?

3. The effectiveness of this discussion of language comes in part from the crisp and imaginative phrasing of Gowers' own language. What is the particular quality that makes each of the following effective: "Some words gatecrash irresistibly" (par. 5); the fourth sentence of par. 8; the last sentence of par. 11? Find similar examples.

4. In this selection some periods and commas come after closing quotation marks in contrast to standard American usage. Can you identify the principle followed by the British printer?

5. Gowers wrote originally for the benefit of British civil servants. Is his advice applicable only to that group?

SUGGESTIONS FOR WRITING

1. Drawing from your own observations, discuss a doctrine of correctness as it might be applied to clothes or to manners at various types of public functions.

2. In light of the discussion of new words by Gowers here and by H. L. Mencken in "Scented Words" (pp. 529-535), try to forecast the future of coinings you have heard or trends you have noticed.

Sabotage
in Springfield

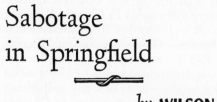

by WILSON FOLLETT

OF DICTIONARIES, as of newspapers, it might be said that the bad ones are too bad to exist, the good ones too good not to be better. No dictionary of a living language is perfect or ever can be, if only because the time required for compilation, editing, and issuance is so great that shadows of obsolescence are falling on parts of any such work before it ever gets into the hands of a user. Preparation of *Webster's Third New International Dictionary of the English Language* began intensively in the Springfield establishment of G. & C. Merriam Company in 1936, but the century was nine months into its seventh decade before any outsider could have his first look at what had been accomplished. His first look is, of course, incompetent to acquaint him with the merits of the new work; these no one can fully discover without months or years of everyday use. On the other hand, it costs only minutes to find out that what will rank as the great event of American linguistic history in this decade, and perhaps in this quarter century, is in many crucial particulars a very great calamity.

2. Why should the probable and possible superiorities of the Third New International be so difficult to assess, the shortcomings so easy? Because the superiorities are special, departmental, and recondite, the shortcomings general and within the common grasp. The new dictionary comes to us with a claim of 100,000 new words or new definitions. These run almost overwhelmingly to scientific and technological terms or meanings that have come into existence since 1934, and especially to words classified as ISV (belonging to the international scientific vocabulary). No one person can possibly use or even comprehend all of them; the coverage in this domain, certainly impressive to the nonspecialist, may or may not command the admiration of specialists. It is said that historians of the graphic arts and of architecture were displeased with the 1934 Webster, both for its omissions and for some definitions of what it included in their fields. Its 1961 successor may have disarmed their reservations; only they can pronounce.

3. But all of us may without brashness form summary judgments about the treatment of what belongs to all of us—the standard, staple, traditional language of general reading and speaking, the ordinary vocabulary and idioms of novelist, essayist, letter writer, reporter, editorial writer, teacher, student, advertiser; in short, fundamental English. And it is precisely in this province that Webster III has thrust upon us a dismaying assortment of the questionable, the perverse, the unworthy, and the downright outrageous.

4. Furthermore, what was left out is as legitimate a grievance to the ordinary reader as anything that has been put in. Think—if you can—of an unabridged dictionary from which you cannot learn who Mark Twain was (though **mark twain** is entered as a leadsman's cry), or what were the names of the apostles, or that the Virgin was Mary the mother of Jesus of Nazareth, or what and where the District of Columbia is!

5. The disappointment and the shock are intensified, of course, because of the unchallenged position earned by the really unabridged immediate predecessor of this strange work. *Webster's New International Dictionary*, Second Edition (1934), consummated under the edi-

torship of William Allan Neilson, at once became the most important reference book in the world to American writers, editors, teachers, students, and general readers—everyone to whom American English was a matter of serious interest. What better could the next revision do than extend the Second Edition in the direction of itself, bring it up to date, and correct its scattering of oversights and errata?

6. The 1934 dictionary has been, heaven knows, no citadel of conservatism, no last bastion of puristical bigotry. But it had made shrewd reports on the status of individual words; it had taken its clear, beautifully written definitions from fit uses of an enormous vocabulary by judicious users; it had provided accurate, impartial accounts of the endless guerrilla war between grammarian and antigrammarian and so given every consultant the means to work out his own decisions. Who could wish the forthcoming revision any better fortune than a comparable success in applying the same standards to whatever new matter the new age imposed?

7. Instead, we have seen a century and a third of illustrious history largely jettisoned; we have seen a novel dictionary formula improvised, in great part out of snap judgments and the sort of theoretical improvement that in practice impairs; and we have seen the gates propped wide open in enthusiastic hospitality to miscellaneous confusions and corruptions. In fine, the anxiously awaited work that was to have crowned cisatlantic linguistic scholarship with a particular glory turns out to be a scandal and a disaster. Worse yet, it plumes itself on its faults and parades assiduously cultivated sins as virtues without precedent.

8. Examination cannot proceed far without revealing that Webster III, behind its front of passionless objectivity, is in truth a fighting document. And the enemy it is out to destroy is every obstinate vestige of linguistic punctilio, every surviving influence that makes for the upholding of standards, every criterion for distinguishing between better usages and worse. In other words, it has gone over bodily to the school that construes traditions as enslaving, the rudimentary principles of syntax as crippling, and taste as irrelevant. This revolution leaves it in the anomalous position of loudly glorifying its own ancestry—which is indeed glorious—while tacitly sabotaging the principles and ideals that brought the preceding Merriam-Webster to its unchallengeable preeminence. The Third New International is at once a resounding tribute of lip service to the Second and a wholesale repudiation of it—a sweeping act of apology, contrition, and reform.

9. The right-about-face is, of course, particularly evident in the vocabulary approved. Within a few days of publication the new dictionary was inevitably notorious for its unreserved acceptance as standard of

wise up, get hep (it uses the second as a definition of the first), *ants in one's pants, one for the book, hugeous, nixie, passel, hepped up* (with *hepcat* and *hepster*), *anyplace, someplace,* and so forth. These and a swarm of their kind it admits to full canonical standing by the suppression of such qualifying status labels as *colloquial, slang, cant, facetious,* and *substandard.* The classification *colloquial* it abolishes outright: "it is impossible to know whether a word out of context is colloquial or not." Of *slang* it makes a chary occasional use despite a similar reservation: "No word is invariably slang, and many standard words can be given slang connotations or used so inappropriately as to become slang." *Cornball* is ranked as slang, *corny* is not.

10. The overall effect signifies a large-scale abrogation of one major responsibility of the lexicographer. He renounces it on the curious ground that helpful discriminations are so far beyond his professional competence that he is obliged to leave them to those who, professing no competence at all, have vainly turned to him for guidance. If some George Ade of the future, aspiring to execute a fable in slang, were to test his attempt by the status labels in Webster III, he would quickly discover with chagrin that he had expressed himself almost without exception in officially applauded English. With but slight exaggeration we can say that if an expression can be shown to have been used in print by some jaded reporter, some candidate for office or his speech writer, some potboiling minor novelist, it is well enough credentialed for the full blessing of the new lexicography.

11. This extreme tolerance of crude neologisms and of shabby diction generally, however, is but one comparatively trifling aspect of the campaign against punctilio. We begin to sound its deeper implications when we plunge into the definitions and the copious examples that illustrate and support them. Under the distributive pronoun *each* we find, side by side: "(each of them is to pay his own fine) (each of them are to pay their own fine)." Where could anyone look for a neater, more succinct way to outlaw the dusty dogma that a pronoun should agree in number with its antecedent? Here is the same maneuver again under another distributive, *everybody*: "usu. referred to by the third person singular (everybody is bringing his own lunch) but sometimes by a plural personal pronoun (everybody had made up their minds)." Or try *whom* and *whomever*: "(a . . . recruit whom he hoped would prove to be a crack salesman) (people . . . whom you never thought would sympathize) . . . (I go out to talk to whomever it is) . . . (he attacked whomever disagreed with him)." It is, then, all right to put the subject of a finite verb in the accusative case—"esp. after a preposition or a verb of which it might mistakenly be considered the object."

^{12.} Shall we look into what our dictionary does with a handful of the more common solecisms, such as a publisher might introduce into a cooked-up test for would-be copy editors? Begin with *center around* (or *about*). It seems obvious that expressions derived from Euclidean geometry should make Euclidean sense. A center is a point; it is what things are around, not what is around them; they center *in* or *on* or *at* the point. The Second Edition defined the Great White Way as "That part of Broadway . . . centering about Times Square"—patently an oversight. Is it the same oversight that produces, in the Third: "heresy . . . 3: a group or school of thought centering around a particular heresy"? We look up *center* itself, and lo: "(a story to tell, centered around the political development of a great state) . . . (more scholarship than usual was centered around the main problems)," followed by several equivalent specimens.

^{13.} Here is *due to*. First we come on irreproachable definitions, irreproachably illustrated, of *due* noun and *due* adjective, and we think we are out of the woods. Alas, they are followed by the manufacture of a composite preposition, *due to*, got up solely to extenuate such abominations as "the event was canceled due to inclement weather." An adjective can modify a verb, then. And here is a glance at that peculiarly incriminating redundancy of the slipshod writer, *equally as*: "equally opposed to Communism as to Fascism." The intolerable *hardly than* or *scarcely than* construction is in full favor: "hardly had the birds dropped than she jumped into the water and retrieved them." The sequence *different than* has the double approbation of editorial use and a citation: conjunctive *unlike* means "in a manner that is different than," and a passage under *different* reads "vastly different in size than it was twenty-five years ago." Adjectival *unlike* and conjunctive *unlike* both get illustrations that implicitly commend the unanchored and grammarless modifier: "so many fine men were outside the charmed circle that, unlike most colleges, there was no disgrace in not being a club man"; "unlike in the gasoline engine, fuel does not enter the cylinder with air on the intake stroke."

^{14.} This small scattering should not end without some notice of that darling of the advanced libertarians, *like* as a conjunction, first in the meaning of *as*, secondly (and more horribly) in that of *as if*. Now, it is well known to the linguistic historian that *like* was so used for a long time before and after Langland. But it is as well known that the language rather completely sloughed off this usage; that it has long been no more than a regional colloquialism, a rarely seen aberration among competent writers, or an artificially cultivated irritant among defiant ones. The *Saturday Evening Post*, in which *like* for *as* is probably more frequent than in any other painstakingly edited magazine, has seldom if

ever printed that construction except in reproducing the speech or tracing the thoughts of characters to whom it might be considered natural.
The arguments for *like* have been merely defensive and permissive. Not
for centuries has there been any real pressure of authority on a writer
to use *like* as a conjunction—until our Third New International Dictionary decided to exert its leverage.

15. How it is exerted will appear in the following: "(impromptu
programs where they ask questions much like I do on the air) . . . (looks
like they can raise better tobacco) (looks like he will get the job) (wore
his clothes like he was . . . afraid of getting dirt on them) (was like he'd
come back from a long trip) (acted like she felt sick) . . . (sounded like
the motor had stopped) . . . (the violin now sounds like an old masterpiece should) (did it like he told me to) . . . (wanted a doll like she saw
in the store window) . . . (anomalies like just had occurred)."

16. By the processes represented in the foregoing and countless others
for which there is no room here, the latest Webster whittles away at one
after another of the traditionary controls until there is little or nothing
left of them. The controls, to be sure, have often enough been overvalued
and overdone by pedants and purists, by martinets and bigots; but more
often, and much more importantly, they have worked as aids toward
dignified, workmanlike, and cogent uses of the wonderful language that
is our inheritance. To erode and undermine them is to convert the language into a confusion of unchanneled, incalculable williwaws, a capri-
cious wind blowing whithersoever it listeth. And that, if we are to judge
by the total effect of the pages under scrutiny—2720 of them and nearly
8000 columns of vocabulary, all compact in Times roman—is exactly
what is wanted by the patient and dedicated saboteurs in Springfield.
They, if they keep their ears to the ground, will hear many echoes of the
despairing cry already wrung from one editorial assistant on a distinguished magazine that still puts its faith in standards: "Why have a Dictionary at all if anything goes?"

17. The definitions are reinforced, it will have been conveyed, with
copious citations from printed sources. These citations occupy a great
fraction of the total space. They largely account for the reduction in the
number of entries (from 600,000 to 450,000) and for the elimination of
the Gazetteer, the Biographical Dictionary, and the condensed key to
pronunciation and symbols that ran across the bottoms of facing pages
—all very material deprivations. Some 14,000 authors, we are told, are
represented in the illustrative quotations—"mostly from the mid-twentieth century."

18. Can some thousands of authors truly worth space in a dictionary
ever be found in any one brief period? Such a concentration can hardly

fail to be, for the purposes of a dictionary, egregiously overweighted with the contemporary and the transient. Any very short period, such as a generation, is a period of transition in the history of English, and any great mass of examples drawn primarily from it will be disproportionately focused on transitional and ephemeral elements. To say that recording English *as we find it today* is precisely the purpose of a new dictionary is not much of a retort. For the bulk of the language that we use has come down to us with but minor, glacially slow changes from time out of mind, and a worthy record of it must stand on a much broader base than the fashions of yesterday.

19. It is, then, a mercy that among the thousands of scraps from recent authors, many of them still producing, we can also find hundreds from Shakespeare, the English Bible, Fielding, Dickens, Hawthorne, Melville, Henry James, Mark Twain, and so on. But the great preponderance of latter-day prose, little of it worth repeating and a good deal of it hardly worth printing in the first place, is likely to curtail by years the useful life of the Third New International.

20. So much is by the way. When we come to the definitions proper we face something new, startling, and formidable in lexicography. The definitions, all of them conformed to a predetermined rhetorical pattern, may be products of a theory—Gestaltist, perhaps?—of how the receiving mind works. The pattern, in the editor's general preface, is described as follows: "The primary objective of precise, sharp defining has been met through development of a new dictionary style based upon completely analytical one-phrase definitions throughout the book. Since the headword in a definition is intended to be modified only by structural elements restrictive in some degree and essential to each other, the use of commas either to separate or to group has been severely limited, chiefly to elements in apposition or in series. The new defining pattern does not provide for a predication which conveys further expository comment."

21. This doctrine of the strictly unitary definition is of course formulated and applied in the interest of a logical integrity and a simplification never before consistently attained by lexical definitions. What it produces, when applied with the rigor here insisted on, is in the first place some of the oddest prose ever concocted by pundits. A typical specimen, from the definition of the simplest possible term: "**rabbit punch** . . . : a short chopping blow delivered to the back of the neck or the base of the skull with the edge of the hand opposite the thumb that is illegal in boxing." When the idea, being not quite so simple, requires the one-phrase statement of several components, the definition usually turns out to be a great unmanageable and unpunctuated blob of words strung out beyond the retentive powers of most minds that would need the defini-

tion at all. Both theory and result will emerge clearly enough from a pair of specimens, the first dealing with a familiar everyday noun, the second with a mildly technical one:

> **groan** . . . 1: a deep usu. inarticulate and involuntary often strangled sound typically abruptly begun and ended and usu. indicative of pain or grief or tension or desire or sometimes disapproval or annoyance.

> **kymograph** . . . 1: a recording device including an electric motor or clockwork that drives a usu. slowly revolving drum which carries a roll of plain or smoked paper and also having an arrangement for tracing on the paper by means of a stylus a graphic record of motion or pressure (as of the organs of speech, blood pressure, or respiration) often in relation to particular intervals of time.

22. About these typical definitions as prose, there is much that any good reader might well say. What must be said is that the grim suppression of commas is a mere crotchet. It takes time to read such definitions anyway; commas in the right places would speed rather than slow the reading and would clarify rather than obscure the sense, so that the unitary effect—largely imaginary at best—would be more helped than hurt. In practice, the one-phrase design without further expository predication lacks all the asserted advantages over a competently written definition of the free conventional sort; it is merely more difficult to write, often impossible to write well, and tougher to take in. Compare the corresponding definitions from the Second Edition:

> **groan** . . . A low, moaning sound; usually, a deep, mournful sound uttered in pain or great distress; sometimes, an expression of strong disapprobation; as, the remark was received with *groans.*

> **kymograph** . . . a An automatic apparatus consisting of a motor revolving a drum covered with smoked paper, on which curves of pressure, etc., may be traced.

23. Everyone professionally concerned with the details of printed English can be grateful to the new Webster for linking the parts of various expressions that have been either hyphenated compounds or separate words—*highlight, highbrow* and *lowbrow, overall, wisecrack, lowercase* and *uppercase,* and so on. Some of the unions now recognized were long overdue; many editors have already got them written into codes of house usage. But outside this small province the new work is a copy editor's despair, a propounder of endless riddles.

24. What, for example, are we to make of the common abbreviations *i.e.* and *e.g.*? The first is entered in the vocabulary as **ie** (no periods, no

space), the second as **e g** (space, no periods). In the preliminary list, "Abbreviations Used in This Dictionary," both are given the customary periods. (Oddly, the list translates its *i.e.* into "that is," but merely expands *e.g.* into "exempli gratia.") Is one to follow the vocabulary or the list? What point has the seeming inconsistency?

25. And what about capitalization? All vocabulary entries are in lowercase except for such abbreviations as ARW (air raid warden), MAB (medical advisory board), and PX (post exchange). Words possibly inviting capitalization are followed by such injunctions as *cap, usu cap, sometimes not cap, usu cap 1st A, usu cap A&B*. (One of the small idiosyncrasies is that "usu.," the most frequent abbreviation, is given a period when roman, denied it when italic.) From **america**, adjective— all proper nouns are excluded—to **american yew** there are over 175 consecutive entries that require such injunctions; would it not have been simpler and more economical to capitalize the entries? A flat *"cap,"* of course, means "always capitalized." But how often is "usually," and when is "sometimes"? We get dictionaries expressly that they may settle such problems for us. This dictionary seems to make a virtue of leaving them in flux, with the explanation that many matters are subjective and that the individual must decide them for himself—a curious abrogation of authority in a work extolled as "more useful and authoritative than any previous dictionary."

26. The rock-bottom practical truth is that the lexicographer cannot abrogate his authority if he wants to. He may think of himself as a detached scientist reporting the facts of the language, declining to recommend use of anything or abstention from anything; but the myriad consultants of his work are not going to see him so. He helps create, not a book of fads and fancies and private opinions, but a Dictionary of the English Language. It comes to every reader under auspices that say, not "Take it or leave it," but rather something like this: "Here in 8000 columns is a definitive report of what a synod of the most trustworthy American experts consider the English language to be in the seventh decade of the twentieth century. This is your language; take it and use it. And if you use it in conformity with the principles and practices here exemplified, your use will be the most accurate attainable by any American of this era." The fact that the compilers disclaim authority and piously refrain from judgments is meaningless: the work itself, by virtue of its inclusions and exclusions, its mere existence, is a whole universe of judgments, received by millions as the Word from on high.

27. And there we have the reason why it is so important for the dictionary maker to keep his discriminations sharp, why it is so damaging if he lets them get out of working order. Suppose he enters a new defini-

tion for no better reason than that some careless, lazy, or uninformed scribbler has jumped to an absurd conclusion about what a word means or has been too harassed to run down the word he really wanted. This new definition is going to persuade tens of thousands that, say, *cohort*, a word of multitude, means one associate or crony "(he and three alleged housebreaking cohorts were arraigned on attempted burglary charges)" or that the vogue word *ambivalence*, which denotes simultaneous love and hatred of someone or something, means "continual oscillation between one thing and its opposite (novels . . . vitiated by an ambivalence between satire and sentimentalism)." To what is the definer contributing if not to subversion and decay? To the swallower of the definition it never occurs that he can have drunk corruption from a well that he has every reason to trust as the ultimate in purity. Multiply him by the number of people simultaneously influenced, and the resulting figure by the years through which the influence continues, and a great deal of that product by the influences that will be disseminated through speech and writing and teaching, and you begin to apprehend the scope of the really enormous disaster that can and will be wrought by the lexicographer's abandonment of his responsibility.

COMMENTARY AND QUESTIONS

This selection and the one following, by Bergen Evans, were written within a few months after the publication of *Webster's Third New International Dictionary*. Both selections appeared in *The Atlantic Monthly:* Follett's in January; Evans' in May of the same year. Bergen Evans, as you will see when you read his essay, defends the Third Edition attacked here by Wilson Follett.

1. As Follett notes in his opening paragraph, the G. & C. Merriam Company, publishers of *Webster's Third New International Dictionary*, is located in Springfield (Massachusetts). This information explains the place name in the title. How early in the selection does Follett reveal that he regards as sabotage what has been done at Springfield?

2. In pars. 5-8 Follett maintains that the Third Edition has not carried on, but has repudiated, the tradition established by the Second Edition. In pars. 9-15 he discusses specific problems of usage; what is the basic charge against the dictionary makers that Follett states here?

3. After lamenting (in pars. 17-19) that the citations in the definitions are drawn largely from mid-twentieth century authors, Follett turns (in pars. 20-22) to an analysis of the definitions themselves, and criticizes the method used. What are the main points in his criticism?

4. After praising the Third Edition (in par. 23) for one practice—that of printing as one word previously hyphenated or separate words—and

condemning it (in par. 24) for another practice—that of handling abbreviations inconsistently, Follett returns (in the process of discussing capitalization in par. 25) to his basic charge: that the dictionary makers have abrogated authority. How is it possible for him to state at the beginning of par. 26 that "the lexicographer cannot abrogate his authority if he wants to"? Does Follett restate his basic charge in par. 27?

But What's
a Dictionary For?

by BERGEN EVANS

THE STORM OF ABUSE in the popular press that greeted the appearance of *Webster's Third New International Dictionary* is a curious phenomenon. Never has a scholarly work of this stature been attacked with such unbridled fury and contempt. An article in the *Atlantic* viewed it as a "disappointment," a "shock," a "calamity," "a scandal and a disaster." The New York *Times,* in a special editorial, felt that the work would "accelerate the deterioration" of the language and sternly accused the editors of betraying a public trust. The *Journal* of the American Bar Association saw the publication as "deplorable," "a flagrant example of lexicographic irresponsibility," "a serious blow to the cause of good English." *Life* called it "a non-word deluge," "monstrous," "abominable," and "a cause for dismay." They doubted that "Lincoln could have modelled his Gettysburg Address" on it—a concept of how things get written that throws very little light on Lincoln but a great deal on *Life.*

2. What underlies all this sound and fury? Is the claim of the G. & C. Merriam Company, probably the world's greatest dictionary maker, that the preparation of the work cost $3.5 million, that it required the efforts of three hundred scholars over a period of twenty-seven years, working

on the largest collection of citations ever assembled in any language—
is all this a fraud, a hoax?

3. So monstrous a discrepancy in evaluation requires us to examine
basic principles. Just what's a dictionary for? What does it propose to do?
What does the common reader go to a dictionary to find? What has the
purchaser of a dictionary a right to expect for his money?

4. Before we look at basic principles, it is necessary to interpose two
brief statements. The first of these is that a dictionary is concerned with
words. Some dictionaries give various kinds of other useful information.
Some have tables of weights and measures on the flyleaves. Some list
historical events, and some, home remedies. And there's nothing wrong
with their so doing. But the great increase in our vocabulary in the past
three decades compels all dictionaries to make more efficient use of their
space. And if something must be eliminated, it is sensible to throw out
these extraneous things and stick to words.

5. Yet wild wails arose. The *Saturday Review* lamented that one can
no longer find the goddess Astarte under a separate heading—though
they point out that a genus of mollusks named after the goddess is included! They seemed to feel that out of sheer perversity the editors of
the dictionary stooped to mollusks while ignoring goddesses and that, in
some way, this typifies modern lexicography. Mr. Wilson Follett, follet-
izing (his mental processes demand some special designation) in the
Atlantic, cried out in horror that one is not even able to learn from the
Third International "that the Virgin was Mary the mother of Jesus"!

6. The second brief statement is that there has been even more progress in the making of dictionaries in the past thirty years than there has
been in the making of automobiles. The difference, for example, between
the much-touted Second International (1934) and the much-clouted
Third International (1961) is not like the difference between yearly
models but like the difference between the horse and buggy and the
automobile. Between the appearance of these two editions a whole new
science related to the making of dictionaries, the science of descriptive
linguistics, has come into being.

7. Modern linguistics gets its charter from Leonard Bloomfield's
Language (1933). Bloomfield, for thirteen years professor of Germanic
philology at the University of Chicago and for nine years professor of
linguistics at Yale, was one of those inseminating scholars who can't be
relegated to any department and don't dream of accepting established
categories and procedures just because they're established. He was as
much an anthropologist as a linguist, and his concepts of language were
shaped not by Strunk's *Elements of Style* but by his knowledge of Cree
Indian dialects.

8. The broad general findings of the new science are:

1. All languages are systems of human conventions, not systems of natural laws. The first—and essential—step in the study of any language is observing and setting down precisely what happens when native speakers speak it.

2. Each language is unique in its pronunciation, grammar, and vocabulary. It cannot be described in terms of logic or of some theoretical, ideal language. It cannot be described in terms of any other language, or even in terms of its own past.

3. All languages are dynamic rather than static, and hence a "rule" in any language can only be a statement of contemporary practice. Change is constant—and normal.

4. "Correctness" can rest only upon usage, for the simple reason that there is nothing else for it to rest on. And all usage is relative.

9. From these propositions it follows that a dictionary is good only insofar as it is a comprehensive and accurate description of current usage. And to be comprehensive it must include some indication of social and regional associations.

10. New dictionaries are needed because English has changed more in the past two generations than at any other time in its history. It has had to adapt to extraordinary cultural and technological changes, two world wars, unparalleled changes in transportation and communication, and unprecedented movements of populations.

11. More subtly, but pervasively, it has changed under the influence of mass education and the growth of democracy. As written English is used by increasing millions and for more reasons than ever before, the language has become more utilitarian and more informal. Every publication in America today includes pages that would appear, to the purist of forty years ago, unbuttoned gibberish. Not that they are; they simply show that you can't hold the language of one generation up as a model for the next.

12. It's not that you mustn't. You *can't.* For example, in the issue in which *Life* stated editorially that it would follow the Second International, there were over forty words, constructions, and meanings which are in the Third International but not in the Second. The issue of the New York *Times* which hailed the Second International as the authority to which it would adhere and the Third International as a scandal and a betrayal which it would reject used one hundred and fifty-three separate words, phrases, and constructions which are listed in the Third International but not in the Second and nineteen others which are condemned in the Second. Many of them are used many times, more than three hundred such uses in all. The Washington *Post,* in an editorial cap-

tioned "Keep Your Old Webster's," says, in the first sentence, "don't throw it away," and in the second, "hang on to it." But the old Webster's labels *don't* "colloquial" and doesn't include "hang on to," in this sense, at all.

13. In short, all of these publications are written in the language that the Third International describes, even the very editorials which scorn it. And this is no coincidence, because the Third International isn't setting up any new standards at all; it is simply describing what *Life,* the Washington *Post,* and the New York *Times* are doing. Much of the dictionary's material comes from these very publications, the *Times,* in particular, furnishing more of its illustrative quotations than any other newspaper.

14. And the papers have no choice. No journal or periodical could sell a single issue today if it restricted itself to the American language of twenty-eight years ago. It couldn't discuss half the things we are interested in, and its style would seem stiff and cumbrous. If the editorials were serious, the public—and the stockholders—have reason to be grateful that the writers on these publications are more literate than the editors.

15. And so back to our questions: what's a dictionary for, and how, in 1962, can it best do what it ought to do? The demands are simple. The common reader turns to a dictionary for information about the spelling, pronunciation, meaning, and proper use of words. He wants to know what is current and respectable. But he wants—and has a right to—the truth, the full truth. And the full truth about any language, and especially about American English today, is that there are many areas in which certainty is impossible and simplification is misleading.

16. Even in so settled a matter as spelling, a dictionary cannot always be absolute. *Theater* is correct, but so is *theatre.* And so are *traveled* and *travelled, plow* and *plough, catalog* and *catalogue,* and scores of other variants. The reader may want a single certainty. He may have taken an unyielding position in an argument, he may have wagered in support of his conviction and may demand that the dictionary "settle" the matter. But neither his vanity nor his purse is any concern of the dictionary's; it must record the facts. And the fact here is that there are many words in our language which may be spelled, with equal correctness, in either of two ways.

17. So with pronunciation. A citizen listening to his radio might notice that James B. Conant, Bernard Baruch, and Dwight D. Eisenhower pronounce *economics* as ECKuhnomiks, while A. Whitney Griswold, Adlai Stevenson, and Herbert Hoover pronounce it EEKuhnomiks. He turns to the dictionary to see which of the two pronunciations is "right" and finds that they are both acceptable.

¹⁸· Has he been betrayed? Has the dictionary abdicated its responsibility? Should it say that one *must* speak like the president of Harvard or like the president of Yale, like the thirty-first President of the United States or like the thirty-fourth? Surely it's none of its business to make a choice. Not because of the distinction of these particular speakers; lexicography, like God, is no respecter of persons. But because so widespread and conspicuous a use of two pronunciations among people of this elevation shows that there *are* two pronunciations. Their speaking establishes the fact which the dictionary must record.

¹⁹· Among the "enormities" with which *Life* taxes the Third International is its listing of "the common mispronunciation" *heighth*. That it is labeled a "dialectal variant" seems, somehow, to compound the felony. But one hears the word so pronounced, and if one professes to give a full account of American English in the 1960s, one has to take some cognizance of it. All people do not possess *Life's* intuitive perception that the word is so "monstrous" that even to list it as a dialect variation is to merit scorn. Among these, by the way, was John Milton, who, in one of the greatest passages in all literature, besought the Holy Spirit to raise him to the "highth" of his great argument. And even the *Oxford English Dictionary* is so benighted as to list it, in full boldface, right alongside of *Height* as a variant that has been in the language since at least 1290.

²⁰· Now there are still, apparently, millions of Americans who retain, in this as in much else, some of the speech of Milton. This particular pronunciation seems to be receding, but the *American Dialect Dictionary* still records instances of it from almost every state on the Eastern seaboard and notes that it is heard from older people and "occasionally in educated speech," "common with good speakers," "general," "widespread."

²¹· Under these circumstances, what is a dictionary to do? Since millions speak the word this way, the pronunciation can't be ignored. Since it has been in use as long as we have any record of English and since it has been used by the greatest writers, it can't be described as substandard or slang. But it is heard now only in certain localities. That makes it a dialectal pronunciation, and an honest dictionary will list it as such. What else can it do? Should it do?

²²· The average purchaser of a dictionary uses it most often, probably, to find out what a word "means." As a reader, he wants to know what an author intended to convey. As a speaker or writer, he wants to know what a word will convey to his auditors. And this, too, is complex, subtle, and forever changing.

²³· An illustration is furnished by an editorial in the Washington *Post* (January 17, 1962). After a ringing appeal to those who "love truth and

accuracy" and the usual bombinations about "abdication of authority" and "barbarism," the editorial charges the Third International with "pretentious and obscure verbosity" and specifically instances its definition of "so simple an object as a door."

24. The definition reads:

> a movable piece of firm material or a structure supported usu. along one side and swinging on pivots or hinges, sliding along a groove, rolling up and down, revolving as one of four leaves, or folding like an accordion by means of which an opening may be closed or kept open for passage into or out of a building, room, or other covered enclosure or a car, airplane, elevator, or other vehicle.

Then follows a series of special meanings, each particularly defined and, where necessary, illustrated by a quotation.

25. Since, aside from roaring and admonishing the "gentlemen from Springfield" that "accuracy and brevity are virtues," the *Post's* editorial fails to explain what is wrong with the definition, we can only infer from "so simple" a thing that the writer takes the plain, downright, man-in-the-street attitude that a door is a door and any damn fool knows that.

26. But if so, he has walked into one of lexicography's biggest booby traps: the belief that the obvious is easy to define. Whereas the opposite is true. Anyone can give a fair description of the strange, the new, or the unique. It's the commonplace, the habitual, that challenges definition, for its very commonness compels us to define it in uncommon terms. Dr. Johnson was ridiculed on just this score when his dictionary appeared in 1755. For two hundred years his definition of a network as "any thing reticulated or decussated, at equal distances, with interstices between the intersections" has been good for a laugh. But in the merriment one thing is always overlooked: no one has yet come up with a better definition! Subsequent dictionaries defined it as a mesh and then defined a mesh as a network. That's simple, all right.

27. Anyone who attempts sincerely to state what the word *door* means in the United States of America today can't take refuge in a log cabin. There has been an enormous proliferation of closing and demarking devices and structures in the past twenty years, and anyone who tries to thread his way through the many meanings now included under *door* may have to sacrifice brevity to accuracy and even have to employ words that a limited vocabulary may find obscure.

28. Is the entrance to a tent a door, for instance? And what of the thing that seals the exit of an airplane? Is this a door? Or what of those sheets and jets of air that are now being used, in place of old-fashioned oak and hinges, to screen entrances and exits. Are they doors? And what

of those accordion-like things that set off various sections of many modern apartments? The fine print in the lease takes it for granted that they are doors and that spaces demarked by them are rooms—and the rent is computed on the number of rooms.

29. Was I gypped by the landlord when he called the folding contraption that shuts off my kitchen a door? I go to the Second International, which the editor of the *Post* urges me to use in preference to the Third International. Here I find that a door is

> The movable frame or barrier of boards, or other material, usually turning on hinges or pivots or sliding, by which an entranceway into a house or apartment is closed and opened; also, a similar part of a piece of furniture, as in a cabinet or bookcase.

This is only forty-six words, but though it includes the cellar door, it excludes the barn door and the accordion-like thing.

30. So I go on to the Third International. I see at once that the new definition is longer. But I'm looking for accuracy, and if I must sacrifice brevity to get it, then I must. And, sure enough, in the definition which raised the *Post*'s blood pressure, I find the words "folding like an accordion." The thing *is* a door, and my landlord is using the word in one of its currently accepted meanings.

31. We don't turn to a work of reference merely for confirmation. We all have words in our vocabularies which we have misunderstood, and to come on the true meaning of one of these words is quite a shock. All our complacency and self-esteem rise to oppose the discovery. But eventually we must accept the humiliation and laugh it off as best we can.

32. Some, often those who have set themselves up as authorities, stick to their error and charge the dictionary with being in a conspiracy against them. They are sure that their meaning is the only "right" one. And when the dictionary doesn't bear them out they complain about "permissive" attitudes instead of correcting their mistake.

33. The New York *Times* and the *Saturday Review* both regarded as contemptibly "permissive" the fact that one meaning of one word was illustrated by a quotation from Polly Adler. But a rudimentary knowledge of the development of any language would have told them that the underworld has been a far more active force in shaping and enriching speech than all the synods that have ever convened. Their attitude is like that of the patriot who canceled his subscription to the *Dictionary of American Biography* when he discovered that the very first volume included Benedict Arnold!

34. The ultimate of "permissiveness," singled out by almost every critic for special scorn, was the inclusion in the Third International of

finalize. It was this, more than any other one thing, that was given as the reason for sticking to the good old Second International—that "peerless authority on American English," as the *Times* called it. But if it was such an authority, why didn't they look into it? They would have found *finalize* if they had.

³⁵· And why shouldn't it be there? It exists. It's been recorded for two generations. Millions employ it every day. Two Presidents of the United States—men of widely differing cultural backgrounds—have used it in formal statements. And so has the Secretary-General of the United Nations, a man of unusual linguistic attainments. It isn't permitting the word but omitting it that would break faith with the reader. Because it is exactly the sort of word we want information about.

³⁶· To list it as substandard would be to imply that it is used solely by the ignorant and the illiterate. But this would be a misrepresentation: President Kennedy and U Thant are highly educated men, and both are articulate and literate. It isn't even a freak form. On the contrary, it is a classic example of a regular process of development in English, a process which has given us such thoroughly accepted words as *generalize, minimize, formalize,* and *verbalize.* Nor can it be dismissed on logical grounds or on the ground that it is a mere duplication of *complete.* It says something that *complete* doesn't say and says it in a way that is significant in the modern bureaucratic world: one usually *completes* something which he has initiated but *finalizes* the work of others.

³⁷· One is free to dislike the word. I don't like it. But the editor of a dictionary has to examine the evidence for a word's existence and seek it in context to get, as clearly and closely as he can, the exact meaning that it conveys to those who use it. And if it is widely used by well-educated, literate, reputable people, he must list it as a standard word. He is not compiling a volume of his own prejudices.

³⁸· An individual's use of his native tongue is the surest index to his position within his community. And those who turn to a dictionary expect from it some statement of the current status of a word or a grammatical construction. And it is with the failure to assume this function that modern lexicography has been most fiercely charged. The charge is based on a naïve assumption that simple labels can be attached in all instances. But they can't. Some words are standard in some constructions and not in others. There may be as many shades of status as of meaning, and modern lexicography instead of abdicating this function has fulfilled it to a degree utterly unknown to earlier dictionaries.

³⁹· Consider the word *fetch,* meaning to "go get and bring to." Until recently a standard word of full dignity ("Fetch me, I pray thee, a little water in a vessel"—I Kings 17:10), it has become slightly tainted. Per-

haps the command latent in it is resented as undemocratic. Or maybe its use in training dogs to retrieve has made some people feel that it is an undignified word to apply to human beings. But, whatever the reason, there is a growing uncertainty about its status, and hence it is the sort of word that conscientious people look up in a dictionary.

40. Will they find it labeled "good" or "bad"? Neither, of course, because either applied indiscriminately would be untrue. The Third International lists nineteen different meanings of the verb *to fetch*. Of these some are labeled "dialectal," some "chiefly dialectal," some "obsolete," one "chiefly Scottish," and two "not in formal use." The primary meaning—"to go after and bring back"—is not labeled and hence can be accepted as standard, accepted with the more assurance because the many shades of labeling show us that the word's status has been carefully considered.

41. On grammatical questions the Third International tries to be equally exact and thorough. Sometimes a construction is listed without comment, meaning that in the opinion of the editors it is unquestionably respectable. Sometimes a construction carries the comment "used by speakers and writers on all educational levels though disapproved by some grammarians." Or the comment may be "used in substandard speech and formerly also by reputable writers." Or "less often in standard than in substandard speech." Or simply "dial."

42. And this very accurate reporting is based on evidence which is presented for our examination. One may feel that the evidence is inadequate or that the evaluation of it is erroneous. But surely, in the face of classification so much more elaborate and careful than any known heretofore, one cannot fly into a rage and insist that the dictionary is "out to destroy . . . every vestige of linguistic punctilio . . . every criterion for distinguishing between better usages and worse."

43. Words, as we have said, are continually shifting their meanings and connotations and hence their status. A word which has dignity, say, in the vocabulary of an older person may go down in other people's estimation. Like *fetch*. The older speaker is not likely to be aware of this and will probably be inclined to ascribe the snickers of the young at his speech to that degeneration of manners which every generation has deplored in its juniors. But a word which is coming up in the scale—like *jazz*, say, or, more recently, *crap*—will strike his ear at once. We are much more aware of offenses given us than of those we give. And if he turns to a dictionary and finds the offending word listed as standard— or even listed, apparently—his response is likely to be an outburst of indignation.

44. But the dictionary can neither snicker nor fulminate. It records.

It will offend many, no doubt, to find the expression *wise up*, meaning to inform or to become informed, listed in the Third International with no restricting label. To my aging ears it still sounds like slang. But the evidence—quotations from the *Kiplinger Washington Letter* and the *Wall Street Journal*—convinces me that it is I who am out of step, lagging behind. If such publications have taken to using *wise up* in serious contexts, with no punctuational indication of irregularity, then it is obviously respectable. And finding it so listed and supported, I can only say that it's nice to be informed and sigh to realize that I am becoming an old fogy. But, of course, I don't have to use it (and I'll be damned if I will! "Let them smile, as I do now, At the old forsaken bough Where I cling").

⁴⁵· In part, the trouble is due to the fact that there is no standard for standard. Ideas of what is proper to use in serious, dignified speech and writing are changing—and with breathtaking rapidity. This is one of the major facts of contemporary American English. But it is no more the dictionary's business to oppose this process than to speed it up.

⁴⁶· Even in our standard speech some words are more dignified and some more informal than others, and dictionaries have tried to guide us through these uncertainties by marking certain words and constructions as "colloquial," meaning "inappropriate in a formal situation." But this distinction, in the opinion of most scholars, has done more harm than good. It has created the notion that these particular words are inferior, when actually they might be the best possible words in an informal statement. And so—to the rage of many reviewers—the Third International has dropped this label. Not all labels, as angrily charged, but only this one out of a score. And the doing so may have been an error, but it certainly didn't constitute "betrayal" or "abandoning of all distinctions." It was intended to end a certain confusion.

⁴⁷· In all the finer shades of meaning, of which the status of a word is only one, the user is on his own, whether he likes it or not. Despite *Life's* artless assumption about the Gettysburg Address, nothing worth writing is written *from* a dictionary. The dictionary, rather, comes along afterwards and describes what *has been* written.

⁴⁸· Words in themselves are not dignified, or silly, or wise, or malicious. But they can be used in dignified, silly, wise, or malicious ways by dignified, silly, wise, or malicious people. *Egghead,* for example, is a perfectly legitimate word, as legitimate as *highbrow* or *long-haired.* But there is something very wrong and very undignified, by civilized standards, in a belligerent dislike for intelligence and education. *Yak* is an amusing word for persistent chatter. Anyone could say, "We were just yakking over a cup of coffee," with no harm to his dignity. But to

call a Supreme Court decision *yakking* is to be vulgarly insulting and so, undignified. Again, there's nothing wrong with *confab* when it's appropriate. But when the work of a great research project, employing hundreds of distinguished scholars over several decades and involving the honor of one of the greatest publishing houses in the world, is described as *confabbing* (as the New York *Times* editorially described the preparation of the Third International), the use of this particular word asserts that the lexicographers had merely sat around and talked idly. And the statement becomes undignified—if not, indeed, slanderous.

49. The lack of dignity in such statements is not in the words, nor in the dictionaries that list them, but in the hostility that deliberately seeks this tone of expression. And in expressing itself the hostility frequently shows that those who are expressing it don't know how to use a dictionary. Most of the reviewers seem unable to read the Third International and unwilling to read the Second.

50. The *American Bar Association Journal*, for instance, in a typical outburst ("a deplorable abdication of responsibility"), picked out for special scorn the inclusion in the Third International of the word *irregardless*. "As far as the new Webster's is concerned," said the *Journal*, "this meaningless verbal bastard is just as legitimate as any other word in the dictionary." Thirty seconds spent in examining the book they were so roundly condemning would have shown them that in it *irregardless* is labeled "nonstand"—which means "nonstandard," which means "not conforming to the usage generally characteristic of educated native speakers of the language." Is that "just as legitimate as any other word in the dictionary"?

51. The most disturbing fact of all is that the editors of a dozen of the most influential publications in America today are under the impression that *authoritative* must mean *authoritarian*. Even the "permissive" Third International doesn't recognize this identification—editors' attitudes being not yet, fortunately, those of the American people. But the Fourth International may have to.

52. The new dictionary may have many faults. Nothing that tries to meet an ever-changing situation over a terrain as vast as contemporary English can hope to be free of them. And much in it is open to honest, and informed, disagreement. There can be linguistic objection to the eradication of proper names. The removal of guides to pronunciation from the foot of every page may not have been worth the valuable space it saved. The new method of defining words of many meanings has disadvantages as well as advantages. And of the half million or more definitions, hundreds, possibly thousands, may seem inadequate or imprecise. To some (of whom I am one) the omission of the label "colloquial" will seem meritorious; to others it will seem a loss.

⁵³· But one thing is certain: anyone who solemnly announces in the year 1962 that he will be guided in matters of English usage by a dictionary published in 1934 is talking ignorant and pretentious nonsense.

COMMENTARY AND QUESTIONS

1. Bergen Evans, professor of English at Northwestern University, here defends *Webster's New Third International Dictionary*. Why does he find it necessary in his opening paragraph to refer to various attacks (including the one by Wilson Follett in the preceding selection)?

2. In pars. 4-5 how does Evans rule out as irrelevant certain complaints against the Third Edition?

3. How do pars. 7-14 develop the statement made in the first sentence of par. 6?

4. In par. 15, after repeating the title-question (first asked in par. 3 of the selection), Evans itemizes in the third sentence the parts of his answer, and these parts furnish the framework for the rest of the selection. In which paragraphs is each of these discussed: "spelling, pronunciation, meaning, and proper use of words"?

5. In the last two sentences of par. 15 Evans states that the reader of a dictionary has a right to the full truth: "that there are many areas in which certainty is impossible and simplification is misleading." In what way is this idea applied in later discussions? (Consider, for example, pars. 16, 18, 27, and 38.)

6. In par. 24 Evans gives a definition of *door* from the Third Edition. Why does he wait until par. 29 to give the parallel definition from the Second Edition?

7. In pars. 34-37 Evans discusses *finalize*. In par. 9 of the selection on "Correctness" (pp. 540-541) Gowers discusses the same word and other words ending in *ise* (the British spelling). Do the two writers have the same attitude on the subject?

8. In par. 52 Evans recognizes the possibility that the Third Edition may have faults. Do you think he should have stated this possibility earlier? On what basis do you think he would defend placing the paragraph in its present position?

SUGGESTIONS FOR WRITING

1. Each of these writers—Sir Ernest Gowers in "Correctness" (pp. 536-545), Wilson Follett in "Sabotage in Springfield" (pp. 546-555), and Bergen Evans in this selection—states or implies a definite attitude towards the question of usage. Making relevant comparisons and contrasts, write an analysis in which you identify the attitude of each.

2. Anyone writing on a controversial subject, especially if he is attacking beliefs stated by equally vocal individuals, is likely to use color-

ful expressions in attempting to point out the absurdity of opposing arguments or objections. Although in cool retrospect a writer may repent a quip or a debating technique he has used, what he has written is a matter of record, and has its own tone. Disregarding the extent to which you agree or disagree with Wilson Follett or Bergen Evans, compare the tone of the two essays. Support all generalizations with specific examples.

Logic and
Logical Fallacies

by ROBERT GORHAM DAVIS

EXPRESSION DOES NOT EXIST apart from thought, and cannot be analyzed or profitably discussed apart from thought. Just as clear and effective organization is essential to good writing, so consistent thinking and coherence of mind underlie consistent writing and coherence of style. The faults and errors which we have discussed under the headings of style and structure are closely bound up with orderly thought, as the student can hardly fail to notice. But some direct suggestions on the modes of consistent thinking and of analyzing and criticizing arguments and assertions ought also to prove useful. The following pages accordingly present some notes on logic and common logical fallacies.

Undefined Terms

2. The first requirement for logical discourse is knowing what the words you use actually mean. Words are not like paper money or counters in a game. Except for technical terms in some of the sciences, they do

From the Harvard *Handbook for English A* (fourth edition, 1947). By permission of the author, of Theodore Morrison, and of Harvard University. Copyright 1940, 1941, 1944, 1947 by the President and Fellows of Harvard College.

not have a fixed face value. Their meanings are fluid and changing, influenced by many considerations of context and reference, circumstance and association. This is just as true of common words such as *fast* as it is of literary terms such as *romantic*. Moreover, if there is to be communication, words must have approximately the same meaning for the reader that they have for the writer. A speech in an unknown language means nothing to the hearer. When an adult speaks to a small child or an expert to a layman, communication may be seriously limited by lack of a mature vocabulary or ignorance of technical terms. Many arguments are meaningless because the speakers are using important words in quite different senses.

3. Because we learn most words—or guess at them—from the contexts in which we first encounter them, our sense of them is often incomplete or wrong. Readers sometimes visualize the Assyrian who comes down like the wolf on the fold as an enormous man dressed in cohorts (some kind of fancy armor, possibly) gleaming in purple and gold. "A rift in the lute" suggests vaguely a cracked mandolin. Failure to ascertain the literal meaning of figurative language is a frequent reason for mixed metaphors. We are surprised to find that the "devil" in "the devil to pay" and "the devil and the deep blue sea" is not Old Nick, but part of a ship. Unless terms mean the same thing to both writer and reader, proper understanding is impossible.

Abstractions

4. The most serious logical difficulties occur with abstract terms. An abstraction is a word which stands for a quality found in a number of different objects or events from which it has been "abstracted" or taken away. We may, for instance, talk of the "whiteness" of paper or cotton or snow without considering qualities of cold or inflammability or usefulness which these materials happen also to possess. Usually, however, our minds carry over other qualities by association. See, for instance, the chapter called "The Whiteness of the Whale" in *Moby Dick*.

5. In much theoretic discussion the process of abstraction is carried so far that although vague associations and connotations persist, the original objects or events from which the qualities have been abstracted are lost sight of completely. Instead of thinking of words like *sincerity* and *Americanism* as symbols standing for qualities that have to be abstracted with great care from examples and test cases, we come to think of them as real things in themselves. We assume that Americanism is Americanism just as a bicycle is a bicycle, and that everyone knows what it means.

We forget that before the question, "Is Father Coughlin sincere?" can mean anything, we have to agree on the criteria of sincerity.

⁶· When we try to define such words and find examples, we discover that almost no one agrees on their meaning. The word *church* may refer to anything from a building on the corner of Spring Street to the whole tradition of institutionalized Christianity. *Germany* may mean a geographical section of Europe, a people, a governing group, a cultural tradition, or a military power. Abstractions such as *freedom, courage, race, beauty, truth, justice, nature, honor, humanism, democracy*, should never be used in a theme unless their meaning is defined or indicated clearly by the context. Freedom for whom? To do what? Under what circumstances? Abstract terms have merely emotional value unless they are strictly defined by asking questions of this kind. The study of a word such as *nature* in a good unabridged dictionary will show that even the dictionary, indispensable though it is, cannot determine for us the sense in which a word is being used in any given instance. Once the student understands the importance of definition, he will no longer be betrayed into fruitless arguments over such questions as whether free verse is "poetry" or whether you can change "human nature."

Name-calling

⁷· It is a common unfairness in controversy to place what the writer dislikes or opposes in a generally odious category. The humanist dismisses what he dislikes by calling it *romantic;* the liberal, by calling it *fascist;* the conservative, by calling it *communistic.* These terms tell the reader nothing. What is *piety* to some will be *bigotry* to others. *Non-Catholics* would rather be called *Protestants* than *heretics.* What is *right-thinking* except a designation for those who agree with the writer? Labor leaders become *outside agitators;* industrial organizations, *forces of reaction;* the Child Labor Amendment, the *youth control bill;* prison reform, *coddling;* progressive education, *fads and frills.* Such terms are intended to block thought by an appeal to prejudice and associative habits. Three steps are necessary before such epithets have real meaning. First, they must be defined; second, it must be shown that the object to which they are applied actually possesses these qualities; third, it must be shown that the possession of such qualities in this particular situation is necessarily undesirable. Unless a person is alert and critical both in choosing and in interpreting words, he may be alienated from ideas with which he would be in sympathy if he had not been frightened by a mere name.

Generalization

8. Similar to the abuse of abstract terms and epithets is the habit of presenting personal opinions in the guise of universal laws. The student often seems to feel that the broader the terms in which he states an opinion, the more effective he will be. Ordinarily the reverse is true. An enthusiasm for Thomas Wolfe should lead to a specific critical analysis of Wolfe's novels that will enable the writer to explain his enthusiasm to others; it should not be turned into the argument that Wolfe is "the greatest American novelist," particularly if the writer's knowledge of American novelists is somewhat limited. The same questions of *who* and *when* and *why* and under what *circumstances* which are used to check abstract terms should be applied to generalizations. Consider how contradictory proverbial wisdom is when detached from particular circumstances. "Look before you leap," but "he who hesitates is lost."

9. Superlatives and the words *right* and *wrong, true* and *untrue, never* and *always* must be used with caution in matters of opinion. When a student says flatly that X is true, he often is really saying that he or his family or the author of a book he has just been reading, persons of certain tastes and background and experience, *think* that X is true. Unless these people are identified and their reasons for thinking so explained, the assertion is worthless. Because many freshmen are taking survey courses in which they read a single work by an author or see an historical event through the eyes of a single historian whose bias they may not be able to measure, they must guard against this error.

Sampling

10. Assertions of a general nature are frequently open to question because they are based on insufficient evidence. Some persons are quite ready, after meeting one Armenian or reading one medieval romance, to generalize about Armenians and medieval romances. One ought, of course, to examine objectively as many examples as possible before making a generalization, but the number is less important than the representativeness of the examples chosen. The Literary Digest Presidential Poll, sent to hundreds of thousands of people selected from telephone directories, was far less accurate than the Gallup Poll which questioned far fewer voters, but selected them carefully and proportionately from all different social groups. The "typical" college student, as portrayed by moving pictures and cartoons, is very different from the "representative"

college student as determined statistically. We cannot let uncontrolled experience do our sampling for us; instances and examples which impress themselves upon our minds do so usually because they are exceptional. In propaganda and arguments extreme cases are customarily treated as if they were characteristic.

11. If one is permitted arbitrarily to select some examples and ignore others, it is possible to find convincing evidence for almost any theory, no matter how fantastic. The fact that the mind tends naturally to remember those instances which confirm its opinions imposes a duty upon the writer, unless he wishes to encourage prejudice and superstition, to look carefully for exceptions to all generalizations which he is tempted to make. We forget the premonitions which are not followed by disaster and the times when our hunches failed to select the winner in a race. Patent medicine advertisements print the letters of those who survived their cure, and not of those who died during it. All Americans did not gamble on the stock exchange in the twenties, and all Vermonters are not thin-lipped and shrewd. Of course the search for negative examples can be carried too far. Outside of mathematics or the laboratory, few generalizations can be made airtight, and most are not intended to be. But quibbling is so easy that resort to it is very common, and the knowledge that people can and will quibble over generalizations is another reason for making assertions as limited and explicitly conditional as possible.

False Analogy

12. Illustration, comparison, analogy are most valuable in making an essay clear and interesting. It must not be supposed, however, that they prove anything or have much argumentative weight. The rule that what is true of one thing in one set of circumstances is not necessarily true of another thing in another set of circumstances seems almost too obvious to need stating. Yet constantly nations and businesses are discussed as if they were human beings with human habits and feelings; human bodies are discussed as if they were machines; the universe, as if it were a clock. It is assumed that what held true for seventeenth century New England or the thirteen Atlantic colonies also holds true for an industrial nation of 130,000,000 people. Carlyle dismissed the arguments for representative democracy by saying that if a captain had to take a vote among his crew every time he wanted to do something, he would never get around Cape Horn. This analogy calmly ignores the distinction between the lawmaking and the executive branches of constitutional democracies. Moreover, voters may be considered much more like the stockholders of a merchant

line than its hired sailors. Such arguments introduce assumptions in a metaphorical guise in which they are not readily detected or easily criticized. In place of analysis they attempt to identify their position with some familiar symbol which will evoke a predictable, emotional response in the reader. The revival during the 1932 presidential campaign of Lincoln's remark, "Don't swap horses in the middle of the stream," was not merely a picturesque way of saying keep Hoover in the White House. It made a number of assumptions about the nature of depressions and the function of government. This propagandist technique can be seen most clearly in political cartoons.

Degree

13. Often differences in degree are more important than differences in kind. By legal and social standards there is more difference between an habitual drunkard and a man who drinks temperately, than between a temperate drinker and a total abstainer. In fact differences of degree produce what are regarded as differences of kind. At known temperatures ice turns to water and water boils. At an indeterminate point affection becomes love and a man who needs a shave becomes a man with a beard. The fact that no men or systems are perfect makes rejoinders and counter-accusations very easy if differences in degree are ignored. Newspapers in totalitarian states, answering American accusations of brutality and suppression, refer to lynchings and gangsterism here. Before a disinterested judge could evaluate these mutual accusations, he would have to settle the question of the degree to which violent suppression and lynching are respectively prevalent in the countries under consideration. On the other hand, differences in degree may be merely apparent. Lincoln Steffens pointed out that newspapers can create a "crime wave" any time they wish, simply by emphasizing all the minor assaults and thefts commonly ignored or given an inch or two on a back page. The great reported increases in insanity may be due to the fact that in a more urban and institutionalized society cases of insanity more frequently come to the attention of authorities and hence are recorded in statistics.

Causation

14. The most common way of deciding that one thing causes another thing is the simple principle: *post hoc, ergo propter hoc*, "After this, therefore because of this." Rome fell after the introduction of Chris-

tianity; therefore Christianity was responsible for the fall of Rome. Such reasoning illustrates another kind of faulty generalization. But even if one could find ten cases in which a nation "fell" after the introduction of Christianity, it still would not be at all certain that Christianity caused the fall. Day, it has frequently been pointed out, follows night in every observable instance, and yet night cannot be called the cause of day. Usually a combination of causes produces a result. Sitting in a draught may cause a cold, but only given a certain physical condition in the person sitting there. In such instances one may distinguish between necessary and sufficient conditions. Air is a necessary condition for the maintenance of plant life, but air alone is not sufficient to produce plant life. And often different causes at different times may produce the same result. This relation is known as plurality of causes. If, after sitting in a stuffy theatre on Monday, and then again after eating in a stuffy restaurant on Thursday, a man suffered from headaches, he might say, generalizing, that bad air gave him headaches. But actually the headache on Monday may have been caused by eye-strain and on Thursday by indigestion. To isolate the causative factor it is necessary that all other conditions be precisely the same. Such isolation is possible, except in very simple instances, only in the laboratory or with scientific methods. If a picture falls from the wall every time a truck passes, we can quite certainly say that the truck's passing is the cause. But with anything as complex and conditional as a nation's economy or human character, the determination of cause is not easy or certain. A psychiatrist often sees a patient for an hour daily for a year or more before he feels that he understands his psychosis.

15. Ordinarily when we speak of cause we mean the proximate or immediate cause. The plants were killed by frost; we had indigestion from eating lobster salad. But any single cause is one in an unbroken series. When a man is murdered, is his death caused by the loss of blood from the wound, or by the firing of the pistol, or by the malice aforethought of the murderer? Was the World War "caused" by the assassination at Sarajevo? Were the Navigation Acts or the ideas of John Locke more important in "causing" the American Revolution? A complete statement of cause would comprise the sum total of the conditions which preceded an event, conditions stretching back indefinitely into the past. Historical events are so interrelated that the isolation of a causative sequence is dependent chiefly on the particular preoccupations of the historian. An economic determinist can "explain" history entirely in terms of economic developments; an idealist, entirely in terms of the development of ideas.

Syllogistic Reasoning

16. The formal syllogism of the type,

> All men are mortal
> John is a man
> Therefore John is mortal,

is not so highly regarded today as in some earlier periods. It merely fixes an individual as a member of a class, and then assumes that the individual has the given characteristics of the class. Once we have decided who John is, and what "man" and "mortal" mean, and have canvassed all men, including John, to make sure that they are mortal, the conclusion naturally follows. It can be seen that the chief difficulties arise in trying to establish acceptable premises. Faults in the premises are known as "material" fallacies, and are usually more serious than the "formal" fallacies, which are logical defects in drawing a conclusion from the premises. But although directly syllogistic reasoning is not much practiced, buried syllogisms can be found in all argument, and it is often a useful clarification to outline your own or another writer's essay in syllogistic form. The two most frequent defects in the syllogism itself are the undistributed and the ambiguous middle. The middle term is the one that appears in each of the premises and not in the conclusion. In the syllogism,

> All good citizens vote
> John votes
> Therefore John is a good citizen,

the middle term is not "good citizens," but "votes." Even though it were true that all good citizens vote, nothing prevents bad citizens from voting also, and John may be one of the bad citizens. To distribute the middle term "votes" one might say (but only if that is what one meant),

> All voters are good citizens
> John is a voter
> Therefore John is a good citizen.

17. The ambiguous middle term is even more common. It represents a problem in definition, while the undistributed middle is a problem in generalization. All acts which benefit others are virtuous, losing money at

poker benefits others, therefore losing at poker is a virtuous act. Here the middle term "act which benefits others" is obviously used very loosely and ambiguously.

Non-sequitur

18. This phrase, meaning "it does not follow," is used to characterize the kind of humor found in pictures in which the Marx Brothers perform. It is an amusing illogicality because it usually expresses, beneath its apparent incongruity, an imaginative, associative, or personal truth. "My ancestors came over on the Mayflower; therefore I am naturally opposed to labor unions." It is not logically necessary that those whose ancestors came over on the Mayflower should be opposed to unions; but it may happen to be true as a personal fact in a given case. Contemporary psychologists have effectively shown us that there is often such a wide difference between the true and the purported reasons for an attitude that, in rationalizing our behavior, we are often quite unconscious of the motives that actually influence us. A fanatical antivivisectionist, for instance, may have temperamental impulses toward cruelty which he is suppressing and compensating for by a reasoned opposition to any kind of permitted suffering. We may expect, then, to come upon many conclusions which are psychologically interesting in themselves, but have nothing to do with the given premises.

Ignoratio elenchi

19. This means, in idiomatic English, "arguing off the point," or ignoring the question at issue. A man trying to show that monarchy is the best form of government for the British Empire may devote most of his attention to the character of George V and the affection his people felt for him. In ordinary conversational argument it is almost impossible for disputants to keep to the point. Constantly turning up are tempting side-issues through which one can discomfit an opponent or force him to irrelevant admisisons that seem to weaken his case.

Begging the Question; Arguing in a Circle

20. The first of these terms means to assume in the premises what you are pretending to prove in the course of your argument. The function of logic is to demonstrate that because one thing or group of things is true,

another must be true as a consequence. But in begging the question you simply say in varying language that what is assumed to be true is assumed to be true. An argument which asserts that we shall enjoy immortality because we have souls which are immaterial and indestructible establishes nothing, because the idea of immortality is already contained in the assumption about the soul. It is the premise which needs to be demonstrated, not the conclusion. Arguing in a circle is another form of this fallacy. It proves the premise by the conclusion and the conclusion by the premise. The conscience forbids an act because it is wrong; the act is wrong because the conscience forbids it.

Arguments ad hominem and ad populum

21. It is very difficult for men to be persuaded by reason when their interest or prestige is at stake. If one wishes to preach the significance of physiognomy, it is well to choose a hearer with a high forehead and a determined jaw. The arguments in favor of repealing the protective tariff on corn or wheat in England were more readily entertained by manufacturers than by landowners. The cotton manufacturers in New England who were doing a profitable trade with the South were the last to be moved by descriptions of the evils of slavery. Because interest and desire are so deeply seated in human nature, arguments are frequently mingled with attempts to appeal to emotion, arouse fear, play upon pride, attack the characters of proponents of an opposite view, show that their practice is inconsistent with their principles; all matters which have, strictly speaking, nothing to do with the truth or falsity, the general desirability or undesirability, of some particular measure. If men are desperate enough they will listen to arguments proper only to an insane asylum but which seem to promise them relief.

22. After reading these suggestions, which are largely negative, the student may feel that any original assertion he can make will probably contain one or several logical faults. This assumption is not true. Even if it were, we know from reading newspapers and magazines that worldly fame is not dimmed by the constant and, one suspects, conscious practice of illogicality. But generalizations are not made only by charlatans and sophists. Intelligent and scrupulous writers also have a great many fresh and provocative observations and conclusions to express and are expressing them influentially. What is intelligence but the ability to see the connection between things, to discern causes, to relate the particular to the general, to define and discriminate and compare? Any man who thinks and feels and observes closely will not want for something to express.

23. And in his expression a proponent will find that a due regard for logic does not limit but rather increases the force of his argument. When statements are not trite, they are usually controversial. Men arrive at truth dialectically; error is weeded out in the course of discussion, argument, attack, and counterattack. Not only can a writer who understands logic show the weaknesses of arguments he disagrees with, but also, by anticipating the kind of attack likely to be made on his own ideas, he can so arrange them, properly modified with qualifications and exceptions, that the anticipated attack is made much less effective. Thus, fortunately, we do not have to depend on the spirit of fairness and love of truth to lead men to logic; it has the strong support of argumentative necessity and of the universal desire to make ideas prevail.

COMMENTARY AND QUESTIONS

This is a chapter from the Harvard University *Handbook for English A*. The first paragraph makes transitional references to earlier chapters. We have omitted here the first sentence and the first word of the second sentence.

1. A method of explaining technical terms is followed rather consistently in this selection. What, for example, is the method used in par. 4?
2. In a textbook on logic, a section on syllogistic reasoning might well be placed first. Why do you think such a discussion is not placed first here instead of being held as late as pars. 16-17?
3. In pars. 14 and 15 Davis points out some of the dangers in loose generalization about causation. How does Thomas Henry Huxley's story (pp. 196-198) about the doubting friend of the man whose spoons were stolen suggest an opposite danger in too much skepticism about generalization?
4. Do pars. 22-23 weaken what has been said earlier in the selection? How are they related to par. 1?

SUGGESTION FOR WRITING

Logical fallacies I have encountered—for example, in newspapers, advertising, or speeches.

PART SEVEN

Narration

ALMOST EVERYBODY LIKES TO READ OR HEAR A STORY. FOR THAT reason lecturers frequently digress from presenting facts and ideas to tell an anecdote or incident intended to illustrate a point. People saying or doing something in a "real" situation—one that can be visualized—are of more immediate interest than facts pyramiding in a notebook or ideas sailing through the thin air of the lecture room.

If there is to be a "story," we must have characters and a situation. Obviously what the characters say or do in the situation makes the story. Superficially what holds most narratives together is a time scheme. He met her on Monday and married her Saturday night, according to a once popular song. What keeps the listener's interest, however, is not the progression of time from Monday to Saturday, but what happened between Monday and Saturday. In most stories what happens between Monday and Saturday shapes itself into a plot, a cause-and-effect chain. Many stories have in addition a theme; some stories have only a theme, without any discernible plot to tie the events together. Whether a story has both theme and plot, it is nearly always based on a problem or a conflict. In simple detective fiction the problem is to determine "whodunit." In more complex fiction the only conflict may be within the mind of one or more characters, and the resolution may involve no tangible action.

Once an author has decided *what* his purpose is—what he wants to say or what effect he wants to create—he must concentrate on *how* to achieve that purpose. His initial problem is determining from what point of view the material is to be presented: shall the story "tell itself" or shall one of the characters act as a narrator? When the point of view is

579

determined, the central problem becomes, as in any kind of writing, the selection and arrangement of details. For the writer of the short narrative, selecting and arranging details is especially important: the shorter the narrative, the more limited must be the scope. To be effective the short narrative must have singleness of purpose. To achieve that singleness the author usually centers the action around one character or theme and restricts the action to one central event. Although he may use several characters and a series of events, he ordinarily subordinates all but one character or theme and passes rapidly over all but one event. Thus the author quickly focuses interest on his purpose, whether that be solving a simple or complex problem or suggesting a subtle, intangible conflict.

A Daring Deed

by MARK TWAIN

WHEN I RETURNED to the pilot-house St. Louis was gone, and I was lost. Here was a piece of river which was all down in my book, but I could make neither head nor tail of it: you understand, it was turned around. I had seen it when coming up-stream, but I had never faced about to see how it looked when it was behind me. My heart broke again, for it was plain that I had got to learn this troublesome river *both ways*.

The pilot-house was full of pilots, going down to "look at the river." What is called the "upper river" (the two hundred miles between St. Louis and Cairo, where the Ohio comes in) was low; and the Mississippi changes its channel so constantly that the pilots used to always find it necessary to run down to Cairo to take a fresh look, when their boats were to lie in port a week; that is, when the water was at a low stage. A deal of this "looking at the river" was done by poor fellows who seldom had a berth, and whose only hope of getting one lay in their being always freshly posted and therefore ready to drop into the shoes of some reputable pilot, for a single trip, on account of such pilot's sudden illness, or some other necessity. And a good many of them constantly ran up and down inspecting the river, not because they ever really hoped to get a berth, but because (they being guests of the boat) it was cheaper to "look at the river" than stay ashore and pay board. In time these fellows grew dainty in their tastes, and only infested boats that had an established reputation for setting good tables. All visiting pilots were useful, for they were always ready and willing, winter or summer, night or day, to go out in the yawl and help buoy the channel or assist the boat's pilots in any way they could. They were likewise welcomed because all pilots are tireless talkers, when gathered together, and as they talk only about the river they are always understood and are always interesting. Your true pilot cares nothing about anything on earth but the river, and his pride in his occupation surpasses the pride of kings.

We had a fine company of these river inspectors along this trip. There were eight or ten, and there was abundance of room for them in our great pilot-house. Two or three of them wore polished silk hats, elaborate shirt-fronts, diamond breastpins, kid gloves, and patent-leather boots. They were choice in their English, and bore themselves with a dig-

From *Life on the Mississippi* by Mark Twain. Reprinted by permission of Harper & Row, Publishers, New York.

nity proper to men of solid means and prodigious reputation as pilots. The others were more or less loosely clad, and wore upon their heads tall felt cones that were suggestive of the days of the Commonwealth.

I was a cipher in this august company, and felt subdued, not to say torpid. I was not even of sufficient consequence to assist at the wheel when it was necessary to put the tiller hard down in a hurry; the guest that stood nearest did that when occasion required—and this was pretty much all the time, because of the crookedness of the channel and the scant water. I stood in a corner; and the talk I listened to took the hope all out of me. One visitor said to another:

"Jim, how did you run Plum Point, coming up?"

"It was in the night, there, and I ran it the way one of the boys on the *Diana* told me; started out about fifty yards above the wood-pile on the false point, and held on the cabin under Plum Point till I raised the reef—quarter less twain—then straightened up for the middle bar till I got well abreast the old one-limbed cottonwood in the bend, then got my stern on the cottonwood, and head on the low place above the point, and came through a-booming—nine and a half."

"Pretty square crossing, ain't it?"

"Yes, but the upper bar's working down fast."

Another pilot spoke up and said:

"I had better water than that, and ran it lower down; started out from the false point—mark twain—raised the second reef abreast the big snag in the bend, and had quarter less twain."

One of the gorgeous ones remarked:

"I don't want to find fault with your leadsmen, but that's a good deal of water for Plum Point, it seems to me."

There was an approving nod all around as this quiet snub dropped on the boaster and "settled" him. And so they went on talk-talk-talking. Meantime, the thing that was running in my mind was, "Now, if my ears hear aright, I have not only to get the names of all the towns and islands and bends, and so on, by heart, but I must even get up a warm personal acquaintanceship with every old snag and one-limbed cottonwood and obscure wood-pile that ornaments the banks of this river for twelve hundred miles; and more than that, I must actually know where these things are in the dark, unless these guests are gifted with eyes that can pierce through two miles of solid blackness. I wish the piloting business was in Jericho and I had never thought of it."

At dusk Mr. Bixby tapped the big bell three times (the signal to land), and the captain emerged from his drawing-room in the forward end of the "texas," and looked up inquiringly. Mr. Bixby said:

"We will lay up here all night, captain."

"Very well, sir."

That was all. The boat came to shore and was tied up for the night. It seemed to me a fine thing that the pilot could do as he pleased, without asking so grand a captain's permission. I took my supper and went immediately to bed, discouraged by my day's observations and experiences. My late voyage's note-booking was but a confusion of meaningless names. It had tangled me all up in a knot every time I had looked at it in the daytime. I now hoped for respite in sleep; but no, it reveled all through my head till sunrise again, a frantic and tireless nightmare.

Next morning I felt pretty rusty and low-spirited. We went booming along, taking a good many chances, for we were anxious to "get out of the river" (as getting out to Cairo was called) before night should overtake us. But Mr. Bixby's partner, the other pilot, presently grounded the boat, and we lost so much time getting her off that it was plain the darkness would overtake us a good long way above the mouth. This was a great misfortune, especially to certain of our visiting pilots, whose boats would have to wait for their return, no matter how long that might be. It sobered the pilot-house talk a good deal. Coming up-stream, pilots did not mind low water or any kind of darkness; nothing stopped them but fog. But down-stream work was different; a boat was too nearly helpless, with a stiff current pushing behind her; so it was not customary to run down-stream at night in low water.

There seemed to be one small hope, however: if we could get through the intricate and dangerous Hat Island crossing before night, we could venture the rest, for we would have plainer sailing and better water. But it would be insanity to attempt Hat Island at night. So there was a deal of looking at watches all the rest of the day, and a constant ciphering upon the speed we were making; Hat Island was the eternal subject; sometimes hope was high and sometimes we were delayed in a bad crossing, and down it went again. For hours all hands lay under the burden of this suppressed excitement; it was even communicated to me, and I got to feeling so solicitous about Hat Island, and under such an awful pressure of responsibility, that I wished I might have five minutes on shore to draw a good, full, relieving breath, and start over again. We were standing no regular watches. Each of our pilots ran such portions of the river as he had run when coming up-stream, because of his greater familiarity with it; but both remained in the pilot-house constantly.

An hour before sunset Mr. Bixby took the wheel, and Mr. W. stepped aside. For the next thirty minutes every man held his watch in his hand and was restless, silent, and uneasy. At last somebody said, with a doomful sigh:

"Well, yonder's Hat Island—and we can't make it."

All the watches closed with a snap, everybody sighed and muttered something about its being "too bad, too bad—ah, if we could *only* have got here half an hour sooner!" and the place was thick with the atmosphere of disappointment. Some started to go out, but loitered, hearing no bell-tap to land. The sun dipped behind the horizon, the boat went on. Inquiring looks passed from one guest to another; and one who had his hand on the door-knob and had turned it, waited, then presently took away his hand and let the knob turn back again. We bore steadily down the bend. More looks were exchanged, and nods of surprised admiration —but no words. Insensibly the men drew together behind Mr. Bixby, as the sky darkened and one or two dim stars came out. The dead silence and sense of waiting became oppressive. Mr. Bixby pulled the cord, and two deep, mellow notes from the big bell floated off on the night. Then a pause, and one more note was struck. The watchman's voice followed, from the hurricane-deck:

"Labboard lead, there! Stabboard lead!"

The cries of the leadsmen began to rise out of the distance, and were gruffly repeated by the word-passers on the hurricane-deck.

"M-a-r-k three! M-a-r-k three! Quarter-less-three! Half twain! Quarter twain! M-a-r-k twain! Quarter-less—"

Mr. Bixby pulled two bell-ropes, and was answered by faint jinglings far below in the engine-room, and our speed slackened. The steam began to whistle through the gauge-cocks. The cries of the leadsmen went on—and it is a weird sound, always, in the night. Every pilot in the lot was watching now, with fixed eyes, and talking under his breath. Nobody was calm and easy but Mr. Bixby. He would put his wheel down and stand on a spoke, and as the steamer swung into her (to me) utterly invisible marks—for we seemed to be in the midst of a wide and gloomy sea—he would meet and fasten her there. Out of the murmur of half-audible talk, one caught a coherent sentence now and then—such as:

"There; she's over the first reef all right!"

After a pause, another subdued voice:

"Her stern's coming down just *exactly* right, by *George!*"

"Now she's in the marks; over she goes!"

Somebody else muttered:

"Oh, it was done beautiful—*beautiful!*"

Now the engines were stopped altogether, and we drifted with the current. Not that I could see the boat drift, for I could not, the stars being all gone by this time. This drifting was the dismalest work; it held one's heart still. Presently I discovered a blacker gloom than that which surrounded us. It was the head of the island. We were closing right down upon it. We entered its deeper shadow, and so imminent seemed the peril that I was likely to suffocate; and I had the strongest impulse to do *something*, anything, to save the vessel. But still Mr. Bixby stood by his wheel, silent, intent as a cat, and all the pilots stood shoulder to shoulder at his back.

"She'll not make it!" somebody whispered.

The water grew shoaler and shoaler, by the leadsman's cries till it was down to:

"Eight-and-a-half! E-i-g-h-t feet! E-i-g-h-t feet! Seven-and—"

Mr. Bixby said warningly through his speaking-tube to the engineer:

"Stand by, now!"

"Ay, ay, sir!"

"Seven-and-a-half! Seven feet! *Six*-and—"

We touched bottom! Instantly Mr. Bixby set a lot of bells ringing, shouted through the tube, "*Now*, let her have it—every ounce you've got!" then to his partner, "Put her hard down! snatch her! snatch her!" The boat rasped and ground her way through the sand, hung upon the apex of disaster a single tremendous instant, and then over she went! And such a shout as went up at Mr. Bixby's back never loosened the roof of a pilot-house before!

There was no more trouble after that. Mr. Bixby was a hero that night; and it was some little time, too, before his exploit ceased to be talked about by river-men.

Fully to realize the marvelous precision required in laying the great steamer in her marks in that murky waste of water, one should know that not only must she pick her intricate way through snags and blind reefs, and then shave the head of the island so closely as to brush the overhanging foliage with her stern, but at one place she must pass almost within arm's reach of a sunken and invisible wreck that would snatch the hull timbers from under her if she should strike it, and destroy a quarter of a million dollars' worth of steamboat and cargo in five minutes, and maybe a hundred and fifty human lives into the bargain.

The last remark I heard that night was a compliment to Mr. Bixby, uttered in soliloquy and with unction by one of our guests. He said:

"By the Shadow of Death, but he's a lightning pilot!"

COMMENTARY AND QUESTIONS

"A Daring Deed," a chapter from *Life on the Mississippi*, is part of Mark Twain's account of his experiences as a cub-pilot. Those experiences he ties together by contrasting his bright dream of enjoying the romantic life of a steamboat pilot with his bitter realization of how hard it is to become one. The three chapters that precede and the two that follow this one are given on pp. 15-36. This chapter contains an example of the simplest kind of narration, an incident recounted to illustrate that Mr. Bixby is "a lightning pilot."

1. The details given on pp. 581-582 emphasize the contrast between the experienced pilots' knowledge of the river and the cub-pilot's lack of knowledge. With relation to the incident itself does the presence of the "river inspectors" serve a more immediate purpose?
2. The climax of the incident appears on pp. 584-585. Could any of the details in the last three paragraphs of the story have been omitted or given earlier?

SUGGESTION FOR WRITING

Select an incident within your field of experience which demonstrated that some person had greater capability or skill or courage than even his friends had realized. Tell this incident in a simple narration, paying some attention to the development of suspense, and letting the events of the story speak for themselves with a minimum of explanation.

The Leader
of the People

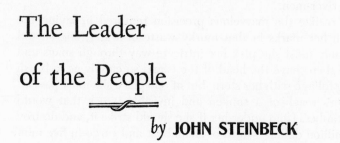

by JOHN STEINBECK

ON SATURDAY AFTERNOON Billy Buck, the ranch-hand, raked together the last of the old year's haystack and pitched small forkfuls over the wire fence to a few mildly interested cattle. High in the air small clouds like puffs of cannon smoke were driven eastward by the March wind. The wind could be heard whishing in the brush on the ridge crests, but no breath of it penetrated down into the ranch-cup.

From *The Long Valley* by John Steinbeck. Copyright 1938 by John Steinbeck. Reprinted by permission of the Viking Press, Inc.

The little boy, Jody, emerged from the house eating a thick piece of buttered bread. He saw Billy working on the last of the haystack. Jody tramped down scuffing his shoes in a way he had been told was destructive to good shoe-leather. A flock of white piegons flew out of the black cypress tree as Jody passed, and circled the tree and landed again. A half-grown tortoise-shell cat leaped from the bunkhouse porch, galloped on stiff legs across the road, whirled and galloped back again. Jody picked up a stone to help the game along, but he was too late, for the cat was under the porch before the stone could be discharged. He threw the stone into the cypress tree and started the white pigeons on another whirling flight.

Arriving at the used-up haystack, the boy leaned against the barbed wire fence. "Will that be all of it, do you think?" he asked.

The middle-aged ranch-hand stopped his careful raking and stuck his fork into the ground. He took off his black hat and smoothed down his hair. "Nothing left of it that isn't soggy from ground moisture," he said. He replaced his hat and rubbed his dry leathery hands together.

"Ought to be plenty mice," Jody suggested.

"Lousy with them," said Billy. "Just crawling with mice."

"Well, maybe, when you get all through, I could call the dogs and hunt the mice."

"Sure, I guess you could," said Billy Buck. He lifted a forkful of the damp ground-hay and threw it into the air. Instantly three mice leaped out and burrowed frantically under the hay again.

Jody sighed with satisfaction. Those plump, sleek, arrogant mice were doomed. For eight months they had lived and multiplied in the haystack. They had been immune from cats, from traps, from poison and from Jody. They had grown smug in their security, overbearing and fat. Now the time of disaster had come; they would not survive another day.

Billy looked up at the top of the hills that surrounded the ranch. "Maybe you better ask your father before you do it," he suggested.

"Well, where is he? I'll ask him now."

"He rode up to the ridge ranch after dinner. He'll be back pretty soon."

Jody slumped against the fence post. "I don't think he'd care."

As Billy went back to his work he said ominously, "You'd better ask him anyway. You know how he is."

Jody did know. His father, Carl Tiflin, insisted upon giving permission for anything that was done on the ranch, whether it was important or not. Jody sagged farther against the post until he was sitting on the ground. He looked up at the little puffs of wind-driven cloud. "Is it like to rain, Billy?"

"It might. The wind's good for it, but not strong enough."

"Well, I hope it don't rain until after I kill those damn mice." He looked over his shoulder to see whether Billy had noticed the mature profanity. Billy worked on without comment.

Jody turned back and looked at the side-hill where the road from the outside world came down. The hill was washed with lean March sunshine. Silver thistles, blue lupins and a few poppies bloomed among the sage bushes. Halfway up the hill Jody could see Doubletree Mutt, the black dog, digging in a squirrel hole. He paddled for a while and then paused to kick bursts of dirt out between his hind legs, and he dug with an earnestness which belied the knowledge he must have had that no dog had ever caught a squirrel by digging in a hole.

Suddenly, while Jody watched, the black dog stiffened, and backed out of the hole and looked up the hill toward the cleft in the ridge where the road came through. Jody looked up too. For a moment Carl Tiflin on horseback stood out against the pale sky and then he moved down the road toward the house. He carried something white in his hand.

The boy started to his feet. "He's got a letter," Jody cried. He trotted away toward the ranch house, for the letter would probably be read aloud and he wanted to be there. He reached the house before his father did, and ran in. He heard Carl dismount from his creaking saddle and slap the horse on the side to send it to the barn where Billy would unsaddle it and turn it out.

Jody ran into the kitchen. "We got a letter!" he cried.

His mother looked up from a pan of beans. "Who has?"

"Father has. I saw it in his hand."

Carl strode into the kitchen then, and Jody's mother asked, "Who's the letter from, Carl?"

He frowned quickly. "How did you know there was a letter?"

She nodded her head in the boy's direction. "Big-Britches Jody told me."

Jody was embarrassed.

His father looked down at him contemptuously. "He *is* getting to be a Big-Britches," Carl said. "He's minding everybody's business but his own. Got his big nose into everything."

Mrs. Tiflin relented a little. "Well, he hasn't enough to keep him busy. Who's the letter from?"

Carl still frowned on Jody. "I'll keep him busy if he isn't careful." He held out a sealed letter. "I guess it's from your father."

Mrs. Tiflin took a hairpin from her head and slit open the flap. Her lips pursed judiciously. Jody saw her eyes snap back and forth over the lines. "He says," she translated, "he says he's going to drive out Saturday to stay for a little while. Why, this is Saturday. The letter must have been delayed." She looked at the postmark. "This was mailed day before yesterday. It should have been here yesterday." She looked up questioningly at her husband, and then her face darkened angrily. "Now what have you got that look on you for? He doesn't come often."

Carl turned his eyes away from her anger. He could be stern with her most of the time, but when occasionally her temper arose, he could not combat it.

"What's the matter with you?" she demanded again.

In his explanation there was a tone of apology Jody himself might have used. "It's just that he talks," Carl said lamely. "Just talks."

"Well, what of it? You talk yourself."

"Sure I do. But your father only talks about one thing."

"Indians!" Jody broke in excitedly. "Indians and crossing the plains!"

Carl turned fiercely on him. "You get out, Mr. Big-Britches! Go on, now! Get out!"

Jody went miserably out the back door and closed the screen with elaborate quietness. Under the kitchen window his shamed, downcast eyes fell upon a curiously shaped stone, a stone of such fascination that he squatted down and picked it up and turned it over in his hands.

The voices came clearly to him through the open kitchen window. "Jody's damn well right," he heard his father say. "Just Indians and crossing the plains. I've heard that story about how the horses got driven off about a thousand times. He just goes on and on, and he never changes a word in the things he tells."

When Mrs. Tiflin answered her tone was so changed that Jody, outside the window, looked up from his study of the stone. Her voice had become soft and explanatory. Jody knew how her face would have changed to match the tone. She said quietly, "Look at it this way, Carl. That was the big thing in my father's life. He led a wagon train clear across the plains to the coast, and when it was finished, his life was done. It was a big thing to do, but it didn't last long enough. Look!" she continued, "it's as though he was born to do that, and after he finished it, there wasn't anything more for him to do but think about it and talk about it. If there'd been any farther west to go, he'd have gone. He's told me so himself. But at last there was the ocean. He lives right by the ocean where he had to stop."

She had caught Carl, caught him and entangled him in her soft tone.

"I've seen him," he agreed quietly. "He goes down and stares off west over the ocean." His voice sharpened a little. "And then he goes up to the Horseshoe Club in Pacific Grove, and he tells people how the Indians drove off the horses."

She tried to catch him again. "Well, it's everything to him. You might be patient with him and pretend to listen."

Carl turned impatiently away. "Well, if it gets too bad, I can always go down to the bunkhouse and sit with Billy," he said irritably. He walked through the house and slammed the front door after him.

Jody ran to his chores. He dumped the grain to the chickens without chasing any of them. He gathered the eggs from the nests. He trotted into the house with the wood and interlaced it so carefully in the woodbox that two armloads seemed to fill it to overflowing.

His mother had finished the beans by now. She stirred up the fire and brushed off the stove-top with a turkey wing. Jody peered cautiously at her to see whether any rancor toward him remained. "Is he coming today?" Jody asked.

"That's what his letter said."

"Maybe I better walk up the road to meet him."

Mrs. Tiflin clanged the stove-lid shut. "That would be nice," she said. "He'd probably like to be met."

"I guess I'll just do it then."

Outside, Jody whistled shrilly to the dogs. "Come on up the hill," he commanded. The two dogs waved their tails and ran ahead. Along the roadside the sage had tender new tips. Jody tore off some pieces and rubbed them on his hands until the air was filled with the sharp wild smell. With a rush the dogs leaped from the road and yapped into the brush after a rabbit. That was the last Jody saw of them, for when they failed to catch the rabbit, they went back home.

Jody plodded on up the hill toward the ridge top. When he reached the little cleft where the road came through, the afternoon wind struck him and blew up his hair and ruffled his shirt. He looked down on the little hills and ridges below and then out at the huge green Salinas Valley. He could see the white town of Salinas far out in the flat and the flash of its windows under the waning sun. Directly below him, in an oak tree, a crow congress had convened. The tree was black with crows all cawing at once.

Then Jody's eyes followed the wagon road down from the ridge where he stood, and lost it behind a hill, and picked it up again on the other side. On that distant stretch he saw a cart slowly pulled by a bay horse. It disappeared behind the hill. Jody sat down on the ground and watched the place where the cart would reappear again. The wind sang on the hilltops and the puff-ball clouds hurried eastward.

Then the cart came into sight and stopped. A man dressed in black dismounted from the seat and walked to the horse's head. Although it was so far away, Jody knew he had unhooked the check-rein, for the horse's head dropped forward. The horse moved on, and the man walked slowly up the hill beside it. Jody gave a glad cry and ran down the road toward them. The squirrels bumped along off the road, and a road-runner flirted its tail and raced over the edge of the hill and sailed out like a glider.

Jody tried to leap into the middle of his shadow at every step. A stone rolled under his foot and he went down. Around a little bend he raced, and there, a short distance ahead, were his grandfather and the cart. The boy dropped from his unseemly running and approached at a dignified walk.

The horse plodded stumble-footedly up the hill and the old man walked beside it. In the lowering sun their giant shadows flickered darkly behind them. The grandfather was dressed in a black broadcloth suit and he wore kid congress gaiters and a black tie on a short, hard collar. He carried his black slouch hat in his hand. His white beard was cropped close and his white eyebrows overhung his eyes like mustaches. The blue eyes were sternly merry. About the whole face and figure there was a granite dignity, so that every motion seemed an impossible thing. Once at rest, it seemed the old men would be stone, would never move again. His steps were slow and certain. Once made, no step could ever be re-traced; once headed in a direction, the path would never bend nor the pace increase nor slow.

When Jody appeared around the bend, Grandfather waved his hat slowly in welcome, and he called, "Why, Jody! Come down to meet me, have you?"

Jody sidled near and turned and matched his step to the old man's step and stiffened his body and dragged his heels a little. "Yes, sir," he said. "We got your letter only today."

"Should have been here yesterday," said Grandfather. "It certainly should. How are all the folks?"

"They're fine, sir." He hesitated and then suggested shyly, "Would you like to come on a mouse hunt tomorrow, sir?"

"Mouse hunt, Jody?" Grandfather chuckled. "Have the people of this generation come down to hunting mice? They aren't very strong, the new people, but I hardly thought mice would be game for them."

"No, sir. It's just play. The haystack's gone. I'm going to drive out the mice to the dogs. And you can watch, or even beat the hay a little."

The stern, merry eyes turned down on him. "I see. You don't eat them, then. You haven't come to that yet."

Jody explained, "The dogs eat them, sir. It wouldn't be much like hunting Indians, I guess."

"No, not much—but then later, when the troops were hunting Indians and shooting children and burning teepees, it wasn't much different from your mouse hunt."

They topped the rise and started down into the ranch cup, and they lost the sun from their shoulders. "You've grown," Grandfather said. "Nearly an inch, I should say."

"More," Jody boasted. "Where they mark me on the door, I'm up more than an inch since Thanksgiving even."

Grandfather's rich throaty voice said, "Maybe you're getting too much water and turning to pith and stalk. Wait until you head out, and then we'll see."

Jody looked quickly into the old man's face to see whether his feelings should be hurt, but there was no will to injure, no punishing nor putting-in-your-place light in the keen blue eyes. "We might kill a pig," Jody suggested.

"Oh, no! I couldn't let you do that. You're just humoring me. It isn't the time and you know it."

"You know Riley, the big boar, sir?"

"Yes. I remember Riley well."

"Well, Riley ate a hole into that same haystack, and it fell down on him and smothered him."

"Pigs do that when they can," said Grandfather.

"Riley was a nice pig, for a boar, sir. I rode him sometimes, and he didn't mind."

A door slammed at the house below them, and they saw Jody's mother standing on the porch waving her apron in welcome. And they saw Carl Tiflin walking up from the barn to be at the house for the arrival.

The sun had disappeared from the hills by now. The blue smoke from the house chimney hung in flat layers in the purpling ranch-cup. The puff-ball clouds, dropped by the falling wind, hung listlessly in the sky.

Billy Buck came out of the bunkhouse and flung a wash basin of soapy water on the ground. He had been shaving in mid-week, for Billy held Grandfather in reverence, and Grandfather said that Billy was one of the few men of the new generation who had not gone soft. Although Billy was in middle age, Grandfather considered him a boy. Now Billy was hurrying toward the house too.

When Jody and Grandfather arrived, the three were waiting for them in front of the yard gate.

Carl said, "Hello, sir. We've been looking for you."

Mrs. Tiflin kissed Grandfather on the side of his beard, and stood still while his big hand patted her shoulder. Billy shook hands solemnly, grinning under his straw mustache. "I'll put up your horse," said Billy, and he led the rig away.

Grandfather watched him go, and then, turning back to the group, he said as he had said a hundred times before, "There's a good boy. I knew his father, old Mule-tail Buck. I never knew why they called him Mule-tail except he packed mules."

Mrs. Tiflin turned and led the way into the house. "How long are you going to stay, Father? Your letter didn't say."

"Well, I don't know. I thought I'd stay about two weeks. But I never stay as long as I think I'm going to."

In a short while they were sitting at the white oilcloth table eating their supper. The lamp with the tin reflector hung over the table. Outside the dining-room windows the big moths battered softly against the glass.

Grandfather cut his steak into tiny pieces and chewed slowly. "I'm hungry," he said. "Driving out here got my appetite up. It's like when we were crossing. We all got so hungry every night we could hardly wait to let the meat get done. I could eat about five pounds of buffalo meat every night."

"It's moving around does it," said Billy. "My father was a government packer. I helped him when I was a kid. Just the two of us could about clean up a deer's ham."

"I knew your father, Billy," said Grandfather. "A fine man he was. They called him Mule-tail Buck. I don't know why except he packed mules."

"That was it," Billy agreed. "He packed mules."

Grandfather put down his knife and fork and looked around the table. "I remember one time we ran out of meat—" His voice dropped to a curious low sing-song, dropped into a tonal groove the story had worn for itself. "There was no buffalo, no antelope, not even rabbits. The hunters couldn't even shoot a coyote. That was the time for the leader to be on the watch. I was the leader, and I kept my eyes open. Know why? Well, just the minute the people began to get hungry they'd start slaughtering the team oxen. Do you believe that? I've heard of parties that just ate up their draft cattle. Started from the middle and worked toward the ends. Finally they'd eat the lead pair, and then the wheelers. The leader of a party had to keep them from doing that."

In some manner a big moth got into the room and circled the hanging kerosene lamp. Billy got up and tried to clap it between his hands. Carl struck with a cupped palm and caught the moth and broke it. He walked to the window and dropped it out.

"As I was saying," Grandfather began again, but Carl interrupted

him. "You'd better eat some more meat. All the rest of us are ready for
our pudding."

Jody saw a flash of anger in his mother's eyes. Grandfather picked
up his knife and fork. "I'm pretty hungry, all right," he said. "I'll tell you
about that later."

When supper was over, when the family and Billy Buck sat in
front of the fireplace in the other room, Jody anxiously watched Grandfather. He saw the signs he knew. The bearded head leaned forward; the
eyes lost their sternness and looked wonderingly into the fire; the big
lean fingers laced themselves on the black knees. "I wonder," he began,
"I just wonder whether I ever told you how those thieving Piutes drove
off thirty-five of our horses."

"I think you did," Carl interrupted. "Wasn't it just before you
went up into the Tahoe country?"

Grandfather turned quickly toward his son-in-law. "That's right.
I guess I must have told you that story."

"Lots of times," Carl said cruelly, and he avoided his wife's eyes.
But he felt the angry eyes on him, and he said, " 'Course I'd like to hear it
again."

Grandfather looked back at the fire. His fingers unlaced and laced
again. Jody knew how he felt, how his insides were collapsed and empty.
Hadn't Jody been called a Big-Britches that very afternoon? He arose
to heroism and opened himself to the term Big-Britches again. "Tell
about Indians," he said softly.

Grandfather's eyes grew stern again. "Boys always want to hear
about Indians. It was a job for men, but boys want to hear about it. Well,
let's see. Did I ever tell you how I wanted each wagon to carry a long
iron plate?"

Everyone but Jody remained silent. Jody said, "No. You didn't."

"Well, when the Indians attacked, we always put the wagons in
a circle and fought from between the wheels. I thought that if every
wagon carried a long plate with rifle holes, the men could stand the
plates on the outside of the wheels when the wagons were in the circle
and they would be protected. It would save lives and that would make
up for the extra weight of the iron. But of course the party wouldn't do
it. No party had done it before and they couldn't see why they should
go to the expense. They lived to regret it, too."

Jody looked at his mother, and knew from her expression that she
was not listening at all. Carl picked at a callus on his thumb and Billy
Buck watched a spider crawling up the wall.

Grandfather's tone dropped into its narrative groove again. Jody
knew in advance exactly what words would fall. The story droned on,

speeded up for the attack, grew sad over the wounds, struck a dirge at the burials on the great plains. Jody sat quietly watching Grandfather. The stern blue eyes were detached. He looked as though he were not very interested in the story himself.

When it was finished, when the pause had been politely respected as the frontier of the story, Billy Buck stood up and stretched and hitched his trousers. "I guess I'll turn in," he said. Then he faced Grandfather. "I've got an old powder horn and a cap and ball pistol down to the bunkhouse. Did I ever show them to you?"

Grandfather nodded slowly. "Yes, I think you did, Billy. Reminds me of a pistol I had when I was leading the people across." Billy stood politely until the little story was done, and then he said, "Good night," and went out of the house.

Carl Tiflin tried to turn the conversation then. "How's the country between here and Monterey? I've heard it's pretty dry."

"It is dry," said Grandfather. "There's not a drop of water in the Laguna Seca. But it's a long pull from '87. The whole country was powder then, and in '61 I believe all the coyotes starved to death. We had fifteen inches of rain this year."

"Yes, but it all came too early. We could do with some now." Carl's eye fell on Jody. "Hadn't you better be getting to bed?"

Jody stood up obediently. "Can I kill the mice in the old haystack, sir?"

"Mice? Oh! Sure, kill them all off. Billy said there isn't any good hay left."

Jody exchanged a secret and satisfying look with Grandfather. "I'll kill every one tomorrow," he promised.

Jody lay in his bed and thought of the impossible world of Indians and buffaloes, a world that had ceased to be forever. He wished he could have been living in the heroic time, but he knew he was not of heroic timber. No one living now, save possibly Billy Buck, was worthy to do the things that had been done. A race of giants had lived then, fearless men, men of a staunchness unknown in this day. Jody thought of the wide plains and of the wagons moving across like centipedes. He thought of Grandfather on a huge white horse, marshaling the people. Across his mind marched the great phantoms, and they marched off the earth and they were gone.

He came back to the ranch for a moment, then. He heard the dull rushing sound that space and silence make. He heard one of the dogs, out in the doghouse, scratching a flea and bumping his elbow against the floor with every stroke. Then the wind arose again and the black cypress groaned and Jody went to sleep.

He was up half an hour before the triangle sounded for breakfast. His mother was rattling the stove to make the flames roar when Jody went through the kitchen. "You're up early," she said. "Where are you going?"

"Out to get a good stick. We're going to kill the mice today."

"Who is 'we'?"

"Why, Grandfather and I."

"So you've got him in it. You always like to have someone in with you in case there's blame to share."

"I'll be right back," said Jody. "I just want to have a good stick ready for after breakfast."

He closed the screen door after him and went out into the cool blue morning. The birds were noisy in the dawn and the ranch cats came down from the hill like blunt snakes. They had been hunting gophers in the dark, and although the four cats were full of gopher meat, they sat in a semi-circle at the back door and mewed piteously for milk. Double-tree Mutt and Smasher moved sniffing along the edge of the brush, performing the duty with rigid ceremony, but when Jody whistled, their heads jerked up and their tails waved. They plunged down to him, wriggling their skins and yawning. Jody patted their heads seriously, and moved on to the weathered scrap pile. He selected an old broom handle and a short piece of inch-square scrap wood. From his pocket he took a shoelace and tied the ends of the sticks loosely together to make a flail. He whistled his new weapon through the air and struck the ground experimentally, while the dogs leaped aside and whined with apprehension.

Jody turned and started down past the house toward the old haystack ground to look over the field of slaughter, but Billy Buck, sitting patiently on the back steps, called to him, "You better come back. It's only a couple of minutes till breakfast."

Jody changed his course and moved toward the house. He leaned his flail against the steps. "That's to drive the mice out," he said. "I'll bet they're fat. I'll bet they don't know what's going to happen to them today."

"No, nor you either," Billy remarked philosophically, "nor me, nor anyone."

Jody was staggered by this thought. He knew it was true. His imagination twitched away from the mouse hunt. Then his mother came out on the back porch and struck the triangle, and all thoughts fell in a heap.

Grandfather hadn't appeared at the table when they sat down. Billy nodded at his empty chair. "He's all right? He isn't sick?"

"He takes a long time to dress," said Mrs. Tiflin. "He combs his whiskers and rubs up his shoes and brushes his clothes."

Carl scattered sugar on his mush. "A man that's led a wagon train across the plains has got to be pretty careful how he dresses."

Mrs. Tiflin turned on him. "Don't do that, Carl! Please don't!" There was more of threat than of request in her tone. And the threat irritated Carl.

"Well, how many times do I have to listen to the story of the iron plates, and the thirty-five horses? That time's done. Why can't he forget it, now it's done?" He grew angrier while he talked, and his voice rose. "Why does he have to tell them over and over? He came across the plains. All right! Now it's finished. Nobody wants to hear about it over and over."

The door into the kitchen closed softly. The four at the table sat frozen. Carl laid his mush spoon on the table and touched his chin with his fingers.

Then the kitchen door opened and Grandfather walked in. His mouth smiled tightly and his eyes were squinted. "Good morning," he said, and he sat down and looked at his mush dish.

Carl could not leave it there. "Did—did you hear what I said?"

Grandfather jerked a little nod.

"I don't know what got into me, sir. I didn't mean it. I was just being funny."

Jody glanced in shame at his mother, and he saw that she was looking at Carl, and that she wasn't breathing. It was an awful thing that he was doing. He was tearing himself to pieces to talk like that. It was a terrible thing to him to retract a word, but to retract it in shame was infinitely worse.

Grandfather looked sidewise. "I'm trying to get right side up," he said gently. "I'm not being mad. I don't mind what you said, but it might be true, and I would mind that."

"It isn't true," said Carl. "I'm not feeling well this morning. I'm sorry I said it."

"Don't be sorry, Carl. An old man doesn't see things sometimes. Maybe you're right. The crossing is finished. Maybe it should be forgotten, now it's done."

Carl got up from the table. "I've had enough to eat. I'm going to work. Take your time, Billy!" He walked quickly out of the dining-room. Billy gulped the rest of his food and followed soon after. But Jody could not leave his chair.

"Won't you tell any more stories?" Jody asked.

"Why, sure I'll tell them, but only when—I'm sure people want to hear them."

"I like to hear them, sir."

"Oh! Of course you do, but you're a little boy. It was a job for men, but only little boys like to hear about it."

Jody got up from his place. "I'll wait outside for you, sir. I've got a good stick for those mice."

He waited by the gate until the old man came out on the porch. "Let's go down and kill the mice now," Jody called.

"I think I'll just sit in the sun, Jody. You go kill the mice."

"You can use my stick if you like."

"No, I'll just sit here a while."

Jody turned disconsolately away, and walked down toward the old haystack. He tried to whip up his enthusiasm with thoughts of the fat juicy mice. He beat the ground with his flail. The dogs coaxed and whined about him, but he could not go. Back at the house he could see Grandfather sitting on the porch, looking small and thin and black.

Jody gave up and went to sit on the steps at the old man's feet.

"Back already? Did you kill the mice?"

"No,sir. I'll kill them some other day."

The morning flies buzzed close to the ground and the ants dashed about in front of the steps. The heavy smell of sage slipped down the hill. The porch boards grew warm in the sunshine.

Jody hardly knew when Grandfather started to talk. "I shouldn't stay here, feeling the way I do." He examined his strong old hands. "I feel as though the crossing wasn't worth doing." His eyes moved up the side-hill and stopped on a motionless hawk perched on a dead limb. "I tell those old stories, but they're not what I want to tell. I only know how I want people to feel when I tell them.

"It wasn't Indians that were important, nor adventures, nor even getting out here. It was a whole bunch of people made into one big crawling beast. And I was the head. It was westering and westering. Every man wanted something for himself, but the big beast that was all of them wanted only westering. I was the leader, but if I hadn't been there, someone else would have been the head. The thing had to have a head.

"Under the little bushes the shadows were black at white noonday. When we saw the mountains at last, we cried—all of us. But it wasn't getting here that mattered, it was movement and westering.

"We carried life out here and set it down the way those ants carry eggs. And I was the leader. The westering was as big as God, and the slow steps that made the movement piled up and piled up until the continent was crossed.

"Then we came down to the sea, and it was done." He stopped and wiped his eyes until the rims were red. "That's what I should be telling instead of stories."

When Jody spoke, Grandfather started and looked down at him. "Maybe I could lead the people some day," Jody said.

The old man smiled. "There's no place to go. There's the ocean to stop you. There's a line of old men along the shore hating the ocean because it stopped them."

"In boats I might, sir."

"No place to go, Jody. Every place is taken. But that's not the worst—no, not the worst. Westering has died out of the people. Westering isn't a hunger any more. It's all done. Your father is right. It is finished." He laced his fingers on his knee and looked at them.

Jody felt very sad. "If you'd like a glass of lemonade I could make it for you."

Grandfather was about to refuse, and then he saw Jody's face. "That would be nice," he said. "Yes, it would be nice to drink a lemonade."

Jody ran into the kitchen where his mother was wiping the last of the breakfast dishes. "Can I have a lemon to make a lemonade for Grandfather?"

His mother mimicked—"And another lemon to make a lemonade for you."

"No, ma'am. I don't want one."

"Jody! You're sick!" Then she stopped suddenly. "Take a lemon out of the cooler," she said softly. "Here, I'll reach the squeezer down to you."

COMMENTARY AND QUESTIONS

1. Although "The Leader of the People" is the fourth part of a long story called *The Red Pony,* it is nevertheless self-contained. By the end of "The Leader of the People" each of the two main characters, Jody and Grandfather, has become aware of something for the first time. What does each learn?

2. How do the following comments and bits of conversation reveal Jody's attitude toward other characters or their attitude toward him?
   a. " 'Big-Britches Jody told me' " (p. 588).
   b. "His mother mimicked—'And another lemon to make a lemonade for you' " (p. 599).
   c. "Jody looked quickly into the old man's face to see whether his feelings should be hurt, but there was no will to injure, no punishing nor putting-in-your-place light in the keen blue eyes" (p. 592).
   d. " 'Well, I hope it don't rain until after I kill those damn mice' " (p. 588).

3. What incidents reveal the attitude of Carl Tiflin and his wife toward each other?

4. When Steinbeck introduces Jody in the second paragraph of "The Leader of the People," he explicitly identifies him as a "little boy." Cite details used by Steinbeck to remind the reader, throughout the story, of Jody's youth.

SUGGESTION FOR WRITING

Explain why you think "The Mouse Hunt" would or would not be a more appropriate title for this story.

By the Waters of Babylon

by STEPHEN VINCENT BENÉT

THE NORTH and the west and the south are good hunting ground, but it is forbidden to go east. It is forbidden to go to any of the Dead Places except to search for metal and then he who touches the metal must be a priest or the son of a priest. Afterwards, both the man and the metal must be purified. These are the rules and the laws; they are well made. It is forbidden to cross the great river and look upon the place that was the Place of the Gods—this is most strictly forbidden. We do not even say its name though we know its name. It is there that spirits live, and demons— it is there that there are the ashes of the Great Burning. These things are forbidden—they have been forbidden since the beginning of time.

My father is a priest; I am the son of a priest. I have been in the Dead Places near us, with my father—at first, I was afraid. When my father went into the house to search for the metal, I stood by the door and my heart felt small and weak. It was a dead man's house, a spirit house. It did not have the smell of man, though there were old bones in a corner. But it is not fitting that a priest's son should show fear. I looked at the bones in the shadow and kept my voice still.

Then my father came out with the metal—a good, strong piece. He looked at me with both eyes but I had not run away. He gave me the metal to hold—I took it and did not die. So he knew that I was truly his son and would be a priest in my time. That was when I was very young—nevertheless, my brothers would not have done it, though they are good hunters. After that, they gave me the good piece of meat and the warm corner by the fire. My father watched over me—he was glad that I should be a priest. But when I boasted or wept without a reason, he punished me more strictly than my brothers. That was right.

After a time, I myself was allowed to go into the dead houses and search for metal. So I learned the ways of those houses—and if I saw bones, I was no longer afraid. The bones are light and old—sometimes they will fall into dust if you touch them. But that is a great sin.

I was taught the chants and the spells—I was taught how to stop the running of blood from a wound and many secrets. A priest must know many secrets—that was what my father said. If the hunters think we do all things by chants and spells, they may believe so—it does not hurt them. I was taught how to read in the old books and how to make the old writings—that was hard and took a long time. My knowledge made me happy—it was like a fire in my heart. Most of all, I liked to hear of the Old Days and the stories of the gods. I asked myself many questions that I could not answer, but it was good to ask them. At night, I would lie awake and listen to the wind—it seemed to me that it was the voice of the gods as they flew through the air.

We are not ignorant like the Forest People—our women spin wool on the wheel, our priests wear a white robe. We do not eat grubs from the tree, we have not forgotten the old writings, although they are hard to understand. Nevertheless, my knowledge and my lack of knowledge burned in me—I wished to know more. When I was a man at last, I came to my father and said, "It is time for me to go on my journey. Give me your leave."

He looked at me for a long time, stroking his beard, then he said at last, "Yes. It is time." That night, in the house of the priesthood, I asked for and received purification. My body hurt but my spirit was a cool stone. It was my father himself who questioned me about my dreams.

He bade me look into the smoke of the fire and see—I saw and told what I saw. It was what I have always seen—a river, and, beyond it, a great Dead Place and in it the gods walking. I have always thought about that. His eyes were stern when I told him—he was no longer my father but a priest. He said, "This is a strong dream."

"It is mine," I said, while the smoke waved and my head felt light. They were singing the Star song in the outer chamber and it was like the buzzing of bees in my head.

He asked me how the gods were dressed and I told him how they were dressed. We know how they were dressed from the book, but I saw them as if they were before me. When I had finished, he threw the sticks three times and studied them as they fell.

"This is a very strong dream," he said. "It may eat you up."

"I am not afraid," I said and looked at him with both eyes. My voice sounded thin in my ears but that was because of the smoke.

He touched me on the breast and the forehead. He gave me the bow and the three arrows.

"Take them," he said. "It is forbidden to travel east. It is forbidden to cross the river. It is forbidden to go to the Place of the Gods. All these things are forbidden."

"All these things are forbidden," I said, but it was my voice that spoke and not my spirit. He looked at me again.

"My son," he said. "Once I had young dreams. If your dreams do not eat you up, you may be a great priest. If they eat you, you are still my son. Now go on your journey."

I went fasting, as is the law. My body hurt but not my heart. When the dawn came, I was out of sight of the village. I prayed and purified myself, waiting for a sign. The sign was an eagle. It flew east.

Sometimes signs are sent by bad spirits. I waited again on the flat rock, fasting, taking no food. I was very still—I could feel the sky above me and the earth beneath. I waited till the sun was beginning to sink. Then three deer passed in the valley, going east—they did not wind me or see me. There was a white fawn with them—a very great sign.

I followed them, at a distance, waiting for what would happen. My heart was troubled about going east, yet I knew that I must go. My head hummed with my fasting—I did not even see the panther spring upon the white fawn. But, before I knew it, the bow was in my hand. I shouted and the panther lifted his head from the fawn. It is not easy to kill a panther with one arrow but the arrow went through his eye and into his brain. He died as he tried to spring—he rolled over, tearing at the ground. Then I knew I was meant to go east—I knew that was my journey. When the night came, I made my fire and roasted meat.

It is eight suns' journey to the east and a man passes by many Dead Places. The Forest People are afraid of them but I am not. Once I made my fire on the edge of a Dead Place at night and, next morning, in the dead house, I found a good knife, little rusted. That was small to what came afterward but it made my heart feel big. Always when I looked for game, it was in front of my arrow, and twice I passed hunting parties of the Forest People without their knowing. So I knew my magic was strong and my journey clean, in spite of the law.

Toward the setting of the eighth sun, I came to the banks of the great river. It was half-a-day's journey after I had left the god-road—we do not use the god-roads now for they are falling apart into great blocks of stone, and the forest is safer going. A long way off, I had seen the water through trees but the trees were thick. At last, I came out upon an open place at the top of a cliff. There was the great river below, like a giant in the sun. It is very long, very wide. It could eat all the streams we know and still be thirsty. Its name is Ou-dis-sun, the Sacred, the Long. No man of my tribe had seen it, not even my father, the priest. It was magic and I prayed.

Then I raised my eyes and looked south. It was there, the Place of the Gods.

How can I tell what it was like—you do not know. It was there, in the red light, and they were too big to be houses. It was there with the red light upon it, mighty and ruined. I knew that in another moment the gods would see me. I covered my eyes with my hands and crept back into the forest.

Surely, that was enough to do, and live. Surely it was enough to spend the night upon the cliff. The Forest People themselves do not come near. Yet, all through the night, I knew that I should have to cross the river and walk in the places of the gods, although the gods ate me up. My magic did not help me at all and yet there was a fire in my bowels, a fire in my mind. When the sun rose, I thought, "My journey has been clean. Now I will go home from my journey." But, even as I thought so, I knew I could not. If I went to the Place of the Gods, I would surely die, but, if I did not go, I could never be at peace with my spirit again. It is better to lose one's life than one's spirit, if one is a priest and the son of a priest.

Nevertheless, as I made the raft, the tears ran out of my eyes. The Forest People could have killed me without fight, if they had come upon me then, but they did not come. When the raft was made, I said the sayings for the dead and painted myself for death. My heart was cold as a frog and my knees like water, but the burning in my mind would not let me have peace. As I pushed the raft from the shore, I began my death song—I had the right. It was a fine song.

"I am John, son of John," I sang. "My people are the Hill People. They are the men.
I go into the Dead Places but I am not slain.
I take the metal from the Dead Places but I am not blasted.

I travel upon the god-roads and am not afraid. E-yah! I have killed
the panther, I have killed the fawn!

E-yah! I have come to the great river. No man has come there before.

It is forbidden to go east, but I have gone, forbidden to go on the great
river, but I am there.

Open your hearts, you spirits, and hear my song.

Now I go to the Place of the Gods, I shall not return.

My body is painted for death and my limbs weak, but my heart is big
as I go to the Place of the Gods!"

All the same, when I came to the Place of the Gods, I was afraid,
afraid. The current of the great river is very strong—it gripped my raft
with its hands. That was magic, for the river itself is wide and calm.
I could feel evil spirits about me, in the bright morning; I could feel
their breath on my neck as I was swept down the stream. Never have I
been so much alone—I tried to think of my knowledge, but it was a
squirrel's heap of winter nuts. There was no strength in my knowledge
any more and I felt small and naked as a new-hatched bird—alone upon
the great river, the servant of the gods.

Yet, after a while, my eyes were opened and I saw. I saw both
banks of the river—I saw that once there had been god-roads across it,
though now they were broken and fallen like broken vines. Very great
they were, and wonderful and broken—broken in the time of the Great
Burning when the fire fell out of the sky. And always the current took
me nearer to the Place of the Gods, and the huge ruins rose before my
eyes.

I do not know the customs of rivers—we are the People of the
Hills. I tried to guide my raft with the pole but it spun around. I thought
the river meant to take me past the Place of the Gods and out into the
Bitter Water of the legends. I grew angry then—my heart felt strong. I
said aloud, "I am a priest and the son of a priest!" The gods heard me—
they showed me how to paddle with the pole on one side of the raft. The
current changed itself—I drew near to the Place of the Gods.

When I was very near, my raft struck and turned over. I can swim
in our lakes—I swam to the shore. There was a great spike of rusted
metal sticking out into the river—I hauled myself up upon it and sat
there, panting. I had saved my bow and two arrows and the knife I found
in the Dead Place but that was all. My raft went whirling downstream
toward the Bitter Water. I looked after it, and thought if it had trod me
under, at least I would be safely dead. Nevertheless, when I had dried
my bowstring and re-strung it, I walked forward to the Place of the Gods.

It felt like ground underfoot; it did not burn me. It is not true
what some of the tales say, that the ground there burns forever, for I

have been there. Here and there were the marks and stains of the Great Burning, on the ruins, that is true. But they were old marks and old stains. It is not true either, what some of our priests say, that it is an island covered with fogs and enchantments. It is not. It is a great Dead Place—greater than any Dead Place we know. Everywhere in it there are god-roads, though most are cracked and broken. Everywhere there are the ruins of the high towers of the gods.

How shall I tell what I saw? I went carefully, my strung bow in my hand, my skin ready for danger. There should have been the wailings of spirits and the shrieks of demons, but there were not. It was very silent and sunny where I had landed—the wind and the rain and the birds that drop seeds had done their work—the grass grew in the cracks of the broken stone. It is a fair island—no wonder the gods built there. If I had come there, a god, I also would have built.

How shall I tell what I saw? The towers are not all broken—here and there one still stands, like a great tree in a forest, and the birds nest high. But the towers themselves look blind, for the gods are gone. I saw a fish-hawk, catching fish in the river. I saw a little dance of white butterflies over a great heap of broken stones and columns. I went there and looked about me—there was a carved stone with cut-letters, broken in half. I can read letters but I could not understand these. They said UBTREAS. There was also the shattered image of a man or a god. It had been made of white stone and he wore his hair tied back like a woman's. His name was ASHING, as I read on the cracked half of a stone. I thought it wise to pray to ASHING, though I do not know that god.

How shall I tell what I saw? There was no smell of man left, on stone or metal. Nor were there many trees in that wilderness of stone. There are many pigeons, nesting and dropping in the towers—the gods must have loved them, or perhaps, they used them for sacrifices. There are wild cats that roam the god-roads, green-eyed, unafraid of man. At night they wail like demons but they are not demons. The wild dogs are more dangerous, for they hunt in a pack, but them I did not meet till later. Everywhere there are the carved stones, carved with magical numbers or words.

I went North—I did not try to hide myself. When a god or a demon saw me, then I would die, but meanwhile I was no longer afraid. My hunger for knowledge burned in me—there was so much that I could not understand. After awhile, I knew that my belly was hungry. I could have hunted for my meat, but I did not hunt. It is known that the gods did not hunt as we do—they got their food from enchanted boxes and jars. Sometimes these are still found in the Dead Places—once, when I was a child and foolish, I opened such a jar and tasted it and found the food sweet. But my father found out and punished me for it strictly, for, often, that food is death. Now, though, I had long gone past what was forbidden, and I entered the likeliest towers, looking for the food of the gods.

I found it at last in the ruins of a great temple in the mid-city. A mighty temple it must have been, for the roof was painted like the sky at night with its stars—that much I could see, though the colors were faint and dim. It went down into great caves and tunnels—perhaps they kept their slaves there. But when I started to climb down, I heard the squeaking of rats, so I did not go—rats are unclean, and there must have been many tribes of them, from the squeaking. But near there, I found food, in the heart of a ruin, behind a door that still opened. I ate only the fruits from the jars—they had a very sweet taste. There was drink, too, in bottles of glass—the drink of the gods was strong and made my head swim. After I had eaten and drunk, I slept on the top of a stone, my bow at my side.

When I awoke, the sun was low. Looking down from where I lay, I saw a dog sitting on his haunches. His tongue was hanging out of his mouth; he looked as if he were laughing. He was a big dog, with a gray-brown coat, as big as a wolf. I sprang up and shouted at him but he did not move—he just sat there as if he were laughing. I did not like that. When I reached for a stone to throw, he moved swiftly out of the way of the stone. He was not afraid of me; he looked at me as if I were meat. No doubt I could have killed him with an arrow, but I did not know if there were others. Moreover, night was falling.

I looked about me—not far away there was a great, broken god-road, leading North. The towers were high enough, but not so high, and while many of the dead-houses were wrecked, there were some that stood. I went toward this god-road, keeping to the heights of the ruins, while the dog followed. When I had reached the god-road, I saw that there were others behind him. If I had slept later, they would have come upon me asleep and torn out my throat. As it was, they were sure enough of me; they did not hurry. When I went into the dead-house, they kept watch at the entrance—doubtless they thought they would have a fine hunt. But a dog cannot open a door and I knew, from the books, that the gods did not like to live on the ground but on high.

I had just found a door I could open when the dogs decided to rush. Ha! They were surprised when I shut the door in their faces—it was a good door, of strong metal. I could hear their foolish baying beyond it but I did not stop to answer them. I was in darkness—I found stairs and climbed. There were many stairs, turning around till my head was dizzy. At the top was another door—I found the knob and opened it. I was in a long small chamber—on one side of it was a bronze door that could not be opened, for it had no handle. Perhaps there was a magic word to open it but I did not have the word. I turned to the door in the opposite side of the wall. The lock of it was broken and I opened it and went in.

Within, there was a place of great riches. The god who lived there must have been a powerful god. The first room was a small ante-room— I waited there for some time, telling the spirits of the place that I came in peace and not as a robber. When it seemed to me that they had had time to hear me, I went on. Ah, what riches! Few, even, of the windows had been broken—it was all as it had been. The great windows that looked over the city had not been broken at all though they were dusty and streaked with many years. There were coverings on the floors, the colors not greatly faded, and the chairs were soft and deep. There were pictures upon the walls, very strange, very wonderful—I remember one of a bunch of flowers in a jar—if you came close to it, you could see nothing but bits of color, but if you stood away from it, the flowers might have been picked yesterday. It made my heart feel strange to look at this pic- ture—and to look at the figure of a bird, in some hard clay, on a table and see it so like our birds. Everywhere there were books and writings, many in tongues that I could not read. The god who lived there must have been a wise god and full of knowledge. I felt I had right there, as I sought knowledge also.

Nevertheless, it was strange. There was a washing-place but no water—perhaps the gods washed in air. There was a cooking-place but no wood, and though there was a machine to cook food, there was no place to put fire in it. Nor were there candles or lamps—there were things that looked like lamps but they had neither oil nor wick. All these things were magic, but I touched them and lived—the magic had gone out of them. Let me tell one thing to show. In the washing-place, a thing said "Hot" but it was not hot to the touch—another thing said "Cold" but it was not cold. This must have been a strong magic but the magic was gone. I do not understand—they had ways—I wish that I knew.

It was close and dry and dusty in their house of the gods. I have said the magic was gone but that is not true—it had gone from the magic things but it had not gone from the place. I felt the spirits about me, weighing upon me. Nor had I ever slept in a Dead Place before—and yet, tonight, I must sleep there. When I thought of it, my tongue felt dry in my throat, in spite of my wish for knowledge. Almost I would have gone down again and faced the dogs, but I did not.

I had not gone through all the rooms when the darkness fell. When it fell, I went back to the big room looking over the city and made fire. There was a place to make fire and a box with wood in it, though I do not think they cooked there. I wrapped myself in a floor-covering and slept in front of the fire—I was very tired.

Now I tell what is very strong magic. I woke in the midst of the night. When I woke, the fire had gone out and I was cold. It seemed to me that all around me there were whisperings and voices. I closed my eyes to shut them out. Some will say that I slept again, but I do not think that I slept. I could feel the spirits drawing my spirit out of my body as a fish is drawn on a line.

Why should I lie about it? I am a priest and the son of a priest. If there are spirits, as they say, in the small Dead Places near us, what spirits must there not be in that great Place of the Gods? And would not they wish to speak? After such long years? I know that I felt myself drawn as a fish is drawn on a line. I had stepped out of my body—I could see my body asleep in front of the cold fire, but it was not I. I was drawn to look out upon the city of the gods.

It should have been dark, for it was night, but it was not dark. Everywhere there were lights—lines of light—circles and blurs of light —ten thousand torches would not have been the same. The sky itself was alight—you could barely see the stars for the glow in the sky. I thought to myself "This is strong magic" and trembled. There was a roaring in my ears like the rushing of rivers. Then my eyes grew used to the light and my ears to the sound. I knew that I was seeing the city as it had been when the gods were alive.

That was a sight indeed—yes, that was a sight: I could not have seen it in the body—my body would have died. Everywhere went the gods, on foot and in chariots—there were gods beyond number and counting and their chariots blocked the streets. They had turned night to day for their pleasure—they did not sleep with the sun. The noise of their coming and going was the noise of many waters. It was magic what they could do—it was magic what they did.

I looked out of another window—the great vines of their bridges were mended and the god-roads went East and West. Restless, restless, were the gods and always in motion! They burrowed tunnels under rivers—they flew in the air. With unbelievable tools they did giant works— no part of the earth was safe from them, for, if they wished for a thing, they summoned it from the other side of the world. And always, as they labored and rested, as they feasted and made love, there was a drum in their ears—the pulse of the giant city, beating and beating like a man's heart.

Were they happy? What is happiness to the gods? They were great, they were mighty, they were wonderful and terrible. As I looked upon them and their magic, I felt like a child—but a little more, it seemed to me, and they would pull down the moon from the sky. I saw them with wisdom beyond wisdom and knowledge beyond knowledge. And yet not all they did was well done—even I could see that—and yet their wisdom could not but grow until all was peace.

Then I saw their fate come upon them and that was terrible past speech. It came upon them as they walked the streets of their city. I have been in the fights with the Forest People—I have seen men die. But this was not like that. When gods war with gods, they use weapons we do not know. It was fire falling out of the sky and a mist that poisoned. It was the time of the Great Burning and the Destruction. They ran about like ants in the streets of their city—poor gods, poor gods! Then the towers began to fall. A few escaped—yes, a few. The legends tell it. But, even after the city had become a Dead Place, for many years the poison was still in the ground. I saw it happen, I saw the last of them die. It was darkness over the broken city and I wept.

All this, I saw. I saw it as I have told it, though not in the body. When I woke in the morning, I was hungry, but I did not think first of my hunger for my heart was perplexed and confused. I knew the reason for the Dead Places but I did not see why it had happened. It seemed to me it should not have happened, with all the magic they had. I went through the house looking for an answer. There was so much in the house I could not understand—and yet I am a priest and the son of a priest. It was like being on one side of the great river, at night, with no light to show the way.

Then I saw the dead god. He was sitting in his chair, by the window, in a room I had not entered before and, for the first moment, I thought that he was alive. Then I saw the skin on the back of his hand —it was like dry leather. The room was shut, hot and dry—no doubt that had kept him as he was. At first I was afraid to approach him—then the fear left me. He was sitting looking out over the city—he was dressed in the clothes of the gods. His age was neither young nor old—I could not tell his age. But there was wisdom in his face and great sadness. You could see that he would have not run away. He had sat at his window, watching his city die—then he himself had died. But it is better to lose one's life than one's spirit—and you could see from the face that his spirit had not been lost. I knew that, if I touched him, he would fall into dust —and yet, there was something unconquered in the face.

That is all of my story, for then I knew he was a man—I knew then that they had been men, neither gods nor demons. It is a great knowledge, hard to tell and believe. They were men—they went a dark road, but they were men. I had no fear after that—I had no fear going home, though twice I fought off the dogs and once I was hunted for two days by the Forest People. When I saw my father again, I prayed and was purified. He touched my lips and my breast, he said, "You went away a boy. You come back a man and a priest." I said, "Father, they were men! I have been in the Place of the Gods and seen it! Now slay me, if it is the law—but still I know they were men."

He looked at me out of both eyes. He said, "The law is not always the same shape—you have done what you have done. I could not have done it in my time, but you come after me. Tell!"

I told and he listened. After that, I wished to tell all the people but he showed me otherwise. He said, "Truth is a hard deer to hunt. If you eat too much truth at once, you may die of the truth. It was not idly that our fathers forbade the Dead Places." He was right—it is better the truth should come little by little. I have learned that, being a priest. Perhaps, in the old days, they ate knowledge too fast.

Nevertheless, we make a beginning. It is not for the metal alone we go to the Dead Places now—there are the books and the writings. They are hard to learn. And the magic tools are broken—but we can look at them and wonder. At least, we make a beginning. And, when I am chief priest we shall go beyond the great river. We shall go to the Place of the Gods—the place Newyork—not one man but a company. We shall look for the images of the gods and find the god ASHING and the others— the gods LICOLN and BILTMORE and MOSES. But they were men who built the city, not gods or demons. They were men. I remember the dead man's face. They were men who were here before us. We must build again.

COMMENTARY AND QUESTIONS

1. Jody in "The Leader of the People" becomes aware of something. But what he learns has, in a sense, a universal application: everybody in the process of growing up has had similar experiences. Do you think what John learns in "By the Waters of Babylon" is equally universal in its application?

2. Does the paragraph on p. 608 beginning "Were they happy?" fit the character and situation or does it seem to be an unwarrantable intrusion of the author's attitude? Do you think Benét has any purpose in writing "By the Waters of Babylon" other than that of holding your interest in John's daring journey? What is the significance of the title?

3. Do you think anything vital would be lost if John's father, and references to him, were omitted?

4. At what point in the story did you suddenly realize the time and setting in which it is placed? Why is the river called *Ou-dis-sun?* Why

does Benét delay John's finding of the dead "god" until rather near the end of the story?

5. Here are two figures of speech used by John: "My body hurt but my spirit was a cool stone" (p. 601); "My heart was cold as a frog and my knees like water, but the burning in my mind would not let me have peace" (p. 603). Find others. Are they appropriate?

6. In writing this story Benét has obviously tried to make the arrangement of words seem to be John's. What techniques has the author used to achieve this purpose? You may find it helpful to contrast this rewriting of the second paragraph of the story with the original:

> When I, the son of a priest, went first with my father to the Dead Places near us, I was afraid. When my father went into the house to search for the metal, my heart felt small and weak as I stood by the door. Although this house of a dead man, a spirit house, did not have the smell of man, there were old bones in a corner. But since it is not fitting that a priest's son should show fear, I kept my voice still when I looked at the bones in the shadow.

SUGGESTIONS FOR WRITING

1. Aldous Huxley's novel *Ape and Essence* is also set in a future time after the virtual destruction of our civilization. Scientists from New Zealand, one of the few places not destroyed, land on the coast of California and investigate the ruins of a civilization. Suppose your town had been destroyed during, to use Benét's phrase, the Great Burning. From the ruins what conclusions do you think an exploring scientist would draw about the life of your town and the things held worthwhile by its citizens?

2. Do you agree with the statement, made in the next-to-last paragraph of "By the Waters of Babylon," that "it is better the truth should come little by little"? Is a simple Yes or No answer possible? In presenting your opinion, discuss situations in which the application of this doctrine would seem to prove or disprove the statement.

Too Young

by EMILY HAHN

"I SIMPLY CAN'T UNDERSTAND your attitude," said Mr. Cross to his wife, in a bewildered tone. He added, "Just what is it you have against the institution of marriage, may I ask?"

Mrs. Cross hesitated. "I have nothing against marriage as such," she said, "but she's too young."

"But she isn't," said Mr. Cross. "She's not a minor in law. She's eighteen."

"I don't care what the law says," Mrs. Cross retorted. "Eighteen is too young."

The Crosses had already been through this exchange several times, with hardly a variation, and Mrs. Cross was tempted to remark that such repetitious conversation did constitute an argument against marriage as such, but she knew it was no time to pick a quarrel. Instead, she injected a new argument. "Everybody knows you English are too eager to marry off your girls," she said. "How can that poor child know what she wants in a husband?"

"I must say this comes very oddly from an American," said her husband. "I thought that in America they started courting—"

"Dating."

"Dating, then, in the cradle."

Mrs. Cross said, "Dating is entirely different." Her voice rose. "This is nothing but a slave mart."

Then she laughed, and so did her husband. After all, they were not arguing about their own daughter. Monica was safe with a friend in Cornwall, spending a week at the seaside, and in any case she was not yet eighteen. The subject of the argument was Mr. Cross's niece, Patricia, the daughter of his brother.

Mrs. Cross continued more good-naturedly. "If Pat had been dating all these years, I wouldn't have a word to say against her engagement now. I'd know she had chosen for herself. But she's seen hardly any men at all until lately. This commander of hers may be an absolute drip —she wouldn't know."

"He's a good chap," said Mr. Cross warmly. "I've met him. And we're leaping to conclusions. It isn't really settled yet, you know."

Mrs. Cross said, "How would you like it if it were Monica? You wouldn't want your own daughter getting married straight out of school, now, would you?"

"Why not?" said Mr. Cross. "I'd probably like it very well."

She stalked out of the room. It seemed to her that she could see Monica's face, still as softly rounded as a child's, under a wedding wreath and veil. The idea saddened her. With relief, she reminded herself that Patricia was the girl who might soon be wearing wreath and veil. Still, Mrs. Cross sighed. She was fond of Patricia, too.

It was Sunday morning. Soon, Patricia and her young man—one must not refer to him yet as a fiancé—were to arrive to spend the day. Pat's parents lived far away, in the North, and on weekends she often came out from London, where she was studying music, to visit her aunt and uncle. Mrs. Cross went into the dining room to set the table, her mind busy once again with Monica and the future. She hoped Pat's engagement, or near engagement, would not put ideas into Monica's head. The cousins had always got on well in spite of the difference in their ages, and there wasn't so much difference in ages anyway—less than a year. Oh, of course Patricia was too young to marry, but if she wasn't— what about Monica? Mrs. Cross shook her head and slammed down a placemat before the young man's chair. Then the sound of Patricia's car arriving took her to the front door, falsely smiling a welcome.

At first sight, there was not much Mrs. Cross could either dislike or like about the commander, whose name was Martin, but he was certainly much older than Patricia. He was on the short side, easy and assured in his ways. He might at least have the grace to be nervous, Mrs. Cross thought severely. Her husband was being unnecessarily cordial, she decided. He pounced on the young people and led the way to the study for drinks. The men had two cocktails apiece, Mrs. Cross had one, and Pat nursed a small sherry. As the men laughed more often and more loudly, Mrs. Cross studied Patricia, whose eyes were fixed solemnly on Martin most of the time. She was slender and fragile, and Mrs. Cross had always felt protective about her—an attitude the girl had always accepted, but without enthusiasm. She was habitually competent and reserved, and it was impossible to guess from her face how she felt about Martin. Mrs. Cross said to herself that she hoped when Monica's day came the child would show more glow about the whole thing. But then, of course, that day was years ahead.

After lunch, the men sat for a while at table, drinking port, and Mrs. Cross hoped for a cozy chat with Patricia. But Patricia went straight up to the attic to sort out sports things she had got into the habit of keeping with the Crosses, and later she and Martin went out for a walk. Mrs. Cross retired to her sitting room, to mend clothes and brood.

She told herself that one must face certain facts. It was no use shutting one's eyes, for example, to the fact that Monica was beginning to show an interest in boys. Mrs. Cross had always realized that the time would come. For one thing, Monica attended a progressive school, where the girls were encouraged to make friends with boys. She belonged to a country-dancing club that met three times a term and had both boy and girl members. Many of Mrs. Cross's friends believed that the school gave the girls too much latitude, and, waiting for Pat and Martin to return for tea, Mrs. Cross wondered if these friends mightn't be right, after all. The school's enlightened attitude might be forcing Monica into maturity too early—all the chatter that seemed to go on there about love; the kudos a girl received if she corresponded regularly with some man. The girls were an excitable lot, judging by Monica's reports, and the news of Patricia's engagement, if engagement it proved to be, would no doubt send them into vicarious transports. Not that they knew Patricia, any of them, but she was Monica's cousin and they knew Monica. There would be no holding girls who set as much store as they evidently did by the fact that Juliet was fourteen.

Patricia and Martin returned, and Mrs. Cross got tea. Afterward, Martin took a train back to London. Pat, who was staying the night, drove him to the station, and Mrs. Cross, now softened by time and tea, returned to her sewing basket and her meditations.

She wondered if she could possibly be mistaken, after all. Yes, she decided, she could. She must be wise, and stop fighting the inevitable. It was extraordinary how much like a mother a mother was capable of behaving. If she didn't watch out, she would become one of those dreadful women who hold on to their children. Too much nature, that was it—too much of whatever keeps hens sitting on their eggs. Eggs must hatch. Hens must get off the nest and find something else to do. Winding a thread around and around a button, Mrs. Cross felt ashamed of her stormy thoughts. She made a vow aloud: "I will not hang on to Monica."

She heard the car returning, and a moment later Patricia ran up the stairs, knocked on the door, and came in. "Well, Auntie," she said, "what do you think of my little man?"

She looked flustered. Mrs. Cross couldn't remember ever having seen her so uncertain. "He seems very nice, dear," she said. "*Is* he your little man, by the way?"

"He wants me to tell you so," said Patricia. She picked up a bowl in which Mrs. Cross kept pins, and ran her fingers around the edge of it as if she were testing it for chips. "He said I should tell you he wants to marry me—just now he said it, at the station."

"I see. Of course you've told your parents?"

"Oh, yes, of course. That is to say, Martin has told them. He did it very properly—special appointment with Daddy and all that." Her fingers went on examining the bowl's edge, circuit after circuit. Her head was bent over it as if she were the original potter, making the vessel.

Mrs. Cross waited for more words, but none came. She asked, "What does your father think about it?"

Pat raised her head and said, with more animation, "He thinks I'm far too young to marry. He said we ought to wait, but Martin doesn't want to wait."

"Will Martin have his way about it, do you suppose?"

"I expect so," said Patricia. "He usually does. And Daddy and Mummy like him, so they'll very likely give way sooner or later."

"I see," said Mrs. Cross again. "Well—it's very exciting, isn't it?"

"Yes," said Patricia. Her tone was flat.

Mrs. Cross said, "I haven't asked how you feel about it yourself."

"Oh, me?" said Patricia. Again she surprised her aunt; her face twisted for a moment, like that of a child about to cry. She did not cry, however. She said calmly, "Actually, I'm not mad keen to be married."

"But my dear, then why do it?"

"Because, why not? I like Martin, and he's mad keen enough for both of us, and no doubt I'll settle in well enough. You see, one's got to get away. One's got to get away from Mummy." Pat paused as if she had shocked herself. She added hastily, "I don't mean to sound disloyal, you understand. I don't mean *my* mother, specifically. Just any mother. Good night."

She nodded and smiled, and backed out through the door.

Monica was at home. She had, in fact, been home from Cornwall three days when, on a calm, lovely August morning, she came in from the garden, flopped down on a chair in her mother's bedroom, and exclaimed rapturously, "The roses!" (Their scent filled the house. All the garden was full of them.) "I've never known such a wonderful summer!" Her face was shimmering. "Mummy. I'm in love."

"Just a minute, darling," said her mother, who was sorting out the clean laundry. "There, now. What did you say?"

"I said I'm in love," said Monica, and looked sidewise at herself in the dressing-table mirror.

"Oh." Mrs. Cross was not quite sure what constituted good manners at such a moment. She sat down on the dressing-table bench and put her hands together in her lap, to keep them from doing anything distracting. "Do you want to tell me about it?" she asked. Even in the maternity ward, she thought wildly, Monica had not looked so babylike. Monica drew a deep breath. "I don't know if I can express it," she said. "What would you like to know?"

Mrs. Cross nearly blurted "Not a thing—I don't want to hear a thing about it." Instead, she raised her eyebrows and said, "You might start by telling me his name. Do I know him?"

Monica shook her head, sniffed the rose-scented air, and looked, with shiny eyes, into the middle distance. "No, you don't. He lives in Cornwall. He's training to be an architect. His name is Allan. He's perfectly beautiful, Mummy, and so sweet and gentle!" Again she drew a deep breath. Mrs. Cross wanted to shake her.

"Age?" she asked.

"Quite old—twenty-four or five, I should think. He makes all the boys I know seem so trivial. When I think of their lives—playing tennis and going to deb dances! And all the time, there's Allan working away at his ideals. I'd do anything to help him. He has wonderful ideas about architecture. We like just exactly the same buildings. Isn't it strange? As if destiny meant us to meet. Mummy, did you ever feel that way about anyone?"

"I did," said Mrs. Cross crisply, "and so did you."

"I? Never."

"You did, too," said Mrs. Cross. "Two years ago, you scared me stiff, writing from school to tell me you had at last met the man you wanted to marry."

No recollection flickered in Monica's wide eyes. She only looked hurt. She said, "This is no time for joking."

"He was a mechanic in the Plymouth garage, at the hotel," Mrs. Cross said. "You told me he looked like an ancient Greek. I never could see it myself."

"That? That didn't count. I was a mere child," said Monica. "You're funny! Fancy remembering, when even I forgot! That was nothing."

She wriggled into a comfortable position on the chair, as if she intended to stay there the rest of the day. In a tranced voice, she answered her mother's questions for a while, and then she stood up abruptly. "I must go and tell Daddy," she said.

"You might as well," said Mrs. Cross wearily.

Monica said, with sudden passion, "Mummy, promise you won't tell anybody about this. Not anybody at all." She ran out, and down the stairs.

Mr. Cross, a man of stern self-discipline, did not come up to discuss the matter with his wife. She did not expect him to do so. It was not until that afternoon, when they happened to be alone together, that he mentioned his talk with Monica, and even then he was carefully off-hand. He said, "This fellow Monica talks about—just who is he?"

It was a simple question, yet it seemed to Mrs. Cross's sensitive ear that he was accusing her. "How do *I* know?" she retorted. "She takes after you. She's secretive."

Mr. Cross did not fire up in response. He said nothing at all for a moment, and then suggested mildly that they pool the information Monica had given them. Forcing herself to be calm, Mrs. Cross agreed, but when they had compared notes, she knew no more than she had known before. The man's name was Allan, he was in his twenties, he aspired to be an architect. "Nothing about his prospects," said Mr. Cross gloomily. "You can't inquire, I suppose, of the people who introduced them? No, it wouldn't do. She swore us to secrecy."

"That's right," said Mrs. Cross.

"It's ridiculous," said her husband. "A penniless fellow. It will be years before he's in any position to support a family. Wherever did she get such notions, at her age? What's the matter with girls nowadays?"

Mrs. Cross did not remind him of Patricia. She rallied only enough to remark that the child would probably forget all about it in due course. Her husband said quietly that he doubted it.

"I've been thinking, Monica," said Mrs. Cross at breakfast several days later. "It does seem a shame for you to hang about the house for the rest of the summer. Would you like to take a little trip somewhere?"

Monica said, "Why—it's so sudden! I don't honestly know what to say." Her mother held her breath while Monica pondered aloud. "Switzerland? No, I don't really—Spain? Mummy, would you come, too?"

"If you'd like me to, I could manage. But aren't there organized tours for young people? I see them advertised in the Sunday papers. Austria seems to be a very popular place."

Monica brightened. "Yes, that sounds splendid. All those castles. Let's find out more."

They investigated. Within four days, Monica had been shipped

off for two weeks in Austria. She had always been an industrious correspondent, and a little heap of envelopes soon collected on the desk
in her room. Mr. Cross looked in the door one morning, to find his wife
eyeing the pile longingly.

"No, no," he said. "One doesn't do that."

Mrs. Cross flushed. "The thought never crossed my mind," she
said. "I was only wondering if there were any Cornish postal marks."

A day or so later, Mrs. Cross had an appointment with her den-
tist, in London. When she came home, late in the afternoon, she walked
straight into her husband's study and sat down.

"If we didn't give our consent, Monica could apply to a judge, or
a magistrate," she said abruptly.

"Been to consult somebody, have you?" Mr. Cross asked.

"Oh, I cited it as a hypothetical case," she said. "Of course, they
could always just elope to Scotland, but, darling, do we want it to come
to that?"

Her husband cleared his throat. "No," he said at last.

"That's what I thought you'd say," said Mrs. Cross. "So let's decide
now. If it does come to anything, we won't oppose it."

"We might try reasoning," Mr. Cross suggested. "Gently, you
know."

"That seldom does any good," said his wife. "Still, if you should
want to try . . ."

Monica came home early one morning, after a night crossing. She
was sunburned and happy, and did not seem especially eager to read
her letters. Both her parents pushed them at her, however, and hovered
over her while she ate an egg and read them. At length, Mrs. Cross
could not control herself any longer.

"How is he?" she asked.

Monica, deep in a letter, asked absently. "Who?"

"What do you mean, who?" her mother snapped. "Allan, naturally."

"Allan? Is there a letter from him?" Monica asked excitedly. She
began to scrabble through the envelopes. "No," she said, sounding disappointed. "But I never really thought he'd write. I'm not even sure he's
got my address."

"You don't correspond?" asked Mr. Cross.

"No," said Monica. "I'd love to, of course, but I hardly like to
write first, and he didn't ask. Look—you haven't been talking to anybody
about Allan, have you? You promised you wouldn't."

"No, darling," said Mrs. Cross.

"That's all right, then," Monica said. "I'd certainly hate for him to know I've been talking. He hasn't a clue to the way I feel."

Mrs. Cross said, "He hasn't?"

"Hardly knows I'm alive," said Monica blithely, and picked up her coffee cup and reached out again for her letters.

COMMENTARY AND QUESTIONS

In this story Emily Hahn develops a contrast between what Monica's state of mind actually is and what her parents think it is. The parents misjudge appearances, and are surprised when they discover their error.

1. The setting of the story is England, at the home of Mr. and Mrs. Cross, not too far from London. How important in the opening conversation is the fact that Mr. Cross is English but Mrs. Cross is American?

2. After Martin's departure Mrs. Cross is stunned by Patricia's lack of enthusiasm and by her explanation of why she will probably marry the young man: "One's got to get away from Mummy." How has Emily Hahn prepared for this scene? (Consider especially the scene, on pp. 613-614, just after the arrival of the young couple.)

3. Why do you think the author doesn't have Martin talk?

4. In a conversation with her mother three days after returning from Cornwall, Monica announces that she's in love with a young architect named Allan. Near the end of the conversation Mrs. Cross reminds her daughter that she felt this way about a mechanic two years before. Does the mother's way of reminding harmonize with the tone she established earlier in the conversation?

5. In the conversation between mother and father following the announcement, Mr. Cross states that Monica is too young to marry. Is there any defense for his being inconsistent with statements about marriage made at the beginning of the story?

6. Throughout the story Mrs. Cross is presented as thinking that a girl of Monica's age is too young to marry. Mr. Cross ultimately agrees, not in the abstract, but about Monica. But both father and mother come to a resigned acceptance of what they judge to be the situation, and agree, while Monica is in Austria, not to oppose the marriage. In the final scene of the story Monica reveals to her parents, and to the reader, that she *is* too young to marry. How is this indicated in the final scene? How has Emily Hahn prepared for this scene in her earlier presentation of Monica, not as her parents think she is, but as she actually is? (Consider, for example, the scene, on pp. 615-617, in which Monica tells her mother about Allan. What is Monica's first remark? How does she receive her mother's reminder of the mechanic?

How does the author describe Monica's actions at the end of this scene?)

7. The story divides itself into five sections: (1) the time before Patricia's visit; (2) the day of her visit; (3) the period following Monica's return from Cornwall; (4) the interval when Monica is in Austria; (5) the morning of her return. In what way would the story be weakened if the first and second sections were omitted?

8. Find expressions used in their conversation that identify Mr. Cross as an Englishman, Mrs. Cross as an American, and Monica as a teenager.

9. To suggest Patricia's state of mind in the conversation with Mrs. Cross, Emily Hahn picks out these physical details: "Her fingers went on examining the bowl's edge, circuit after circuit. Her head was bent over it as if she were the original potter, making the vessel" (p. 615). Find other examples of this technique.

SUGGESTION FOR WRITING

Making relevant comparisons and contrasts, analyze the parent-child relationships in "The Leader of the People," "By the Waters of Babylon," and "Too Young."

Tobermory

by SAKI (H. H. Munro)

IT WAS A CHILL, rain-washed afternoon of a late August day, that indefinite season when partridges are still in security or cold storage, and there is nothing to hunt—unless one is bounded on the north by the Bristol Channel, in which case one may lawfully gallop after fat red stags. Lady Blemley's house-party was not bounded on the north by the Bristol Channel, hence there was a full gathering of her guests round the tea-table on this particular afternoon. And, in spite of the blankness of the season and the triteness of the occasion, there was no trace in the company of that fatigued restlessness which means a dread of the pianola and a subdued hankering for auction bridge. The undisguised open-mouthed attention of the entire party was fixed on the homely negative personality of Mr. Cornelius Appin. Of all her guests, he was the one who had come to Lady Blemley with the vaguest reputation. Some one had said he was "clever," and he had got his invitation in the moderate expectation, on the part of his hostess, that some portion at least of his cleverness would be contributed to the general entertainment. Until tea-time that day she had been unable to discover in what direction, if any, his cleverness lay. He was neither a wit nor a croquet champion, a hypnotic force nor a begetter of amateur theatricals. Neither did his exterior suggest the sort of man in whom women are willing to pardon a generous measure of mental deficiency. He had subsided into mere Mr. Appin, and the Cornelius seemed a piece of transparent baptismal bluff. And now he was claiming to have launched on the world a discovery beside which the invention of gunpowder, of the printing-press, and of steam locomotion were inconsiderable trifles. Science had made bewildering strides in many directions during recent decades, but this thing seemed to belong to the domain of miracle rather than to scientific achievement.

"And do you really ask us to believe," Sir Wilfrid was saying, "that you have discovered a means for instructing animals in the art of human speech, and that dear old Tobermory has proved your first successful pupil?"

"It is a problem at which I have worked for the last seventeen years," said Mr. Appin, "but only during the last eight or nine months have I been rewarded with glimmerings of success. Of course I have experimented with thousands of animals, but latterly only with cats, those wonderful creatures which have assimilated themselves so marvellously with our civilization while retaining all their highly developed feral instincts. Here and there among cats one comes across an outstanding superior intellect, just as one does among the ruck of human beings, and when I made the acquaintance of Tobermory a week ago I saw at once that I was in contact with a 'Beyond-cat' of extraordinary intelligence. I had gone far along the road to success in recent experiments; with Tobermory, as you call him, I have reached the goal."

Mr. Appin concluded his remarkable statement in a voice which he strove to divest of a triumphant inflection. No one said "Rats," though Clovis's lips moved in a monosyllabic contortion which probably invoked those rodents of disbelief.

"And do you mean to say," asked Miss Resker, after a slight pause, "that you have taught Tobermory to say and understand easy sentences of one syllable?"

"My dear Miss Resker," said the wonder-worker patiently, "one teaches little children and savages and backward adults in that piece-meal fashion; when one has once solved the problem of making a beginning with an animal of highly developed intelligence one has no need for those halting methods. Tobermory can speak our language with perfect correctness."

This time Clovis very distinctly said, "Beyond-rats!" Sir Wilfrid was more polite, but equally sceptical.

"Hadn't we better have the cat in and judge for ourselves?" suggested Lady Blemley.

Sir Wilfrid went in search of the animal, and the company settled themselves down to the languid expectation of witnessing some more or less adroit drawing-room ventriloquism.

In a minute Sir Wilfrid was back in the room, his face white beneath its tan and his eyes dilated with excitement.

"By Gad, it's true!"

His agitation was unmistakably genuine, and his hearers started forward in a thrill of awakened interest.

Collapsing into an armchair he continued breathlessly: "I found him dozing in the smoking-room, and called out to him to come for his tea. He blinked at me in his usual way, and I said, 'Come on, Toby; don't keep us waiting'; and, by Gad! he drawled out in a most horribly natural voice that he'd come when he dashed well pleased! I nearly jumped out of my skin!"

Appin had preached to absolutely incredulous hearers; Sir Wilfrid's statement carried instant conviction. A Babel-like chorus of startled exclamation arose, amid which the scientist sat mutely enjoying the first fruit of his stupendous discovery.

In the midst of the clamour Tobermory entered the room and made his way with velvet tread and studied unconcern across to the group seated round the tea-table.

A sudden hush of awkwardness and constraint fell on the company. Somehow there seemed an element of embarrassment in addressing on equal terms a domestic cat of acknowledged mental ability.

"Will you have some milk, Tobermory?" asked Lady Blemley in a rather strained voice.

"I don't mind if I do," was the response, couched in a tone of even indifference. A shiver of suppressed excitement went through the listeners, and Lady Blemley might be excused for pouring out the saucerful of milk rather unsteadily.

"I'm afraid I've spilt a good deal of it," she said apologetically.

"After all, it's not my Axminster," was Tobermory's rejoinder.

Another silence fell on the group, and then Miss Resker, in her best district-visitor manner, asked if the human language had been difficult to learn. Tobermory looked squarely at her for a moment and then fixed his gaze serenely on the middle distance. It was obvious that boring questions lay outside his scheme of life.

"What do you think of human intelligence?" asked Mavis Pellington lamely.

"Of whose intelligence in particular?" asked Tobermory coldly.

"Oh, well, mine for instance," said Mavis, with a feeble laugh.

"You put me in an embarrassing position," said Tobermory, whose tone and attitude certainly did not suggest a shred of embarrassment. "When your inclusion in this house-party was suggested Sir Wilfrid protested that you were the most brainless woman of his acquaintance, and that there was a wide distinction between hospitality and the care of the feeble-minded. Lady Blemley replied that your lack of brain-power was the precise quality which had earned you your invitation, as you were the only person she could think of who might be idiotic enough to buy their old car. You know, the one they call 'The Envy of Sisyphus,' because it goes quite nicely up-hill if you push it."

Lady Blemley's protestations would have had greater effect if she had not casually suggested to Mavis only that morning that the car in question would be just the thing for her down at her Devonshire home.

Major Barfield plunged in heavily to effect a diversion.

"'How about your carryings-on with the tortoise-shell puss up at the stables, eh?"

The moment he had said it every one realized the blunder.

"One does not usually discuss these matters in public," said Tobermory frigidly. "From a slight observation of your ways since you've been in this house I should imagine you'd find it inconvenient if I were to shift the conversation on to your own little affairs."

The panic which ensued was not confined to the Major.

"Would you like to go and see if cook has got your dinner ready?" suggested Lady Blemley hurriedly, affecting to ignore the fact that it wanted at least two hours to Tobermory's dinner-time.

"Thanks," said Tobermory, "not quite so soon after my tea. I don't want to die of indigestion."

"Cats have nine lives, you know," said Sir Wilfrid heartily.

"Possibly," answered Tobermory; "but only one liver."

"Adelaide!" said Mrs. Cornett, "do you mean to encourage that cat to go out and gossip about us in the servants' hall?"

The panic had indeed become general. A narrow ornamental balustrade ran in front of most of the bedroom windows at the Towers, and it was recalled with dismay that this had formed a favourite promenade for Tobermory at all hours, whence he could watch the pigeons—and heaven knew what else besides. If he intended to become reminiscent in his present outspoken strain the effect would be something more than disconcerting. Mrs. Cornett, who spent much time at her toilet table, and whose complexion was reputed to be of a nomadic though punctual disposition, looked as ill at ease as the Major. Miss Scrawen, who wrote fiercely sensuous poetry and led a blameless life, merely displayed irritation; if you are methodical and virtuous in private you don't necessarily want every one to know it. Bertie van Tahn, who was so depraved at seventeen that he had long ago given up trying to be any worse, turned a dull shade of gardenia white, but he did not commit the error of dashing out of the room like Odo Finsberry, a young gentleman who was understood to be reading for the Church and who was possibly disturbed at the thought of scandals he might hear concerning other people. Clovis had the presence of mind to maintain a composed exterior; privately he was calculating how long it would take to procure a box of fancy mice through the agency of the *Exchange and Mart* as a species of hush-money.

Even in a delicate situation like the present, Agnes Resker could not endure to remain too long in the background.

"Why did I ever come down here?" she asked dramatically.

Tobermory immediately accepted the opening.

"Judging by what you said to Mrs. Cornett on the croquet-lawn yesterday, you were out for food. You described the Blemleys as the dullest people to stay with that you knew, but said they were clever enough to employ a first-rate cook; otherwise, they'd find it difficult to get anyone to come down a second time."

"There's not a word of truth in it! I appeal to Mrs. Cornett—" exclaimed the discomfited Agnes.

"Mrs. Cornett repeated your remark afterwards to Bertie van Tahn," continued Tobermory, "and said, 'That woman is a regular Hunger Marcher; she'd go anywhere for four square meals a day,' and Bertie van Tahn said—"

At this point the chronicle mercifully ceased. Tobermory had caught a glimpse of the big yellow Tom from the Rectory working his way through the shrubbery towards the stable wing. In a flash he had vanished through the open French window.

With the disappearance of his too brilliant pupil Cornelius Appin found himself beset by a hurricane of bitter upbraiding, anxious inquiry, and frightened entreaty. The responsibility for the situation lay with him, and he must prevent matters from becoming worse. Could Tobermory impart his dangerous gift to other cats? was the first question he had to answer. It was possible, he replied, that he might have initiated his intimate friend the stable puss into his new accomplishment, but it was unlikely that his teaching could have taken a wider range as yet.

"Then," said Mrs. Cornett, "Tobermorry may be a valuable cat and a great pet; but I'm sure you'll agree, Adelaide, that both he and the stable cat must be done away with without delay."

"You don't suppose I've enjoyed the last quarter of an hour, do you?" said Lady Blemley bitterly. "My husband and I are very fond of Tobermory—at least, we were before this horrible accomplishment was infused into him; but now, of course, the only thing is to have him destroyed as soon as possible."

"We can put some strychnine in the scraps he always gets at dinner-time," said Sir Wilfrid, "and I will go and drown the stable cat myself. The coachman will be very sore at losing his pet, but I'll say a very catching form of mange has broken out in both cats and we're afraid of it spreading to the kennels."

"But my great discovery!" expostulated Mr. Appin; "after all my years of research and experiment—"

"You can go and experiment on the short-horns at the farm, who are under proper control," said Mrs. Cornett, "or the elephants at the Zoological Gardens. They're said to be highly intelligent, and they have this recommendation, that they don't come creeping about our bedrooms and under chairs, and so forth."

An archangel ecstatically proclaiming the Millennium, and then finding that it clashed unpardonably with Henley and would have to be indefinitely postponed, could hardly have felt more crestfallen than Cornelius Appin at the reception of his wonderful achievement. Public opinion, however, was against him—in fact, had the general voice been consulted on the subject it is probable that a strong minority vote would have been in favour of including him in the strychnine diet.

Defective train arrangements and a nervous desire to see matters brought to a finish prevented an immediate dispersal of the party, but dinner that evening was not a social success. Sir Wilfrid had had rather a trying time with the stable cat and subsequently with the coachman. Agnes Resker ostentatiously limited her repast to a morsel of dry toast, which she bit as though it were a personal enemy; while Mavis Pellington maintained a vindictive silence throughout the meal. Lady Blemley kept up a flow of what she hoped was conversation, but her attention was fixed on the doorway. A plateful of carefully dosed fish scraps was in readiness on the sideboard, but sweets and savoury and dessert went their way, and no Tobermory appeared either in the dining-room or kitchen.

The sepulchral dinner was cheerful compared with the subsequent vigil in the smoking-room. Eating and drinking had at least supplied a distraction and cloak to the prevailing embarrassment. Bridge was out of the question in the general tension of nerves and tempers, and after Odo Finsberry had given a lugubrious rendering of "Mélisande in the Wood" to a frigid audience, music was tacitly avoided. At eleven the servants went to bed, announcing that the small window in the pantry had been left open as usual for Tobermory's private use. The guests read steadily through the current batch of magazines, and fell back gradually on the "Badminton Library" and bound volumes of *Punch*. Lady Blemley made periodic visits to the pantry, returning each time with an expression of listless depression which forestalled questioning.

At two o'clock Clovis broke the dominating silence.

"He won't turn up tonight. He's probably in the local newspaper office at the present moment, dictating the first instalment of his reminiscences. Lady What's-her-name's book won't be in it. It will be the event of the day."

Having made this contribution to the general cheerfulness, Clovis went to bed. At long intervals the various members of the house-party followed his example.

The servants taking round the early tea made a uniform announcement in reply to a uniform question. Tobermory had not returned.

Breakfast was, if anything, a more unpleasant function than dinner had been, but before its conclusion the situation was relieved. Tobermory's corpse was brought in from the shrubbery, where a gardener had just discovered it. From the bites on his throat and the yellow fur which coated his claws it was evident that he had fallen in unequal combat with the big Tom from the Rectory.

By midday most of the guests had quitted the Towers, and after lunch Lady Blemley had sufficiently recovered her spirits to write an extremely nasty letter to the Rectory about the loss of her valuable pet.

Tobermory had been Appin's one successful pupil, and he was destined to have no successor. A few weeks later an elephant in the Dresden Zoological Garden, which had shown no previous signs of irritability, broke loose and killed an Englishman who had apparently been teasing it. The victim's name was variously reported in the papers as Oppin and Eppelin, but his front name was faithfully rendered Cornelius.

"If he was trying German irregular verbs on the poor beast," said Clovis, "he deserved all he got."

COMMENTARY AND QUESTIONS

1. Does this story have a central character?
2. Could the last two paragraphs be omitted without changing the emphasis of the story?
3. As Tobermory offers information in response to comments and questions, almost every character in the story becomes aware that he has something to hide. How does Saki want you to consider the faults, both revealed and hidden—as social blunders or primarily as moral aberrations? Consider the characters individually before you generalize an answer.
4. Explain the following allusions: "the Cornelius seemed a piece of transparent baptismal bluff" (p. 621); "Babel-like chorus" (p. 622); "'The Envy of Sisyphus'" (p. 623).
5. If the statement (p. 626) that "after lunch Lady Blemley had sufficiently recovered her spirits to write an extremely nasty letter to the Rectory about the loss of her valuable pet" is an example of irony of character or situation, explain that kind of irony as distinguished from irony as a figure of speech.

SUGGESTIONS FOR WRITING

1. In defense of Cornelius Appin, scientist.
2. Strychnine for Tobermory and his teacher.
3. If Tobermory knew my friends.

The Unspoiled Reaction

by MARY McCARTHY

IN THE THEATER LOBBY everyone at first mistook her for another patron (a grandmother, perhaps), though the fact that she wore an unstylish closefitting hat, antique earrings, and no coat and had a generally anxious, false, and flustered air should have announced her status: she was a hostess, or, rather, one of those *entrepreneuses* masquerading as hostesses who are inevitably associated with benefits, club luncheons, lectures, alumnae teas, with all gatherings whose intention is not primarily pleasure.

Here, in the theater, on a rainy Monday morning, she was an anomaly, for in New York, in the Times Square neighborhood, relations between management and customer are, by common consent, austerely professional. Consequently her intervention at the door came as a perceptible shock to each parent and child; it demanded a slight adjustment of focus. "Haven't we seen you before?" She addressed the child, and the face that turned up to her in each case showed bewilderment and pleasure. Only a moment before, the child had been an anonymous consumer bent on mass gratification; this magic question turned him back into his human self, and the child, unless he were totally hardened, blushed.

"What is your name?" the lady continued, and now even the parent was drawn in and smiled tenderly, sharing for an instant with this unknown but plainly intuitive person the holy miracle of his child's identity. Sometimes the children answered, speaking their own names softly, with reverence; more often, shyness and delight held them tongue-tied, and the parent supplied the information. "It's for Sunny," the lady added, in a sort of whispered nudge at the parent, who came to himself with a start. The explanation, if it told him nothing else (who or what was Sunny, anyway?), told him unmistakably that he had been a fool just now—he ought to have suspected the utilitarian motive. Angry and disillusioned, he passed into the poorly lit auditorium, the remnants of the smile, the fond, fatuous smile, still tugging at the corners of his mouth.

But at once the sight of so many empty places (hardly twenty persons were seated in a cluster down in front) brought a sentiment of pity for the woman outside. Clearly, these puppeteers were in a bad way; not even the rain, not even Monday, not even the too high price of admission, could explain or palliate the smallness of the house. An air of failure hung over the whole undertaking, infecting the audience itself with the poison of financial sickness, so that even the most healthy, the most fortunate parents and children, sitting there in little groups in the bad light, with the dismal smell of damp wool and dead cigarettes all about them, had the look of derelicts huddled together.

So strong indeed was the sense of misery that the more sensitive parents felt an impulse to remove their children from this house of death and were only prevented by the practical difficulties (how to explain?) and by the habit of chivalry toward the poor and ill-favored. If the rat does *not* leave the sinking ship, his only recourse is to identify himself with its fortunes; so the parents, having committed themselves to this unhappy enterprise, immediately experienced the symptoms of solidarity. They began to tell themselves that the attendance could have been worse (after all, it *was* Monday and it *was* raining), to clock off each new arrival with a feeling of personal triumph, and finally to lean forward in their seats and will people into the theater as passengers in a decrepit car lean forward to will the car up a long grade.

These exercises in kinesthetic magic, in which, from their clenched fists and closed eyes, one would say nearly the whole audience was engaging, were cut short by another woman, younger and more openly managerial than the first, a progressive school teacher in genus if not in actuality, one accustomed to giving orders in the form of requests. "Will you please take an outside seat?" she said, leaning over and tapping surprised parents on the shoulder.

Some mothers and fathers did as they were bid at once, almost apologetically. Others were slow and showed even a certain disposition to stand on their rights. Still others (the most well-fed and polished) pretended not to hear. "This does not apply to me," their deaf backs declared.

When it became plain that she was not going to be obeyed without further explanation (for her little air of authority had stirred up latent antagonism in an audience which had disposed itself to pity but not to be ruled by her), she walked down an empty row and took hold of the back of a seat, in the manner of an informal lecturer. "We like to have the children together in the middle," she announced with that excess of patience that suggests that patience is really out of place. "These puppet plays are intended for *children*. We want to reach the children as a group. We want them to be free of adult influences. We want an unspoiled reaction."

This fetched even the most stubborn, for it hinted to every adult in the audience that he was the snake in this paradise of innocence, that there was something intrinsically disgusting in the condition of being grown-up. There was a great shuffling of coats, hats, and handbags. Mothers dropped packages on the floor, a little girl cried, but at length the resettlement was accomplished, and the sheep were separated from the goats.

Whenever a new party came in, the earlier arrivals would, out of a kind of concerted malice, allow the parent to get herself well lodged in the center block of seats before breaking it to her that she was out of place. Indeed, the greater part of the audience was disinclined to make the revelation at all; its original feelings of mistrust had returned; it saw something ugly in this arbitrary manipulation of the natural order of seating, this planned spontaneity. Though it looked forward to the confounding of the newcomer, it would not take the side of the management; in an attitude of passive hooliganism it waited for the dark.

But disaffected as it was, the audience contained the inevitable minority of enthusiastic coöperators who rejoice in obeying with ostentatious promptness any command whatsoever, who worship all signs, prohibitions, warnings, and who constitute themselves volunteer deputies of any official person they can find in their neighborhood. These coöperators nudged, tapped, poked, signaled, relayed admonitory whispers along rows of children, until every misplaced adult became conscious of the impropriety of his position and retreated, in confusion, to the perimeter of the house. By the time the curtain went up, the adults formed three sides of a box which contained the children but left the cover open to receive the influences of the stage.

II

Almost at once the object of the first lady's question became apparent. Laboriously, the curtains of the miniature stage parted and an unusually small puppet, dressed as a boy, was revealed, bowing and dancing in a veritable tantrum of welcome. This was Sunny. "Hello, boys and girls," he began in the shrieky voice that is considered *de rigueur* for puppets and marionettes. "Welcome to our theater." "Hello, Sunny," replied a self-assured child, patently the son of one of the coöperators. He had been here before, and he did what was expected of him. "Hello, John, how are you today?" the puppet screamed in answer, and now he passed from child to child, speaking to each by name.

The children, for the most part, looked at each other in wonder and astonishment. They were at a loss to account for the puppet's knowing them; they did not relate cause and effect and doubtless had already forgotten the question and answer in the lobby. After the first consternation, the voices that answered the gesticulating creature grew louder and firmer. The children were participating. Each one was anxious to show himself more at home than his neighbor, and soon they were treating the puppet with positive familiarity, which he encouraged, greeting every bold remark from the audience with peals of shrill artificial laughter. Before the actual play began he had drawn all but the very youngest and shyest into an atmosphere of audacity.

Along the sides of the human box, the parents were breathing easier. Gladly they divested themselves of their original doubts. It was enough that the children were entering into the spirit of the thing. That reciprocity between player and audience, lost to us since the medieval mysteries, and mourned by every theoretician of the drama, was here re-covered, and what did it matter if the production was a mockery, a car-toon of the art of drama? What did it matter that the children's innocence had been taken advantage of, that the puppet who seemed to know them knew only their names? And as for the seating arrangements, perhaps in the modern world all spontaneity had to be planned; as with crop control and sex, the "unspoiled reaction" did not come of itself; it was the end-product of a series of maneuvers.

The curtains closed on Sunny, with the children yelling, "Good-bye." The main attraction, "Little Red Riding Hood," was about to begin, when a party of late-comers made its way down the aisle. There were eight or ten children and a dispirited-looking young teacher. They took places in the very first row and were a little slow getting seated. The children kept changing places, and the teacher was either ineffectual or a principled anti-disciplinarian, for she made no real effort to interpose her authority.

The curtains on the stage above them moved, as if with impatience, and a human hand and then a face, grotesquely enlarged to eyes ad-justed to the scale of puppets, appeared and then quickly withdrew. This apparition was terrifying to everyone but those for whom it was in-tended, the school children in front, who had as yet no standard of com-parison and continued their bickering unperturbed. The face had come and gone so abruptly that nobody could be sure whether it belonged to a man or a woman; it left the audience with a mere sense of some disem-bodied anger—a deity was displeased. Could this be Sunny? the parents wondered.

At length, the party in the front row composed itself. Little Red Riding Hood and her basket were revealed as the curtains lurched back. To the left of the puppet stage, a little box opened, and there was Sunny, ready with a prologue, adjuring the children to watch out for Little Red Riding Hood as if she were their own little sister. The box closed, the action began, and the children took Sunny at his word. From the house a series of warnings and prophecies of disaster followed the little red puppet out its door. "Look out," the children called. "Don't obey your Mummy." "Eat the basket yourself."

In all these admonitions none were louder than the party in the front row. These children, indeed, appeared to be the ideal audience for Sunny and his troupe; they were the unspoiled reaction in test-tube pur-ity. While other boys and girls hung back, murmured their comments, or simply parroted the cries of the bolder children, the ones down in front were inventive and various in their advice—so much so that it seemed hardly possible that the play could go on without the actors' taking cognizance of what these untrammeled children were saying, and one almost expected Little Red Riding Hood to sail off from her lines into pure improvisation, and a kind of *commedia dell' arte* to ensue. But the puppets kept rigidly to the text, oblivious of interruptions and suggestions, and the usual situation was reversed—it was not the audience which was unresponsive but the players.

By the middle of the second scene, when the wolf had made his appearance, the whole theater was in a condition of wild excitement. Some children were taking the side of the wolf, urging him to make a good dinner, and some, traditionalists even in unrestraint, remained loyal to the grandmother. The contest on the stage was transported into the pit.

III

At the end of the second scene, Sunny came out once more, and now the boldness of the children perfectly matched the provocations of the puppet. Saucy answer met impudent question. Sunny was beside himself; from time to time, a witticism from the house would capsize him altogether and he would lie panting on the stage, gasping out the last exhausted notes of the hee-hee-hee. Liberty and equality reached such a pitch of frenzy that it seemed the most natural thing in the world that a boy from the front row should climb up onto the stage to speak directly to Sunny.

The audience watched him go without the slightest sense of a breach of decorum. The puppet, however, drew back into his box at the approach of the child. Slowly, his cloth body began to wriggle and twist in any uncanny pantomime of distaste and fear. The child put out his hand to touch the puppet, and now the doll was indubitably alive. A shudder ran through it; it shrank back against the curtains and doubled itself up, as though to leave no intimate surface exposed to the violator's touch.

As the hand still pursued and it seemed as if no power on earth could prevent the approaching indignity, the puppet cried out. But its voice had changed; the falsetto shriek had become a human scream. "Sunny doesn't like that," called an agonized woman's voice from behind the curtain. The note of hysteria struck home to the boy, separating him from his intention. He leaped back, stumbled toward the stairs, slipped on them, and fell into the orchestra pit. Two of the fathers rushed forward. The teacher joined them, peering anxiously over the brink. The child was retrieved, unhurt, and firmly put back into his seat. In the commotion, Sunny had disappeared.

Fortunately, the children hardly missed him. For the moment, they were more interested in the mechanics of the little boy's fall than in its cause. "What is an orchestra pit?" they called out to the mothers who had tried to explain, and some got out of their seats, proposing to investigate. "Afterwards, afterwards," the mothers' voices ordered. "The show is going to begin again."

But was it? The parents, glancing at each other, wondered. Had they not witnessed, just now, one of those ruptures which are instantly and irrevocably permanent, since they reveal an aversion so profound that no beginning, i.e., no cause can be assigned to it, and hence no end, no solution can be predicted? Like guests sitting around a dinner table which the hostess has just quitted to pack her trunk in a fury, the parents fidgeted, waiting for a sign which would tell them that it was not really necessary to go home to meet again the emptiness of their own devices, yet knowing perfectly well that the only thing to do was to go and go at once, before anything else happened. But inertia, the great minimizer, provided them with the usual excuses. They told themselves that they were letting their imaginations run away with them, that nothing of any consequence had happened—an incompetent teacher had let her charge misbehave.

And as the minutes passed and the curtains did not move, the sentiment of the audience turned sharply against the teacher. "Damn fool of a woman," murmured the father of a boy to the pretty mother of a girl. "I certainly wouldn't send a child to *her* school," replied the mother, brightening up. As if aware of the whispers of criticism, the teacher stiffened in her seat and stared blindly forward, feigning unconsciousness.

In the middle of the house, the children were also turning the experience over, clumsily trying to fix the blame, but they were not so adroit, so practiced as their parents, and small frowns of dissatisfaction wrinkled their brows. "Was that little boy naughty?" called a little girl's voice, at last. "Yes," answered her mother, without a moment's hesitation. "Oh," said the little girl, but her look remained troubled.

"And *now*, boys and girls—" It was Sunny, cordial as ever, and the third scene was about to start. There was no doubt that the puppet was himself again; he bowed, he clapped his hands, he danced, he screeched, in his old dionysiac style. Bygones were bygones, all was forgiven, childhood was off on another spree.

Yet the children at first were wary and glanced toward their parents, seeking instruction, for they no longer knew what was expected of them. The parents nodded encouragement, and as the children still hesitated, the adults screwed their own faces into grimaces of pleasure, till everywhere the children looked, on the sides of the audience or, above them, on the stage, there was a large, energetic smile bidding them enjoy themselves. The more docile children began to laugh, rather mechanically; others joined in, and in a few moments the crisis was past and the mood of abandon tentatively reestablished. The play proceeded, and before long the children were barking and howling like wolves, the timid little girl was whimpering with terror, and the parents were quietly rejoicing in the fact that another morning had been got through without serious damage to the children or emotional cost to themselves.

The last scruple died as Little Red Riding Hood was rescued and the play came safely to an end. The curtains closed, but the children were not quite disposed to go. They remained clapping and shouting in their seats, while their parents gathered up hats and coats.

At this moment, when all danger seemed past and former fears groundless and even morbid, the same little boy in the front row jumped up and asked his teacher a question. "Yes," she said, in a voice that penetrated the whole auditorium, "I think it will be all right for you to go backstage now."

Something in the teacher's tone arrested everyone; even those parents who had succeeded in getting their children halfway up the aisle now paused to watch as the party in the front row made a little procession up the stairs. The drama was not quite over; a reconciliation must follow between the puppet and the child; the child must handle the puppet, but ceremoniously, backstage, and with the puppet's permission.

Indulgently, the audience waited. The little procession reached the stage. Other children, emboldened, were starting down the aisle after it, when the curtains parted. There, her white hair disheveled, her well-bred features working with rage, stood the woman everyone had met in the lobby and who was now instantly identifiable as the apparition of anger, the face between the curtains. "Get out, get out of here, get out." She barred the way of the approaching group. "You dreadful, horrible children."

The voice, screaming, was familiar too; it was, of course, Sunny's. "You horrible, horrible children," she repeated, her *r*'s trilling out in a kind of reflex of gentility. The children turned and ran, and she pursued them to the stairs, a trembling figure of terrible malevolence, in whom could be discerned, as in a triple exposure, traces of the gracious hostess and the frolicsome puppet.

From behind the curtains came someone to seize her. A man from the box office ran down the aisle to pacify the teacher, who, now seeing herself on firm ground, was repeating over and over again, "That is no way to talk to a child." The audience did not wait to see the outcome. In shame and silence, it fled out into the rain, pursued by the sound of weeping which intermingled with the word *child*, as pronounced by the teacher in a tone of peculiar piety and reverence, her voice genuflecting to it as though to the Host.

COMMENTARY AND QUESTIONS

1. This story is unlike any of the others preceding it. In "Tobermory" there is an obvious and immediate problem to be solved: getting rid of Tobermory. The attitude of Lady Blemley's group toward Cornelius Appin is not hard to determine. What do you think the author's purpose is in "The Unspoiled Reaction"? In seeking an answer to this question you may find it helpful to do two things: (a) trace the attitude toward the puppeteers, as it is stated or implied throughout the story, which is held by each of these—the parents, the children, the teacher; (b) trace the attitude toward children, as it is stated or implied throughout the story, which is held by each of these—the puppeteers, the teacher, the parents.
2. What is the significance of the title for each of these—the children, Sunny, Sunny's puppeteer, the teacher, the parents?
3. About how many of the characters are you given sufficient information for you to visualize them as individuals, each with a distinctive physical appearance? Just how important is physical appearance in this story?
4. Do you think the author should have, or could have, used more conversation?
5. Do the following expressions fit into the atmosphere of the story: *entrepreneuses* (p. 627); *de rigueur* (p. 630); *commedia dell' arte* (p. 632)?

SUGGESTION FOR WRITING

Suppose you were a newspaper reporter or an editorial writer who happened to drop in at the theater of the puppeteers on the particular day of this story. Write either a factual account of what happened or an editorial based on what you saw.

The Golden Age

by JOHN CHEEVER

OUR IDEAS OF CASTLES, formed in childhood, are inflexible, and why try to reform them? Why point out that in a real castle thistles grow in the courtyard, and the threshold of the ruined throne room is guarded by a nest of green adders? Here are the keep, the drawbridge, the battlements and towers that we took with our lead soldiers when we were down with the chicken pox. The first castle was English, and this one was built by the king of Spain during an occupation of Tuscany, but the sense of imaginative supremacy—the heightened mystery of nobility—is the same. Nothing is inconsequential here. It is thrilling to drink Martinis on the battlements, it is thrilling to bathe in the fountain, it is even thrilling to climb down the stairs into the village after supper and buy a box of matches. The drawbridge is down, the double doors are open, and early one morning we see a family crossing the moat, carrying the paraphernalia of a picnic.

They are Americans. Nothing they can do will quite conceal the touching ridiculousness, the clumsiness of the traveler. The father is a tall young man, a little stooped, with curly hair and fine white teeth. His wife is pretty, and they have two sons. Both boys are armed with plastic machine guns, which were recently mailed to them by their grandparents. It is Sunday, bells are ringing, and who ever brought the bells into Italy? Not the *vaca* in Florence but the harsh country bells that bing and bang over the olive groves and the cypress alleys in such an alien discord that they might have come in the carts of Attila the Hun. This urgent jangling sounds over the last of the antique fishing villages—really one of the last things of its kind. The stairs of the castle wind down into a place that is lovely and remote. There are no bus or train connections to this place, no *pensions* or hotels, no art schools, no tourists or souvenirs; there is not even a post card for sale. The natives wear picturesque costumes, sing at their work, and haul up Greek vases in their fishing nets. It is one of the last places in the world where you can hear shepherds' pipes, where beautiful girls with loose bodices go unphotographed as they carry baskets of fish on their heads, and where serenades are sung after dark. Down the stairs come the Americans into the village.

The women in black, on their way to church, nod and wish them good morning. "*Il poeta*," they say, to each other. Good morning to the poet, the wife of the poet, and the poet's sons. Their courtesy seems to embarrass the stranger. "Why do they call you a poet?" his older son asks, but Father doesn't reply. In the piazza there is some evidence of the fact that the village is not quite perfect. What has been kept out by its rough roads has come in on the air. The village boys roosting around the fountain have their straw hats canted over their foreheads, and match-sticks in their teeth, and when they walk they swagger as if they had been born in a saddle, although there is not a saddle horse in the place. The blue-green beam of the television set in the café has begun to trans-form them from sailors into cowboys, from fishermen into gangsters, from shepherds into juvenile delinquents and masters of ceremonies, their bladders awash with Coca-Cola, and this seems very sad to the Amer-icans. *E colpa mia,* thinks Seton, the so-called poet, as he leads his family through the piazza to the quays where their rowboat is moored.

The harbor is as round as a soup plate, the opening lies between two cliffs, and on the outermost, the seaward cliff, stands the castle, with its round towers, that the Setons have rented for the summer. Regarding the nearly perfect scene, Seton throws out his arms and exclaims, "Jesus, what a *spot!*" He raises an umbrella at the stern of the rowboat for his wife, and quarrels with the boys about where they will sit. "You sit where I tell you to sit, Tommy!" he shouts. "And I don't want to hear another word *out* of you." The boys grumble, and there is a burst of machine-gun fire. They put out to sea in a loud but not an angry uproar. The bells are silent now, and they can hear the wheezing of the old church organ, its lungs rotted with sea fog. The inshore water is tepid and extraordi-narily dirty, but out past the mole the water is so clear, so finely colored that it seems like a lighter element, and when Seton glimpses the shadow of their hull, drawn over the sand and rocks ten fathoms down, it seems that they float on blue air.

There are thongs for oarlocks, and Seton rows by standing in the waist and putting his weight against the oars. He thinks that he is quite adroit at this—even picturesque—but he would never, even at a great distance, be taken for an Italian. Indeed, there is an air of criminality, of shame about the poor man. The illusion of levitation, the charming tran-quillity of the day—crenelated towers against that blueness of sky that seems to be a piece of our consciousness—are not enough to expunge his sense of guilt but only to hold it in suspense. He is a fraud, an imposter, an aesthetic criminal, and, sensing his feelings, his wife says gently, "Don't worry, darling, no one will know, and if they do know, they won't care." He is worried because he is not a poet, and because this perfect day is, in a sense, his day of reckoning. He is not a poet at all, and only hoped to be better understood in Italy if he introduced himself as one. It is a harmless imposture—really an aspiration. He is in Italy only because he wants to lead a more illustrious life, to at least broaden his powers of reflection. He has even thought of writing a poem—something about good and evil.

There are many other boats on the water, rounding the cliff. All the idlers and beach boys are out, bumping gunwales, pinching their girls, and loudly singing phrases of *canzone*. They all salute *il poeta*. Around the cliff the shore is steep, terraced for vineyards, and packed with wild rosemary, and here the sea has beaten into the shore a chain of sandy coves. Seton heads for the largest of these, and his sons dive off the boat as he approaches the beach. He lands, and unloads the umbrella and the other gear.

Everyone speaks to them, everyone waves, and everyone in the village but the few churchgoers is on the beach. The Setons are the only strangers. The sand is a dark-golden color, and the sea shines like the curve of a rainbow—emerald, malachite, sapphire, and indigo. The striking absence of vulgarity and censoriousness in the scene moves Seton so that his chest seems to fill up with some fluid of appreciation. This is simplicity, he thinks, this is beauty, this is the raw grace of human nature! He swims in the fresh and buoyant water, and when he has finished swimming he stretches out in the sun. But now he seems restless, as if he were troubled once more about the fact that he is not a poet. And if he is not a poet, then what is he?

He is a television writer. Lying on the sand of the cove, below the castle, is the form of a television writer. His crime is that he is the author of an odious situation comedy called "The Best Family." When it was revealed to him that in dealing with mediocrity he was dealing not with flesh and blood but with whole principalities and kingdoms of wrongdoing, he threw up his job and fled to Italy. But now "The Best Family" has been leased by Italian television—it is called "La Famiglia Tosta" over here—and the asininities he has written will ascend to the towers of Siena, will be heard in the ancient streets of Florence, and will drift out of the lobby of the Gritti Palace onto the Grand Canal. This Sunday is his début, and his sons, who are proud of him, have spread the word in the village. *Poeta!*

His sons have begun to skirmish with their machine guns. It is a harrowing reminder of his past. The taint of television is on their innocent shoulders. While the children of the village sing, dance, and gather wild flowers, his own sons advance from rock to rock, pretending to kill. It is a mistake, and a trivial one, but it flusters him, although he cannot bring himself to call them to him and try to explain that their adroitness at imitating the cries and the postures of the dying may deepen an international misunderstanding. They are misunderstood, and he can see the women wagging their heads at the thought of a country so barbarous that even little children are given guns as playthings. *Mamma mia!* One has seen it all in the movies. One would not dare walk on the streets of New York because of gang warfare, and once you step out of New York you are in a wilderness, full of naked savages.

The battle ends, they go swimming again, and Seton, who has brought along some spearfishing gear, for an hour explores a rocky ledge that sinks off the tip of the cove. He dives, and swims through a school of transparent fish, and farther down, where the water is dark and cold, he sees a large octopus eye him wickedly, gather up its members, and slip into a cave paved with white flowers. There at the edge of the cave he sees a Greek vase, an amphora. He dives for it, feels the rough clay on his fingers, and goes up for air. He dives again and again, and finally brings the vase triumphantly into the light. It is a plump form with a narrow neck and two small handles. The neck is looped with a scarf of darker clay. It is broken nearly in two. Such vases, and vases much finer, are often found along that coast, and if they are of no value they stand on the shelves of the café, the bakery, and the barbershop, but the value of this one to Seton is inestimable—as if the fact that a television writer could reach into the Mediterranean and bring up a Greek vase were a hopeful cultural omen, proof of his own worthiness. He celebrates his find by drinking some wine, and then it is time to eat. He polishes off the bottle of wine with his lunch, and then, like everyone else on the beach, lies down in the shade and goes to sleep.

Just after Seton had waked and refreshed himself with a swim, he saw the strangers coming around the point in a boat—a Roman family, Seton guessed, who had come up to Tarlonia for the weekend. There were a father, a mother, and a son. Father fumbled clumsily with the oars. The pallor of all three of them, and their attitudes, set them apart from the people of the village. It was as if they had approached the cove from another continent. As they came nearer, the woman could be heard asking her husband to bring the boat up on the beach.

The father's replies were short-tempered and very loud. His patience was exhausted. It was not easy to row a boat, he said. It was not as easy as it looked. It was not easy to land in strange coves where, if a wind came up, the boat could be dashed to pieces and he would have to buy the owner a new boat. Boats were expensive. This tirade seemed to embarrass the mother and tire the son. They were both dressed for bathing and the father was not, and, in his white shirt, he seemed to fit that much less into the halcyon scene. The purple sea and the graceful swimmers only deepened his exasperation, and, red-faced with worry and discomfort, he called out excited and needless warnings to the swimmers, fired questions at the people on the shore (How deep was the water? How safe was the cove?), and finally brought his boat in safely. During this loud performance, the boy smiled slyly at his mother and she smiled slyly back. They had put up with this for so many years! Would it never end? Fuming and grunting, the father dropped anchor in two feet of water, and the mother and the son slipped over the gunwales and swam away.

Seton watched the father, who took a copy of *Il Tempo* out of his pocket and began to read, but the light was too bright. Then he felt anxiously in his pockets to see if the house keys and the car keys had taken wing and flown away. After this, he scraped a little bilge out of the boat with a can. Then he examined the worn oar thongs, looked at his watch, tested the anchor, looked at his watch again, and examined the sky, where there was a single cloud, for signs of a tempest. Finally, he sat down and lit a cigarette, and his worries, flying in from all points of the compass, could be seen to arrive on his brow. They had left the hot-water heater on in Rome! His apartment and all his valuables were perhaps at that very moment being destroyed by the explosion. The left front tire on the car was thin and had probably gone flat, if the car itself had not been stolen by the brigands that you found in these remote fishing villages. The cloud in the west was small, to be sure, but it was the kind of cloud that heralded bad weather, and they would be tossed mercilessly by the high waves on their way back around the point, and would reach the *pensione* (where they had already paid for dinner) after all the best cutlets had been eaten and the wine had been drunk. For all he knew, the president might have been assassinated in his absence, the lira devalued. The government might have fallen. He suddenly got to his feet and began to roar at his wife and son. It was time to go, it was time to go. Night was falling. A storm was coming. They would be late for dinner. They would get caught in the heavy traffic near Fregene. They would miss all the good television programs. . . .

His wife and his son turned and swam back toward the boat, but they took their time. It was not late, they knew. Night was not falling, and there was no sign of a storm. They would not miss dinner at the *pensione*. They knew from experience that they would reach the *pensione* long before the tables were set, but they had no choice. They climbed

aboard while the father weighed anchor, shouted warnings to the swimmers, and asked advice from the shore. He finally got the boat into the
bay, and started around the point.

They had just disappeared when one of the beach boys climbed to
the highest rock and waved a red shirt, shouting, *"Pesce cane! Pesce
cane!"* All the swimmers turned, howling with excitement and kicking up
a heavy surf, and swam for the shore. Over the bar where they had been
one could see the fin of a shark. The alarm had been given in time, and
the shark seemed surly as he cruised through the malachite-colored
water. The bathers lined the shore, pointing out the menace to one another, and a little child stood in the shallows shouting, *"Brutto! Brutto!
Brutto!"* Then everyone cheered as down the path came Mario, the best
swimmer in the village, carrying a long spear gun. Mario worked as a
stonemason, and for some reason—perhaps his industriousness—had
never fitted into the scene. His legs were too long or too far apart, his
shoulders were too round or too square, his hair was too thin, and that
luxuriance of the flesh that had been dealt out so generously to the other
bucks had bypassed poor Mario. His nakedness seemed piteous and
touching, like a stranger surprised in some intimacy. He was cheered and
complimented as he came through the crowd, but he could not even muster a nervous smile, and, setting his thin lips, he strode into the water and
swam to the bar. But the shark had gone, and so had most of the sunlight.
The disenchantment of a dark beach moved the bathers to gather their
things and start for home. No one waited for Mario; no one seemed to
care. He stood in the dark water with his spear, ready to take on his
shoulders the safety and welfare of the community, but they turned their
backs on him and sang as they climbed the cliff.

To hell with "La Famiglia Tosta," Seton thought. To hell with it.
This was the loveliest hour of the whole day. All kinds of pleasure—
food, drink, and love—lay ahead of him, and he seemed, by the gathering
shadow, gently disengaged from his responsibility for television, from the
charge of making sense of his life. Now everything lay in the dark and
ample lap of night, and the discourse was suspended.

The stairs they took went past the ramparts they had rented,
which were festooned with flowers, and it was on this stretch from here
up to the drawbridge and the portal, that the triumph of the King, the
architect, and the stonemasons was most imposing, for one was involved in
the same breath with military impregnability, princeliness, and beauty.
There was no point, no turning, no tower or battlement where these
forces seemed separate. All the ramparts were finely corniced, and at
every point where the enemy could have been expected to advance, the
great, eight-ton crest of the Christian King of Spain proclaimed the

blood, the faith, and the good taste of the defender. Over the main portal, the crest had fallen from its fine setting of sea gods with tridents and had crashed into the moat, but it had landed with its blazonings upward, and the quarterings, the cross, and the marble draperies could be seen in the water.

Then, on the wall, among the other legends, Seton saw the words *"Americani, go home, go home."* The writing was faint; it might have been there since the war, or its faintness might be accounted for by the fact that it had been done in haste. Neither his wife nor his children saw it, and he stood aside while they crossed the drawbridge into the courtyard, and then he went back to rub the words out with his fingers. Oh, who could have written it? He felt mystified and desolate. He had been invited to come to this strange country. The invitations had been clamorous. Travel agencies, shipping firms, airlines, even the Italian government itself had besought him to give up his comfortable way of life and travel abroad. He had accepted the invitations, he had committed himself to their hospitality, and now he was told, by this ancient wall, that he was not wanted.

He had never before felt unwanted. It had never been said. He had been wanted as a baby, wanted as a young man, wanted as a lover, a husband and father, wanted as a scriptwriter, a raconteur and companion. He had, if anything, been wanted excessively, and his only worry had been to spare himself, to spread his sought-after charms with prudence and discretion, so that they would do the most good. He had been wanted for golf, for tennis, for bridge, for charades, for cocktails, for boards of management—and yet this rude and ancient wall addressed him as if he were a pariah, a nameless beggar, an outcast. He was most deeply wounded.

Ice was stored in the castle dungeon, and Seton took his cocktail shaker there, filled it, made some Martinis, and carried them up to the battlements of the highest tower, where his wife joined him to watch the light ring its changes. Darkness was filling in the honeycombed cliffs of Tarlonia, and while the hills along the shore bore only the most far-fetched resemblance to the breasts of women, they calmed Seton's feelings and stirred in him the same deep tenderness.

"I might go down to the café after dinner," his wife said, "just to see what sort of a job they did with the dubbing."

She did not understand the strength of his feelings about writing for television; she had never understood. He said nothing. He supposed that, seen at a distance, on his battlement, he might have been taken for what he was not—a poet, a seasoned traveler, a friend of Elsa Maxwell's, a prince or a duke—but this world lying all about him now did not really have the power to elevate and change him. It was only himself—the author of "The Best Family"—that he had carried at such inconvenience and expense across borders and over the sea. The flowery and massive setting had not changed the fact that he was sunburned, amorous, hungry, and stooped, and that the rock he sat on, set in its place by the great King of Spain, cut into his rump.

At dinner, Clementina, the cook, asked if she might go to the village and see "La Famiglia Tosta." The boys, of course, were going with their mother. After dinner, Seton went back to his tower. The fishing fleet had begun to go out past the mole, their torches lighted. The moon rose and blazed so brightly on the sea that the water seemed to turn, to spin in the light. From the village he could hear the *bel canto* of mothers calling their girls, and, from time to time, a squawk from the television set. It would all be over in twenty minutes, but the sense of wrongdoing *in absentia* made itself felt in his bones. Oh, how could one stop the advance of barbarism, vulgarity and censoriousness? When he saw the lights his family carried coming up the stairs, he went down to the moat to meet them. They were not alone. Who was with them? Who were these figures ascending? The doctor? The mayor? And a little girl carrying gladioli. It was a delegation—and a friendly one, he could tell by the lightness of their voices. They had come to praise him.

"It was so beautiful, so comical, so true to life!" the doctor said.

The little girl gave him the flowers, and the mayor embraced him lightly. "Oh, we thought, *Signore*," he said, "that you were merely a poet."

COMMENTARY AND QUESTIONS

The main strand of action in this story is rather easy to follow. An American and his family have rented a castle in an Italian village, where, seeking to escape from his role of television writer, he wants to be known as a poet. He is shamed to think of the debasement that will follow the introduction into Italy of his television program. But at the end of the story he finds himself honored by the villagers because he is not a mere poet but a writer of the script for "La Famiglia Tosta."

1. The impact of the story comes from the suggested contrast between life as it might be and as it is. The phrase which forms the title reflects an attitude of mind. Not infrequently a nation or a people, dissatisfied with the present, looks back to some period in the past when, it is assumed, life was perfect, for everything was as it should be: all men were heroic, or at least were innocently good; evil did not exist, or at least was never triumphant. Accompanying this view

of the past nearly always is the hope or dream that the Golden Age may come again. How is the title of the story reflected in Seton's attitude towards the village and its people, and in his view of himself as *il poeta*?

2. The reader first glimpses the Seton family as they leave the castle on the way to picnic on the beach of a sandy cove. They are greeted by the native women: "Good morning to the poet, the wife of the poet, and the poet's sons" (p. 637). Why doesn't Seton reply when his elder son asks, "Why do they call you a poet?"

3. As Seton rows the boat, standing in native fashion, his wife seeks to reassure him: "Don't worry, darling, no one will know, and if they do know, they won't care" (p. 637). What does she mean by her comment? What do the sons think of the fact that this Sunday is the day of the debut in Italy of their father's television program?

4. Why is Seton so pleased with himself when he secures the Greek vase? How has the description in the second paragraph of the story prepared for this scene?

5. While the Americans are at the beach, another family of outsiders ("a Roman family, Seton guessed") appears. The father of the Roman family is unable on this holiday occasion, as his actions are interpreted, to enjoy the happiness of the moment because of his frets and worries about things that may or may not take place. To what extent is Seton like the Roman father? Does the relation of the Roman father to his family parallel the relation of Seton to his family? To what extent might the Roman family resemble the characters in "The Best Family"?

6. When Mario first appears on the beach, after the shark has been sighted, how is he received by the crowds of natives? What is there unheroic about his appearance and about what happens following his arrival? To what extent do the first two sentences of the story apply to this scene? Is the reaction of the villagers toward Seton (anxious to protect them against the "wrongdoing" of television) parallel to their attitude toward Mario ("ready to take on his shoulders the safety and welfare of the community")?

7. At the end of the day, after the debut of "La Famiglia Tosta," it will no longer be possible for Seton to hide from the villagers the fact that he is a television writer. Why is he so "deeply wounded" by the inscription on the castle wall, *Americani, go home, go home*? Is it the author of "The Best Family" that is wounded, or *il poeta*? Do the first two sentences of the story help to explain his anxiety?

8. What is the significance of the attributes ("so beautiful, so comical, so true to life") selected for praise by the doctor at the end of the story when he characterizes the television program he has just seen?

9. Why is it appropriate in this story for there to be so little dialogue?

10. The effect of Cheever's carefully wrought style is achieved in part by his choice of a single evocative verb—"straw hats canted over their foreheads"—or of a disarmingly simple figure of speech—"The harbor is as round as a soup plate." Find other examples.

SUGGESTION FOR WRITING

Returning to "castles formed in childhood."

The Destructors

by GRAHAM GREENE

IT WAS ON THE EVE of August Bank Holiday that the latest recruit became the leader of the Wormsley Common Gang. No one was surprised except Mike, but Mike at the age of nine was surprised by everything. "If you don't shut your mouth," somebody once said to him, "you'll get a frog down it." After that Mike had kept his teeth tightly clamped except when the surprise was too great.

The new recruit had been with the gang since the beginning of the summer holidays, and there were possibilities about his brooding silence that all recognized. He never wasted a word even to tell his name until that was required of him by the rules. When he said "Trevor" it was a statement of fact, not as it would have been with the others a statement of shame or defiance. Nor did anyone laugh except Mike, who finding himself without support and meeting the dark gaze of the newcomer opened his mouth and was quiet again. There was every reason why T., as he was afterwards referred to, should have been an object of mockery —there was his name (and they substituted the initial because otherwise they had no excuse not to laugh at it), the fact that his father, a former architect and present clerk, had "come down in the world" and that his mother considered herself better than the neighbors. What but an odd quality of danger, of the unpredictable, established him in the gang without any ignoble ceremony of initiation?

The gang met every morning in an impromptu car park, the site of the last bomb of the first blitz. The leader, who was known as Blackie, claimed to have heard it fall, and no one was precise enough in his dates to point out that he would have been one year old and fast asleep on the down platform of Wormsley Common Underground Station. On one side of the car park leaned the first occupied house, No. 3, of the shattered Northwood Terrace—literally leaned, for it had suffered from the blast of the bomb and the side walls were supported on wooden struts. A smaller bomb and some incendiaries had fallen beyond, so that the house stuck up like a jagged tooth and carried on the further wall relics of its neighbor, a dado, the remains of a fireplace. T., whose words were almost confined to voting "Yes" or "No" to the plan of operations proposed each day by Blackie, once startled the whole gang by saying broodingly, "Wren built that house, Father says."

"Who's Wren?"

"The man who built St. Paul's."

"Who cares?" Blackie said. "It's only Old Misery's."

Old Misery—whose real name was Thomas—had once been a builder and decorator. He lived alone in the crippled house, doing for himself: once a week you could see him coming back across the common with bread and vegetables and once as the boys played in the car park he put his head over the smashed wall of his garden and looked at them.

"Been to the loo," one of the boys said, for it was common knowledge that since the bombs fell something had gone wrong with the pipes of the house and Old Misery was too mean to spend money on the property. He could do the redecorating himself at cost price, but he had never learned plumbing. The loo was a wooden shed at the bottom of the narrow garden with a star-shaped hole in the door: it had escaped the blast which had smashed the house next door and sucked out the window frames of No. 3.

The next time the gang became aware of Mr. Thomas was more surprising. Blackie, Mike, and a thin yellow boy, who for some reason was called by his surname Summers, met him on the common coming back from the market. Mr. Thomas stopped them. He said glumly, "You belong to the lot that play in the car park?"

Mike was about to answer when Blackie stopped him. As the leader he had responsibilities. "Suppose we are?" he said ambiguously.

"I got some chocolates," Mr. Thomas said. "Don't like 'em myself. Here you are. Not enough to go round, I don't suppose. There never is," he added with somber conviction. He handed over three packets of Smarties.

The gang were puzzled and perturbed by this action and tried to explain it away. "Bet someone dropped them and he picked 'em up," somebody suggested.

"Pinched 'em and then got in a bleeding funk," another thought aloud.

"It's a bribe," Summers said. "He wants us to stop bouncing balls on his wall."

"We'll show him we don't take bribes," Blackie said, and they sacrificed the whole morning to the game of bouncing that only Mike was young enough to enjoy. There was no sign from Mr. Thomas.

Next day T. astonished them all. He was late at the rendezvous, and the voting for that day's exploit took place without him. At Blackie's suggestion the gang was to disperse in pairs, take busses at random, and see how many free rides could be snatched from unwary conductors (the operation was to be carried out in pairs to avoid cheating). They were drawing lots for their companions when T. arrived.

"Where you been, T.?" Blackie asked. "You can't vote now. You know the rules."

"I've been *there*," T. said. He looked at the ground, as though he had thoughts to hide.

"Where?"

"At Old Misery's." Mike's mouth opened and then hurriedly closed again with a click. He had remembered the frog.

"At Old Misery's?" Blackie said. There was nothing in the rules against it, but he had a sensation that T. was treading on dangerous ground. He asked hopefully, "Did you break in?"

"No. I rang the bell."

"And what did you say?"

"I said I wanted to see his house."

"What did he do?"

"He showed it to me."

"Pinch anything?"

"No."

"What did you do it for then?"

The gang had gathered round: it was as though an impromptu court were about to form and to try some case of deviation. T. said, "It's a beautiful house," and still watching the ground, meeting no one's eyes, he licked his lips first one way, then the other.

"What do you mean, a beautiful house?" Blackie asked with scorn.

"It's got a staircase two hundred years old like a corkscrew. Nothing holds it up."

"What do you mean, nothing holds it up? Does it float?"

"It's to do with opposite forces, Old Misery said."

"What else?"

"There's paneling."

"Like in the Blue Boar?"

"Two hundred years old."

"Is Old Misery two hundred years old?"

Mike laughed suddenly and then was quiet again. The meeting was in a serious mood. For the first time since T. had strolled into the car park on the first day of the holidays his position was in danger. It only needed a single use of his real name and the gang would be at his heels.

"What did you do it for?" Blackie asked. He was just, he had no jealousy, he was anxious to retain T. in the gang if he could. It was the word "beautiful" that worried him—that belonged to a class world that you could still see parodied at the Wormsley Common Empire by a man wearing a top hat and a monocle, with a haw-haw accent. He was tempted to say, "My dear Trevor, old chap," and unleash his hell hounds. "If you'd broken in," he said sadly—that indeed would have been an exploit worthy of the gang.

"This was better," T. said. "I found out things." He continued to stare at his feet, not meeting anybody's eye, as though he were absorbed in some dream he was unwilling—or ashamed—to share.

"What things?"

"Old Misery's going to be away all tomorrow and Bank Holiday."

Blackie said with relief, "You mean we could break in?"

"And pinch things?" somebody asked.

Blackie said, "Nobody's going to pinch things. Breaking in—that's good enough, isn't it? We don't want any court stuff."

"I don't want to pinch anything," T. said. "I've got a better idea."

"What is it?"

T. raised eyes, as gray and disturbed as the drab August day. "We'll pull it down," he said. "We'll destroy it."

Blackie gave a single hoot of laughter and then, like Mike, fell quiet, daunted by the serious implacable gaze. "What'd the police be doing all the time?" he said.

"They'd never know. We'd do it from inside. I've found a way in." He said with a sort of intensity, "We'd be like worms, don't you see, in an apple. When we came out again there'd be nothing there, no staircase, no panels, nothing but just walls, and then we'd make the walls fall down—somehow."

"We'd go to jug," Blackie said.

"Who's to prove? and anyway we wouldn't have pinched anything." He added without the smallest flicker of glee, "There wouldn't be anything to pinch after we'd finished."

"I've never heard of going to prison for breaking things," Summers said.

"There wouldn't be time," Blackie said. "I've seen housebreakers at work."

"There are twelve of us," T. said. "We'd organize."

"None of us know how . . ."

"I know," T. said. He looked across at Blackie, "Have you got a better plan?"

"Today," Mike said tactlessly, "we're pinching free rides . . ."

"Free rides," T. said. "You can stand down, Blackie, if you'd rather . . ."

"The gang's got to vote."

"Put it up then."

Blackie said uneasily, "It's proposed that tomorrow and Monday we destroy Old Misery's house."

"Here, here," said a fat boy called Joe.

"Who's in favor?"

T. said, "It's carried."

"How do we start?" Summers asked.

"He'll tell you," Blackie said. It was the end of his leadership. He went away to the back of the car park and began to kick a stone, dribbling it this way and that. There was only one old Morris in the park, for few cars were left there except lorries: without an attendant there was no safety. He took a flying kick at the car and scraped a little paint off the rear mudguard. Beyond, paying no more attention to him than to a stranger, the gang had gathered around T.; Blackie was dimly aware of the fickleness of favor. He thought of going home, of never returning, of letting them all discover the hollowness of T.'s leadership, but suppose after all what T. proposed was possible—nothing like it had ever been done before. The fame of the Wormsley Common car park gang would surely reach around London. There would be headlines in the papers. Even the grown-up gangs who ran the betting at the all-in wrestling and the barrow boys would hear with respect of how Old Misery's house had been destroyed. Driven by the pure, simple, and altruistic ambition of fame for the gang, Blackie came back to where T. stood in the shadow of Misery's wall.

He was giving orders with decision: it was as though this plan had been with him all his life, pondered through the seasons, now in his fifteenth year crystallized with the pain of puberty. "You," he said to Mike, "bring some big nails, the biggest you can find, and a hammer. Anyone else who can, better bring a hammer and a screw driver. We'll need plenty of them. Chisels too. We can't have too many chisels. Can anbody bring a saw?"

"I can," Mike said.

"Not a child's saw," T. said. "A real saw."

Blackie realized he had raised his hand like any ordinary member of the gang.

"Right, you bring one, Blackie. But now there's a difficulty. We want a hacksaw."

"What's a hacksaw?" someone asked.

"You can get 'em at Woolworth's," Summers said.

The fat boy called Joe said gloomily, "I knew it would end in a collection."

"I'll get one myself," T. said. "I don't want your money. But I can't buy a sledge hammer."

Blackie said, "They are working on No. 15. I know where they'll leave their stuff for Bank Holiday."

"Then that's all," T. said. "We meet here at nine sharp."

"I've got to go to church," Mike said.

"Come over the wall and whistle. We'll let you in."

II

On Sunday morning all were punctual except Blackie, even Mike. Mike had a stroke of luck. His mother felt ill, his father was tired after Saturday night, and he was told to go to church alone with many warnings of what would happen if he strayed. Blackie had difficulty in smuggling out the saw, and then in finding the sledge hammer at the back of No. 15. He approached the house from a lane at the rear of the garden, for fear of the policeman's beat along the main road. The tired evergreens kept off a stormy sun: another wet Bank Holiday was being prepared over the Atlantic, beginning in swirls of dust under the trees. Blackie climbed the wall into Misery's garden.

There was no sign of anybody anywhere. The loo stood like a tomb in a neglected graveyard. The curtains were drawn. The house slept. Blackie lumbered nearer with the saw and the sledge hammer. Perhaps after all nobody had turned up: the plan had been a wild invention: they had woken wiser. But when he came close to the back door he could hear a confusion of sound, hardly louder than a hive in swarm: a clickety-clack, a bang bang bang, a scraping, a creaking, a sudden painful crack. He thought: it's true, and whistled.

They opened the back door to him and he came in. He had at once the impression of organization, very different from the old happy-go-lucky ways under his leadership. For awhile he wandered up and down stairs looking for T. Nobody addressed him: he had a sense of great urgency and already he could begin to see the plan.

The interior of the house was being carefully demolished without touching the outer walls. Summers with hammer and chisel was ripping out the skirting boards in the ground floor dining room: he had already smashed the panels of the door. In the same room Joe was heaving up the parquet blocks, exposing the soft wood floorboards over the cellar. Coils of wire came out of the damaged skirting and Mike sat happily on the floor, clipping the wires.

On the curved stairs two of the gang were working hard with an inadequate child's saw on the banisters—when they saw Blackie's big saw they signaled for it wordlessly. When he next saw them a quarter of the banisters had been dropped into the hall. He found T. at last in the bathroom—he sat moodily in the least cared for room in the house, listening to the sounds coming up from below.

"You've really done it," Blackie said with awe. "What's going to happen?"

"We've only just begun," T. said. He looked at the sledge hammer and gave his instructions. "You stay here and break the bath and the wash basin. Don't bother about the pipes. They come later."

Mike appeared at the door. "I've finished the wire, T.," he said.

"Good. You've just got to go wandering round now. The kitchen's in the basement. Smash all the china and glass and bottles you can lay hold of. Don't turn on the taps—we don't want a flood—yet. Then go into all the rooms and turn out drawers. If they are locked get one of the others to break them open. Tear up any papers you find and smash all the ornaments. Better take a carving knife with you from the kitchen. The bedroom's opposite here. Open the pillows and tear up the sheets. That's enough for the moment. And you, Blackie, when you've finished in here crack the plaster in the passage up with your sledge hammer."

"What are you going to do?" Blackie asked.

"I'm looking for something special," T. said.

It was nearly lunch time before Blackie had finished and went in search of T. Chaos had advanced. The kitchen was a shambles of broken glass and china. The dining room was stripped of parquet, the skirting was up, the door had been taken off its hinges, and the destroyers had moved up a floor. Streaks of light came in through the closed shutters where they worked with the seriousness of creators—and destruction is a form of creation. A kind of imagintion had seen this house as it had now become.

Mike said, "I've got to go home for dinner."

"Who else?" T. asked, but all the others on one excuse or another had brought provisions with them.

They squatted in the ruins of the room and swapped unwanted sandwiches. Half an hour for lunch and they were at work again. By the time Mike returned, they were on the top floor, and by six the superficial damage was completed. The doors were all off, all the skirtings raised, the furniture pillaged and ripped and smashed—no one could have slept in the house except on a bed of broken plaster. T. gave his orders—eight o'clock next morning, and to escape notice they climbed singly over the garden wall, into the car park. Only Blackie and T. were left: the light had nearly gone and when they touched a switch, nothing worked—Mike had done his job thoroughly.

"Did you find anything special?" Blackie asked.

T. nodded. "Come over here," he said, "and look." Out of both pockets he drew bundles of pound notes. "Old Misery's savings," he said. "Mike ripped out the mattress, but he missed them."

"What are you going to do? Share them?"

"We aren't thieves," T. said. "Nobody's going to steal anything from this house. I kept these for you and me—a celebration." He knelt down on the floor and counted them out—there were seventy in all. "We'll burn them," he said, "one by one," and taking it in turns they held a note upward and lit the top corner, so that the flame burned slowly toward their fingers. The gray ash floated above them and fell on their heads like age. "I'd like to see Old Misery's face when we are through," T. said.

"You hate him a lot?" Blackie asked.

"Of course I don't hate him," T. said. "There'd be no fun if I hated him." The last burning note illuminated his brooding face. "All this hate and love," he said, "it's soft, it's hooey. There's only things, Blackie," and he looked round the room crowded with the unfamiliar shadows of half things, broken things, former things. "I'll race you home, Blackie," he said.

III

Next morning the serious destruction started. There were two casualties—Mike and another boy whose parents were off to Southend and Brighton in spite of the slow warm drops that had begun to fall and the rumble of thunder in the estuary like the first guns of the old blitz. "We've got to hurry," T. said.

Summers was restive. "Haven't we done enough?" he said. "I've been given a bob for slot machines. This is like work."

"We've hardly started," T. said. "Why, there's all the floors left, and the stairs. We haven't taken out a single window. You voted like the others. We are going to *destroy* this house. There won't be anything left when we've finished."

They began again on the first floor picking up the top floorboards next the outer wall, leaving the joists exposed. Then they sawed through the joists and retreated into the hall as what was left of the floor heeled and sank. They had learned with practice and the second floor collapsed more easily. By the evening an odd exhilaration seized them as they looked down the great hollow of the house. They ran risks and made mistakes: when they thought of the windows it was too late to reach them. "Cor," Joe said and dropped a penny down into the dry rubble-filled well. It cracked and span among the broken glass.

"Why did we start this?" Summers asked with astonishment; T. was already on the ground, digging at the rubble, clearing a space along the outer wall. "Turn on the taps," he said. "It's too dark for anyone to see now and in the morning it won't matter." The water overtook them on the stairs and fell through the floorless rooms.

It was then they heard Mike's whistle at the back. "Something's wrong," Blackie said. They could hear his urgent breathing as they unlocked the door.

"The bogies?" Summers asked.

"Old Misery," Mike said. "He's on his way." He put his head between his knees and retched. "Ran all the way," he said with pride.

"But why?" T. said. "He told me . . ." He protested with the fury of the child he had never been, "It isn't fair."

"He was down at Southend," Mike said, "and he was on the train coming back. Said it was too cold and wet." He paused and gazed at the water. "My, you've had a storm here. Is the roof leaking?"

"How long will he be?"

"Five minutes. I gave Ma the slip and ran."

"We better clear," Summers said. "We've done enough anyway."

"Oh no, we haven't. Anybody could do this—" "This" was the shattered hollowed house with nothing left but the walls. Yet walls could be preserved. Façades were valuable. They could build inside again more beautifully than before. This could again be a home. He said angrily, "We've got to finish. Don't move. Let me think."

"There's no time," a boy said.

"There's got to be a way," T. said. "We couldn't have got this far . . ."

"We've done a lot," Blackie said.

"No. No we haven't. Somebody watch the front."

"We can't do any more."

"He may come in at the back."

"Watch the back too." T. began to plead, "Just give me a minute and I'll fix it. I swear I'll fix it." But his authority had gone with his ambiguity. He was only one of the gang. "Please," he said.

"Please," Summers mimicked him and then suddenly struck home with the fatal name. "Run along home, Trevor."

T. stood with his back to the rubble like a boxer knocked groggy against the ropes. He had no words as his dreams shook and slid. Then Blackie acted before the gang had time to laugh, pushing Summers backward. "I'll watch the front, T.," he said, and cautiously he opened the shutters of the hall. The gray wet common stretched ahead, and the lamps gleamed in the puddles. "Someone's coming, T. No, it's not him. What's your plan, T.?"

"Tell Mike to go out to the loo and hide close beside it. When he hears me whistle he's got to count ten and start to shout."

"Shout what?"

"Oh, 'help,' anything."

"You hear, Mike," Blackie said. He was the leader again. He took a quick look between the shutters. "He's coming, T."

"Quick, Mike. The loo. Stay here, Blackie, all of you."

"Where are you going, T.?"

"Don't worry. I'll see to this."

Old Misery came limping off the common. He had mud on his shoes and he stopped to scrape them on the pavement's edge. He didn't want to soil his house, which stood jagged and dark between the bomb sites, saved so narrowly as he believed from destruction. Even the fanlight had been left unbroken by the bomb's blast. Somewhere somebody whistled. Old Misery looked sharply round. He didn't trust whistles. A child was shouting: it seemed to come from his own garden. Then a boy ran into the road from the car park. "Mr. Thomas," he called, "Mr. Thomas."

"What is it?"

"I'm terribly sorry, Mr. Thomas. One of us got taken short and we thought you wouldn't mind and now he can't get out."

"What do you mean, boy?"

"He's got stuck in your loo."

"He'd no business . . . Haven't I seen you before?"

"You showed me your house."

"So I did. So I did. That doesn't give you the right to . . ."

"Do hurry, Mr. Thomas. He'll suffocate."

"Nonsense. He can't suffocate. Wait till I put my bag in."

"I'll carry your bag."

"Oh no, you don't. I carry my own."

"This way, Mr. Thomas."

"I can't get in the garden that way. I've got to go through the house," he protested.

"But you *can* get in the garden this way, Mr. Thomas. We often do."

"You often do?" He followed the boy with a scandalized fascination. "When? What right . . .?"

"Do you see . . . ? the wall's low."

"I'm not going to climb walls into my own garden. It's absurd."

"This is how we do it. One foot here, one foot there, and over." The boy's face peered down, an arm shot out, and Mr. Thomas found his bag taken and deposited on the other side of the wall.

"Give me back my bag," Mr. Thomas said. From the loo a boy yelled and yelled. "I'll call the police."

"Your bag's all right, Mr. Thomas. Look. One foot there. On your right. Now just above. To your left." Mr. Thomas climbed over his own garden wall. "Here's your bag."

"I'll have the wall built up," Mr. Thomas said, "I'll not have you boys coming over here, using my loo." He stumbled on the path, but the boy caught his elbow and supported him. "Thank you, thank you, my boy," he murmured automatically.

Somebody shouted again through the dark. "I'm coming, I'm coming," Mr. Thomas called. He said to the boy beside him, "I'm not unreasonable. Been a boy myself. As long as things are done regular, I don't mind you playing round the place Saturday mornings. Sometimes I like company. Only it's got to be regular. One of you asks leave and I say Yes. Sometimes I'll say No. Won't feel like it. And you come in at the front door and out at the back. No garden walls."

"Do get him out, Mr. Thomas."

"He won't come to any harm in my loo," Mr. Thomas said, stumbling slowly down the garden. "Oh my rheumatics," he said. "Always get 'em on Bank Holiday. I've got to go careful. There's loose stones here. Give me your hand. Do you know what my horoscope said yesterday? 'Abstain from any dealings in first half of week. Danger of serious crash.' That might be on this path," Mr. Thomas said. "They speak in parables and double meanings." He paused at the door of the loo. "What's the matter in there?" he called. There was no reply.

"Perhaps he's fainted," the boy said.

"Not in my loo. Here, you, come out," Mr. Thomas said and giving a great jerk at the door he nearly fell on his back when it swung easily open. A hand first supported him and then pushed him hard. His head hit the opposite wall and he sat heavily down. His bag hit his feet. A hand whipped the key out of the lock and the door slammed. "Let me out," he called and heard the key turn in the lock. "A serious crash," he thought and felt dithery and confused and old.

A voice spoke to him softly through the star-shaped hole in the door. "Don't worry, Mr. Thomas," it said, "we won't hurt you, not if you stay quiet."

Mr. Thomas put his head between his hands and pondered. He had noticed that there was only one lorry in the car park, and he felt certain that the driver would not come for it before the morning. Nobody could hear him from the road in front, and the lane at the back was seldom used. Anyone who passed there would be hurrying home and would not pause for what they would certainly take to be drunken cries. And if he did call "Help," who, on a lonely Bank Holiday evening, would have the courage to investigate? Mr. Thomas sat on the loo and pondered with the wisdom of age.

After a while it seemed to him that there were sounds in the silence—they were faint and came from the direction of his house. He stood up and peered through the ventilation hole—between the cracks in one of the shutters he saw a light, not the light of a lamp but the wavering light that a candle might give. Then he thought he heard the sound of hammering and scraping and chipping. He thought of burglars—perhaps they had employed the boy as a scout, but why should burglars engage in what sounded more and more like a stealthy form of carpentry? Mr. Thomas let out an experimental yell, but nobody answered. The noise could not even have reached his enemies.

IV

Mike had gone home to bed, but the rest stayed. The question of leadership no longer concerned the gang. With nails, chisels, screw drivers, anything that was sharp and penetrating, they moved around the inner walls worrying at the mortar between the bricks. They started too high, and it was Blackie who hit on the damp course and realized the work could be halved if they weakened the joints immediately above. It was a long, tiring, unamusing job, but at last, it was finished. The gutted house stood there balanced on a few inches of mortar between the damp course and the bricks.

There remained the most dangerous task of all, out in the open at the edge of the bomb site. Summers was sent to watch the road for passers-by, and Mr. Thomas sitting on the loo heard clearly now the sound of sawing. It no longer came from his house and that a little reassured him. He felt less concerned. Perhaps the other noises too had no significance.

A voice spoke to him through the hole. "Mr. Thomas."

"Let me out," Mr. Thomas said sternly.

"Here's a blanket," the voice said, and a long gray sausage was worked through the hole and fell in swathes over Mr. Thomas' head.

"There's nothing personal," the voice said. "We want you to be comfortable tonight."

"Tonight," Mr. Thomas repeated incredulously.

"Catch," the voice said. "Penny buns—we've buttered them, and sausage rolls. We don't want you to starve, Mr. Thomas."

Mr. Thomas pleaded desperately. "A joke's a joke, boy. Let me out and I won't say a thing. I've got rheumatics. I got to sleep comfortable."

"You wouldn't be comfortable, not in your house, you wouldn't. Not now."

"What do you mean, boy?" but the footsteps receded. There was only the silence of night: no sound of sawing. Mr. Thomas tried one more yell, but he was daunted and rebuked by the silence—a long way away an owl hooted and made off again on its muffled flight through the soundless world.

At seven next morning the driver came to fetch his lorry. He climbed into the seat and tried to start the engine. He was vaguely aware of a voice shouting, but it didn't concern him. At last the engine responded and he backed the lorry until it touched the great wooden shore that supported Mr. Thomas' house. That way he could drive right out and down the street without reversing. The lorry moved forward, was momentarily checked as though something were pulling it from behind, and then went on to the sound of a long rumbling crash. The driver was astonished to see bricks bouncing ahead of him, while stones hit the roof of his cab. He put on his brakes. When he climbed out the whole landscape had suddenly altered. There was no house beside the car park, only a hill of rubble. He went round and examined the back of his car for damage and found a rope tied there that was still twisted at the other end round part of a wooden strut.

The driver again became aware of somebody shouting. It came from the wooden erection which was the nearest thing to a house in that desolation of broken brick. The driver climbed the smashed wall and unlocked the door. Mr. Thomas came out of the loo. He was wearing a gray blanket to which flakes of pastry adhered. He gave a sobbing cry. "My house," he said. "Where's my house?"

"Search me," the driver said. His eye lit on the remains of a bath and what had once been a dresser and he began to laugh. There wasn't anything left anywhere.

"How dare you laugh," Mr. Thomas said. "It was my house. My house."

"I'm sorry," the driver said, making heroic efforts, but when he remembered the sudden check to his lorry, the crash of bricks falling, he became convulsed again. One moment the house had stood there with such dignity between the bomb sites like a man in a top hat, and then, bang, crash, there wasn't anything left—not anything. He said, "I'm sorry. I can't help it, Mr. Thomas. There's nothing personal, but you got to admit it's funny."

COMMENTARY AND QUESTIONS

On the level of plot structure, this is a rather simple story: a gang of London boys brings about the destruction of a house at the instigation of a comparatively new member, T. Depth, however, is given to the story by two contrasts—between the attitude of T. and that of the rest of the gang toward the act of destruction, and between the reaction of the owner, Mr. Thomas, and that of the lorry-driver to the act—and by the similarity between T.'s spirit of impersonal objectivity and the lorry-driver's.

1. As a means of analyzing the first contrast, consider such questions as these: What incidents are introduced early in the story that help to explain the gang's willingness to follow T.'s suggestion to destroy Old Misery's house? In what way does it become apparent at the time of the burning of the pound notes that Blackie has misinterpreted T.'s attitude toward the exploit? Why is T. unwilling to stop when Old Misery unexpectedly returns?

2. In what way can the lorry-driver's reaction at the end of the story be compared to someone's laughing when a man slips on a banana peel?

3. As part of his apology to Mr. Thomas, the lorry-driver says, "There's nothing personal." When has this expression been used earlier in the story?

4. Should the lorry-driver have been given a name?

5. Each of the following passages states or implies a contrast between two situations or two ways of looking at things. Explain each contrast and relate it to the story's central action.
   a. "He had at once the impression of organization, very different from the old happy-go-lucky ways under his leadership" (p. 650).
   b. " 'Haven't we done enough?' he said. 'I've been given a bob for slot machines. This is like work' " (p. 652).

c. "He stumbled on the path, but the boy caught his elbow and supported him. 'Thank you, thank you, my boy,' he murmured automatically" (p. 655).

6. Changes in leadership of the gang occur at moments of tension. Under what circumstances does T. gain and then lose the leadership? How is the second sentence of section IV to be explained: "The question of leadership no longer concerned the gang"?

7. Blackie is characterized thus at one point (p. 648): "He was just, he had no jealousy. . . ." To what extent do Blackie's actions substantiate this generalization? What details in the story suggest his most powerful motivations?

8. How is the picture of Mike suggested in the first paragraph of the story filled out by these passages:
   a. ". . . they sacrificed the whole morning to the game of bouncing that only Mike was young enough to enjoy" (p. 647).
   b. " 'Today,' Mike said tactlessly, 'we're pinching free rides . . .' " (p. 649).
   c. " 'Old Misery's savings,' he said. 'Mike ripped out the mattress, but he missed them' " (p. 652).
   d. "Mike said, 'I've got to go home for dinner' " (p. 651).

9. Part of a short-story writer's problem is to get through the initial exposition quickly. How long does it take Greene to give the setting and introduce the main characters?

10. In the third paragraph and in the final paragraph of the story Greene uses two similes to describe Mr. Thomas' house: "the house stuck up like a jagged tooth"; "the house had stood there with such dignity between the bomb sites like a man in a top hat." How is each simile appropriate to its place in the story?

SUGGESTIONS FOR WRITING

1. Why is this story not likely to encourage anyone to do similar acts of destruction?
2. Should the writer of a story always include explicit moral judgments on the action?
3. "Destruction is a form of creation."
4. The power of group loyalty for constructive and destructive action.
5. "There's nothing personal, but you got to admit it's funny."

Blackberry Winter

by ROBERT PENN WARREN

It was getting into June and past eight o'clock in the morning, but there was a fire—even if it wasn't a big fire, just a fire of chunks—on the hearth of the big stone fireplace in the living room. I was standing on the hearth, almost into the chimney, hunched over the fire, working my bare toes slowly on the warm stone. I relished the heat which made the skin of my bare legs warp and creep and tingle, even as I called to my mother, who was somewhere back in the dining room or kitchen, and said: "But it's June, I don't have to put them on!"

"You put them on if you are going out," she called.

I tried to assess the degree of authority and conviction in the tone, but at that distance it was hard to decide. I tried to analyze the tone, and then I thought what a fool I had been to start out the back door and let her see that I was barefoot. If I had gone out the front door or the side door she would never have known, not till dinner time anyway, and by then the day would have been half gone and I would have been all over the farm to see what the storm had done and down to the creek to see the flood. But it had never crossed my mind that they would try to stop you from going barefoot in June, no matter if there had been a gully-washer and a cold spell.

Nobody had ever tried to stop me in June as long as I could remember, and when you are nine years old, what you remember seems forever; for you remember everything and everything is important and stands big and full and fills up Time and is so solid that you can walk around and around it like a tree and look at it. You are aware that time passes, that there is a movement in time, but that it is not what Time is. Time is not a movement, a flowing, a wind then, but is, rather, a kind of climate in which things are, and when a thing happens it begins to live and keeps on living and stands solid in Time like the tree that you can walk around. And if there is a movement, the movement is not Time itself, any more than a breeze is climate, and all the breeze does is to shake a little the leaves on the tree which is alive and solid. When you are nine, you know that there are things that you don't know, but you know that when you know something you know it. You know how a thing has been and you know that you can go barefoot in June. You do not understand that voice from back in the kitchen which says that you cannot go bare-foot outdoors and run to see what has happened and rub your feet over the wet shivery grass and make the perfect mark of your foot in the smooth, creamy, red mud and then muse upon it as though you had suddenly come upon that single mark on the glistening auroral beach of the world. You have never seen a beach, but you have read the book and how the footprint was there.

The voice had said what it had said, and I looked savagely at the black stockings and the strong, scuffed brown shoes which I had brought from my closet as far as the hearth rug. I called once more, "But it's June," and waited.

"It's June," the voice replied from far away, "but it's blackberry winter."

I had lifted my head to reply to that, to make one more test of what was in that tone, when I happened to see the man.

The fireplace in the living room was at the end; for the stone chimney was built, as in so many of the farmhouses in Tennessee, at the end of a gable, and there was a window on each side of the chimney. Out of the window on the north side of the fireplace I could see the man. When I saw the man I did not call out what I had intended, but, engrossed by the strangeness of the sight, watched him, still far off, come along the path by the edge of the woods.

What was strange was that there should be a man there at all. That path went along the yard fence, between the fence and the woods which came right down to the yard, and then on back past the chicken runs and on by the woods until it was lost to sight where the woods bulged out and cut off the back field. There the path disappeared into the woods. It led on back, I knew, through the woods and to the swamp, skirted the swamp where the big trees gave way to sycamores and water oaks and willows and tangled cane, and then led on to the river. Nobody ever went back there except people who wanted to gig frogs in the swamp or to fish in the river or to hunt in the woods, and those people, if they didn't have a standing permission from my father, always stopped to ask permission to cross the farm. But the man whom I now saw wasn't, I could tell even at that distance, a sportsman. And what would a sportsman have been doing down there after a storm? Besides, he was coming from the river, and nobody had gone down there that morning. I knew that for a fact, because if anybody had passed, certainly if a stranger had passed, the dogs would have made a racket and would have been out on him. But this man was coming up from the river and had come up through the woods. I suddenly had a vision of him moving up the grassy path in the woods, in the green twilight under the big trees, not making any sound on the path, while now and then, like drops off the eaves, a big drop of water would fall from a leaf or bough and strike a stiff oak leaf lower down with a small, hollow sound like a drop of water hitting tin. That sound, in the silence of the woods, would be very significant.

When you are a boy and stand in the stillness of woods, which can be so still that your heart almost stops beating and makes you want to stand there in the green twilight until you feel your very feet sinking into and clutching the earth like roots and your body breathing slow through its pores like the leaves—when you stand there and wait for the next drop to drop with its small, flat sound to a lower leaf, that sound seems to measure out something, to put an end to something, to begin something, and you cannot wait for it to happen and are afraid it will not happen, and then when it has happened, you are waiting again, almost afraid.

But the man whom I saw coming through the woods in my mind's eye did not pause and wait, growing into the ground and breathing with the enormous, soundless breathing of the leaves. Instead, I saw him moving in the green twilight inside my head as he was moving at that very moment along the path by the edge of the woods, coming toward the house. He was moving steadily, but not fast, with his shoulders hunched a little and his head thrust forward, like a man who has come a long way and has a long way to go. I shut my eyes for a couple of seconds, thinking that when I opened them he would not be there at all. There was no place for him to have come from, and there was no reason for him to come where he was coming, toward our house. But I opened my eyes, and there he was, and he was coming steadily along the side of the woods. He was not yet even with the back chicken yard.

"Mama," I called.

"You put them on," the voice said.

"There's a man coming," I called, "out back."

She did not reply to that, and I guessed that she had gone to the kitchen window to look. She would be looking at the man and wondering who he was and what he wanted, the way you always do in the country, and if I went back there now she would not notice right off whether or not I was barefoot. So I went back to the kitchen.

She was standing by the window. "I don't recognize him," she said, not looking around at me.

"Where could he be coming from?" I asked.

"I don't know," she said.

"What would he be doing down at the river? At night? In the storm?"

She studied the figure out the window, then said, "Oh, I reckon maybe he cut across from the Dunbar place."

That was, I realized, a perfectly rational explanation. He had not been down at the river in the storm, at night. He had come over this morning. You could cut across from the Dunbar place if you didn't mind breaking through a lot of elder and sassafras and blackberry bushes which had about taken over the old cross path, which nobody ever used any more. That satisfied me for a moment, but only for a moment. "Mama," I asked, "what would he be doing over at the Dunbar place last night?"

Then she looked at me, and I knew I had made a mistake, for she was looking at my bare feet. "You haven't got your shoes on," she said.

But I was saved by the dogs. That instant there was a bark which I recognized as Sam, the collie, and then a heavier, churning kind of bark which was Bully, and I saw a streak of white as Bully tore round the corner of the back porch and headed out for the man. Bully was a big, bone-white bull dog, the kind of dog that they used to call a farm bull dog but that you don't see any more, heavy chested and heavy headed, but with pretty long legs. He could take a fence as light as a hound. He had just cleared the white paling fence toward the woods when my mother ran out to the back porch and began calling, "Here you, Bully! Here you!"

Bully stopped in the path, waiting for the man, but he gave a few more of those deep, gargling, savage barks that reminded you of something down a stone-lined well. The red clay mud, I saw, was splashed up over his white chest and looked exciting, like blood.

The man, however, had not stopped walking even when Bully took the fence and started at him. He had kept right on coming. All he had done was to switch a little paper parcel which he carried from the right hand to the left, and then reach into his pants pocket to get something. Then I saw the glitter and knew that he had a knife in his hand, probably the kind of mean knife just made for devilment and nothing else, with a blade as long as the blade of a frog-sticker, which will snap out ready when you press a button in the handle. That knife must have had a button in the handle, or else how could he have had the blade out glittering so quick and with just one hand?

Pulling his knife against the dogs was a funny thing to do, for Bully was a big, powerful brute and fast, and Sam was all right. If those dogs had meant business, they might have knocked him down and ripped him before he got a stroke in. He ought to have picked up a heavy stick, something to take a swipe at them with and something which they could see and respect when they came at him. But he apparently did not know much about dogs. He just held the knife blade close against the right leg, low down, and kept on moving down the path.

Then my mother had called, and Bully had stopped. So the man let the blade of the knife snap back into the handle, and dropped it into his pocket, and kept on coming. Many women would have been afraid with the strange man who they knew had that knife in his pocket. That is, if they were alone in the house with nobody but a nine-year-old boy. And my mother was alone, for my father had gone off, and Dellie, the cook, was down at her cabin because she wasn't feeling well. But my mother wasn't afraid. She wasn't a big woman, but she was clear and brisk about everything she did and looked everybody and everything right in the eye from her own blue eyes in her tanned face. She had been the first woman in the county to ride a horse astride (that was back when she was a girl and long before I was born), and I have seen her snatch up a pump gun and go out and knock a chicken hawk out of the air like a busted skeet when he came over her chicken yard. She was a steady and self-reliant woman, and when I think of her now after all the years she has been dead, I think of her brown hands, not big, but somewhat square for a woman's hands, with square-cut nails. They looked, as a matter of fact, more like a young boy's hands than a grown woman's. But back then it never crossed my mind that she would ever be dead.

She stood on the back porch and watched the man enter the back gate, where the dogs (Bully had leaped back into the yard) were dancing and muttering and giving sidelong glances back to my mother to see if she meant what she had said. The man walked right by the dogs, almost brushing them, and didn't pay them any attention. I could see now that he wore old khaki pants, and a dark wool coat with stripes in it, and a gray felt hat. He had on a gray shirt with blue stripes in it, and no tie. But I could see a tie, blue and reddish, sticking in his side coat-pocket. Everything was wrong about what he wore. He ought to have been wearing blue jeans or overalls, and a straw hat or an old black felt hat, and the coat, granting that he might have been wearing a wool coat and not a jumper, ought not to have had those stripes. Those clothes, despite the fact that they were old enough and dirty enough for any tramp, didn't belong there in our back yard, coming down the path, in Middle Tennessee, miles away from any big town, and even a mile off the pike.

When he got almost to the steps, without having said anything, my mother, very matter-of-factly, said, "Good morning."

"Good morning," he said, and stopped and looked her over. He did not take off his hat, and under the brim you could see the perfectly unmemorable face, which wasn't old and wasn't young, or thick or thin. It was grayish and covered with about three days of stubble. The eyes were a kind of nondescript, muddy hazel, or something like that, rather bloodshot. His teeth, when he opened his mouth, showed yellow and uneven. A couple of them had been knocked out. You knew that they had been knocked out, because there was a scar, not very old, there on the lower lip just beneath the gap.

"Are you hunting work?" my mother asked him.

"Yes," he said—not "yes, mam"—and still did not take off his hat.

"I don't know about my husband, for he isn't here," she said, and didn't mind a bit telling the tramp, or whoever he was, with the mean knife in his pocket, that no man was around, "but I can give you a few things to do. The storm has drowned a lot of my chicks. Three coops of them. You can gather them up and bury them. Bury them deep so the dogs won't get at them. In the woods. And fix the coops the wind blew over. And down yonder beyond that pen by the edge of the woods are some drowned poults. They got out and I couldn't get them in. Even after it started to rain hard. Poults haven't got any sense."

"What are them things—poults?" he demanded, and spat on the brick walk. He rubbed his foot over the spot, and I saw that he wore a black, pointed-toe low shoe, all cracked and broken. It was a crazy kind of shoe to be wearing in the country.

"Oh, they're young turkeys," my mother was saying. "And they haven't got any sense. I oughtn't to try to raise them around here with so many chickens, anyway. They don't thrive near chickens, even in separate pens. And I won't give up my chickens." Then she stopped herself and resumed briskly on the note of business. "When you finish that, you can fix my flower beds. A lot of trash and mud and gravel has washed down. Maybe you can save some of my flowers if you are careful."

"Flowers," the man said, in a low, impersonal voice which seemed to have a wealth of meaning, but a meaning which I could not fathom. As I think back on it, it probably was not pure contempt. Rather, it was a kind of impersonal and distant marveling that he should be on the verge of grubbing in a flower bed. He said the word, and then looked off across the yard.

"Yes, flowers," my mother replied with some asperity, as though she would have nothing said or implied against flowers. "And they were very fine this year." Then she stopped and looked at the man. "Are you hungry?" she demanded.

"Yeah," he said.

"I'll fix you something," she said, "before you get started." She turned to me. "Show him where he can wash up," she commanded, and went into the house.

I took the man to the end of the porch where a pump was and

where a couple of wash pans sat on a low shelf for people to use before they went into the house. I stood there while he laid down his little parcel wrapped in newspaper and took off his hat and looked around for a nail to hang it on. He poured the water and plunged his hands into it. They were big hands, and strong looking, but they did not have the creases and the earth-color of the hands of men who work outdoors. But they were dirty, with black dirt ground into the skin and under the nails. After he had washed his hands, he poured another basin of water and washed his face. He dried his face, and with the towel still dangling in his grasp, stepped over to the mirror on the house wall. He rubbed one hand over the stubble on his face. Then he carefully inspected his face, turning first one side and then the other, and stepped back and settled his striped coat down on his shoulders. He had the movements of a man who has just dressed up to go to a church or a party—the way he settled his coat and smoothed it and scanned himself in the mirror.

Then he caught my glance on him. He glared at me for an instant out of the bloodshot eyes, then demanded in a low, harsh voice, "What you looking at?"

"Nothing," I managed to say, and stepped back a step from him.

He flung the towel down, crumpled, on the shelf, and went toward the kitchen door and entered without knocking.

My mother said something to him which I could not catch. I started to go in again, then thought about my bare feet, and decided to go back of the chicken yard, where the man would have to come to pick up the dead chicks. I hung around behind the chicken house until he came out.

He moved across the chicken yard with a fastidious, not quite finicking motion, looking down at the curdled mud flecked with bits of chicken-droppings. The mud curled up over the soles of his black shoes. I stood back from him some six feet and watched him pick up the first of the drowned chicks. He held it up by one foot and inspected it.

There is nothing deader looking than a drowned chick. The feet curl in that feeble, empty way which back when I was a boy, even if I was a country boy who did not mind hog-killing or frog-gigging, made me feel hollow in the stomach. Instead of looking plump and fluffy, the body is stringy and limp with the fluff plastered to it, and the neck is long and loose like a little string of rag. And the eyes have that bluish membrane over them which makes you think of a very old man who is sick about to die.

The man stood there and inspected the chick. Then he looked all around as though he didn't know what to do with it.

"There's a great big old basket in the shed," I said, and pointed to the shed attached to the chicken house.

He inspected me as though he had just discovered my presence, and moved toward the shed.

"There's a spade there, too," I added.

He got the basket and began to pick up the other chicks, picking each one up slowly by a foot and then flinging it into the basket with a nasty, snapping motion. Now and then he would look at me out of the bloodshot eyes. Every time he seemed on the verge of saying something, but he did not. Perhaps he was building up to say something to me, but I did not wait that long. His way of looking at me made me so uncomfortable that I left the chicken yard.

Besides, I had just remembered that the creek was in flood, over the bridge, and that people were down there watching it. So I cut across the farm toward the creek. When I got to the big tobacco field I saw that it had not suffered much. The land lay right and not many tobacco plants had washed out of the ground. But I knew that a lot of tobacco round the country had been washed right out. My father had said so at breakfast.

My father was down at the bridge. When I came out of the gap in the osage hedge into the road, I saw him sitting on his mare over the heads of the other men who were standing around, admiring the flood. The creek was big here, even in low water; for only a couple of miles away it ran into the river, and when a real flood came, the red water got over the pike where it dipped down to the bridge, which was an iron bridge, and high over the floor and even the side railings of the bridge. Only the upper iron work would show, with the water boiling and frothing red and white around it. That creek rose so fast and so heavy because a few miles back it came down out of the hills, where the gorges filled up with water in no time when a rain came. The creek ran in a deep bed with limestone bluffs along both sides until it got within three quarters of a mile of the bridge, and when it came out from between those bluffs in flood it was boiling and hissing and steaming like water from a fire hose.

Whenever there was a flood, people from half the county would come down to see the sight. After a gully-washer there would not be any work to do anyway. If it didn't ruin your crop, you couldn't plow and you felt like taking a holiday to celebrate. If it did ruin your crop, there wasn't anything to do except to try to take your mind off the mortgage, if you were rich enough to have a mortgage, and if you couldn't afford a mortgage you needed something to take your mind off how hungry you would be by Christmas. So people would come down to the bridge and look at the flood. It made something different from the run of days.

There would not be much talking after the first few minutes of trying to guess how high the water was this time. The men and kids just stood around, or sat their horses or mules, as the case might be, or stood up in the wagon beds. They looked at the strangeness of the flood for an hour or two, and then somebody would say that he had better be getting on home to dinner and would start walking down the gray, puddled limestone pike, or would touch heel to his mount and start off. Everybody always knew what it would be like when he got down to the bridge, but people always came. It was like church or a funeral. They always came, that is, if it was summer and the flood unexpected. Nobody ever came down in winter to see high water.

When I came out of the gap in the bodock hedge, I saw the crowd, perhaps fifteen or twenty men and a lot of kids, and saw my father sitting his mare, Nellie Gray. He was a tall, limber man and carried himself well. I was always proud to see him sit a horse, he was so quiet and straight, and when I stepped through the gap of the hedge that morning, the first thing that happened was, I remember, the warm feeling I always had when I saw him up on a horse, just sitting. I did not go toward him, but skirted the crowd on the far side, to get a look at the creek. For one thing, I was not sure what he would say about the fact that I was barefoot. But the first thing I knew, I heard his voice calling, "Seth!"

I went toward him, moving apologetically past the men, who bent their large, red or thin, sallow faces above me. I knew some of the men, and knew their names, but because those I knew were there in a crowd, mixed with the strange faces, they seemed foreign to me, and not friendly. I did not look up at my father until I was almost within touching distance of his heel. Then I looked up and tried to read his face, to see if he was angry about my being barefoot. Before I could decide anything from that impassive, high-boned face, he had leaned over and reached a hand to me. "Grab on," he commanded.

I grabbed on and gave a little jump, and he said, "Up-see-daisy!" and whisked me, light as a feather, up to the pommel of his McClellan saddle.

"You can see better up here," he said, slid back on the cantle a little to make me more comfortable, and then, looking over my head at the swollen, tumbling water, seemed to forget all about me. But his right hand was laid on my side, just above my thigh, to steady me.

I was sitting there as quiet as I could, feeling the faint stir of my father's chest against my shoulders as it rose and fell with his breath, when I saw the cow. At first, looking up the creek, I thought it was just another big piece of driftwood steaming down the creek in the ruck of water, but all at once a pretty good-size boy who had climbed part way up a telephone pole by the pike so that he could see better yelled out, "Golly-damn, look at that-air cow!"

Everybody looked. It was a cow all right, but it might just as well have been driftwood; for it was dead as a chunk, rolling and roiling down the creek, appearing and disappearing, feet up or head up, it didn't matter which.

The cow started up the talk again. Somebody wondered whether it would hit one of the clear places under the top girder of the bridge and get through or whether it would get tangled in the drift and trash that had piled against the upright girders and braces. Somebody remembered how about ten years before so much driftwood had piled up on the bridge that it was knocked off its foundations. Then the cow hit. It hit the edge of the drift against one of the girders, and hung there. For a few seconds it seemed as though it might tear loose, but then we saw that it was really caught. It bobbed and heaved on its side there in a slow, grinding, uneasy fashion. It had a yoke around its neck, the kind made out of a forked limb to keep a jumper behind fence.

"She shore jumped one fence," one of the men said.

And another: "Well, she done jumped her last one, fer a fack."

Then they began to wonder about whose cow it might be. They decided it must belong to Milt Alley. They said that he had a cow that was a jumper, and kept her in a fenced-in piece of ground up the creek. I had never seen Milt Alley, but I knew who he was. He was a squatter and lived up the hills a way, on a shirt-tail patch of set-on-edge land, in a cabin. He was pore white trash. He had lots of children. I had seen the children at school, when they came. They were thin-faced, with straight, sticky-looking, dough-colored hair, and they smelled something like old sour buttermilk, not because they drank so much buttermilk but because that is the sort of smell which children out of those cabins tend to have. The big Alley boy drew dirty pictures and showed them to the little boys at school.

That was Milt Alley's cow. It looked like the kind of cow he would have, a scrawny, old, sway-backed cow, with a yoke around her neck. I wondered if Milt Alley had another cow.

"Poppa," I said, "do you think Milt Alley has got another cow?"

"You say 'Mr. Alley,' " my father said quietly.

"Do you think he has?"

"No telling," my father said.

Then a big gangly boy, about fifteen, who was sitting on a scraggly little old mule with a piece of croker sack thrown across the sawtooth spine, and who had been staring at the cow, suddenly said to nobody in particular, "Reckin anybody ever et drownt cow?"

He was the kind of boy who might just as well as not have been the son of Milt Alley, with his faded and patched overalls ragged at the bottom of the pants and the mud-stiff brogans hanging off his skinny, bare ankles at the level of the mule's belly. He had said what he did, and then looked embarrassed and sullen when all the eyes swung at him. He hadn't meant to say it, I am pretty sure now. He would have been too proud to say it, just as Milt Alley would have been too proud. He had just been thinking out loud, and the words had popped out.

There was an old man standing there on the pike, an old man with a white beard. "Son," he said to the embarrassed and sullen boy on the mule, "you live long enough and you'll find a man will eat anything when the times comes."

"Time gonna come fer some folks this year," another man said.

"Son," the old man said, "in my time I et things a man don't like to think on. I was a sojer and I rode with Gin'l Forrest, and them things we et when the time come. I tell you. I et meat what got up and run when you taken out yore knife to cut a slice to put on the fire. You had to knock it down with a carbeen butt, it was so active. That-air meat would jump like a bullfrog, it was so full of skippers."

But nobody was listening to the old man. The boy on the mule turned his sullen sharp face from him, dug a heel into the side of the mule and went off up the pike with a motion which made you think that any second you would hear mule bones clashing inside that lank and scrofulous hide.

"Cy Dundee's boy," a man said, and nodded toward the figure going up the pike on the mule.

"Reckin Cy Dundee's young-uns seen times they'd settle fer drownt cow," another man said.

The old man with the beard peered at them both from his weak, slow eyes, first at one and then at the other. "Live long enough," he said, "and a man will settle fer what he kin git."

Then there was silence again, with the people looking at the red, foam-flecked water.

My father lifted the bridle rein in his left hand, and the mare turned and walked around the group and up the pike. We rode on up to our big gate, where my father dismounted to open it and let me myself ride Nellie Gray through. When he got to the lane that led off from the drive about two hundred yards from our house, my father said, "Grab on." I grabbed on, and he let me down to the ground. "I'm going to ride down and look at my corn," he said. "You go on." He took the lane, and I stood there on the drive and watched him ride off. He was wearing cowhide boots and an old hunting coat, and I thought that that made him look very military, like a picture. That and the way he rode.

I did not go to the house. Instead, I went by the vegetable garden and crossed behind the stables, and headed down for Dellie's cabin. I wanted to go down and play with Jebb, who was Dellie's little boy about two years older than I was. Besides, I was cold. I shivered as I walked, and I had gooseflesh. The mud which crawled up between my toes with every step I took was like ice. Dellie would have a fire, but she wouldn't make me put on shoes and stockings.

Dellie's cabin was of logs, with one side, because it was on a slope, set on limestone chunks, with a little porch attached to it, and had a little whitewashed fence around it and a gate with plow-points on a wire to clink when somebody came in, and had two big white oaks in the yard and some flowers and a nice privy in the back with some honeysuckle growing over it. Dellie and Old Jebb, who was Jebb's father and who lived with Dellie and had lived with her for twenty-five years even if they never had got married, were careful to keep everything nice around their cabin. They had the name all over the community for being clean and clever Negroes. Dellie and Jebb were what they used to call "white-folks' niggers." There was a big difference between their cabin and the other two cabins farther down where the other tenants lived. My father kept the other cabins weatherproof, but he couldn't undertake to go down and pick up after the litter they strewed. They didn't take the trouble to have a vegetable patch like Dellie and Jebb or to make pre-serves from wild plum, and jelly from crab apple the way Dellie did. They were shiftless, and my father was always threatening to get shed of them. But he never did. When they finally left, they just up and left on their own, for no reason, to go and be shiftless somewhere else. Then some more came. But meanwhile they lived down there, Matt Rawson and his family, and Sid Turner and his, and I played with their children all over the farm when they weren't working. But when I wasn't around they were mean sometimes to Little Jebb. That was because the other tenants down there were jealous of Dellie and Jebb.

I was so cold that I ran the last fifty yards to Dellie's gate. As soon as I had entered the yard, I saw that the storm had been hard on Dellie's flowers. The yard was, as I have said, on a slight slope, and the water running across had gutted the flower beds and washed out all the good black woods-earth which Dellie had brought in. What little grass there was in the yard was plastered sparsely down on the ground, the way the drainage water had left it. It reminded me of the way the fluff was plas-tered down on the skin of the drowned chicks that the strange man had been picking up, up in my mother's chicken yard.

I took a few steps up the path to the cabin, and then I saw that the drainage water had washed a lot of trash and filth out from under Dellie's house. Up toward the porch, the ground was not clean any more. Old pieces of rag, two or three rusted cans, pieces of rotten rope, some hunks of old dog dung, broken glass, old paper, and all sorts of things like that had washed out from under Dellie's house to foul her clean yard. It looked just as bad as the yards of the other cabins, or worse. It was worse, as a matter of fact, because it was a surprise. I had never thought of all that filth being under Dellie's house. It was not anything against Dellie that the stuff had been under the cabin. Trash will get under any house. But I did not think of that when I saw the foulness which had washed out on the ground which Dellie sometimes used to sweep with a twig broom to make nice and clean.

I picked my way past the filth, being careful not to get my bare feet on it, and mounted to Dellie's door. When I knocked, I heard her voice telling me to come in.

It was dark inside the cabin, after the daylight, but I could make out Dellie piled up in bed under a quilt, and Little Jebb crouched by the hearth, where a low fire simmered. "Howdy," I said to Dellie, "how you feeling?"

Her big eyes, the whites surprising and glaring in the black face, fixed on me as I stood there, but she did not reply. It did not look like Dellie, or act like Dellie, who would grumble and bustle around our kitchen, talking to herself, scolding me or Little Jebb, clanking pans, making all sorts of unnecessary noises and mutterings like an old-fashioned black steam thrasher engine when it has got up an extra head of steam and keeps popping the governor and rumbling and shaking on its wheels. But now Dellie just lay up there on the bed, under the patchwork quilt, and turned the black face, which I scarcely recognized, and the glaring white eyes to me.

"How you feeling?" I repeated.

"I'se sick," the voice said croakingly out of the strange black face which was not attached to Dellie's big, squat body, but stuck out from under a pile of tangled bedclothes. Then the voice added: "Mighty sick."

"I'm sorry," I managed to say.

The eyes remained fixed on me for a moment, then they left me and the head rolled back on the pillow. "Sorry," the voice said, in a flat way which wasn't question or statement of anything. It was just the empty word put into the air with no meaning or expression, to float off like a feather or a puff of smoke, while the big eyes, with the whites like the peeled white of hard-boiled eggs, stared at the ceiling.

"Dellie," I said after a minute, "there's a tramp up at the house. He's got a knife."

She was not listening. She closed her eyes.

I tiptoed over to the hearth where Jebb was and crouched beside him. We began to talk in low voices. I was asking him to get out his train and play train. Old Jebb had put spool wheels on three cigar boxes and put wire links between the boxes to make a train for Jebb. The box that was the locomotive had the top closed and a length of broom stick for a smoke stack. Jebb didn't want to get the train out, but I told him I would go home if he didn't. So he got out the train, and the colored rocks, and fossils of crinoid stems, and other junk he used for the load, and we began to push it around, talking the way we thought trainmen talked, making a chuck-chucking sound under the breath for the noise of the locomotive and now and then uttering low, cautious toots for the whistle. We got so interested in playing train that the toots got louder. Then, before he thought, Jebb gave a good, loud *toot-toot,* blowing for a crossing.

"Come here," the voice said from the bed.

Jebb got up slow from his hands and knees, giving me a sudden, naked, inimical look.

"Come here!" the voice said.

Jebb went to the bed. Dellie propped herself weakly up on one arm, muttering, "Come closer."

Jebb stood closer.

"Last thing I do, I'm gonna do it," Dellie said. "Done tole you to be quiet."

Then she slapped him. It was an awful slap, more awful for the kind of weakness which it came from and brought to focus. I had seen her slap Jebb before, but the slapping had always been the kind of easy slap you would expect from a good-natured, grumbling Negro woman like Dellie. But this was different. It was awful. It was so awful that Jebb didn't make a sound. The tears just popped out and ran down his face, and his breath came sharp, like gasps.

Dellie fell back. "Cain't even be sick," she said to the ceiling. "Git sick and they won't even let you lay. They tromp all over you. Cain't even be sick." Then she closed her eyes.

I went out of the room. I almost ran getting to the door, and I did run across the porch and down the steps and across the yard, not caring whether or not I stepped on the filth which had washed out from under the cabin. I ran almost all the way home. Then I thought about my mother catching me with the bare feet. So I went down to the stables.

I heard a noise in the crib, and opened the door. There was Big Jebb, sitting on an old nail keg, shelling corn into a bushel basket. I went in, pulling the door shut behind me, and crouched on the floor near him. I crouched there for a couple of minutes before either of us spoke, and watched him shelling the corn.

He had very big hands, knotted and grayish at the joints, with cal-

loused palms which seemed to be streaked with rust with the rust coming
up between the fingers to show from the back. His hands were so strong
and tough that he could take a big ear of corn and rip the grains right off
the cob with the palm of his hand, all in one motion, like a machine.
"Work long as me," he would say, "and the good Lawd'll give you a hand
lak cass-ion won't nuthin' hurt." And his hands did look like cast iron, old
cast iron streaked with rust.

He was an old man, up in his seventies, thirty years or more older
than Dellie, but he was strong as a bull. He was a squat sort of man,
heavy in the shoulders, with remarkably long arms, the kind of build
they say the river natives have on the Congo from paddling so much in
their boats. He had a round bullet-head, set on powerful shoulders. His
skin was very black, and the thin hair on his head was now grizzled like
tufts of old cotton batting. He had small eyes and a flat nose, not big, and
the kindest and wisest old face in the world, the blunt, sad, wise face of
an old animal peering tolerantly out on the goings-on of the merely
human creatures before him. He was a good man, and I loved him next
to my mother and father. I crouched there on the floor of the crib and
watched him shell corn with the rusty cast-iron hands, while he looked
down at me out of the little eyes set in the blunt face.

"Dellie says she's mighty sick," I said.

"Yeah," he said.

"What's she sick from?"

"Woman-mizry," he said.

"What's woman-mizry?"

"Hit comes on 'em," he said. "Hit just comes on 'em when the
time comes."

"What is it?"

"Hit is the change," he said. "Hit is the change of life and time."

"What changes?"

"You too young to know."

"Tell me."

"Time come and you find out everything."

I knew that there was no use in asking him any more. When I
asked him things and he said that, I always knew that he would not tell
me. So I continued to crouch there and watch him. Now that I had sat
there a little while, I was cold again.

"What you shiver fer?" he asked me.

"I'm cold. I'm cold because it's blackberry winter," I said.

"Maybe 'tis and maybe 'tain't," he said.

"My mother says it is."

"Ain't sayen Miss Sallie doan know and ain't sayen she do. But
folks doan know everything."

"Why isn't it blackberry winter?"

"Too late fer blackberry winter. Blackberries done bloomed."

"She said it was."

"Blackberry winter just a leetle cold spell. Hit come and then hit go away, and hit is growed summer of a sudden lak a gunshot. Ain't no tellen hit will go way this time."

"It's June," I said.

"June," he replied with great contempt. "That what folks say. What June mean? Maybe hit is come cold to stay."

"Why?"

" 'Cause this-here old yearth is tahrd. Hit is tahrd and ain't gonna perduce. Lawd let hit come rain one time forty days and forty nights, 'cause He was tahrd of sinful folks. Maybe this-here old yearth say to the Lawd, Lawd, I done plum tahrd, Lawd, lemme rest. And Lawd say, Yearth, you done yore best, you give 'em cawn and you give 'em taters, and all they think on is they gut, and, Yearth, you kin take a rest."

"What will happen?"

"Folks will eat up everything. The yearth won't perduce no more. Folks cut down all the trees and burn 'em 'cause they cold, and the yearth won't grow no more. I been tellen 'em. I been tellen folks. Sayen, maybe this year, hit is the time. But they doan listen to me, how the yearth is tahrd. Maybe this year they find out."

"Will everything die?"

"Everthing and everbody, hit will be so."

"This year?"

"Ain't no tellen. Maybe this year."

"My mother said it is blackberry winter," I said confidently, and got up.

"Ain't sayen nuthin' agin Miss Sallie," he said.

I went to the door of the crib. I was really cold now. Running, I had got up a sweat and now I was worse.

I hung on the door, looking at Jebb, who was shelling corn again.

"There's a tramp came to the house," I said. I had almost forgotten the tramp.

"Yeah."

"He came by the back way. What was he doing down there in the storm?"

"They comes and they goes," he said, "and ain't no tellen."

"He had a mean knife."

"The good ones and the bad ones, they comes and they goes. Storm or sun, light or dark. They is folks and they comes and they goes lak folks."

I hung on the door, shivering.

He studied me a moment, then said, "You git on to the house. You ketch yore death. Then what yore mammy say?"

I hesitated.

"You git," he said.

When I came to the back yard, I saw that my father was standing by the back porch and the tramp was walking toward him. They began talking before I reached them, but I got there just as my father was saying, "I'm sorry, but I haven't got any work. I got all the hands on the place I need now. I won't need any extra until wheat thrashing."

The stranger made no reply, just looked at my father.

My father took out his leather coin purse, and got out a half-dollar. He held it toward the man. "This is for half a day," he said.

The man looked at the coin, and then at my father, making no motion to take the money. But that was the right amount. A dollar a day was what you paid them back in 1910. And the man hadn't even worked half a day.

Then the man reached out and took the coin. He dropped it into the right side pocket of his coat. Then he said, very slowly and without feeling: "I didn't want to work on your —— farm."

He used the word which they would have frailed me to death for using.

I looked at my father's face and it was streaked white under the sunburn. Then he said, "Get off this place. Get off this place or I won't be responsible."

The man dropped his right hand into his pants pocket. It was the pocket where he kept the knife. I was just about to yell to my father about the knife when the hand came back out with nothing in it. The man gave a kind of twisted grin, showing where the teeth had been knocked out above the new scar. I thought that instant how maybe he had tried before to pull a knife on somebody else and had got his teeth knocked out.

So now he just gave that twisted, sickish grin out of the unmemorable, grayish face, and then spat on the brick path. The glob landed just about six inches from the toe of my father's right boot. My father looked down at it, and so did I. I thought that if the glob had hit my father's boot something would have happened. I looked down and saw the bright glob, and on one side of it my father's strong cowhide boots, with the brass eyelets and the leather thongs, heavy boots splashed with good red mud and set solid on the bricks, and on the other side the pointed-toe, broken, black shoes, on which the mud looked so sad and out of place. Then I saw one of the black shoes move a little, just a twitch first, then a real step backward.

The man moved in a quarter circle to the end of the porch, with my father's steady gaze upon him all the while. At the end of the porch, the man reached up to the shelf where the wash pans were to get his little newspaper-wrapped parcel. Then he disappeared around the corner of the house and my father mounted the porch and went into the kitchen without a word.

I followed around the house to see what the man would do. I wasn't afraid of him now, no matter if he did have the knife. When I got around in front, I saw him going out the yard gate and starting up the drive toward the pike. So I ran to catch up with him. He was sixty yards or so up the drive before I caught up.

I did not walk right up even with him at first, but trailed him, the way a kid will, about seven or eight feet behind, now and then running two or three steps in order to hold my place against his longer stride. When I first came up behind him, he turned to give me a look, just a meaningless look, and then fixed his eyes up the drive and kept on walking.

When we had got around the bend in the drive which cut the house from sight, and were going along by the edge of the woods, I decided to come up even with him. I ran a few steps, and was by his side, or almost, but some feet off to the right. I walked along in this position for a while, and he never noticed me. I walked along until we got within sight of the big gate that let on the pike.

Then I said: "Where did you come from?"

He looked at me then with a look which seemed almost surprised that I was there. Then he said, "It ain't none of yore business."

We went on another fifty feet.

Then I said, "Where are you going?"

He stopped, studied me dispassionately for a moment, then suddenly took a step toward me and leaned his face down at me. The lips jerked back, but not in any grin, to show where the teeth were knocked out and to make the scar on the lower lip come white with the tension.

He said: "Stop following me. You don't stop following me and I cut yore throat, you little son-of-a-bitch."

Then he went on to the gate, and up the pike.

That was thirty-five years ago. Since that time my father and mother have died. I was still a boy, but a big boy, when my father got cut on the blade of a mowing machine and died of lockjaw. My mother sold the place and went to town to live with her sister. But she never took hold after my father's death, and she died within three years, right in middle life. My aunt always said, "Sallie just died of a broken heart, she was so devoted." Dellie is dead, too, but she died, I heard, quite a long time after we sold the farm.

As for Little Jebb, he grew up to be a mean and ficey Negro. He killed another Negro in a fight and got sent to the penitentiary, where he is yet, the last I heard tell. He probably grew up to be mean and ficey from just being picked on so much by the children of the other tenants, who were jealous of Jebb and Dellie for being thrifty and clever and being white-folks' niggers.

Old Jebb lived forever. I saw him ten years ago and he was about a hundred then, and not looking much different. He was living in town then, on relief—that was back in the Depression—when I went to see him. He said to me: "Too strong to die. When I was a young feller just comen on and seen how things wuz, I prayed the Lawd. I said, Oh, Lawd, gimme strength and meke me strong fer to do and to indure. The Lawd hearkened to my prayer. He give me strength. I was in-duren proud fer being strong and me much man. The Lawd give me my prayer and my strength. But now He done gone off and fergot me and left me alone with my strength. A man doan know what to pray fer, and him mortal."

Jebb is probably living yet, as far as I know.

That is what has happened since the morning when the tramp leaned his face down at me and showed his teeth and said: "Stop following me. You don't stop following me and I cut yore throat, you little son-of-a-bitch." That was what he said, for me not to follow him. But I did follow him, all the years.

COMMENTARY AND QUESTIONS

As long as the events of a day in 1910 are being narrated, this story seems deceptively ingenuous. But when the reader comes to the final section of the story and realizes that Seth, the narrator, has been recounting from the standpoint of maturity what happened thirty-five years ago, the events of that earlier time and the way in which they are presented take on a heightened significance. During the recounting of the earlier events an explicit contrast is drawn between the orderly and predictable way of life represented by the father and the mother and the breaking of normal patterns represented by the stranger. By the end of the story another contrast becomes apparent: between the narrator's expectation of stability when he was nine years old and his realization with the passing of time that life is not stable.

1. In what ways are the father and the stranger contrasted? What actions and manners of the stranger does the nine-year-old boy find odd or even ridiculous? When does the boy lose his fear of the stranger?

2. In what way does the mother fulfill the confidence of her son as the stranger approaches the house for the first time? Are you surprised by what happens to her (briefly noted in the final section of the

story) after the father's death? (Notice that in the earlier scene
Warren gives the reader knowledge of her death [p. 664]: ". . . when
I think of her now after all the years she has been dead, I think of
her brown hands. . . .")

3. In the incident of the drowned cow (pp. 668-670), what contrasts
   are suggested by these items: the father's reprimanding Seth for not
   saying "Mr. Alley"; the Dundee boy's asking, "Reckin anybody ever
   et drownt cow?"

4. Why is the boy Seth shocked by the sight of the filth washed down
   from underneath Dellie's cabin, and even more shocked by Dellie's
   slapping her son?

5. In the final section of the story, what is the narrator's explanation of
   Little Jebb's becoming "a mean and ficey Negro"? What is the irony
   of this outcome, and why is it appropriate to the story?

6. The question of where the stranger came from arouses young Seth's
   curiosity. Is the boy satisfied with his mother's answer to the question? What attitude is implicit in this comment by Big Jeb as he discusses the stranger: "The good ones and the bad ones, they comes
   and they goes. Storm or sun, light or dark. They is folks and they
   comes and they goes lak folks" (p. 675)?

7. How does Big Jebb's evaluation of human wisdom in the final section
   of the story ("A man doan know what to pray fer, and him mortal")
   differ from the implicit evaluation of his own wisdom revealed in
   his talk with the boy Seth in the corn crib?

8. As viewed by young Seth in 1910, the stranger obviously represents
   a pattern of life entirely different from and less desirable than that
   represented by the father and the mother. But thirty-five years later
   the narrator reports that he has "followed" the stranger "all the
   years." Do you think the author should have devoted more than the
   last few paragraphs to the years between 1910 and 1945?

9. As the story opens, Seth is being told by his mother to put on his
   shoes and stockings. During the course of the story, what use is made
   of the fact that he did not put them on?

10. In the fourth paragraph (pp. 660-661) there is a rather long com-
    ment on Time. Considering the development of the story, do you
    think this passage is appropriate?

SUGGESTIONS FOR WRITING

1. "Live long enough and a man will settle fer what he kin git" (p. 670).

2. Both Mike in "The Destructors" (pp. 645-658) and young Seth in
   this story are identified as being nine years old. In what ways are
   the methods of presenting the two characters similar? In what ways
   are they dissimilar?

Index

681